GED TEST PREP

GED TEST PREP

LEARNINGEXPRESS®

NEW YORK

Library of Congress Control Number: 2008920450

Printed in the United States of America

9 8 7 6 5 4 3 2 1

First Edition

ISBN: 978-1-57685-605-5

For more information or to place an order, contact LearningExpress at:
  55 Broadway
  8th Floor
  New York, NY 10006

Or visit us at:
  www.learnatest.com

Contents ▶

CONTENTS

CONTENTS

Preparing for the GED

ONGRATULATIONS ON YOUR decision to take the GED, exams that can make a dramatic difference in your life. Of course, you want to be prepared for these important exams—that's why you bought this book. There's a lot more to good preparation than just taking a practice exam or two. That's why this book gives you the opportunity to review the knowledge and build the skills you will need for the exams.

But first things first. Before you begin studying the different subjects tested on the GED, you need to learn as much as you can about the exams. That way, you will know exactly *how* to prepare. Chapter 1 will tell you all about the GED, including the structure of the exams, eligibility requirements, testing information, scoring, and fees.

Your time is valuable, and you will want to make the most of your study time. That's why the rest of this section is devoted to study strategies and test-taking skills. Chapter 2 reviews basic, effective study techniques. Chapter 3 shows you how to better learn and remember material. Chapter 4 provides tips and strategies for tackling standardized tests like the GED. Read the chapters in this section carefully so you can create an effective study plan and study wisely.

All about the GED

Planning to take the GED? Here's what you need to know to get started. This chapter covers the basic information about these important exams. You will learn how the exams are structured, how to register, and how the exams are scored.

Edward dropped out of high school at 16 when his mother became ill and could no longer work or take care of Edward and his younger brother. He began working full time and never finished high school.

Rajesh came to the United States with the equivalent of a tenth-grade education from his native country. He dreamed of becoming a computer programmer but had to work full time. He often worked extra shifts to help make ends meet.

Marie was a certified nurse in her native Caribbean country. But when she immigrated, she found out her nursing certification was not valid in the United States. She could not apply to a U.S. nursing program without a high school diploma.

TODAY, AFTER TAKING the GED and earning their high school diplomas, Edward, Rajesh, and Marie—like thousands of others who take the GED each year—are able to pursue the education and careers of their dreams. For more than half a century, the GED diploma has given millions of people the opportunity to find better employment, enroll in colleges and training programs, improve their standard of living, and feel better about themselves and their futures.

▶ What the Tests Are About

The General Educational Development (GED) examination is a series of exams covering the broad range of knowledge and skills students are expected to master in high school. They are exams for people who wish to earn a high school diploma but who have been unable to graduate in the traditional manner. Passing the GED certifies that you have a high school level education and entitles you to a GED diploma, the equivalent of a high school diploma. For hundreds of thousands of people each year, the GED is an important stepping stone to a better job and continued education.

Did You Know?

The GED was originally developed for veterans returning from World War II to help them complete their educations and earn their high school credentials. The first test was administered more than 65 years ago, in 1942.

The GED is jointly administered by the General Education Development Testing Service, a program of the American Council on Education (ACE) Center for Adult Learning and Education Credentials, and the education department of each participating state or province. The GED exams are actually a battery of *five* exams that measure knowledge in five content and skills areas: writing, reading comprehension (understanding literature), social studies, mathematics, and science.

GED Components

The GED is actually a battery of five separate exams:
- ◆ Language Arts, Writing (Parts I and II)
- ◆ Social Studies
- ◆ Science
- ◆ Language Arts, Reading
- ◆ Mathematics (Parts I and II)

The complete battery of GED exams takes a total of seven hours and five minutes. The level of difficulty is set so that only two-thirds of traditional high school seniors will pass. On average, at least two-thirds of adults who take all five exams earn their diploma, and many states report even higher pass rates.

In many testing centers, you can take the GED one exam at a time until you complete all five exams. In others, you must take the entire battery of exams in one or two sessions.

The questions on the GED are all multiple choice with two important exceptions. Part II of the Language Arts, Writing Test requires you to write an essay, and about 25% of math questions are "alternate format" questions that may include short written responses. You will learn details about each exam, including the specific material covered and the kind of questions to expect, throughout the rest of this book.

GED Fact Box

According to the American Council on Education, which oversees the GED Testing Service:
- ◆ Test takers who pass the GED outperform 40% of high school seniors on the exam.
- ◆ Approximately 90% of U.S. colleges recognize the GED, and over 95% of U.S. employers offer GED graduates the same hiring, compensation, and promotion opportunities as employees with a traditional high school diploma.
- ◆ Approximately 1 in 20 first-year college students are GED graduates.

▶ Who Takes the GED—and Why

The people who take the GED each year are a very diverse group who come from a rich variety of backgrounds. As different as their situations and experiences may be, their main reasons for taking the GED are the same. Passing the GED:

- ■ enables them to apply to colleges and universities
- ■ allows them to apply for jobs or promotions that require a high school diploma

- demonstrates to others the importance of education
- is a significant accomplishment that improves self-esteem

▶ GED Eligibility Requirements

GED candidates must first meet certain eligibility requirements set by the ACE and participating states and territories. You are eligible to take the GED if you meet the following conditions:

1. You are not enrolled in high school AND
2. You have not graduated from high school AND
3. You have not received or qualified for a high school level equivalency credential.
4. You are at least 16 years of age AND
5. You meet the requirements of your state, province, or territory regarding age, residency, and the length of time since leaving school.

▶ Testing Centers and Registration

There are approximately 3,400 GED testing centers around the world. These centers are typically operated by local school boards, community colleges, and/or centers for adult education. Test takers outside the United States, Canada, or their territories may be able to take the GED at a Thomson Prometric facility.

Because test centers are run locally, registration procedures, fees, and test times vary. You need to contact the center where you would like to take the exams to find specific registration, fee, and test time information.

If you live inside the United States, Canada, or their territories, you can find the testing center nearest you by:

1. Calling 1-800-62-MY-GED OR
2. Checking in the blue pages of your local telephone book (look for "GED Testing" under the state department of education listing) OR
3. Going to www.acenet.edu/resources/GED/center_locator.cfm. From there, select your specific area to find out how to contact your local testing center.

▶ International Testing

If you live outside the United States, Canada, or their territories, you can still take the GED through one of Thomson Prometric's testing centers. Thomson Prometric, in partnership with the ACE, offers a computer-based GED, which was revised as of January 1, 2008. (Note, all partial completed scores taken prior to then are invalid.) If you reside outside the United States, Canada, or their territories and wish to take the online exam, you must be at least 17 years old. Thomson Prometric processes U.S. high school equivalency diploma applications through the Maine Department of Education; diplomas will be issued from the U.S. state of Maine.

For more information on international testing for the GED, contact 866-776-6387 or Thomson Prometric, 1000 Lancaster Street, Suite 200, Baltimore, MD 21202. Ask for the Regional Registration Center in your country or province. Visit their website at www.prometric.com or email additional questions to ged@prometric.com.

Thomson Prometric has approximately 200 testing centers around the world.

- Australia/New Zealand
- China
- Europe
- India
- Indonesia
- Japan
- Korea
- Latin America/Caribbean
- Middle East/North Africa
- Pakistan
- Southeast Asia
- Sub-Sahara/Africa
- Taiwan
- Thailand

Testing centers are open year-round but hours vary from country to country.

▶ Spanish and French Versions of the GED

In addition to the standard English version of the GED, there are also Spanish and French versions, initially developed for Puerto Rico and Canada, respectively. These tests are now authorized for use throughout the United States but may not be available in all areas and are *not* available at international testing centers (international GED candidates must take the English version). A new version of both the Spanish and French GEDs went into effect on January 1, 2004.

The Spanish GED

The structure and content of the Spanish GED is essentially the same as the English GED, with the important exception that the examples and test questions are based on Spanish language and culture. In the Language Arts, Reading Exam, all excerpts are from Spanish-language writers with an emphasis on writers from the Caribbean and Central and South America. In the Language Arts, Writing Exam, grammar questions focus on issues specific to the Spanish language, such as gender agreement and multiple-object pronouns. The essay is scored by readers whose first language is Spanish or who are secondary or college-level Spanish instructors.

The French GED

The French GED also follows the English GED in format and structure. Like the Spanish GED, it draws its questions and context from French language and culture. Most measurement questions use the metric system. Essays on the French exam are scored by readers whose first language is French or who have taught French at the secondary or college level.

▶ Special Accommodations

Special testing accommodations are available for GED candidates with documented disabilities that may affect their ability to pass the GED. These accommodations include, but are not limited to:

- testing in English-language Braille
- testing by audiocassette
- large-print test editions
- extended time
- frequent, supervised breaks
- use of a talking calculator or scribe
- private testing rooms
- vision enhancing technologies
- use of video equipment
- use of sign-language interpreter
- one-on-one testing

Dictionaries and spell checkers are *not* permitted, nor is having someone read the questions aloud to the candidate.

If you need special accommodations to take the GED, request the appropriate form from your local testing center. You may download these forms from www.gedtest.org.

Once you have completed the form and provided the necessary documentation, return the form to your GED testing center. Be sure to request and complete this form well in advance of your test date to allow sufficient time for processing.

▶ GED Testing Fees

Fees for the GED vary widely. In some states, you can take the GED exams at no charge; in others, all testing centers charge the same fee (usually $20–$90); and in others, individual testing centers determine their own fees (also usually $20–$90).

▶ When the Tests Are Offered

Each test center determines when and how often it will offer the GED exams. Some centers may offer the tests only two or three times a year; others offer them much more frequently. Contact your local testing center to see when the tests will be offered. If the dates and times are inconvenient, check other centers nearby. Their offerings may better fit your schedule.

▶ How the Tests Are Scored

Each of the five GED exams is scored separately on a standard scale of 200 to 800 points. Each correct answer is worth one point, but because the individual tests have different numbers of questions, the score for each test is converted to this 200–800 standard. This allows the scores on all five tests to be compared. The Language Arts, Writing Exam score is a statistical combination of the scores for the multiple-choice questions and the essay, but a high score on Part I is no longer enough to pass the exam. Candidates must pass *both* parts of the test in order to pass the Language Arts, Writing Exam.

The GED score reflects an estimate of your skills and knowledge in each content area as compared to recent high school graduates. Your score will be reported in two ways: a number from 200–800 and a percentage. The percentage indicates how your score compares with the performance of graduating high school students. If your percentile rank is 85, for example, that means you have scored better than 85% of graduating high school seniors. Here's a more detailed example:

GED TESTS	SCORE
Language Arts, Writing	606
Social Studies	688
Science	490
Language Arts, Reading	621
Mathematics	552
Average Overall Score	**591**
Percentile Rank	**81%**

What Is a Passing Score?

The minimum score required to pass the GED and earn the GED diploma is set by individual states, provinces, and territories. The passing score is usually a combination of both a *minimum score per test* and a *minimum average score overall*. Most testing jurisdictions use the passing score set by the GED Testing Service:

- a minimum score of **410** on each test
- a minimum average score of **450** overall

If you answer approximately 60–65% of the questions correctly, you should receive a standard score of about 410 points per exam.

Enough to Pass

In most states, you must score 410 on each exam and an average score of 450 overall in order to pass the GED.

Getting Your Scores

How and when you get your GED results will also vary from testing center to testing center. Most centers, however, will mail your results for all tests except Language Arts, Writing in 2–4 weeks. Scoring of the essay part of the exam typically takes longer, so you may have to wait 4–6 weeks for those test results. Some centers may also post test scores or provide a number to call for test results.

Getting Your Diploma

Most states will automatically issue your diploma if you pass the GED. The names of candidates with passing scores are forwarded to the state department of education, and you can expect to receive your diploma in the mail in approximately 6–8 weeks.

Retaking the GED

Fortunately, if you do not pass the full battery of exams or would like to improve your score, you can retake the GED. Most states allow you to retake the tests two or three times within a specified time period. Often, you can retest only after you have completed all five exams.

Check with your state or province to find out the regulations regarding retesting. Also, be sure to check with your testing center regarding fees for retaking the exams. These fees are usually significantly lower than the initial exam fee, typically between $5–$30.

▶ The Structure of the GED

Each of the five GED exams contains 40–50 multiple-choice questions, with the exception of the mathematics exam, which also contains 25% "alternate format" questions (this will be explained further in Chapter 41). The Language Arts, Writing Exam also contains an essay section. The time allotted for each exam varies from 45 minutes (essay) to 90 minutes (math exam). The table on the next page describes the basic structure of the exams, including length, number of questions, and type of questions. You will learn more about the kinds of questions on each exam as you read Parts III–VII.

You will find out much more about each of the GED exams in the chapters ahead. But first, it's time to review study skills and create your study plan.

GED EXAMS	NUMBER OF QUESTIONS	SUBTOPIC/TYPE OF QUESTION	TIME LENGTH
Language Arts, Writing, Part I	50	Multiple choice: 30% sentence structure 30% usage 25% mechanics 15% organization	75 minutes
Language Arts, Writing, Part II	1	Essay	45 minutes
Social Studies	50	Multiple choice: 40% history (25% national history, 15% world history) 25% civics and government 20% economics 15% geography	70 minutes
Science	50	Multiple choice: 45% life science 35% physical science 20% Earth and space science	80 minutes
Language Arts, Reading	40	Multiple choice: 30–35% analysis 30–35% synthesis 20% comprehension 15% application 75% literary texts 25% nonfiction	65 minutes
Mathematics, Parts I and II (Note: A standard calculator is permitted for Part I of the math test. Calculators are provided at the test site. No calculators are permitted for Part II.)	50	Multiple choice (80%) and alternate format (20%): 75% calculations 25% set-up (determining the correct way to solve the problem) 20–30% geometry and measurement 20–30% number operations and number sense 20–30% algebra, functions, and patterns 20–30% data analysis, statistics, and probability	90 minutes
Total:	240 + essay		7 hours, 5 minutes

CHAPTER

2 ▶ Study Skills

How much time you spend studying each week is important. But *how* you study is the key to your success. This chapter shows you how to set up an effective learning environment, determine your learning style, and create an effective study plan.

MAYBE IT'S BEEN a while since you last studied for an exam, or maybe you have never had to prepare for standardized tests like the GED. In any case, you may be unsure about the best way to get ready for these important exams. Fortunately, there are many strategies that can help you learn and remember the material you need to know to succeed on the GED. There are several important steps to take *before* you begin to study.

▶ Environment and Attitude

To study means "to give one's attention to learning a subject; to look at with careful attention." Notice that the word *attention* comes up twice in this definition. To study well, you need to be able to focus all your attention on the material. So, the first step is to make sure you have the right kind of learning environment and attitude.

The Right Mood

Studying can bring wonderful rewards. You can gain new knowledge. You can do well on tests—like the GED—that enable you to achieve your academic and professional goals. But it can still be difficult to get in the mood to study. After all, studying can be hard work, and you might be worried about whether you will pass the exam. You may have many other things you would rather do, or you might just have trouble getting started. These are all reasons that may lead you to procrastinate and put off work that you need to do. But procrastinating can cause lots of trouble at test time. If you procrastinate too much or for too long, you won't be prepared for the exams.

One of the best ways to beat procrastination is to use a *reward system*. Everyone likes to be rewarded for a job well done, and if there's going to be a reward at the end of the work, it's easier to get started. So promise yourself a small reward for each study session. For example, you might promise yourself a trip to the gym or a phone call to a good friend as a reward for an hour of study. You might promise to treat yourself to a movie after you finish a chapter or give yourself a nutritious snack after you finish a difficult lesson. You can also think about the reward you will give yourself when you pass the GED. Make sure this reward is a big one!

You can also get in the mood for studying by thinking about the short- and long-term rewards you will receive for your hard work. Keep in mind the benefits you will receive from your GED study time:

- You will gain or reinforce important knowledge and skills in five fundamental subject areas.
- You will be able to apply to U.S. colleges and universities.
- You will be eligible for jobs and training programs that require a high school diploma.
- You will get the education you need for a successful future.

Remember that while you are preparing for the GED, your attitude is very important. It can dramatically affect how much you learn and how well you learn it. Make sure that you have a positive attitude. You will study, you will learn, and you will do well. Your study time will be time well spent.

Mood Booster

Whenever you need help getting motivated to study, try saying the following out loud:
- I know more today than I did yesterday.
- I will know more after I study than I know now.
- Every minute I spend studying will help me achieve my goals.

The Right Conditions

You can have the best attitude in the world, but if you are tired or distracted, you are going to have difficulty studying. To be at your best, you need to be focused, alert, and calm. That means you need to study under the right conditions.

Everyone is different, so you need to know what conditions work best for you. Here are some questions to consider:

1. What time of day do you work best—morning, afternoon, or evening? How early in the day or late in the night can you think clearly?
2. Do you work best in total silence? Or do you prefer music or other noise in the background?
3. If you prefer music, what kind? Classical music often helps people relax because the music is soft and there are no words. But you may prefer music that energizes you, such as rock and roll. Others work best with music that has special meaning to them and puts them in a positive state of mind.
4. Where do you like to work? Do you feel most comfortable sitting at the kitchen counter? At the dining room table? At a desk in your office or bedroom? (Try to avoid studying in bed. You will probably be relaxed, but you may be *too* comfortable and fall asleep.) Or do you prefer to study out of the house, at the library or a local coffee shop?
5. What do you like to have around you when you work? Do you feel most comfortable in your favorite chair? Do you like to have pictures of family and friends around?
6. What kind of lighting do you prefer? Does soft light make you sleepy? Do you need bright light? If it's too bright, you may feel uncomfortable. If it's too dark, you may feel sleepy. Remember that poor lighting can also strain your eyes and give you a headache.
7. How does eating affect you? Do you feel most energized right after a meal? Or does eating tend to make you feel sleepy? Which foods give you a lot of energy? Which slow you down?
8. Can you put problems or other pressing concerns out of your mind to focus on a different task? How can you minimize distractions so you can fully focus on your work?

Think carefully about each of these questions. Write down your answers so you can develop a good study plan. For example, say you work best in the morning but need total silence to work. If you have children, you would be wise to schedule your study time early in the morning before the kids are up or first thing after they leave for school. If you wait until they are in bed, you will have a quiet house, but you may be too tired to study well. Similarly, if you have trouble concentrating when you are hungry, schedule study time shortly after meals, or be sure to start your study sessions with a healthy snack.

The Right Tools

Help make your study session successful by having the right learning tools by your side. As you study for the GED, have:

- a good English dictionary, such as *Merriam-Webster's Collegiate Dictionary, Eleventh Edition*
- paper or legal pads
- pencils (and a pencil sharpener) or pens
- a highlighter, or several highlighters in different colors
- index or other note cards
- folders or notebooks
- a calendar or personal digital assistant, such as a Palm Pilot®
- a calculator
- graph paper

As you gather your supplies, keep your personal preferences in mind. Perhaps you like to write with a certain kind of pen or on a certain kind of paper. If so, make sure you have that pen or paper with you when you study. It will help you feel more comfortable and relaxed as you work.

Learning How You Learn

Imagine that you need directions to a restaurant you have never been to before. Which of the following would you do to find out how to get there?

- Look at a map.
- Ask someone to tell you directions.
- Draw a map or copy someone's written directions.
- List step-by-step directions.

Most people learn in a variety of ways. They learn by seeing, hearing, doing, and organizing information from the world around them. But most of us tend to use one way more than others. That's our *dominant* (strongest) learning style. How you would handle getting directions, for example, suggests which learning style you use most often:

- **Visual.** Visual learners learn best by *seeing*. If you would look at a map for directions, you are probably a visual learner. You understand ideas best when they are in pictures or graphs. You may learn better by using different colors as you take notes. Use a highlighter (or several, in different colors) as you read to mark important ideas. Mapping and diagramming ideas are good learning strategies for visual learners.
- **Auditory.** Auditory learners learn best by *listening*. If you would ask someone to tell you directions, you are probably an auditory learner. You would probably rather listen to a lecture than read a textbook, and you may learn better by reading aloud. Try recording your notes and listening to them as one of your main study strategies.
- **Kinesthetic.** Kinesthetic learners learn best by *doing*. (*Kinesthetic* means *feeling the movements of the body*.) They like to keep their hands and bodies moving. If you would draw a map or copy down directions, you are probably a kinesthetic learner. You will benefit from interacting with the material you are studying. Underline, take notes, and create note cards. Recopying material will help you remember it.
- **Sequential.** Sequential learners learn best by *organizing*. If you would create a step-by-step list of driving directions, you are probably a sequential learner. You may learn better by creating outlines and grouping ideas together into categories.

Think carefully about how you learn. Which is your dominant learning style? Keep it in mind as you read about learning strategies in Chapter 3.

Whatever your general learning style, most of us learn to speak and understand language best by *listening*. If English is not your native language and you need to improve your reading and writing skills, take some time to build your listening skills, too. The more familiar you become with the sounds and rhythms of the language, the more quickly you will learn. Spend as much time as possible around people speaking English. Go to places where you will see and hear English, such as to plays or to the movies. The more you hear the language, the more comfortable you will be thinking in that language. This will make it easier to understand written English and to write effectively.

Of course, the best thing you can do to improve your English writing and comprehension skills is to *read*. Read as much as you can in English to learn the structure and style of the language. Rent movies based on novels. Watch the film to build your listening skills, and then read the book to improve your reading comprehension and writing skills. Good novel/movie combinations to try are those by John Grisham, including:

A Time to Kill
The Client
The Firm
The Pelican Brief

Of course, there's more to movie adaptations than legal thrillers. Here are some more good choices, from classics to contemporary, from American to world literature:

Angela's Ashes by Frank McCourt
The Cider House Rules by John Irving
The Color Purple by Alice Walker
The Commitments by Roddy Doyle
The Count of Monte Cristo by Alexander Dumas
Doctor Zhivago by Boris Leonidovich Pasternak
Gone With the Wind by Margaret Mitchell
The Joy Luck Club by Amy Tan
The Shipping News by E. Annie Proulx
Snow Falling on Cedars by David Guterson
To Kill a Mockingbird by Harper Lee

You can also read English versions of books that you have already read in your native language. The plot and characters will already be familiar to you, so you will be able to understand more as you read.

▶ Creating a Study Plan

Sometimes, we put off work because the task just seems too big to handle. But you can make any task manageable by creating a project plan. Follow these four steps to create a successful study plan for the GED:

1. **Get the correct information.** Your first step is to find as much as you can about the exams. Get all the details about the GED. Contact your local testing center to find out:

- specific state eligibility requirements (make sure you are eligible to take the exams)
- when the exams will be offered
- where they will be held
- what you need to do to register
- when you need to register
- how much the exams cost
- if you must take all the exams at once or if you can take individual exams

In addition to these administrative matters, you need to learn as much as possible about the exams. What exactly will be tested on the exams? What subjects? What kinds of questions? Chapter 1 provides general information about the basic structure of the GED exams. Parts III–VII each begin with a summary of the content covered on each exam and the type of questions you will be asked on the exams. Be sure to read these sections carefully.

2. **Find out what you already know and what you need to learn.** To create an effective study plan, you need to have a good sense of exactly what you need to study. Chances are, you already know much of the material well. Some of it you may only need to review. And some of it you may need to study in detail. Take the diagnostic exams in Part II

to get an idea of how you would do on the exam. How did you score? What do you seem to know well? What do you need to review? What do you need to study in detail?

3. **Set a time frame.** Once you have a good sense of how much studying is ahead, create a detailed study schedule. Use a calendar to set specific deadlines. If deadlines make you nervous, give yourself plenty of time for each task. Otherwise, you might have trouble keeping calm and staying on track.

To create a good schedule, break your studying into small tasks that will get you to your learning goals. A study plan that says "Learn everything by May 1" isn't going to be helpful. However, a study plan that sets dates for learning specific material in March and April *will* enable you to learn everything by May 1. For example, take a look at the following five-month study plan created by a GED candidate who needs to focus on all GED exams:

Week 1	Take all subject diagnostic exams.
Week 2	Study math. Focus: measurement and number relations.
Week 3	Study math. Focus: algebra, geometry, word problems, and data analysis.
Week 4	Take first GED math practice exam. Review errors.
Week 5	Study science. Focus: unifying concepts and processes, science as inquiry, life sciences, and physical sciences.
Week 6	Study science. Focus: science and technology, personal and social perspectives in science, history and nature of science, and Earth and space sciences.
Week 7	Take first GED science practice exam. Review errors.
Week 8	Study social studies. Focus: civics and government and economics.
Week 9	Study social studies. Focus: world history and geography.

Week 10	Take first GED social studies practice exam. Review errors.
Week 11	Study grammar/writing. Focus: sentence structure, usage, mechanics, and organization.
Week 12	Study grammar/writing. Focus: writing an effective essay.
Week 13	Take first GED writing practice exam. Review errors.
Week 14	Study reading. Focus: reading comprehension strategies and reading literature.
Week 15	Study reading. Focus: fiction, nonfiction, and poetry.
Week 16	Take first GED reading practice exam. Review errors.
Week 17	Review math, science, and social studies.
Week 18	Review writing and reading.
Week 19	Take second practice exams for all subjects. Review errors.

Notice how this schedule builds in time to review *each subject* and establishes different topics to focus on each week.

As you set your deadlines, think carefully about your day-to-day schedule. How much time can you spend on studying each week? Exactly when can you fit in the time to study? Be sure to be realistic about how much time you have and how much you can accomplish. Give yourself the study time you need to succeed.

4. **Stick to your plan.** Make sure you have your plan written on paper and post your plan where you can see it. (Don't just keep it in your head!) Look at it regularly so you can remember what and when to study. Checking your plan regularly can also help you see how much progress you have made along the way.

It's very important that you *don't give up* if you fall behind. Unexpected events may interrupt your plans. You may have to put in extra time at work, you may have to deal with a problem at home, or you may even come down with the flu. Or, it might

By creating a study plan, you can avoid **cramming**—trying to learn everything at the last minute. Cramming can make you very nervous, and for good reason. If you wait until a few days before the tests, chances are, you won't be able to learn everything. And if you stay up all night trying to get everything done, you will be too tired to study effectively.

Create a study plan that spaces out your learning goals. Give yourself plenty of time to learn and time to review. Learn at a pace that is comfortable for you.

just take you longer to get through a task than you planned. That's okay. Stick to your schedule as much as possible, but remember that sometimes, "life gets in the way."

For example, if you have a family problem that's keeping you from concentrating, you may need to postpone your studies to resolve that problem. And that's okay—as long as you reschedule your study time. Better to study later when you can concentrate than to waste time "studying" when you are unable to focus.

So if you miss one of your deadlines, don't despair. Instead, just pick up where you left off. Try to squeeze in a little extra time in the next few weeks to catch up. If that doesn't seem possible, simply adjust your schedule. Change your deadlines so that they are more realistic. Just be sure you still have enough time to finish everything before the exams.

▶ How Do You Know What You Know?

One of the keys to successful studying is knowing what you know, and knowing what you don't know. Practice tests are one good way to measure this, but there are also other ways.

One of the best ways to measure how well you know something is to see how well you can explain it to someone else. If you *really* know the material, you should be able to help someone else understand it. Use your learning style to explain it. For example, if you are an auditory learner, talk it out. If you are a visual learner, create diagrams and tables to demonstrate your knowledge. Rewrite your notes or make up your own quizzes with questions and answers like those on the exam. Provide an explanation along with the correct answer.

How do you know what you *don't* know? If you feel uncertain or uncomfortable during a practice test or when you have difficulty explaining it to someone else, you probably need to study more. Write down all of your questions and uncertainties. If you write down what you don't know, you can focus on searching for answers. When you get the answers, you can write them out next to the question and review them periodically. Notice how many questions you answer along the way—you will be able to see yourself making steady progress.

If you are avoiding certain topics, it's a good sign that you don't know those topics well enough for the exams. Make up your mind to tackle these areas at your next study session. Don't procrastinate!

Sometimes, it's just plain hard to get started on a big project. If you are having trouble getting going, start with an easy task, such as creating flash cards for review. That way, you will be able to accomplish something quickly and easily. And that will motivate you to move on to harder tasks. Or, try starting your study session by reviewing or copying your notes from last session. This way, you will better remember what you have already learned while you ease into study mode.

3 ▶ Learning Strategies

Once you have created an effective learning environment and a detailed study plan, you can begin to review the material that will be tested on the GED. But how can you remember all that you need to know? This chapter reviews several key learning strategies, including effective note-taking, outlining, and memory techniques.

HOW SUCCESSFUL YOU are at studying usually has less to do with how much you know and how much you study than with *how* you study. That's because some study techniques are much more effective than others. You can spend hours and hours doing practice tests, but if you don't carefully review your answers, much of your time will be wasted. You need to learn from your mistakes and study what you don't know. The best method is to use several of the following proven study techniques. They can help you make the most of your learning style and store information in your long-term memory.

▶ Asking Questions

Asking questions is a powerful study strategy because it forces you to get actively involved in the material you want to learn. That, in turn, will help you better understand and remember the material. And there's another important benefit—asking and answering your own questions will help you be comfortable with the format of the exam.

For example, when you are reading a short story, you can ask yourself questions like those you might see on the GED, such as:

1. What is the theme of the story?
2. What is the narrator's attitude toward her mother?

3. Why is the setting important?
4. Which adjective best describes the narrator?
5. What is the narrator's main motivation for her actions?
6. What is the significance of the empty basket?
7. What is the narrator's relationship to the woman in the window?

Similarly, if you are analyzing a diagram of the human ear, you can ask:

1. What is immediately below the auditory tube?
2. What is the scientific name of the ear drum?
3. Where is the incus located?
4. What parts of the ear must a sound wave travel through to get to the pharynx?
5. How many bones are in the middle ear cavity?

Of course, you may not be able to answer all of your questions right away. You may need to do some extra work to find the answer.

▶ Highlighting and Underlining

Here's a good habit to get into: Whenever you read, have a pen, pencil, or highlighter in your hand. That way, as you read, you can mark the words and ideas that are most important to learn or remember. Highlighting and underlining help make key ideas stand out. Important information is then easy to find when you need to take notes or review.

The key to effective highlighting or underlining is to *be selective*. Don't highlight or underline everything. If you highlight every other sentence, nothing will stand out for you on the page. Highlight only the key words and ideas.

But how do you know what you should highlight or underline? As you study for the GED, you should highlight or underline:

- words that are defined in the text
- main ideas
- key details that support or explain main ideas
- words, grammar rules, and other items that you need to remember
- ideas or concepts that are new to you

- unfamiliar vocabulary words and idiomatic expressions (so that you can look them up and learn their meaning)

▶ Taking Notes

Taking notes is a terrific study strategy. It helps you understand, organize, and remember information. The secret to taking good notes is knowing what you should write down. As with highlighting, the key is to be selective. Take notes about the same things you would underline, especially main ideas, rules, and other items you need to learn. Whenever possible, include examples so that you can *see* the concept clearly. For example, below are some notes on the structure of an animal cell:

Animal Cell Structure
Three parts: *plasma membrane, cytoplasm, nucleus.*
Plasma membrane: Isolates cell from the environment, regulates movement of materials in and out of cell, communicates with other cells.
Cytoplasm: Includes water, salts, and enzymes that catalyze reactions. Contains *organelles* such as *mitochondrion*, which capture energy from food molecules.
Nucleus: Includes *nuclear envelope* (isolates nucleus), *nuclear pores* (regulate the passage of materials, including water, ions, proteins, and RNA; controls flow of information to and from DNA), *chromatin* (DNA and associated proteins) and, at innermost core, *nucleolus* (site of ribosome assembly).

▶ Making Notes

Making notes is often as important as *taking* notes. Making notes means that you *respond* to what you read. There are several ways you can respond (talk back) to the text:

- **Write questions.** If you come across something you don't understand, write a question. *What does this mean? Why did the author choose this word? Why is this the best title? How is this different from previous examples? Why is the information in this* *chart important? What was the impact of this discovery?* Then, answer all your questions.

- **Make connections.** Any time you make connections between ideas, you improve your chances of remembering that material. For example, if you are studying the Industrial Revolution, you might make connections between a number of key inventions by imagining how cotton might move from a farm in Georgia to a shirt in a British store: *cotton gin, steamboat, steam engine.*

  Similarly, when you are reviewing the Constitution, you might make a connection between the Nineteenth Amendment (granting women the right to vote) and your only female cousin's age (she's 19). (If you then picture your 19-year-old cousin in a 1920s flapper outfit in a voting booth, you'll have a much better chance of remembering which amendment granted women the right to vote.)

- **Write your reactions.** Your reactions work much like connections, and they can help you remember information. For example, if you are reviewing the Constitution, you might note the following:

  Why did it take 50 years after the Fifteenth Amendment, granting people of all races the right to vote, for the Nineteenth Amendment, granting both genders the right to vote, to be passed?

▶ Outlining and Mapping Information

Outlines are great tools, especially for sequential learners. They help you focus on what's most important by making it easier to review key ideas and see relationships among those ideas. With an outline, you can see how supporting information is related to main ideas.

The basic outline structure is this:

I. Topic
  A. Main idea
    1. Major supporting idea
      a. Minor supporting idea
        i. Additional supportive information

Outlines can have many layers and variations, but this is the general form. Here are the notes for animal cell structure presented in outline format:

Animal Cell Structure

I. Three parts: *plasma membrane, cytoplasm, nucleus*
  A. *Plasma membrane*
    1. Isolates cell from the environment
    2. Regulates movement of materials in and out of cell
    3. Communicates with other cells
  B. *Cytoplasm*
    1. Includes water, salts, and enzymes that catalyze reactions
    2. Contains *organelles*
      a. Example: *mitochondrion*, which captures energy from food molecules
  C. *Nucleus*
    1. *Nuclear Envelope*
      a. Isolates nucleus (like plasma membrane)
    2. *Nuclear Pores*
      a. Regulate the passage of materials into the nucleus
        i. Water, ions, proteins, and RNA
      b. Controls flow of information to and from DNA
    3. *Chromatin*
      a. Clusters of DNA and associated proteins
    4. *Nucleolus*
      a. Site of ribosome assembly

Mapping information is similar to making an outline. The difference is that maps are less structured. You don't have to organize ideas from top to bottom. Instead, with a map, the ideas can go all over the page. The key is that you still show how the ideas are related. The next page shows the same example in a map instead of an outline.

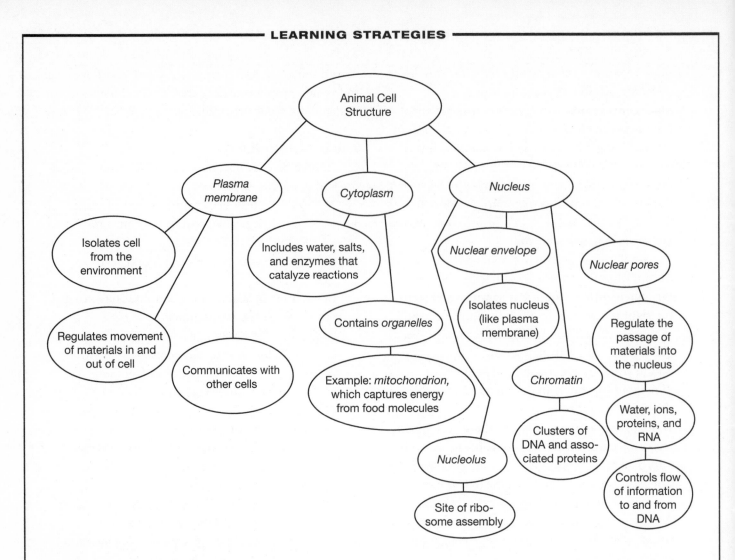

► Making Flash Cards

Flash cards are a simple but very effective study tool. First, buy or cut out small pieces of paper (3 × 5 index cards work well). On one side, put a question or word you need to learn. On the back, put the answer. You can use different colors and pictures, especially if you are a visual learner.

For example, if you are studying the history of life on Earth, you could make flash cards like the following:

Front of Card	Back of Card
Precambrian Age	4,600–590 million years ago 3,500 million years ago: origin of first living cells
Paleozoic Age	590–248 million years ago Algae, invertebrates, fish, fungi, plants, insects, first amphibians and reptiles, conifers

Mesozoic Age	248–65 million years ago Origin of mammals and dinosaurs, birds, flowering plants; separation of continents
Cenozoic Age	65 million years ago–present Flourishing of birds, mammals, insects, flowering plants Evolution of *Homo sapiens*

▶ Memorizing vs. Remembering

Imagine that you need to memorize a list of homonyms for the GED. You go over and over the list until you are sure you know them. Then you take a practice exam. Suddenly, you can't seem to remember the list. The words are used in context (within sentences), and they are not in the order you memorized. You fail the practice exam.

What happened? The problem is not that you didn't study. The problem is that you didn't study wisely. You focused on *memorizing*, not *remembering*. You didn't learn the words in *context*. You didn't *use* the words or *practice* them by writing sample sentences with the correct spelling. That's why, on the exam, you couldn't remember them.

It's true that "repetition is the key to mastery." Try repeating a new phone number over and over, for example. Eventually you will remember it. But it may only stay in your *short-term* memory. In a few days (or maybe even a few hours), you are likely to forget the number. You need to *use it* to really learn it and store the information in your *long-term* memory.

While there are some tricks you can use to help remember things in the short term, your best bet is to *use* what you are learning as much as possible and as soon as possible. For example, you can use new vocabulary words or idioms in your conversations throughout the day; you can also teach the new word or idiom to others. Likewise, you can share something you learn about world history or life sciences with a friend.

Here are some general strategies to help you remember information as you prepare for the GED:

- **Learn information in small chunks.** Our brains process small chunks of information better than large ones. If you have a list of 20 scientific vocabulary words, for example, break that list into four lists of five words each.
- **Spread out your memory work.** Don't try to remember too much at one time. For example, if you break up those 20 words into four lists, don't try to do all four lists, one after another. Instead, try studying one list each day in several short, spaced-out sessions. For example, spend 20 minutes in the morning studying the new words. Review the words again for 15 minutes at lunchtime. Take another 15 minutes while you are waiting at the bus stop on your way home. Add another ten-minute review before bed. This kind of *distributed practice* is very effective. It's also a sneaky way to add more study time to your schedule. And, it provides lots of repetition without tiring your brain.
- **Make connections.** You learn best when you make connections to things you already know. (See "Make connections" on page 17.)
- **Use visual aids,** especially if you are a visual learner. Help yourself "see" in your mind what you need to learn. For example, if you are studying the Great Depression, you can imagine yourself living in that time period. This can help you remember many facts about the Great Depression.
- **Use your voice,** especially if you are an auditory learner. Say aloud what you need to learn; you can even sing it if you like, especially if you can make a rhyme (for example, you might say "speak, spoke,

spoken; break, broke, broken" to memorize some irregular verbs). Anytime you are learning grammar and structure, say a sample sentence aloud several times. Try different variations, too. For example, if you are trying to memorize the irregular past tense of a verb like *tear*, you can say a sentence like:

> *My dress has a tear. It's torn.*
> *Her dress has a tear, too. It's also torn.*

Thinking of the sentence helps; *hearing* it aloud helps even more. And if you also *write it down*, you take an extra step toward sealing the material in your memory.

- **Use *mnemonics*.** Mnemonics are tricks to help you remember information. The most common trick is to create an *acronym*. Say you need to remember a list of words. Take the first letter from each word, then make a word from those letters. For example, imagine you want to remember the three main civilizations of the early Americas: the Aztecs, the Incas, and the Mayans. You could use the acronym AIM to help you remember.

Another trick is to make a sentence using the first letter (or first two letters) of each word you want to remember. For example, if you want to memorize the order of the major historical ages—Precambrian, Paleozoic, Mesozoic, and Cenozoic—you could write the following sentence:

> *I promised Patty my car.*

Of course, the sillier the better (the easier to remember). So you might try something crazy, like:

> *Prancing pandas make cookies.*

There are all kinds of other mnemonic tricks you can make up on your own. For example, to distinguish between the homonyms *where* and *wear*, you might remember the sentence:

> *You wear an earring in your ear.*

If you remember that *wear* includes the word *ear*, you can remember which meaning goes with which word.

Sleep on It

A rested and relaxed brain learns information best. Whenever possible, study right before you go to sleep or first thing after you wake up. Try not to do anything else in between. If you study for an hour and then watch TV for an hour before bed, you won't remember as much as if you studied for an hour and then went right to bed. Right before and after sleep, you are usually in your most relaxed state—and that makes it easier for you to learn.

CHAPTER

4 ▶ Test-Taking Strategies

You have reviewed techniques to help you study effectively. Now it's time to review techniques that will help you perform well on an exam. This chapter covers several key strategies for taking standardized tests like the GED. You will learn how to prevent and treat test anxiety, how to approach multiple-choice questions, and how to keep yourself healthy for the exams.

KNOWING THE MATERIAL you will be tested on improves your chances of succeeding. But it doesn't guarantee that you will do your best on the test. That's because the GED doesn't *just* test your knowledge of science, math, social studies, reading, and writing in the English language. Like all standardized tests, it also measures your test-taking skills.

▶ Learn about the Exams

One sure way to increase your chances of test success is to find out as much as you can about the exams. If you don't know what to expect, you won't know how to study. It is likely that you will be extra anxious about the exams, too. The more you know about the exams you are going to take, the better you can prepare—and the more relaxed you will be on test day.

You already know that the GED has five separate exams: *Math; Science; Social Studies; Language Arts, Writing;* and *Language Arts, Reading.* You know that most of the questions are multiple choice and that you'll have to write an essay. You know how much time you have to complete each section. But until you look at actual sample questions, you still don't *really* know what to expect. For example, on the Language Arts, Reading Exam, what kind of passages will you read? What kind of questions will you be asked about those passages?

Getting sample tests and working with skill builders like this book can help you in many ways. You will get used to the kind of questions you will be asked and the level of difficulty of those questions. You will also become familiar with the format and comfortable with the length of the exam.

▶ Handling Test Stress

Test anxiety is like the common cold. Most people suffer from it periodically. It won't kill you, but it can make your life miserable for several days.

Like a cold, test anxiety can be mild or severe. You may just feel an underlying nervousness about the upcoming exam, or you may be nearly paralyzed with worry, especially if there's a lot riding on the exams. Whatever the case, if you have test anxiety, you need to deal with it. Fortunately, there are many strategies to help prevent and treat test anxiety.

Prevention

The best "cure" for test anxiety is to *prevent* it from happening in the first place. Test anxiety is often caused by a lack of preparation. If you learn all you can about the test and create and follow a study plan, you should be in good shape when it comes to exam time. Here are some other, more general strategies:

- **Establish and stick to routine.** Routines help us feel more comfortable and in control. Whenever possible, study at the same time and in the same place. Make your test preparation a habit that's hard to break. Studying for the GED will become easier as it becomes routine. You will be more likely to avoid distractions, and others will know not to disturb you during your GED study time. Set routines for other aspects of your life, too, such as exercise and paying the bills.
- **Keep your general stress level low.** If there are a lot of other stresses in your life, chances are, a big test will make those other stresses seem more difficult to manage. Remember to keep things in perspective. If something is beyond your control, don't waste your energy worrying about it. Instead, think of how you can handle what *is* in your control.

- **Stay confident.** Remind yourself that you are smart and capable. You can take these exams—and you can do well on them. Remember, you know more today than you did yesterday.
- **Stay healthy.** When your body is run down or ill, your brainpower will suffer, too. And you are much more likely to be overtaken by worries. Take care of yourself throughout the test-preparation process. (See more information on page 23–24.)

Treatment

If it's too late to prevent test anxiety, don't panic. You can still treat it effectively. Here are some strategies to help reduce test stress:

- **Face your fears.** Admit that you are worried about the exam and examine the reasons why. Your fears won't change the fact that you have to take it, but they can paralyze you and keep you from studying and doing well on the exam. Acknowledge your fears, put them in perspective, and refuse to let your fears hurt you.

  One very helpful strategy is to write your fears down. When you put your worries on paper, they often seem more manageable than when they are bouncing around in your brain and keeping you up at night. Once you write down your fears, you can then brainstorm solutions. For example, imagine you are worried about not being able to find enough time to get your work done and finish studying. Once you put this fear down on paper, you can begin to figure out how to squeeze in the hours you will need to get everything done. And you will feel more in control.
- **Keep things in perspective.** Yes, the GED is a big deal. But even if you don't pass the exams, is it the end of the world? Will your family stop loving you? Will you be less of a person? Of course not. And you can always take the exams again later.

  Perspective is very important to performance. Of course you should be serious about succeeding. But don't lose sight of other important aspects of your life.
- **Be sufficiently prepared.** Anxiety often comes from feeling insecure in a new situation. But if you prepare well, using this and other books, the GED will not be new to you. And if you follow your

study plan, you will know how to answer the questions you will face on the exams. If you have fallen behind, remember that it's not too late to catch up.

- **Stop making excuses.** Excuses may give you some comfort in the short term, but they don't take away test anxiety—and they won't help you do well on the exams. In fact, excuses often make things worse by making you feel guilty and powerless. Don't let yourself feel like a victim. You may have a lot of things going on in your life and many things may interfere with your studies, but you have the power to choose how you deal with your circumstances.

- **Imagine yourself succeeding.** Highly successful people will often tell you that one of their secrets is *visualization*. In their mind's eyes, they *see* themselves succeeding. They imagine the situations they will face, and they imagine themselves handling those situations beautifully.

  Visualization is a very powerful tool. It's a way of telling yourself that *you believe you can do it.* The power of this kind of belief is staggering. If you believe you can accomplish something, you are far more likely to accomplish it. Likewise, if you believe you *can't* do something, you are far more likely to *fail* to achieve that goal. Positive visualization will make it easier for you to study and manage your entire test-preparation process.

  Anyone can use the power of visualization. Picture yourself sitting calmly through the exam, answering one question after another correctly. See yourself getting excellent test results in the mail. Imagine yourself telling family and friends how well you did on the exams. Picture yourself receiving the college acceptance letter or job offer you desire.

- **Stick to your study plan.** Test anxiety can paralyze you if you let it. And before you know it, you have missed several deadlines on your study plan. Guess what? That will only make your test anxiety worse. As soon as you feel your stomach start to flutter with test anxiety, go back to your study plan. Make an extra effort to stick to your schedule.

▶ Be Healthy

It's difficult to do your best on a test when you are not feeling well. Your mind *and* body need to be in good shape for the exam. If you let your body get run down, you may become ill. That, in turn, will set you back on your study schedule. And that may lead to test anxiety, which can make you feel run down again. This is a downward spiral you need to avoid. If you do feel run down, take a day or two to rest and feel better. Maybe you will be two days behind your study schedule, but when you continue, your studying will be more effective. As long as it's not a constant problem for you and as long as you are not using illness to avoid studying, you will do yourself a favor by resting.

Take good care of yourself throughout the entire test-preparation process and especially in the week before the exam. Here are some specific suggestions for staying healthy:

1. **Get enough rest.** Some of us need eight or more hours of sleep each night. Others are happy with just five or six. You know what your body needs for you to feel clearheaded and energized. Make sleep a priority so that you are able to concentrate on the day of the exams. If you have trouble sleeping, try one of the following strategies:
   - Get extra exercise during the day. A tired body will demand more sleep.
   - Get up and study. If you study in the night when you can't sleep, you can cut out study time from the next day so you can take a nap or get to bed earlier. (Of course, sometimes studying will help you fall asleep in the first place.)
   - Relax with a hot bath, a good book, or sleep-inducing foods. A glass of warm milk, for example, may help you fall back asleep.
   - Do some gentle stretching or seated forward bends. Try to touch your toes with your legs outstretched. This posture stretches tense muscles, improves circulation, and helps relax the whole body. Or, practice a few simple relaxation poses from yoga: child's pose, corpse pose, or cat stretch (see www.yoga.com for details).

- Spend a few minutes deep breathing. Fill your lungs slowly and completely. Hold your breath for a few seconds and then release slowly and completely. You can practice deep breathing any time you need to relax or regain focus.
- Write down your worries. Again, putting your fears on paper can help make them more manageable.

2. **Eat well.** Keeping a healthy diet is often as hard as getting enough rest when you are busy preparing for a test. But how you eat can have a tremendous impact on how you study and how you perform on the exams. You may think you are saving time by eating fast food instead of cooking a healthy meal. But in reality, you are depriving your body of the nutrition it needs to be at its best. You may think that a couple of extra cups of coffee a day are a good thing because you can stay up later and study. But in reality, you are "tricking" your brain into thinking that it's awake and making yourself more dependent on caffeine.

Foods to avoid—especially at test time—include high-sugar, high-calorie, low-nutrition foods, such as doughnuts, chips, and cookies. Instead, find healthy substitutes such as the following:

INSTEAD OF . . .	EAT . . .
doughnuts	low-sugar, multigrain cereal
chips	carrot sticks
cookies	natural granola bar
ice cream	low-fat yogurt
sugary soda	fresh-squeezed fruit juice
giant-sized coffee	green tea

3. **Get exercise.** You hardly have the time to study, so how can you find the time to exercise? As difficult as it may be, it's important to squeeze exercise into your busy schedule. Even light exercise, such as a brisk walk to the store, can dramatically improve your brainpower. For one thing, exercising can help you clear your head, especially if you are preoccupied with many things and need to get focused on your work. For another, if you exercise,

you will have more energy during the day and sleep better at night. That means all your study time will be more productive. In addition, your exercise time can actually double as study time. For example, you can review material while you are riding an exercise bike. You can compose an essay in your head as you race-walk around the park. If you exercise with a friend who is also studying for the GED, you can quiz each other on exam material. And here's another bonus: Exercise helps relieve stress. So, especially if you are dealing with test anxiety, make exercise a priority.

▶ Multiple-Choice Test Strategies

Multiple choice is the most popular question format for standardized tests like the GED and understandably so: Multiple-choice questions are easy and fast to grade. They are also popular because they are generally considered *objective:* They are questions based solely on information and don't allow the test taker to express opinions.

Multiple-choice questions have three parts:

Stem: the question

Options: the answer choices

Distracters: the incorrect answer choices

Here's an example:

Stem: The narrator knew her mother was lying because
Options:
   a. her mother was acting strangely.
   b. what her mother said goes against her mother's character.
   c. her mother was always lying.
   d. she has ESP (extrasensory perception).

In this question, the correct answer is **b.** The other options are all distracters.

Here are some strategies to help you answer multiple-choice questions correctly:

1. **Identify key words in the stem.** These are the words that help you search for the correct answer. For example, in the stem:

   Clinically depressed patients have all of the following symptoms EXCEPT

   the key words are "clinically depressed," "symptoms," and "except." You need to look in the passage for the symptoms of clinical depression. And you need to find the answer that is *not* specifically mentioned in the passage.

2. **Immediately eliminate all answers you know are incorrect.** This will help you find the correct answer. It is an especially important step if you have to guess at the answer.

3. **Beware of distracter techniques.** Test developers will often put in look-alike options, easily confused options, and silly options. For example, in the question about the narrator's mother, choice **a** may be true according to the passage, but it may be that the narrator's mother often acts strangely, or that there's another reason that she is acting in this way. A careful reading of the story would show that what the mother said contradicts her usual values. Choice **d** is the silliest option and is the one you should probably eliminate first.

4. **Read stems carefully** to be sure you understand *exactly* what is being asked. Watch for tricky wording such as "All of the following are true EXCEPT." You will find distracters that are accurate and may sound right but do not apply to that stem. For example, if you don't notice the "except" on the clinical depression question stem, you might choose a distracter that *is* a symptom of clinical depression. The answer would be accurate but wrong because you did not read the question carefully.

5. **Beware of absolutes.** Carefully read any stem that includes words like *always, never, none,* or *all.* An answer may sound perfectly correct and the general principle may be correct. However, it may not be true in all circumstances.

Should You Guess?

If you aren't sure about the answer to a multiple-choice question, should you guess? On the GED, you will not be penalized for any incorrect answers. So YES, you should guess when you do not know the answer. But whenever possible, make it an *educated guess.* Eliminate any answers you know are incorrect. On the GED, multiple-choice questions have five options, only one of which is right. That gives you a 20% chance of guessing correctly.

▶ Almost There: Strategies for the Final Days before the Exams

Your months of preparation will soon pay off. You have worked hard, and the exams are just a week or two away. Here are some tips for making sure things go smoothly in the homestretch.

The week before the exams:
- Be sure you know exactly where you are taking the exams. Get detailed directions. Take a practice drive so you know exactly how long it will take you to get there.
- Review everything you have learned.
- Get quality sleep each night.
- Practice visualization—*see* yourself performing well on the GED.

The day before the exams:
- Get to bed early.
- Get light exercise. Don't work out too hard. You don't want to be sore or physically exhausted the day of the exams.
- Get everything you will need ready: pencils/pens, admission materials/documentation, any mints or snacks you would like to bring along.
- Make a list of everything you need to bring so you don't forget anything in the morning.

The day of the exams:

- Get up early. Make sure you set your alarm. Ask a family member or friend to make sure you are up on time.
- Eat a light, healthy breakfast, such as yogurt and granola or a low-fat, low-sugar cereal and fruit.
- Dress comfortably. Wear layers so that you can take off a shirt or sweater if you are too warm in the test room.
- Don't drastically alter your diet. For example, if you drink coffee every morning, don't skip it—you could get a headache. However, don't go for that second cup or super-sized portion. Too much caffeine can make you jittery during the exams, and you can "crash" when the caffeine wears off.

At the test site:

- Chat with others, but *not* about the exams. That might only make you more nervous.
- Think positively. Remember, you are prepared.
- Avoid squeezing in a last-minute review. Instead, visualize your success and plan your reward for when the tests are over.
- Make sure you read and understand all directions clearly. How should you fill out the answer sheet? What should you do if you want to change an answer? What is the time limit? What if you have technical difficulties during the exams? Don't hesitate to ask questions about *anything* that is unclear.

After the tests:

- Celebrate!

II ▶ Diagnosing Strengths and Weaknesses

OLLOWING ARE diagnostic exams for each of the GED subject areas. The answer key at the end of each exam will help you to identify the areas where you most need work.

Before taking these diagnostics, find a quiet place where you will not be interrupted. You should have several sheets of blank paper and three or four sharpened pencils. (Because the actual GED must be answered in pencil, it is a good idea to accustom yourself to working in pencil rather than pen.)

You may wish to have a clock nearby. If you were taking these diagnostics under actual test conditions, you would be allowed the following time for each exam:

Writing—75 minutes (Part I); 45 minutes (Part II)
Reading—65 minutes
Science—80 minutes
Social Studies—70 minutes
Mathematics—90 minutes

For that reason, you may want to time yourself just to get an idea of how many questions in each subject that you can complete in the allotted time. However, you should continue working until you have completed each exam. Work quickly, carefully, and do not spend a great length of time on any single question. If a certain question gives you difficulty, skip it, making a mark next to it in the margin. You can come back to the question later, if you wish. When taking the actual exam, you would come back to skipped questions, if time permitted. It is good practice, then, to learn how to pace yourself when answering questions.

Multiple-choice questions are followed by five possible answers. Try to work out the answer for yourself before looking at the choices. Otherwise, you may be tricked by answers that appear reasonable, but are actually incorrect.

CHAPTER

5 ▶ GED Language Arts, Writing Diagnostic Exam

▶ Part I

Directions: In each of the following passages, the paragraphs are lettered and the sentences are numbered. Read each passage carefully and then answer the questions that follow.

Please use the following to answer questions 1–7.

A

(1) Wouldn't you love to have a pet tarantula to startle and astonish your friends? (2) Perhaps you would rather amaze people walking down the street with your sleek and adorable pet ferret. (3) A fluffy cat or a playful dog seem a bit mundane compared to an outrageous exotic pet. (4) These exotic pets can be fascinating, but prospective owners must make careful evaluations before taking responsibility for one of these unusual companions.

B

(5) Before deciding to adopt an exotic pet, you should make sure that your pet will be legal. (6) Investigate the local state and national laws that prohibit or limit owning specific species. (7) Once you are sure your pet would be legal, you must also consider whether or not you have provided for all of the pet's needs.

1. Sentence 1: Wouldn't you love to have a pet tarantula to startle and astonish your friends?

Which revision should be made to the placement of sentence 1?

a. Move sentence 1 to follow sentence 2.
b. Move sentence 1 to the end of paragraph A.
c. Move sentence 1 to the beginning of paragraph B.
d. Remove sentence 1.
e. No correction is necessary.

2. Sentence 2: Perhaps you would rather amaze <u>people walking down</u> the street with your sleek and adorable pet ferret.

Which of the following is the best way to write the underlined portion of this sentence? If the original is the best way, choose option **a**.

a. people walking down
b. people, walking down
c. people who are walking down
d. people instead of walking down
e. people by walking down

3. Sentence 3: A fluffy cat or a playful dog seem a bit mundane compared to an outrageous exotic pet.

What correction should be made to this sentence?

a. Insert a comma after <u>cat</u>.
b. Change <u>seem</u> to <u>seems</u>.
c. Insert a comma after <u>dog</u>.
d. Insert a comma after <u>mundane</u>.
e. No correction is necessary.

4. Sentence 4: These exotic pets can be <u>fascinating, but prospective owners</u> must make careful evaluations before taking responsibility for one of these unusual companions.

Which of the following is the best way to write the underlined portion of this sentence? If the original is the best way, choose option **a**.

a. fascinating, but prospective owners
b. fascinating but perspective owners
c. fascinating. But prospective owners
d. fascinating; But perspective owners
e. fascinating; but prospective owners

5. Sentence 5: Before deciding to adopt an exotic pet, you should make sure that your pet will be legal.

If you rewrote sentence 5 beginning with <u>You should make sure that your pet will be legal</u> the next word should be

a. adopt.
b. pet.
c. when.
d. after.
e. before.

6. Sentence 6: Investigate the <u>local state and national laws</u> that prohibit or limit owning specific species.

Which of the following is the best way to write the underlined portion of this sentence? If the original is the best way, choose option **a**.

a. local state and national laws
b. local, state, and national laws
c. local state, and national laws
d. local state and national, laws
e. local, state, and national, laws

7. Sentence 7: Once you are sure your pet would be legal, you must also consider whether or not you have provided for all of the pet's needs.

What correction should be made to this sentence?

a. Change <u>would be</u> to <u>was</u>.
b. Change <u>whether</u> or <u>weather</u>.
c. Change <u>pet's</u> to <u>pets</u>.
d. Change <u>have provided</u> to <u>can provide</u>.
e. No correction is necessary.

Please use the following to answer questions 8–14.

A

(1) When the Digital Video Disc (DVD) format was launched in April of 1997, some experts predict a rapid failure. (2) These analysts thought that consumers which were used to VHS recordings would be unwilling to shift to another format, no matter how superior. (3) The DVD, however, has had one of histories most successful product introductions. (4) Sales statistics indicate that viewers have been favorable impressed by the high quality of the DVD's digital image. (5) Consumers bought 315,000

DVD players the first year they were on the market; one million players were sold the following year. (6) Today, manufacturers have sold more than 17 million players and predicted that the market for these devices will only increase. (7) The power, precision, and capacity of this flourishing technology are now being praised by the skeptics who once anticipated a format flop.

8. Sentence 1: When the Digital Video Disc (DVD) format was launched in April of 1997, some experts predict a rapid failure.

What correction should be made to this sentence?

a. Change <u>April</u> to <u>april</u>.
b. Remove the comma after <u>1997</u>.
c. Change <u>experts</u> to <u>expert's</u>.
d. Change <u>predict</u> to <u>predicted</u>.
e. No correction is necessary.

9. Sentence 2: These analysts thought that <u>consumers which were used to</u> VHS recordings would be unwilling to shift to another format, no matter how superior.

Which of the following is the best way to write the underlined portion of this sentence? If the original is the best way, choose option **a.**

a. consumers which were used to
b. consumers, which were used to
c. consumers who were used to
d. consumers often used to
e. consumers being used to

10. Sentence 3: The DVD, however, has had one of histories most successful product introductions.

What correction should be made to this sentence?

a. Remove the comma after <u>DVD</u>.
b. Change <u>has had</u> to <u>has</u>.
c. Change <u>histories</u> to <u>history's</u>.
d. Change <u>most successful</u> to <u>more successfully</u>.
e. Change <u>introductions</u> to <u>introduction</u>.

11. Sentence 4: Sales statistics indicate that viewers have been favorable impressed by the high quality of the DVD's digital image.

What correction should be made to this sentence?

a. Change <u>indicate</u> to <u>indicates</u>.
b. Change <u>indicate</u> to <u>would have indicated</u>.
c. Change <u>favorable</u> to <u>favorably</u>.
d. Change <u>DVD's</u> to <u>DVDs</u>.
e. No correction is necessary.

12. Sentence 5: Consumers bought 315,000 DVD players the first year they were on the <u>market; one million players</u> were sold the following year.

Which of the following is the best way to write the underlined portion of this sentence? If the original is the best way, choose option **a.**

a. market; one million players
b. market, one million players
c. market one million players
d. market because one million players
e. market and one million players

13. Sentence 6: Today, manufacturers have sold more than 17 million <u>players and predicted</u> that the market for these devices will only increase.

Which of the following is the best way to write the underlined portion of this sentence? If the original is the best way, choose option **a.**

a. players and predicted
b. players and predict
c. players; predicted
d. players; predict
e. players and predicts

14. Sentence 7: The power, precision, and capacity of this flourishing technology are now being praised by the skeptics who once anticipated a format flop.

If you rewrote sentence 7 beginning with <u>Skeptics who once anticipated a format flop</u>, the next words should be

a. won't praise.
b. should praise.
c. might praise.
d. have praised.
e. now praise.

Please use the following to answer questions 15–21.

A

(1) Whether you are evaluating an entire team or just one speaker, you must remain impartial. (2) To be a good debate judge, there is one thing you must do. (3) Content refers to the logic of the arguments, the effectiveness of any factual support, and the thoroughness of the rebuttals. (4) Although you may have strong feelings about the issues you should be careful not to let your opinions interfere with your assessment.

B

(5) As you listen to the debate, you may find it helpful to consider the two attributes of delivery and content. (6) Delivery refers to the speakers style and clarity. (7) Think about the speaker's use of wit, repetition, and other rhetorical devices, to grab and hold the audience's attention.

15. Sentence 1: Whether you are evaluating an entire team or just one speaker, you must remain impartial.

If you rewrote sentence 1 beginning with <u>You must remain impartial</u> the next word should be
   a. whenever.
   b. whether.
   c. because.
   d. evaluating.
   e. and.

16. Sentence 2: To be a good debate judge, there is one thing you must do.

Which revision should be made to the placement of sentence 2?
   a. Move sentence 2 to follow sentence 3.
   b. Move sentence 2 to the beginning of paragraph A.
   c. Move sentence 2 to the beginning of paragraph B.
   d. Move sentence 2 to follow sentence 4.
   e. No revision is necessary.

17. Sentence 3: Content refers to the logic of the arguments, the effectiveness of any factual support, and the thoroughness of the rebuttals.

Which revision should be made to the placement of sentence 3?
   a. Move sentence 3 to follow sentence 1.
   b. Move sentence 3 to the end of paragraph A.
   c. Move sentence 3 to follow sentence 6.
   d. Move sentence 3 to the end of paragraph B.
   e. No revision is necessary.

18. Sentence 4: Although you may have strong feelings about the issues you should be careful not to let your opinions interfere with your assessment.

What correction should be made to this sentence?
   a. Insert a semicolon after <u>issues</u>.
   b. Insert a comma after <u>issues</u>.
   c. Insert a comma after <u>feelings</u>.
   d. Change the period to a question mark.
   e. No correction is necessary.

19. Sentence 5: As you listen to the debate, you may find it helpful to consider the two attributes of delivery and content.

What correction should be made to this sentence?
   a. Remove the comma after <u>debate</u>.
   b. Change the comma after <u>debate</u> to a semicolon.
   c. Insert a comma after <u>attributes</u>.
   d. Insert a comma after <u>delivery</u>.
   e. No correction is necessary.

20. Sentence 6: Delivery refers to the <u>speakers style and clarity</u>.

Which of the following is the best way to write the underlined portion of this sentence? If the original is the best way, choose option **a.**
   a. speakers style and clarity
   b. speakers, style, and clarity
   c. speakers style clarity
   d. speakers's style and clarity
   e. speaker's style and clarity

21. Sentence 7: Think about the speaker's use of wit, repetition, and other rhetorical devices, to grab and hold the audience's attention.

What correction should be made to this sentence?
a. Remove the comma after <u>repetition</u>.
b. Remove the comma after <u>devices</u>.
c. Change <u>audience's</u> to <u>audiences</u>.
d. Change <u>audience's</u> to <u>audiences'</u>.
e. No correction is necessary.

Please use the following to answer questions 22–29.

MEMO
To: All Employees of InterCorp
From: The Shipping Department

A

(1) This memo outlines the new shipping policies which will take affect on Monday, April 12. (2) Consult the following guidelines for interoffice, overnight, and express mail.

B

(3) Interoffice mail will now be delivered three times daily, rather then twice a day. (4) Please clearly identify the recipient's name and office location and use the yellow address labels or envelopes for interoffice mail.

C

(5) Packages for overnight delivery must be received by the shipping Department no later than 5:00 P.M. (6) Allow at least one additional hour if you are dropping off items that need to be packed. Such as books, videotapes, or loose papers. (7) Be sure to fill out the overnight express form complete and accurate.

D

(8) Packages for express mail, that usually arrives in two to five business days, will be mailed the day after they are brought to the shipping department.

22. Sentence 1: This memo outlines the new shipping policies which will take affect on Monday, April 12.

What correction should be made to this sentence?
a. Change <u>outlines</u> to <u>outline</u>.
b. Change <u>affect</u> to <u>effect</u>.
c. Change <u>Monday</u> to <u>monday</u>.
d. Delete the comma after <u>Monday</u>.
e. No correction is necessary.

23. Sentence 2: Consult the following guidelines for <u>interoffice, overnight, and express mail.</u>

Which of the following is the best way to write the underlined portion of this sentence? If the original is the best way, choose option **a.**
a. interoffice, overnight, and express mail.
b. interoffice overnight, and express mail.
c. interoffice, overnight, and express, mail.
d. interoffice overnight and express mail.
e. interoffice; overnight; and express mail.

24. Sentence 3: Interoffice mail will now be delivered three times daily, rather then twice a day.

What correction should be made to this sentence?
a. Change <u>be</u> to <u>have been</u>.
b. Change <u>delivered</u> to <u>deliver</u>.
c. Remove the comma after <u>daily</u>.
d. Change <u>then</u> to <u>than</u>.
e. No correction is necessary.

25. Sentence 4: Please clearly identify the recipient's name and office location and use the yellow address labels or envelopes for interoffice mail.

If you rewrote sentence 4 beginning with <u>Please use the yellow address labels or envelopes for interoffice mail</u>, the next words should be
a. and clearly.
b. but clearly.
c. because clearly.
d. not clearly.
e. or clearly.

26. Sentence 5: Packages for overnight delivery must be received by the shipping Department no later than 5:00 P.M.

What correction should be made to this sentence?

a. Change Packages to Package.
b. Change Department to department.
c. Insert a comma after received.
d. Insert a comma after Department.
e. No correction is necessary.

27. Sentence 6: Allow at least one additional hour if you are dropping off items that need to be packed. Such as books, videotapes, or loose papers.

Which of the following is the best way to write the underlined portion of this sentence? If the original is the best way, choose option **a.**

a. packed. Such as books
b. packed such as books
c. packed. Books
d. packed; such as books
e. packed, such as books

28. Sentence 7: Be sure to fill out the overnight express form complete and accurate.

Which of the following is the best way to write the underlined portion of this sentence? If the original is the best way, choose option **a.**

a. form complete and accurate.
b. form, complete and accurate.
c. form completely and accurately.
d. form complete and accurately.
e. form, be complete and accurate.

29. Sentence 8: Packages for express mail, that usually arrive in two to five business days, will be mailed the day after they are brought to the shipping department.

What correction should be made to this sentence?

a. Change that to which.
b. Change arrive to arrives.
c. Change days to day's.
d. Remove the comma after mail.
e. No correction is necessary.

Please use the following to answer questions 30–36.

A

(1) Of the two types of eclipse, the most common is the lunar eclipse, which occurs when a full moon passes through Earth's shadow. (2) The disc-shaped moon slowly disappears completely or turns a coppery red color. (3) Solar and lunar eclipses both occur from time to time.

B

(4) During a solar eclipse, the moon passes between the Earth and Sun. (5) As the moon moves into alignment, it blocks the light from the Sun creating an eerie darkness. (6) When the moon is perfectly in position, the Sun's light is visible as a ring, or corona, around the dark disc of the moon. (7) A lunar eclipse can be viewed from anywhere on the nighttime half of Earth, a solar eclipse can only be viewed from a zone that is only about 200 miles wide and covers about one-half of a percent of Earth's total area.

30. Sentence 1: Of the two types of eclipse, the most common is the lunar eclipse, which occurs when a full moon passes through Earth's shadow.

What correction should be made to this sentence?

a. Change most to more.
b. Change occurs to occur.
c. Change which to that.
d. Change Earth's to Earths'.
e. No correction is necessary.

31. Sentence 2: The disc-shaped moon slowly disappears completely or turns a coppery red color.

If you rewrote sentence 2, beginning with The disc-shaped moon slowly turns a coppery red color, the next word should be

a. and.
b. but.
c. when.
d. because.
e. or.

32. Which revision would improve the effectiveness of paragraph A?
a. Remove sentence 1.
b. Move sentence 2 to the beginning of the paragraph.
c. Remove sentence 2.
d. Move sentence 3 to the beginning of the paragraph.
e. No revision is necessary.

33. Sentence 4: During a solar eclipse, the moon passes between the Earth and Sun.
What correction should be made to this sentence?
a. Change the comma after <u>eclipse</u> to a semicolon.
b. Change <u>passes</u> to <u>pass</u>.
c. Insert a comma after <u>passes</u>.
d. Insert a comma after <u>Earth</u>.
e. No correction is necessary.

34. Sentence 5: As the moon moves into alignment, it blocks the light from <u>the Sun creating</u> an eerie darkness.
Which of the following is the best way to write the underlined portion of this sentence? If the original is the best way, choose option **a.**
a. the Sun creating
b. the Sun. Creating
c. the Sun and creates
d. the Sun; creating
e. the Sun which creates

35. Sentence 6: When the moon is perfectly in position, the Sun's light is visible as a ring, or corona, around the dark disc of the moon.
What correction should be made to this sentence?
a. Remove the comma after <u>position</u>.
b. Change <u>Sun's</u> to <u>Suns'</u>.
c. Remove the comma after <u>ring</u>.
d. Remove the comma after <u>corona</u>.
e. No correction is necessary.

36. Sentence 7: A lunar eclipse can be viewed from anywhere on the nighttime half of <u>Earth, a solar eclipse</u> can only be viewed from a zone that is only about 200 miles wide and covers about one-half of a percent of Earth's total area.
Which of the following is the best way to write the underlined portion of this sentence? If the original is the best way, choose option **a.**
a. Earth, a solar eclipse
b. Earth a solar eclipse
c. Earth; a solar eclipse
d. Earth, because a solar eclipse
e. Earth, when a solar eclipse

Please use the following to answer questions 37–43.

A
(1) A district attorney, often abbreviated as DA, is a government lawyer who investigate and tries criminal cases. (2) District attorneys work hand in hand with police investigators. (3) Police officers do not earn as much money as district attorneys. (4) The police are responsible for identifying and arresting suspects, and they also gather evidence, such as fingerprints. (5) District attorneys assemble this evidence and decides how to present it in court. (6) During a trial, the DA interrogates witnesses trying to uncover inconsistencies or missing details. (7) Although today's juries are quite sophisticated, district attorneys frequently need to explain complex technologies, such as DNA sampling. (8) A DA can help jurors avoid confusion and reach a verdict.

37. Sentence 1: A district attorney, often abbreviated as DA, is a government lawyer who investigate and tries criminal cases.
What correction should be made to this sentence?
a. Remove the comma after <u>attorney</u>.
b. Remove the comma after <u>DA</u>.
c. Change <u>is</u> to <u>are</u>.
d. Change <u>investigate</u> to <u>investigates</u>.
e. No correction is necessary.

38. Sentence 2: District attorneys work hand in hand with police investigators.

What correction should be made to this sentence?
a. Change <u>attorneys</u> to <u>attorney</u>.
b. Change <u>work</u> to <u>works</u>.
c. Insert a comma after <u>hand in hand</u>.
d. Change <u>investigators</u> to <u>investigator</u>.
e. No correction is necessary.

39. Sentence 5: District attorneys assemble this evidence and decides how to present it in court.

Which correction should be made to this sentence?
a. Change <u>attorneys</u> to <u>attorney</u>.
b. Change <u>assemble</u> to <u>assembles</u>.
c. Change <u>decides</u> to <u>decide</u>.
d. Change <u>present</u> to <u>presents</u>.
e. No correction is necessary.

40. Sentence 6: During a trial, the DA interrogates <u>witnesses trying to uncover</u> inconsistencies or missing details.

Which of the following is the best way to write the underlined portion of this sentence? If the original is the best way, choose option **a.**
a. witnesses trying to uncover
b. witnesses and trying to uncover
c. witnesses. Trying to uncover
d. witnesses who are trying to uncover
e. witness and tries to uncover

41. Sentence 7: Although today's juries are quite sophisticated, district attorneys frequently need to explain complex technologies, such as DNA sampling.

If you rewrote sentence 7 beginning with <u>District attorneys frequently need to explain complex technologies, such as DNA sampling</u>, the next words should be
a. because today's juries.
b. if today's juries.
c. when today's juries.
d. even though today's juries.
e. for today's juries.

42. Sentence 8: A DA can help jurors avoid confusion and reach a verdict.

The most effective revision of sentence 8 would begin with which group of words?
a. Even though explaining the facts in the case, a
b. By clearly explaining the facts in the case, a
c. Being able to explain the facts in the case, a
d. Having to explain the facts in the case, a
e. Failing to explain the facts in the case, a

43. Which revision would improve the effectiveness of the paragraph?
a. Move sentence 5 to follow sentence 1.
b. Move sentence 2 to follow sentence 6.
c. Remove sentence 3.
d. Begin a new paragraph with sentence 7.
e. No revision is necessary.

Please use the following to answer questions 44–50.

A

(1) Many investors today feel that mutual funds offers an unparalleled investment opportunity. (2) A mutual fund is a company that brings together money, from many people and invests it in stocks, bonds, or other securities. (3) The fund's portfolio—its combined holdings—are selected by a professional money manager. (4) Investors who buy the fund's shares can benefit from the manager's experience and knowing the market.

B

(5) Some mutual funds, such as a money market fund, focuses on relatively low-risk investments. (6) However, stock funds, which focus on buying shares in other companies, offer a greater potential risk and a greater potential profit. (7) Investors should remember that mutual funds always carry some risk—they are not guaranteed or insured by any bank or government agency.

44. Sentence 1: Many investors today feel that mutual funds offers an unparalleled investment opportunity.

What correction should be made to this sentence?

a. Change <u>Many</u> to <u>More</u>.
b. Change <u>feel</u> to <u>feels</u>.
c. Change <u>offers</u> to <u>offer</u>.
d. Insert a comma after <u>unparalleled</u>.
e. No correction is necessary.

45. Sentence 2: A mutual fund is a company that brings together <u>money, from many people</u> and invests it in stocks, bonds, or other securities.

Which of the following is the best way to write the underlined portion of this sentence? If the original is the best way, choose option **a.**

a. money, from many people
b. money; from many people
c. money, from many people,
d. money from many people
e. money. From many people

46. Sentence 3: The fund's portfolio—its combined holdings—are selected by a professional money manager.

What correction should be made to this sentence?

a. Change <u>fund's</u> to <u>funds'</u>.
b. Change <u>its</u> to <u>it's</u>.
c. Change <u>are</u> to <u>is</u>.
d. Insert a comma after <u>money</u>.
e. No correction is necessary.

47. Sentence 4: Investors who buy the fund's shares can benefit from the manager's experience <u>and knowing the market.</u>

Which of the following is the best way to write the underlined portion of this sentence? If the original is the best way, choose option **a.**

a. and knowing the market.
b. and knowledge of the market.
c. and, knowing the market.
d. and knowing about the market.
e. and knowing of the market.

48. Sentence 5: Some mutual funds, such as a money market fund, focuses on relatively low-risk investments.

What correction should be made to this sentence?

a. Remove comma after <u>funds</u>.
b. Remove comma after <u>fund</u>.
c. Change <u>focuses</u> to <u>focus</u>.
d. Change <u>relatively low-risk</u> to <u>relatively-low-risk</u>.
e. No correction is necessary.

49. Sentence 6: However, stock funds, which focus on buying shares in other companies, offer a <u>greater potential risk and</u> a greater potential profit.

Which of the following is the best way to write the underlined portion of this sentence? If the original is the best way, choose option **a.**

a. greater potential risk and
b. greater potential risk; and
c. greater, potential risk and
d. greatest potential risk and
e. greater potentially risky and

50. Sentence 7: Investors should remember that mutual funds always carry some risk—they are not guaranteed or insured by any bank or government agency.

If you rewrote sentence 7 beginning with <u>Investors should remember that mutual funds are not guaranteed or insured by any bank or government agency</u>, the next word should be

a. so.
b. because.
c. if.
d. unless.
e. for.

▶ Answers

1. e. This sentence is a good topic sentence for these paragraphs. The placement suggested by the other answer choices would introduce a lack of unity and coherence.

2. e. In the original sentence, the phrase *walking down the street with your sleek and adorable pet ferret* is a dangling modifier. The phrase should refer to the subject of the sentence, *you*, not *people*, because *you* are the one walking with the ferret. Choice **e** makes this relationship clear. The other answer choices do not improve the dangling modifier.

3. b. A compound subject composed of two singular nouns joined by the conjunction *or* takes a singular verb. In this sentence, the subject is *A fluffy cat or a playful dog*. The verb should be singular: *seems*. The other answer choices introduce errors into the sentence.

4. a. The punctuation of the sentence is correct as it is. The comma separates two independent clauses joined by the conjunction *but*. The other ways of punctuating this sentence are incorrect.

5. e. When you rewrite the sentence, you must keep the sequence of events the same as the original sentence. In order to keep the sense of the original, the next clause in the rewritten sentence will be <u>*before* deciding to adopt an exotic pet</u>. The other words suggested would introduce clauses with different meanings.

6. b. The use of serial commas helps readers understand that there are three levels of laws: local, state, and national. The other punctuations suggested are not clear or accurate.

7. d. Tenses must follow a logical progression. Because the first clause of the sentence suggests a future action, the verb in the second clause must reflect this tense. Because you have not yet adopted the pet, *have provided* is not accurate. *Can provide* is a more logical verb here. The other changes introduce errors into the sentence.

8. d. Because the first clause of the sentence is in the past tense, the verb in the second clause needs to be in the past tense. *Predict* should be changed to *predicted* for consistency. The other changes introduce errors.

9. c. Because the noun *consumers* refers to people, the following clause, which modifies *consumers*, should begin with *who*, not *which*.

10. c. In this sentence, *history's* should be a possessive noun, not a plural noun. The meaning refers to one of the most successful introductions *in history*, not to more than one different history. The other changes introduce errors.

11. c. In order to make sense, *favorable* should be changed to an adverb, *favorably*, to modify the adjective *impressed*. The other changes introduce errors.

12. a. The semicolon in the original sentence correctly separates two related sentences. The other changes introduce errors.

13. b. The verb tense in the second clause makes more sense when changed to *predict* because it then refers to a current prediction about future sales. When the tense is in the past, as in the original sentence, it refers to a nonsensical past prediction.

14. e. To keep the meaning of the original sentence, the next phrase should indicate that skeptics have changed their minds, so you should begin the rest of the sentence with *now praise*. The other words introduce other relationships that are not suggested by the original sentence.

15. b. To keep the meaning of the sentence the same, the next clause should be *whether you are evaluating an entire team or just one speaker*. Using one of the other words to start your sentence will create a sentence with a different meaning.

16. b. Sentence 2 makes an ideal topic sentence for paragraph A. It belongs at the beginning of the paragraph because it leads directly into sentence 1.

17. c. This sentence interrupts the unity and coherence of paragraph A. It belongs in paragraph B. Sentence 5 refers to delivery and content. Sentence 6 deals with the first attribute, delivery. Sentence 3 deals with content, and it should follow sentence 6.

18. b. The adverb clause introduced by the conjunction *although* must be followed by a comma. The comma separates the introductory subordinate clause from the independent clause. The other changes introduce errors.

19. e. The punctuation in this sentence is correct. The comma separates an introductory dependent clause from an independent clause. The suggested changes introduce errors.

20. e. In this sentence, *speaker's* is a possessive noun referring to the style and clarity of the speaker.

21. b. The comma after *devices* is unnecessary. The infinitive phrase *to grab and hold the audience's attention* does not need to be set off with a comma. The other changes introduce errors.

22. b. In this sentence, the word *effect* is used as a noun meaning "result." The word *affect* is usually a verb meaning "to influence." Here, *effect* is the correct word.

23. a. The original sentence correctly uses commas to separate three items in a series.

24. d. *Than* is used in comparisons. It is often confused with the adverb *then*, which usually refers to time. In this sentence, the phrase *rather than* compares two situations.

25. a. The two parts of this sentence are related by an additive conjunction. When you rewrite the sentence, you can keep this relationship by using the conjunction *and*.

26. b. The word *department* should not be capitalized because it is not a proper noun. The other changes introduce errors.

27. e. The phrase *Such as books, videotapes, or loose papers* is not a complete sentence. It gives examples of the kinds of items that need to be packed and should be set off from the rest of the preceding sentence by a comma.

28. c. The words *completely* and *accurately* are adverbs that modify the verb *fill out*. Therefore, the adverb forms are correct.

29. a. The independent clause set off by commas should be introduced by *which*, not *that*.

30. a. Use the comparative when comparing only two things. Here, you are comparing two types of eclipses, so *more* is correct. The other changes introduce errors.

31. e. The clauses are joined by the conjunction *or* in the original sentence. Maintaining this conjunction maintains the original relationship between ideas.

32. d. Placing sentence 3 at the beginning of the paragraph would make the paragraph more effective because sentence 3 makes a good topic sentence. It also leads directly into sentence 1.

33. e. The punctuation in this sentence is correct. The comma separates an introductory clause. No commas are needed after the verb or between two items in a series. The verb *passes* correctly agrees with the singular subject *moon*.

34. c. The original sentence has a dangling modifier. It is the moon's movement, not the Sun, that creates an eerie darkness. Choice **c** makes this meaning clear. The other choices do not adequately correct the poorly placed modifier.

35. e. The suggested corrections introduce errors. The comma after the introductory phrase is correct. *Sun's* is correctly punctuated as a singular possessive noun. The comma after *ring* introduces the appositive *or corona*. The comma after the word *corona* indicates the end of the appositive.

36. c. The two related sentences should be separated by a semicolon. The other answers suggest incorrect punctuation or introduce inaccurate relationships between the sentences.

37. d. The subject of the clause *who investigate and tries criminal cases* is the singular noun *lawyer*, so the verb *investigate* needs to be changed to the plural form, *investigates*.

38. e. The corrections suggested introduce errors. The plural subject *attorneys* correctly matches the plural verb *work*. The final prepositional phrase *with police investigators* does not need to be set off with commas. The plural *investigators* is also correct.

39. c. The verb *decide* should be plural to match the plural subject, *attorneys*. The other changes introduce errors.

40. e. The original sentence contains a confusing modifier. The witnesses are not trying to uncover inconsistencies or missing details, the DA is. This meaning is made clear by the change suggested in choice **e**.

41. d. To maintain the original meaning, you need to use a conjunction that shows that DAs need to explain technologies regardless of the fact that juries today are sophisticated. The phrase *even though* suggests this meaning.

42. b. Only the words *By clearly explaining* tell how a DA can help jurors avoid confusion and reach a verdict. The other answers do not fit the logic of the sentence.

43. c. Sentence 3 has almost no relationship to the rest of the paragraph. The paragraph would be more effective if sentence 3 were removed.

44. c. The verb *offers* takes a singular subject. The subject of the sentence is *funds*, which is plural. The verb must agree with the subject in number.

45. d. The prepositional phrase *from many people* should not be set off with any punctuation.

46. c. The subject of this sentence is the singular *portfolio*, so the verb should also be singular. *Is* is the correct verb.

47. b. To be parallel, the final joined ideas should both be nouns. Changing *knowing the market* to *knowledge of the market* creates this parallelism.

48. c. The plural subject, *funds*, should be followed by the plural verb *focus*.

49. a. This sentence is correctly punctuated. Two ideas in a series do not need to be separated by commas or other punctuation marks.

50. a. The meaning of the rewritten sentence should suggest that investors should remember that mutual funds are not guaranteed and, as a result, always carry some risk. The conjunction *so* conveys this relationship between ideas.

▶ Part II

Answer the following essay prompt. When preparing your essay, you should take the following steps:

1. *Carefully read the directions and the essay topic.*
2. *Plan your essay in detail before you start to write.*
3. *Use scratch paper to make any notes.*
4. *Write your essay in the space provided.*
5. *Review your work thoroughly. Make any changes that will improve your essay.*
6. *Check your paragraphs, sentence structure, spelling, punctuation, capitalization, and usage. Make any necessary corrections.*

Prompt:

Research tells us that what children learn in their earliest years is very important to their future success in school. Because of this, public schools all over the country are starting to offer Pre-Kindergarten classes.

What are the benefits of starting school early? What are some of the problems you see in sending four-year-olds to school? Write a composition in which you weigh the pros and cons of public school education for Pre-Kindergartners. Give reasons and specific examples to support your opinion. There is no specific word limit for your composition, but it should be long enough to give a clear and complete presentation of your ideas.

▶ Sample Score 4 Essay

Today, more and more four-year-olds are joining their big brothers and sisters on the school bus and going to Pre-Kindergarten. Although the benefits of starting school early are clear, it is also clear that Pre-K is not for every child.

The students who are successful in Pre-K are ahead when they start kindergarten. Pre-K teaches them to play well with others. Even though it does not teach skills like reading and writing, it does help to prepare students for "real" school. Pre-K students sing songs, dance, paint and draw, climb and run. They learn to share and to follow directions. They tell stories and answer questions, and as they do, they add new words to their vocabularies. Pre-K can also give students experiences they might not get at home. They might take trips to the zoo or the farm, have visits from musicians or scientists, and so on. These experiences help the students better understand the world.

There are, however, some real differences among children of this age. Some four-year-olds are just not ready for the structure of school life. Some have a hard time leaving home, even for three or four hours a day. Other children may already be getting a great preschool education at home or in daycare.

While you weigh the advantages and disadvantages of Pre-K, it is safe to say that each child is different. For some children, it is a wonderful introduction to the world of school. But others may not or should not be forced to attend Pre-K.

Evaluation of Sample Score 4 Essay: This paper is clearly organized and has stated a definite point of view. The paper opens with an introduction and closes with a conclusion. The introduction and conclusion combine an expression of the writer's opinion. Connections to the writer's opinion are made throughout the paper. The following examples are given in the paper.

<u>Pros</u>	<u>Cons</u>
Prepares students for real school	**Real differences among children of this age**
Examples:	Examples:
Learn to play with others	Not ready for structure of school life
Sing, dance, paint, draw, climb, run	Have a hard time leaving home
Learn to share	Getting a great education at home or in daycare
Learn to follow directions	
Add words to vocabulary	
Gives students new experiences	
Examples:	
Trips to zoo or farm	
Visits from musicians or scientists	

▶ Sample Score 3 Essay

Just like everything in life, there are pros and cons to early childhood education. Pre-K classes work for many children, but they aren't for everyone.

The pluses of Pre-K are obvious. Pre-K children learn many skills that will help them in kindergarten and later on. Probably the most important thing they learn is how to follow directions. This is a skill they will need at all stages of their life.

Other pluses include simple tasks like cutting, coloring in the lines, and learning capital letters. Many children don't get these skills at home. They need Pre-K to prepare them for kindergarten.

The minuses of Pre-K are not as obvious, but they are real. Children at this young age need the comfort of home. They need to spend time with parents, not strangers. They need that security. If parents are able to, they can give children the background they need to do well in school.

Other minuses include the fact that a lot of four-year-old children can't handle school. They don't have the maturity to sit still, pay attention, or share with others. Given another year, they may mature enough to do just fine in school. Sometimes it's better just to wait.

So there are definitely good things about Pre-K programs in our public schools, and I would definitely want to see one in our local schools. However, I think parents should decide whether their children are ready for a Pre-K education or not.

Evaluation of Sample Score 3 Essay: This paper has an identifiable organization plan, with pros and cons listed in order. The development is easy to understand if not somewhat simplistic. The language of the paper is uneven, with some vague turns of phrase—"Just like everything in life," "definitely some good things." However, the essay is clear and controlled, and generally follows written conventions. If the writer had included more developed and explicit examples and used more varied words, this paper might earn a higher score.

Pros	Cons
Children learn skills.	**Children need their homes.**
Examples:	Reasons:
Follow directions	They need security.
Cut	**Parents can give them**
Draw	**needed background.**
Learn capital letters	**Some four-year-olds**
	can't handle school.
	Examples:
	Can't sit still
	Can't pay attention
	Can't share with others

▶ Sample Score 2 Essay

Is early childhood education a good idea? It depends on the child you're talking about. Some children probally need more education in the early years and need something to do to keep out of trouble. Like if there isnt any good nursry school or day care around it could be very good to have Pre-Kindergarten at the school so those children could have a good start on life. A lot of skills could be learned in Pre-Kindergarten, for example they could learn to write their name, cut paper, do art, etc.

Of course theres some kids who wouldnt do well, acting out and so on, so they might do better staying home than going to Pre-Kindergarten, because they just arent ready for school, and maybe wouldnt even be ready for kindergarten the next year either. Some kids just act younger than others or are too baby-ish for school.

So I would suport Pre-Kindergarten in our schools, it seems like a good idea to have someplace for those kids to go. Even if some kids wouldnt do well I think enough kids would do well, and it would

make a diference in their grades as they got older. All those skills that they learned would help them in the future. If we did have Pre-Kindergarten it would help their working parents too, knowing their kids were someplace safe and learning importent things for life.

Evaluation of Sample Score 2 Essay: Although the writer of this paper has some good points to make, a lack of language skills and a certain disconnectedness of thought keep the paper from scoring well. The paper begins with a vague introduction of the topic and ends with a paragraph that expresses the author's opinion, but the rest of the paper is disorganized. The reasons given do not always have examples to support them, and the examples that are given are weak.

Pros	Cons
Keeps kids out of trouble	**Some kids aren't ready**
Teaches skills	**for school.**
Examples:	Examples:
Write name	Act babyish
Cut paper	Act out
Do art	

▶ Sample Score 1 Essay

What are benefits? What are some of problems with sending four-year-olds to school? Well, for one problem, its hard to see how little kids would do with all those big kids around at the school. They might get bullyed or lern bad habits, so I wouldnt want my four year old around those big kids on the bus and so on. Its hard to see how that could be good for a four year old. In our area we do have Pre-Kindergarten at our school but you dont have to go there a lot of kids in the program, I think about 50 or more, you see them a lot on the play ground mostly all you see them do is play around so its hard to see how that could be too usefull. They could play around at home just as easy. A reason for not doing Pre-Kindergarten is then what do you learn in Kindergarten. Why go do the same thing two years when you could just do one year when your a little bit bigger (older). I wonder do the people who want Pre-Kindergarten just want there kids out of the house or a baby sitter for there kids. Its hard to see why do we have to pay for that. I dont even know if Kindergarten is so usefull anyway, not like first grade where you actually learn something. So I would say theres lots of problems with Pre-Kindergarten.

Evaluation of Sample Score 1 Essay: This paper barely responds to the prompt. It gives reasons not to support Pre-K instruction, but it does not present any benefits of starting school early. The writer repeats certain phrases ("It's hard to see") to no real effect, and the faulty spelling, grammar, and punctuation significantly impede understanding. Several sentences wander off the topic entirely ("there a lot of kids in the program, I think about 50 or more, you see them a lot on the play ground." "I dont even know if Kindergarten is so usefull anyway, not like first grade where you actually learn something."). Instead of opening with an introduction, the writer simply lifts phrases from the prompt. The conclusion states the writer's opinion, but the reasons behind it are illogical and vague. Rather than organizing the essay in paragraph form, the writer has written a single, run-on paragraph. The lack of organization, weak language skills, and failure to address the prompt earn this essay a 1.

CHAPTER

6 ▶ GED Language Arts, Reading Diagnostic Exam

Directions: Read each passage carefully and answer the multiple-choice questions that follow. Choose the one best answer to each question.

Please use the following to answer questions 1–6.

What Happens When Four Men Struggle to Stay Alive After Their Ship Sinks?

None of them knew the color of the sky. Their eyes glanced level, and were fastened upon the waves that swept toward them. These waves were of the hue of slate, save for the tops, which were foaming white, and all of the men knew the colors of the sea.

The cook squatted in the bottom as he bent to bail out the boat.

The oiler, steering with one of two oars in the boat, sometimes raised himself suddenly to keep clear of water that swirled in over the stern. It was a thin little oar and it seemed often ready to snap.

The correspondent, pulling at the other oar, watched the waves and wondered why he was there.

The injured captain, lying in the bow, was at this time buried in that profound dejection and indifference which comes, temporarily at least, to even the bravest and most enduring when, willy nilly, the firm fails, the army loses, the ship goes down.

As each slatey wall of water approached, it shut all else from the view of the men in the boat, and it was not difficult to imagine that this particular wave was the final outburst of the ocean. There was a terrible grace in the move of the waves, and they came in silence, save for the snarling of the crests.

In disjointed sentences the cook and the correspondent argued as to the difference between a life-saving station and a house of refuge. The cook had said: "There's a house of refuge just north of the Mosquito Inlet Light, and as soon as they see us, they'll come off in their boat and pick us up."

"As soon as who sees us?" said the correspondent.

"The crew," said the cook.

"Houses of refuge don't have crews," said the correspondent. "As I understand them, they are only places where clothes and grub are stored for the benefit of shipwrecked people. They don't carry crews."

"Oh, yes, they do," said the cook.

"No, they don't," said the correspondent.

"Well, we're not there yet, anyhow," said the oiler, in the stern.

"Bully good thing it's an on-shore wind," said the cook. "If not, where would we be? Wouldn't have a show."

In the meantime the oiler and the correspondent sat together in the same seat, and each rowed an oar. Then the oiler took both oars; then the correspondent took both oars; then the oiler, then the correspondent.

The captain, rearing cautiously in the bow, after the dinghy soared on a great swell, said that he had seen the lighthouse at Mosquito Inlet.

"See it?" said the captain.

"No," said the correspondent slowly, "I didn't see anything."

"Look again," said the captain. He pointed. "It's exactly in that direction."

"Think we'll make it, captain?"

"If this wind holds and the boat don't swamp, we can't do much else," said the captain.

—Stephen Crane, from "The Open Boat" (1898)

1. Why did none of the four men know the color of the sky?
   a. They were keeping their eyes on the waves.
   b. They did not know what shade of gray the sky was.
   c. They were too tired to look at the sky.
   d. The sky was the same color as the water.
   e. The waves were too high to see the sky.

2. Why does the cook say ". . . good thing it's an on-shore wind. If not, where would we be"?
   a. An off-shore wind stirs up taller and more dangerous waves.
   b. An on-shore wind would blow them in toward land.
   c. He is trying to cheer up his companions by telling a lie.
   d. He doesn't know in which direction the land really is.
   e. He is echoing what the captain has said.

3. Why was the captain depressed and dejected?
   a. He was sad about losing his ship.
   b. He feared that a storm was coming.
   c. He was afraid that the waves would sink the dinghy.
   d. He knew that the wind was blowing the dinghy away from land.
   e. He was weak and tired from rowing.

4. Later in the story, the author writes: "It would be difficult to describe the subtle brotherhood of men that was here established on the seas. . . . [T]here was this comradeship that the correspondent, for instance, who had been taught to be cynical of men, knew even at the time was the best experience of his life. But no one said that it was so. No one mentioned it."

   Which of the following is most likely the reason that the correspondent thought that this experience was the best of his life?
   a. He realized that the captain was the wisest man he had ever met.
   b. He discovered that working on a ship at sea was a wonderful life.
   c. He realized that the best things in life happen accidentally.
   d. He discovered the value of comradeship in the face of life-threatening danger.
   e. He realized that he and the other survivors would drown, no matter what they did.

5. Which of the following statements best compares the correspondent's and the cook's views about a house of refuge?

a. Both men believe that crews from a house of refuge will rescue them.

b. The correspondent says that a house of refuge has a crew, but the cook says it does not.

c. Both men are sure that there are no houses of refuge along the coast.

d. The cook says that a house of refuge has a crew, but the correspondent says it does not.

e. Both men are doubtful that they will ever find a house of refuge.

6. How do you think the correspondent would react if the boat sprung a serious leak? He would probably

a. become very frightened and upset the boat.

b. ignore all orders from the captain.

c. leap overboard and swim away.

d. tell everyone to jump overboard.

e. help the crew to bail out the water and keep the boat afloat.

Please use the following to answer questions 7–11.

How Can One Photograph Have an Impact?

Gordon Parks' first professional photograph, which he titled "American Gothic" after a well-known painting by Grant Wood, remains one of the most powerful images of minorities created in the years leading up to the Civil Rights Movement. The composition of Parks' photograph echoes that of Wood's painting, but while the painting depicts a rigidly stoic farmer and his wife holding a pitchfork against the backdrop of a rustic American farm, the photograph shows an African-American charwoman (a woman hired to clean) holding a broom and mop against the backdrop of a looming American flag. The woman's gaze is direct yet not accusatory; her glance is slightly averted, suggesting a natural tendency to avoid confrontation. The power of the image comes from the contrast of the subject's almost painfully deep expression with the glorious ideals symbolized by the American flag.

Parks captured this memorable image in 1942 on his first day working for the Farm Security Administration (FSA). This government agency was established by President Franklin D. Roosevelt to aid workers during the harsh years of the Depression. Photographers like Parks were hired to create images that could communicate the plight of these Americans. As an African American, Parks had many first-hand experiences of discrimination and prejudice. Yet he was still surprised by the attitudes he encountered when he began working for the FSA in Washington, D.C. He was forced to enter restaurants from rear entrances and forbidden from even going into some theaters and other locations. Parks' new boss, Roy Stryker, suggested that he talk with some African-American residents in Washington and use his camera to record their experiences.

Parks followed his mentor's advice, which led him to Ella Watson, the subject of "American Gothic." Parks met her while she was cleaning floors in the FSA building. She told him of her life, which included many instances of bigotry and extreme hardship. When she agreed to let the young photographer take her picture, Watson stepped into one of the most recognized and influential photographs of our time.

But when Parks brought the photograph to Stryker, he was both impressed and cautious. "You're getting the idea," Stryker commented, "but you're going to get us all fired." Parks accepted Stryker's appraisal, recognizing that the photograph might be too sensational for large-scale publication. So it was both surprise and pride that Parks felt when he saw "American Gothic" on the front page of the *Washington Post*. Ella Watson's face spoke volumes about her past, and Parks' piercing composition added an unavoidable editorial commentary.

—Stanley Isaacs

7. Why did Gordon Parks choose the name "American Gothic" for his photograph?

a. because the photograph was dark and mysterious

b. because the photograph exactly duplicated the images of Grant Wood's painting with the same name

c. because the photograph had a composition similar to Grant Wood's painting

d. because he admired Grant Wood's life and work

e. because Ella Watson bore an uncanny resemblance to the farmer's wife in Grant Wood's painting

8. Why did the Farm Security Administration hire photographers like Gordon Parks?

   a. to create advertisements that would recruit new farmers

   b. to produce photographs showing the conditions of life of American workers

   c. to take photographs that could be sold as souvenirs or mementos

   d. to make photojournalism more influential than print journalism

   e. to provide direct aid to struggling farmers and other workers

9. Based on your understanding of this excerpt, which of these generalizations about Gordon Parks' work is most likely to be true?

   a. All of Parks' photographs are portraits of celebrities.

   b. Parks' most important works are all parodies or satires of existing artwork.

   c. Parks prefers to take photographs of ordinary working people.

   d. Parks spends most of his time on fashion photography.

   e. Parks is famous for his photographs of landscapes in the American West.

10. How do you think Gordon Parks would have responded to an assignment to capture images of poverty in inner city regions? He would have

   a. looked for a way to fulfill the assignment without photographing people.

   b. rejected the assignment because the message of the photographs would be too disturbing.

   c. tried to find unusual, but compelling, images that embodied his feelings on the topic.

   d. photographed only wealthy people in order to show how their wealth affected others.

   e. limited himself to photographing women who had experienced the hardships of poverty.

11. Talking about his career choices, Parks has said, "I picked up a camera because it was my choice of weapons against what I hated most about the universe: racism, intolerance, poverty."

Using what you know from the excerpt and this quotation, why does Parks say that a camera is a "weapon"? Parks believes that a camera

   a. creates pictures that often get people fired.

   b. is a tool an artist uses to capture beauty and light.

   c. can capture and destroy the soul of people who are photographed.

   d. is dangerous because it can be used to create propaganda.

   e. can create photographs that lead to social and political change.

Please use the following to answer questions 12–17.

What Happens When Two Schemers Bungle a Kidnapping?

It looked like a good thing: but wait till I tell you. We were down South, in Alabama—Bill Driscoll and myself—when this kidnapping idea struck us.

There was a town down there called Summit. Bill and me had a joint capital of about six hundred dollars, and we needed just two thousand dollars more to pull off a fraudulent town-lot scheme in Western Illinois.

We selected for our victim the only child of a prominent citizen named Ebenezer Dorset. The father was respectable and tight, a mortgage fancier [the narrator means "financier," someone who lends money to people who want to buy property]. The kid was a boy of ten. Bill and me figured that Ebenezer would melt down for a ransom of two thousand dollars to a cent.

About two miles from Summit was a little mountain. On the rear elevation of this mountain was a cave. There we stored provisions.

One evening after sundown, we drove in a buggy past old Dorset's house. The kid was in the street, throwing rocks at a kitten on the opposite fence.

"Hey, little boy!" says Bill, "would you like to have a bag of candy and a nice ride?"

The boy catches Bill neatly in the eye with a piece of brick.

"That will cost the old man an extra five hundred dollars," says Bill.

The boy put up a fight, but, at last, we got him down in the bottom of the buggy and drove away. We took him up to the cave. After dark I drove the buggy to the little village where we had hired it, and walked back to the mountain.

There was a fire burning behind the big rock at the entrance of the cave, and the boy was watching a pot of boiling coffee, with two buzzard tail-feathers stuck in his red hair. He points a stick at me when I come up, and says:

"Ha! Do you dare to enter the camp of Red Chief, the terror of the plains?"

"He's all right now," says Bill, rolling up his trousers and examining some bruises on his shins. "I'm Old Hank, the Trapper, Red Chief's captive, and I'm to be scalped at daybreak. By Geronimo! That kid can kick hard."

Yes, sir, that boy seemed to be having the time of his life. He immediately christened me Snake-eye, the Spy, and announced that I was to be broiled at the stake at the rising of the sun.

"Red Chief," says I to the kid, "would you like to go home?"

"Aw, what for?" says he. "I don't have any fun at home. I hate to go to school. I like to camp out. You won't take me back home again, Snake-eye, will you? I never had such fun in all my life."

We went to bed around eleven o'clock. I fell into a troubled sleep.

Just at daybreak, I was awakened by a series of awful screams from Bill. Red Chief was sitting on Bill's chest, with one hand twined in Bill's hair. In the other he had the sharp case-knife we used for slicing bacon; and he was trying to take Bill's scalp, according to the sentence that had been pronounced upon him the evening before.

I got the knife away from the kid and made him lie down again. But, from that moment, Bill's spirit was broken. He never closed an eye again in sleep as long as that boy was with us.

I dozed off for a while, but along toward sun-up I remembered that Red Chief had said I was to be burned at the stake at the rising of the sun. I wasn't nervous or afraid; but I sat up and lit my pipe and leaned against a rock.

"What you getting up so soon for, Sam?" asked Bill.

"Me?" says I. "Oh, I got a kind of a pain in my shoulder. I thought sitting up would rest it."

"You're a liar!" says Bill. "You're afraid. You was to be burned at sunrise, and you was afraid he'd do it. And he would, too, if he could find a match."

"Ain't it awful, Sam?" says Bill. "Do you think anybody will pay out money to get a little imp like that back home?"

—O. Henry, from "The Ransom of Red Chief" (1907)

12. Why do Sam and Bill want to kidnap the son of Ebenezer Dorset?
  a. They know that Ebenezer will pay them a ransom just to avoid publicity.
  b. They have failed to kidnap any other children from Summit.
  c. They need $100 and know that Ebenezer will pay that sum.
  d. Ebenezer's son is sickly and weak and will be easy to kidnap.
  e. They think that he is wealthy enough to pay a good deal of money to get his only son back.

13. Which of these lines of dialogue shows how the author uses nonstandard, informal grammar?
  a. "Do you dare to enter the camp of Red Chief?"
  b. "Red Chief, would you like to go home?"
  c. "I never had such fun in my life."
  d. "Oh, I got a kind of pain in my shoulder."
  e. "You was to be burned at sunrise."

14. How is Red Chief different from a typical kidnapping victim?
  a. Red Chief acts scared and pleads to go home.
  b. Red Chief scares and hurts his kidnappers.
  c. Red Chief doesn't like being kept hidden in a cave.
  d. Red Chief is afraid his father will not be able to meet the ransom.
  e. Red Chief is afraid he will be killed by his kidnappers.

15. Which words best describe the tone of the excerpt?
  a. dark and mysterious
  b. lighthearted and cheerful
  c. bitter and angry
  d. humorous and ironic
  e. objective and realistic

16. Later in the story, after another day spent with Red Chief, Sam and Bill write a ransom note to Ebenezer. They sign the note, "Two Desperate Men." Normally criminals use this phrase to indicate that they will do anything—even kill—to get what they want. Based on this information and the excerpt, why is this phrase ironic in this passage?
   a. It shows that they cannot deal with Red Chief and are willing to do anything to get out of the situation.
   b. It shows that they will kill Red Chief.
   c. They are wanted for crimes in other states.
   d. They are hungry and urgently need food.
   e. A storm is coming and they need more shelter than the cave can offer.

17. If Sam were to ask Bill to join him in another risky moneymaking scheme, how do you think Bill would respond? He would probably
   a. agree because he owes Sam a lot of money.
   b. agree because he enjoys doing risky things.
   c. refuse because he doesn't trust Sam anymore.
   d. refuse because he doesn't want to go to jail.
   e. be unable to decide because he isn't used to doing anything on his own.

Please use the following to answer questions 18–23.

How Can Having a Dream Change Your View of Life?

He Had His Dream

(1) He had his dream, and all through life,
     Worked up to it through toil and strife.
     Afloat fore'er before his eyes,
     It colored for him all his skies:
(5) The storm-cloud dark
     Above his bark,
     The calm and listless vault of blue
     Took on its hopeful hue,
     It tinctured every passing beam—
(10) He had his dream.

     He labored hard and failed at last,
     His sails too weak to bear the blast,
     The raging tempests tore away
     And sent his beating bark astray.
(15) But what cared he
     For wind or sea!
     He said, "The tempest will be short,

My bark will come to port."
He saw through every cloud a gleam—
(20) He had his dream.

                              —Paul Laurence Dunbar

18. What is the meaning of the word *bark* in lines 6, 14, and 18?
   a. heart
   b. storm
   c. ocean
   d. tree
   e. boat

19. Which of the following is true about the form of the poem?
   a. Almost every pair of lines rhymes, and all have the same rhythm pattern.
   b. The poem has two stanzas, and each follows the same rhyme and rhythm pattern.
   c. The poem has no rhyming lines and no regular rhythm pattern.
   d. Every other line of each stanza rhymes and has the same rhythm pattern.
   e. Every pair of lines rhymes, but there is no regular rhythm pattern.

20. What is the main image presented by this poem?
   a. a hardworking man facing difficulties
   b. a ship being battered by a storm at sea
   c. a strong west wind
   d. a peaceful harbor
   e. a foolish man

21. Which word best describes the man who *had his dream*?
   a. realistic
   b. optimistic
   c. sarcastic
   d. pessimistic
   e. analytic

22. Which of these sayings best expresses the message of this poem?
   a. A bird in the hand is worth two in the bush.
   b. A friend in need is a friend indeed.
   c. Necessity is the mother of invention.
   d. Keep your mind on your goal and never give up.
   e. Wishing won't make it so.

23. In one of his most famous speeches, Dr. Martin Luther King, Jr., declared, "I have a dream." In the speech, Dr. King spoke of his hope to achieve a society in which people of all races are treated equally. How does the message of King's speech compare to the theme of Dunbar's poem?
   a. Both writers emphasize the importance of pursuing a positive goal.
   b. Both writers share their personal experiences about racial equality.
   c. Neither writer actually believes that dreams can ever be truly fulfilled.
   d. Neither writer accepts personal responsibility for taking steps to achieve a goal.
   e. Both writers believe that dreams are important, but reality is unimportant.

Please use the following to answer questions 24–29.

What Happens When a Neighbor Asks for a Favor?

He laughs and asks, "Do I have a silly laugh?"

"No," I say, "no." But he does. Jorge does have a silly laugh. Faw faw fawwww. Faw faw fawwww. With squeaks. You'd actually get up and change seats in a movie theater if you were sitting behind somebody who had this laugh, because how could you watch the movie with that going on?

"People have told me I have a silly laugh."

"Oh no," I say, "no." My words are specific, chosen. Each no is its own precise lie. One means "No, you don't have a silly laugh." The next means "No, you shouldn't listen to your friends." Another means "No, I wouldn't say that since, after all, you're doing me a favor by driving me to school." I could lie more explicitly, but the words just come out "no, no, no."

"I'm glad your sister got sick," he says, and wham! The awkward implications of his statement land like a dead fish on the dashboard. After a moment of embarrassed silence, Jorge realizes what he has just said and nervously offers an explanation. "I mean, I'm not glad she got sick. When I said I was glad she got sick, I didn't mean it. What I meant was that I'm glad she couldn't drive you to school. I mean, I'm not glad she couldn't, but I'm glad that I get to, you know? Because I've been wanting to meet you ever since you moved in."

I nod. I should say something like "yes, me too," or "I've wanted to get to know you too, Jorge," but those lies catch in my throat.

The silence in the car becomes thicker as we slow to a halt. Outside the window, a worker is redirecting traffic onto the shoulder while a construction crew prepares to dig up a big chunk of the highway. Inside the car, Jorge works to fill the silence with more hot air.

"I mean, we are neighbors now, so we should know more about each other, right? Good neighbors make good fencers," Jorge says and laughs again. Faw faw fawwww.

The workers in the pit are revving a heavy drill, getting ready to bore the innocent pavement. I know how the pavement feels.

—Eric Reade

24. What event probably occurred before the beginning of this excerpt?
   a. Jorge drove the narrator to school for several days.
   b. The narrator's sister recovered from her illness.
   c. Jorge asked whether or not he has a silly laugh.
   d. The narrator asked Jorge for a ride to school.
   e. The narrator noticed road construction on the way to school.

25. Why does the narrator lie to Jorge in the opening lines of this excerpt? The narrator
   a. wants to avoid the awkwardness that would come from telling the truth.
   b. hopes to become close friends with Jorge.
   c. is a compulsive liar who is unable to distinguish between lies and the truth.
   d. plans to tell Jorge the truth about his laugh when they reach the school.
   e. wants to punish Jorge for his poor jokes.

26. Which words best describe the narrator's attitude when Jorge attempts to get better acquainted with him?
   a. angry and hostile
   b. upset and frightened
   c. eager and interested
   d. distant and cautious
   e. cold and uncaring

27. Why does this author include some sentence fragments, such as *With squeaks*?
    a. to suggest that the characters are poorly educated
    b. to indicate that the narrator speaks with a regional dialect
    c. to imitate everyday speech patterns
    d. to show the limitations of formal writing conventions
    e. to illustrate common grammatical errors

28. Later in the story, one of the characters says, "Road construction always reminds me of going to the dentist. I mean, it isn't exactly the same thing, but all that drilling and shouting, right?" The character who probably says this is
    a. the narrator, because the quotation describes the road construction.
    b. the narrator, because the quotation contains formal diction.
    c. Jorge, because the quotation reflects his use of language.
    d. Jorge, because the quotation contains a colorful and precise metaphor.
    e. someone new, because the words are entirely unlike those Jorge or the narrator use.

29. The title of this story is "Discomfort and Joy." What does this title suggest will happen to the tension between the two characters in the car? The tension will probably
    a. build to a violent climax.
    b. be resolved, leading to a better relationship between the narrator and Jorge.
    c. disappear as soon as the drilling at the road construction site stops.
    d. increase steadily as the car gets closer to the school.
    e. turn out to have been in the narrator's imagination all the time.

Please use the following to answer questions 30–34.

JULIET: Now, good sweet nurse,—O Lord, why look'st thou sad?
   Though news be sad, yet tell them merrily;
   If good, thou shamest the music of sweet news
   By playing it to me with so sour a face.

NURSE: I am a-weary, give me leave awhile:
   Fie, how my bones ache! what a jaunce [trip] I have had!

JULIET: I would thou hadst my bones, and I thy news.
   Nay, come, I pray thee, speak; good, good nurse, speak.

NURSE: Can you not stay awhile?
   Do you not see that I am out of breath?

JULIET: How are thou out of breath, when thou hast breath
   To say to me that thou art out of breath?
   The excuse that thou dost make in this delay
   Is longer than the tale thou dost excuse.
   Is thy news good, or bad? . . .
   What says he of our marriage? what of that?

NURSE: Lord, how my head aches! what a head have I!
   It beats as it would fall in twenty pieces. . . . Oh my back, my back! . . .

JULIET: I'faith, I am sorry that thou are not well.
   Sweet, sweet, sweet nurse, tell me, what says my love? . . .

NURSE: Is this the poultice [medicated bandage] for my aching bones? . . .
   Have you got leave to go to shrift [confession to a priest] to-day?

JULIET: I have.

NURSE: Then hie you hence to Friar Laurence's cell;
   There stays a husband to make you a wife . . .
   Hie you to church; I must another way,
   To fetch a ladder, by the which your love
   Must climb a bird's nest soon when it is dark . . .
   Go; I'll to dinner; hie you to the cell.

JULIET: Hie to high fortune! Honest nurse, farewell.

—William Shakespeare,
from *Romeo and Juliet* (1597)

30. What is Juliet's response to the nurse when the nurse complains that she is out of breath?
a. She says that if the nurse has breath enough to complain, she can't be out of breath.
b. She says that the nurse is out of breath because she is ill.
c. She is worried that the nurse will faint.
d. She tells the nurse to rest and come back later.
e. She says that if the nurse is out of breath, she should sit down and rest.

31. What is the real reason the nurse keeps complaining about her head and her back?
a. She does not want to tell Juliet bad news.
b. She was told by Romeo not to tell Juliet anything.
c. She is afraid that Juliet will run away.
d. She is teasing Juliet by withholding information about what Romeo has told her.
e. The nurse is truly suffering aches and pains as a result of going to meet Romeo.

32. Why did Juliet send the nurse to meet Romeo?
a. to find out whether anyone from her family has been spying on Romeo
b. to find out whether Romeo is all right
c. to find out when and where Romeo plans to marry her
d. to tell him that she no longer wants to marry him
e. to give the nurse something to do while Romeo is in the garden

33. Why does the nurse ask if Juliet has permission to go to confession?
a. The nurse thinks Juliet should wait for Friar Laurence to come and visit her.
b. The nurse wants to make sure that Juliet has an excuse to see Friar Laurence.
c. The nurse is angry because Juliet has been disobedient.
d. The nurse wants Juliet to stay with her until Romeo arrives.
e. The nurse doesn't want Juliet to go to confession without her.

34. Which of the following events seems most likely, based on the information in this excerpt?
a. Juliet's parents will prevent her from going to see Friar Laurence.
b. Romeo will be killed before he and Juliet are married.
c. Juliet will have an accident before she gets to see Friar Laurence.
d. Friar Laurence will secretly marry Romeo and Juliet.
e. Juliet will flee with Romeo to another country.

Please use the following to answer question 35.

Earlier in the play, this conversation takes place between Romeo and the nurse.

> **ROMEO:** Bid her devise
> Some means to come to shrift this afternoon;
> And there she shall at Friar Laurence' cell
> Be . . . married.
>
> **NURSE:** This afternoon, sir?
> Well, she shall be there.
>
> **ROMEO:** And stay, good nurse, behind the abbey wall
> Within this hour my man shall be with thee,
> And bring thee cords made like a tackled stair . . .

35. Based on this conversation and the excerpt, which is the best conclusion?
a. The nurse is secretly spying on Romeo and Juliet on orders from Juliet's parents.
b. The nurse will not provide the ladder Romeo has asked for to climb to Juliet's chamber.
c. Romeo does not trust the nurse.
d. The nurse wants to help Juliet marry Romeo.
e. The nurse does not want Romeo to succeed in marrying Juliet.

Please use the following to answer questions 36–40.

What Will Workshop Participants Learn?

COMMUNICATION WORKSHOP OVERVIEW
Welcome to the Communication Workshop. At today's conference, we'll be discussing many aspects of business communication. You'll learn many useful strategies you can use to make your workplace discussions

effective and productive. This list presents some of the key concepts we'll discuss during the seminar.

1. **Listen, Listen, Listen**

   You have to listen before you can respond. It sounds simple, but you'd be surprised how often people jump into a conversation without really listening to what others are saying. Focus on what the other person is saying, not what you want to say in response. Another useful strategy is to summarize what you just heard a speaker say before adding your own comments. This technique can help you correct any misunderstandings, too.

2. **Use Professional Language**

   Remember that a workplace is a professional setting. No matter how strongly you feel about a subject, you should choose your words carefully. Some words and phrases that might be suitable at home are just not appropriate at work.

3. **Be Specific**

   The more specific you are, the more clearly you communicate. Instead of saying "The quarterly report is a mess," take the time to describe the exact problems that you have identified. A general statement is much more likely to be misinterpreted or misunderstood than a specific one.

4. **Avoid Negative Statements**

   You can think of this as the *No "No" Rule*. Work is often about problem solving, but too many negative statements can create a gloomy and pessimistic work atmosphere. You'll get much better reactions if you balance negative statements with positive ones. You might feel like shouting "There's no way we'll ever meet this deadline!" but you'll help your team a lot more if you say "Last time we had a deadline like this it seemed impossible, but we pulled together and got the job done!"

5. **Use Notes**

   Notes can help you keep your business communications focused and productive. Before a meeting, jot down a list of the topics you want to cover or questions you want to ask. During or after a meeting, write a quick summary that covers the main points discussed. You can e-mail your notes

to everyone who participated in the discussion, so that you all have the same record.

36. Which of the following summaries best describes the subject of this conference?
   a. making decisions based on effective communication
   b. using business skills to promote efficiency
   c. avoiding negative statements to create a positive work environment
   d. using communication skills to manipulate consumers
   e. ways to improve your business communications skills

37. According to this excerpt, which of the following statements is the best example of effective business communication?
   a. "You and I never see eye to eye on anything."
   b. "Yesterday's meeting was totally useless."
   c. "Let's try to resolve the inconsistencies in this report."
   d. "I'll never do a favor for the production department again."
   e. "There's no point in even discussing this anymore."

38. From this overview, which conclusion can you draw about the leaders of the company sponsoring this workshop? The company leaders
   a. have recently identified a sharp decline in productivity.
   b. believe in the importance of communication among employees.
   c. think that employees should be seen and not heard.
   d. plan to sponsor communication workshops for other businesses.
   e. hope to increase the number of employees in management.

39. How is this excerpt organized?
   a. statements of opinion supported by factual evidence
   b. bulleted items followed by step-by-step directions
   c. general topics divided into narrower subtopics
   d. rules followed by elaborations and explanations
   e. anecdotes supported by statistical data

40. In addition to the Communication Workshop Overview, each participant was also given an organized chart in which to take notes on the conference. Which of the following conclusions about the leaders of the workshop is supported by this information and the excerpt? The workshop leaders

a. believe that note-taking is the most important communication skill of all.

b. do not trust the participants to remember anything they hear.

c. want to help employees develop the beneficial habit of note-taking.

d. think that note-taking can take the place of verbal communication.

e. will score participants on the quality and completeness of their notes.

▶ Answers

1. a. The first paragraph implies that the reason the men did not know the color of the sky was that they were too busy watching the waves. This was the only way to avoid being hit by a wave that would capsize their frail lifeboat (choice **a**). Choices **b**, **c**, **d**, and **e** might seem plausible, but they are not supported in the passage.

2. b. An on-shore wind blows from the ocean toward the land. Choice **a** is incorrect because an off-shore wind comes from land and would blow the boat farther out to sea. There is no evidence in the text to support choices **c**, **d**, or **e**. All the sailors know the direction in which the land lies, and a little bit later, the captain does see signs of land.

3. a. The text makes it clear that the captain is dejected because his ship has sunk. Choice **b** is incorrect because nothing in the text suggests that a storm is coming. Choice **c** is incorrect because no one, least of all the captain, has given up hope of surviving the waves. Choice **d** is incorrect because the wind is blowing toward shore, not away from it. Choice **e** is not correct since the correspondent and the oiler, not the captain, are rowing. The captain is in charge of the dinghy and its small crew.

4. d. The author clearly states that the comradeship of men struggling together to save their lives is the best experience of his life. None of the other choices is supported by the excerpt. The correspondent never speaks of the captain as a wise man (choice **a**). There is no reference in the excerpt to life on the ship before the sinking (choice **b**), or to accidental occurrences (choice **c**). And no one in the boat ever voices the fear that they will all drown (choice **e**).

5. d. In the conversation between the correspondent and the cook, it is the cook who says that a house of refuge has a crew. The correspondent says it doesn't. So choice **d** is the correct answer. The passage does not support any of the other answers.

6. e. There is no evidence that the correspondent would do anything but help the others to keep the boat afloat (choice **e**). He has been calm throughout the ordeal, and it is unlikely that he would suddenly do anything to upset the boat (choice **a**). He has always followed the captain's orders, so it is unlikely that the correspondent would ignore the captain if there were a leak (choice **b**). He would not abandon the boat to save himself (choice **c**), nor would he try to take command and give an order to jump overboard (choice **d**).

7. c. The text explains how Parks' photograph echoes the composition of Grant Wood's famous painting. There is no indication that the photograph is dark and mysterious (choice **a**), or that Ella Watson resembled the farmer's wife in Grant Wood's painting (choice **e**). Although Parks may have admired Grant Wood (choice **d**), the text does not support that choice, and the essay clearly shows that the images in the photograph differ from the images in the painting (choice **b**). Only choice **c** fits the information given.

8. b. The excerpt clearly states that the FSA hired photographers to communicate the plight of Americans in difficulty, so choice **b** is the best answer.

9. c. It is safe to assume that Parks continued to create photographic images of ordinary working people, so choice **c** presents a valid generalization. The other choices make assumptions that are not based on evidence in the excerpt.

10. c. Parks would probably use the same approach to the new assignment that he used to create "American Gothic," so he would probably try to share his feelings on the subject of poverty by showing unusual, but compelling, images. Choice **a** makes no sense since Parks was a photographer. Choices **b** and **d** are incorrect because part of Parks' mission was to show the hardships of life. Choice **e** is incorrect because there is no evidence in the text that Parks concentrates on women only.

11. e. Parks calls a camera a weapon because it can create influential images like "American Gothic." It is a weapon that contributes directly to social and political change, so choice **e** is the best answer. Although choices **a**, **b**, and **d** may be valid points, they do not fit in with Parks' quote about wanting to expose the world's evils. Choice **c** is nonsensical.

12. e. The text clearly states that Ebenezer Dorset is a prominent citizen who lends money to people needing mortgages. He is therefore a fairly well-to-do person. So choice **e** is the correct choice. None of the other answers is supported by the text.

13. e. The only one of the five choices that contains nonstandard grammar is choice **e**. The line "You was to be burned at sunrise" contains an error in subject-verb agreement. The sentence should be "You were to be burned at sunrise." None of the other choices contains any grammar errors.

14. b. The irony in this passage is that Red Chief does not act like the usual kidnapping victim. Rather than being frightened and mistreated, he scares his captors and inflicts pain on Bill repeatedly. So choice **b** is the correct answer. None of the other choices is supported by the text. They describe typical kidnapping victims, not Red Chief.

15. d. The tone of the excerpt is humorous and ironic. The basic irony (the opposite of what was expected) in the situation is that the roles of kidnappers and victim are reversed. The kidnappers suffer at the hands of their victim. Their victim is enjoying camping out and playing, but Bill and Sam are miserable. Choice **d** is the correct answer because none of the other choices accurately describes the tone reflected in the situation or the language used.

16. a. The correct answer is choice **a**. Choice **b** is incorrect because the two never threaten to kill Red Chief. Choices **c**, **d**, and **e** are not supported by evidence in the text.

17. c. In this excerpt, Bill seems to be the one getting the worst treatment from Red Chief. His statement at the end of the passage shows that he's worried that they will never be able to get rid of the child. Choice **a** is incorrect because there is no evidence that Bill owes anyone money. Choice **b** may be true, but there is no evidence in the excerpt that Bill enjoys taking risks. Choice **d** is incorrect because Bill shows no sign of being worried about going to jail for his illegal acts. Choice **e** might be true, but there is no evidence that Bill is not capable of doing anything for himself.

18. e. The context of the poem makes it clear that "bark" here means *boat* or *ship*. The images of the first and second stanza depict a boat that is tossed and battered by a storm.

19. b. The poem is divided into two stanzas that follow the same pattern. Pairs of lines rhyme, but the rhythms vary from couplet to couplet, so choices **a**, **c**, and **d** are incorrect. Although the rhythms vary from couplet to couplet, each stanza follows the same rhythmic pattern, making choice **e** incorrect as well. So, choice **b** is the correct answer.

20. b. Although the poem is about a man motivated by a goal or dream, the image presented to the reader is that of a ship at sea struggling to survive battering winds and water. Thus, choice **b** is correct. The other choices are either literal interpretations, or name small parts of the whole.

21. b. The man's dream allows him to remain optimistic (choice **b**) despite the difficulties of his life, as symbolized by the metaphor of the storms at sea. Since he "labored hard and failed at last," the dreamer cannot be called realistic (choice **a**). Nothing about the dreamer and his dream is sarcastic (choice **c**), and his hopefulness against all odds makes him the opposite of pessimistic (choice **d**). Lastly, he is not particularly analytic (choice **e**); if he were, he might realize the impossibility of his dream.

22. d. The poem describes how having a dream helped a man maintain optimism in the face of challenges. The saying that best expresses this idea is choice **d**. Choice **e** is precisely the opposite of this idea. Choice **a** means that one should be satisfied with what one can attain, which also goes against the theme of striving against all odds. Choices **b** and **c** have nothing to do with the content of the poem.

23. a. Dunbar is not relating a personal experience, so choice **b** cannot be correct. Dunbar's protagonist and King himself certainly do believe that dreams can be fulfilled, which makes choice **c** incorrect. Personal responsibility in the form of hard work is key to Dunbar's protagonist, and personal responsibility in the form of working toward social change is important to King, so choice **d** does not fit either. The contrast between reality and dreams (choice **e**) is important to both writers. Dunbar's poem shows how pursuing a goal can make a life rewarding and joyful; King's speech showed how pursuing a dream can lead to social and political change.

24. d. Jorge is driving the narrator to school because the narrator's sister is ill and unable to do so. Therefore, it is most likely that the narrator asked Jorge for this favor. Choice **d** is the best answer. The awkwardness of the conversation indicates that this is the first time this has happened, so choice **a** cannot be correct. If the narrator's sister had recovered from her illness (choice **b**), the entire scene would not have taken place. Jorge asked whether or not he has a silly laugh as the scene begins, not before the scene begins (choice **c**). Last, the narrator notices the road construction (choice **e**) toward the end of the passage.

25. a. The narrator admits that Jorge has an annoying laugh but does not share this information with Jorge because Jorge is doing the narrator a favor. The narrator's motivation is to avoid social awkwardness. The narrator makes it clear in the passage that he has no desire to be friends with Jorge (choice **b**), and there is no indication that he intends to speak to Jorge once they reach the school (choice **d**). His failure to tell Jorge the truth is a kindness rather than a punishment (choice **e**), and there is no support for the notion that he is a compulsive liar (choice **c**); in fact, he agonizes over the difference between his words and his thoughts. Choice **a** is the correct answer.

26. d. The narrator is neither angry nor hostile (choice **a**); his refusal to confront Jorge with the truth is clear indication of that. He is not frightened of Jorge (choice **b**), although he finds their conversation uncomfortable. Because of his negative feelings toward Jorge, he tries hard not to appear eager and interested (choice **c**), but his careful consideration of Jorge's feelings keeps him from seeming cold and uncaring (choice **e**). The narrator remains somewhat distant and detached during the conversation taking place within the car. The narrator is also very cautious about revealing any personal feelings. Choice **d** is the correct choice.

27. c. Sentence fragments could indicate an uneducated character (choice **a**), but the sentence construction in other places is sophisticated. Because the characters are on their way to school, this choice seems unlikely. There is no support in the passage for the notion that the author intends to show limitations of formal writing conventions or to illustrate common grammatical errors. A fictional piece such as this one would not be the place to do so, making choices **d** and **e** implausible. The writer uses some sentence fragments because this is the way people speak to each other in everyday conversations. However, there is no indication that this speech reflects a regional dialect (choice **b**), so choice **c** is the best answer.

28. c. Although the narrator first notices the road construction, this quotation is not typical of his brief responses to Jorge's remarks, so choice **a** cannot be correct. The quotation does not, in fact, contain formal diction, so choice **b** is also incorrect. Although the comparison of road construction to dentistry is colorful, it is not particularly precise, and this figurative language is not typical of Jorge's previous quotes, so choice **d** is not the best answer. Despite this, the quotation does sound like Jorge, so attributing it to a new character (choice **e**) would be illogical. The quotation reflects Jorge's casual and wordy way of speaking, including the phrase "I mean," which he uses several times earlier in the story, making choice **c** the best answer.

29. b. The excerpt from "Discomfort and Joy" suggests discomfort as the awkwardness during the conversation in the car builds. The tension is certainly not imagined (choice **e**), although the narrator feels it more strongly than Jorge does. Although the tension may build, as in choices **a** and **d**, the word *joy* indicates a resolution that is not violent—or even abrupt, as in choice **c**. Therefore, it is likely that the story will go on to include something that gently relieves tension between the narrator and Jorge and brings some sense of *joy*, so the best answer is choice **b**.

30. a. Juliet tells the nurse that she can't be so out of breath if she has breath enough to tell Juliet that she is out of breath. The text does not support any of the other choices.

31. d. It is clear from the dialogue between Juliet and her nurse that the nurse purposely delays telling Juliet what Romeo has said. Juliet asks, "What says he of our marriage?" and "what says my love?" but gets no direct answer. The nurse wants to tease Juliet a bit before telling her the news. Choice **d** is the correct answer. None of the other answers is supported by information in the excerpt.

32. c. The dialogue in the excerpt makes it clear that Juliet has sent the nurse to find out from Romeo when and where he plans to marry her. She clearly wants to marry him, so choice **d** is incorrect. Romeo is not in the garden, and sending the nurse was not simply a way to get rid of her, so choice **e** is not correct. Juliet may or may not suspect that her family is spying or that Romeo may not be all right, but there is no evidence in the text for either of these choices. So choices **a** and **b** are incorrect.

33. b. Before telling Juliet to go and see Friar Laurence, the nurse first asks whether Juliet has permission to go to shrift (confession). She wants to make sure that Juliet has an excuse for going to the Friar's cell where the secret wedding is to take place. Choices **a**, **c**, **d**, and **e** are not supported by evidence from the excerpt.

34. d. There is nothing in the excerpt to suggest that Juliet's parents will learn about or prevent Juliet's plans to marry Romeo, so choice **a** is not correct. There is nothing in the excerpt to suggest that anything will happen to Juliet, that Romeo will be killed, or that Juliet and Romeo have plans to escape to another place, so choices **b**, **c**, and **e** are not correct. Choice **d** is the correct answer.

35. d. Information from these two excerpts makes it clear that the nurse is doing whatever she can to further the marriage plans of Romeo and Juliet. So choice **d** is the correct answer. The nurse says that she is to provide a ladder, as Romeo had asked, so choice **b** is incorrect. Romeo certainly trusts the nurse; otherwise, he would not confide in her. So choice **c** is incorrect. Nothing in either passage suggests that the nurse is spying on the couple for Juliet's parents, or that the nurse does not want Juliet to marry Romeo. So choices **a** and **e** are incorrect.

36. e. The overall subject of the conference is improving your business communications skills (choice **e**). The other summaries are either inaccurate (choices **a** and **d**) or define the topic too narrowly (choice **c**), or too broadly (choice **b**).

37. c. Choice **c** uses professional, positive language to identify a specific problem. The other answer choices include negative language and/or vague statements and do not support good communication skills.

38. b. The fact that the leaders of the company authorized this communications workshop suggests that they believe in the importance of employee communication. The other choices are not supported by the text.

39. d. Each numbered item presents a rule, which is then elaborated on or explained. Therefore, choice **d** is the best choice.

40. c. The fact that the leaders provide a note-taking chart, combined with the support for effective note-taking in the overview, suggests that the leaders want to help employees learn how to take effective notes. The other conclusions are not supported by the text.

GED Science Diagnostic Exam

Directions: Read the following questions carefully and choose the best answer for each question. Some questions may refer to a passage, illustration, or graph.

1. In an acid base reaction, an acid reacts with a base to produce water and a salt. The pH scale can be used to describe the acidity of a liquid. Look at the following diagram.

Which two liquids could undergo an acid base reaction?
a. bleach and ammonia
b. lye and ammonia
c. blood and saliva
d. bleach and vinegar
e. stomach acid and beer

2. According to Newton's laws of motion, an object set in motion remains in motion unless a force acts on it. If you suspend an object from a string and make it swing, the object will swing for a while, then slow down and stop. Why does the suspended object stop swinging?

    a. because an object at rest remains at rest unless a force acts upon it

    b. because the mass of the object is too small to maintain the motion

    c. because energy is the ability to do work

    d. because gravity is pulling it toward the Earth

    e. because energy of motion is converted to heat through friction with air

3. In an exothermic process, heat is released to the surroundings. An example of an exothermic process is burning wood. An endothermic process requires the input of heat from the surroundings. An example of an endothermic process is boiling water. Which of the following is an endothermic process?

    a. detonation of an explosive

    b. melting ice

    c. burning paper

    d. the formation of helium on the Sun

    e. freezing water

4. Ice floats on water because

    a. ice is less dense than water.

    b. water conducts heat better than ice.

    c. ice has a lower temperature.

    d. heat from the Earth's core travels upward, cooling the bottom first.

    e. it needs energy from the Sun to melt.

5. Which of the following is NOT true about gravity?

    a. The more massive two objects are, the greater the gravitational force between them.

    b. Gravitational force between two objects depends only on the mass of the larger object.

    c. Gravitational force between two objects depends on the distance between them.

    d. People can jump higher on the moon than on Earth because the gravitational force between a person and the moon is lower than the gravitational force between a person and the Earth.

    e. A gravitational force exists between the moon and the Sun.

6. Change of phase is a process whereby matter changes form (solid, liquid, gas). Which one of the following constitutes a phase change?

    a. condensation of water vapor

    b. photosynthesis

    c. digestion of food

    d. dry-cleaning

    e. exhaling

7. Two negatively charged spheres

    a. repel each other.

    b. attract each other.

    c. neither attract nor repel each other.

    d. can either attract or repel each other depending on their position.

    e. attract each other only when the distance between them is small.

8. Which statement about energy and/or matter is INCORRECT?

    a. Matter and energy can't be destroyed.

    b. Matter and energy can't be created.

    c. All matter tends toward more disordered states.

    d. Energy can be stored and transferred.

    e. Heat energy is composed of heat atoms.

9. In addition to magnifying the image of an object, a microscope inverts the image left to right. The image of the object observed through the microscope is also upside down. Looking through the eyepiece, you would therefore see the upside-down mirror image of the object under the microscope lens. What would the following object look like if observed through the microscope?

10. People wear woolen gloves in the winter because gloves
   a. generate heat energy through radiation.
   b. increase the temperature of cold air through convection.
   c. decrease the loss of body heat to surroundings through insulation.
   d. increase the amount of heat energy generated by the body through conduction.
   e. transform cold wind energy into thermal energy.

11. Different colors of light correspond to different wavelengths. Wavelengths are often quoted in nanometers (nm). The wavelengths of the visible part of the spectrum are shown in the following diagram.

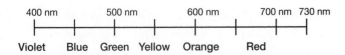

According to the diagram, blue-green light would most likely have a wavelength of
   a. 670 nm.
   b. 550 nm.
   c. 350 nm.
   d. 475 nm.
   e. 700 nm.

12. What always stays the same when a chemical reaction takes place?
   a. the number of atoms
   b. the number of molecules
   c. the amount of gas
   d. the amount of solid matter
   e. the amount of disorder

13. Which of the following is NOT true about sunlight?
   a. It is a form of radiation.
   b. It is used as an energy source in solar powered calculators.
   c. It contains the colors of the rainbow.
   d. Its speed is infinite.
   e. It can be absorbed by plants.

14. In order to protect themselves from being eaten, animals resort to camouflage and chemical defense. Animals camouflage by mimicking the appearance of their environment. Animals that have chemical defenses contain chemicals noxious to predators. Which of these is NOT an example of camouflage or chemical defense?
   a. A walking stick insect looks just like a twig.
   b. A skunk has an awful smell.
   c. Feathers of the pitohui bird in New Guinea contain a deadly toxin.
   d. Roses have thorns.
   e. A harlequin crab looks just like the sea cucumber it lives on.

15. Osmosis is the movement of water across a selectively permeable membrane in order to equalize the concentration (the amount of protein per milliliter of water) on two sides of the membrane. Consider the following diagram. The container is divided into two compartments, A and B, by a selectively permeable membrane. Each circle represents 100 protein molecules that can't pass through the membrane. The amount of water on two sides of the membrane is initially equal. What will happen as a result of osmosis?

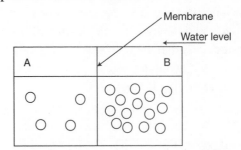

   a. Protein will flow from compartment B to compartment A.
   b. Protein will flow from compartment A to compartment B.
   c. Water will flow from compartment B to compartment A.
   d. Water will flow from compartment A to compartment B.
   e. Both water and protein will flow from compartment B to compartment A.

16. Which of the following statements about human genetics is TRUE?
   a. Half of the chromosomes in a human are inherited from the mother, and half from the father.
   b. A human looks 50% like the father, and 50% like the mother.
   c. Fraternal twins are genetically more similar than siblings who are not twins.
   d. Exposure to X-rays can have no effect on a human's chromosomes.
   e. Genes are particles found in the nucleus of DNA atom.

17. Identical twins have exactly the same genes. Identical twins result when
   a. an egg fertilized by one sperm divides in two.
   b. two eggs are fertilized with two sperm cells.
   c. one egg divides in two and is fertilized by two sperm cells.
   d. the same sperm cell fertilizes two eggs.
   e. the same egg is fertilized by two sperm cells.

18. In peas, the gene for green color is dominant over the gene for yellow color. We will specify the gene for yellow peas as **y**, and the gene for green peas as **Y**. Each pea has two genes for color (one from each parent), and donates only one gene for color to its offspring. Peas that are yellow have the genotype **yy**. Any other genotype leads to green peas. Consider the following Punnett square:

	Parent	
	Y	**y**
y	Yy	yy
y	Yy	yy

(left label: Parent)

The offspring of these two parents
   a. could never be yellow.
   b. could never be green.
   c. could be either green or yellow.
   d. could be yellow-green.
   e. could be yellow, but could never have yellow offspring.

19. Which of the following is NOT true?
   a. All organisms are made of atoms.
   b. All organisms are made of molecules.
   c. All organisms are made of one or more cells.
   d. All organisms have genetic material.
   e. All organisms have a cell wall.

20. In humans, a pair of chromosomes (one from each parent) determines the sex of the offspring. Females have two X chromosomes, while males have an X chromosome and a Y chromosome. The offspring always gets an X chromosome from the mother, so in humans, it is the father that determines the sex of the offspring by supplying either an X chromosome to yield a female, or a Y chromosome to yield a male. In birds, like in humans, a pair of chromosomes determines the sex. Birds that have two W chromosomes are male. Birds that have a W chromosome and a Z chromosome are female. Which statement is TRUE about birds?
   a. The male bird determines the sex of the offspring by supplying a W chromosome or a Z chromosome.
   b. The male bird determines the sex of the offspring by supplying one of his W chromosomes.
   c. The male bird determines the sex of the offspring by supplying an X chromosome or a Y chromosome.
   d. The female bird determines the sex of the offspring by supplying an X chromosome or a Y chromosome.
   e. The female bird determines the sex of the offspring by supplying it with the W chromosome or a Z chromosome.

21. A species may live in association with another species. Such an arrangement is called symbiosis. Symbiosis in which both species benefit is called mutualism. If the symbiosis is beneficial to one species and neither beneficial nor harmful to the other, it is called commensalism. If one species benefits at the expense of the other, the relationship is called parasitism. A tick that attaches to the skin of a human or animal and feeds on its blood is an example of
  a. commensalism.
  b. parasitism.
  c. competition.
  d. coevolution.
  e. mutualism.

Questions 22–24 are based on the following passage.

An island in the Adriatic Sea was overpopulated with snakes. Sailors who came to the island brought and let loose mongooses, animals that feed on snakes. The population of snakes started decreasing, since the mongooses were eating them. The mongoose population started increasing since there was ample food around. The mongooses were not native to the island and there were no predators on the island to keep the mongoose population in check. At some point, there were hardly any snakes left on the island, and people started populating it. The mongoose, facing a shortage of snakes, started eating chickens that people kept for their eggs and meat. However, people caught on, and protected the chickens from getting eaten. The mongoose population decreased. There are still some on the island, but their number is now at equilibrium, kept in check by the availability of food.

22. The passage illustrates
  a. the interdependence of organisms.
  b. the fragility of an ecosystem.
  c. the ability of humans to change an ecosystem.
  d. the relationship between the population of predator and prey.
  e. all of the above

23. There were hardly any snakes left on the island because
  a. the mongooses had eaten them.
  b. the people had killed them.
  c. there was no predator for the mongooses.
  d. the sailors brought them prey.
  e. the chickens didn't taste as good to the mongooses.

24. Which statement best describes the change in population of mongooses on the island?
  a. The population was zero before sailors brought a few. The few then multiplied, and the number of mongooses on the island is still steadily growing.
  b. The population was zero before sailors brought a few. The few then multiplied, increasing the number of mongooses. When the snakes were almost gone, the mongoose population started decreasing.
  c. The population was small before sailors brought more mongooses, increasing the gene pool. The number of mongooses kept growing, until the people started protecting the chickens.
  d. The population was small before sailors brought more snakes, increasing the food supply for the mongoose. The number of mongooses kept growing, until the snake population was almost gone. The mongooses died out, since they ran out of food.
  e. The population was initially large, but when a predator was brought by sailors, the number of mongooses decreased.

Questions 25–27 are based on the following passage.

A bottling company fills several barrels with sugar, water, and other natural ingredients. During the mixing process yeast is added. The mixture is then left to ferment a long period of time, then bottled, then sold.

25. Which of the following is a reasonable predicted outcome based on the process description?
  a. CO_2 levels and mixture temperature rise.
  b. CO_2 levels and mixture temperature drop.
  c. NH_3 will be produced.
  d. The mixture will evaporate.
  e. Nothing at all will happen.

26. Of the following, which beverage is most likely being produced in this process?
  a. soda
  b. wine
  c. distilled water
  d. fruit juice
  e. a new sports drink

27. Which type of respiration is at work in this example?
  a. abiotic
  b. anaerobic
  c. aerobic
  d. photosynthetic
  e. bidirectional

28. In the early nineteenth century, almost all peppered moths collected by biologists in the U.K. were pale and mottled. Only rarely was a collector able to find a dark peppered moth. After the industrial revolution, when furnaces filled the air with dark soot, the light peppered moth became rare and the dark peppered moth was most common in industrial cities. A reasonable explanation for this change is that the dark moth was less likely to be seen and eaten by birds against the dark background. This explanation illustrates the principle of
  a. conservation of energy.
  b. natural selection.
  c. gene flow.
  d. male competition.
  e. acquired traits.

29. All of the following are mammals EXCEPT
  a. humans.
  b. rabbits.
  c. whales.
  d. penguins.
  e. rats.

30. All of the following are primates EXCEPT
  a. humans.
  b. gorillas.
  c. whales.
  d. chimpanzees.
  e. orangutans.

31. A solar eclipse occurs when the moon blocks our view of the Sun. Select the diagram that best represents the position of the Sun, the Earth, and the moon during a solar eclipse (not drawn to scale), as well as the correct orbits.

a.

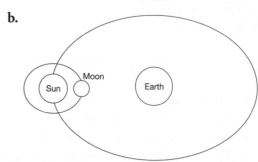

b.

c.

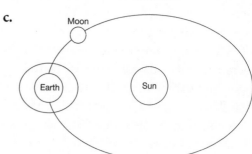

d.

e.

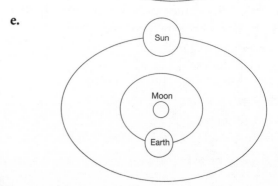

32. Convection currents of molten rock within the Earth's mantle cause all of the following EXCEPT
   a. sunlight.
   b. movement of plates on the Earth's crust.
   c. volcanic eruptions.
   d. earthquakes.
   e. flow of molten rock from cracks along the bottom of the ocean.

33. Which of the following does NOT cause changes in the Earth's surface such as the formation of mountains and valleys?
   a. collision of plates
   b. moving apart of plates
   c. volcanic eruptions
   d. erosion
   e. ozone

34. The United States is in the northern hemisphere. Which statement(s) about the southern hemisphere are true?
   I. It is always warm in the southern hemisphere.
   II. When it's summer in the northern hemisphere, it is winter in the southern hemisphere.
   III. In the southern hemisphere, the Sun sets in the east.
   IV. When it's winter in the northern hemisphere, it is summer in the southern hemisphere.
   a. statement I only
   b. statement II only
   c. statements II, III, and IV
   d. statements II and IV
   e. statements I, II, and IV

35. Humidity is a measure of
   a. air temperature.
   b. the amount of water vapor in air.
   c. air pressure.
   d. cloudiness.
   e. air resistance.

36. The Milky Way is estimated to be about 100,000 light-years across its larger diameter. A light-year is a measure of
   a. time since the Big Bang.
   b. distance.
   c. brightness.
   d. the number of stars in a galaxy.
   e. speed of light.

Questions 37–38 are based on the following passage.

According to scientists, the Sun has existed for 4.6 billion years. The Sun produces energy by a nuclear conversion of hydrogen into helium. When hydrogen runs out, according to this theory, the Sun will expand, engulfing the Earth and other planets. Not to worry—the expansion will not affect us, since the Sun has enough hydrogen for another 4.6 billion years. When it expands, the Sun will become what is called a red giant star. In another 500 million years, the Sun will shrink to the current size of the Earth and will be called a white dwarf, cooling down for several billion years.

37. According to the passage, the Sun will eventually
   a. expand and then shrink.
   b. shrink and then expand.
   c. shrink and then run out of helium.
   d. expand because it ran out of helium.
   e. shrink because it ran out of hydrogen.

38. Based on this theory, the Sun will at some point be a
   a. blue star.
   b. red dwarf star.
   c. red giant star.
   d. asteroid.
   e. galaxy.

39. Webbed feet enable ducks to swim better by
   a. making the ducks aerodynamic.
   b. increasing the surface area with which ducks propel water.
   c. preventing particles from being stuck between the duck's toes.
   d. making the duck less dense.
   e. increasing the rate of heat loss, so that ducks can cool down faster.

40. Which one of the following statements is an OPINION, rather than a fact?
   a. All organisms are made of one or more cells.
   b. It's wrong to kill any organism.
   c. All organisms need energy.
   d. Some organisms reproduce asexually.
   e. Some organisms can breathe underwater.

41. Here are a few experimental observations and known facts:

I.   A scummy substance often forms in solutions of an amino acid in water.

II. When the water is purified and exposed to UV radiation, the scummy substance does not form in the amino acid solution.

III. UV radiation kills bacteria.

What would be a valid hypothesis based on I, II, and III?

a. The scummy substance is a form of the amino acid.

b. The scummy substance would not appear if water were treated by a method, other than UV radiation, that kills bacteria.

c. The scummy substance is caused by organisms that humans are unable to detect.

d. The amino acid would not form the scummy substance in another galaxy.

e. UV light contributes to global warming.

42. Hypertension, or high blood pressure, is a condition that can lead to heart attack and stroke. A scientist graphed the following data collected from a study on hypertension. What is a logical conclusion based on the data?

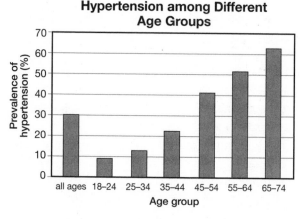

Hypertension among Different Age Groups

a. The prevalence of hypertension is higher than average in the 35–44 age group.

b. The prevalence of hypertension is highest in the 45–54 age group.

c. The prevalence of hypertension increases with age.

d. No teenager suffers from hypertension.

e. All senior citizens suffer from hypertension.

Questions 43–44 are based on the following passage.

Is Pluto a Planet?

Based on perturbations in Neptune's orbit, the search for a ninth planet was conducted and Pluto was discovered in 1930. However, the term *planet* never had an official meaning until August 2006. As defined, a planet is an object that orbits the Sun, dominating the neighborhood around its orbit, and must be large enough to have amassed a round shape due to the force of its own gravity. Pluto orbits around the Sun and is large enough to cite its gravitational force as the reason for its roundness. Pluto does not dominate its neighborhood because it is not all that much larger than its moon, Charon. Many believe that Pluto should be regarded as a planet because it has been classified as one for more than 70 years since its discovery.

43. In reference to the statements below, which answer choice correctly explains Pluto's classification?

I. Pluto orbits the Sun.

II. Pluto is large enough to have amassed a round shape due to the force of its own gravity.

III. Pluto dominates its region.

a. Pluto is a planet because statement I is true.

b. Pluto is a planet because both statement I and II are true.

c. Pluto is not a planet because statement I is false.

d. Pluto is not a planet because statement II is false.

e. Pluto is not a planet because statement III is false.

44. A group of scientists wish to justify classifying Pluto as a planet. Based on the information in the passage, which of the following strategies would best help them to accomplish this?

a. Prove that Pluto has been regarded as a planet for more than 70 years.

b. Use evidence to show that Pluto meets the 2006 definition.

c. Redefine the term *planet*.

d. Use data to show how similar Pluto's atmosphere is to Mercury's.

e. Use data to show that Pluto is neither an asteroid nor a comet.

45. The instrument shown here can be used to study

    a. cell organelles.
    b. the flight pattern of birds.
    c. the movement of stars in other galaxies.
    d. old manuscripts.
    e. human vision defects.

Questions 46–47 are based on the following passage.

Farm animals can carry salmonella, a kind of bacteria that can cause severe food poisoning. However, animals that are fed antibiotics can carry especially deadly strains of salmonella. In Minnesota in 1983, 11 people were hospitalized with salmonella poisoning. This number itself was not striking at all. Forty thousand Americans are hospitalized with salmonella poisoning every year. What was striking about the cases in Minnesota was that each patient had severe symptoms and that all of the patients were infected with the same, rare strain of salmonella, resistant to several common antibiotics. A young scientist, Scott Holmberg, noted that eight patients were taking the same antibiotics for sore throats. He ruled out the possibility that the antibiotics themselves were infected with the bacteria because three of the patients were not taking antibiotics at all. He later showed that the people were infected with salmonella prior to taking the antibiotics, but that the antibiotics triggered the onset of salmonella poisoning. He postulated that salmonella suddenly flourished when the patients took antibiotics, because the antibiotics killed off all other competing bacteria. He was also able to trace the antibiotic-resistant salmonella to the beef that was imported to Minnesota from a farm in South Dakota at which cattle were routinely fed antibiotics and at which one calf had died of the same strain of salmonella.

46. As a result of this finding, the Food and Drug Administration should
    a. carefully regulate the prescription of antibiotics for sore throats.
    b. prevent the export of meat from South Dakota to Minnesota.
    c. limit the practice of feeding antibiotics to cattle.
    d. take the antibiotic that caused salmonella off the market.
    e. require a special prescription for antibiotics resistant to salmonella.

47. Based on the passage, which one of the following statements is FALSE?
    a. Salmonella poisoning is a common bacterial infection.
    b. Some strands of bacteria are resistant to antibiotics.
    c. Antibiotics kill off bacteria that are not resistant to antibiotics.
    d. Antibiotics transmit salmonella.
    e. Farm animals can carry salmonella.

48. Which of the following is the most common result of prolonged excessive alcohol consumption?
    a. heart attack
    b. brain tumor
    c. lung cancer
    d. liver damage
    e. cataracts

49. Which of the following could be transmitted through kissing?
    a. lung cancer
    b. a brain tumor
    c. the flu
    d. diabetes
    e. lupus

50. Through friction, energy of motion is converted to heat. You use this in your favor when you
    a. wear gloves to make your hands warm.
    b. rub your hands together to make them warm.
    c. soak your hands with hot water to make them warm.
    d. place your hands near a fireplace to make them warm.
    e. hold a cup of tea to make your hands warm.

▶ Answers

1. d. Acid base reactions occur betweeen an acid and a base. Choice **d** is correct because it contains the only pair of liquids in which one is clearly acidic (vinegar—pH 3) and the other is clearly basic (bleach—pH 9). In choice **a**, both bleach and ammonia are basic. In choice **b**, both lye and ammonia are basic. In choice **c**, blood and saliva are very close to being neutral, and we would not expect an acid base reaction to occur. In choice **e**, both stomach acid and beer are acidic.

2. e. The object set in motion slows down and stops swinging because the force of friction acts on it. The kinetic energy of the object is converted to heat energy through friction with air. Statements **a**, **c**, and **d** are true, but are not the reason why the object stops swinging. An object having any mass can maintain motion, so choice **b** is incorrect.

3. b. An endothermic process requires the input of heat energy. The only one that requires input of energy (heat) is melting ice (ice melts when heated), making choice **b** correct. The rest of the processes listed give off heat, so they are exothermic.

4. a. Density is the measure of mass per volume. If one substance has less mass per a given volume than another, it is less dense. Things that float are less dense than the substance in which they float; if they were more dense, they would sink. This makes choice **a** correct. None of the other choices offers a valid scientific explanation as to why the ice would float.

5. b. The statement in choice **b** is false because the gravitational force between two objects depends on the masses of both objects. All the other statements are true and consistent with Newton's law of gravitation. Because you are looking for the statement that is NOT true, choice **b** is the correct answer.

6. a. When water vapor condenses, gas changes to liquid, so choice **a** is correct. Choices **b**, **c**, and **d** involve chemical reactions, and can't be considered physical processes. Through exhaling, choice **e**, air is pushed out of the lungs, but there is no phase change.

7. a. Two negative charges always repel each other, as stated in choice **a**. The choices that state that these would attract (choices **b**, **d**, and **e**) are incorrect. Since choice **c** states that they neither attract nor repel each other, it is also incorrect.

8. e. The statement in choice **e** is false because energy is not composed of matter (atoms). All other statements are true. Both matter and energy can neither be created nor destroyed (making both **a** and **b** true statements). In the universe, there is always a tendency for increased entrophy (disorder), making **c** a true statement. Choice **d** states that energy can be stored and transferred, which is true. Since you are looking for an incorrect statement, choice **e** is the correct answer.

9. b. Only choice **b** represents what the object looks like when it is inverted left to right (mirror image) and then flipped upside down. The second step (flipping the E upside down after inverting it from left to right) does not actually change how the inverted figure appears to us, because there is an axis of symmetry.

10. c. Gloves provide insulation, so choice **c** is correct. Insulators prevent the loss of heat, and this is why gloves keep our hands warm. Gloves can't generate heat, so we know that gloves that are outside would be cold, so choice **a** is incorrect. Gloves can't have an effect on the temperature, so choice **b** is incorrect. They also don't affect the amount of energy your body produces (as in choice **d**) or transform energy in any way (as in choice **e**).

11. d. The wavelength of blue-green should be between the wavelength of blue light and green light. The wavelength of blue light is about 450 nm and the wavelength of green light is at about 500 nm. 475 nm is midway between these wavelengths, making choice **d** the only plausible answer.

12. a. The number of atoms stays constant through-out a chemical reaction, so choice **a** is correct. The number of molecules can change, so choice **b** is incorrect. For example, in photosynthesis, 6 molecules of carbon dioxide and 6 molecules of water (a total of 12 molecules) can react to form 1 molecule of glucose and 6 molecules of oxygen (total of 7 molecules). Similarly, the amount of gas and solid can change (making choices **c** and **d** incorrect). The amount of disorder in the universe is always increasing, so it does not have to stay constant through a reaction, making choice **e** incorrect.

13. d. The statement in choice **d** is false because light has a finite speed. It is very large, but it is not infinite. The rest of the statements are true.

14. d. Thorns are a form of defense, but are neither camouflage nor a chemical defense. Since the question asks to find the choice that is NOT an example of camouflage or a chemical defense, choice **d** is the correct answer. Choices **a** and **e** are examples of camouflage. Choices **b** and **c** are examples of chemical defense.

15. d. The concentration of protein in compartment B is higher. Because of the nature of the membrane, the protein can't pass through it. This makes choices **a**, **b**, and **e** incorrect. The only way for concentration to reach the same level in two compartments is for water to flow from A to B. This movement of water is represented in choice **d**. Choice **c** is incorrect because it has the water flowing in the opposite direction.

16. a. Every human normally inherits 23 chromosomes from the mother and 23 chromosomes from the father, making choice **a** correct. Inheriting 23 chromosomes from the mother and 23 chromosomes from the father doesn't mean that humans look exactly 50% like the father and 50% like the mother (as in choice **b**), since one parent's genes can be more dominant, and since genes from two parents sometimes produce a blended effect. Fraternal twins happen to be in the womb at the same time, but genetically, they are not any more similar than two siblings who are not twins, making choice **c** incorrect. Fraternal twins come from two different eggs fertilized by two different sperm cells. Exposure to X-rays can alter chromosomes, so choice **d** is incorrect.

Genes are not particles. DNA is not an atom and it doesn't have a nucleus, thus choice **e** is incorrect. Genes are found in the nucleus of a cell and are made of DNA.

17. a. In order for twins to have the same genes, they need to come from one egg and one sperm cell, and it is the egg that divides into two after being fertilized by a sperm cell, so choice **a** is correct. Choice **b** represents what happens in the case of fraternal twins.

18. c. According to the Punnett square, the combination of genes of Parent I with the genes of Parent II results in either offspring with yy (which is yellow) or Yy (which is green), making **c** correct, and all the other choices incorrect.

19. e. The statement in choice **e** is false, so **e** is the correct answer. Animal cells do not have a cell wall. The other statements are true.

20. e. In humans, the sperm determines the sex of the offspring because the male has two different chromosomes. In birds, the female is the one with two different chromosomes, so she determines the sex of the offspring, thus choice **e** is correct, and **a** and **b** are incorrect. Birds have Ws and Zs, not Xs and Ys like humans, so choices **c** and **d** are incorrect.

21. b. The text in the question defines parasitism as when one species benefits at the expense of the other. The tick is a parasite. It benefits, while the animal it feeds off of suffers; thus, choice **b** is correct.

22. e. Statements **a** through **d** were illustrated in the passage. Mongooses depend on snakes for food, choice **a**. The balance in the ecosystem was disturbed when a new predator was introduced, choice **b**. Humans entirely changed the ecosystem when they brought the mongooses, choice **c**. When the population of mongooses increased, the population of snakes decreased, causing a drop in the population of mongooses, choice **d**.

23. a. There was no mention of choice **b** in the passage. Choice **c** is true, but not as directly related to snake disappearance as choice **a**. Choice **d** is false. Sailors did not bring prey for the snakes; they brought a predator. There isn't enough information to support choice **e**, and even if it were true, it wouldn't be directly related to the disappearance of snakes.

24. b. Choice **b** accurately states what happened based on the passage. There is no support for other statements in the passage.

25. a. According to the process description, fermentation is taking place during this process, and during fermentation CO_2 levels rise due to anaerobic respiration. Also, heat is produced during the process, causing a rise in temperature. Thus, choice **a** is correct.

26. b. As stated in the process description, fermentation is taking place and the process involves sugar and water. This would indicate that alcohol is also a byproduct of this process, making wine, choice **b**, the only logical choice.

27. b. When yeast is involved in a chemical process that uses sugar to make CO_2 and alcohol, the process that occurs is anaerobic respiration (choice **b**). Aerobic respiration would consume oxygen and yield CO_2, which, in this example, is not the case.

28. b. *Natural selection* is the process whereby the members of the species who are best able to survive and reproduce in an environment thrive, passing their genes on to next generations. The pollution in the environment selected for a new advantageous trait: the dark color of peppered moths.

29. d. Penguins are birds. They hatch from eggs and have wings. They are not mammals; they don't give birth to or breastfeed their young. Since you are looking for the choice that is *not* a mammal, choice **d** is the correct answer. All the other answer choices are mammals.

30. c. Whales are not primates. Primates have five digits on each hand and foot, binocular vision, and flexible shoulder joints. Since you are looking for the choice that is *not* a primate, choice **c** is the correct answer. All the other answer choices are primates.

31. a. The diagram in choice **a** corresponds to the correct arrangement of the Earth, the moon, and the Sun during a solar eclipse. The moon is located between the Earth and the Sun, blocking the Earth's view of the Sun. It also corresponds to the correct orbits, with the moon orbiting around the Earth, and the Earth around the Sun. Choice **b** is incorrect because it shows the Sun orbiting around the Earth, and

the moon around the Sun. Choice **c** is incorrect because the Earth, moon, and Sun are not aligned as they should be during an eclipse, and the moon is not orbiting around the Earth. Choice **d** shows correct orbits, but the moon is not blocking the Sun from the Earth's view. In fact, choice **d** corresponds to a lunar eclipse. Choice **e** is incorrect because it shows the Earth and the Sun orbiting around the moon.

32. a. Sunlight is caused by nuclear reactions on the Sun, not by convection currents of molten rock within the Earth's mantle, so choice **a** is the correct answer. All of the other items listed are, indeed, caused by the convection currents of molten rock within the Earth's mantle.

33. e. Ozone (choice **e**) cannot directly change the surface of the Earth, whereas the processes in choices **a** through **d** can.

34. d. When it's summer in the northern hemisphere, it is winter in the southern hemisphere, and vice versa, thus statements II and IV are correct. That makes choice **d** the correct answer; **b** is incorrect. On average, the southern hemisphere is not warmer than northern hemisphere, so statement I is incorrect, and all answer choices containing I are incorrect (**a** and **e**). The Sun always sets in the west, everywhere on Earth, so statement III is incorrect, and choices containing III are incorrect (**c**).

35. b. Humidity is a measure of the amount of water vapor in air; therefore, choice **b** is correct.

36. b. A light-year is a measure of the distance that light travels in a year (about 5.88 trillion miles), so choice **b** is correct.

37. a. The passage states that the Sun will first expand (not shrink, so choices **b**, **c**, and **e** are incorrect) when it runs out of hydrogen (not helium, so choice **d** is incorrect), and then 500 million years later it will shrink. Thus, choice **a** is correct.

38. c. Choice **c** is the correct answer based on the passage: *When it expands, the Sun will become what is called a red giant star.*

39. b. Webbed feet enable ducks to swim better by increasing the surface area on their feet, so choice **b** is correct. In swimming, being hydrodynamic, not aerodynamic (choice **a**), is important. Stuck particles between a duck's toes, choice **c**, would most likely not be a frequent problem. Webbed feet would not affect the duck's density (choice **d**) by much. The rate of heat loss (choice **e**) may be slightly higher because of larger surface area, but heat loss is not essential for swimming.

40. b. Choice **b** contains a statement that can't be tested by scientific means. All of the other statements can.

41. b. Choice **a** is not consistent with observation II. Choices **c** and **d** are not testable, and are therefore invalid. Choice **e** is not relevant to the observations.

42. c. Choice **c** contains the only statement supported by the graph. Notice that the height of the bars in the graph get taller from left to right, starting with the bar labeled 18–24. Thus, as age increases, the prevalence of hypertension increases. The *all ages* bar would be the average. Since the bar for the 35–44 age group is shorter than the average, choice **a** is incorrect. The highest bar is the 65–74 bar, so **b** is incorrect. We cannot tell if a teenager has suffered from hypertension for sure, but because there is a bar for 18–24, it is possible that some have, so choice **d** is not logical. Similarly, just because some senior citizens suffer from hypertension, it would not be logical to assume that all do, so choice **e** is incorrect.

43. e. The weakest argument is choice **e** because it is justified with authority, tradition, and past belief, rather than scientific facts. People have been wrong in the past, and noting that something has been done a certain way for years does not mean that there are no better ways. Thus, **e** is not a convincing scientific argument.

44. e. Pluto is not a planet according to the 2006 definition because it does not meet all three criteria. Statements I, II, and III would all need to be true in order for Pluto to be classified as a planet. The passage states: "Pluto orbits around the Sun and is large enough to cite its gravitational force as the reason for its roundness." Statement I and statement II are both true. The passage also states: "Pluto does not dominate its neighborhood because it is not all that much larger than its moon, Charon." Thus, statement III is false. Because one of the three criteria is not met, and the one that is not met is specified in statement III, choice **e** is correct.

45. c. Because the current definition of *planet* established criteria that Pluto does not meet, the only way to establish Pluto as a planet would be to change the definition. Choice **a** is a weak strategy because it attempts to justify the classification with tradition and past belief, rather than scientific facts. Choice **b** is also weak because there is no evidence to support the 2006 definition—in fact, all evidence contradicts the classification of Pluto as a planet. Choices **d** and **e**, though referring to true information, neither show that Pluto meets the current definition of the term *planet*, nor do they suggest a redefining of the term, and would both be unhelpful strategies.

46. c. Choice **a** is already being done: A prescription is needed to get the antibiotics. And since the antibiotics weren't directly making people ill (choice **d**), these measures wouldn't be necessary. There is nothing that indicates that all meat from South Dakota has salmonella or that meat from everywhere else is always healthy, so choice **b** would not be necessary. Choice **e** is incorrect because antibiotics are not resistant to salmonella; some salmonella is resistant to antibiotics. Only choice **c** would make sense, so this is the correct answer.

47. d. The statement in choice **d** is false. Antibiotics do not transmit samonella. The problem arose because the samonella was resistant to the antibiotics. All of the other answer choices contain true statements.

48. d. While alcohol damages other tissues, most alcoholics first experience liver failure, so choice **d** is correct. One of the functions of the liver is to rid the body of toxins. Alcohol is a toxin to the body.

49. c. Only certain contagious diseases can be transmitted through kissing, and the flu, choice **c**, is contagious. Health problems associated with the other choices are not contagious. One can't get lung cancer, a brain tumor, diabetes, or lupus by kissing someone who has it.

50. b. Only the action in choice **b** involves friction (of one hand against the other), so this is the correct answer. Choice **a** demonstrates insulation. Choices **c**, **d**, and **e** involve the transfer of heat energy from one place to another, and not the generation of heat through the energy of motion.

GED Mathematics Diagnostic Exam

▶ Part I

You are about to begin Part I of this diagnostic exam. You may use your calculator for these questions.

1. Ms. Klein bought 4 pounds of beef and $3\frac{1}{2}$ pounds of chicken for $13.98. If the beef cost $2.76 per pound, what was the cost of the chicken per pound?
   a. $0.72
   b. $0.80
   c. $0.84
   d. $0.87
   e. $0.92

Question 2 is based on the following figure.

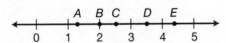

2. Which point on the number line represents the closest approximation to the square root of 12?
   a. *A*
   b. *B*
   c. *C*
   d. *D*
   e. *E*

3. A house and a lot cost $120,000. If the house cost 3 times as much as the lot, how much did the house cost?
- **a.** $30,000
- **b.** $40,000
- **c.** $60,000
- **d.** $90,000
- **e.** $100,000

4. Latrice made three long-distance calls. According to her phone bill, the calls were 19 minutes, 24 minutes, and 8 minutes in length. If Latrice pays 9 cents per minute on all long-distance calls, how much was she billed for the three calls?
- **a.** $2.70
- **b.** $4.59
- **c.** $5.10
- **d.** $13.77
- **e.** $15.30

5. Evaluate: $3[2(3 + 9) - 10]$
- **a.** 42
- **b.** −42
- **c.** 720
- **d.** −720
- **e.** 12

Question 6 is based on the following figure.

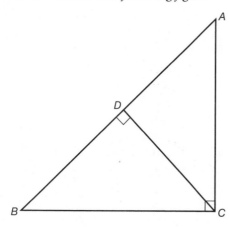

6. $\triangle ABC$ is a right triangle, and $\overline{CD} \perp \overline{AB}$. If the measure of $\angle CAD = 40°$, what is the measure of $\angle DCB$?
- **a.** 10°
- **b.** 20°
- **c.** 40°
- **d.** 50°
- **e.** 90°

7. The gauge on a water tank shows that the tank is $\frac{1}{3}$ full of water. In order to fill the tank, 16 gallons of water are added. How many gallons of water does the tank hold when full?
- **a.** 20
- **b.** 24
- **c.** 30
- **d.** 32
- **e.** 48

Question 8 is based on the following figure.

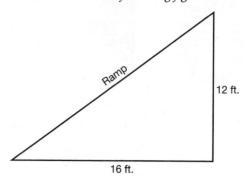

8. What is the length in feet of the ramp?
- **a.** 13
- **b.** 17
- **c.** 20
- **d.** 24
- **e.** Not enough information is given.

9. At a luncheon, 48 half-pints of fruit juice are served. What is the cost, at $3.50 per gallon, of these servings of fruit juice?
- **a.** $6.00
- **b.** $7.00
- **c.** $10.50
- **d.** $12.50
- **e.** $15.00

Question 10 is based on the following figure.

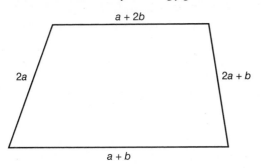

10. What is the perimeter of the figure?
   a. $6a + b$
   b. $5a + 5b$
   c. $6a + 4b$
   d. $3a + 5b$
   e. $3a + 5b$

Question 11 is based on the following figure.

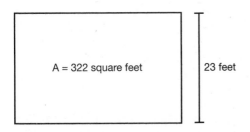

11. A rectangular dining room has a floor area of 322 square feet. If the length of the room is 23 feet, what is the perimeter?
   a. 28 feet
   b. 37 feet
   c. 45 feet
   d. 60 feet
   e. 74 feet

Question 12 is based on the following table.
This table gives the instructions that accompany an income tax form.

IF YOUR TAXABLE INCOME IS:		
At Least	But Not More Than	Your Tax Is
0	$3,499	2% of amount
$3,500	$4,499	$70 plus 3% of any amount above $3,500
$4,500	$7,499	$100 plus 5% of any amount above $4,500
$7,500		$250 plus 7% of any amount above $7,500

12. How much tax is due on a taxable income of $5,800?
   a. $120
   b. $135
   c. $150
   d. $165
   e. $175

Question 13 is based on the following graph.

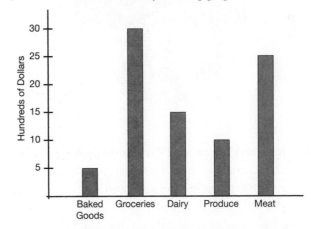

13. By how many dollars do the sales in the meat department exceed the sales in the dairy department?
   a. $100
   b. $1,000
   c. $1,500
   d. $1,800
   e. $10,000

Question 14 is based on the following graph.

Distribution of Expenses for Sales of $240,000 Ace Manufacturing Company

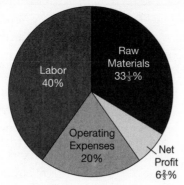

14. How many dollars were spent for labor?
a. $4,800
b. $9,600
c. $48,000
d. $96,000
e. $960,000

Question 15 is based on the following graph.

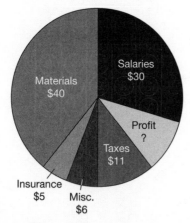

15. The graph shows what happens to each $100 taken in by a small business. How many dollars out of each $100 taken in represent profit?
a. $5
b. $6
c. $7
d. $7.50
e. $8

16. What is the median value of $268; $1,258; $654; $1,258; $900; $1,558; and $852?
a. $1,258
b. $960
c. $900
d. $913
e. $852

17. What is the mode of the following numbers: 14, 17, 14, 12, 13, 15, 22, and 11?
a. 13.5
b. 14
c. 14.75
d. 16.5
e. Not enough information is given.

18. A bag contains 12 red, 3 blue, 6 green, and 4 yellow marbles. If a marble is drawn from the bag at random, what is the probability that the marble will be either blue or yellow?
a. 7%
b. 12%
c. 16%
d. 25%
e. 28%

19. Danny worked 40 hours and earned $6.30 per hour. His friend Erica earned $8.40 per hour at her job. How many hours would Erica have to work in order to equal Danny's earnings for 40 hours?
a. 20
b. 25
c. 30
d. 252
e. Not enough information is given.

20. The number of students in a class is x. One day, 5 students were absent. What fractional part of the class was present?
a. $\frac{x}{5}$
b. $\frac{5}{x}$
c. $\frac{5}{(x-5)}$
d. $\frac{(x+5)}{5}$
e. $\frac{(x-5)}{5}$

21. Given the equation $x^2 + x - 6 = 0$, which of the following gives a complete solution of the equation?
a. 2
b. 2 and –3
c. –2 and 3
d. 2 and 3
e. 3 and –3

22. Henry has $5 more than Oliver and has the same amount of money as Murray. Together, they have $85. How much money does Oliver have?
a. $10
b. $12
c. $15
d. $25
e. Not enough information is given.

23. A box of cereal is priced at x cents per box. A customer has a coupon for 15 cents off. If the store reduces prices by doubling the value of each coupon, how much, in cents, does the customer pay for the box of cereal?
a. $x - 15$
b. $x - 30$
c. $x + 15$
d. $x + 30$
e. Not enough information is given.

24. If 1 dollar is worth x euros, what is the value, in dollars, of y euros?
a. xy
b. $\frac{x}{y}$
c. $\frac{y}{x}$
d. $\frac{1}{xy}$
e. $x + y$

25. If your hourly wage is $12.50 and you need to earn at least $250, how many hours will you have to work?
a. 10 hours
b. 12 hours
c. 15 hours
d. 18 hours
e. 20 hours

▶ **Part II**

You are about to begin Part II of this diagnostic exam. In this section, you must answer an additional 25 questions. Unlike Part I, you may NOT use your calculator for these questions, so be sure to put it away to simulate the actual GED testing experience.

26. A bed and breakfast charges $48.00 per day for a double room. In addition, there is a 5% tax. How much does a couple pay for several days' stay?
a. $144.00
b. $151.20
c. $156.20
d. $158.40
e. Not enough information is given.

27. The distance between two heavenly bodies is 63,150,000,000 miles. What is this number expressed in scientific notation?
a. 631.5×10^8
b. 63.15×10^9
c. 6315×10^7
d. 6.315×10^{10}
e. 6.315×10^{-10}

28. Andrea bought a used mountain bike for $250. She gave the bike a new paint job; replaced the tires, chain, and gear assembly; and sold the bike for 150% of the price she paid. For what amount, in dollars, did she sell the bike? Mark your answer in the following grid.

29. The sum of three consecutive even integers is 90. What is the greatest number in the series?
a. 26
b. 28
c. 30
d. 32
e. 34

30. Which of the following integers is NOT evenly divisible by 3?
a. 18,423
b. 7,690
c. 351
d. 128,502
e. 90

31. Evaluate: $-5(-6 \times 11) + 7^2$
Mark your answer in the following grid.

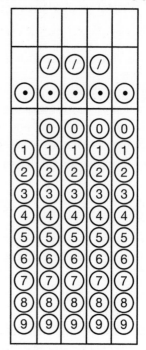

Question 32 is based on the following figure.

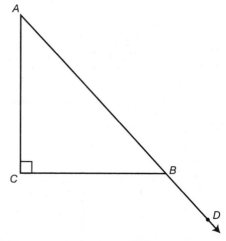

32. If $\overline{AC}$ is perpendicular to $\overline{CB}$ and m∠CBD = 125°, then m∠A equals
a. 15°
b. 20°
c. 35°
d. 45°
e. Not enough information is given.

Question 33 is based on the following figure.

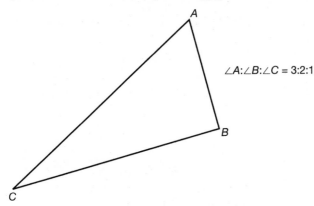

$\angle A : \angle B : \angle C = 3 : 2 : 1$

33. The measures of the angles of a triangle are in the ratio 3:2:1. What is the measure of the largest angle of the triangle?
   a. 65°
   b. 70°
   c. 72°
   d. 80°
   e. 90°

Question 34 is based on the following figure.

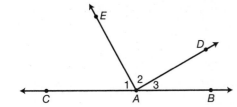

34. If m∠1 = 36° and m∠2 = 2(m∠3), then m∠3 equals
   a. 36°
   b. 40°
   c. 44°
   d. 48°
   e. Not enough information is given.

Question 35 is based on the following graph.

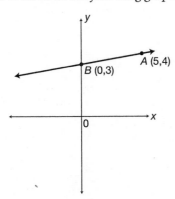

35. What is the slope of the line passing through points *A* (5,4) and *B* (0,3)?
   a. $\frac{1}{10}$
   b. $\frac{1}{5}$
   c. $\frac{3}{5}$
   d. $\frac{4}{5}$
   e. 5

Question 36 refers to the following graph.

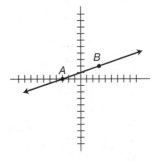

36. What is the slope of the line that passes through points *A* and *B* on the coordinate graph? Mark your answer in the following grid.

	/	/	/	
⊙	⊙	⊙	⊙	⊙
	0	0	0	0
1	1	1	1	1
2	2	2	2	2
3	3	3	3	3
4	4	4	4	4
5	5	5	5	5
6	6	6	6	6
7	7	7	7	7
8	8	8	8	8
9	9	9	9	9

37. Ajani finds that the distance between two land-marks on a map is $6\frac{1}{2}$ inches. If the map scale reads $\frac{3}{4}$ inch = 120 miles, what is the actual distance, in miles, between the two landmarks? Mark your answer in the following grid.

38. On a coordinate plane, a vertical line is drawn through the point (–3,4). On the same plane, a horizontal line is drawn through the point (2,–1). At what point on the plane will the two lines intersect? Mark your answer in the following coordinate grid.

Questions 39–41 refer to the following graph.

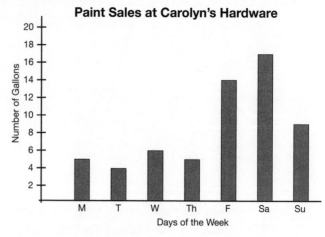

Paint Sales at Carolyn's Hardware

39. How many gallons of paint were sold on Wednesday?
   a. 3
   b. 4
   c. 5
   d. 6
   e. 7

40. How much more paint was sold on Saturday than on Monday?
   a. 6 gallons
   b. 8 gallons
   c. 10 gallons
   d. 11 gallons
   e. 12 gallons

41. What was the total amount, in gallons, of paint sold by the store that week? Mark your answer in the following grid.

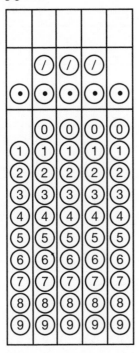

Questions 42 and 43 refer to the following graph.

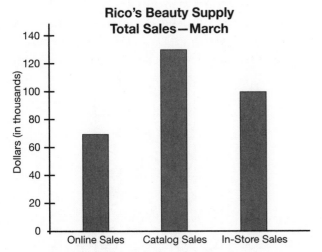

**Rico's Beauty Supply
Total Sales—March**

42. Customers of Rico's Beauty Supply can make purchases online, from a catalog, or in the store. About how much more did the company make from catalog sales than from online sales in March?
- **a.** $35,000
- **b.** $65,000
- **c.** $130,000
- **d.** $195,000
- **e.** $650,000

43. Approximately what fraction of the company's total sales came from in-store sales?
- **a.** $\frac{2}{3}$
- **b.** $\frac{1}{3}$
- **c.** $\frac{1}{2}$
- **d.** $\frac{1}{4}$
- **e.** $\frac{1}{6}$

44. What was Edmundo's mean score for a round of golf in August if his scores for each round were 78, 86, 82, 81, 82, and 77?
- **a.** 77
- **b.** 78
- **c.** 81
- **d.** 82
- **e.** Not enough information is given.

45. Norm borrows $8,000 for 5 years to make improvements to his home office. If the simple interest rate is 13%, how much will he pay in interest? Mark your answer in the following grid.

46. The solution $x = -5$ makes which of the following equations true?
   a. $14 - x = 9$
   b. $\frac{x}{5} = 1$
   c. $x + 3 = 8$
   d. $\frac{30}{x} = 6$
   e. $12x = -60$

47. Marc had $572.18 in his checking account. After writing a check, he had $434.68. Which of the following equations could be used to find the amount of the check (c)?
   a. $572.18 + c = 434.68$
   b. $572.18 - c = 434.68$
   c. $572.18c = 434.68$
   d. $572.18 - 2c = 434.68$
   e. $434.68 + c = 572.18$

48. What is the value of the expression $3(2x - y) + (3 + x)^2$, when $x = 4$ and $y = 5$? Mark your answer in the following grid.

49. A display of canned yams has a sign that reads "5 cans for $3." At the same rate, how much would the store charge, to the nearest whole cent, for 8 cans? Mark your answer in the following grid.

50. Deb has 12 times as many CDs as John. If Deb gives John 24 CDs, she'll have 4 times as many CDs as John. How many CDs do Deb and John have together? Mark your answer in the following grid.

▶ Answers

1. c. The beef costs 4($2.76) = $11.04. The chicken costs $13.98 − $11.04 = $2.94. To find the cost per pound of chicken, divide $2.94 by $3\frac{1}{2}$ or by $\frac{7}{2}$; $2.94 \div \frac{7}{2} = 2.94 \div \frac{7}{2} = 0.84$.

2. d. Since $3^2 = 9$ and $4^2 = 16$, $\sqrt{12}$ is between 3 and 4. Only point D lies between 3 and 4.

3. d. Let x = cost of lot and $3x$ = cost of house.
$x + 3x = 120,000$
$4x = 120,000$
$x = 120,000 \div 4 = 30,000$
$3x = 3(30,000) = \$90,000$

4. b. Add the times and multiply by 9 cents. 19 + 24 + 8 = 51 minutes. $51 \times .09 = \$4.59$.

5. a. Follow the order of operations:
$3[2(3 + 9) − 10] =$
$3[2(12) − 10] =$
$3[24 − 10] =$
$3[14] =$
42

6. c. Since m$\angle ACB$ = 90° and m$\angle CAD$ = 40°, then m$\angle B$ = 180 − 90 − 40 = 50°. In BCD, m$\angle CDB$ = 90° and m$\angle B$ = 50°. Therefore, m$\angle DCB$ = 180 − 90 − 50 = 40°.

7. b. If the tank is $\frac{1}{3}$ full, it is $\frac{2}{3}$ empty. Let x = the capacity of the tank; $\frac{2}{3}x = 16$, so $x = 16 \div \frac{2}{3} = 16 \times \frac{3}{2} = 24$.

8. c. Let x = the length of the ramp. Use the Pythagorean theorem to obtain the equation:
$x^2 = 12^2 + 16^2 = 144 + 256 = 400$
$x = \sqrt{400} = 20$

9. c. 48 half-pints = 24 pints. Since 2 pt. = 1 qt., 12 qt. = 3 gal., 3($3.50) = $10.50.

10. c. To find the perimeter of the figure, find the sum of the lengths of its sides.
$2a + a + b + 2a + b + a + 2b = 6a + 4b$.

11. e. Let x = the width of the room; $23x = 322$; $x = 322 \div 23 = 14$. Perimeter = 23 + 14 + 23 + 14 = 74 feet.

12. d. $5,800 − $4,500 = $1,300. Your tax is $100 + 5% of $1,300 = 100 + 0.05(1,300) = 100 + 65 = $165.

13. b. Meat department sales = $2,500
Dairy department sales = $1,500
Difference = $1,000

14. d. 40% of the total expenses of $240,000 went for labor; 0.40($240,000) = $96,000.

15. e. Add the amounts given: 11 + 6 + 5 + 40 + 30 = $92. $100 − $92 leaves $8 for profit.

16. c. The median is the middle amount when the numbers are arranged in order. Arrange the amounts in order, and find the middle amount, $900.

17. b. The mode is the number that occurs most often. Only 14 occurs more than once in the data set.

18. e. Add the total marbles: 12 + 3 + 6 + 4 = 25. The total blue and yellow marbles are 3 + 4, or 7. $\frac{7}{25}$ of the marbles might be blue or yellow. $\frac{7}{25} = 0.28$, or 28%.

19. c. Danny earned a total of 40($6.30) = $252. To find the number of hours Erica would take to earn $252, divide $252 by $8.40; $252 \div 8.4 = 30$.

20. e. If the class has x students and 5 students are absent, then $x − 5$ students are present: $\frac{(x-5)}{5}$.

21. b. If x is replaced by the answer choices, only 2 and −3 make the expression true.
$(2)^2 + 2 − 6 = 0 \qquad (−3)^2 + −3 − 6 = 0$
$4 + −4 = 0 \qquad\quad 9 + −3 − 6 = 0$
$\qquad\qquad\qquad\qquad 9 + −9 = 0$
$0 = 0 \qquad\qquad\quad 0 = 0$

22. d. Set up an equation with Oliver's money as the unknown, and solve. Oliver = x, Henry = $5 + x$, and Murray = $5 + x$. Therefore,
$O + H + M = 85$
$x + 2(5 + x) = 85$
$x + 10 + 2x = 85$
$3x + 10 = 85$
$3x = 75$
$x = 25$

23. b. Because the coupon has double value, the reduction is 2(.15) = 30 cents. The cost of the cereal is x − 30 cents.

24. c. If you don't see that you need to divide y by x, set up a proportion. Let z = number of dollars needed to purchase y euros.
$$\frac{\text{dollars}}{\text{euros}} = \frac{1}{x} = \frac{z}{y}$$
$$y\left(\frac{1}{x}\right) = \left(\frac{z}{y}\right)y$$
$$\frac{y}{x} = z$$

25. e. $12.50x \geq $250; $x \geq 20$ hours

26. e. You cannot compute the cost unless you are told the number of days that the couple stays at the bed and breakfast. This information is not given.

27. d. To express a number in scientific notation, express it as the product of a number between 1 and 10 and a power of 10. In this case, the number between 1 and 10 is 6.315. In going from 6.315 to 63,150,000,000, you move the decimal point 10 places to the right. Each such move represents a multiplication by 10^{10}, and $63,150,000,000 = 6.315 \times 10^{10}$.

28. 375.

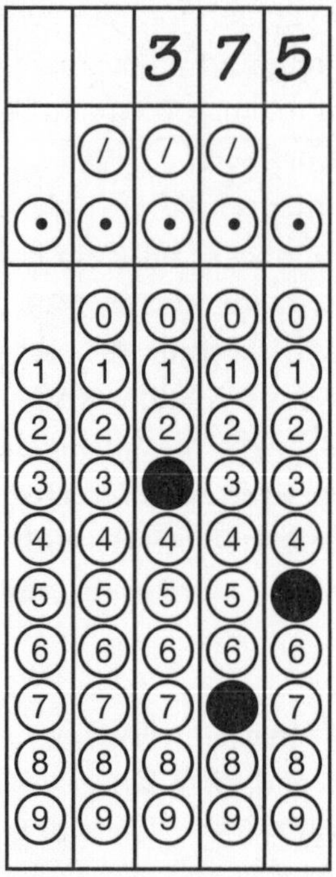

Multiply $250 by 1.5, which equals $375. Do not grid the dollar symbol.

29. d. The three numbers can be represented by x, $x + 2$, and $x + 4$. Solve the equation:
$x + x + 2 + x + 4 = 90$
$3x + 6 = 90$
$3x = 84$
$x = 28$
The three numbers are 28, 30, 32. The question asks for the largest of these.

30. b. According to the rules of divisibility, when the sum of the digits of any number equals a multiple of 3, then the entire number is evenly divisible by three. The sum of the digits of 7,690 = 22, which is not evenly divisible by 3.

31. 379.

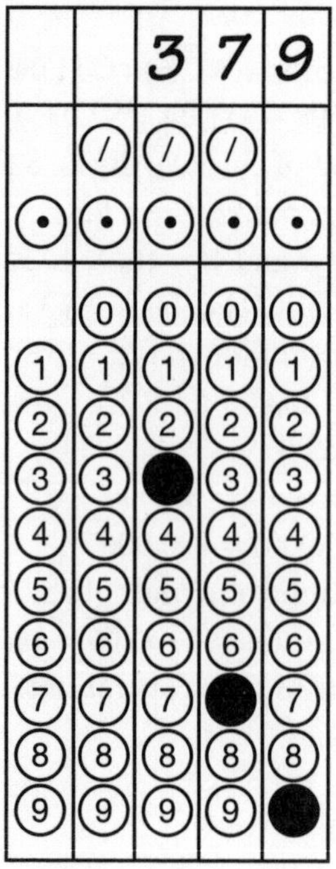

Perform operations within the parentheses first:
$-6 \times 11 = -66$
Then solve the exponent: $7^2 = 7 \times 7 = 49$
Simplify: $-5(-66) + 49$
$330 + 49 = 379$

32. c. $m\angle CBD = 125$
$m\angle ABC = 180 - 125 = 55$
$m\angle A + m\angle ABC = 90$
$m\angle A + 55 = 90$
$m\angle A = 90 - 55 = 35$

33. e. Let x, $2x$, and $3x$ be the measures of the three angles. Then:
$x + 2x + 3x = 180$
$6x = 180$
$x = 180 \div 6 = 30$
$3x = 3(30) = 90$

34. d. Let $x = m\angle 3$ and $2x = m\angle 2$
$m\angle 1 + m\angle 2 + m\angle 3 = 180$
$36 + 2x + x = 180$
$3x + 36 = 180$
$3x = 180 - 36 = 144$
$x = 144 \div 3 = 48°$

35. b. Slope $= \frac{y_1 - y_2}{x_1 - x_2}$; in this case, $y_1 = 4$, $y_2 = 3$, $x_1 = 5$, and $x_2 = 0$. Slope $= \frac{(4-3)}{5-0} = \frac{1}{5}$.

36. $\frac{1}{3}$.

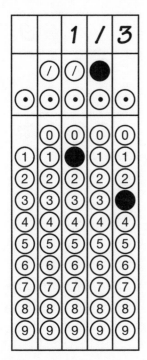

37. 1040.

The coordinates of point *A* are (−3,0). The coordinates of point *B* are (3,2). Use the slope formula:

$$\frac{y_2 - y_1}{x_2 - x_1}$$

Substitute and solve:

$$\frac{2 - 0}{3 - (-3)} = \frac{2}{6}, \text{ or } \frac{1}{3}$$

Set up the proportion and solve: *x* = the number of miles between the two landmarks.

$$\frac{(\frac{3}{4})}{120} = \frac{(6\frac{1}{2})}{x}$$

$6\frac{1}{2} \times 120 = 780$, and

$380 \div \frac{3}{4} = 1,040$

The answer is 1,040 miles. Remember that you do not grid commas, so the answer is 1040.

38. (–3,–1).

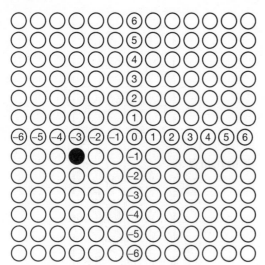

The vertical line is parallel to the *y*-axis, and all of its points have the *x*-coordinate –3. The horizontal line is parallel to the *x*-axis, and all of its points have the *y*-coordinate –1. Therefore, the coordinates are –3 and –1.

39. d. The top of the bar for Wednesday is at 6 on the vertical scale.

40. e. The top of the bar for Monday is halfway between 4 and 6, so 5 gallons were sold on Monday. The top of the bar for Saturday is halfway between 16 and 18, so 17 gallons were sold on Saturday. The difference between 17 and 5 is 12.

41. 60.

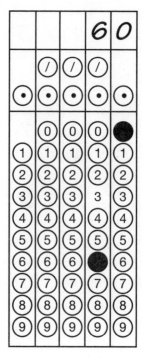

The tops of the bars for Monday through Sunday are at 5, 4, 6, 5, 14, 17, and 9. These add up to 60.

42. b. $130,000 (catalog sales) – $65,000 (online sales) = $65,000

43. b. $130,000 + $65,000 + $100,000 = $295,000, which is about $300,000. Working with compatible numbers, $100,000 out of $300,000 is $\frac{1}{3}$.

44. c. Mean = average. Add the scores and divide by the number of scores.
78 + 86 + 82 + 81 + 82 + 77 = 486
486 ÷ 6 = 81

45. 5200.

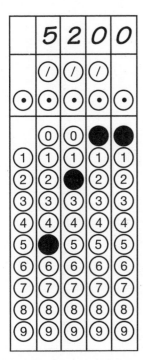

I = *prt* Multiply: $8,000 × 0.13 × 5 = $5,200. Remember that you do not grid commas or dollar signs.

46. e. Try −5 for *x* in each equation. Only choice **e** is true when −5 is substituted for *x*.

$$12x = -60$$
$$12(-5) = -60$$
$$-60 = -60$$

47. b. When you subtract the check from the amount in the checking account, the result will be the current balance; $572.18 − *c* = $434.68

48. 58.

Substitute the values for *x* and *y* in the expression, then simplify.

$$3(2 \times 4 - 5) + (3 + 4)^2 = 3(3) + 7^2 = 9 + 49 = 58$$

49. 4.8 or 4.80.

Set up the proportion $\frac{5}{3} = \frac{8}{x}$, where *x* is the cost of 8 cans of yams; $3 \times 8 = 24$, and $24 \div 5 = 4.80.

50. 195.

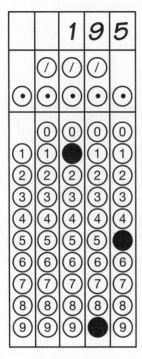

Set up the two equations that represent what you know.

$D = (12J)$

$(D) - 24 = 4(J + 24)$

Substitute $12J$ for D:

$(12J) - 24 = 4J + 96$

$8J = 120$

$J = 15$

If $J = 15$, $(12J) = 180 = D$

$D + J = 180 + 15 = 195$

GED Social Studies Diagnostic Exam

CHAPTER

9

Directions: Read each question carefully. The questions are multiple choice and may be based on a passage, table, or illustration. Select the one best answer to the question. Note: On the GED, you are not permitted to write in the test booklet. Make any notes on a separate piece of paper.

Please use the following to answer questions 1–4.

Voter Turnout in National Elections: 1980—2000

Year	Voting-age population	Voter turnout	Turnout as percentage of voting-age population
2000	205,822,000	105,380,929	51.2
1998	200,929,000	73,117,022	36.4
1996	196,511,000	96,456,345	49.1
1994	193,650,000	75,105,860	38.8
1992	189,529,000	104,405,155	55.1
1990	185,812,000	67,859,189	36.5
1988	182,778,000	91,594,693	50.1
1986	178,566,000	64,991,128	36.4
1984	174,466,000	92,652,680	53.1
1982	169,938,000	67,615,576	39.8
1980	164,597,000	86,515,221	52.6

Note: Bolded years represent years in which presidential elections were held.

1. In which year was voter turnout highest in terms of percentage of the voting-age population?
   a. 2000
   b. 1996
   c. 1994
   d. 1992
   e. 1988

2. Suppose you had been responsible for deciding how many ballots to print for the 2002 election. Based on the pattern shown, how many ballots do you think you would have needed?
   a. the same number as for 2000
   b. twice as many as for 2000
   c. about half as many as for 2000
   d. about three-quarters as many as for 2000
   e. about one and one-half times as many as for 2000

3. How does the change in voter turnout between 1984 and 1986 compare with the change between 1988 and 1990?
   a. In both cases, voter turnout increased by several percentage points.
   b. In both cases, voter turnout declined by several percentage points.
   c. In the first case, voter turnout went up; in the second, it declined.
   d. In the first case, voter turnout declined; in the second, it rose.
   e. In the first case, voter turnout rose; in the second, it was unchanged.

4. Which conclusion is best supported by the information in the table?
   a. Turnout is higher in presidential election years.
   b. Turnout declined sharply throughout the 1990s.
   c. Turnout steadily increased during the 1980s and 1990s.
   d. Turnout rose sharply throughout the 1980s.
   e. Turnout is highest in years that end in 0.

Please use the following to answer question 5.

Portuguese Sea Routes to the East

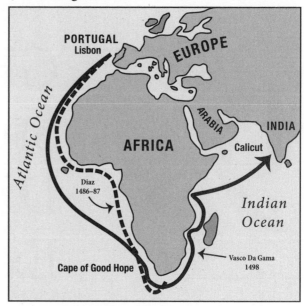

■ ■ ■ **Bartolomeu Diaz**
▬▬▬ **Vasco Da Gama**

5. What did the Portuguese explorer Bartolomeu Diaz achieve on his voyage of 1486–87?
   a. He purchased spices and jewels in India and brought them back to Portugal.
   b. He proved the existence of a sea route around southern Africa to the Indian Ocean.
   c. He crossed Africa on foot and reached Arabia.
   d. He managed to reach Calicut in India in only two years.
   e. He circled the globe and proved once and for all that the world was round.

Please use the following to answer questions 6–7.

The term **standard of living** is used to describe the minimum level of necessities and luxuries of life to which a person or a group is accustomed. The average (mean) standard of living in a country may be measured by dividing the GNP (the value of the goods and services produced in the national economy in a given year) by the number of citizens in the country. The resulting figure is the *per capita GNP*. Per capita GNP tells how much each person would receive if all the goods and services produced in the country during the year were divided equally.

An individual's standard of living, of course, may improve or decline depending on circumstances. Retirement from employment, for instance, often leads to a decline in the standard of living as retirees attempt to live on a percentage of their former income. The average standard of living in a country may be subject to change due to political upheaval, forces of nature, or global economics.

6. Which of these circumstances would almost certainly improve a person's standard of living?
   a. divorcing a spouse
   b. having a child
   c. receiving a college diploma
   d. experiencing a layoff
   e. filing tax forms on time

7. Country *X* has a larger gross national product than Country *Y*. To find out whether the standard of living is higher in Country *X*, what else would you need to know?
   a. the number of school-age children in Countries *X* and *Y*
   b. the size of the populations of Countries *X* and *Y*
   c. the number of retirees in Countries *X* and *Y*
   d. the number of unemployed workers in Countries *X* and *Y*
   e. the climates of Countries *X* and *Y*

8. "The United States was born in the country and moved to the city in the nineteenth century."
   —Anonymous
   To what great movement does this quotation refer?
   a. western expansion
   b. colonization
   c. industrialization
   d. imperialism
   e. populism

Please use the following to answer questions 9–12.

Roman Conquest of Gaul (Gallia), 58–51 B.C.

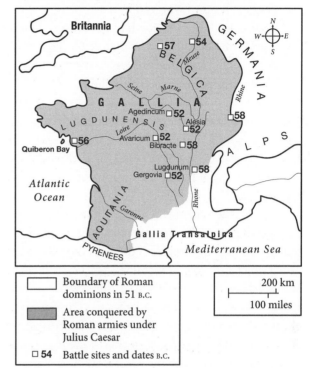

9. Complete the following sentence. A battle took place along the _____ River in 54 B.C.
   a. Garonne
   b. Rhine
   c. Seine
   d. Meuse
   e. Marne

10. Which answer lists battles in chronological order, according to the map?
   a. Avaricum, Lugdunum, Quiberon Bay
   b. Gergovia, Quiberon Bay, Lugdunum
   c. Alesia, Lugdunum, Quiberon Bay
   d. Quiberon Bay, Agedincum, Bibracte
   e. Bibracte, Quiberon Bay, Gergovia

11. Which conclusion is best supported by the information presented in the map?
   a. The Romans conquered Aquitania and Belgica.
   b. The Romans began their war of conquest in the north and worked their way south.
   c. The battle at Lugdunum lasted several months.
   d. Following the conquest of Gaul, the Romans planned to cross the Pyrenees.
   e. The climate in Belgica affected the Roman armies.

12. What do the Loire and Garonne rivers have in common?
 a. They both flow from west to east.
 b. They both flow from north to south.
 c. They both empty into the Atlantic Ocean.
 d. They both empty into the Mediterranean Sea.
 e. They are each over 1,000 miles long.

Please use the following to answer questions 13–16.

The following is an excerpt from the 1954 Supreme Court Decision Brown et al v. Board of Education of Topeka et al.

In each of these cases, minors of the Negro race, through their legal representatives, seek the aid of the courts in obtaining admission to the public schools of their community on a nonsegregated basis. In each instance, they had been denied admission to schools attended by white children under laws requiring or permitting segregation according to race. This segregation was alleged to deprive the plaintiffs of the equal protection of the laws under the Fourteenth Amendment. [. . .] A three-judge federal district court denied relief to the plaintiffs on the so-called "separate but equal" doctrine announced by this court in *Plessy v. Ferguson, 163 U.S.537.* Under that doctrine, equality of treatment is accorded when the races are provided substantially equal facilities, even though these facilities be separate. [. . .] The plaintiffs contend that segregated public schools are not "equal" and cannot be made "equal," and that hence they are deprived of the equal protection of the laws.

[. . .] We come then to the question presented: Does segregation of children in public schools solely on the basis of race, even though the physical facilities and other "tangible" factors may be equal, deprive the children of the minority group of equal educational opportunities? We believe that it does.

[. . .] Segregation of white and colored children has a detrimental effect upon the colored children. [. . .] We conclude that in the field of public education the doctrine of "separate but equal" has no place. Separate educational facilities are inherently unequal.

—Chief Justice Earl Warren, writing for the majority of the Court

13. According to Justice Warren, what is the question the Court must answer?
 a. Is segregation by race in public schools unfair to minority children?
 b. Should the Court demand equal facilities in segregated schools?
 c. Does the Court have authority over public school systems?
 d. Should Congress pass laws ending all segregation by race?
 e. Does the Constitution give control of education to the states?

14. The majority on this Court would most likely approve of which of the following?
 a. creating "minorities-only" seating sections in theaters and sports arenas
 b. passing laws that give majority racial groups special rights in the field of education
 c. establishing separate leagues for minority players in baseball
 d. making sure that public colleges do not bar minority students on the basis of race
 e. creating separate voting districts for minorities

15. According to the passage, which is true of the Fourteenth Amendment?
 a. It authorizes the separation of races in public schools.
 b. It provides for the establishment of a nationwide public school system.
 c. It specifies standard nationwide voting procedures.
 d. It is unreasonable and should be repealed.
 e. It requires that people receive the equal protection of the laws.

16. What reason did the Court give for rejecting the doctrine of "separate but equal"?
 a. Federal district courts have no power over public school systems.
 b. Schools can be segregated but still have equal facilities.
 c. Private schools offer equal educational opportunities to all children.
 d. Segregated schools are unequal by their very nature.
 e. Educational achievement is difficult to measure.

Please use the following to answer questions 17–20.

Unemployment Rates in Selected Countries, 1995

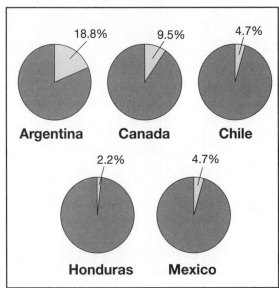

18.8% — Argentina
9.5% — Canada
4.7% — Chile
2.2% — Honduras
4.7% — Mexico

Key:
Percent Unemployed
Percent Employed
Total = 100%

17. What was Canada's approximate rate of unemployment in 1995?
a. 40%
b. 25%
c. 10%
d. 3%
e. less than 1%

18. Which two countries had about the same unemployment rate?
a. Chile and Mexico
b. Canada and Argentina
c. Chile and Argentina
d. Argentina and Mexico
e. Honduras and Canada

19. High unemployment is generally associated with a low growth rate and a low level of inflation. Based on the graphs, which country would you expect to have the lowest level of inflation?
a. Argentina
b. Chile
c. Honduras
d. Mexico
e. Canada

20. Which conclusion can you fairly draw from these data?
a. Workers travel to Chile from Mexico to earn higher wages.
b. A laborer from Honduras could easily find work in Argentina.
c. Honduras is the poorest nation in the western hemisphere.
d. Unemployment is directly related to a country's wealth.
e. Chile and Argentina, though neighbors, have different economic conditions.

21. "The history of the world is the record of a man in quest of his daily bread and butter."
—Hendrik Willem van Loon
Which of these methods of looking at history would van Loon find most valuable?
a. gender studies
b. historical geography
c. autobiography
d. economic history
e. anthropology

Please use the following to answer questions 22–24.

The core of the Iroquois empire extended from the Hudson River to the Genesee River in present-day central New York State, and from Lake Ontario to what is now the Pennsylvania–New York border. By 1700, the Iroquois had extended their territory westward, spreading some 800 miles between the Appalachians and the Mississippi River.

The power of the Iroquois began in the 1500s, when Hiawatha brought together the Five Iroquois Nations of the New York valley and formed the Iroquois League to try and keep the peace. Although the league lasted 300 years, the so-called "Great Peace" would not last. One important reason for the destruction of the peace was the fur trade.

As the French began systematic fur-trading, the Algonquians became their main suppliers of beaver pelts. Meanwhile, Dutch traders created a similar pact with the Iroquois. In a short time, both Algonquian and Iroquois territories were denuded of wildlife, and a struggle for trapping grounds ensued. The Iroquois routed the Algonquians, who fled eastward to the seashore. The French turned to the Hurons to replace the Algonquians as trading partners, but the Dutch urged their Iroquois allies to break the Huron monopoly. By the mid-1600s, the Iroquois had succeeded in destroying the Huron civilization and sending the survivors west to the plains.

22. According to this passage, why did Hiawatha create the Iroquois League?
   a. to secure a lasting peace among the Five Iroquois Nations
   b. to strengthen his bargaining position in negotiations with the Dutch
   c. to form a buffer against invasion by the Algonquians
   d. to extend the boundaries of the Iroquois empire
   e. to strengthen ties between the Huron and the Iroquois

23. Which conclusion about the fur trade is best supported by the information presented?
   a. The fur trade built friendship among the tribes.
   b. European traders were generous to their American Indian partners.
   c. The fur trade improved the standard of living for all.
   d. Fur traders traveled all the way to the Rocky Mountains.
   e. The fur trade was a negative influence on tribal life.

24. According to this passage, why did the Iroquois make war on the Hurons?
   a. They wanted the Hurons' land to use for farming.
   b. They had been attacked by the Hurons' French partners.
   c. They feared that the Hurons would join forces with the Algonquians.
   d. They were encouraged to do so by the Dutch.
   e. They disapproved of the Hurons' treaty with the French.

Please use the following to answer question 25.

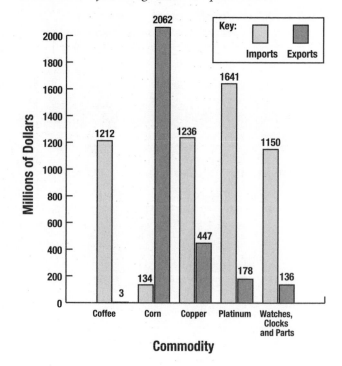

25. According to the chart, which of the following items, if found in a store in the United States, would most likely be entirely American made?
   a. copper tubing
   b. a platinum wedding band
   c. a package of frozen corn
   d. a can of coffee
   e. an alarm clock

GOING THROUGH THE FORM OF UNIVERSAL SUFFERAGE.
Boss. "You have the *Liberty of Voting* for any one you please; but we have the *Liberty of Counting* in any way we please."
"Do your Duty as Citizens, and leave the rest to take its course."—*The New York Times.*

26. What is the main point of the above political cartoon, "Going Through the Form of Universal Suffrage"?
  a. Voting is a privilege to be earned by the citizenry.
  b. Voters should always cast their ballots strictly along party lines.
  c. Universal suffrage is meaningless when political bosses control the ballot box.
  d. Voting is the right of every working person.
  e. Once the citizens have done their duty, democracy is ensured.

27. According to the respected American historian Frederick Jackson Turner, America's western frontier finally closed in the year 1890. Which of the following facts from the 1890 census is the best evidence for Jackson's statement?
  a. In 1890, 35% of Americans lived in cities.
  b. In 1890, there was no longer any single large area in the West without settlers.
  c. In 1890, the population of Los Angeles reached 50,000.
  d. In 1890, Chicago had become the second largest city in the United States.
  e. In 1890, more than 10% of the U.S. population was foreign born.

Please use the following to answer questions 28–30.

The Neolithic Era saw significant climatic changes that allowed for the beginning of farming in many parts of the world.

The Rise of Farming in the Neolothic Era

9000 B.C.	collection of wild cereals, domestication of dog, pig, goat
8000 B.C.	cereal cultivation, first villages, pottery, cattle-keeping groups
7000 B.C.	linen textiles, copper ornaments, root crops, domestication of sheep and cattle
6000 B.C.	smelting, irrigation, plowing
5000 B.C.	woolen textiles, domestication of horse and donkey, tree crops, maize, rice cultivation
4000 B.C.	domestication of llama by New World peoples, cotton textiles, wheeled vehicles, sailboats

28. How did people's lives change when they began cultivating cereal crops?
   a. They stopped being afraid of wild animals.
   b. They started painting on the walls of caves.
   c. They started using fire to cook their food.
   d. They started using axes and other tools.
   e. They started settling down in villages.

29. Is it reasonable to conclude that cattle were used for plowing before horses were?
   a. No, because horses were domesticated before cattle were.
   b. No, because cattle were still wild when plowing was introduced.
   c. Yes, because horses were not yet domesticated when plowing was introduced.
   d. Yes, because cattle were more common than horses were.
   e. No, because llamas might just as easily have been used.

30. Which statement based on the diagram is an opinion rather than a fact?
   a. The wheel was invented long after people settled down in villages.
   b. Dugout canoes preceded sailboats by thousands of years.
   c. Olive trees and fruit trees were first cultivated around 5000 B.C.
   d. In the New World, the llama served a purpose similar to a sheep or cow in the Old World.
   e. Irrigation was the Neolithic era's most important innovation.

Please use the following to answer question 31.

Residency Requirements for Voting

State	Residency Requirement
California	Must be a registered voter 29 days before an election; 20-day residency requirement
Colorado	25-day residency requirement
Illinois	30-day residency requirement
Kansas	14-day residency requirement
Missouri	No durational residency requirement; must be registered by the fourth Wednesday prior to election

31. An election is to be held on Tuesday, November 6. In which of these states would someone who moved to the state on Monday, October 1, and registered immediately be allowed to vote?
   a. California only
   b. California and Kansas only
   c. all the states listed except Missouri
   d. all the states listed except Illinois
   e. all the states listed

Please use the following to answer question 32.

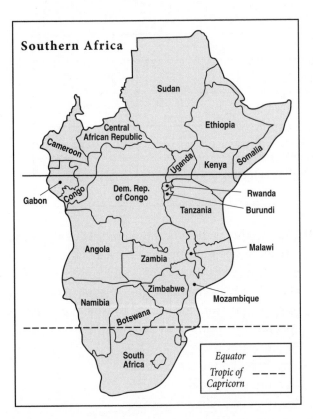

Southern Africa

Sudan

Ethiopia

Central African Republic

Cameroon

Uganda Kenya Somalia

Gabon Congo Dem. Rep. of Congo Rwanda

Tanzania Burundi

Angola Zambia Malawi

Zimbabwe

Namibia Mozambique

Botswana

South Africa

Equator ————
Tropic of - - - - -
Capricorn

32. Which countries lie entirely between the Tropic of Capricorn and the Equator?
a. Namibia and Botswana
b. Angola and Malawi
c. South Africa and Kenya
d. Angola and South Africa
e. Botswana and Mozambique

Please use the following to answer question 33.

As damaging as it was in terms of American lives lost, World War II had an even greater effect on the lives of British, French, and Soviet soldiers and civilians. This chart compares the losses.

Country	Military Losses	Civilian Losses
United States	292,131	fewer than 10
Britain	397,762	70,000
France	210,671	173,260
Soviet Union	14,500,000	7,700,000

33. Which of the following most likely explains why civilian losses were so much lower in the United States than in Europe?
a. The U.S. military was better able to protect its civilians.
b. Outside of certain Alaskan islands, no fighting took place on U.S. soil.
c. U.S. civilians were not allowed to witness battles.
d. More U.S. civilians were drafted into the armed forces.
e. The United States was far more sparsely populated.

34. A civil war is defined as a war between factions or regions of the same country. Based on this definition, which of these is NOT a civil war?
a. the 1642 struggle between supporters of the king and parliamentarians in England
b. the 1918 conflict between the anticommunist White Army and the Red Army of the Soviets in Russia
c. the war between the Hutu and Tutsi peoples in present-day Rwanda
d. the 1904 conflict between Russia and Japan over control of Manchuria and Korea
e. the war during the 1920s between the Irish republicans and the Irish Free State forces in Ireland

Please use the following to answer question 35.

Famous Explorers of the Middle Ages

Name	Nationality	Journeys	Date
Eric the Red	Norwegian	to Greenland from Iceland	c. 982
Leif Ericsson	Norwegian	may have reached mainland North America	c. 1000
Marco Polo	Italian	Sri Lanka, China, India, Iran, Sumatra	1271–1295
Odoric of Pordenone	Italian	Turkey, Iran, across Central Asia, Indian and South Pacific oceans	c. 1314–c. 1330

35. Which of the following most likely explains why the Norwegian explorers traveled west whereas the Italian explorers traveled east?
  a. The Italians were looking for wealth, but the Norwegians were looking for land.
  b. Geography made it easier to travel eastward from Italy and westward from Norway.
  c. Italian explorers had already visited North America.
  d. Norwegian explorers had nothing to trade with the people of Asia.
  e. Explorers from northern Europe could not cope with the climate of the Far East.

36. Sovereignty is the power or authority of a government. At one time, people believed that governments ruled by divine right, with power granted by God. Today's democratic governments receive their sovereignty from the people. By what means do the people demonstrate sovereignty in a democracy?
  a. crowning a king
  b. serving in the armed forces
  c. voting on issues
  d. attending religious services
  e. obeying the law

Please use the table at the bottom of this page to answer question 37.

37. Which country belongs to OPEC and ASEAN but not the Arab League?
  a. Indonesia
  b. Algeria
  c. Iraq
  d. Kuwait
  e. Brunei

International Organization	Members
Arab League	Algeria, Bahrain, Comoros, Djibouti, Egypt, Iraq, Jordan, Kuwait, Lebanon, Libya, Mauritania, Morocco, Oman, Qatar, Saudi Arabia, Somalia, Sudan, Syria, Tunisia, United Arab Emirates, Yemen, Palestine Liberation Organization
Organization of Petroleum Exporting Countries (OPEC)	Algeria, Indonesia, Iran, Iraq, Kuwait, Libya, Nigeria, Qatar, Saudi Arabia, United Arab Emirates, Venezuela
Association of Southeast Asian Nations (ASEAN)	Brunei, Burma, Cambodia, Indonesia, Laos, Malaysia, Philippines, Singapore, Thailand, Vietnam

Please use the following to answer question 38.

First Phase of the Korean Conflict, 1950

June 25	North Korea invades South Korea.
June 27	The United Nations asks member nations to aid South Korea.
June 1	Allied troops from the United States and other UN members begin arriving in South Korea.
October 19	Allied troops capture Pyongyang, the North Korean capital.
October 25	China enters the war on the side of North Korea.
November 26	Allied troops begin to retreat.

38. What is the most likely reason for the Allied retreat on November 26?

a. The arrival of Chinese troops greatly increased enemy strength.

b. Chinese forces withdrew from the Korean peninsula.

c. The United Nations called for a general end to the conflict.

d. South Korea agreed to a truce with North Korea.

e. The capture of Pyongyang was the only goal of the Allied advance.

Please use the following to answer question 39.

U.S. Immigrants, 1880–1920 by Ethnic Origin

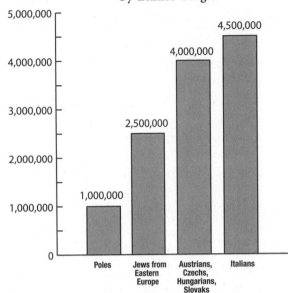

39. Which conclusion regarding immigration to the United States is supported by information in the graph?

a. The Italians were the largest immigrant group during this period.

b. Italians and Poles immigrated because of religious persecution.

c. Italians and Poles immigrated at the same rate and number.

d. During this period, the population of Italy was greater than that of Poland.

e. Most immigrants during this period were Jews.

Please use the following to answer questions 40–41.

Laissez-faire economics refers to the idea that people are most productive when governments leave them alone to do whatever they please. The term was coined by the Physiocrats, a group of eighteenth-century French thinkers. The Physiocrats believed that the government should do nothing to hinder free competition among producers and sellers. They also thought that there should be no restrictions on foreign trade, and that countries that practiced free trade would grow rich. However, other economists, called Mercantilists, believed just the opposite. The Mercantilists thought that the government should try to control foreign trade to make it more profitable. Of course, neither the Physiocrats nor the Mercantilists ever imagined today's world of multinational corporations. Today, *laissez-faire* can sometimes mean leaving corporations free to form unfair monopolies. Nevertheless, free trade remains popular in major exporting countries such as the United States.

40. What is the author's attitude toward *laissez-faire* economics?

   a. It is the most useful economic policy ever invented.

   b. It was wrong from the start.

   c. It should immediately be applied in the United States.

   d. It is not always the best policy in today's world.

   e. It involves too much government interference in business.

41. How did the Physiocrats differ from the Mercantilists?

   a. The Mercantilists favored farming; the Physiocrats favored industry.

   b. The Physiocrats favored government regulation; the Mercantilists did not.

   c. The Physiocrats favored the wealthy; the Mercantilists favored the poor.

   d. The Physiocrats favored monopolies; the Mercantilists did not.

   e. The Mercantilists favored government regulation; the Physiocrats did not.

Please use the following to answer question 42.

Euro Conversion Rates

On January 1, 1999, 11 European countries began phasing in the "euro" to replace their national currencies. The following table shows the value of one euro in each of the 11 countries' currencies.

1 euro =

13.76	Austrian schillings
40.34	Belgian francs
2.20	Dutch guilders
5.95	Finnish markkas
6.56	French francs
1.96	German marks
0.79	Irish punts
1,936.27	Italian lire
40.34	Luxembourg francs
200.48	Portuguese escudos
166.39	Spanish pesetas

42. Which conclusion is best supported by the information in the table?

   a. A German mark is worth less than a Finnish markka.

   b. An Irish punt is the currency with the greatest value of the euro.

   c. Belgium and Luxembourg share a government.

   d. It takes more than 200 euros to equal one Portuguese escudo.

   e. One euro is worth more Finnish markkas than French francs.

Please use the following to answer question 43.

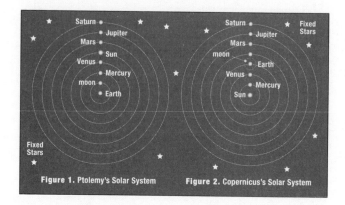

Figure 1. Ptolemy's Solar System   **Figure 2.** Copernicus's Solar System

43. In 150 A.D. the Greek astronomer Ptolemy taught that the solar system was structured as shown in Figure 1. Much later, in the sixteenth century, the Polish astronomer Nicolai Copernicus proposed the structure shown in Figure 2. What is the biggest difference between Ptolemy's and Copernicus's ideas?

   a. Ptolemy thought that Mars and Venus were comets, but Copernicus said they were planets.

   b. Ptolemy thought that the Earth was at the center of the solar system, but Copernicus said that the Sun was at the center.

   c. Ptolemy thought that Saturn was the most distant planet, but Copernicus said that there was another planet beyond Saturn.

   d. Ptolemy thought that the Sun was at the center of the solar system, but Copernicus said that the Earth was at the center.

   e. Ptolemy thought that the orbits of the planets were circular, but Copernicus said they were oval in shape.

Please use the following to answer question 44.

Earliest Civilizations

	Egypt	**Sumer**	**India**	**China**
Start Date	3000 B.C.	3200 B.C.	2500 B.C.	2100 B.C.
Location	Nile River valley	Euphrates River valley (Iraq)	Indus River valley	Huang Ho River valley
Main Sites	Memphis, Thebes	Ur, Eridu	Harappa, Mohenjo-Daro	Zhengzhou, Anyang
Types of Writing	hieroglyphics	cuneiform	Indus writing	Chinese characters
Forms of Government	monarchy	monarchy	unknown	monarchy

44. Which conclusion is best supported by the information presented in the chart?
   a. All early civilizations were monarchies.
   b. Egypt is the oldest of the world's civilizations.
   c. Many of the world's earliest civilizations developed in river valleys.
   d. All early civilizations used a type of writing called hieroglyphics.
   e. Civilization began in China and spread westward across Asia.

Please use the following to answer question 45.

- **Monroe Doctrine, 1823:** The United States vows to oppose any attempt by European countries to establish colonies in Latin America or elsewhere in the western hemisphere.
- **Good Neighbor Policy, 1933:** The United States and Latin American countries pledge not to interfere in each other's internal affairs.
- **Marshall Plan, 1948:** The United States helps European countries to recover from the destruction of World War II.
- **Alliance for Progress, 1961:** The United States vows to help promote economic and social development in Latin America.

45. Which item on the list does not fit with the others?
   a. The Good Neighbor Policy, because it involved the United States.
   b. The Monroe Doctrine, because it involves Latin America.
   c. The Good Neighbor Policy, because it was introduced after 1900.
   d. The Alliance for Progress, because it did not have warlike aims.
   e. The Marshall Plan, because it did not involve Latin America.

46. The eighteenth-century slave trade was a "triangular" trade. A ship would travel from Europe to West Africa carrying cotton fabrics, hardware, and guns. In Africa, these items would be traded for slaves. The ship would then carry the slaves to the West Indies and the southern American colonies. Finally, the ship would return to Europe carrying sugar and tobacco.
   Which of the following would you most likely find on board an eighteenth-century slave ship sailing from the West Indies to Great Britain?
   a. slaves
   b. cotton fabrics
   c. sugar
   d. guns
   e. hardware

Please use the following to answer questions 47–50.

CALIFORNIA VOTER GUIDE
California Legislative Races

The California State Legislature is made up of two houses: the Senate and the Assembly. The Senate is the upper house. There are 40 senators, each representing about 800,000 people. The Assembly is the lower house. There are 80 assembly members, each representing about 400,000 people. Senators and assembly members receive an annual salary of $99,000 plus per diem; legislative leaders receive a slightly higher salary.

Assembly members are elected to two-year terms and are limited to serving three terms. Senators are elected to four-year terms and are limited to serving two terms. California's legislative districts are "nested," so that two Assembly districts comprise one Senate district.

The California Voter Foundation has compiled information on each of this year's 80 state Assembly races and 20 state Senate races. (Half the Senate seats are up for election in each election year—this year the odd-numbered seats are up.) In this guide you will find a list of the candidates running in each district, their party affiliation, and contact information. You will also learn how to access candidates' websites, which typically feature campaign literature, endorsement lists, position papers, and information about how to contribute or volunteer.

47. Based on the guide, which statement is true about California legislators?
   a. Each senator represents more people than each assembly member.
   b. Each assembly member represents more people than each senator.
   c. Senators have term limits, but assembly members do not.
   d. Assembly members have term limits, but senators do not.
   e. Senators make twice as much money as assembly members do.

48. Why won't voters choose all of California's state senators in the next election?
   a. Some Senate seats have term limits.
   b. Typically only half of eligible voters vote.
   c. California's legislative districts are "nested."
   d. Only half the Senate seats are up for election in any election year.
   e. There are half as many senators as assembly members.

49. A California assembly member was first elected in 1996 and reelected in 1998. Which of the following would be true of her 2000 campaign for reelection to the Assembly?
   a. It is illegal under the laws of California.
   b. If she won in 2000, she would be allowed to run for the Assembly again in 2002.
   c. She would be running for her final term in the Assembly in 2000.
   d. She would be required to change her party affiliation to run for the Assembly again.
   e. She would run uncontested and win the seat in the Assembly.

50. Based on the guide, if you live in an odd-numbered district, which of the following is true?
   a. You need only vote for a senator in the coming election.
   b. You may vote for both an assembly member and a senator in the coming election.
   c. You need only vote for an assembly member in the coming election.
   d. You are represented only by a senator.
   e. You are represented only by an assembly member.

► Answers

1. d. The fourth column of the table shows voter turnout as a percentage of the voting-age population. According to the table, that percentage was highest in 1992, which is choice **d**. Choices **a**, **b**, **c**, and **e** are all years when the voter turnout percentage was lower.

2. d. The table shows a distinct pattern in voter turnout: in every other election, turnout goes up; then, in the next election, it declines. Based on this pattern, 2000 was an "up" year, and turnout most likely declined in 2002. Furthermore, the pattern appears to be that turnout in each "down" year is about three-quarters of turnout in the preceding "up" year (turnout in 1990 was 73% of turnout in 1988; turnout in 1994 was 72% of turnout in 1992; turnout in 1998 was 76% of turnout in 1996). Based on this pattern, for 2002 you would have needed to print about three-quarters as many ballots as were used in 2000, which is choice **d**. Choices **a**, **b**, **c**, and **e** do not fit this pattern.

3. b. The pattern shown in the table is that in every other election, turnout goes up; then, in the next election, it declines. The years 1984 and 1988 were both "up" years, followed in 1986 and 1990 by "down" years. Choice **b** is the only one that fits this pattern. Nothing in the table supports choices **a**, **c**, **d**, or **e**.

4. a. The pattern shown in the table is that in every other election, turnout goes up; then, in the next election, it declines. The "up" years, 1980, 1984, 1988, 1992, 1996, and 2000, were all presidential election years, so choice **a** is the correct answer. There is no evidence in the table to support the conclusions in choices **b**, **c**, **d**, or **e**.

5. b. The map shows that Diaz sailed south from Portugal, rounded the southern tip of Africa, and entered the Indian Ocean. Choices **a** and **d** cannot be correct because, unlike his fellow explorer Vasco da Gama, Diaz never reached India. Choice **c** cannot be correct because Diaz made a sea voyage, not a land journey. Choice **e** cannot be correct because Diaz did not circle the globe. Choice **b** is the only conclusion that can fairly be drawn from the information from the map: Diaz's voyage proved that there is a sea route around southern Africa to the Indian Ocean.

6. c. The passage says that an individual's standard of living may improve or decline depending on personal circumstances, such as retirement. However, choice **a**, divorcing a spouse, is no guarantee of improvement; in fact, many divorced people experience a decline in living standards. Choice **b**, having a child, is also no guarantee of improvement, and choice **d**, experiencing a layoff, often leads to a decline in living standards. Choice **e**, filing tax forms on time, has no effect one way or the other. Only choice **c**, receiving a college diploma, will almost certainly lead to a higher standard of living, since it is reasonable to conclude that an improvement in education level will result in increased income.

7. b. According to the passage, the average standard of living in a country is calculated by dividing the country's gross national product (GNP) by the number of inhabitants. Thus, to compare the standards of living in Country X and Country Y, you would need to know the GNP of each country and also the number of people in each country so that you could calculate and compare per capita GNP. None of the information described in choices **a**, **c**, **d**, and **e** would be helpful in calculating per capita GNP.

8. c. The United States was indeed "born in the country" in the sense that, at its start, the nation was overwhelmingly rural. However, the nineteenth century in the United States was the time of the Industrial Revolution. During this period, factories were built in the cities, and great numbers of people left the farms and small towns to become city-dwelling factory workers. This is the movement to which the quote refers, so **c** is the best answer. Choice **a** is incorrect because westward expansion refers to the acquisition of new territories in the West by the United States during the nineteenth century; that migration resulted in an increase in the nation's rural population. Choice **b** is incorrect because colonization refers to the settlement of English colonies along the Eastern Seaboard in the seventeenth and eighteenth centuries. Choice **d** is incorrect because imperialism refers to the takeover of territories in Africa, Asia, and the Pacific, mainly by European countries during the nineteenth and early twentieth centuries. Choice **e** is incorrect because populism was a nineteenth-century political movement that represented mainly farming interests; it called for government control of monopolies and cartels.

9. d. According to the map of the Roman conquest of Gaul, a battle took place in 54 B.C. along the Meuse River in the region then called Belgica. Therefore, choice **d** is correct. The information on the map does not support any of the other choices.

10. e. According to the map of the Roman conquest of Gaul, various battles were fought between 58 and 51 B.C. Keep in mind that B.C. dates run "backward"; for example, 58 B.C. came seven years before 51 B.C. Choice **e** is correct because it is the only one that lists three battles in proper time order from earliest to latest: Bibracte (58 B.C.), Quiberon Bay (56 B.C.), and Gergovia (52 B.C.). None of the other choices lists battles in the proper time order.

11. a. Of the conclusions presented, the map supports only the one stated in choice **a**, that the Romans conquered Aquitania and Belgica. The battle dates show no particular pattern of conquest starting in the north and working south, so there is no support for choice **b**. There is no way to tell how long the battle of Lugdunum lasted, so there is no support for choice **c**. There is no information about what the Romans planned after conquering Gaul, so there is no support for choice **d**. There is also no information about the effect of the climate on the Roman army, so there is no support for choice **e**.

12. c. The map shows that the Loire and Garonne rivers both flow into the Atlantic Ocean, so choice **c** is correct. They both flow generally from east to west (a river flows toward the larger body of water it feeds), so choices **a** and **b** are incorrect. They do not flow into the Mediterranean Sea, so choice **d** is incorrect. Based on the map scale, neither is anywhere near 1,000 miles long, so choice **e** is incorrect.

13. a. The passage says, "We come now to the question presented: Does segregation of children in public schools solely on the basis of race [. . .] deprive the children of the minority group of equal educational opportunities?" Choice **a**, "Is segregation by race in public schools unfair to minority children?", is a paraphrase of this portion of the passage; therefore, choice **a** is the best answer. The questions presented in the other choices may be relevant to the issue of segregation in schools, but they are not the one that the Court has decided it must answer in this case.

14. d. Justice Warren, writing for the Court majority, says, "In the field of public education the doctrine of 'separate but equal' has no place." Although the case involved education at the precollege level, Warren's statement applies to all publicly funded education, including state-run universities; therefore, choice **d** is the best answer. In light of Justice Warren's argument, it is unlikely that the Court would approve of creating separate facilities of the types described in choices **a**, **c**, and **e**. Based on the principle of equal protection of the laws in the Fourteenth Amendment, it is highly unlikely that the Court would approve of special rights for majority racial groups, which rules out choice **b**.

15. e. The passage says, "This segregation was alleged to deprive the plaintiffs of the equal protection of the laws under the Fourteenth Amendment." It is thus logical to conclude that the Fourteenth Amendment requires that people receive the equal protection of the laws. Thus, choice **e** is correct. There is no support in the passage for any of the other answer choices.

16. d. The Court concluded that the doctrine of "separate but equal" should be rejected because "segregation of white and colored children has a detrimental effect upon the colored children," and as a result, "separate educational facilities are inherently unequal." Choice **d** is a good paraphrase of this portion of the Court decision. The Court's decision says nothing about the power of federal courts over public school systems (choice **a**), the opportunities offered by private schools (choice **c**), or the measurement of educational achievement (choice **e**). Choice **b** is incorrect because it states the exact opposite of the Court's conclusion.

17. c. In the circle graph for Canada, the shaded portion is about 10% of the whole. Therefore, unemployment was about 10%, and choice **c** is correct. The other choices show percentages that are either much larger or much smaller than the 10% shown on the graph.

18. a. In the circle graphs for Chile and Mexico, the shaded portions are about the same; each is about 5%; therefore, choice **a** is the best answer. All of the other choices list pairs of countries that had visibly different unemployment rates in 1995.

19. a. If high unemployment is associated with low inflation, then the country with the highest unemployment rate is likely to have the lowest level of inflation. Of the countries shown, Argentina has the highest unemployment rate; thus, choice **a** is the correct answer. The other choices all list countries that have lower unemployment rates than Argentina.

20. e. The circle graphs show similar unemployment rates in Chile and Mexico, so there is no reason to think that demand for workers is any higher in Chile than it is in Mexico. Thus, it is unlikely that workers from Mexico could earn higher wages in Chile. Choice **a** is incorrect. The graphs also show that unemployment in Argentina is very high, so chances are slim that a laborer from Honduras could easily find work in Argentina; thus, choice **b** is incorrect. Choices **c** and **d** are incorrect because the graphs do not provide enough information to support either conclusion. The only fair conclusion is choice **e**, that Chile and Argentina have very different unemployment rates and therefore different economic conditions.

21. d. The quotation implies that the most important aspect of history is economic history, "the record of man in quest of his daily bread and butter." Thus, choice **d** is the best answer. Each of the disciplines named in the other answer choices may incorporate economics into a larger discipline of study, but they do not focus on economic issues and therefore would not be the most valuable method of looking at history for van Loon's purpose.

22. a. The passage says that Hiawatha brought together the Five Iroquois Nations in a league "designed to keep the peace." Thus, choice **a**, "to secure a lasting peace," is the correct answer. Choice **b** is incorrect because Hiawatha lived before the arrival of the Dutch. Choices **c** and **e** are incorrect because nothing in the passage suggests that the Iroquois were afraid of an Algonquian invasion or that they sought better ties with the Hurons. Choice **d** is incorrect because the passage says that the league was formed to keep the peace, not as a means of extending Iroquois power.

23. e. Competition for the fur trade caused war among the Iroquois, Algonquians, and Hurons, so choice **e**, that "the fur trade was a negative influence on tribal life," is a fair conclusion to draw from the passage. For the same reason, choice **a** must be incorrect. Nothing in the passage supports choices **b**, **c**, or **d**.

24. d. According to the passage, the Dutch urged their Iroquois allies to attack the Hurons to break the Huron monopoly over the fur trade. Therefore, choice **d** is the best answer. The other choices are incorrect because there is no support for them in the passage.

25. c. The graph shows that the United States imports large quantities of coffee, copper, platinum, and watches and clocks. It also shows that the United States exports only very small amounts of these same commodities. These two facts suggest that the United States does not produce large amounts of these particular items. The United States exports a great deal of corn, however, and imports very little; therefore, it is reasonable to conclude that the United States produces most of the corn available on its domestic market. And it follows that if you bought a package of frozen corn in a store in the United States, that corn would likely be American made. Therefore, choice **c** is the best answer. All of the other choices are incorrect based on the information in the graph.

26. c. The cartoon shows men voting while a political boss and his cronies watch. The boss's comment, provided in the caption, makes it clear that voting is an empty exercise when a boss will declare his candidate elected, no matter what the vote count. Choice **c** is the best answer because it reflects the point of the cartoon. None of the other choices is supported by the cartoon or its caption.

27. b. The frontier referred to the hypothetical boundary between settled areas of the United States and open territory that had not yet been settled by people. With no single area in the West without settlers in 1890, the frontier, in effect, no longer existed. Therefore, choice **b** is the best answer. Choice **c**, which refers to the population of Los Angeles, might at first seem relevant; however, it is not legitimate to draw conclusions about a vast region based on the population of a single city within that region. None of the other choices supports Jackson's claim.

28. e. According to the time line, the cultivation of cereal crops occurred around 8000 B.C. At that time, the most significant development was the appearance of villages in which people settled. Therefore, choice **e** is the best answer. None of the other choices applies to the appropriate time period. Choice **a** refers to domestication of animals, which had occurred earlier in 9000 B.C. Wall painting, choice **b**, is never mentioned in the time line; nor is the use of fire for cooking, choice **c**. The use of tools, choice **d**, can be inferred from information about textiles in 7000 B.C. and smelting and plowing in 6000 B.C., but there is no evidence in the time line that it occurred before 8000 B.C.

29. c. The time line makes it clear that plowing occurred before the domestication of the horse, so it is reasonable to conclude that cattle were used for plowing. Thus, choice **c** is the best answer. The other choices are incorrect because each one is based on a misreading of the information in the time line.

30. e. Choice **e** is the correct answer because it is the only opinion among the five choices. The words *most important* give a clue that the statement is a value judgment, not a fact. All the other answers are facts, not opinions.

31. e. None of the states in the chart has a residency requirement of more than 30 days. The time from October 1 to November 6 is more than 30 days. If someone registered immediately, the registration requirements of California and Missouri would have been met. Thus, choice **e** is the best answer.

32. b. Among the choices, the only two countries listed that lie entirely between the Tropic of Capricorn and the Equator are Angola and Malawi, choice **b**. None of the other choices meets that requirement.

33. b. During World War II, no fighting took place on U.S. soil except in the Aleutian Islands off Alaska. No battles took place in Great Britain either, but British soldiers fought in the major battles in Europe. So did French and Soviet soldiers, and all these countries suffered civilian losses from German bombing and/or occupation. Thus, choice **b** is the best answer. The other answer choices are opinions that are either not supported by fact or can be refuted by fact.

34. d. Choices **a**, **b**, **c**, and **e** refer to civil conflicts between factions or groups within a country. The only conflict between two different countries is the one between Russia and Japan. Therefore, choice **d** is the best answer.

35. b. Choice **b** is the mostly likely explanation. The difference in the geography of these two countries most likely explains why Norwegians sailed west and Italians sailed east. There is no factual support for choices **a** and **c**. Choices **d** and **e** are speculations without any basis in fact.

36. c. Choice **c** is the best answer. None of the other choices is relevant to democracies. In a democracy, only by voting do people choose who will represent them in government.

37. a. The only country that belongs to OPEC and ASEAN but not to the Arab League is Indonesia, choice **a**. The countries named in the other answer choices do not meet these specifications.

38. a. The proximity in time between China's entering the conflict and the retreat of Allied troops
suggests that China's entrance into the war was
the cause for the Allied retreat. Therefore,
choice **a** is the best answer. Choice **b** contradicts
the facts. Choices **c** and **d** did not occur. Choice
e is not true; the capture of the North Korean
capital alone would have meant little without a
victory over North Korea.

39. a. The only fact supported by the graph is choice
a. About 4.5 million Italians immigrated to the
United States during that period. No informa-
tion in the chart supports choice **b**, **c**, **d**, or **e**.

40. d. The last two sentences in the passage suggest
that *laissez-faire* economics can lead to problems, such as unfair monopolies that hinder
competition. Therefore, choice **d** is a fair statement of the author's attitude. None of the other
choices states the author's position. When
answering questions about the author's attitude, beware of answers that make absolute
statements such as choice **a** ("most useful economic policy ever invented") or state strong
opinions that would be difficult to support,
such as choice **b** ("wrong from the start").

41. e. The only choice that correctly states the difference between the Physiocrats' and Mercan-
tilists' views is choice **e**. Mercantilists favored
government regulation in trade; Physiocrats
favored government noninterference.

42. b. One euro is worth about $\frac{4}{5}$ of an Irish punt.
Choice **a** is incorrect because the German mark
is actually worth more than a Finnish markka.
A markka is equal to about $\frac{1}{6}$ of a euro; a
German mark is equal to about $\frac{1}{2}$ of a euro. The
table provides no information about governments, so choice **c** cannot be correct. Choice **d**
is incorrect because it takes more than 200
escudos to equal one euro. Choice **e** is incorrect: one euro is worth more French francs
(6.56) than Finnish markkas (5.95).

43. b. The only statement that is true about the Ptole-
maic and Copernican views of the solar system
is choice **b**. Choice **a** is incorrect because both
considered Mars and Venus planets. Choice **c** is
incorrect because both figures show Saturn as
the most distant of the six planets. Choice **d** is
incorrect because Ptolemy placed Earth at the
center and Copernicus placed the Sun at the
center. Choice **e** is incorrect because both show
the orbits to be circular.

44. c. Choice **a** is incorrect because the chart gives no
information about the type of government of
the Indian civilization. Choice **b** is incorrect
because the civilization of Sumer is the oldest
shown in the chart. Choice **d** is also incorrect;
only one of the four civilizations mentioned
used hieroglyphics. Choice **e** is incorrect because
Chinese civilization began later than the others,
not earlier. Thus, choice **c** is the best answer.

45. e. It is the only answer that describes a policy that
does *not* deal with Latin America.

46. c. Ships sailing from the West Indies to Europe
carried sugar and tobacco. Thus, choice **c** is the
best answer. Choice **a**, slaves, were carried from
Africa to the West Indies. Choices **b**, **d**, and **e**
were carried from Europe to West Africa.

47. a. Each senator represents 800,000 people, but
each assembly member represents 400,000, so
choice **a** is the best answer. Choice **b** contradicts
those figures. Choices **c** and **d** are incorrect
because both senators and assembly members
have term limits. Choice **e** is incorrect because
each legislator, whether a senator or an assembly member, makes the same salary.

48. d. The only answer choice supported by the text is
choice **d**. All Senate seats have term limits, so
choice **a** is incorrect. Choices **b**, **c**, and **e** are
irrelevant to the question.

49. c. Assembly members are elected to two-year terms
and may serve for three terms. Thus, an assembly member who served two terms from 1996 to
2000 would be allowed to serve one more term
only. Therefore, choice **c** is the best answer.

50. b. Odd-numbered Senate seats are up for election
this year, so you would vote for a Senator and
an Assembly member, since there is an election
for Assembly members every two years. Therefore, choice **b** is the best answer.

III ▶ The GED Language Arts, Writing Exam

IN THIS SECTION, you will learn about the GED Language Arts, Writing Exam: what the test is like, what kinds of questions to expect, and how to tackle those questions. You will also review the fundamental grammar and writing skills you need to do well on the exam.

Before you begin with Chapter 10, take a few minutes to do the pretest that follows. The passage and questions are similar to those you will find on the GED. When you are finished, check the answer key carefully to assess your results. Your pretest score will help you determine how much preparation you need and the areas in which you need the most careful review and practice.

▶ Pretest: GED Language Arts, Writing

Directions: In the following passage, the paragraphs are lettered and the sentences are numbered. Read the passage carefully and then answer the multiple-choice questions that follow. Choose the best answer for each question. To practice the timing of the exam, take 15 minutes to complete this pretest. Record your answers on the answer sheet provided. Make sure you mark the answer in the circle that corresponds to the question.

Note: On the GED, you are not permitted to write in the test booklet. Make any notes on a separate piece of paper.

ANSWER SHEET

1. (a) (b) (c) (d) (e)
2. (a) (b) (c) (d) (e)
3. (a) (b) (c) (d) (e)
4. (a) (b) (c) (d) (e)
5. (a) (b) (c) (d) (e)
6. (a) (b) (c) (d) (e)
7. (a) (b) (c) (d) (e)
8. (a) (b) (c) (d) (e)
9. (a) (b) (c) (d) (e)
10. (a) (b) (c) (d) (e)

Questions 1–10 refer to the following passage.

Batman

A

(1) Year after year, one of the most popular Halloween costumes for children and adults alike is Batman. (2) In fact, this superhero, was created in 1939 and known worldwide, continues to be one of the most popular comic strip characters ever created.

B

(3) Batman was the brainchild of comic book artist Bob Kane. (4) Who was just 22 years old when he was asked to create a new superhero for DC Comics. (5) Superman was a phenomenal success, and DC Comics wanted another hero, just as powerful, to appeal to it's readers. (6) Kane's idea for Batman reportedly came from

Leonardo da Vinci's famous sketch of a man flying with batlike wings and the heroes in the *Shadow* and *Zorro* series who wore masks.

C

(7) Kane's Batman was a success that was big right from the start. (8) The masked hero soon moved from comic books to its own newspaper strip, and in 1943, Batman episodes were aired on the radio. (9) In 1966, live-action Batman shows hit the TV screen. (10) The series was wildly popular, and the syndicated show still airs today on channels like the Cartoon Network.

D

(11) Batman is really Bruce Wayne a millionaire who witnessed the murder of his parents as a child. (12) Why was Batman so popular? (13) The answer may lie in the background Kane gave his character. (14) He vowed to avenge their deaths and the bringing of criminals to justice. (15) He didn't have any supernatural powers. (16) Instead, he devotes his life to training his body and mind to fight crime and used his wealth to develop high-tech crime-fighting tools and weapons, like his famous Batmobile. (17) Thus, Kane created a superhero who is just as human as the rest of us. (18) In Batman, Kane gave us an image of our own superhero potential.

1. Sentence 2: In fact, <u>this superhero, was created in 1939 and known worldwide, continues</u> to be one of the most popular comic strip characters ever created.

    Which is the best way to write the underlined portion of this sentence? If the original is the best way, choose option **a.**
    a. this superhero, was created in 1939 and known worldwide, continues
    b. this superhero, having been created in 1939 and known worldwide, continues
    c. this superhero, created in 1939 and known worldwide, continues
    d. this superhero, was created in 1939 and known worldwide, and continuing
    e. this superhero, who was created in 1939 and being known worldwide, continues

2. Sentences 3 and 4: Batman was the brainchild of comic book artist <u>Bob Kane. Who was</u> just 22 years old when he was asked to create a new superhero for DC Comics.

Which is the best way to write the underlined portion of these sentences? If the original is the best way, choose option **a**.

a. Bob Kane. Who was
b. Bob Kane; who was
c. Bob Kane. Kane was
d. Bob Kane, who was
e. Bob Kane, while he was

3. Sentence 5: Superman was a phenomenal success, and DC Comics wanted another hero, just as powerful, to appeal to it's readers.

Which correction should be made to sentence 5?

a. Change <u>hero</u> to <u>Hero</u>.
b. Change <u>it's</u> to <u>its</u>.
c. Replace <u>Superman was</u> with <u>Superman is</u>.
d. Insert a comma after <u>Comics</u>.
e. No correction is necessary.

4. Sentence 6: Kane's idea for Batman reportedly came from Leonardo da Vinci's famous sketch of a man flying with batlike wings and the heroes in the *Shadow* and *Zorro* series who wore masks.

Which revision should be made to sentence 6?

a. Change <u>man flying</u> to <u>flying man</u>.
b. Replace <u>batlike wings</u> with <u>having wings like a bat</u>.
c. Start a new sentence after <u>wings</u>.
d. Change <u>reportedly came from</u> to <u>was reported coming from</u>.
e. Move <u>who wore masks</u> to follow <u>the heroes</u>.

5. Sentence 7: Kane's Batman <u>was a success that was big</u> right from the start.

Which is the best way to write the underlined portion of sentence 7? If the original is the best way, choose option **a**.

a. was a success that was big
b. was a big success
c. was successful in a big way
d. was successfully big
e. is a successful thing

6. Sentence 11: Batman is really Bruce Wayne a millionaire who witnessed the murder of his parents as a child.

Which correction should be made to sentence 11?

a. Insert a comma after <u>Wayne</u>.
b. Replace <u>who</u> with <u>that</u>.
c. Change <u>witnessed</u> to <u>saw</u>.
d. Replace <u>as a child</u> with <u>during his childhood</u>.
e. No correction is necessary.

7. Sentence 11: Batman is really Bruce Wayne a millionaire who witnessed the murder of his parents as a child.

Which revision should be made to the placement of sentence 11?

a. Move sentence 11 to follow sentence 7.
b. Move sentence 11 to the end of paragraph C.
c. Move sentence 11 to follow sentence 12.
d. Move sentence 11 to follow sentence 13.
e. Move sentence 11 to follow sentence 14.

8. Sentence 14: He vowed to avenge their deaths <u>and the bringing of criminals to justice</u>.

Which is the best way to write the underlined portion of this sentence? If the original is the best way, choose option **a**.

a. and the bringing of criminals to justice
b. and brought criminals to justice
c. and will bring criminals to justice
d. and bring criminals to justice
e. and that he would bring criminals to justice

9. Sentence 16: Instead, he devotes his life to training his body and mind to fight crime and used his wealth to develop high-tech crime-fighting tools and weapons, like his famous Batmobile.

Which correction should be made to sentence 16?

a. Change <u>devotes</u> to <u>devoted</u>.
b. Replace <u>to fight</u> with <u>fighting</u>.
c. Change <u>high-tech</u> to <u>high, tech</u>.
d. Insert a comma after <u>body</u>.
e. No correction is necessary.

10. Sentence 18: In Batman, Kane gave us an image of our own superhero potential.

The most effective revision of sentence 18 would begin with which group of words?

a. However, Batman was someone in whom Kane
b. Therefore, in Batman, we are given
c. More importantly, in Batman, Kane gives us
d. On the other hand, in Batman, we see
e. Thankfully, it is in Batman that we have

▶ Answers

1. c. The nonessential information in this sentence is best set off by commas, and choice **c** is the only version that is grammatically correct. Choice **a** is incorrect because the information set off by commas is incomplete (*was* should be deleted, or *who* should be inserted before *was*). Choice **b** is incorrect because the verb phrase *having been created* is incorrect; the correct helping verb would be *had,* not *having,* and the clause would require *which* before *had.* Choice **d** is incorrect for the same reason as choice **a**; also, the verb *continuing* should be in the past tense. Choice **e** is incorrect because the verb *being* should be either the present or past tense, not a present participle.

2. d. Sentence 4 is best attached to sentence 3 as a nonessential *who* clause, thus providing extra information regarding the creation of Batman. Choice **a** is incorrect because sentence 4 is a sentence fragment. Choice **b** is incorrect because a semicolon can be used only between two complete sentences (independent clauses), and sentence 4 is an incomplete sentence. Choice **c** is correct, but it unnecessarily repeats *Kane;* combining the sentences with a *who* clause eliminates the repetition. Choice **e** is incorrect because it is wordy and awkward.

3. b. *It's* is the contraction of *it is;* the sentence needs the possessive form, *its.* Choice **a** is incorrect because *hero* is not a specific noun and should not be capitalized. Choice **c** is incorrect because the verb *was* needs to remain in the past tense. Choice **d** is incorrect because commas should not separate subjects and verbs unless a complete phrase or clause is inserted. Choice **e** is incorrect because *it's* needs to be corrected.

4. e. The modifier *who wore masks* should be moved after *heroes* to be as close as possible to the noun it modifies. Choice **a** is incorrect because *flying* should be as close as possible to the prepositional phrase *with batlike wings;* reversing *man* and *flying* would indicate that the man was a flying man, not a man who flew with batlike wings. Choice **b** is incorrect because *batlike wings* is a more concise modifier than *having wings like a bat*; also, the verb *having* cannot follow *flying with.* Choice **c** is incorrect because the new sentence beginning with *and* would be a fragment (incomplete sentence). In choice **d**, the verb phrase *was reported coming from* is incorrect.

5. b. This is the most concise and correct way to convey this idea. Choice **a** is unnecessarily wordy. Choice **c** is too informal (*in a big way* is slang). Choice **d** is awkward and states that the size was a success, not that the comic strip was a success. Choice **e** is incorrect because *thing* is too general; a more precise noun should be used.

6. a. The information after *Wayne* is a nonessential descriptive clause that needs to be set off by a comma. Choice **b** is incorrect because *who* should be used when referring to people; *that* should be used to refer to things. Choice **c** is incorrect because *witnessed* is a more precise word than *saw.* Choice **d** is incorrect because it is more wordy and also suggests a longer time frame, as if the murder occurred over time. Choice **e** is incorrect because the comma after *Wayne* is necessary.

7. d. Sentence 11 is the first sentence describing Batman's background, so the most logical and effective place for this information is after sentence 13: *The answer may lie in the background Kane gave his character.* Choice **a** is incorrect because paragraph C describes Batman's success, not his background. Choice **b** is incorrect for the same reason. Choice **c** is incorrect because the sentence doesn't directly answer the question asked in sentence 12; sentence 13 needs to state the answer (Batman's background) first. Choice **e** is incorrect because we need to know that Batman's parents were murdered before we learn that he vowed to avenge their deaths; we would not know whose murder Batman was avenging.

8. d. This choice uses parallel structure and is correct and concise. Choice **a** is incorrect because it requires the verbs *avenge* and *bring* to be in their infinitive forms. Choice **b** is incorrect for the same reason; *brought* is in the past tense, not the infinitive form. Likewise, choice **c** uses the future tense (*will bring*), so it is incorrect. Choice **e** is grammatically correct, but it is wordy and less effective than the parallel structure in choice **d**.

9. a. The tenses are inconsistent (present tense *devotes* and past tense *used*). The other sentences about Batman's background are in the past tense, so *devotes* should be changed to the past tense *devoted*. Choice **b** is incorrect because *to* is necessary to show the relationship between *mind* and *fight*; a gerund (*fighting*) would not make sense here. Choice **c** is incorrect because *high* and *tech* work together to create one modifier, so the hyphen between them is necessary. Choice **d** is incorrect because there are only two items in the list (*body* and *mind*), so there should not be a comma between them. Choice **e** is incorrect because the inconsistent verb tense needs to be corrected.

10. c. The most effective transitional phrase to begin this sentence is *more importantly.* The idea expressed in this sentence—that Batman gives us *an image of our own superhero potential*—is the most powerful explanation for why so many people were drawn to the Batman character. Choice **a** is incorrect because the idea in sentence 18 does not contrast with the idea in sentence 17. While choice **b** is logical (the idea in sentence 18 is an "effect" of the idea in sentence 17), choice **c** is more appropriate in the context. Choice **d** is incorrect because sentence 18 does not contrast the idea in sentence 17. Choice **e** is incorrect because it is wordy, and the transitional word *thankfully* seems out of place in both style and context.

▶ Pretest Assessment

How did you do on the pretest? If you answered seven or more questions correctly, you have earned the equivalent of a passing score on Part I of the GED Language Arts, Writing Exam. But that doesn't mean you should skip Chapter 10. This pretest is not designed to give you an exact measure of how you would do on the GED. Rather, it is designed to help you determine where to focus your study efforts. Remember that this pretest does not cover all of the material that may be included on the GED Language Arts, Writing Exam and does not include an essay.

10 ▶ About the GED Language Arts, Writing Exam

To prepare effectively for the GED Language Arts, Writing Exam, you need to know exactly what the test is like. This chapter explains the structure of the exam, including the types of questions and passages you will see on the test.

▶ What to Expect on the GED Language Arts, Writing Exam

As you know, the GED Language Arts, Writing Exam has two parts. **Part I** consists of 50 multiple-choice questions that measure your knowledge in four key writing areas:

- sentence structure—30%
- usage—30%
- mechanics—25%
- organization—15%

You will have 75 minutes to complete this part of the test. Each question will have five options; only one will be correct.

Because there's a lot more to writing an effective essay than good grammar or logical organization, and because effective writing is essential if you are to succeed in college or in the workplace, the GED Language Arts, Writing Exam also includes an essay. **Part II** consists of one essay topic. You will have 45 minutes to write an essay in response to that prompt.

A lot of people are intimidated by essay exams. After all, you are being asked to write well under pressure, and if you don't pass the essay exam, you don't pass the GED Language Arts, Writing Exam. But there is some good news about this part of the GED Language Arts, Writing Exam. For one thing, the essay doesn't have to be long. In fact, because you have only 45 minutes, you are only expected to write about five paragraphs. (In contrast, most college-level essays are expected to be at least three to five pages!) For another, you are given only one essay prompt. That means you don't have to spend any time deciding which question to answer. You only have to decide how you will answer that question.

In addition, no matter what writing prompt you get, you will be able to answer the question. All of the essay topics are general enough for anyone to write about. None of them will require you to have any kind of specialized knowledge or experience.

If you finish your essay in less than 45 minutes, you can return to Part I for the remainder of the test time. This can give you the opportunity to double-check your answers, especially those where you guessed at the answer.

One Test, Two Parts

The GED Language Arts, Writing Exam consists of two separate parts:

▶ Part I: Multiple-choice questions on sentence structure, usage, mechanics, and organization (75 minutes)
▶ Part II: An essay of approximately 250 words (45 minutes)

You must pass *both* parts to pass the GED Language Arts, Writing Exam.

Questions in Context

Unlike many other standardized English exams, the questions on Part I of the GED Language Arts, Writing Exam do not test writing knowledge and skills in isolation. Instead, all questions are asked in context. You may be used to seeing grammar or usage tests with questions like the following:

Identify the correct spelling of the word below:
  a. embellesh
  b. embelish
  c. embillish
  d. embellish
  e. imbellish

On the GED Language Arts, Writing Exam, however, each question refers to specific words, sentences, or paragraphs taken from a complete passage. All of the questions in the pretest use this format, and you can expect all of the questions in Part I to look like this as well:

Sentence 8: Be sure to be honest and not embellish the truth in you are resume.

Which correction should be made to sentence 8?
  a. Change Be sure to Make it sure.
  b. Insert a comma after honest.
  c. Change honest to honesty.
  d. Replace you are with your.
  e. Change be honest to being honest.

(The correct answer for both examples is **d**.)

To answer this kind of question, you will often need to read and understand the entire sentence and often surrounding sentences as well. A smaller portion of the questions will require you to read and understand the surrounding paragraphs in order to select the correct answer. You may also need a sense of the author's purpose and writing strategies. This is especially true of revision questions that ask you to find the best place for sentences or decide the best place to start a new paragraph.

Kinds of Passages

On Part I of the GED Language Arts, Writing Exam, questions will be drawn from reading passages that are between 200–300 words and 12–22 sentences long. Most passages will have three to five paragraphs. Part I will have three different types of reading passages:

1. **informational**, with topics such as home computers, recreational activities, historical events, family matters, health, and careers
2. **business communications**, such as memos, letters, reports, meeting minutes, e-mails, applications, and executive summaries
3. **how-to documents** that provide directions or instructions on matters such as finding a job, acing an interview, buying a computer, choosing a college, etc.

Types of Multiple-Choice Questions

The questions on Part I will be one of three types: *correction* (45%), *revision* (35%), and *construction shift* (20%).

1. **Correction.** These questions will present you with a sentence (or sentences) and ask you to identify the correction that should be made to the sentence(s). Correction questions test your editing skills: how well you can correct errors in sentence structure, usage, and mechanics. These questions are typically worded like this:

    Which correction should be made to sentence 4?

2. **Revision.** These questions will also present you with a sentence (or sentences) and ask you to identify the revision that should be made to the sentence(s). To **revise** means to look at something again (to *re-examine*) in order to improve it or amend it. This is quite different from editing for grammatical mistakes. Revision questions will focus on changes that *clarify ideas* rather than correct errors. Revision questions will also deal with improving organization, fluency, and overall impact. Revision questions are typically worded like this:

    The most effective revision of sentence 3 would begin with which group of words?
    Which revision should be made to the placement of sentence 9?

3. **Construction shift.** These questions will present you with a sentence (or sentences) with part of the sentence(s) underlined. You will be asked to identify the best way to rewrite the underlined portion of a sentence or the best way to combine sentences. These questions may be a matter of editing or revision. For example, connecting two sentences properly may correct a sentence fragment. Construction shift questions are typically worded like this:

    Which is the best way to write the underlined portion of the sentence? If the original is the best way, choose option a.
    Which is the most effective combination of sentences 2 and 3?

Types of Essay Prompts

Part II of the GED Language Arts, Writing Exam is, of course, the essay. The test will include one writing **prompt**—a topic and direction for your essay. The prompts are designed to be general enough for all test candidates to respond in a short (200–300 word) essay that explains or describes an idea, situation, or experience. (In other words, you should write a factual piece based upon your own opinions, knowledge, and experiences, not a fictitious story.)

The essay prompt on Part II will typically be one of three types:

1. **A narrative prompt** that asks you to describe an experience and why it is significant to you. Here's an example:

    Sometimes events take an unexpected turn and things turn out differently than we imagined. Tell about a time when something unexpected happened to you. In your essay, describe what was supposed to happen and how things actually turned out. Use supporting details throughout your essay.

2. **A persuasive prompt** that asks you to take a position on an issue and explain why you have taken that position. Here's an example:

    The Internet includes many websites with images and content that are inappropriate for children. Other sites on the Internet promote violence or intolerance against certain groups of people. Should websites like these be censored? In your essay, state your position on this issue and explain why you take that position. Use your personal observations, experiences, and knowledge to support your essay.

3. **An expository prompt** that asks you to explain or describe your response to a specific situation or question. These topics can vary widely. Here is an example:

    Our relationship with our neighbors is very important. Sometimes these relationships are the source of great joy in our lives; other times, they can be the source of great trouble. In your opinion, what makes a good neighbor? In your essay, identify the characteristics of a good neighbor and explain why these characteristics are important for people living side by side. Use your personal observations, experiences, and knowledge to support your essay.

The importance of responding accurately to the prompt cannot be understated. **If you do not write on the assigned topic,** *you will not receive a score for the essay exam.*

▶ How the Tests Are Scored

You will receive one point for each correct answer on Part I. Part II is scored on a scale of 1 (lowest) to 6 (highest). The ACE uses a special formula to combine these scores and then convert them to the standard 200–800 scale. Thus, you will receive one score for both parts of the GED Language Arts, Writing Exam. Individual essay scores are not reported. For the combined score, the multiple-choice results represent 65% and the essay represents 35%.

Passing Score

A test taker must earn a score of 2 or higher on Part II in order to receive a composite score (multiple choice and essay) and obtain a passing score. If the test taker receives an essay score of 1 or 1.5, there will be no composite score, and the candidate must retake *both* the multiple-choice and essay parts of the exam.

Individual states may set a composite passing score that is higher than the current minimum GED passing score (410); however, this score cannot be set lower than the GED minimum.

Part II, the essay, is scored by two independent readers. The scores of the independent readers are combined and averaged.

The essay is graded holistically, which means that the readers assess the essay's overall effectiveness, not just its grammatical correctness. You can still earn a high score if you have a few comma splices or misspelled words (after all, you aren't allowed to use a dictionary). If your essay

- has a clear main idea
- maintains focus
- develops its ideas

- provides strong support
- is logically organized
- adheres to the conventions of standard written English

you are well on your way to a passing score.

Follow Directions

Your essay will not be scored if you leave the page blank, if your essay is illegible, or if you write on a topic other than the one that was assigned. **It is therefore extremely important that you respond to the prompt you are given. Do not write about a different topic.**

Also, make sure you write your essay on the lined pages in the answer booklet. Only the writing in that booklet will be scored.

While scoring an essay is far more subjective than correcting a multiple-choice exam, the ACE has developed a detailed **scoring rubric** to guide readers through the essay scoring process. This rubric lists the specific criteria that an essay should meet for each score. What follows is a scoring rubric modeled after the official scoring guide for Part II of the GED Language Arts, Writing Exam. Be sure to review the scoring guide carefully. The more you know about what is expected of your essay, the better you will be able to meet those expectations.

Sample Essay Scoring Rubric

The essay exam is scored on a four-point scale from 4 (high) to 1 (low). The four levels of writing are:

4. Effective
3. Adequate
2. Marginal
1. Inadequate

The overall evaluation will be based on the following five areas:

1. Response to the assigned topic
2. Organization of the essay
3. Demonstration of the development and details
4. Conventions of language (grammar, usage, mechanics)
5. Word choice

A "4" Essay

- presents a well-developed main idea and a clear focus that responds to the assigned prompt
- exhibits a logical and clear organizational plan
- offers support that is specific, substantive, and/or highly illustrative
- consistently follows sentence structure and the conventions of Edited American English (EAE)
- exhibits accurate, diverse, and appropriate word choice

A "3" Essay

- uses the writing prompt to establish a main idea
- exhibits a sufficient organizational plan
- demonstrates a reasonably focused development with some relevant details and examples
- generally controls sentence structure and the conventions of Edited American English (EAE)
- exhibits appropriate word choice

A "2" Essay

- responds to the prompt, but the focus may shift
- exhibits some indication of organizational plan
- demonstrates some development, but details and examples may be redundant or generalized
- exhibits inconsistency in sentence structure and the conventions of Edited American English (EAE)
- exhibits a narrow range of word choice, frequently including inappropriate choices

A "1" Essay

- lacks a clear purpose or presents more than one purpose
- shows evidence of insufficient organizational plan
- is significantly underdeveloped or offers inadequate or inappropriate support
- exhibits minimal or no control of sentence structure and the conventions of Edited American English (EAE)
- exhibits weak or inappropriate word choice

A "0" score will be given to essays that are blank, illegible, or develop a topic other than the one assigned in the prompt.

Write Neatly, Please

Though the quality of your writing should be the only thing that matters, the quality of your *handwriting* counts, too. You must write neatly enough for the readers to understand each word. It won't matter how wonderful your essay is if the readers can't understand what you have written.

11 ▶ Sentence Structure

To help you do well and feel comfortable during the exam, Chapters 11–16 review the four writing areas covered on Part I of the GED Language Arts, Writing Exam: sentence structure, usage, mechanics, and organization. In this chapter, you will learn the components of sentences and how they work together to express ideas.

SENTENCE STRUCTURE REFERS to the way we compose sentences: how we string subjects, verbs, objects, and modifiers together in clauses and phrases. Awkward or incorrect placement of phrases and clauses can result in sentences that are confusing or unclear, or say things that you don't mean. Sentence structure is also important to style. If sentence structure is too simple or repetitive, the writing becomes monotonous for the reader. (Sentence variety will be addressed in the review for Part II.)

▶ Subjects, Predicates, and Objects

When we write, we express our ideas in sentences. But what is a sentence, anyway?

The **sentence** is our basic unit of written expression. It consists of two essential parts—a **subject** and a **predicate**—and it must express a complete thought. The subject of a sentence tells us *who* or *what* the sentence is about—who or what is performing the action of the sentence. The predicate tells us something *about* the subject—what the subject is or does. Thus, in the following sentence:

The phone is ringing.

The word *phone* is the subject. It tells us what the sentence is about—who or what performs the action of the sentence. The verb phrase *is ringing* is the predicate. It tells us the action performed by (or information about) the subject.

The subject of a sentence can be **singular** or **compound** (plural):

I slept all day.   *Kendrick and I worked all night.*
singular subject   compound subject (two subjects performing the action)

The predicate can also be singular or compound:

I bought a present.   *I bought a present and wrapped it beautifully.*
singular predicate   compound predicate (two actions performed by the subject)

In many sentences, someone or something "receives" the action expressed in the predicate. This person or thing is called the **direct object**. In the following sentences, the subject and predicate are separated by a slash (/) and the direct object is underlined:

I / bought a present. (The present receives the action of being bought.)
Jane / loves ice cream. (Ice cream receives the action of being loved by Jane.)

Sentences can also have an **indirect object**: a person or thing who "receives" the direct object. In the following sentences, the direct object is underlined and the indirect object is in bold:

*I / gave **Sunil** a present.* (Sunil receives the present; the present receives the action of being given.)
*The reporter / asked **the president** a question.* (The president receives the question; the question receives the action of being asked.)

▶ Independent and Dependent Clauses

A **clause** contains a subject and a predicate and may also have direct and indirect objects. An **independent clause** expresses a complete thought; it can stand on its own as a sentence. A **dependent clause**, on the other hand, cannot stand alone because it expresses an incomplete idea. When a dependent clause stands alone, the result is a **sentence fragment**.

Independent clause: *She was excited.*
Dependent clause: *Because she was excited.*

Notice that the dependent clause is incomplete; it needs an additional thought to make a complete sentence, such as:

She spoke very quickly because she was excited.

The independent clause, however, can stand alone. It is a complete thought.

Subordinating Conjunctions

What makes a dependent clause dependent is a **subordinating conjunction** such as the word *because*. Subordinating conjunctions connect clauses and help show the relationship between those clauses. Here is a list of the most common subordinating conjunctions:

after	even though	that	when
although	if	though	where
as, as if	in order that	unless	wherever
because	once	until	while
before	since		

When a clause begins with a subordinating conjunction, it is dependent. It must be connected to an independent clause to become a complete thought:

I never knew true happiness   *until I met you.*
independent clause   dependent clause

After Johnson quit,   *I had to work overtime.*
dependent clause   independent clause

A sentence with both a dependent clause (DC) and independent clause (IC) is called a **complex sentence**. Both of the previous sentences are complex sentences.

Conjunctive Adverbs

A very common grammar mistake is to think that words such as *however* and *therefore* are subordinating conjunctions. *However* and *therefore* belong to a group of words called **conjunctive adverbs**. These words also signal relationships between parts of a sentence. When they are used with a semicolon, they can combine independent clauses.

also	indeed	now
anyway	instead	otherwise
besides	likewise	similarly
certainly	meanwhile	still
finally	moreover	then
furthermore	namely	therefore
however	nevertheless	thus
incidentally	next	undoubtedly

Here are some examples:

I didn't go to the party; <u>instead</u>, I stayed home and watched a good film.

Samantha is a fabulous cook; <u>indeed</u>, she may even be better than Jacque.

I need to pay this bill immediately. <u>Otherwise</u>, my phone service will be cut off.

▶ Compound Sentences and Coordinating Conjunctions

When two independent clauses are combined, the result is a **compound sentence** like the following:

He was late, so he lost the account.

The most common way to join two independent clauses is with a comma and a coordinating conjunction: *and, but, or, nor, for, so, yet.* Independent clauses can also be joined with a semicolon if the ideas in the sentences are closely related.

I am tall, and he is short.
[IC, coordinating conjunction + IC]

I am tall; he is short.
[IC; IC]

I was late, yet I still got the account.
[IC, coordinating conjunction + IC]

PART OF SPEECH	FUNCTION	EXAMPLES
noun	names a person, place, thing, or concept	*water, Byron, telephone, Main Street, tub, virtue*
pronoun	takes the place of a noun so that the noun does not have to be repeated	*I, you, he, she, us, they, this, that, themselves, somebody, who, which*
verb	describes an action, occurrence, or state of being	*wait, seem, be, visit, renew*
helping verb (also called *auxiliary verb*)	combines with other verbs (main verbs) to create verb phrases that help indicate tenses	forms of *be, do,* and *have; can, could, may, might, must, shall, should, will, would*
adjective	describes nouns and pronouns; can also identify or quantify	*green, round, old, surprising; that* (e.g., *that elephant*); *several* (e.g., *several elephants*)
adverb	describes verbs, adjectives, other adverbs, or entire clauses	*dreamily, quickly, always, very, then*
preposition	expresses the relationship in time or space between words in a sentence	*in, on, around, above, between, underneath, beside, with, upon* (see the following list)

Prepositions: A Short List

Prepositions are extremely important; they help us understand how objects relate to each other in space and time. Recognizing them can help you quickly check for subject-verb agreement and other grammar issues. Here is a list of the most common prepositions. See page 140 for notes about the most common prepositional idioms.

about	at	besides	except	like	outside	to	with
above	before	between	for	near	over	toward	without
across	behind	beyond	from	of	since	under	
after	below	by	in	off	through	until	
against	beneath	down	inside	on	throughout	up	
around	beside	during	into	out	till	upon	

▶ Sentence Boundaries

Expressing complete ideas and clearly indicating where sentences begin and end are essential to effective writing. Two of the most common grammatical errors with sentence boundaries are fragments and run-ons.

Incomplete Sentences (Fragments)

As we stated earlier, a complete sentence must (1) have both a **subject** (who or what performs the action) and a **verb** (a state of being or an action), and (2) express a complete thought. If you don't complete a thought, or if you are missing a subject or verb (or both), then you have an **incomplete sentence** (also called a sentence **fragment**). To correct a fragment, add the missing subject or verb or otherwise change the sentence to complete the thought.

Incomplete: Which is simply not true. [No subject. (*Which* is not a subject.)]
Complete: *That* is simply not true.

Incomplete: For example, the French Revolution. [No verb.]
Complete: *The best example is* the French Revolution.

Incomplete: Even though the polar icecaps are melting. [Subject and verb, but not a complete thought.]
Complete: <u>Some people still don't believe in global warming</u> even though the polar icecaps are melting.

Run-on Sentences

A **run-on** sentence occurs when one sentence "runs" right into the next without proper punctuation between them. Usually, there's either no punctuation at all or just a comma between the two thoughts. But commas alone are not strong enough to separate two complete ideas. Here are some examples of run-ons:

Let's go it's getting late.
Whether or not you believe me it's true, I didn't lie to you.

There are five ways to correct run-on sentences:

1. With a period
2. With a comma and a coordinating conjunction: *and, or, nor, for, so, but, yet*
3. With a semicolon
4. With a dash
5. With a subordinating conjunction to create a dependent clause: *although, because, during, while,* etc.

Here's a run-on sentence corrected with each of these techniques:

Run-on:	The debate is over, now it is time to vote.	
Period:	The debate is over. Now it is time to vote.	
Comma + conjunction:	The debate is over, and now it is time to vote.	
Semicolon:	The debate is over; now it is time to vote.	
Dash:	The debate is over—now it is time to vote.	
Subordinating conjunction:	Since the debate is over, it is time to vote.	

▶ Parts of Speech: A Brief Review

A word's *function* and *form* is determined by its **part of speech**. The word *calm*, for example, can be either a verb (*calm* down) or an adjective (a *calm* afternoon); it changes to *calmly* when it is an adverb (they discussed the matter *calmly*). Be sure you know the different parts of speech and the job each part of speech performs in a sentence. The table on the page 125 offers a quick reference guide for the main parts of speech.

▶ Phrases and Modifiers

Sentences are often "filled out" by **phrases** and **modifiers**. Phrases are groups of words that *do not* have both a subject and predicate; they might have either a subject or a verb, but not both, and sometimes neither. Modifiers are words and phrases that qualify or describe people, places, things, and actions. The most common phrases are **prepositional phrases**, which consist of a preposition and a noun or pronoun (e.g., *in the attic*). Modifiers include **adjectives** (e.g., *slow, blue, excellent*) and **adverbs** (e.g., *cheerfully, suspiciously*). In the following examples, the prepositional phrases are underlined and the modifiers are in bold:

He was **very** late <u>for an important</u> meeting <u>with a</u> **new** client.

He **brazenly** took her wallet <u>from her purse</u> when she got up <u>from the table</u> to go <u>to the **ladies'** room.</u>

Placement of Modifiers

As a general rule, words, phrases, or clauses that describe nouns and pronouns should be as close as possible to the words they describe. *The relaxing music,* for example, is better (clearer, more concise and precise) than *the music that is relaxing.* In the first sentence, the modifier *relaxing* is right next to the word it modifies (*music*).

When modifiers are not next to the words they describe, you not only often use extra words, but you might also end up with a **misplaced** or **dangling modifier** and a sentence that means something other than what was intended. This is especially true of phrases and clauses that work as modifiers. Take a look at the following sentence, for example:

Racing to the car, I watched him trip and drop his bag.

Who was racing to the car? Because the modifier *racing to the car* is next to *I*, the sentence says that *I* was doing the racing. But the verb *watched* indicates that *he* was the one racing to the car. Here are two corrected versions:

I watched as he raced to the car and dropped his bag.
I watched as, racing to the car, he dropped his bag.

In the first sentence, the phrase *racing to the car* has been revised to *raced to the car* and given the appropriate subject, *he*. In the second sentence, *racing to the car* is right next to the modified element (*he*).
Here's another example:

Growling ferociously, I watched as the lions approached each other.

It's quite obvious that it was the lions, not the speaker, that were growling ferociously. But because the modifier (*growling ferociously*) isn't right next to what it modifies (*the lions*), the sentence actually says that *I* was growling ferociously. Here's the corrected version:

I watched as the lions, growling ferociously, approached each other.

Again, the sentence is clearer now because the modifier is right next to what it modifies.

Sometimes these errors can be corrected simply by moving the modifier to the right place (next to what it modifies). Other times, you may need to add a subject and verb to clarify who or what is modified by the phrase. Here are some more examples of misplaced and dangling modifiers and their corrections:

Incorrect: *Worn and tattered, Uncle Joe took down the flag.*

Correct: *Uncle Joe took down the flag, which was worn and tattered. OR Uncle Joe took down the worn, tattered flag.*

Incorrect: *While making breakfast, the smoke alarm went off and woke the baby.*

Correct: *While I was making breakfast, the smoke alarm went off and woke the baby. OR The smoke alarm went off and woke the baby while I was making breakfast.*

▶ Parallel Structure

Parallel structure is an important part of effective writing. It means that words and phrases in the sentence follow the same grammatical pattern. This makes ideas easier to follow and expresses ideas more gracefully. Notice how parallelism works in the following examples:

Not parallel: *We came, we saw, and it was conquered by us.*
(The first two clauses use the active *we + past tense verb* construction; the third uses a passive structure with a prepositional phrase.)

Parallel: *We came, we saw, we conquered.*
(All three clauses start with *we* and use a past tense verb.)

Not parallel: *Please be sure to throw out your trash, place your silverware in the bin, and your tray should go on the counter.*
(Two verbs follow the *to + verb + your + noun* pattern; the third puts the noun first, then the verb.)

Parallel: *Please be sure to throw out your trash, place your silverware in the bin, and put your tray on the counter.*
(All three items follow the *to + verb + your + noun* [*+ prepositional phrase*] pattern.)

Parallelism is most often needed in lists, as in the previous examples, and in the *not only/but also* sentence pattern.

Hermione's nervousness was exacerbated not only by the large crowd, but also by the bright lights.
(Each phrase has a preposition, an adjective, and a noun.)

Their idea was not only the most original; it was also the most practical.
(Each phrase uses the superlative form of an adjective—see page 139 for more information on superlatives.)

▶ Active and Passive Voice

In most cases, effective writing will use the **active voice** as much as possible. In an active sentence, the subject performs the action:

James filed the papers yesterday.
Jin Lee sang the song beautifully.

In a **passive** sentence, on the other hand, the subject is passive. Rather than performing the action, the subject is *acted upon*:

The papers were filed by James yesterday.
The song was sung beautifully by Jin Lee.

Active sentences are more direct, powerful, and clear. They often use fewer words and have less room for confusion. There are times when the passive voice is preferred, such as when the source of the action is not known or when the writer wants to emphasize the recipient of the action rather than the performer of the action:

Protective gear must be worn by everyone entering this building.

As a general rule, however, sentences should be active whenever possible.

12 ▶ Usage

On the GED Language Arts, Writing Exam, questions about usage will cover topics such as subject-verb agreement, correct verb tense and conjugation, and proper pronoun use. This chapter will review these grammar rules and more so that you will be prepared for the exam.

U SAGE REFERS TO the rules that govern the form of the words we use and how we string those words together in sentences. Correct grammar and usage are essential for clear and effective communication. In this section, you will review the following areas of basic grammar and usage:

1. Verb conjugation and usage
2. Consistent verb tense
3. Subject-verb agreement
4. Gerunds and infinitives
5. Pronoun cases
6. Pronoun agreement
7. Comparative and superlative adjectives and adverbs
8. Prepositional idioms

▶ Verbs

Verbs are the "heart" of a sentence. They express the action or *state of being* of the subject, telling us what the subject is doing, thinking, or feeling.

> She **yelled** out the window. (action)
> I **am** happy to be here. (state of being)
> We **feel** very lucky **to be** alive. (state of being)
> I **should ask** Winston what he **thinks**. (action)

Verbs have five basic forms:

1. **Infinitive:** the base form of the verb plus the word *to*.

   > to go   to be   to dream   to admire

   To indicate tenses of regular verbs (when the action of the verb did occur, is occurring, or will occur), we use the base form of the verb and add the appropriate tense endings.

2. **Present tense:** the verb form that expresses what is happening now.

   > I **am** sorry you **are** not coming with us.

   > Jessica **does** yoga every morning.

   The present tense of regular verbs is formed as follows:

	SINGULAR	PLURAL
first person (*I/we*)	base form (*believe*)	base form (*believe*)
second person (*you*)	base form (*believe*)	base form (*believe*)
third person (*he/she/it/they*)	base form + -s/-es (*believes*)	base form (*believe*)

3. **Present participle:** the verb form that describes what is happening now. It ends in *-ing* and is accompanied by a helping verb such as *is*.

   > Jessica <u>is doing</u> a difficult yoga pose.

   > The leaves <u>are falling</u> from the trees.

Note: Words that end in *-ing* don't always function as verbs. Sometimes they act as nouns and are called **gerunds**. They can also function as adjectives (called **participial phrases**).

Present participle
(verb):   He <u>is loading</u> the boxes into the car.

Gerund
(noun):   This parking area is for <u>loading</u> only.

Participial phrase
(adjective):   The <u>loading</u> dock is littered with paper.

(You will learn more about gerunds later in this section.)

4. **Past tense:** the verb form that expresses what happened in the past.

   > It <u>snowed</u> yesterday in the mountains.

   > I <u>felt</u> better after I <u>stretched</u> and <u>did</u> some deep breathing.

5. **Past participle:** the verb form that describes an action that happened in the past and is used with a helping verb, such as *has, have,* or *had.*

   > It <u>has</u> not <u>snowed</u> all winter.

   > I <u>have waited</u> as long as I can.

Regular Verbs

Most English verbs are "regular"—they follow a standard set of rules for forming the present participle, past tense, and past participle.

- The present participle is formed by adding *-ing*.
- The past and past participle are formed by adding *-ed*.
- If the verb ends with the letter *e*, just add *d*.
- If the verb ends with the letter *y*, for the past tense, change the *y* to an *i* and add *-ed*.

PRESENT	PRESENT PARTICIPLE	PAST	PAST PARTICIPLE
ask	asking	asked	asked
dream	dreaming	dreamed	dreamed
protect	protecting	protected	protected
spell	spelling	spelled	spelled
whistle	whistling	whistled	whistled

A handful of English verbs have the same present, past, and past participle form. Here is a partial list of those verbs and several examples:

SAME PRESENT, PAST, AND PAST PARTICIPLE FORM

bet	hit	set
bid	hurt	shut
burst	put	spread
cost	quit	upset
cut	read	

Present: *I **read** the newspaper every morning.*

Past: *I **read** the newspaper yesterday morning.*

Past participle: *I **have read** the newspaper every morning since 1992.*

Irregular Verbs

About 150 English verbs are **irregular**. They don't follow the standard rules for changing tense. We can divide these irregular verbs into three categories:

1. irregular verbs with the same *past* and *past participle* forms
2. irregular verbs with three distinct forms
3. irregular verbs with the same *present* and *past participle* forms

The following table lists a few examples of irregular verbs.

PRESENT	PAST	PAST PARTICIPLE
Same past and past participle forms:		
bite	bit	bit
dig	dug	dug
hear	heard	heard
leave	left	left
Three distinct forms:		
begin	began	begun
ring	rang	rung
sing	sang	sung
spring	sprang	sprung
Same present and past participle forms:		
come	came	come
overcome	overcame	overcome
run	ran	run

In English, as in many other languages, the essential verb *to be* is highly irregular:

SUBJECT	PRESENT	PAST	PAST PARTICIPLE
I	am	was	have been
you	are	were	have been
he, she, it	is	was	has been
we	are	were	have been
they	are	were	have been

Helping Verbs

Helping verbs (also called **auxiliary verbs**) are essential to clear communication. They help indicate exactly when an action took place or will take place. They also suggest very specific meanings, such as the subject's ability or intention to do something. The following table lists the helping verbs, their forms, and their meanings.

PRESENT & FUTURE	PAST	MEANING	EXAMPLES
will, shall	would	intention	*She will meet us at the hotel.* *They said they would call first.*
can	could	ability	*I can be there in ten minutes.* *Rose could find only one glove.*
may, might, can, could	could, might	permission	*May I tag along?* *Could we get together after the meeting?*
should	should + have + past participle	recommendation	*We should leave before the snow starts.* *They should have known better.*
must, have (to)	had (to)	necessity	*I must go to the dentist.* *I had to have two teeth pulled.*
should	should + have + past participle	expectation	*They should be on the next train.* *They should have been on that train.*
may, might	might + have + past participle	possibility	*They may be lost.* *They might have gotten lost.*

Subjunctive Mood

The **subjunctive mood** is one of the verb forms we often forget to use in conversation, and therefore we often neglect to use it correctly in our writing. Like helping verbs, the subjunctive is used to express a specific meaning, indicating something that is wished for or that is contrary to fact. It is formed by using *were* instead of *was* as in the following examples:

If she <u>were</u> a little more experienced, she would get the promotion. (She is not a little more experienced.)

If I <u>were</u> rich, I would travel the world. (Unfortunately, I am not rich.)

Troublesome Verbs

Three verb pairs are particularly troublesome, even for native speakers of English:

lie / lay
sit / set
rise / raise

The key to knowing which verb to use is remembering which verb takes an object. In each pair, one verb is **transitive**—an object "receives" the action—while the other is **intransitive**—the subject itself "receives" or performs the action. For example, *lie* is an action that the subject of the sentence "performs" on itself: *I will lie down.* The transitive verb *lay*, on the other hand, is an action that the subject of the sentence performs upon an object: *I lay the baby down in the crib.* In the following examples, the subjects are in bold and the objects are underlined.

lie: to rest or recline (intransitive—subject only)
lay: to put or place (transitive—needs an object)

I will lie down for a while.
*Will **you** please lay the <u>papers</u> down on the table?*

sit: to rest (intransitive—subject only)
set: to put or place (transitive—needs an object)

*Why don't **we** sit down and talk this over?*
***He** will set the <u>record</u> straight.*

rise: to go up (intransitive—subject only)
raise: to move something up (transitive—needs an object)

*The **sun** will rise at 5:48 A.M. tomorrow.*
***He** raised the <u>rent</u> to $750 per month.*

The basic forms of these verbs can also be a bit tricky. The following table shows how each verb is conjugated.

PRESENT	PRESENT PARTICIPLE (WITH *AM, IS, ARE*)	PAST	PAST PARTICIPLE (WITH *HAVE, HAS, HAD*)
lie, lies	lying	lay	lain
lay, lays	laying	laid	laid
sit, sits	sitting	sat	sat
set, sets	setting	set	set
rise, rises	rising	rose	risen
raise, raises	raising	raised	raised

Now that you have reviewed verb conjugation and tense formation, it's time to talk about two key issues with verb usage: consistent tense and subject-verb agreement.

Consistent Tense

One of the quickest ways to confuse readers, especially if you are telling a story or describing an event, is to shift verb tenses. To help readers be clear about *when* actions occur, make sure verbs are consistent in tense. If you begin telling the story in the present tense, for example, keep the story in the present tense; do not inadvertently mix tenses as you write. Be clear about changing tense, and make sure that it makes sense in the context of the story (for example, a story that takes place in the present tense might use the past tense to talk about actions that happened before the story started). Otherwise, you will leave your readers wondering whether actions are taking place in the present or took place in the past.

<u>Incorrect</u>:	*She <u>left</u> the house and <u>forgets</u> her keys again.*
<u>Correct</u>:	*She <u>left</u> the house and <u>forgot</u> her keys again.*

Incorrect: *When we <u>work</u> together, we <u>got</u> better results.*

Correct: *When we <u>work</u> together, we <u>get</u> better results.* OR
When we <u>worked</u> together, we <u>got</u> better results.

Agreement

In English grammar, **agreement** means that sentence elements are balanced. Verbs, for example, should *agree* with their subjects: If the subject is singular, the verb should be singular; if the subject is plural, the verb should be plural.

Incorrect: *They doesn't have a chance against Coolidge.*
(plural subject, singular verb)

Correct: *They don't have a chance against Coolidge.*
(plural subject, plural verb)

Of course, to make sure subjects and verbs agree, you need to be clear about who or what is the subject of the sentence. For example, what is the subject in the following sentence, and which is the correct verb?

Only one of the students [was/were] officially registered for the class.

In this sentence, the subject is *one*, not *students*. Though it seems like *students* are performing the action of being completed, *students* can't be the subject because it is part of a prepositional phrase (*of the students*), and **subjects are never found in prepositional phrases**. Thus, the verb must be singular (*was*, not *were*) to agree with *one*. In addition, it is only **one** of the students—not all—who was registered, so again, the verb must be singular.

Here are some other important guidelines for subject-verb agreement:

- If a compound, singular subject is connected by *and*, the verb must be plural.

  Both <u>Vanessa and Xui want</u> to join the committee.

- If a compound, singular subject is connected by *or* or *nor*, the verb must be singular.

Neither <u>Vanessa nor Xiu wants</u> to join the committee.

- If one plural and one singular subject are connected by *or* or *nor*, the verb agrees with the closest subject.

  Neither Vanessa nor <u>the treasurers</u> want to join the committee.

  Neither the treasurers nor <u>Vanessa</u> wants to join the committee.

- In an **inverted sentence**, the subject comes *after* the verb, so the first step is to clearly identify the subject. (Sentences that begin with *there is* and *there are*, for example, as well as questions, are inverted sentences.) Once you correctly identify the subject, then you can make sure your verb agrees. The correct subjects and verbs are underlined.

  Incorrect: *There's plenty of reasons to go.*

  Correct: *There <u>are</u> plenty of <u>reasons</u> to go.*

  Incorrect: *What's the side effects of this medication?*

  Correct: *What <u>are</u> the side <u>effects</u> of this medication?*

Gerunds and Infinitives

Gerunds and **infinitives** have given many students of English a grammar headache, but they are not so difficult to master. Gerunds, as we noted earlier, *look* like verbs because they end in *-ing*, but they actually function as nouns in sentences:

Tracy loves <u>camping</u>.

Here, the "action" Tracy performs is *loves*. The *thing* (noun) she enjoys is *camping*. In the following sentence, however, *camping* is the *action* Tracy performs, so it is functioning as a verb, not as a gerund:

Tracy <u>is camping</u> in the Pine Barrens next week.

Words ending in *-ing* can also function as adjectives:

Some of our <u>camping</u> gear needs to be replaced before our trip.

Here's another example of how the same word can have three different functions:

Verb:	*He is <u>screaming</u> loudly.*
Gerund (noun):	*That <u>screaming</u> is driving me crazy!*
Adjective:	*The <u>screaming</u> boy finally stopped.*

What this means is that you can't count on word endings to determine a word's part of speech. Lots of words that look like verbs may not be. It's how they function in the sentence that counts.

Infinitives are the base (unconjugated) form of the verb preceded by *to*: *to be, to delay, to manage.* They are often part of a verb chain, but they are not the main verb (main action) of a sentence:

Priya likes <u>to write</u> poems.

In this example, *likes* is the main verb; what Priya likes (the action she likes to take) is *to write* poems.

When to Use Infinitives and Gerunds

In many situations, you may be uncertain whether to use an infinitive or a gerund. Which is correct: *I like to swim* or *I like swimming*? In this case, both are correct; *like, hate,* and other verbs that express preference can be followed by either a gerund or infinitive. But other verbs can only be followed by one or the other. Here are a few helpful guidelines:

- Always use a **gerund** after a preposition.

  Keza thought that by <u>taking</u> the train, she would save money and time.

  Noriel was afraid of <u>offending</u> her host, but she couldn't eat the dinner.

- Always use a **gerund** after the following verbs:

admit	dislike	practice
appreciate	enjoy	put off
avoid	escape	quit
can't help	finish	recall
consider	imagine	resist
delay	keep	risk
deny	miss	suggest
discuss	postpone	tolerate

We should discuss <u>buying</u> a new computer.

I am going to quit <u>smoking</u>.

- In general, use an **infinitive** after these verbs:

agree	decide	need	refuse
ask	expect	offer	venture
beg	fail	plan	want
bother	hope	pretend	wish
claim	manage	promise	

Aswad promises <u>to be</u> back by noon.

Fatima failed <u>to keep</u> her promise.

- When a noun or pronoun immediately follows these verbs, use an **infinitive**:

advise	expect	require
allow	force	tell
ask	like	urge
cause	need	want
command	order	warn
convince	persuade	
encourage	remind	

I'd like you <u>to reconsider</u> my offer.

The committee needs you <u>to organize</u> this event.

▶ Pronouns

Pronouns, as we noted earlier, replace nouns. This keeps us from having to repeat names and objects over and over. But pronouns can be a bit tricky at times. This section reviews the different kinds of pronouns and the rules they follow.

Personal Pronouns

Personal pronouns refer to specific people or things. They can be either singular (*I*) or plural (*we*); they can be subjects (*I*) or objects (*me*).

	SUBJECT	OBJECT
singular	I	me
	you	you
	he	him
	she	her
	it	it
plural	we	us
	they	them

Pronoun mistakes are often made by using the subject form when you really need the object form. Here are two guidelines to follow:

- Always use the object pronoun in a prepositional phrase. **Pronouns and nouns in prepositional phrases are always objects.**

    He promised to bring a souvenir for Betty and me.

    Please keep this between us.

- Always use the subject pronoun in a *than* construction (comparison). When a pronoun follows *than*, it is usually part of a clause that omits the verb in order not to repeat unnecessarily.

    I realize that Alonzo is more talented than I. [than I am]

    Sandra is much more reliable than he. [than he is]

Indefinite Pronouns

Unlike personal pronouns, **indefinite pronouns**, such as *anybody* and *everyone*, don't refer to a specific person. The following indefinite pronouns are **always singular** and require singular verbs:

anyone, anybody	everyone, everybody
no one, nobody	someone, somebody
either, neither	each
one	

Everybody has a chance to win.
Neither child admits to eating the cookies.
Has anyone seen my keys?

The following indefinite pronouns are **always plural**:

both   few   many   several

Both sound like good options.
Only a few are left.

These indefinite pronouns can be singular or plural, depending upon the noun or pronoun to which they refer:

all   any   most   none   some

Some of the money is counterfeit.
Some of the coins are valuable.
None of the animals have been fed.
All of the bread is moldy.

Pronoun-Antecedent Agreement

Just as subjects (both nouns and pronouns) must agree with their verbs, pronouns must also agree with their **antecedents**—the words they replace. For example:

Children will often believe everything their parents tell them.

The word *children* is the antecedent and is replaced by *their* and *them* in the sentence. Because *children* is plural, the pronouns must also be plural.

Indefinite pronouns can also be antecedents. Singular indefinite pronouns require singular pronouns:

Everyone has <u>his or her</u> own reasons for coming.
<u>Neither</u> of the physicists could explain what she saw.

A Bad Habit

One of the most common mistakes we make when speaking and writing is an error of pronoun-antecedent agreement. We often say sentences like the following:

Did everyone bring their notebooks?

Most people make this mistake because it's easier (shorter and faster) to say *their*—but it's not correct. When the antecedent is singular, the pronouns must be singular, too:

Did everyone bring his or her notebook?

Plural indefinite pronouns, on the other hand, require plural pronouns, just like they need plural verbs:

both   few   many   several

<u>Both</u> of them have finished <u>their</u> work.
Only a <u>few</u> are still in <u>their</u> original cases.

Finally, those pronouns that can be either singular or plural, depending upon the noun or pronoun to which they refer, should take the pronoun that matches their referent. If the antecedent is singular, the pronoun and verb must also be singular. If the antecedent is plural, they must be plural:

all   any   most   none   some

All of the chocolate is gone. It was delicious!
All of the cookies are gone. They were delicious!

None of the information is accurate; it's all out of date.
None of the facts are accurate; they are all out of date.

Pronoun Consistency

Just as you need to be consistent in verb tense, you should also be consistent in your pronoun *point of view*. Pronouns can be:

	SINGULAR	PLURAL
First person	I, me	we, us, our
Second person	you	you (all)
Third person	he, she, it	they, them, their
	one	

A passage that begins in the third-person plural should continue to use that third-person plural point of view.

<u>Incorrect:</u> *We have tested our hypothesis and the team believes it is correct.*

<u>Correct:</u> *We have tested our hypothesis and we believe it is correct.*

<u>Incorrect:</u> *If you prepare carefully, one can expect to pass the exam.*

<u>Correct:</u> *If you prepare carefully, you can expect to pass the exam. OR*
If one prepares carefully, one can expect to pass the exam.

Possessive Pronouns

The **possessive pronouns** *its*, *your*, *their*, and *whose* are often confused with the contractions *it's* (*it is* or *it has*), *you're* (*you are*), *they're* (*they are*), and *who's* (*who is*). Because we use apostrophes to show possession in nouns (*Louise's* truck, the *rug's* pattern), many people make the mistake of thinking that pronouns use apostrophes for possession, too. But possessive pronouns *do not* take apostrophes. When a pronoun has an apostrophe, it always shows **contraction**.

POSSESSIVE PRONOUN	MEANING	EXAMPLE
its	belonging to it	*The dog chased its tail.*
your	belonging to you	*Your time is up.*
their	belonging to them	*Their words were comforting.*
whose	belonging to who	*Whose tickets are these?*

CONTRACTION		
it's	it is	*It's time to eat.*
you're	you are	*You're not going to believe your eyes.*
they're	they are	*They're getting their tickets now.*
who's	who has who is	*Who's got my tickets?* *Who's sitting in front?*

The pronouns *who, that,* and *which* are also often confused. Here are the general guidelines for using these pronouns correctly:

- Use **who** or **whom** when referring to people:

  She is the one who should make that decision, not me.

- Use **that** when referring to things:

  This is the most important decision that she will make as director.

- Use **which** when introducing clauses that are not essential to the information in the sentence, unless they refer to people. In that case, use **who**.

  Emily married Sonny, who has been in love with her since first grade.

  Antoinette, who is a computer programmer, would be a good match for Daniel.

  The film, which is a comedy, won several awards.

▶ Adjectives and Adverbs

Adjectives and adverbs help give our sentences color; they describe things and actions. **Adjectives** describe nouns and pronouns and tell us *which one, what kind,* and *how many.* See the following table.

WHICH ONE?	WHAT KIND?	HOW MANY?
that book	*romance* novel	*several* chapters
the *other* class	*steep* expense	*multiple* choices
the *last* song	*jazzy* melody	*six* awards

Adverbs, on the other hand, describe verbs, adjectives, and other adverbs. They tell us *where, when, how,* and *to what extent.* See the table below.

WHERE?	WHEN?	HOW?	TO WHAT EXTENT?
The plane flew *south*.	Jude arrived *early*.	She sang *beautifully*.	Anthony is *very* talented.
Put the chair *here*.	She registered *late*.	The system is behaving *erratically*.	Eleanor is still *extremely* ill.

Remember to keep modifiers as close as possible to what they modify.

Fewer/Less, Number/Amount

As a rule, use the adjective *fewer* to modify plural nouns or things that can be counted. Use *less* for singular nouns that represent a quantity or a degree. Most nouns to which an *-s* can be added require the adjective *fewer*.

Use <u>less salt</u> this time.   Use <u>fewer eggs</u> this time.

I had <u>less reason</u> to go this time.   I had <u>fewer reasons</u> to go this time.

Good/Bad, Well/Badly

These pairs of words—*good/well, bad/badly*—are often confused. The key to proper usage is to understand their function in the sentence. *Good* and *bad* are adjectives; they should be used to modify only nouns and pronouns. *Well* and *badly* are adverbs; they should be used to modify verbs.

I was surprised by how <u>good</u> Sebastian's <u>cake</u> was.

Jennelle hasn't been <u>feeling well</u> lately.

Her <u>attitude</u> is <u>good</u>, but she didn't <u>do well</u> in the interview.

Comparisons

An important function of adjectives and adverbs is comparisons. When you are comparing *two* things, use the **comparative form** (*-er*) of the modifier. If you are comparing more than two things, use the **superlative form** (*-est*) of the modifier.

To create the **comparative** form, either:

1. add *-er* to the modifier OR
2. place the word *more* or *less* before the modifier.

In general, add *-er* to short modifiers (one or two syllables). Use *more* or *less* with modifiers of more than two syllables.

cheaper   less expensive

smarter   more intelligent

To create the **superlative** form, either:

1. add *-est* to the modifier OR
2. place the word *most* or *least* before the modifier.

Again, as a general rule, add *-est* to short modifiers (one or two syllables). Use *most* or *least* with modifiers that are more than two syllables.

Wanda is <u>more experienced</u> than I, but I am the <u>most familiar</u> with the software.

Ahmed is clearly the <u>smartest</u> student in the class.

Double Comparisons and Double Negatives

Be sure to avoid **double comparisons**. Don't use both *-er/-est* and *more/less* or *most/least* together.

<u>Incorrect:</u>   She has the <u>most longest</u> hair I've ever seen.
<u>Correct:</u>   She has the <u>longest</u> hair I've ever seen.

<u>Incorrect:</u>   Minsun is <u>more happier</u> now.
<u>Correct:</u>   Minsun is <u>happier</u> now.

Likewise, be sure to avoid **double negatives**. When a negative word such as *no* or *not* is added to a statement that is already negative, a double negative—and potential confusion—results. *Hardly* and *barely* are also negative words. Remember, one negative is all you need.

<u>Incorrect:</u>   He doesn't have <u>no</u> idea what she's talking about.
<u>Correct:</u>   He does<u>n't</u> have any idea what she's talking about.
    He has <u>no</u> idea what she's talking about.

<u>Incorrect:</u>   I can't hardly wait to see you.
<u>Correct:</u>   I can <u>hardly</u> wait to see you.
    I ca<u>n't</u> wait to see you.

▶ Prepositional Idioms

Another aspect of usage that may be covered on the GED Language Arts, Writing Exam is prepositional idioms: the specific word/preposition combinations that we use in the English language, such as *take care of* and *according to*. What follows is a list of some of the most common prepositional idioms. Review the list carefully to be sure you are using prepositional idioms correctly.

according to	concerned with	in accordance with	regard to
afraid of	congratulate on	incapable of	related to
anxious about	conscious of	in conflict	rely on/upon
apologize to (someone)	consist of	inferior to	respect for
apologize for (something)	depend on/upon	insist on/upon	responsible for
approve of	equal to	in the habit of	satisfied with
ashamed of	except for	in the near future	similar to
aware of	fond of	interested in	sorry for
blame (someone) for (something)	from now on	knowledge of	suspicious of
bored with	from time to time	next to	take care of
capable of	frown on/upon	of the opinion	thank (someone) for (something)
compete with	full of	on top of	tired of
complain about	glance at (something)/ glance through (something, e.g., a book)	opposite of	with regard to
composed of	grateful to (someone)	prior to	
concentrate on	grateful for (something)	proud of	

13 ▶ Mechanics

When do you need a comma? When should you use a dash or semi-colon? How do you know when something should be capitalized? These questions and more will be answered in this chapter. You will review the basic rules of mechanics so that you can answer GED Language Arts, Writing questions about spelling, capitalization, and punctuation.

MECHANICS REFERS TO the rules that govern *punctuation marks, capitalization,* and *spelling.* Like the rules that govern usage, the rules that govern sentence mechanics help us keep our sentences and their meanings clear.

Since the GED Language Arts, Writing Exam was revised in 2002, the only spelling that is tested is the spelling of homonyms, possessives, and contractions. Correct use of punctuation will be tested, but comma questions will generally be limited to instances where a comma is necessary to eliminate or prevent confusion.

▶ Punctuation

Punctuation marks are the symbols used to separate sentences, express emotions, and show relationships between objects and ideas. Correct punctuation makes your meaning clear and adds drama and style to your sentences. Poor punctuation, on the other hand, can lead to a great deal of confusion for your readers and can send a message other than the one you intended. For example, take a look at the following two versions of the same sentence:

Don't bother Xavier.
Don't bother, Xavier.

These sentences use the same words, but have very different meanings because of punctuation. In the first sentence, the comma indicates that the speaker is telling *the reader* not to bother Xavier. In the second sentence, the speaker is telling *Xavier* not to bother. Here's another example of how punctuation can drastically affect meaning:

You should eat Zak so you can think clearly during your interview.

Because this sentence is missing some essential punctuation, the sentence says something very different from what the author intended. The speaker isn't telling *the reader* to eat Zak; rather, she's telling *Zak* to eat. The sentence should be revised as follows:

You should eat, Zak, so you can think clearly during your interview.

Punctuation helps to create meaning, and it also has another important function: It enables writers to express a variety of tones and emotions. For example, take a look at these two versions of the same sentence:

Wait—I'm coming with you!
Wait, I'm coming with you.

The first sentence clearly expresses more urgency and excitement thanks to the dash and exclamation point. The second sentence, with its comma and period, does not express emotion; the sentence is neutral.

Punctuation Guidelines

There are many rules for punctuation, and the better you know them, the more correctly and effectively you can punctuate your sentences. The following table lists the main punctuation marks and guidelines for when to use them:

YOUR PURPOSE:	USE THIS PUNCTUATION:	EXAMPLE:
End a sentence	period [.]	*Most sentences end in a period.*
Connect complete sentences (two independent clauses)	semicolon [;]	*A semicolon can connect two sentences; it is an excellent way to show that two ideas are related.*
	comma [,] *and a* conjunction [*and, or, nor, for, so, but, yet*]	*Leslie is coming, but Huang is staying home.*
	dash [—] (less common, but more dramatic)	*Hurry up—we're late!*
Connect items in a list	comma [,] but if one or more items in that list already have a comma, use a semicolon [;]	*His odd shopping list included batteries, a box of envelopes, and a can of spam.* *The castaways included a professor, who was the group's leader; an actress; and a millionaire and his wife.*
Introduce a list of three or more items	colon [:]	*There are three things I want to do before I die: go on a cruise, go skydiving, and surf.* *Colons have three functions: introducing long lists, introducing quotations, and introducing explanations.*

Introduce an explanation (what follows "explains" or "answers" what precedes)	**colon [:]**	*You know what they say about real estate: Location is everything.*
Introduce a quotation (words directly spoken)	**colon [:] or comma [,]**	*She yelled, "Let's get out of here!"*
Indicate a quotation	**quotation marks [" "]**	*"To be or not to be?" is one of the most famous lines from Hamlet.*
Indicate a question	**question mark [?]**	*What time is it?* *"How much longer?" he asked.*
Connect two words that work together as one object or modifier	**hyphen [-]**	*Mother-in-law, turn-of-the-century poet, French-fried potatoes*
Separate a word or phrase for emphasis	**dash [—]**	*Never lie—never.* *We're late—very late!*
Separate a word or phrase that is relevant but not essential information	**commas [,]**	*Elaine, my roommate, is from Chicago.* *Her nickname as a child, her mother told me, was "Boo-boo."*
Separate a word or phrase that is relevant but secondary information	**parentheses [( )]**	*There is an exception to every rule (including this one).*
Show possession or contraction	**apostrophe [']**	*Why is Lisa's wallet in Ben's backpack?*

Comma Rules

Many mechanics questions will deal with commas, the most common punctuation mark within sentences. The presence and placement of commas can dramatically affect meaning and can make the difference between clarity and confusion. The previous chart lists four comma uses, but there are several others. What follows is a complete list of comma rules. If you know them, then you can be sure your sentences are clear. You will also be able to tell whether or not a comma is needed to correct a sentence.

Use a comma:

1. with a coordinating conjunction to separate two complete sentences. Note that a comma is *not* required if both parts of the sentence are four words or less.

   Let's eat first, and then we will go to a movie.

   I'm definitely older, but I don't think I'm much wiser.

   I love him and he loves me.

2. to set off introductory words, phrases, or clauses.

   Next year, I will stick to my New Year's resolutions.

   Wow, that sure looks good!

   Because the game was canceled, Jane took the kids bowling.

3. to set off a direct address, interjection, or transitional phrase.

> *Well, Jeb, it looks like we will be stuck here for a while.*

> *His hair color is a little, um, unusual.*

> *My heavens, this is spicy chili!*

> *Sea horses, for example, are unusual in that the males carry the eggs.*

4. between two modifiers that could be replaced by *and*.

> *He is a mean, contemptible person.*
> (Both *mean* and *contemptible* modify *person*.)

> Incorrect: *Denny's old, stamp collection is priceless.*
> Correct: *Denny's old stamp collection is priceless.*
> (You cannot put "and" between *old* and *stamp*; *old* describes *stamp* and *stamp* modifies *collection*. They do not modify the same noun.)

5. to set off information that is relevant but not essential (nonrestrictive).

> Essential, not set off:
> *The woman <u>who wrote</u> Happy Moon is coming to our local bookstore.*
> (We need this information to know which woman we're talking about.)

> Nonessential, set off by commas:
> *The dog, lost and confused, wandered into the street.*
> (The fact that the dog was lost and confused is not essential to the sentence.)

> Essential, not set off:
> *Witnesses <u>who lie under oath</u> will be prosecuted.*

> Nonessential, set off by commas:
> *Leeland, who at first refused to testify, later admitted to lying under oath.*

6. to separate items in a series.

> *The price for the cruise includes breakfast, lunch, dinner, and entertainment.*

> *The recipe calls for fresh cilantro, chopped onions, diced tomatoes, and lemon juice.*

7. to set off most quotations. As a general rule, short quotations are introduced by commas while long quotations (several sentences or more) are introduced by colons. All speech in dialogue should be set off by commas.

> *"Let's get going," he said impatiently.*

> *Rene Descartes is famous for the words, "I think, therefore I am."*

> *Joseph said, "Please forgive me for jumping to conclusions."*

8. to set off parts of dates, numbers, titles, and addresses.

> *She was born on April 30, 2002.*

> *Please print 3,000 copies.*

> *Tiberio Mendola, MD, is my new doctor.*

> *Please deliver the package to me at 30 Willow Road, Trenton, NJ.*

9. to prevent confusion, as in cases when a word is repeated.

> *What it is, is a big mistake.*

> *After I, comes J.*

Capitalization

Capitalization is an important tool to help us identify (1) the beginning of a new sentence and (2) proper nouns and adjectives. Here are six rules for correct capitalization:

1. Capitalize the first word of a sentence.

> *Please close the door.*

> *What are you trying to say?*

If you are quoting a full sentence within your own sentence, use a capital letter, unless you introduce the quote with *that*.

> *The author notes, "A shocking three out of four students admitted to cheating."*

> *The author notes that "a shocking three out of four students admitted to cheating."*

If you have a full sentence within parentheses, that sentence should be capitalized as well (and the end punctuation mark should be within the parentheses).

> *He was expelled for repeatedly violating the school's code of conduct (including several instances of stealing and cheating).*

> *He was expelled for repeatedly violating the school's code of conduct. (He was caught stealing and cheating several times.)*

2. Capitalize proper nouns. A **proper noun** is the name of a specific person, place, or thing (as opposed to a *general* person, place, or thing). See the table on this page.

3. Capitalize the days of the week and months of the year, but not the seasons.

> *It was a warm spring day in May.*

> *Wednesday is the first official day of autumn.*

4. Capitalize the names of countries, nationalities, geographical regions, languages, and religions.

> *He has traveled to Brazil and Tunisia.*

> *She is half Chinese, half French.*

> *She is from the South.*
> (But, *Drive south for five miles.*)

> *We speak Spanish at home.*

> *He is a devout Catholic.*

5. Capitalize titles that come *before* proper names.

> | *Judge Lydia Ng* | *Lydia Ng, judge in the Fifth District* |
> | --- | --- |
> | *Professor Lee Chang* | *Lee Chang, professor of physical science* |
> | *Vice President Tilda Stanton* | *Tilda Stanton, vice president* |

6. Capitalize titles of **publications**, including books, stories, poems, plays, articles, speeches, essays, and other documents, and **works of art**, including films, paintings, and musical compositions.

> *Pablo Picasso's painting* Guernica *captures the agony of the Spanish Civil War.*

> *Read Susan Sontag's essay "On Photography" for class tomorrow.*

> *The Declaration of Independence is a sacred document.*

CAPITALIZE (SPECIFIC)	DON'T CAPITALIZE (GENERAL)
Jennifer Johnson (specific person)	the lady
Algebra 101 (specific class)	my math class
Main Street (specific street)	on the street
Frosted Flakes (specific brand)	good cereal
Caspian Sea (specific sea)	deep sea/ocean
Lincoln Memorial (specific monument)	impressive memorial/monument
USS *Cole* (specific ship)	naval destroyer
Dade High School (specific school)	our high school
Precambrian Age (specific time period)	long ago
Microsoft Corporation (specific company)	that company

▶ Spelling

As noted earlier, spelling questions on the GED Language Arts, Writing Exam will be limited to homonyms, contractions, and possessives. The spelling of these words is reviewed in the following section.

Contractions and Possessives

Confusion between contractions and possessives results in some of the most common spelling mistakes.

Contractions are words that use an apostrophe to show that a letter or letters have been omitted from the word(s). **Possessive pronouns** indicate ownership of objects and ideas. They DO NOT take an apostrophe.

POSSESSIVE PRONOUN	MEANING	EXAMPLE
its	belonging to it	The dog chased its tail.
your	belonging to you	Your time is up.
their	belonging to them	Their words were comforting.
whose	belonging to who	Whose tickets are these?

CONTRACTION	MEANING	EXAMPLE
it's	it is	It's time to eat.
you're	you are	You're not going to believe your eyes.
they're	they are	They're getting their tickets now.
who's	who is, who has	Who's got my tickets?

Homonyms

Homonyms are words that sound alike but have different spellings and meanings. Here are some of the most common homonyms:

accept	to take or receive
except	leave out
affect	*(verb)* to have an influence
effect	*(noun)* the result or impact of something
all ready	fully prepared
already	previously
bare	*(adj)* uncovered; *(verb)* to uncover
bear	*(noun)* animal; *(verb)* to carry or endure
brake	*(verb)* to stop; *(noun)* device for stopping
break	*(verb)* to fracture or rend; *(noun)* a pause or temporary stoppage
buy	*(verb)* to purchase
by	*(preposition)* next to or near; through
desert	*(noun)* dry area; *(verb)* to abandon
dessert	sweet course at the end of a meal
every day	each day
everyday	ordinary; daily
hear	*(verb)* to perceive with the ears
here	*(adverb)* in this place

know	to understand, be aware of
no	negative—opposite of *yes*
loose	*(adj)* not tight; not confined
lose	*(verb)* to misplace; to fail to win
may be	might be (possibility)
maybe	perhaps
morning	the first part of the day
mourning	grieving
passed	past tense of *pass* (to go by)
past	beyond; events that have already occurred
patience	quality of being patient; able to wait
patients	people under medical care
personal	*(adj)* private or pertaining to the individual
personnel	*(noun)* employees
presence	condition of being
presents	gifts
principal	most important; head of a school
principle	fundamental truth
right	correct; opposite of *left*
rite	ceremony
write	produce words on a surface
scene	setting or view
seen	past participle of *see*
than	used to compare (*he is taller than I*)
then	at that time, therefore (*first this, then that; if you think it's good, then I'll do it*)
their	possessive form of *they*
there	location; in that place
through	in one side and out the other; by means of
threw	past tense of *throw*
to	*(preposition)* in the direction of
too	*(adverb)* in addition; excessive
two	number
waist	part of the body
waste	*(verb)* to squander; *(noun)* trash
weak	feeble
week	seven days
weather	climatic conditions
whether	introducing a choice
which	what, that
witch	practitioner of witchcraft

14 ▶ Organization

The GED Language Arts, Writing Exam includes questions about organization: how ideas are arranged in a text. This chapter reviews key strategies and patterns writers use to effectively organize their ideas.

O N THE GED Language Arts, Writing Exam, questions about organization are designed to measure your ability to organize ideas effectively. You may be asked to identify the best sequence of sentences or paragraphs, the best place to move a sentence or paragraph, or the best sentence or paragraph to eliminate to improve a paragraph's unity or coherence.

This section reviews three aspects of organization:

1. essay structure and organizational patterns
2. effective paragraphs
3. transitions

▶ Essay Structure and Organizational Patterns

Most nonfiction texts have the basic underlying structure of *main idea → support*. They begin with a **main idea** (sometimes called the **thesis** or **theme** of the text) that controls the whole passage. It is this idea that the text will develop. The rest of the text then provides support for that idea in the form of examples, definitions, reasons, and so on. Most **paragraphs** function this way, too. In fact, you can think of a paragraph as a mini-essay.

On this basic level of *main idea → support,* everything in the passage or paragraph should support or develop that main idea. When sentences or paragraphs lose focus, when they stray from that controlling idea, the passage or paragraph loses its effectiveness.

Writers can use several different strategies for organizing their support. One of these strategies often serves as the overall organizing principle for the text while individual sections may use other techniques as well. For example, imagine an essay comparing and contrasting two film versions of *Frankenstein.* The support will be organized by comparison and contrast. But the writer may also use other organizational techniques within that comparison and contrast structure. For example, she may use order of importance when explaining what makes one version better than the other.

The four most common organizational patterns are:

1. chronological order
2. order of importance
3. comparison and contrast
4. cause and effect

To answer many of the questions about organization on the GED Language Arts, Writing Exam, you will need to be able to determine the writer's purpose and be able to recognize organizational patterns on both the essay and paragraph level. By identifying the organizational pattern, you can determine where to insert sentences or paragraphs and if any sentences or paragraphs are misplaced, such as a sentence that is out of chronological order.

Chronological Order

When writers use time as their main organization principle, it is called **chronological order**. They describe events in the order in which they did happen, will happen, or should happen. Much of what you read is organized in this way, including historical texts, instructions and procedures, and essays about personal experiences.

Passages organized by chronology typically use a lot of **transitional words** and phrases to help us follow the passage of time. The transitions help us see when things happened and in what order. They help us follow along when the passage shifts from one period of time to another. Transitional words and phrases keep events linked together in the proper order. (Transitions are covered in more detail on pages 152–153.)

Here is a list of some of the most common chronological transitions:

first, second, third, etc.		before
after	next	now
then	when	as soon as
immediately	suddenly	soon
during	while	meanwhile
later	in the meantime	at last
eventually	finally	afterward

The third paragraph of the Batman text from page 112 uses this organizational pattern. The transitions are underlined:

Kane's Batman was a big success right from the start. The masked hero <u>soon</u> moved from comic books to its own newspaper strip, and <u>in 1943</u>, Batman episodes were aired on the radio. <u>In 1966</u>, live-action Batman shows hit the TV screen. The series was wildly popular, and the syndicated show <u>still</u> airs today on channels like the Cartoon Network.

Order of Importance

With this organizational pattern, ideas are arranged by rank instead of time. What's most important comes first or last, depending upon the writer's purpose.

Organizing ideas from most important to least important puts the most essential information first. Many writers do this when they are offering advice or when they want to be sure readers get the most important information right away. Newspaper articles, for example, generally use this structure. They begin with the most important information (the *who, what, when, where,* and *why* about the event) so readers don't have to read the whole article to get those key facts. Details and background information come later in the article.

When writers move from least to most important, they save their most important idea or piece of information for last. Writers often use this approach when they are presenting an argument. That's because this kind of structure is usually more convincing than the most-to-least organizational pattern. The more controversial the argument, the more important this structure. Many writers "save the best for last" because that's where "the best" often has the most impact.

Transitions are very important for this organizational pattern, too. Here's a list of the most common transitions writers use with the order of importance structure. Most of these work for both the most-to-least important and least-to-most important formats:

first and foremost	most important
more important	moreover
above all	first, second, third
last but not least	

Comparison and Contrast

When you show how two or more things are similar, you are making a **comparison**. When you show how two or more things are different, you are **contrasting** them. As an organizational technique, this pattern allows you to place two (or more) items side by side and see how they measure up against each other. How are they similar or different? And why does it matter? For example, a writer comparing and contrasting the 1931 and 1994 film versions of *Frankenstein* might aim to show that the 1994 version is far truer to the book because it portrays Victor Frankenstein as just as much of a monster as the creature he creates.

As with the other organizational patterns, one of the keys to a good comparison and contrast is strong transitions. Here are some words and phrases that show similarity:

similarly	in the same way	likewise
like	in a like manner	just as
and	also	both

The following words and phrases, on the other hand, show difference:

but	on the other hand	yet
however	on the contrary	in contrast
conversely	while	unlike

Cause and Effect

The fourth most common organizational pattern is cause and effect. A **cause** is a person or thing that makes something happen (creates an effect). An **effect** is an event or change created by an action (or cause). A passage about cause explains *why* something took place. You might ask, for example, "What caused the Cold War?" A passage about effect, on the other hand, explains *what happened after* something took place. What happened as a result of the Cold War?

Just as certain key words indicate whether you are comparing or contrasting, other key words indicate whether things are causes or effects. Here is a partial list of words and phrases that indicate cause and effect:

WORDS INDICATING CAUSE	WORDS INDICATING EFFECT
because (of)	therefore
created (by)	so
since	hence
caused (by)	consequently
	as a result

▶ Effective Paragraphs

Sentences are the building blocks of paragraphs, and paragraphs are the building blocks of essays. Effective organization in an essay depends upon unity within those paragraphs.

In an essay, all paragraphs should work together to support one main idea. The same is true of a paragraph. A **paragraph** is, by definition, a series of sentences about one main idea. If there's more than one main idea, you should have more than one paragraph.

A **paragraph** is one or more sentences about one main idea. Indicate a new paragraph by skipping a line or by indenting the first line.

A **topic sentence** is a sentence that states the main idea of a paragraph.

In an essay, the controlling idea is usually expressed in a thesis statement. On the paragraph level, this controlling idea is often expressed in a **topic sentence**. This topic sentence is commonly found at the beginning of the paragraph, but it can also be at the end. Less frequently, the topic sentence is found somewhere in the middle of the paragraph or is simply implied. In the first paragraph that follows, the topic sentence is at the beginning; in the second example, the topic sentence is at the end.

Many people are afraid of snakes, but most snakes aren't as dangerous as people think they are. There are more than 2,500 different species of snakes around the world. Only a small percentage of those species are poisonous, and only a few species have venom strong enough to kill a human being. Furthermore, snakes bite only 1,000–2,000 people in the United States each year, and only ten of those bites (that's less than 1%) result in death. Statistically, many other animals are far more dangerous than snakes. In fact, in this country, more people die from dog bites each year than from snake bites.

There are more than 2,500 different species of snakes around the world. Only a small percentage of those species are poisonous, and only a few species have venom strong enough to kill a human being. Furthermore, snakes bite only 1,000–2,000 people in the United States each year, and only ten of those bites (that's less than 1%) result in death. Statistically, many other animals are far more dangerous than snakes. In fact, in this country, more people die from dog bites each year than from snake bites. *So although many people are afraid of snakes, most snakes aren't as dangerous as people think they are.*

In addition to a logical order and controlling idea, strong paragraphs also need focus. Is there a piece of the passage that seems to digress? Would removing a sentence or paragraph improve the focus of the text? Would adding another sentence make it clear how a certain sentence relates to the main idea of the passage?

For example, notice how the following paragraph loses focus:

(1) Electronic mail (e-mail) is very convenient, but should not be used for every business occasion and must be carefully managed. (2) E-mail messages should be concise and limited to one topic. (3) The re: line should clearly state what the e-mail is about, and the first sentence or two of the e-mail should clearly convey the main point of the message. (4) It is important to be concise in business. (5) It is also important to be very polite. (6) Say what you need to say as succinctly as possible. (7) When complex issues need to be addressed, phone calls are still best.

Sentences 4, 5, and 6, while true, do not fit the focus of this paragraph about e-mail. The paragraph would be much stronger if these sentences were omitted.

▶ Transitions

Transitions are the words and phrases used to move from one idea to the next. They help words flow smoothly and show readers how ideas relate to one another. Transitional words and phrases connect ideas within sentences and between sentences, within paragraphs and between paragraphs. They are essential to good writing. Notice, for example, the difference between the following two paragraphs. In the first version, the transitions have been omitted. In the second version, they are underlined.

Why do we punish those who commit crimes? There are two main theories of punishment: retribution and deterrence. Retribution argues that people who commit crimes deserve to be punished and that the punishment should fit the crime. It is an "eye for an eye" philosophy. Deterrence theory posits that punishing offenders will help prevent future crimes.

Why do we punish those who commit crimes? There are two main theories of punishment: retribution and deterrence. The first, retribution, argues that people who commit crimes deserve to be punished and that the punishment should fit the crime. In other words, it is an "eye for an eye" philosophy. Deterrence theory, on the other hand, posits that punishing offenders will help prevent future crimes.

With the appropriate transitions, the second paragraph reads much more smoothly and makes its ideas clearer.

Certain transitions work best for specific functions. For example, *for example* is a great transition to use when introducing a specific example. Here's a brief list of some of the most common transitional words and phrases:

IF YOU WANT TO:	USE THESE TRANSITIONAL WORDS AND PHRASES:		
introduce an example	for example	for instance	that is
	in other words	in particular	specifically
	in fact	first (second) of all	
show addition	and	in addition	also
	again	moreover	furthermore
show emphasis	indeed	in fact	certainly
acknowledge another point of view	although	though	granted
	despite	even though	
show rank	more important	above all	first and foremost
show cause and effect	because	therefore	as a result
	thus	consequently	since
show comparison	likewise	similarly	like
show contrast	unlike	however	on the other hand
	whereas	instead	rather
show the passage of time	then	next	during
	after	before	soon
	meanwhile	while	later

15 ▶ Writing an Effective Essay

Part II of the GED Language Arts, Writing Exam has only one question—an essay prompt. But this test is just as important as Part I, and you must pass the essay test to pass the entire GED Language Arts, Writing Exam. This chapter will tell you how to write an effective essay for the GED. You will learn six steps to take during an essay exam, including how to brainstorm and organize ideas and how to write with style.

ON PART II OF the GED Language Arts, Writing Exam, you will be asked to write a short essay about a general topic. You will have 45 minutes to demonstrate how effectively you can express your ideas in writing.

A strong GED essay will have these five key elements:

1. A clear main idea (thesis). Do you have something to say?
2. Sufficient development. Have you explained your ideas?
3. Strong support. Have you supported your ideas?
4. Effective organization. Have you presented your ideas and support in a logical order?
5. Grammatical correctness. Have you followed the conventions of standard written English?

As a general guide, you will need to write about four or five paragraphs to have a sufficiently developed essay. That includes an introductory paragraph that states your main idea, two or three paragraphs developing and supporting that main idea, and a brief concluding paragraph. Your essay should be approximately 250–300 words.

▶ General Writing Strategies

To do well on the essay, you need to have a solid grasp of general writing strategies. These strategies are those basic techniques writers use to develop a readable and engaging text. They include the ability to:

- write in a way that is appropriate for audience and purpose
- provide appropriate and sufficient support
- craft effective introductions and conclusions
- use effective transitions
- revise for more effective writing

Audience and Purpose

Effective writing has at its core a constant awareness of and attention to **audience** and **purpose**. Good writers are always thinking about their readers: Who are they? What do they know about the subject? What prejudices or preconceived notions might they have? What will keep their attention?

Good writers are also always thinking about purpose. Is their goal to teach a lesson? Provide information? Entertain? Answer a question? Convince or persuade?

Writing for Your Audience

Knowing your audience will help you make a couple of key writing decisions. First, it helps you determine your *level of formality*. Will you use slang or very formal language? It depends upon your relationship with your reader. On the GED, you will be expected to write for a *general audience*. That is, you should assume your readers are "everyday" people with a wide variety of interests and backgrounds. You will need an appropriate level of formality for this audience. Treat your readers with respect, but do not put them off by sounding too formal or pretentious. Avoid slang (too informal) or jargon (technical or specialized language). Let your writing be natural without being too informal.

Your audience also determines the *level of detail* and *specificity* in your essay. Because you are writing for a general audience and not friends, you cannot assume that readers know the context of your ideas and experiences. For example, if you are arguing that Internet sites should be censored, do not assume that readers have seen the kind of sites you are talking about—or even that they have been on the Internet. You will need to briefly describe those sites to give your readers sufficient context.

Knowing Your Purpose

As important as knowing whom you are writing for is knowing *why* you are writing. What is the goal of your essay? What are you hoping to convey through your writing? The more clearly you can articulate your purpose while you outline your essay, the more effective your writing and revising states will be.

Here are some verbs you might find helpful for describing your purpose:

show	*describe*	*explain*
prove	*convince*	*demonstrate*
compare	*contrast*	*review*
inform	*summarize*	*propose*
defend	*explore*	*encourage*

Of course, your specific goals will be guided by the prompt you receive on Part II. In a narrative essay, for example, your main purpose will be to describe. In a persuasive essay, your main purpose will probably be to convince. In an expository essay, you may aim to inform, compare, propose, or explain, depending upon your topic.

As you think about how to write your essay, think about how you would fill in the blank in the following sentence:

My goal in this essay is to _____.

Beginnings, Middles, and Ends

As you know, essays have three distinct parts:

- beginning (introduction)
- middle (body)
- end (conclusion)

You will be expected to have all three parts in your essay.

Introductions

First impressions count, and that's why introductions are so important in writing. A good introduction:

1. indicates what the essay is about (its topic) and what the writer is going to say about the topic (its main idea)
2. grabs the reader's attention
3. establishes the tone of the passage

Techniques for grabbing attention include opening with:

- a question
- a quotation
- a surprising fact or statement
- an imaginary situation or scenario
- an anecdote
- interesting background information
- a new twist on a familiar phrase

For example, a more attention-grabbing introduction to the Batman passage in the pretest might be something like the following:

> *Pow! Bam! Zap! Batman triumphs again, saving the citizens of Gotham City from evil.*

This opening plays upon a convention of comic strips and the Batman television series. And because it is unique and uses exclamation points, it generates interest and excitement in the reader.

Conclusions

Conclusions, too, should be powerful. After all, people tend to remember most what comes first and last, and the final words have the power to ring in readers' ears for a long time afterward. A good conclusion will:

1. restate the main idea
2. provide a sense of closure (not "open a new can of worms" by introducing a new topic)
3. arouse readers' emotions to make the ending and main idea memorable

The Batman text, again, provides a good example.

> *In Batman, Kane gave us an image of our own superhero potential.*

This concluding sentence sums up what makes Batman so popular, rounding out the passage in a way that makes readers think about their own similarities to Batman and what sort of superheroes they could be.

Many of the same introductory techniques can be used to help make conclusions memorable:

- a quotation
- a question
- an anecdote
- a prediction
- a solution or recommendation
- a call to action

For example, the conclusion to an essay about a healthy diet might end with a call to action:

> *Take a good, long look in your refrigerator and pantry. What unhealthy foods call your icebox and cabinets their home? Find them, get rid of them, and stock up on foods that will help you live a longer, healthier life.*

▶ Effective Essays and the Writing Process

Experienced writers know that good writing doesn't happen all at once. Rather, it develops in stages. That's because writing is a process, not just a product. And it's difficult to get a good product without going through each step in the writing process.

The writing process can be divided into three basic steps:

1. planning
2. drafting
3. revising and editing

When you are under pressure to write a winning essay in just 45 minutes, you may be tempted to skip these steps and just write your essay in one shot. You may end up with a successful essay with this approach. But your chances of doing well on Part II of the GED Language Arts, Writing Exam—indeed, on any writing task—will increase dramatically if you take the time to work through each step. Even though you only have 45 minutes, the ten minutes you spend planning and proofreading your essay will be time well spent. In fact, for essay exams, the planning stage is so important that it has been divided into six separate steps in the following section.

How to Divide Your Time on an Essay Exam

When your time is limited, how long should you spend on each step in the writing process? On an essay exam, use this general rule for dividing your time:

$\frac{1}{4}$ of the time: planning
$\frac{1}{2}$ of the time: writing
$\frac{1}{4}$ of the time: revising and editing

Your 45 minutes on the GED essay can be divided as follows:

10 minutes planning
25 minutes writing
10 minutes revising and editing

▶ Six Steps to a Strong Essay

These six steps will help you write a strong, effective essay on the GED Language Arts, Writing Exam.

Step 1: Understand the Writing Prompt

Before you can begin to plan your essay, you need to be sure you understand the kind of essay you need to write. As noted earlier, it is essential that you respond accurately to the writing prompt you are given on the exam. If you write about a different topic, *you will not receive credit for your essay*. It's therefore critical to understand exactly what the prompt is asking you to do.

Earlier in this section, we divided the essay prompts into three types: narrative, persuasive, and expository. How do you know which kind of essay the prompt is asking for? Each prompt will have key words that can help you understand what to do. These key words include terms such as:

tell   describe   identify   explain

Notice, for example, the underlined key words in the following prompts:

The Internet includes many websites with images and content that are inappropriate for children. Other sites on the Internet promote violence or intolerance against certain groups of people. Should websites like these be censored? In your essay, state your position on this issue and explain why you take that position. Use your personal observations, experiences, and knowledge to support your essay.

Sometimes events take an unexpected turn and things end up differently than we imagined. Tell about a time when something unexpected happened to you. In your essay, describe what was supposed to happen and how things actually turned out. Use supporting details throughout your essay.

You are on your way to a successful essay if:

1. **You understand what kind of essay to write:** narrative (tell a story), persuasive (make an argument), or expository (explain an idea or respond to a situation or scenario).
2. **You follow the directions exactly and directly answer the questions** in the prompt. In the first example, you must state your position on the issue raised in the prompt—censorship of certain types of Internet sites. In the second example, you must tell a story about a specific kind of experience—a time when something unexpected happened.

Step 2: Formulate a Clear Thesis

Before you begin to write, you need to decide what you are going to write about. Once you are sure you understand the prompt, how will you answer the question it asks? Your answer will form the core of your essay. It will be the main idea that controls everything you write and determine the kind of support you will provide. In other words, your answer to the question in the prompt is your **thesis**—your main idea. It is the "argument" that you are going to make and the idea you need to support.

A thesis does not just repeat or paraphrase the question or prompt. It does not simply make general statements about the topic or state how others might respond to the question. A good thesis takes a clear, personal position. For example, look again at the following prompt:

Our relationship with our neighbors is very important. Sometimes these relationships are the source of great joy in our lives; other times, they can be the source of great trouble. In your opinion, what makes a good neighbor? In your essay, identify the characteristics of a good neighbor and explain why these characteristics are important for people living side by side. Use your personal observations, experiences, and knowledge to support your essay.

The following sentences are not thesis statements (they do not answer the question).

- There are all kinds of neighbors.
- What makes a good neighbor?
- There are many characteristics of a good neighbor.

These, however, are thesis statements. They respond directly to the question.

- Good neighbors are helpful and kind.
- The best kind of neighbors help when asked and otherwise mind their own business.
- Good neighbors are friendly, helpful, and respectful of boundaries.

Step 3: Brainstorm Support for Your Thesis

Once you have decided how to answer the question(s) in the prompt, decide how you will *support* your answer. On your piece of scrap paper, list at least three to five reasons, examples, or specific details to support your thesis or events to develop your story.

Because you are still in the planning stage, write down whatever comes to mind. You don't have to include everything you list in your essay. And the more ideas you put down, the more freedom you will have to pick the best (strongest) support for your thesis.

For example, here's how you might brainstorm support for the previous prompt:

Thesis: Good neighbors are friendly, helpful, and respectful of boundaries.

Why?
Friendly neighbors are pleasant to have around, make it nice to live where you live.

Helpful is important—know you can count on them for small favors, when you are in need. Need to respect boundaries, not to take what is yours, not to get too involved in your life—otherwise they will not be welcome.

Examples:
Friendly—my neighbor Selma and her family—always saying hello, often chatting, cookies at Christmas.
Helpful—lending tools to Dad, borrowing sugar etc., babysitting.
Respecting boundaries—don't just walk in, don't be nosy; they're your neighbors, not your family.

Listing is just one brainstorming strategy. You can also *map* your ideas. This is especially effective if you are a visual learner, as shown on page 160.

Freewriting

If you are totally stuck and can't think of how to answer your question or how to support your thesis, try **freewriting**. This brainstorming technique is what it says—*free writing*. Write down whatever comes to mind about the question or topic. Don't worry about grammar or structure. Write in your own language if you like. Just write. If you keep your hands moving for even two or three minutes, you are bound to come up with some good ideas.

Step 4: Create a Detailed Outline

The next step is your opportunity to make sure the essay you write is both well organized and well developed. By creating a detailed outline, you can:

- put your ideas in a logical, effective order
- fill in any gaps in your support

Basic Outline Structure

Essays follow this basic structure:

1. introduction (states thesis)
2. body (explains and supports thesis)
3. conclusion (brings closure and restates thesis)

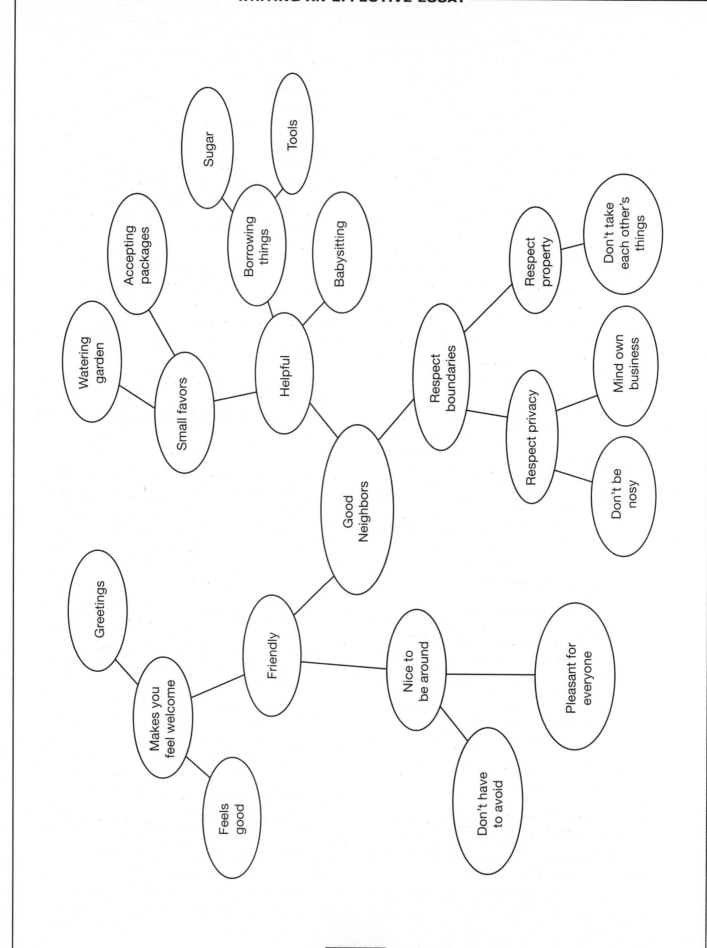

Your outline should follow this basic structure, too. Because you are writing a very short essay, you should have at least one point in your outline for each paragraph. Thus, the "body" section of your outline should be broken down into the individual supporting ideas for your essay:

1. introduction
2. support 1
3. support 2
4. support 3
5. conclusion

This basic outline has three supporting points. If each outline item has one paragraph, you will have a total of five paragraphs in your essay. While there's no set rule about how many points or how many paragraphs you should have in your essay, this is a good guide to follow. Three supporting paragraphs will generally give you enough support to make a strong case (if you are writing a persuasive essay), to sufficiently explain your ideas (expository essay), or to tell your story (narrative essay).

Three-Part Essay Structure

Introduction: Tell your readers what you are going to tell them. (State your thesis.)
Body: Tell them. (Develop your ideas and provide specific support for your thesis.)
Conclusion: Tell them what you have told them. (Restate your thesis.)

Organizing Your Support

Obviously, you know where to put your introductory and concluding paragraphs. But how do you organize the ideas in the body of your essay? Which of the four organizational patterns you reviewed earlier—chronology, comparison and contrast, cause and effect, and order of importance—should you use for your support? (See pages 149–151 for a review of organizational patterns.)

If you are responding to a narrative prompt, **chronological order** is clearly your best choice. Describe the events in the order in which they happened. Be sure to use strong transitions and details as you tell your story.

If you are responding to a persuasive prompt, **order of importance** is probably the most effective pattern to

use. Because the prompt asks you to take a position, your main support will consist of the reasons that you took this particular stance. A logical and effective way to present those reasons is by rank. Organize ideas from the least important to the most important reason, from the least compelling to the most compelling example.

If you are responding to an expository prompt, your organizational pattern will depend upon your purpose. Often, order of importance will be your most effective choice. This is true for the good neighbor prompt. Notice, for example, how you might organize the support from the previous brainstorm:

Introduction: Good neighbors are friendly, helpful, and respectful of boundaries.

1. Friendly neighbors are pleasant to have around, make it nice to live where you live.
   Ex: My neighbor Selma and her family

2. Helpful is important—know you can count on them for small favors, when you are in need.
   Ex: lending and borrowing things

3. Need to respect boundaries, not take what is yours, not get too involved in your life—otherwise, they will not be welcome. (It's okay to not be friendly and not be helpful, I can live with that—but it's not okay to not respect boundaries.)
   Ex: physical boundaries (yard, house) and social boundaries (private family business)

Here, the characteristics that make good neighbors are organized by order of importance. The most important characteristic and most compelling examples come last.

Strong Supporting Paragraphs

Outlining your ideas not only sets up an effective organization. It can also show you if your essay is sufficiently developed. For an essay to be effective, *each paragraph* must be effective, too. And that means each paragraph must be sufficiently developed.

While there is no magic formula, there are some general guidelines regarding paragraph length. A paragraph with just one sentence—unless that sentence is specifically set off to create a special effect—is too short. It doesn't sufficiently develop its idea. A paragraph with ten sentences, on the other hand, is probably too long. There's likely to be more than one idea developed in that paragraph. (Remember, a paragraph, by definition, is a group of sentences about the same idea.) For an essay of this type, paragraphs of three or four sentences each should be enough to explain and provide specific details and examples for each of your supporting ideas.

To help you develop your paragraphs, expand your outline. For each main supporting idea, list at least one specific detail or example. Imagine each paragraph as a mini-essay, with its own thesis (topic sentence) and support (specific examples and details). Notice, for example, how the previous outline can be expanded as follows:

Introduction: Good neighbors are friendly, helpful, and respectful of boundaries.

1. Friendly neighbors are pleasant to have around, make it nice to live where you live.
   Ex: my neighbor Selma and her family—
   - always saying hello
   - often chatting
   - cookies at Christmas

2. Helpful is important—know you can count on them for small favors, when you are in need.
   Ex:
   - borrowing sugar etc.
   - Hank lending tools to Dad
   - Selma helping Mom sew curtains

3. Need to respect boundaries, not to take what is yours, not to get too involved in your life—otherwise they will not be welcome. (It's okay to not be friendly and not be helpful, I can live with that—but it's not okay to not respect boundaries.)
   Ex:
   - physical boundaries: don't just walk in; it's not your house, don't take things
   - old neighbors, the Wilcoxes, taking things from our shed w/o asking
   - social boundaries: don't be nosy; it's not your family; respect privacy
     - what happened when Uncle Andy's neighbors got too nosy
     - neighbors got involved in divorce
     - made painful experience more complicated and confusing for everyone

Notice now how clearly the order of importance of the organizational pattern stands out, especially in the last section. And because this outline is so detailed, it offers a guide for just about every sentence in the body of the essay.

Step 5: Write Your Essay

Now that you have a clear, detailed outline, you can begin to write. If you can quickly think of a catchy way to begin your essay, terrific. If not, don't spend precious minutes trying to come up with the perfect opening line. You don't have the time. Remember, you have only 45 minutes for the whole essay—planning, writing, and editing. You need to start writing as soon as you organize your thoughts. One good way to jump right in is to **paraphrase** (repeat in your own words) the key discussion note stated in the prompt and then state your thesis. Here's an example of this kind of introduction:

It is very important to have good relationships with our neighbors. In my opinion, there are three characteristics that make it easy to live side by side with someone. Neighbors should be friendly, they should be helpful, and they should respect boundaries.

Notice how this introduction also **outlines** the three main topics that will be developed in the body of the essay: being friendly, being helpful, and respecting boundaries.

Once you have written your introduction, write the body of your essay paragraph by paragraph, following your outline. Make sure each paragraph has a clear topic sentence and specific support. Don't forget about transitions between paragraphs. Key words and phrases such as *more importantly*, *similarly*, etc. help guide your reader through your argument. (See "Transitions" on page 152 to review transitional words and phrases.)

After your supporting paragraphs, write a brief conclusion. Restate your thesis, but not in exactly the same words. Don't introduce any new topics. Instead, make readers feel as if you have covered your topic thoroughly and that they have gotten something meaningful from reading your essay. Here's an example:

When you live side by side with someone, it's important to have a good relationship. To be a good neighbor, you need to be friendly and helpful. Most important, you need to respect boundaries. Your house is your house; your life is your life. It doesn't belong to your neighbor.

Writing with Style

Style refers to the manner in which something is done. For example, we all buy and wear clothes that fit our own personal style—the way we like to look and feel when we are dressed. The same is true of our writing; each person has his or her own individual style, and the more you understand stylistic techniques, the more effectively you can express yourself in writing.

Style in writing is created by several different elements, including:

- word choice
- consistent and appropriate tone
- variety in sentence structure and use of punctuation and other techniques for effect

Word Choice

One of the most important decisions writers make is a constant one: **word choice.** As you write, you are always, in every sentence, thinking about the right words to express your ideas. The "right" word has three essential characteristics:

1. It expresses the idea you wish to convey.
2. It is exact (precise).
3. It is appropriate for the audience and tone.

Notice how effective word choice cuts back on wordiness and creates much more powerful sentences in the following example:

He *walked very quickly* into the room.

He *rushed* into the room.
He *raced* into the room.
He *burst* into the room.

Each of these italicized verbs has much more impact than the verb *walked* and its two modifiers, *very quickly*. These exact verbs create a vivid picture; they tell us exactly how he entered the room.

Exact nouns will improve your sentences, too. Here's an example of a general sentence made more precise:

The *machine* made a loud *noise* and then stopped.
The *generator* made a loud *bang* and then stopped.

The second sentence, with its exact nouns, tells us what kind of machine it was and what kind of noise it made, giving us a much clearer picture of what happened.

Adjectives, too, should be precise. Instead of writing:

I am *very tired.*

Try an exact adjective:

I am *exhausted.*

Exhausted means *very tired*—and it's a much more powerful word to convey your idea.

Appropriate Level of Formality

Word choice determines level of formality, and vice versa. Would you say to your boss, "Yo, wassup?" Probably not. But you certainly might talk that way to your friends. We're usually careful to use the right level of formality when we talk to someone. The same should be true of writing. Writers must decide how formal or informal they should be when they write, and they make this decision based on their audience and their purpose.

Level of formality can range from the very informal (slang) to the very formal (esoteric, ceremonial) to everything in between. Writers use word choice and sentence structure to manipulate the level of formality. Here's an example:

A: *It was so cool. I mean, I never saw anything like it before. What a great flick! You have to check it out.*

B: *It was really an impressive film, unlike anything I've ever seen before. You should definitely go see it.*

These two sentences are drastically different in style and in particular in the level of formality. Though they both tell the same story and both use the personal first-person *I*, there's clearly a different relationship to the reader. From the word choice and style—the short sentences, the very casual language—we can tell that the writer of passage A has a more informal, more friendly relationship with the reader than the writer of passage B.

The emotion of the writer in passage A is much more transparent, too, because the language is more informal and natural. You get the idea that passage A is addressed to a close friend, while passage B might be addressed to a colleague or supervisor.

In your essay, be sure to write at an appropriate level of formality. Do not use slang, but do not be excessively formal, either.

Consistent and Appropriate Tone

An appropriate and consistent tone is another essential element of effective writing. **Tone** is the mood or attitude conveyed by words or speech. Think, for example, of all the different ways to say *sure* or *hello*. It's how you say the word that conveys so much of its meaning.

When you listen to others, it's usually pretty easy to hear the tone of their voice. But how do you establish tone in writing?

When you speak, you create tone by how quickly or slowly you say a word, how loudly or softly you say it, and how you use facial expressions and body language. When you write, though, your readers can't hear how your words sound. And they certainly can't see your facial expressions or body language. But you can use word choice, punctuation, and style to establish tone. For example, recall this pair of sentences from the punctuation review:

> *Wait, I'm coming with you.*
> *Wait—I'm coming with you!*

Here, it's the punctuation that changes the tone. The first sentence is calm and neutral. The second sentence, on the other hand, is emotional and excited.

There are endless varieties of tones when you speak. Likewise, there are endless varieties of tone in writing. Here's a list of some of the more common words used to describe tone:

cheerful	hopeful	sad	gloomy
apologetic	critical	sincere	insincere
sarcastic	ironic	playful	demanding
bossy	indifferent	anxious	respectful
disrespectful	foreboding	uncertain	threatening
matter-of-fact	somber	grateful	annoyed
humorous	mocking	defeated	uplifting
timid	joyful	secure	insecure
hesitant	bold	rude	proud
complimentary	angry	confident	mischievous

As you write, choose words that convey your desired tone. For example, if you are describing a humorous event, you might use the phrase *topsy-turvy* rather than *chaotic* or *disorganized*. Similarly, if you are describing an unpleasant event, you might use the word *tumultuous* or *helter-skelter* to convey the same idea.

Variety in Sentence Structure and Rhetorical Techniques for Emphasis

A strong essay will demonstrate an ability to manipulate sentence structure and punctuation for effect. Sentence structure, as noted earlier, is an important element of style. If all of your sentences have the same pattern, you will end up with writing that is monotonous and dry, like the following passage:

> *She is a teacher. She lives in Montana. She has a ranch there. She goes to California a lot. She has family there. She has two pets, a cat and a dog.*

Unsophisticated and quite dull, isn't it? That's because all of the sentences are short and share the same structure; they all start with *she* and a present tense verb. This is quite different from parallel structure. **Parallelism** means using a repeating sentence pattern to create rhythm within a sentence or paragraph. This kind of repetition, on the other hand, creates monotony and shows a lack of flexibility in creating sentence patterns. Here is the same paragraph, revised to show variety in sentence structure:

> *She is a teacher and lives on a ranch in Montana with her cat and dog. Because she has family in California, she travels there frequently.*

Notice how much more interesting this paragraph is now. The seven sentences have been combined into two, and only one sentence starts with *she*. Many of the short sentences have been turned into modifiers that make for more varied sentence patterns.

Sentence structure and punctuation can also be used to manipulate emphasis. The best place to put sentence elements that you want to emphasize is at the end (the "save the best for last" approach). What comes last is what lingers longest in the readers' ears.

He is tall, dark, and handsome. [The emphasis is on *handsome*. If *tall* is the most important characteristic, then that should come last.]

She is smart, reliable, and experienced. [The emphasis is on *experienced*; if *smart* is the most important characteristic, then that should be last in the list.]

You can also use a dash to set off part of a sentence for emphasis:

He is tall, dark, handsome—and married.

Here, the stress on the last element is heightened by the dash, which emphasizes the sense of disappointment in the sentence.

Don't Repeat Yourself

On the sentence level, in general, less is more. The fewer words you use to get your point across, the better. **Redundancy** is the unnecessary repetition of ideas. **Wordiness** is the use of several words when a few can express the same idea more clearly and concisely. Avoid both of these as you write your essay.

Wordiness and redundancy typically result from three causes:

▶ The use of unnecessary words or phrases

Redundant: Turn left at the <u>green-colored</u> house.
Correct: Turn left at the <u>green</u> house.

▶ Unnecessary repetition of nouns or pronouns

Redundant: <u>Riva she</u> couldn't believe her ears.
Correct: <u>Riva</u> couldn't believe her ears.

▶ The use of wordy phrases instead of adverbs

Wordy: She spoke <u>in a very convincing manner</u>.
Concise: She spoke <u>convincingly</u>.

Don't skimp on details, but try not to waste words.

Step 6: Proofread Carefully

In the three-step writing process, the third step is to revise and edit. What exactly is the difference between revising and editing, anyway?

To **revise** means to carefully read over your essay and make changes to improve it. Revising focuses on improving the **content** (*what* you say) and **style** (*how* you say it). In other words, when you revise, you concentrate on the "big picture": your ideas and how you organize and present them in your essay. Editing, on the other hand, deals with **grammar** (correct sentences), **mechanics** (correct spelling, capitalization, and punctuation), and **usage** (correct use of words and idioms).

Editing is very important; your writing should be as clear and correct as possible. But as a general rule, it doesn't make much sense to carefully proofread each sentence only to realize that you need to rewrite several paragraphs.

However—and this is a big "however"—the guidelines are a little different on a timed essay exam, especially when the time is so short. Because your time is so limited, revising should actually take place *before* you write, while you are outlining your essay. As you outline, make sure you have a clear thesis that addresses the writing prompt, sufficient and relevant support, and logical organization. You probably won't have time to rewrite paragraphs or add new ones. That's why it's crucial to outline so carefully. But you will probably have a few minutes to change word order, adjust word choice, and correct grammatical and mechanical mistakes. And this final "polishing" step can help make your ideas come across much more clearly for your readers.

▶ Sample Essay

You have seen the brainstorming and outline for the good neighbor prompt. Now, here is a complete essay. This essay would score a "6" on Part II of the GED Language Arts, Writing Exam.

No matter where you live, you have neighbors. The kind of neighbors you have can make a big difference in how happy you are. I'm lucky to have wonderful neighbors. The people who live next to me are friendly, they are helpful, and they respect boundaries.

Friendly neighbors help to make it nice to live where you do. Grumpy, unpleasant neighbors don't usually do you any harm, but they don't make you feel good, either. A friendly neighbor makes you feel welcome. For example, our neighbors, Mr. and Mrs. Ulerio and their children, are very friendly. Whenever we see them they say a cheerful hello and ask how we're doing. Mr. and Mrs. Ulerio often chat with my parents, and every Christmas, Mrs. Ulerio and her daughter Jessica bring us homemade cookies. They make us feel like they're glad to have us next door.

Good neighbors aren't just friendly, they're also helpful. If we run out of sugar while baking or need one more egg for a recipe, we know we can run over to the Ulerios' or our other neighbors, the Zurowskis'. Mr. Zurowski is particularly helpful to my dad. My dad doesn't have a lot of tools, but Mr. Zurowski does, and he's always willing to lend them to my dad. He also helps my dad with projects once in a while, like fixing the roof on the dog house. There have also been plenty of times when we stayed with Mrs. Ulerio while our parents were out.

Perhaps the most important aspect of being a good neighbor is respecting boundaries. I think most of us could live with neighbors who are unfriendly or never offer a helping hand. But few of us will tolerate neighbors who don't respect our property and our privacy. Our old neighbors, for example, used to come and take toys and lawn equipment from our shed without asking. Sometimes, we'd have to go to their house and ask for our things back because they didn't return them. Even worse, my Uncle Andy's neighbors were extremely nosey and gossipy. They got involved in Uncle Andy's divorce and made the experience more complicated and painful for everyone.

Good neighbors like mine are hard to find. I hope I will always have neighbors like the Ulerios and Zurowskis. They are kind, they know when to help, and they respect our property and privacy.

16 ▶

Tips and Strategies for the GED Language Arts, Writing Exam

You have reviewed what you need to know for the GED Language Arts, Writing Exam. Now you will learn some specific tips and strategies to use.

ONE OF THE myths about writing is that either you have writing talent, or you don't. True, some people have a special gift for effective writing. But good writing is a skill, and like other skills, it is something that *everyone* can learn.

Throughout this chapter, you will review the structure of the writing exam and specific tips you can use to improve your score on the test. Read this chapter carefully, and then review your notes from the whole GED Language Arts, Writing section. When you are ready, move on to the practice questions that follow.

▶ The GED Language Arts, Writing Exam in a Nutshell

The GED Language Arts, Writing Exam consists of two parts. Part I (75 minutes) will ask you 50 questions about sentence structure, usage, mechanics, and organization. These questions will be drawn from informational passages, business documents such as memos, and how-to texts. You will be asked the best way to correct or revise sentences or paragraphs.

Part II (45 minutes) will ask you to write an essay of about 250 words (four to five paragraphs). Your essay prompts may ask you to write a narrative essay (tell a story), a persuasive essay (argue a point of view), or expository essay (explain or describe your response to a question). Essays are scored holistically, taking into account the overall effectiveness of the essay.

▶ Sentence Structure

Sentence structure refers to the way we put words together in sentences. Chapter 11 reviewed the building blocks of sentences: subjects, predicates, and objects; independent and dependent clauses; sentence boundaries; parts of speech; and parallel structure.

Approximately one-third of the questions on Part I will be about sentence structure. Here are some tips for tackling questions about sentence structure:

1. Look for words that signal relationships and make connections: subordinating conjunctions, coordinating conjunctions, and conjunctive adverbs. These words help describe the relationship between ideas and determine sentence boundaries and punctuation.
2. Look carefully at word order. Are modifiers close to the things they modify?
3. Look for grammatical patterns. Is there—or should there be—parallel structure at work in the sentence?
4. Consider sentence combining possibilities. Could sentences be combined effectively?
5. If you suspect a sentence fragment, isolate that sentence and see if it makes sense on its own. If not, it probably needs to be combined with another sentence or revised to be complete.
6. If you suspect a run-on sentence, look at each clause. Is it independent? If so, is there strong enough punctuation or connecting words between the clauses?

▶ Usage

Another third of the questions on Part I will be about usage: the rules that govern the form of the words we use and how we put those words together in sentences. Chapter 12 reviewed the usage rules you should know for the exam. Here are some specific tips for questions about usage.

Verbs

Because verbs are the driving force in every sentence, and because verbs can take so many different forms, you can be sure that many usage questions will be about verbs. Here are five tips to help you prepare for those questions:

1. Memorize *irregular* and *troublesome* verb forms.
2. Remember that verbs should be *consistent in tense*.
3. Make sure that verbs *agree* with their subjects.
4. Make sure the correct *helping verbs* are used to convey the intended meaning.
5. Use *infinitives* and *gerunds* correctly.

Indefinite Pronouns

To remember singular indefinite pronouns, note that *someone, anyone, everyone*, and *no one* all contain the word *one*. *One*, of course, is singular. Indefinite pronouns beginning with *some, any, every* and *no* are all singular.

Agreement

When it comes to agreement, think of sentences as a scale with subjects on one side and verbs on the other, or with antecedents on one side and pronouns on the other. The subjects and verbs need to agree in order for the scale to be balanced. Likewise, the pronouns need to agree with their antecedents to balance the scale.

Pronouns

It's so easy to make a mistake with pronouns and contractions because we show possession of nouns with an apostrophe (*Ralph's car*). With pronouns, however, possession does not require an apostrophe. If you get confused, think of a possessive pronoun that doesn't get confused with contractions, like *my* or *our*. These do not have apostrophes; other possessive pronouns shouldn't, either.

And here's one way to remember to use *that* when referring to *things*: Both words begin with the letter *t*.

Prepositional Idioms

If prepositional idioms tend to give you problems, try writing sentences with the idioms to give yourself extra practice. Create a worksheet for yourself or someone else who may also need extra idiom review.

▶ Mechanics

About one-fourth of the questions on Part I will be about mechanics: the rules that govern punctuation, capitalization, and spelling. Chapter 13 reviewed punctuation guidelines, rules for correct capitalization, and spelling for contractions and possessive pronouns as well as homonyms. Here are some specific tips for handling questions about mechanics.

Punctuation

Remember that punctuation marks are used to separate sentences, show the relationships between ideas, reveal tone, and clarify meaning. Each punctuation mark has a specific function and should only be used in specific situations. Take the time to memorize the uses for each punctuation mark. Here are some tips to help you learn them:

1. Pay attention to how punctuation is used as you read. Now that you know the rules, the more you see them in action, the easier it will be to remember them.
2. Write your own sentences with each punctuation mark and each comma rule. Notice how punctuation can change the impact and meaning of sentences.
3. Teach the punctuation rules to someone else.

Capitalization

When capitalization is the issue, ask yourself whether the word in question is *specific* or *general.* If it is a specific person, place, or thing, then it probably should be capitalized. Remember, in this regard, *specific* means *particular* or *individual,* not *detailed.* For example, a poodle is a specific type of dog, but it is not capitalized because it doesn't refer to a specific (individual or particular) dog. *Rover,* however, should be capitalized because Rover is a specific (particular, individual) dog.

Contractions

Whenever you come across a question with a contraction, read it as two words. If it doesn't make sense, then you need a possessive pronoun, not a contraction. Eliminate the apostrophe.

Homonyms

Unfortunately, the only thing you can do to prepare for questions about homonyms is to memorize the correct meanings and spellings. Try using mnemonic devices to remember which word is which. For example:

stationary vs. stationery: Remember that "stationery" is the one to write on because it's spelled with an "er" like the lett**er** you are writing.

▶ Organization

Finally, a smaller portion of the questions on Part I will be about organization: how writers arrange their ideas. Chapter 14 reviewed essay structure and organizational patterns, effective paragraphs, and transitions. When you encounter a question about organization, these guidelines can help you identify the correct answer.

1. Identify the organizational pattern. How are the ideas in the passage or paragraph organized? Then consider: Is there any sentence or paragraph that seems to be out of place in the pattern?
2. Identify the main idea of the paragraph or passage. What thought holds the paragraph or passage together? Is there a topic sentence expressing that thought? Then consider: Is there any sentence (or portion of a sentence) that doesn't fit under the controlling idea?
3. Look for transitions in the paragraph or passage. Are there strong transitions leading you from one idea to the next? Would the paragraph or passage be more effective if more (or more appropriate) transitions were added?

▶ Part II: The Essay

Chapter 15 described the steps you should take to write well on an essay exam. You learned that when you must write under pressure, *good planning* and *time management* are the keys to success. At test time, remember this guideline for using your time on the exam:

$\frac{1}{4}$ time (10–15 minutes): planning

$\frac{1}{2}$ time (20–25 minutes): writing

$\frac{1}{4}$ time (10–15 minutes): revising and editing

The Six Steps for Essay Exam Writing

When you are writing for an exam, follow these six steps:

Step 1: Understand the writing prompt.
Step 2: Formulate a clear thesis.
Step 3: Brainstorm support for your thesis.
Step 4: Create a detailed outline.
Step 5: Write the essay.
Step 6: Proofread carefully.

The following tips can help you write a successful essay for the GED Language Arts, Writing Exam:

1. Make sure you understand the prompt. What kind of essay are you being asked to write?

2. Make sure you directly answer the prompt. Remember, you will receive a zero if you do not write on the assigned topic.

3. Remember that you only have 45 minutes, so it's important not to waste any time. If you are stuck and can't seem to get started, try *freewriting* or another *brainstorming* technique. This will help you get some ideas down on paper and get your thoughts flowing.

4. Remember that in a brainstorm, there's no such thing as a stupid idea; write down anything that comes to mind. When you're ready to outline, you can eliminate ideas that don't fit.

5. On Part II, it's important to write for a general audience. That means two things:

   a. You must provide *context* for your readers. Don't assume that your readers know what you know. For example, if you are writing about your favorite film, you must provide some essential information about that film for your readers, including the basic plot and characters.

   b. You must use an appropriate level of *formality*. Avoid **jargon** (technical or specialized language) and slang. Don't try to use big words just to sound more intelligent. Often, simple words are the most clear and effective. Besides, you may end up misusing vocabulary and saying things you don't mean.

6. Make sure you have a clear purpose. Know what you want to accomplish in your essay. What is your goal? Before you begin to write, draft a thesis statement. Remember that a thesis must say something *about* the subject.

7. Remember that first impressions count. Get your reader's attention and state your thesis clearly in your introduction.

8. Remember that writing is a process, and that *effective planning* is perhaps the most important part of that process. Plan your essay carefully. Use your outline to organize your ideas and make sure you have provided strong and sufficient support. If you don't have at least two supporting ideas, you should rethink your essay. If you are making an argument, use order of importance (least to most important) to organize your ideas.

9. Make sure to provide strong transitions throughout your essay. Use transitional words and phrases to connect sentences and ideas.

10. Remember that *style* is important. When you revise:

    a. Try to make a few word choice changes so that your writing has more impact. Use precise, vivid verbs and nouns.

    b. Check for wordiness and redundancy. Don't repeat yourself or use bulky constructions such as *in this day and age* (*today* is more concise and appropriate).

    c. Be sure you have some variety in sentence structure. If your essay has a sing-songy or monotonous rhythm, combine sentences and add introductory phrases so that your sentence patterns are more diverse.

11. Even if you have only a few minutes left at the end of the exam, take the time to review what you have written. If you make only one or two minor corrections, you have still made an improvement in your essay.

IV ▶ The GED Language Arts, Reading Exam

I N THIS SECTION, you will learn about the GED Language Arts, Reading Exam. You will find out what the exam is like, what kinds of passages and questions to expect, and how to tackle those questions. You will also review the genres and elements of literature and the fundamental reading comprehension skills you need to do well on this exam.

Before you begin this chapter, take a few minutes to do the following pretest. The passages and questions are the same type you will find on the GED Language Arts, Reading Exam. When you are finished, check the answer key carefully to assess your results. Your pretest score will help you determine how much preparation you need and the areas in which you need the most careful review and practice.

► Pretest: GED Language Arts, Reading

Directions: Read the following passages carefully. Choose the one best answer to each question.

To practice the timing of the exam, take approximately 15 minutes to complete this pretest. Record your answers on the answer sheet provided here.

Note: On the GED, you are not permitted to write in the test booklet. Make any notes on a separate piece of paper.

ANSWER SHEET

1. ⓐ ⓑ ⓒ ⓓ ⓔ
2. ⓐ ⓑ ⓒ ⓓ ⓔ
3. ⓐ ⓑ ⓒ ⓓ ⓔ
4. ⓐ ⓑ ⓒ ⓓ ⓔ
5. ⓐ ⓑ ⓒ ⓓ ⓔ
6. ⓐ ⓑ ⓒ ⓓ ⓔ
7. ⓐ ⓑ ⓒ ⓓ ⓔ
8. ⓐ ⓑ ⓒ ⓓ ⓔ
9. ⓐ ⓑ ⓒ ⓓ ⓔ
10. ⓐ ⓑ ⓒ ⓓ ⓔ

Questions 1–5 refer to the following poem.

How Does the Speaker Feel about Eagles?

The Eagle

(1) He clasps the crag with crooked hands;
Close to the sun in lonely lands,
Ringed with the azure world, he stands.

The wrinkled sea beneath him crawls;
(5) He watches from his mountain walls,
And like a thunderbolt he falls.
— Alfred Lord Tennyson, "The Eagle" (1851)

1. The "he" that the speaker refers to in the poem is
   a. the poet.
   b. the speaker.
   c. an eagle.
   d. a man on a mountain.
   e. the reader.

2. In line 6, the speaker compares the eagle to a thunderbolt. This comparison suggests that the eagle
   a. was hit by a thunderbolt.
   b. is as powerful as a thunderbolt.
   c. is as loud as a thunderbolt.
   d. is flying during a storm.
   e. is out of control.

3. The poet's goal is most likely to
   a. make the reader feel as lonely as the eagle.
   b. paint a detailed picture of an eagle on a mountain.
   c. convey the magnificence and power of eagles.
   d. convince the reader to get involved in saving endangered species.
   e. tell a story about a special eagle.

4. Line 6 tells us that the eagle "falls" from the mountain. The eagle is most likely
   a. falling because it got hit by a lightning bolt.
   b. dying.
   c. going to look for another eagle.
   d. going down toward the sea where it is not so close to the sun.
   e. going after an animal that it spotted from the mountain.

5. If the poet could belong to a contemporary organization, which group might he join?
   a. NAACP
   b. The World Wildlife Fund
   c. National Human Rights Organization
   d. International Mountain Climbers Club
   e. The Vegetarian Society

Questions 6–10 refer to the following excerpt.

What Is Bothering John Wade?

(1) In late November of 1968 John Wade extended his tour for an extra year. He had no meaningful choice. After what happened at Thuan Yen, he'd lost touch with some defining part of himself. He couldn't
(5) extricate himself from the slime. "It's a personal decision," he wrote Kathy. "Maybe someday I'll be able to explain it, but right now I can't leave this place. I have to take care of a few things; otherwise I won't ever get home. Not the right way."

(10) Kathy's response, when it finally came, was enigmatic. She loved him. She hoped it wasn't a career move.

Over the next months John Wade did his best to apply the trick of forgetfulness. He paid attention to
(15) his soldiering. He was promoted twice, first to spec four, then to buck sergeant, and in time he learned to comport himself with modest dignity under fire. It wasn't valor, but it was a start. In the first week of December he received a nasty flesh wound in the
(20) mountains west of Chu Lai. A month later he took a half pound of shrapnel in the lower back and thighs. He needed the pain. He needed to reclaim his own virtue. At times he went out of his way to confront hazard, walking point or leading night patrols, which
(25) were acts of erasure, a means of burying one great horror under the weight of many smaller horrors.

Sometimes the trick almost worked. Sometimes he almost forgot.

In November of 1969 John Wade returned home
(30) with a great many decorations. Five months later he married Kathy in an outdoor ceremony, pink and white balloons bobbing from the trees, and just before Easter they moved into the apartment in Minneapolis.

(35) "We'll be happy," Kathy said, "I know it."
John laughed and carried her inside.

—Tim O'Brien,
from *In the Lake of the Woods* (1994)

6. John Wade extends his tour of duty in Vietnam because
   a. he is required to serve another year.
   b. he is looking for something he lost.
   c. he doesn't want to see Kathy.
   d. he needs to come to terms with something he's done.
   e. he needs to heal from his physical wounds.

7. After he extends his tour, John Wade sometimes "went out of his way to confront hazard" (lines 23–24). He does this because
   a. he wants to die.
   b. he hopes it will help him forget.
   c. he thinks he is invincible.
   d. he hopes it will get him another promotion.
   e. he wants Kathy to think he is brave.

8. The excerpt tells us that John Wade "did his best to apply the trick of forgetfulness" (lines 13–14) and that "Sometimes the trick almost worked. Sometimes he almost forgot" (lines 27–28). What is it that John is trying to forget?
   a. Kathy, because his love for her distracts him from his soldiering
   b. his career plans, because he might never come home
   c. something terrible that took place in Thuan Yen
   d. something terrible he did at Chu Lai
   e. something terrible that happened to him as a child

9. Kathy tells John, "We'll be happy . . . I know it." The excerpt suggests that
   a. John has healed emotionally and physically, and Kathy is right.
   b. John may be healed physically, but not emotionally.
   c. Kathy is lying to herself and did not really want to marry John.
   d. Kathy is worried that John does not really love her.
   e. Kathy knows John can't be happy without her.

10. The excerpt suggests that reading this story can help us
  a. know what to do if we are ever in a combat situation.
  b. understand how difficult it is to have a happy marriage.
  c. realize that sometimes bad things are best forgotten.
  d. understand the importance of bravery in combat.
  e. understand the experience of Vietnam veterans.

▶ Answers

1. c. The poem describes an eagle sitting on a mountain crag. Though the word *eagle* does not appear in the poem, it is the title of the poem, indicating to readers that the lines that follow will be about an eagle. The title rules out the poet (choice **a**), the speaker of the poem (choice **b**), and the reader (choice **e**) as answers. It is possible that the lines could be describing a man (choice **d**), but again, the title makes it clear that the poem is about an eagle.

2. b. This simile suggests the power of the eagle. Thunderbolts are powerful, a force of nature beyond human control. By comparing an eagle's determined flight (plummeting toward the sea), the poet captures the bird's power. The speaker does not tell us that the bird was hit by a thunderbolt (choice **a**); he compares the bird to a thunderbolt. Thunderbolts are loud (choice **c**), but the comparison is made to how the eagle falls (flies), not how it sounds, so **c** is incorrect. There is no evidence of a storm in the poem, so choice **d** is incorrect. The controlled meter and rhyme of the poem and the sense of purpose conveyed in line 5 ("He watches from his mountain walls") suggest that the eagle will fly when it is ready, when it spots prey. It does not suggest that the bird is out of control, so choice **e** is incorrect.

3. c. The poem's word choice conveys the feeling of the eagle's power and magnificence. The eagle is "ringed with the azure world" as if he is wearing a crown; the phrase "he stands" is set off to suggest his strength and the fact that he is set apart from others in his power and beauty. He is compared to a thunderbolt, a powerful and magnificent force of nature. Choice **a** is incorrect because though the speaker mentions that the bird lives "in lonely lands," the tone of the poem doesn't convey a feeling of loneliness. The focus is on the eagle's actions (clasping, standing, watching, falling). Choice **b** is incorrect because there are few details about the appearance of the eagle himself. His environment is described (high up on a mountain), but we do not know what the eagle looks like. Choice **d** is incorrect because there is no attempt to persuade readers to get involved in saving endangered species. Appreciating eagles may lead someone to get so involved, but that is not the goal of the poem. The poem also does not tell a story—there is very little action and no conflict—so choice **e** is incorrect.

4. e. Line 5 states that the eagle "watches from his mountain walls." This suggests that he is looking for something, perhaps prey, and waiting for the right moment to swoop down toward the sea. Choice **a** is incorrect because there is no suggestion of a storm; the thunderbolt is used only as a comparison. Choice **b** is incorrect because there is no evidence that the eagle is dying. There are several active verbs in the poem that convey the eagle's strength. There is no evidence that the eagle is searching for another eagle (choice **c**) or that he simply wants to get away from the sun (choice **d**). Because he falls "like a thunderbolt," there is a suggestion of definite purpose in the eagle's action.

5. b. The poem conveys a respect for eagles, suggesting that the poet cares deeply about animals. The organization he would most likely join is the World Wildlife Fund. The poem does not convey how the poet feels about civil rights, human rights, mountain climbing, or eating meat, so choices **a**, **c**, **d**, and **e** are incorrect.

6. d. The first paragraph reveals that John Wade needs to come to terms with something he's done. The lines "After what happened at Thuan Yen, he'd lost touch with some defining part of himself" and his letter to Kathy ("It's a personal decision . . . right now I can't leave this place. I have to take care of a few things; otherwise I won't ever get home. Not the right way.") tell us that he was involved in something deeply disturbing at Thuan Yen. It is clear from the first paragraph that he chose to extend his tour, so choice **a** is incorrect. He is looking for something he lost, but only metaphorically, not physically, so choice **b** is incorrect. There's no evidence that he doesn't want to see Kathy, so choice **c** is incorrect. He doesn't get his physical wounds until after he extends his tour, so choice **e** is also incorrect.

7. b. The full sentence reads, "At times he went out of his way to confront hazard, walking point or leading night patrols, which were acts of erasure, a means of burying one great horror under the weight of many smaller horrors." The great horror is what happened at Thuan Yen; thus, he confronts danger in order to bury (forget) that horror. Choice **a** is incorrect because there is no evidence that he wants to die; he was trying to forget, not get killed. He wanted pain, but not death. Choice **c** is incorrect because the passage suggests that he was actually a bit of a coward: "in time he learned to comport himself with modest dignity under fire. It wasn't valor, but it was a start." There is no evidence that he is seeking to get promoted, so choice **d** is incorrect. He gets promoted because he "paid attention to his soldiering" as a means of forgetting. There is no suggestion that he is trying to impress Kathy, so choice **e** is incorrect.

8. c. The main clue again comes from lines 3–5: "After what happened at Thuan Yen, he'd lost touch with some defining part of himself. He couldn't extricate himself from the slime." This event is what drives him to try to forget, to try to come home "the right way." There is no evidence that he is distracted by Kathy, so choice **a** is incorrect. Choice **b** is incorrect because the passage does not discuss his career plans other than Kathy's brief mention that she hopes his extended tour "is not a career move." Choice **d** is incorrect because at Chu Lai he gets wounded in December; this is a month after he extends his tour in an effort to forget. There is no evidence that he is trying to forget something from his childhood, so choice **e** is also incorrect.

9. b. Lines 27–28 tell us that "Sometimes the trick almost worked. Sometimes he almost forgot." This suggests that he was unable to forget, unable to heal. This in turn suggests that John is still emotionally disturbed and that he and Kathy may have a difficult marriage. Choice **a** is therefore incorrect. The passage tells us that Kathy loved John (line 11), and there is no evidence that she might be lying to herself, that she is afraid he doesn't love her, or that he can't be happy without her. Choices **c**, **d**, and **e** are therefore incorrect.

10. e. The excerpt is about a Vietnam soldier who experiences something horrible during the war and is having difficulty coming to terms with what he's seen and done. There is no advice about how to behave in a combat situation, so choice **a** is incorrect. The excerpt ends on the day of their marriage, so choice **b** is incorrect. The excerpt suggests that John needs to accept what happened, not forget it, so choice **c** is incorrect. The focus in the excerpt is on John's pain, not his performance in battle (in fact, there are no details about any battles), so choice **d** is also incorrect.

▶ Pretest Assessment

How did you do on the pretest? If you answered seven or more questions correctly, you have earned the equivalent of a passing score on the GED Language Arts, Reading Exam. But remember, this pretest is only ten questions. On the GED Language Arts, Reading Exam, you must answer 40 questions about texts from a wide variety of genres and time periods. Even if you passed this pretest, read the following chapters carefully. Use the pretest to help you determine where you need to focus your study efforts.

17 ▶ About the GED Language Arts, Reading Exam

In this chapter, you will learn all about the GED Language Arts, Reading Exam, including what kind of questions and reading passages to expect.

▶ What to Expect on the GED Language Arts, Reading Exam

The GED Language Arts, Reading Exam tests your ability to understand both literary and nonfiction texts. You will be asked to read these texts and then answer 40 multiple-choice questions about those passages. One-quarter (25%) of those questions will be based on nonfiction passages; the other 75% will be based on literary texts, including stories, poems, and plays. You will have 65 minutes for this exam.

Types of Passages
The reading passages on the GED, except poems, are typically between 300–400 words. Most of the passages will be excerpts from larger works. Each exam will include:

- one *poem* of 8–25 lines
- one excerpt from a *play*
- one *commentary* on the arts (most likely about a visual art experience, such as a film, museum exhibit, or painting)
- one *business-related document* (such as an excerpt from an employee manual)
- one or more excerpts from *fiction* (novels and short stories) and *nonfiction* prose (essays, editorials/ articles, autobiography/memoir)

The passages include literature from a wide range of historical periods and literary movements. You can expect texts from three different time periods:

- pre-1920 (ancient and classical literature)
- 1920–1960 (modern literature)
- 1960–present (contemporary literature)

The passages on the GED Language Arts, Reading Exam are also carefully chosen to reflect the rich diversity of writers and themes in literature. For example, your test may include a poem by a American Indian man, an excerpt from a story by a Chinese-American woman, and an excerpt from a play about civil war in Africa.

Defining Literature

Technically, the term **literature** means *any written or published text.* This can include everything from a classic such as Mark Twain's *Huckleberry Finn* to your latest grocery shopping list. Of course, most of us don't curl up next to a warm fire with our favorite shopping list or give a computer manual to a friend as a birthday gift. These texts serve a function, but they do not necessarily provide us with the pleasure of a literary text.

Literary **texts** are fundamentally different from *functional* **texts**. Literary texts are valued for:

- the message they convey
- the beauty of their forms
- their emotional impact

While a functional text may have a practical message and convey important or useful information, it does not typically convey a message about values or human nature as literary texts do. A functional text also usually follows a standard format and has little emotional impact.

One generally thinks of **fiction** (invented stories) when thinking of literary texts, but literary texts can also be nonfiction (true stories). For example, Maya Angelou's autobiography *I Know Why the Caged Bird Sings* is literary, not functional, although it is the true story of her life. Similarly, "The Knife," an essay by Richard Selzer, describes his true experiences and reflections as a surgeon. His amazement at the beauty and complexity of the human body and the beauty of his descriptions and style make it unquestionably a literary text.

Literary Genres

There are many different types or genres of literature. On the GED Language Arts, Reading Exam, you can expect literature from these genres:

Fiction:
- novels
- short stories
- poems
- drama

Nonfiction:
- autobiography/memoir
- essays
- commentary on the arts
- business-related documents

Seventy-five percent of the passages on the GED Language Arts, Reading Exam are described as "literary" and 25% as "nonfiction." Of course, nonfiction texts can also be literary. The nonfiction referred to here is the commentary on the arts and the business-related documents. Each exam will have between seven and nine passages, with four to six questions for each passage. Five to seven of those passages will be literary (one or more poems, excerpts from plays, and excerpts from stories or novels, and possibly one or more excerpts from literary nonfiction text such as autobiographies or essays). Two to three of those passages will be functional nonfiction (commentary and business documents).

Test Statistics

- 65 minutes
- 40 questions
- 7–9 reading passages
- 4–6 questions per passage
- 5–7 literary passages
- 2–3 nonfiction (functional) texts

Types of Questions

There are four types of multiple-choice questions on the GED Language Arts, Reading Exam:

1. **Comprehension questions (20%)** test your basic understanding of what you read. They may ask you to restate information, summarize ideas, identify specific facts or details, draw basic conclusions about the information presented, or identify implications of the ideas you have just read about. For example, question 1 from the pretest is a comprehension question:

   The "he" that the speaker refers to in the poem is
   a. the poet.
   b. the speaker.
   c. an eagle.
   d. a man on a mountain.
   e. the reader.

2. **Analysis questions (30–35%)** test your ability to break down information and explore relationships between ideas (e.g., a main idea and a supporting detail); distinguish between fact and opinion; compare and contrast items and ideas; recognize unstated assumptions; identify cause and effect relationships; and make basic inferences. For example, question 7 from the pretest is an analysis question:

   After he extends his tour, John Wade sometimes "went out of his way to confront hazard" (lines 23–24). He does this because
   a. he wants to die.
   b. he hopes it will help him forget.
   c. he thinks he is invincible.
   d. he hopes it will get him another promotion.
   e. he wants Kathy to think he is brave.

3. **Synthesis questions (30–35%)** ask you to develop theories and hypotheses about the texts. In terms of reading comprehension, this is essentially an extension of the inference-making skill. Questions may ask you to determine the author's purpose or intent, infer cause and effect, infer how the author or a character feels about a related issue, or determine the effect of a particular technique. For example, question 3 from the pretest is a synthesis question:

   The poet's goal is most likely to
   a. make the reader feel as lonely as the eagle.
   b. paint a detailed picture of an eagle on a mountain.
   c. convey the magnificence and power of eagles.
   d. convince the reader to get involved in saving endangered species.
   e. tell a story about a special eagle.

4. **Application questions (15%)** ask you to use the ideas from a passage in a different context. For example, question 5 from the pretest is an application question:

   If the poet could belong to a contemporary organization, which group might he join?
   a. NAACP
   b. The World Wildlife Fund
   c. National Human Rights Organization
   d. International Mountain Climbers Club
   e. The Vegetarian Society

Doing well on the GED Language Arts, Reading Exam requires both solid reading comprehension skills and an understanding of the types and elements of literature. The rest of the chapters in this section will review reading comprehension strategies, the elements of each of the types of passages you will find on the exam, and specific tips for understanding each kind of text.

18▶ Reading Comprehension Strategies

Reading, like writing, is based on a few fundamental skills. This chapter reviews five essential reading comprehension strategies, including finding the main idea and drawing logical conclusions from the text.

To UNDERSTAND WHAT you read, you use a combination of skills that together enable you to obtain meaning from a text. These skills can be grouped into five essential reading comprehension strategies:

1. Determining the main idea or theme
2. Identifying specific supporting facts and details
3. Distinguishing between fact and opinion
4. Making inferences
5. Identifying cause and effect relationships

▶ Determining the Main Idea or Theme

Standardized reading comprehension tests always have questions about the main idea of the passage. But just what is the main idea, anyway, and why is it so important? And how is the main idea different from the theme?

Often, students confuse the main idea, or theme, of a passage with its topic. But they are two very different things. The **topic** or **subject** of a passage is what the passage is *about*. **Main idea** and **theme**, on the other hand, are what the writer wants to say *about that subject.* For example, take another look at the poem you read in the pretest, "The Eagle":

The Eagle

He clasps the crag with crooked hands;
Close to the sun in lonely lands,
Ringed with the azure world, he stands.

The wrinkled sea beneath him crawls;
He watches from his mountain walls,
And like a thunderbolt he falls.
—Alfred Lord Tennyson, "The Eagle" (1851)

This poem is *about* an eagle, so an eagle is the topic of the poem. But that is not the theme of the poem. Main ideas and themes must express an attitude or an idea; they need to say something *about* their subject and they should be stated in complete sentences.

> **Topic/Subject:** what the passage is about
> **Main Idea:** the overall fact, feeling, or thought a writer wants to convey about his or her subject
> **Theme:** the overall meaning, idea, or emotional impact of a work of fiction, poetry, or drama

---

Main idea and theme are so important because they are what the text *adds up to.* The main idea or theme is what holds all of the ideas in the passage together; it is the writer's main point. Indeed, it is why the writer writes in the first place: to express this idea.

In "The Eagle," the action and word choice in the poem reveal how the poet feels about his subject. The image of a noble eagle standing on a mountain crag and then suddenly plummeting toward the sea captures the writer's respect for this awesome bird. This reverence for the power and beauty of the eagle is the theme of the poem.

To hold all of the ideas in the passage together, a main idea or theme needs to be sufficiently general. That is, it needs to be broad enough for all of the other ideas in the passage to fit underneath, like people underneath an umbrella. For example, look at the following choices for the theme of "The Eagle":

a. Eagles often live on mountains.
b. Eagles can swoop down from the sky very quickly.
c. Eagles are powerful, majestic birds.

The only answer that can be correct is **c**, because this is the idea that the whole poem adds up to. It's what holds together all of the ideas in the poem. Choices **a** and **b** are both too specific to be the theme. In addition, they do not express *attitude* or feelings. They simply state specific facts.

Finding the Main Idea in Nonfiction

Most nonfiction texts follow a very basic pattern of **general idea → specific support**. That is, the writer will state the main idea he or she wants to convey about the topic and then provide support for that idea, usually in the form of specific facts and details. This format can be diagrammed as follows:

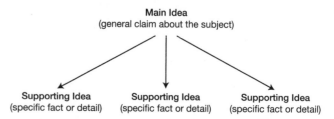

In the following paragraph, for example, notice how the first sentence states a main idea (makes a general claim about surveillance cameras). The rest of the paragraph provides specific facts and details to show why this statement is true:

> Surveillance cameras can provide two immensely important services. One, they can help us find those who commit crimes, including thieves, kidnappers, vandals, and even murderers. Two, they can serve as a powerful deterrent to crime. A thief who plans to steal a car may think twice if he knows he will be caught on video. A woman who hopes to kidnap a child may abandon her plans if she knows she will be captured on film.

This main idea → support structure works on two levels: for the text as a whole and for each individual section or paragraph within the text.

Distinguishing Main Ideas from Supporting Ideas

If you're not sure whether something is a main idea or a supporting idea, ask yourself the following question: Is the sentence making a *general statement*, or is it providing *specific information*? In the following paragraph, for example, most of the sentences except one are too specific to be the main idea of the paragraph. Only one sentence—the first—is general enough to serve as an "umbrella" or "net" for the whole paragraph.

> Many people are afraid of snakes, but most snakes aren't as dangerous as people think they are. There are more than 2,500 different species of snakes around the world. Only a small percentage of those species are poisonous, and only a few species have venom strong enough to kill a human being. Furthermore, snakes bite only 1,000–2,000 people in the United States each year, and only ten of those bites (that's less than 1%) result in death. Statistically, many other animals are far more dangerous than snakes. In fact, in this country, more people die from dog bites each year than from snake bites.

Notice how the first sentence makes a general claim about snakes (that they "aren't as dangerous as people think they are"). Then the rest of the sentences in the paragraph provide details and specific facts that support the main idea.

Writers often provide clues that can help you distinguish between main ideas and their support. Here are some of the most common words and phrases used to introduce specific examples:

for example	*for instance*	*in particular*
in addition	*furthermore*	*some*
others	*specifically*	

These signal words usually mean that a supporting fact or idea will follow. If you are having trouble finding the main idea of a paragraph, try eliminating sentences that begin with these phrases. (Notice that one of the sentences in the snake paragraph begins with one of these transitional words.)

Topic Sentences

In nonfiction texts, the main idea is supported by ideas expressed in paragraphs. Each of these paragraphs also has its own main idea. In fact, that's the definition of a **paragraph**: *a group of sentences about the same idea.* The sentence that expresses the main idea of a paragraph is called a **topic sentence**. The first sentence

in both the surveillance camera and snake paragraphs state their main ideas. Those sentences are therefore the topic sentences for those paragraphs.

Topic sentences are often located at the beginning of paragraphs, but not always. Sometimes writers begin with specific supporting ideas and lead up to the main idea. In this case, the topic sentence would probably be at the end of the paragraph. Notice how we can rewrite the snake paragraph to put the topic sentence at the end of the passage:

> There are more than 2,500 different species of snakes around the world. Only a small percentage of those species are poisonous, and only a few species have venom strong enough to kill a human being. Snakes bite only 1,000–2,000 people in the United States each year, and only ten of those bites (that's less than 1%) result in death. Statistically, many other animals are far more dangerous than snakes. In fact, in this country, more people die from dog bites each year than from snake bites. Clearly, snakes aren't as dangerous as people think they are.

Sometimes the topic sentence is not found at the beginning or end of a paragraph but rather somewhere in the middle. Other times, there isn't a clear topic sentence at all. But that doesn't mean the paragraph doesn't have a main idea. It's there, but the author has chosen not to express it in a clear topic sentence. In that case, you will have to look carefully at the paragraph for clues about the main idea.

Finding an Implied Main Idea

When the main idea is **implied**, there is no topic sentence, so finding the main idea requires some good detective work. If you look carefully at what is said and at the *structure, word choice, style,* and *tone* of the passage, you can figure out the main idea. (These terms will be discussed in more detail later in the chapter.)

For example, take a look at the following paragraph:

> This summer I read *The Windows of Time*. Though it's over 100 pages long, I read it in one afternoon. I couldn't wait to see what happened to Evelyn, the main character. But by the time I got to the end, I wondered if I should have spent my afternoon doing something else. The ending was so awful that I completely forgot I'd enjoyed most of the book.

There's no topic sentence here, but you should still be able to find the main idea. Look carefully at what the writer says and how she says it. What is she suggesting?

a. *The Windows of Time* is a terrific novel.
b. *The Windows of Time* is disappointing.
c. *The Windows of Time* is full of suspense.
d. *The Windows of Time* is a lousy novel.

The correct answer is choice **b**, the novel is disappointing. How can you tell that this is the main idea? First, we can eliminate choice **c**, because it's too specific to be a main idea. It deals only with one specific aspect of the novel (its suspense).

Choices **a**, **b**, and **d**, on the other hand, all express a larger idea—a general assertion about the quality of the novel. But only one of these statements can actually serve as a "net" for the whole paragraph. Notice that while the first few sentences *praise* the novel, the last two *criticize* it. (The word "but" at the beginning of the third sentence signals that the positive review is going to turn negative.) Clearly, this is a mixed review. Therefore, the best answer is **b**. Choice **a** is too positive and doesn't account for the "awful" ending. Choice **d**, on the other hand, is too negative and doesn't account for the suspense and interest in the main character. But choice **b** allows for both positive and negative—when a good thing turns bad, one often feels disappointed.

Here's another example. In this passage, word choice is more important, so read carefully.

Fortunately, none of Toby's friends had ever seen the apartment where Toby lived with his mother and sister. Sandwiched between two burnt-out buildings, his two-story apartment building was by far the ugliest one on the block. It was a real eyesore: peeling orange paint (orange!), broken windows, crooked steps, crooked everything. He could just imagine what his friends would say if they ever saw this poor excuse for a building.

Which of the following expresses the main idea of this paragraph?
a. Toby wishes he could move to a nicer building.
b. Toby wishes his dad still lived with them.
c. Toby worries about what his friends would think of where he lives.
d. Toby is sad because he doesn't have any friends.

From the description, we can safely assume that Toby doesn't like his apartment building and wishes he could move to a nicer building (choice **a**). But that idea isn't general enough to cover the whole paragraph, because it doesn't say anything about his friends. Choice **d** doesn't say anything about his building, so it's not broad enough either. Besides, the first sentence states that Toby has friends. We know that Toby lives only with his mother and little sister, so we might assume that he wishes his dad still lived with them (choice **b**). But there's nothing in the paragraph to support that assumption and this idea doesn't include the two main topics of the paragraph—Toby's building and Toby's friends.

What the paragraph *adds up* to is that Toby is embarrassed about his building, and he's glad none of his friends have seen it (choice **c**). This is the main idea. The paragraph opens with the word "fortunately," so we know that he thinks it's a good thing none of them have been there. Plus, look at the word choice. Notice how the building is described. It's "by far the ugliest on the block," which is saying a lot since it's stuck between two burnt-out buildings. The writer calls it an "eyesore," and repeats "orange" with an exclamation point to emphasize how ugly the color is. Everything's "crooked" in this "poor excuse for a building." He's ashamed of where he lives and worries about what his friends would think if they saw it.

Determining Theme in Literature

Theme is the overall message or idea that the writer wants to convey. Like a main idea, the theme is different from the subject in that the theme *says something about the subject*. For example, take John Donne's poem "Death Be Not Proud." The *subject* of the poem is death. But the *theme* of the poem says something about death. The poem's message is that death is a gift for those who believe in God.

Sonnet 72. "Death be not proud, though some have called thee"

(1) DEATH be not proud, though some have called thee
Mighty and dreadful, for, thou art not so,
For those whom thou think'st, thou dost overthrow,
Die not, poor death, nor yet canst thou kill me.
(5) From rest and sleep, which but thy pictures bee,
Much pleasure, then from thee, much more must flow,
And soonest our best men with thee do go,
Rest of their bones, and soul's delivery.
Thou art slave to fate, chance, kings, and desperate men,
(10) And dost with poison, war, and sickness dwell,

And poppy, or charms can make us sleep as well,
And better then thy stroke; why swell'st thou then?
One short sleep past, we wake eternally,
And death shall be no more; Death, thou shalt die.

The main idea of a text is the thought that holds everything together. Likewise, the theme of a work of literature is the thought that holds together the characters and action. It's the idea that guides every choice the writer makes throughout the text.

For example, look at the poem "A Poison Tree," from William Blake's *Songs of Innocence and Experience*. The poem has four **stanzas** (groups of lines in a poem, much like a paragraph is a group of lines in an essay or story). Read the poem carefully and read it out loud, too, because poetry is meant to be *heard* as well as read.

A Poison Tree

(1) I was angry with my friend:
     I told my wrath, my wrath did end.   *wrath = anger*
     I was angry with my foe;   *foe = enemy*
     I told it not, my wrath did grow.

(5) And I water'd it in fears,
     Night & morning with my tears;
     And I sunned it with smiles,   *deceitful = causing others*
     And with soft deceitful wiles.   *to believe what is not true*
                                       wiles = trickery, deceit

     And it grew both by day and night,
(10) Till it bore an apple bright.
     And my foe beheld it shine,   *beheld = saw*
     And he knew that it was mine.

     And into my garden stole
     When the night had veil'd the pole;   *veiled = hidden*
(15) In the morning glad I see
     My foe outstretch'd beneath the tree.

To understand Blake's theme, you need to look carefully at *what* happened and then look at *why* it happened. In the first stanza, Blake sets up two situations. First, the speaker (the "voice" or "narrator" of the poem) is angry with his friend (line 1) and he tells his friend about it (line 2). As a result, the anger goes away (line 2—"my wrath did end"). But he acts differently with his enemy. He doesn't tell his foe about his anger (line 4) and, as a result, the anger grows (line 4).

In the second stanza, the speaker "water'd" his wrath in fears and "sunned" his wrath with smiles and wiles. Blake isn't being literal here; rather, he's drawing a comparison between the speaker's anger to something that grows with water and sun. It's like some kind of plant. How do you know exactly what it is? Blake tells you in two key places: in the title and in the last line. The poem is called "The Poison Tree." "Tree" is mentioned again in the last line of the poem.

The kind of comparison is called a **metaphor**, and it is an important clue to the meaning of the poem. Blake could have compared the speaker's anger to anything, but he chose to compare it to a tree. Trees have deep, strong roots and often flower or bear fruit. (This tree bears an apple.) They need some nurturing (sun and water) to grow.

In the third stanza, the foe sees the speaker's apple. In the fourth, he sneaks into the speaker's garden at night. Finally, at the end of the poem, the foe is killed by the poisonous apple (the apple poisoned by the speaker's wrath).

That is what happens in the poem, but what does it all add up to? What does it mean? In other words, what is the theme?

Look again at the action. Cause and effect are central to the theme of this poem. What does the speaker do? He tells his friend about his anger. What *doesn't* the speaker do? He *doesn't* tell his enemy about his anger. What happens to his anger, then? It grows and grows and it offers fruit that tempts his enemy. And what happens to his enemy? He steals the apple, but it is the fruit of anger. It is poisonous and it kills him. Thus, the idea that best summarizes the idea of the poem is this: If you don't talk about your anger, it can be deadly. This is the message or "lesson" of the poem.

In many poems, the theme is an idea, while in others, the theme is an emotion. That is, the poet wants readers to feel an emotion very strongly. Poets can accomplish this through language. "The Eagle" is a good example of a poem whose theme is emotional. The next poem, written by Stephen Crane in 1899, combines both action and language to convey theme. Read the poem out loud at least twice.

A Man Said to the Universe

A man said to the universe:
"Sir, I exist!"
"However," replied the universe,
"The fact has not created in me
A sense of obligation."

Look carefully at the language in the poem. What kinds of words has the poet chosen? Are they warm, friendly words, or are they cold, distancing words? Do they make you feel comfortable, welcome? Or uncomfortable, rejected? Are they specific or general? Do you feel like there's a personal relationship here? Or are things formal, official?

Crane's word choice helps convey his theme. The words "sir," "fact," and "obligation" are cold and formal. There's no sense of personal relationship between the man and the universe. This is heightened by the general nature of the poem. It's just "a man"—not anyone specific, not anyone you know. Not anyone the universe knows, either. It's also written in the third-person point of view. The poem would have a different effect if it began, "*I* said to the universe."

The tone of the poem is cold and uncaring. That combined with action and word choice conveys Crane's theme: The universe is indifferent to humans (however one might wish it were otherwise).

▶ Identifying Specific Facts and Details

On standardized tests, you will often be asked to identify specific facts and details from what you read. This is true of the GED Language Arts, Reading Exam as well.

The idea behind this kind of question isn't for you to *memorize* everything in the passage. Rather, these questions test (1) how carefully you read, (2) your ability to know where to look for specific information within a passage, and (3) your ability to distinguish between main idea and support. Some questions may ask you to identify how an author supports his or her argument or what sort of examples are used to illustrate an idea. Others will ask you to identify or restate a specific fact or detail from the text. For example, take another look at the snakes paragraph:

Many people are afraid of snakes, but most snakes aren't as dangerous as people think they are. There are more than 2,500 different species of snakes around the world. Only a small percentage of those species are poisonous, and only a few species have venom strong enough to kill a human being. Furthermore, snakes bite only 1,000–2,000 people in the United States each year, and only ten of those bites

(that's less than 1%) result in death. Statistically, many other animals are far more dangerous than snakes. In fact, in this country, more people die from dog bites each year than from snake bites.

How many species of snakes are there worldwide?
a. between 1,000–2,000
b. less than 100
c. less than 2,500
d. more than 2,500

There are several numbers in this passage, and if you didn't read carefully, you could easily choose the wrong answer. The correct answer is **d**, more than 2,500. This fact is stated in the second sentence.

The best way to find this information is to **use the key words from the question** as your guide. In this example, the key words are *how many* and *species.* These two items tell you to look for a sentence in the passage that has both a number and the word *species.* Then you can find the sentence that provides the correct information. You don't have to reread the entire passage—in fact, you can't, because you will run out of time for other questions. Instead, *skim* through the paragraphs looking for your key words.

In addition, you can use the *structure* of the passage to help you find the correct information. If you read carefully, you probably noticed that the paragraph talks about species first, then venom, then bites. Thus, you can use your understanding of the structure to guide you to the place to find the correct answer.

▶ Distinguishing between Fact and Opinion

On the GED Language Arts, Reading Exam, you may not be asked directly to identify whether a statement is a fact or an opinion. But distinguishing between fact and opinion is an important reading comprehension skill, one you will use when reading both fiction and nonfiction texts, especially commentary.

Facts are:
- things *known* for certain to have happened
- things *known* for certain to be true
- things *known* for certain to exist

Opinions, on the other hand, are:

- things *believed* to have happened
- things *believed* to be true
- things *believed* to exist

The key difference between fact and opinion lies in the difference between *believing* and *knowing*. Opinions may be *based* on facts, but they are still what people think and believe, not what they know. Opinions are debatable; two different people could have two different opinions about the matter. Facts, however, are not debatable. Two different people would have a hard time debating a fact. They might not agree on how to *interpret* the facts, but they would have to agree on the facts themselves.

Consider this example: "Poems are more fun to read than stories." This statement is debatable. You could argue that stories are more fun to read than poems, or that they are both equally enjoyable, or even that they are both dreadfully boring. All of these statements are opinions. But "poems are written in verse" is not debatable; it's impossible to disagree with this statement. It's something known to be true. Thus, it's a fact.

Asking Questions

A good test for whether something is fact or opinion, then, is to ask yourself two questions:

- Can this statement be debated?
- Is this something known to be true?

If you can answer "yes" to the first question, it's probably an opinion. If you can answer "yes" to the second question, it's probably a fact. For example, look at the following sentence:

Tim O'Brien is a contemporary American novelist and short story writer.

Does this topic sentence express a fact or an opinion? Well, is it debatable? Can someone disagree? No. It's a matter of fact, something that can be proven by a quick trip to the library or search on the Internet. On the other hand, look at the following claim:

Tim O'Brien is one of the best contemporary American novelists and short story writers.

Now, is this statement something known to be true, or is it debatable? Clearly, different people can have different opinions on this issue. It's an opinion.

Looking for Clues

Writers often provide clues when they are expressing a fact or an opinion. *In fact,* for example, is a clear signal that the writer is going to present a fact. Opinions are often stated using words such as *should* or *ought,* as in the following examples:

- We *should* apologize for being rude.
- He *ought* to return those library books right away.

Words that show judgment or evaluation, such as *good, bad, interesting,* and *important,* usually signal an opinion, too. Here are some examples:

- She is a great teacher.
- This was the most significant development in the history of science.

Words and Phrases That Often Signal Opinions		
should	*ought*	*had better*
good	*bad*	*great*
excellent	*terrible*	*interesting*
fascinating	*important*	*insignificant*
boring	*remarkable*	*disappointing*

People can, and often do, have opinions on just about anything. But some opinions are more reasonable than others. A *reasonable* opinion is one that is supported by relevant facts. In fact, that's what most nonfiction writing is all about. Writers make a claim about their subject, and that claim is often an opinion. Then they offer facts to support that opinion.

Good writers offer support for their opinions because they know that opinions are debatable. They know readers will want to see *why* they think what they do. Most of their evidence will come in the form of facts. Of course, this doesn't mean that readers will agree with the writer's opinion. But an opinion supported by facts is much stronger than an opinion that stands alone or that is supported only by other opinions.

▶ Making Inferences

Inferences are conclusions that are drawn based upon evidence. For example, if you look up at the sky and see heavy black rain clouds, you might logically infer that it is going to rain. Reading comprehension tests like the GED Language Arts, Reading Exam will often ask you to draw conclusions based upon what you read in the passage.

The key to drawing the right conclusions (making the right inferences) is to look for clues in the context. Some of the best clues come from the writer's **word choice**.

Word Choice

Often the best clues to meaning come from the specific words a writer chooses to describe people, places, and things. The writer's word choice (also called **diction**) can reveal a great deal about how he or she (or a character) feels about the subject.

To see how word choice reveals the writer's attitude, read the two sentences below:

> **A:** Myra stared at Bill as he talked to his ex-wife, Irene.
>
> **B:** Myra glared at Bill as he talked to his ex-wife, Irene.

It's not hard to see the difference between these sentences. In sentence A, the writer says that Myra *stared* at Bill while he talked to his ex-wife. Sentence B, on the other hand, uses the word *glared*. Both sentences say that Myra was looking steadily at Bill. But there is a difference. One sentence is much stronger than the other because one word is much stronger than the other. *To stare* is to look directly and fixedly at someone or something. *To glare* is to stare fixedly and angrily. Thus, the writer of sentence B is able to tell us not only what is happening (that Myra is staring at Bill) but also what she is feeling (anger) by using effective word choice.

Denotation and Connotation

Even words that seem to mean the same thing have subtly different meanings and sometimes not-so-subtle effects. For example, look at the words *slim* and *thin*. If you say your aunt is *thin,* that means one thing. If you say she is *slim,* that means something a little bit different. That's because *slim* has a different connotation than *thin.* **Connotation** is a word's *suggested* or implied meaning; it's what the word makes you think or feel. *Slim* and *thin* have almost the same **denotation**—their dictionary definition—but *slim* suggests more grace and class than *thin. Slim* is a very positive word. It suggests that your aunt is healthy and fit. *Thin,* however, does not. *Thin* suggests that your aunt may be a little bit too skinny for her health. *Thin* and *slim,* then, have different connotations. So the word you choose to describe your aunt can tell others a lot.

Searching for Clues

Word choice, actions, and other clues can help you make inferences about other things, too, such as the relationship between characters. For example, if the stage directions for a play note that two characters fidget and keep their distance while talking to each other, you can infer that they are uncomfortable with each other and the conversation.

The key to drawing correct inferences is paying attention to details and making sure there is evidence to back up your assertions. Sometimes we draw conclusions based on what we want to believe, not on the evidence in the text. Look at words and actions, at what is said (or not said) and how it is said, and draw your conclusions from there.

▶ Identifying Cause and Effect Relationships

A **cause** is a person or thing that makes something happen. An **effect** is the change created by an action or cause. Cause tells you why something happened; effect tells you what happened as a result of that action.

Many questions on the GED Language Arts, Reading Exam will ask you to identify cause and effect relationships. In nonfiction passages, you may be asked to identify causes and effects of historical events or personal actions. When the causes and/or effects are explicit in the passage, then this type of question is really a matter of finding specific facts and details. However, cause and effect are often implied, especially in literary texts, and you will have to draw your own conclusions about cause and effect. In literary texts, for example, you will often be asked to determine why characters do what they do and feel what they feel.

Inferring Cause

Writers suggest cause in many ways. Sometimes, the clues are mostly action clues—what people say and do. For example, if a character had gone out looking for work and comes home looking dejected, you can infer that the dejection is caused by not having any luck finding a job.

Clues can also come in the form of details, word choice, and style. For example, look at the following passage:

Dennis was scared—really scared. His knees were weak. He looked down, twenty feet, to the water below. He looked up again, quickly. He tried to think of something else. He tried to reassure himself. "It's only twenty feet!" he said aloud. But that only made it sound worse. Twenty feet! He felt dizzy and hot.

This writer could have simply said, "Dennis was scared. He was afraid of heights." Instead, she *suggests* the cause of Dennis's fear by *showing* you how Dennis feels. This way, you are able to see for yourself what Dennis is going through. And through these details, you can conclude that he is afraid of heights. The repetition of "twenty feet" is another clue, and so is the sentence structure. Notice that the sentences are short and choppy. In fact, they sound a little panicky. This helps to reflect how Dennis feels.

The following is an excerpt from a short story. Read the passage carefully to see if you can determine why the characters do what they do.

Why Are Stan and Anne Fighting?

Anne tensed when she heard the front door open. She waited in the kitchen near the dirty dishes in the sink. She knew Stan would look there first. Taking a deep breath, she thought about what she would say to him. She waited.

A moment later, Stan stepped into the kitchen. She watched him gaze around the room, watched his eyes focus on the sink, watched his face harden when he saw the dishes piled high. Pointing angrily at the dishes, he said coldly, "What are those filthy things still doing in the sink? How many times have I told you I want this house clean when I come home?!"

"Oh, every day. You tell me every single day. In fact, you tell me every day exactly what I should do and how I should do it. Do you think you own me?"

"I do own this house, that's for sure. And I want my house clean!" Stan shouted.

"Then hire a maid," Anne said bitterly.

"What?"

"You heard me. Hire a maid. If you can find someone who can stand to work for you. You're never satisfied. And have you ever once said 'thank you'?"

Stan looked at Anne for a moment. His eyes were cold and hard. Then he turned and walked out of the room.

This passage raises several questions about cause and effect. Why does Stan get mad? Why didn't Anne do the dishes? Why is Anne mad at Stan? The actions and words of the characters and the word choice tell us what is going on under the surface.

Stan's face "hardens" with anger when he sees the dishes in the sink. You can tell he expects the kitchen to be clean when he comes home. When he walks in, he looks around the kitchen as if he's inspecting it. Then he sees the dishes and his face hardens. He asks why the dishes are still in the sink. Further, he tells Anne he expects a clean house when he comes home.

You can tell Anne wants to start a fight from the first paragraph. She purposely waits in the kitchen near the dirty dishes. She knows Stan is going to be mad about the dishes when he sees them. As she waits, she thinks about what she is going to say to him.

Anne's response to Stan tells you why she's mad. She's tired of him telling her what to do "every single day." She feels like he owns her. She's also frustrated because he's "never satisfied." And she's mad because he has never "once said 'thank you.'"

Inferring Effects

Just as writers can imply cause, they can also suggest effects. In the passage you just read, Anne clearly had a specific goal. She purposely decided not to do the dishes because she wanted to start a fight. Why? What do you think Anne was hoping to get from the fight? What effect do you think she was looking for?

a. that Stan would do the dishes himself for once
b. that Stan would hire a maid so she could relax
c. that Stan would stop being so bossy and start appreciating her housework

How can you tell that choice **c** is the best answer? You have to look carefully at the passage. Anne says, "You tell me every day exactly what I should do and how I should do it. Do you think that you own me?" This shows that Stan is very bossy—and that Anne doesn't like it. She also says, "If you can find someone who can stand to work for you. You're never satisfied. And have you ever once said 'thank you'?" This suggests that Stan's very hard to please, and that he doesn't appreciate the things Anne does. Anne has clearly had enough of this.

The passage doesn't directly say so, but from these clues, you can conclude that Anne was hoping for a change in Stan. That's why she didn't do the dishes. That's why she picked a fight. She wanted him to know how she felt and why she felt that way. She wanted him to change.

But will she get the effect she hoped for? Take another look at the passage, paying close attention to the end. What do you think? Will Anne get her wish? Will Stan change his ways? Why do you think so?

Most likely, Anne won't get her wish. How can you tell? The end of the passage offers a strong clue. Look at Stan's reaction. He doesn't even respond to Anne; he simply shuts down the conversation. He chooses to walk away instead of trying to work things out.

Maybe Stan walks away because he wants to give Anne a chance to calm down. Maybe he was going to come back later to talk it out. But this isn't likely. How do you know? Again, the ending offers an important clue. At the end of the story, Stan's eyes are "cold and hard." This suggests that he is pretty set in his ways. You shouldn't expect him to change.

19 ▶ Reading Literature

On the GED Language Arts, Reading Exam, you will find many different kinds of literature from many different time periods. This chapter shows you how to read actively and describes the three time periods included on this exam.

READING LITERATURE IS a search for meaning. Even in the most functional texts, your job as a reader is to discover what the writer wants to say. In most functional texts, writers make a point of making their goals and main ideas very clear to their readers. Literary texts, however, are much more subtle in expressing their themes. For both types of texts, and especially for literary texts, you will understand more if you read *actively.*

▶ Active Reading

Though reading often seems like a rather passive activity, there are many things you can (and should) do as you read. These active reading strategies will help you better comprehend and more fully enjoy what you read.

Before You Read

To help you better understand what you read, take a few steps before you begin to read.

1. **Read the title carefully.** This will give you a clue to the subject and theme of the text. For example, if the excerpt is from a novel called *Crime and Punishment,* you can get a pretty good idea of one of the central issues of the novel.

Note: On the GED Language Arts, Reading Exam, each passage will typically be preceded by a question. This is not the title of the text, though it may look that way. You will need to look at the end of the passage for the author's name, title of the text, and date of publication. The question still serves the same purpose as a title, though: It gives you a strong clue about the main theme of the passage and what information you should get from reading the text.

2. **Note the name of the author and date of publication**, if provided. If it's an author you have read before, you may already know something about the passage or the kinds of themes the writer deals with. Even if you have never read the author before, you may still have some knowledge about the writer. (You probably know, for example, that Stephen King writes horror novels, even if you have never read one of his books.) The date of publication can help you prepare for the historical context of the piece and set up your reading expectations. Consider what you know about the time period in which the text was written—the historical, political, social, and religious contexts.

3. **Read the questions about the passage**. By reading the questions *before* you read the passage, you help "train" your mind to look for those answers as you read. But be sure not to read just for those answers. Often, the answer comes only from understanding the whole, especially with literary texts (and with poetry in particular).

As You Read

1. **Mark up the text**. Whenever possible, underline key words and ideas in the text. Record your questions and reactions in the margins or on a separate piece of paper. When you are not permitted to write on the text—and you will *not* be allowed to write in the GED test booklet—use a piece of scrap paper to write down key words, questions, and reactions.

2. **Be observant**. Look carefully at the words, the structure, everything you see. Did you notice, for example, that the word *shame* was repeated five times in a passage? Or did you notice that the writer capitalized the words *love* and *hate*? In literary texts, meaning is conveyed not just through words but also through form, and writers are always making choices that will help convey their ideas.

▶ Time Periods

To cover the breadth of literary forms and themes, the texts are selected from three different time periods: pre-1920, 1920–1960, and 1960–present. The emphasis is on works from more recent history, with approximately two-thirds of the texts from the last 80 years. This is in part because the last century has seen a great deal of experimentation and change in literary forms, and also because modern and contemporary literature and themes are likely to be most familiar to, and have the most profound impact upon, today's readers.

Pre-1920: Ancient and Classical Literature

This period, of course, covers a very large time span. Texts may be as old as a seventeenth-century Shakespearian sonnet or a fifth-century B.C. Greek tragedy. Many different literary movements fit into this time period, including Renaissance literature (1450–1600), Romanticism (1800s), and Realism (late 1800s–early 1900s).

While knowing about these literary periods may be helpful, you do not need this knowledge to do well on the exam. As different as these older texts may be, the reason we still read them (the reason they are *classics*) is that they have characters and themes that still matter to today's readers. As different as life may have been in ancient Greece or sixteenth-century Italy, today's readers can still relate to Oedipus's desire to be a good leader and find his true father.

Still, older texts *are* different from today's texts, and because of differences in language and style and their historical contexts, they can be more challenging to understand. Here are a few things to keep in mind as you read older texts:

1. **Setting.** Historical context is important. Note when the text was written and try to identify the specific time and place in which the story takes place. Try to recall any significant facts about the social, political, and religious contexts of that time. For example, if a story is set in Virginia in 1860,

you know that this is just one year before the outbreak of the American Civil War, and tensions
between the North and South over slavery are running high.

2. **Style.** In many older texts, you will find longer and
more complex sentences and a more formal style
than in contemporary texts. Don't let this daunt
you. Simply take it one sentence at a time. You can
also try paraphrasing the text in contemporary
terms (how would you write it if you were writing
for a classmate?).

3. **Vocabulary.** Because word usage and writing styles
change over time, you are likely to find some words
and phrases that are unfamiliar. Look carefully at
context (the words and sentences surrounding the
unfamiliar word) for clues to meaning. You will
not be expected to know these words and you will
not find questions about their meaning unless the
meaning can be determined from context.

4. **Theme.** Most themes will be timeless: the depth of
love, the pain of betrayal, how easily power cor-
rupts. Though the setting may be very specific and
may provide the circumstances for the theme, the
theme is likely to be one that can apply to many
different time periods and places. Look for an
overarching idea that someone today could still
write about.

1920–1960: Modern Literature

While scholars may differ on exactly when the "modern"
period begins and ends, they do agree on the defining
events of the time period: World War I (1914–1917),
the Great Depression (1929–1939), World War II
(1939–1945) and the beginning of the Cold War.

The setting, style, and vocabulary of modern texts
will not differ greatly from contemporary works. But literature is always a product of its time, so historical context is important. As you read works from this time
period, remember the key events and how they affected
society. Following are some general notes about the modern period that can help you better understand the concerns of modern writers and their themes:

- questioning of authority and tradition, especially
traditional roles; greater emphasis on the rights
and importance of the individual
- demand for equal rights of all individuals
- tremendous advances in science and technology;
increasing mechanization and specialization
- Sigmund Freud's psychoanalysis: new understanding of the self and of hidden motivations and
desires
- great politico-economic battle: capitalism versus
communism
- experimentalism in form, style, and theme as ways
of more accurately reflecting the reality of our
human experience (e.g., stream of consciousness
writing, fragmented texts)
- great sense of uncertainty and loss; the incredible
scale of World War I (an estimated 37 million
dead) left a generation feeling lost, fragmented,
and insecure. This was increased by World War II
(World War I, after all, was supposed to be the war
that ended all wars) and was further intensified by
the dawn of the nuclear age.

1960–Present: Contemporary Literature

Contemporary literature will present settings, characters,
and themes in language that will be very familiar to most
readers. Contemporary literature will include a broader
range of voices and acknowledgement of writers and
themes that in the past had often been marginalized (left
out). Some key defining moments, issues, and characteristics of our contemporary period include:

- the civil rights, women's rights, and gay rights
movements
- space exploration
- globalization and increasing interdependence
- the end of the Cold War and the expansion of
democracy
- the computer revolution and the beginning of the
Information Age; advances in and increasing
dependence upon technology
- questioning of reality (artificial intelligence, virtual
reality)
- the AIDS epidemic
- environmentalism
- multiculturalism and celebration of roots

20 ▶ Fiction

The kind of literature that students are most familiar with (and therefore most comfortable with) is fiction. This chapter reviews the eight core elements of fiction, including plot, character, setting, and theme.

THE WORD *FICTION* comes from the Latin word *fingere,* which means "to make or shape." Works of **fiction** tell about characters and events created in and shaped by the author's imagination. Fiction includes the genres listed earlier: novels, short stories, poems, and plays. But because poems and plays have their own special characteristics and conventions, they will be covered in separate sections. The focus here is on prose fiction. **Prose** is writing that is not in poetic form (verse) or dramatic form (stage or screen play).

There are eight important elements of fiction:

1. plot
2. character
3. setting
4. tone
5. point of view
6. language and style
7. symbolism
8. theme

▶ Plot

Plot refers to the series of events in a story—the order in which the actions take place. A story's plot always revolves around some kind of *conflict*. The conflict may be between two characters, between the main character and an idea or force (e.g., nature or racism), or between the character and him- or herself.

Plot is often arranged **chronologically** (in time order), but authors sometimes vary the order of events to help build suspense and to control how much we know about the characters. For example, an author may use **flashbacks** to describe events that took place earlier in the timeline of action—events that might help us understand the character and his or her traits or motivations.

Plots usually follow a five-part "pyramid" pattern, though the pyramid should be lopsided, since the climax typically occurs near the end of the story:

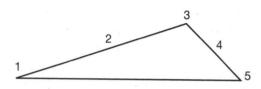

1. **Exposition** introduces readers to the people, places, and basic circumstances or situation of the story.
2. **Complication** (sometimes referred to as "rising action") is the series of events that "complicate" the story and build up to the climax.
3. **Climax** is the "highpoint" of the story, the moment of greatest tension (the peak of the pyramid). This is often the turning point of the story, when a character must make a difficult decision or take some kind of action.
4. **Falling action** occurs when the missing pieces of the puzzle are filled in (for example, secrets are revealed, mysteries solved, confessions made). The story "settles down."
5. **Resolution** or **denouement** is the conclusion of the story in which conflicts are resolved (at least to some degree), questions are answered, and characters are set to move on with a new understanding or under new circumstances.

▶ Character

Characters are the people created by the author to tell the story. They perform the actions, speak the words, and convey the ideas of the story. As readers, we see what the characters think, do, and say, and we try to understand why they think, do, and say these things.

Characters can be round or flat. **Round characters** are fully developed, complex, three-dimensional creatures. They are dynamic characters who embody contradictions and undergo change or growth of some sort throughout the story. **Flat characters**, on the other hand, are one-dimensional, undeveloped, and static. They are typically defined by one main characteristic and do not change. They are often *stereotypes* or *symbolic*.

Just as every story has a conflict, every story has a protagonist and an antagonist. The **protagonist** is the "hero" or main character of the story, the one who faces the conflict and undergoes change. The **antagonist** is the person, force (such as a disease or natural disaster), or idea (such as prejudice or crippling self-doubt) that works against the protagonist.

In fiction, characters reveal themselves through **dialogue** and **action**. In dialogue, characters tell us what they think, feel, and believe. How a character talks can provide information about the character's background (for example, a Southern dialect may mean that a character grew up in the South) and education (for example, a character who speaks with a highly sophisticated vocabulary may have spent several years in an institution of higher learning). Action undertaken by characters moves the story forward while creating dynamic, round characters.

▶ Setting

The **setting** is the *time* and *place* in which the story unfolds. This gives the story a particular social and historical context. What was happening in the world at that time? What was happening in that particular place at that time? Remember that the setting of a piece of fiction is not the same as the publication date. Many stories written during contemporary times have settings dating back hundreds of years. When considering the setting, we should consider the political, social, and overall historical contexts of the time and place. For example, if a story takes place in 1762 in Boston, there are certain historical expectations. You can expect tensions to be high between

Americans and the British. You can expect certain details of daily life, such as carriages, torches, and outhouses. If the story does not meet those expectations (if, for example, a character rides into town in a convertible), you need to consider why the author has broken those expectations.

Setting can be specific or universal. Some stories, for example, can take place anywhere and any time; the plot and characters are not unique to any historical circumstances. Other stories, like a story of the American Revolution, must take place in a certain place and time. Some of the story's themes (e.g., the importance of freedom) are considered universal.

► Tone

Setting is often important in creating the tone of the story. **Tone** is the mood or attitude conveyed in the writing. For example, notice how Edgar Allen Poe uses setting to establish an appropriately gloomy tone for his horror tale "The Fall of the House of Usher":

> During the whole of a dull, dark, and soundless day in the autumn of the year, when the clouds hung oppressively low in the heavens, I had been passing alone, on horseback, through a singularly dreary tract of country; and at length found myself, as the shades of the evening drew on, within view of the melancholy House of Usher.

Poe's word choice—*dull, dark, soundless, oppressively, alone, dreary, melancholy*—work together to create a dark and somewhat mysterious tone for the story.

Often the most important tone in fiction is irony. **Situational irony** occurs when there is incongruity between what is expected to happen and what actually occurs. For example, in Guy de Maupassant's classic short story "The Necklace," Madame Loisel spends ten years of her life struggling to pay off the debt she owes for a necklace she bought to replace the one she had borrowed from a friend and lost. In the last lines of the story, Madame Loisel runs into that old friend and learns that she sacrificed in vain:

> "You remember the diamond necklace you lent me for the ball at the Ministry?"
> "Yes. Well?"
> "Well, I lost it."

"How could you? Why, you brought it back."

"I brought you another one just like it. And for the last ten years we have been paying for it. You realize it wasn't easy for us; we had no money. . . . Well, it's paid for at last, and I'm glad indeed."

Madame Forestier had halted.

"You say you bought a diamond necklace to replace mine?"

"Yes. You hadn't noticed it? They were very much alike."

And she smiled in proud and innocent happiness.

Madame Forestier, deeply moved, took her two hands.

"Oh, my poor Mathilde! But mine was imitation. It was worth at the very most five hundred francs! . . ."

► Point of View

Point of view refers to the person who is telling us the story. All stories have a **narrator**—the person who describes the characters and events. *Note: The author is NOT the narrator. In fiction, the narrator is always a "character" created by the author to tell the tale.*

A **first-person narrator** tells the story from his or her own point of view using *I*. With this point of view, you see and hear the story from someone directly involved in the action. This is a very subjective and personal point of view. Here's an example:

> I wiped my eyes and looked in the mirror. I was surprised at what I saw. I had on a beautiful red dress, but what I saw was even more valuable. I was strong. I was pure. I had genuine thoughts inside that no one could see, that no one could ever take away from me. I was like the wind.
> —Amy Tan, from *The Joy Luck Club* (1989)

In a story told from the **second-person point of view**, the writer uses the pronoun *you*, and thus the reader becomes a character in the story, thinking the thoughts and performing the actions of the main character:

> Moss Watson, the man you truly love like no other, is singing December 23 in the Owonta Opera production of *Amahl and the Night Visitors*. He's playing Kaspar, the partially deaf Wise Man. Wisdom, says Moss, arrives in all forms. And you think, Yes,

sometimes as a king and sometimes as a hesitant phone call that says the king'll be late at rehearsal and don't wait up, and then when you call back to tell him to be careful not to let the cat out when he comes home, you discover there's been no rehearsal there at all.

—Lorrie Moore, "Amahl and the Night Visitors," from *Self Help* (1985)

With a **third-person narrator**, the author uses the pronouns *he, she,* and *they* to tell the story. This narrator is removed from the action, so the story is more objective. Third-person narrators are often **omniscient**: They know everything about the characters and tell us what the characters think and feel. Here's an example:

To tell the truth, he found it at first rather hard to get used to these privations, but after a while it became a habit and went smoothly enough—he even became quite accustomed to being hungry in the evening; on the other hand, he had spiritual nourishment, for he carried ever in his thoughts the idea of his future overcoat. His whole existence had in a sense become fuller, as though he had married, as though some other person were present with him, as though he were no longer alone, but an agreeable companion had consented to walk the path of life hand in hand with him, and that companion was no other than the new overcoat with its thick wadding and its strong, durable lining.

—Nikolai Gogol, from "The Overcoat" (1842)

Third-person narration can also be **limited**. This means the author still uses the third-person pronouns (*he, she*), but only imparts the thoughts and feelings of one character in the story. In this way, third-person limited point of view is very similar to first-person narration, but it does give as intimate a feeling as first-person narration does.

▶ Language and Style

One of the main things that draws us to certain writers is their language and style. *How* do they tell the story? What sort of words and sentences do the writers use to tell the tale? Language and style consist of diction (the specific words the writer uses), **figurative language** (similes, metaphors, imagery, and personification), **level of description and detail**, and **sentence structure**.

A **simile** makes a comparison using *like* or *as: Your eyes <u>are like</u> shining sapphires.* A **metaphor** is more powerful. It makes the comparison directly: *Your eyes <u>are</u> shining sapphires.*

Personification is the attribution of human characteristics to animals or objects. For example, in the poem "The Eagle" from the pretest, the eagle is described as "clasp[ing] the crag with crooked hands." Eagles do not actually have hands. This is personification.

Imagery is the representation of sensory experience through language. Imagery helps us see, hear, taste, smell, and touch in our imaginations. Notice the powerful imagery and the similes in the passage below, from Sandra Cisneros' *The House on Mango Street* (1984):

Everybody in our family has different hair. My Papa's hair is like a broom, all up in the air. And me, my hair is lazy. It never obeys barrettes or bands. Carlos' hair is thick and straight. He doesn't need to comb it. Nenny's hair is slippery—slides out of your hand. And Kiki, who is the youngest, has hair like fur.

But my mother's hair, my mother's hair, like little rosettes, like little candy circles all curly and pretty because she pinned it in pincurls all day, sweet to put your nose into when she is holding you, holding you and you feel safe, is the warm smell of bread before you bake it, is the smell when she makes room for you on her side of the bed still warm with her skin, and you sleep near her, the rain outside falling and Papa snoring. The snoring, the rain, and Mama's hair that smells like bread.

However, **style** is more than just figurative language. It is the overall manner of writing, including sentence structure and the level of formality, which is managed through word choice. It is also a matter of how much description and detail the author likes to provide. Notice, for example, the drastically different styles of the two science fiction writers in the next example. One uses very long sentences and sophisticated, formal vocabulary. The other is much more casual, with shorter sentences and more everyday vocabulary.

From Mary Shelley's *Frankenstein* (1818):

It is with considerable difficulty that I remember the original era of my being; all the events of that period appear confused and indistinct. A strange multiplicity of sensations seized me, and I saw, felt, heard, and smelt at the same time; and it was, indeed, a long time before I learned to distinguish between the operations of my various senses.

From Kurt Vonnegut's *Slaughterhouse Five* (1969):

Listen:
Billy Pilgrim has come unstuck in time.

Billy has gone to sleep a senile widower and awakened on his wedding day. He has walked through a door in 1955 and come out another one in 1941. He has gone back through that door to find himself in 1963. He has seen his birth and death many times, he says, and pays random visits to all the events in between.

He says.

▶ Symbolism

In fiction, writers often use **symbolism** to help convey the themes of their stories. A **symbol** is a person, place, or thing invested with special meaning or significance. It is a person, place, or thing that is both itself and a representation of something else (usually an idea). Flags are an everyday example of symbolism. A flag is a decorated piece of cloth, but it is also much more than that; it represents a group of people and the ideas that hold those people together. Colors are also highly symbolic. White may be used to represent purity or innocence; red to represent passion or bloodshed; purple to represent royalty. Birds often represent freedom, and an olive branch represents peace.

In "The Necklace," the necklace Madame Loisel loses becomes a symbol of what happens when we want desperately to be something or someone we are not, of what we can suffer when we are too proud to tell the truth to others.

▶ Theme

All of these elements add up to express the story's theme. As noted earlier, theme in literature is like the thesis of an expository essay, but it is a bit more complex. You won't find a thesis statement in a short story or novel. Instead, you have to evaluate the whole and consider the questions the story has raised, the points it has made, and the positions it has taken. Indeed, stories can have several themes. The key is to ask yourself what the story adds up to in the end. What seems to be the message the writer wants to convey through all that has occurred? What ideas can you take away from the characters and events you just experienced?

In *Frankenstein*, for example, you might state the themes this way:

- People must be responsible for what they create.
- We should not "play God" and attempt to control or overrule nature.
- Everyone needs to be loved, and we bring destruction upon ourselves when we reject others.

All three of these themes and more come from the story—from all elements of fiction working together in the novel to convey the writer's ideas.

21 ▶ Poetry

Poetry shares many of the same elements as fiction, but poetry is a unique genre with its own styles and conventions. This chapter explains what makes poems different from stories and how to read and understand poems.

POETRY IS OFTEN easy to recognize but not as easy to define. Poems are usually short, and often rhyme, but not always. The beauty (and, for many, the difficulty) of poetry is its brevity. The writer must convey an idea or emotion in a very short space. Because there are so few words in a poem, every word counts, and poems are often layered with meaning. That's where a poem gets its power.

One fundamental difference between poetry and prose is structure. Poems, of course, are written in verse. They are meant to be *heard* as well as read. The meaning in a poem comes not just from the words, but also from how the words *sound* and how they are arranged on the page.

▶ Types of Poems

While poems are often categorized by structure (e.g., sonnets or ballads), a more fundamental way to classify poems is by their general purpose. Poems can be emotive, imagistic, narrative, and argumentative. They can also mourn or celebrate.

An **emotive** poem aims to capture a mood or emotion and to make readers feel that mood or emotion. Here is an untitled poem by the Russian poet Alexander Pushkin:

I have loved you; even now I may confess,
Some embers of my love their fire retain
but do not let it cause you more distress,
I do not want to sadden you again.

Hopeless and tongue-tied, yet, I loved you dearly
With pangs the jealous and the timid know;
So tenderly I loved you—so sincerely;
I pray God grant another love you so.

An **imagistic** poem aims to capture a moment and help us experience that moment sensually (through our senses). Here is a powerful two-line imagistic poem by Ezra Pound:

In a Station of the Metro
The apparition of these faces in the crowd;
Petals on a wet, black bough.

Narrative poems tell stories, while **argumentative** poems explore an idea (such as love or valor). Here's a poem by Robert Frost that does both:

The Road Not Taken
Two roads diverged in a yellow wood,
And sorry I could not travel both
And be one traveller, long I stood
And looked down one as far as I could
To where it bent in the undergrowth;

Then took the other, as just as fair,
And having perhaps the better claim,
Because it was grassy and wanted wear;
Though as for that the passing there
Had worn them really about the same,

And both that morning equally lay
In leaves no step had trodden black.
Oh, I kept the first for another day!
Yet knowing how way leads on to way,
I doubted if I should ever come back.

I shall be telling this with a sigh
Somewhere ages and ages hence:
Two roads diverged in a wood, and I—I took the
    one less traveled by,
And that has made all the difference.

Elegies and odes are two other common types of poems. An **elegy** is a poem that laments the loss of someone or something. An **ode**, on the other hand, celebrates a person, place, thing, or event. Here are a few lines from John Keats' (1795–1821) famous "Ode on a Grecian Urn":

Ah, happy, happy boughs! that cannot shed
    Your leaves, nor ever bid the spring adieu;
And, happy melodist, unwearied,
    For ever piping songs for ever new;
More happy love! more happy, happy love!
    For ever warm and still to be enjoy'd,
        For ever panting, and for ever young;

Word Choice in Poetry

Because of their brevity, poets are especially careful about word choice. They often rely on figurative language to convey larger ideas, allowing images to convey ideas rather than sentences. Poets will also often use words that can have multiple meanings or associations.

▶ Elements of Sound

Though not all poems use rhyme, this is the most recognized element of sound in poetry. A **rhyme** is the repetition of identical or similar stressed sounds at the end of a word. Rhymes create rhythm and suggest a relationship between the rhymed words.

There are several different types of rhymes:

- **Exact rhymes** share the same last syllables (the last consonant and vowel combination). For example:
    cat, hat
    laugh, staff
    refine, divine
- **Half-rhymes** share only the final consonant(s)
    cat, hot
    adamant, government
- **Eye rhymes** look like a rhyme because the word endings are spelled the same, but the words don't sound the same
    bough, through
    enough, though

Alliteration is another important element of sound, and one that is often used in prose as well. **Alliteration** is the repetition of sounds. The sound is most often found at the beginning of words but can also be found throughout words. For example, the words *pitter patter* use alliteration at the beginning (repetition of the *p* sound), in the middle (repetition of the *t* sound), and at the end (repetition of the *r* sound). Notice the alliteration of the *k* sound in the first line and the *l* sound in the second line of "The Eagle":

He **c**lasps the **c**rag with **c**rooked hands;
Close to the sun in **l**onely **l**ands,

Some sounds, such as *l, s, r, m, n,* and vowel sounds (*a, e, i, o,* and *u*) are soft and create a pleasant, musical effect. Other sounds, such as *b, g, k,* and *p,* are much harder sounds, less pleasant and more forceful. Writers will use sound to help create the right tone and reflect the theme of the poem. By using the *k* and *l* sounds together in the first two lines, Tennyson suggests the duality of the eagle: its serene beauty and its awesome power.

Onomatopoeia is another element of sound. An **onomatopoeia** is a word that sounds like its meaning; the sound is the definition of the word. *Buzz, hiss, moan,* and *screech* are a few examples. These two lines from Robert Frost's 1916 poem "Out, Out," for example, use onomatopoeia:

And the saw snarled and rattled, snarled and
    rattled,
As it ran light, or had to bear a load.

Rhythm

One of the most important ways poets establish rhythm in their poems is through meter. **Meter** is the number of syllables in a line and how the stress falls on those syllables. In **iambic meter**, one of the most common metrical patterns, the stress falls on every other syllable, creating a steady *da-dum, da-dum, da-dum* rhythm to the poem. Each "drum beat" (da-dum) is called a **foot**. Here is Robert Frost again to demonstrate iambic tetrameter (four feet per line). Read these lines from "Stopping by Woods on a Snowy Evening" out loud to hear how the rhythm works. The stressed syllables are in bold type.

Whose **woods** these **are** I **think** I **know**.
His **house** is **in** the **vill**age, **though**;

He **will** not **see** me **stop**ping **here**
To **watch** his **woods** fill **up** with **snow**.

▶ Elements of Structure

You won't find a GED Language Arts, Reading question asking you to identify the rhyme scheme or meter of a poem, and you won't be asked to determine whether a poem is free verse or a sonnet. But knowing these poetic forms and techniques can help you better understand the poems you read. In poetry more than any other type of literature, form is part of the poem's meaning.

Line Breaks and Stanzas

Because poems are written in verse, poets must decide how much information belongs on each line and when those lines should be broken into **stanzas** (poetic "paragraphs"). First, it's important to remember that when you read a poem out loud, you should pause only when *punctuation* tells you to pause. Do not pause at the end of each line or even at the end of a stanza unless there is a comma, period, or other punctuation mark that requires pause. That way, you can hear the flow of the words as the poet intended.

When you *look* at a poem, however, you need to take into consideration the important visual element of line breaks and stanzas. Line breaks and stanzas have two purposes: 1) to call attention to the words at the end of each line and 2) to set aside each group of words as a distinct idea. Thus, while poetic sentences sometimes cut across line breaks and even sometimes stanzas, the visual separation of words within those sentences helps poets set off particular words and ideas for emphasis. Any word at the end of a line, for example, will stand out. And poets can space words all across the page, as in the following example:

Sleeping
Sleeping, and it was
                            dark
outside. Inside,
I was
                            wondering
alone,
                            wandering
in a dream
of you.

Notice how the spacing here ties the words *dark*, *wondering*, and *wandering* together, pairs the words *inside* and *outside*, and sets off *alone*.

Rhymed and Metered Verse

Poems can be **rhymed verse**, **metered** (or **blank**) **verse**, or **free verse**. Rhymed and metered/blank poems are very confined by their structure; the lines must follow a rhyme scheme or metrical pattern (or both, if the poem is both rhymed and metered). Word choice (diction) is especially controlled by rhyme scheme and metrical pattern. Poets must find words that both convey just the right idea, have the right ending to fit the rhyme scheme, *and* have the right number of syllables and the right stresses to fit the metrical pattern.

Three common types of rhymed and metered verse include the **sonnet**, the **ballad**, and the **villanelle**. These forms all have specific rhyme schemes and metrical patterns that poets must follow. A sonnet, for example, is composed of 14 lines usually written in iambic pentameter (five feet per line). The rhyme scheme will vary depending on the type of sonnet. An Italian sonnet, for example, will divide the poem into two stanzas, one with eight lines, the other with six, using the following rhyme scheme: **abbaabba cdcdcd** (or *cdecde* or *cdccdc*). A Shakespearian sonnet, on the other hand, separates the lines into three **quatrains** (a quatrain is a stanza of four lines) and ends with a **couplet** (a pair of rhyming lines) with the following rhyme scheme: *abab cdcd efef gg*.

A **ballad** is a poem that usually tells a story and is often meant to be sung. The rhyme scheme is typically *abcb defe ghih*, etc. Ballads tend to emphasize action rather than emotions or ideas and often have a steady, sing-songy meter.

One of the most complex rhyme schemes is the villanelle. A **villanelle** has five three-line stanzas with an *aba* rhyme scheme and a final quatrain with an *abaa* rhyme. There are only two rhymes in the poem, and line one must be repeated in lines six, 12, and 18 while line three must be repeated in lines nine, 15, and 19.

Blank or metered verse is guided only by meter, not rhyme. Thus, the lines have a set number of syllables without any rhyme scheme. A haiku is an example of blank verse. **Haikus** are unrhymed poems of three lines and 17 syllables. Line one has five syllables; line two has seven; and line three has five. Here is an example:

The Falling Flower
What I thought to be
Flowers soaring to their boughs
Were bright butterflies.

—Moritake (1452–1540)

Free Verse

Free verse is poetry that is free from the restrictions of meter and rhyme. But that doesn't mean that free verse poems are haphazard or simply thrown together. Rather than fitting a traditional metrical pattern or rhyme scheme, free verse poems often use a thematic structure or repetitive pattern. "Sleeping" is one example, setting off words to isolate some and associate others. A more structured free verse poem is Kenneth Fearing's 1941 poem "Ad." The poem is structured like a help-wanted ad designed to recruit soldiers for World War II.

Wanted: Men;
Millions of men are *wanted at once* in a big new field
Wages: *Death.*

The last line of the poem sums up the compensation for the soldiers.

Thus, the structure of the poem helps reflect its theme: The absurdity of running an advertisement for men to kill and be killed, of calling war "a big new field" to make it sound exciting, reflects the poet's feelings about the war—that it, too, is absurd, and that it is absurd to ask men to kill each other and to die.

22 ▶ Drama

Like fiction and poetry, drama has its own conventions and forms. Understanding these conventions and forms can help you understand the drama excerpts you will find on the GED Language Arts, Reading Exam. This chapter reviews the elements of drama and strategies for understanding this genre.

BEFORE BOOKS AND movies, even before language, people were acting out their experiences. Drama is the oldest form of storytelling and one of the oldest ways of making sense of the human experience.

▶ How Drama Is Different

Drama has the same elements of fiction: *plot, character, setting, point of view, tone, language and style, symbolism,* and *theme.* However, drama differs from poetry and prose in a number of significant ways. The most obvious and important difference is that drama is *meant to be performed;* it is literature that is designed for a live audience. (The exception is a small minority of plays called **closet dramas**, which are plays meant only to be read, not performed.) This makes plays the most immediate and energetic genre of literature, because there is an active exchange of energy and emotion during the performance.

In drama, **action** is the driving force of the plot. "The essence of a play is action," said Aristotle, the first literary critic of the Western world. Because of the immediacy of a play and the short time span in which the action must occur, things happen more quickly than they might in a novel. There is less time for digressions; everything must be related to the unfolding of events on the stage.

Drama also presents us with a unique point of view. Because there is no narrator, the story isn't filtered through someone's point of view. Even if there is a narrator on stage telling us the story, we still see the action for ourselves. This **dramatic point of view** allows us to come to our own conclusions about the characters and their actions.

The action of a play takes place in a real physical space, so **setting** is particularly important in drama. The setting might be realistic, minimalist, or symbolic; the play can occur in "real time" or take place over several years in the characters' lives. For example, in Samuel Beckett's famous play *Waiting for Godot,* the stage is intentionally bare. The stage directions call only for a tree and a low mound on which one of the characters sits. The emptiness on stage reflects the emptiness that echoes throughout the play: the characters wait, and wait, and do nothing; they wait for someone who does not come.

▶ Dramatic Irony

In a play, we must listen carefully for the tone that characters use when they speak. But the controlling tone of a play is often **dramatic irony**. Dramatic irony occurs when a character's speech or actions have an unintended meaning known to the audience but not to the character. For example, in Henrik Ibsen's classic 1879 play *A Doll's House,* we find Torvald Helmer lecturing his wife about the evils of lying. He uses Krogstad, whom Helmer had just fired for committing forgery, as an example. But he doesn't know what we know. Several years before, Nora had forged her father's signature to borrow money she needed to help Helmer through a serious illness. Because Helmer hates the idea of borrowing money, she kept the forgery and the loan a secret. But now Krogstad has threatened to reveal the secret if he does not get his job back. Notice how powerful the irony is in the passage below, especially when Helmer takes Nora's hand:

> NORA: But tell me, was it really such a crime that this Krogstad committed?
> HELMER: Forgery. Do you have any idea what that means?
> NORA: Couldn't he have done it out of need?
> HELMER: Yes, or thoughtlessness, like so many others. I'm not so heartless that I'd condemn a man categorically for just one mistake.

NORA: No, of course not, Torvald!
HELMER: Plenty of men have redeemed themselves by openly confessing their crimes and taking their punishment.
NORA: Punishment—?
HELMER: But now Krogstad didn't go that way. He got himself out by sharp practices, and that's the real cause of his moral breakdown.
NORA: Do you really think that would—?
HELMER: Just imagine how a man with that sort of guilt in him has to lie and cheat and deceive on all sides, has to wear a mask even with the nearest and dearest he has, even with his own wife and children. And with the children, Nora—that's where it's most horrible.
NORA: Why?
HELMER: Because that kind of atmosphere of lies infects the whole life of a home. Every breath the children take in is filled with the germs of something degenerate.
NORA: [coming closer behind him] Are you sure of that?
HELMER: Oh, I've seen it often enough as a lawyer. Almost everyone who goes bad early in life has a mother who's a chronic liar.
NORA: Why just—the mother?
HELMER: It's usually the mother's influence that's dominant, but the father's works in the same way, of course. Every lawyer is quite familiar with it. And still this Krogstad's been going home year in, year out, poisoning his own children with lies and pretense; that's why I call him morally lost. [Reaching his hands out toward her.] So my sweet little Nora must promise me never to plead his cause. Your hand on it. Come, come, what's this? Give me your hand. There, now. All settled. I can tell it'd be impossible for me to work alongside of him. I literally feel physically revolted when I'm anywhere near such a person.

▶ The Dramatic Stage

Drama comes from the Greek word *dran,* which means *to do* or *to act.* Because dramas are performed, these elements of the performance are essential elements of drama:

- dialogue
- stage directions
- live audience

Dialogue

In fiction, the story is heard through the voice of a narrator; in poetry, through the voice of the speaker of the poem. In drama, as noted earlier, there is no narrator; instead, the characters speak directly to each other or to the audience. The story is driven forward by the words and actions of the characters, without the filter of a narrator. Through **dialogue** (two or more characters speaking to each other), **monologue** (a character speaking directly to the audience), and **soliloquy** (a character "thinking aloud" on stage), we learn what the characters think and feel about themselves, each other, and the things that are happening around them. Characters can also speak in an **aside**, which is like a blend between a monologue and a soliloquy. In an aside, the actor shares a quick thought with the audience but not with the other characters. This privileges the audience with knowledge that the other characters do not have.

The exchange between Nora and Helmer is an example of dialogue. Here is an excerpt from one of the most famous soliloquies of all time:

> HAMLET: To be, or not to be: that is the
> question:
> Whether 'tis nobler in the mind to suffer
> The slings and arrows of outrageous fortune,
> Or to take arms against a sea of troubles,
> And by opposing end them? To die: to sleep;
> No more; and by a sleep to say we end
> The heart-ache and the thousand natural shocks
> That flesh is heir to, 'tis a consummation
> Devoutly to be wish'd. To die, to sleep;
> To sleep: perchance to dream: ay, there's the rub;
> For in that sleep of death what dreams may come
> When we have shuffled off this mortal coil,
> Must give us pause:
> —William Shakespeare, from *Hamlet*

Stage Directions

Stage directions are the playwright's instructions to the director and actors. They often include specific details about how the characters should look, the tone of voice they should use when they speak, significant gestures or actions they should take, and the setting, including costumes, props, and lighting. Stage directions can help us understand tone and reinforce the theme of the play. For example, the stage directions for *Waiting for Godot*, as we noted earlier, are intentionally few; the emptiness of the stage is meant to echo the play's exploration of the emptiness in our lives. Similarly, the stage directions in Susan Glaspell's 1916 play *Trifles* show us how uneasy the women feel when they begin to piece together the puzzle of Mr. Wright's murder. When Mrs. Peters finds the bird that Mr. Wright killed, she remembers how she felt in a similar situation and understands how Mrs. Wright could have killed her husband:

> MRS. PETERS: [In a whisper] When I was a
> girl—my kitten—there was a boy took a
> hatchet, and before my eyes—and before I could
> get there—[Covers her face an instant.] If they
> hadn't held me back I would have—[Catches
> herself, looks upstairs where steps are heard, falters weakly]—hurt him.

Audience

Audience, of course, is the third essential element of drama, for without an audience, a play cannot be fully brought to life. Of course, this does not mean one cannot find great meaning and enjoyment out of simply reading a play. While missing out on the visual effects and the energy of the theater, reading a play can often offer greater enjoyment because the reader has the option to reread lines and imagine the scenes in his or her own mind. To bring the play to life, however, one needs to pay extra attention to the stage directions to see how things are supposed to happen and how the actors are supposed to behave.

▶ Types of Plays

The symbol of the theater is two masks, one with a great smile, the other with a frown and a tear.

For many years, drama, which originated in religious celebrations of the ancient Greeks, was either tragic or comic. Today, of course, plays can be tragedies, comedies, and everything in between. But you will better understand all those "in betweens" if you understand the extremes and the traditions from which they come.

Tragedy

In drama, a **tragedy** is a play that presents a noble character's fall from greatness. In Greek drama, the characters are all kings, queens, and other nobles. In the course of a typical Greek tragedy, the main character does something (or doesn't do something) that leads to a dramatic fall from grace. This fall usually happens because of the character's tragic flaw (though the character often tries to blame fate).

A **tragic flaw** is a characteristic that drives the character to make a poor decision or do something he or she shouldn't do. Often the flaw is also part of what makes the character great. Pride is often a tragic flaw, and so is absolutism. For example, in Sophocles' ancient play *Antigone,* Creon puts the welfare of the state before the welfare of any individual, and he is respected and revered for his powerful leadership and devotion to the state. But he refuses to make an exception when his niece Antigone breaks the law, and as a result Antigone, Creon's son (Antigone's fiancée), and Creon's wife all kill themselves by the end of the play. Only Creon is left to survey the destruction he brought upon his family.

While a tragedy will often move us to tears, it is not entirely depressing. A true tragedy is **cathartic**, allowing us to feel and release strong emotions by experiencing the pain and sadness of the characters, by watching human beings make mistakes and suffer—without actually making mistakes or suffering ourselves. The hope comes from how tragic heroes deal with that suffering and loss. A **tragic hero** like Creon, for example, accepts responsibility for those mistakes, and Antigone ends with the hope that Creon has learned from the tragedy and will therefore be a better (more flexible, more just, more compassionate) leader in the future.

Comedy

On the other end of the spectrum is the **comedy**. As a rule, comedies have happy endings. Instead of ending in death, destruction, or separation, comedies end in happiness, reconciliation, and union (e.g., marriage).

The humor in comedies can come from many sources, such as miscommunications, missed timing, and mistaken identities (all things that can also be the source of tragedy). Humor may also arise from **puns** (plays on the meaning of words) and double meanings as well as overturned expectations. For example, in Woody Allen's 1968 one-act play *Death Knocks*, the Grim Reaper—normally portrayed as a somber, frightening, powerful character of few words and fearful actions—climbs through Nat Ackerman's window and asks for a glass of water. This Grim Reaper is no ominous character who unwillingly takes us from life. Rather, he is a hassled, clumsy, casual character who has to check whether he's got the right address. Instead of being afraid of death, we laugh at it, especially at Death's attempt to make a dramatic entrance:

> DEATH: I climbed up the drainpipe. I was trying to make a dramatic entrance. I see the big windows and you're awake reading. I figure it's worth a shot. I'll climb up and enter with a little—you know . . . [Snaps fingers.] Meanwhile, I get my heel caught on some vines, the drainpipe breaks, and I'm hanging by a thread. Then my cape begins to tear. Look, let's just go. It's been a rough night.

A **melodrama** is a "tragedy" that has been given a happy ending, thus ruining the effect of a true tragedy. **Tragicomedies** are more common. These are true tragedies (with a tragic ending), but interspersed throughout are comic scenes that help alleviate the intensity of the emotion the tragedy arouses.

Today's Theater

Unlike the Greek tragedies of long ago, today's dramas do not center around extraordinary people (kings and queens) and extraordinary events (wars, plagues, and other major historical events). Rather, most dramas focus on "normal" people and the everyday situations and challenges they face. For example, John Guare's play *Six Degrees of Separation* is about our need to connect with others and the lengths we may go to alleviate loneliness and fit in.

Many of today's dramatists also believe that plays should acknowledge that they *are* plays and should not attempt to be realistic. At the same time, they attempt to portray human nature as realistically as possible. As a result, the **antihero** has emerged as a regular onstage presence. This character inspires pity more than admiration, for he or she often ruins more than he or she repairs. In Arthur Miller's *Death of a Salesman,* for example, Willy Loman is a deluded salesman who believes that success means being liked by as many people as possible. When he loses his job and realizes that he has been living a lie—and that he has raised his sons to live the same kind of lie—he commits suicide. He is a pitiful character who does not redeem himself. But his son, Biff, will change his life as a result of what he has learned throughout the play. He is the true tragic hero.

▶ Vocabulary Review

As you encounter dramatic passages on the GED Language Arts, Reading Exam, keep in mind the following ideas that pertain to drama:

comedy: a play ending in resolution, or union

dialogue: conversations between characters

dramatic irony: the audience is aware of something the characters onstage are not aware of

monologue: a lengthy speech made by one character

soliloquy: a lengthy speech that reveals a character's thoughts

stage directions: written directions showing specific actions of characters

tragedy: a play ending in the tragic fall of a main character

23▶ Nonfiction

From essays to commentary to reports and memos, nonfiction texts are written for many different purposes and have many different functions. This chapter describes the kinds of nonfiction texts you will see on the GED Language Arts, Reading Exam.

ONFICTION TEXTS CAN be literary or functional. The literary nonfiction you might see on the GED Language Arts, Reading Exam includes essays and autobiography/memoir. The functional texts you will see include commentary on the arts and business communications.

▶ How Nonfiction Is Different

While nonfiction texts may be *imaginative*, they differ from fiction because they are not about imagined people and events. Rather, nonfiction texts deal with real people and real events.

There are other important differences between fiction and nonfiction. In nonfiction, there is no narrator, so there is no "filter" between the author and the reader. In a nonfiction text, the author is speaking to the reader directly, expressing his or her point of view. Thus, the voice in a nonfiction text is the unique voice of the author.

Point of view is important in nonfiction. Remember, point of view establishes a certain relationship with the reader. First-person texts are more personal but also more subjective. Third-person texts are more objective but less personal. The point of view an author chooses will depend upon his or her purpose and audience. For example, an annual report would likely use the third person, which is appropriate for a formal business document, while an essay about a personal experience would probably use the first-person point of view and explore the impact of that experience on the writer.

▶ Essays

There are many different types of **essays**. The four most common types are:

1. **descriptive:** describing a person, place, or thing
2. **narrative:** telling a story or describing an event
3. **expository:** exploring and explaining an idea or position
4. **persuasive:** arguing a specific point of view

There are essays about every imaginable topic, from what it is like to grow up poor (or rich, or bilingual) to why we should (or should not) clone human beings. The basic structure of an essay is *main* idea *support.* Even if the writer is describing an experience, he or she has a reason for telling that story, and that reason—why the writer thinks the story is important enough to tell— is the main idea.

Essays will often make their main idea clear in a **thesis statement**. This statement is likely to come at the beginning of the essay. Notice here how the author states his thesis at the end of the opening paragraph of his essay:

> When you think of former president Bill Clinton, what's the first thing that comes to mind? Unfortunately, for many people, the first thing they think of is Monica Lewinsky. Like millions of people around the globe, I was horrified by how much the Whitewater investigation delved into Mr. Clinton's private affairs. No one needed to know the sort of details that were revealed by Ken Starr's investigation. But while I don't want to know the details, *I do believe we have a right to know what sort of lives our politicians are living. I believe their behavior in private is a reflection of their true values and how they will behave in office.*

One type of writing that you may see in essays (as well as other forms of literature) is satire. **Satire** is a form of comedy in which the writer exposes and ridicules someone or something in order to inspire change. Satires rely heavily on **verbal irony**, in which the intended meaning is the opposite of the expressed meaning. Satirists also use **hyperbole**, which is extreme exaggeration, as well as sarcasm and understatement in order to convey their ideas.

Jonathan Swift's 1729 essay "A Modest Proposal" is one of the most famous examples of satire. In the essay, Swift proposes that the Irish, who are starving, eat their own children to prevent "the children of poor people in Ireland from being a burden to their parents or country." Here's a brief excerpt:

> I have been assured by a very knowing American of my acquaintance in London, that a young healthy child well nursed is at a year old a most delicious, nourishing, and wholesome food, whether stewed, roasted, baked or boiled; and I make no doubt that it will equally serve in a fricassee or ragout.

Of course, Swift is not really suggesting that the Irish become cannibals. He is using this ridiculous proposal to criticize the British for oppressing the Irish, especially poor Irish Catholics, who often had many children. The outrageous nature of Swift's proposal reflects his feelings about the absurdity of British rule in Ireland at the time and the British government's inability to find a satisfactory solution to the Irish famine.

▶ Autobiography and Memoir

In an **autobiography** or **memoir**, the author will—very subjectively, of course—tell the story of his or her life. The difference between autobiographies and memoirs is that memoirs tend to be less comprehensive and more exploratory—they will cover less ground and spend more time examining the impact of people and events. Authors may write to clarify an experience, teach a lesson, or make a statement about a historical event or social movement. As you read an autobiography or memoir, look for what the author feels has shaped him. Why has he chosen to relate these particular events; describe these particular people?

For example, here is a brief excerpt from Frank McCourt's best-selling 1996 memoir, *Angela's Ashes*:

> Next day we rode to the hospital in a carriage with a horse. They put Oliver in a white box that came with us in the carriage and we took him to the graveyard. They put the white box into a hole in the ground and covered it with earth. My mother and Aunt Aggie cried, Grandma looked angry, Dad, Uncle Pa Keating, and Uncle Pat Sheehan looked sad but did not cry

and I thought that if you're a man you can cry only when you have the black stuff that is called the pint.

I did not like the jackdaws that perched on trees and gravestones and I did not want to leave Oliver with them. I threw a rock at a jackdaw that waddled over toward Oliver's grave. Dad said I shouldn't throw rocks at jackdaws, they might be somebody's soul. I didn't know what a soul was but I didn't ask him because I didn't care. Oliver was dead and I hated jackdaws. I'd be a man someday and I'd come back with a bag of rocks and I'd leave the graveyard littered with dead jackdaws.

▶ Commentary on the Arts

The purpose of **commentary** is to illuminate or explain other works of literature and art. These texts review and analyze a work of art (performance art, visual art, and literature) and generally have two goals: 1) to help us understand the work of art and 2) to evaluate its success or value. A book review, for example, will typically offer some background on the author, summarize the basic plot of the story, and describe the main characters and their chief conflicts. It will also point out what makes the novel good (e.g., the characters are especially endearing, the plot has surprising twists and turns, the descriptions are particularly lush, the structure is very unique) or bad (e.g., the plot is trite, the characters are flat and unbelievable, the writing is clumsy, the chapters are disorganized). Thus, commentary can help you determine whether or not a work of art is something you should experience, and if you do experience it, the commentary can help you make more sense of your experience.

The commentary on the GED Language Arts, Reading Exam can be of any sort, including reviews of books, movies, concerts/musical performances, dance productions, musicals, television shows, plays, paintings, sculptures, photography, or multimedia arts. But you are most likely to see commentary on a visual art piece or experience.

When you read commentary, one of the most important skills to have is the ability to distinguish between fact and opinion. While commentators do deal with facts, commentary is by nature highly subjective; they are sharing their personal reactions to a work of art. A good commentator will always explain why he or she feels the way he or she does about a work of art. For example, a movie critic might praise a film because the story was original and moving, the actors convincing, and the special effects stunning.

Remember, however, that the reviewer's feelings about the film are *opinions*, no matter how well the author might defend them. There are many non-debatable facts about a work of art such as a film, including when it was made, how long it took to make, who made it, how much it cost, the events in the plot, how the special effects were created, etc. But the reviewer's judgment of these facts is a matter of debate, and therefore a matter of opinion. You might find the story in a movie interesting while your friend finds it boring.

As you read commentary, pay attention to word choice. Even in sentences that seem to express facts, commentators can express their opinion. For example, look at the following sentences. They have the same meaning but convey different attitudes:

Raquel Ramirez *plays* the role of Ophelia.
Raquel Ramirez *shines* in the role of Ophelia.

▶ Business-Related Documents

There is one business document on every exam. These texts can range from employee handbooks and training manuals to letters, memos, reports, and proposals.

Business documents are unlike the other nonfiction texts because they:

- are meant for a specific audience
- have a specific, business-related purpose

While essays, autobiographies, and commentary are meant for a general reader, business documents (with the exception of annual reports) are designed for a much smaller and more specific audience. Memos and letters, for example, are often addressed to only one individual.

The purpose of each business document, too, is very specific. A memo may provide an agenda for a meeting or a reminder about forms that need to be completed; a proposal may describe a plan to improve or expand business; a training manual will show employees how to perform specific tasks.

The purpose of the document will usually be made very clear right from the start. As the saying goes, in business, time is money, and in order to save the reader time, writers of business communications state their purpose clearly at the beginning of the document. For example, notice how the main idea of the following letter is stated in the second sentence:

Dear Ms. Ng:

Thank you for your recent application for an automobile loan from Crown Bank. Unfortunately, we are unable to process your application because information is missing from your application form.

We need the following information to complete the loan application process:

1. the number of years in your current residence
2. your driver's license number
3. the name and telephone number of your insurance provider

Please provide this information to us as soon as possible. You may call me at 800-123-4567, extension 22, or fax me at 222-123-4567. Please put application code **XT121** on your correspondence.

Thank you for your prompt attention to this matter. I look forward to completing your loan application.

Sincerely,
Victor Wilson
Junior Loan Analyst
Crown Bank

Readability Techniques

To maximize time and clarity, business-related documents will use several **readability techniques**. These include *chunking information* and *using headings and lists*.

Business writers often organize information into small, manageable "chunks" of data. That is, they will group sentences or paragraphs according to the specific topics or ideas they discuss and set those sentences apart with line breaks and/or headings.

Headings and subheadings provide "titles" within the text to guide readers topic by topic through the document. Headings show readers how ideas are related and help readers find specific information in the document. (Notice, for example, how headings are used throughout this book.)

To make information easier to process, business writers will also use bulleted or numbered lists as often as possible, especially when providing instructions. It is easier to see the items in a list when they are separated and listed vertically rather than running together horizontally in a regular sentence or paragraph. For example, notice how much easier it is to absorb the information in the bulleted list than in the following narrative:

To apply for a permit, you must bring proof of residency, a photo identification, a copy of your birth certificate, and proof of insurance.

To apply for a permit, you must bring:
- proof of residency
- a photo identification
- a copy of your birth certificate
- proof of insurance

Whether the text is a business document or a personal essay, remember that writers always write for a reason. Think about the writer's purpose. Why is he or she writing? Look for clues in both content (including specific facts and details) and style (including word choice and tone). Check for topic sentences and thesis statements that express the author's main idea.

24 ▶ Tips and Strategies for the GED Language Arts, Reading Exam

In the following chapters, you will review a lot of material to prepare for the GED Language Arts, Reading Exam. Now here are some specific tips and strategies for handling the questions you will see on the exam.

▶ The GED Language Arts, Reading Exam in a Nutshell

This GED Language Arts, Reading Exam consists of 40 multiple-choice questions about texts from three different time periods: pre-1920, 1920–1960, and 1960–present. Each exam will include a poem, an excerpt from a play, a commentary on the arts, a business-related document such as a memo or report, and at least one excerpt from a work of fiction. Each passage (except the poem) will be approximately 300–400 words long.

Questions will test your basic comprehension (20%) of the texts, your ability to analyze the texts (30–35%), your ability to "synthesize" (draw inferences from) ideas from the texts (30–35%), and your ability to apply information or ideas from the texts to different contexts (15%). You may be asked about the main idea or theme of a text, about a character's feelings or motivations, or the significance of a symbol. You may be asked to identify a specific fact or detail or to predict the effect of an action described or implied in the text. You might be asked about the effect of a rhetorical technique or to identify the tone of a passage.

▶ Getting Ready for the Exam

The GED Language Arts, Reading Exam covers a lot of material. It tests your comprehension not just of functional texts but also of the many genres and time periods of literature. Between now and test time, one of the best things you can do is to read as much as possible, especially the genres with which you are least familiar. The more comfortable you are with literature, the easier it will be to understand what you read, and the more comfortable you will be at test time.

As you read various texts, remember that you don't necessarily have to *like* what you read. Hopefully, you will find the experience enjoyable and rewarding. But if you don't like every poem you read, that's okay. Different writers have different styles, and sometimes the writer's style and subject matter may simply not appeal to you. What matters is that you are able to *appreciate* the text and understand what the author is trying to say. Whether you like the writer's style or not, whether the subject matter thrills you or bores you, keep reading and developing your reading comprehension skills. You may find some authors and texts that have a profound impact on you. You might also develop a love for a genre that will last throughout your life.

▶ Finding the Main Idea

Remember that the main idea is the thought that controls the text. What is the author trying to say? What point does he or she want to get across? The main idea may be explicitly stated in a topic sentence (for a paragraph) or a thesis statement (for a complete text). It can also be implied. In literature, the main idea is called the theme. The **theme** is the "sum" of all of the elements of literature, including *plot, character, symbolism, tone, language,* and *style.*

Here are some specific tips for finding the main idea:

1. Remember that themes and main ideas are general and should cast a "net" over the whole passage or text.
2. Consider the author's purpose. What do you think the writer is trying to accomplish with this text? Why do you think he or she wrote it?
3. Try to fill in the blanks:
   - This story (poem, play, essay, etc.) is about _____ (insert topic).
   - The writer seems to be saying _____ (general thematic statement) about this topic.

   If you can support your statement with specific evidence from the text, and if that statement is general enough to encompass the whole passage,

you have probably successfully identified the main idea or one of the themes of the text. (Literary texts, especially long ones such as novels, can have more than one theme.)

4. Try giving the text a new title that conveys the main idea or theme. What would you call the passage?

▶ Finding Specific Facts and Details

Specific facts and details are often used to support the main idea of a text. Here are some tips for questions about specific facts and details:

1. Remember the difference between main ideas and their support. Note the specific examples, facts, and details the writer uses to develop his or her ideas.
2. Look for **key words** in the question to tell you exactly what information to look for in the passage.
3. Think about the **structure** of the passage and where that information is likely to be located.

▶ Distinguishing between Fact and Opinion

An important reading comprehension skill is also a critical thinking skill: the ability to distinguish between fact and opinion. It is often important to know whether a writer is stating a fact or expressing an opinion. Here are two quick tips for distinguishing between the two:

1. When you are unsure whether something is a fact or opinion, ask yourself, *Is this statement debatable? Can others take a different position?*
2. Look for signal words and other clues that the author is expressing a fact or an opinion. Signal words include phrases such as *I believe* and words such as *should* and *ought.*
3. Remember that good writers will usually provide facts to support their opinions.

► Making Inferences

The ability to draw logical conclusions from a text is essential to reading comprehension and to doing well on the GED Language Arts, Reading Exam. Remember that your conclusions must be based on evidence from the text. If a writer wants you to infer something, he or she will give you clues so you can make that inference. If you have a hunch about what the writer is trying to say, search for evidence in the text to support your ideas.

Here are some more specific tips for making effective inferences:

1. Pay careful attention to *word choice, details, actions,* and *structure.* If the writer wants you to infer something, he or she will leave you clues to guide you to the right conclusion.
2. Test your inference. Double back to find specific evidence that will support your conclusion.

Inferring Cause and Effect

1. Look for basic clues like transitions that signal cause and effect: *since, because, therefore, as a result,* etc.
2. Make sure you can establish a direct link between cause and effect. Remember that many effects have more than one cause and that there is often a chain of causes that lead to a specific event.
3. Again, make sure you have evidence to support your inferences about cause and effect.

► Reading Fiction

When you read a work of fiction, remember the eight elements of fiction that work together to create meaning:

1. plot
2. character
3. setting
4. point of view
5. tone
6. language and style
7. symbolism
8. theme

Here are some specific tips for handling questions about fiction on the GED Language Arts, Reading Exam:

1. Pay attention to details, especially details about characters and setting.
2. Use your mind's eye to visualize people, places, and actions.
3. Think about *motivations.* Why do the characters say what they say, feel what they feel, do what they do? Many of the questions will be about the reasons for characters' thoughts and actions.
4. Remember that stories aim to help us better understand our world and ourselves. Think about what message the story might be sending that would meet this goal.

► Reading Drama

Drama is literature that is meant to be performed. But you can still be greatly entertained and moved by simply reading a play. Here are some tips for understanding dramatic excerpts on the GED Language Arts, Reading Exam:

1. Remember to read any stage directions carefully. These notes from the playwright can provide important clues to the characters' emotions as they speak and to the relationships between characters. Stage directions about setting are also important clues to the play's theme.
2. As with fiction, think about *motivations.* Why do the characters say what they say and do what they do? What has happened between the characters or to the characters to make them feel, say, and do these things?
3. Use the stage directions and other clues to "stage" the play in your head. Create a "theater of the mind" and imagine the action taking place on stage. Try to hear the characters saying their lines and see them moving about on the stage.

► Reading Poetry

Every GED Language Arts, Reading Exam will include at least one poem. Remember that while there are many different types of poems, most poems aim to tell a story, capture a moment, embody an emotion, or make an argument. In a poem, word choice is limited by the poem's length and often by structure and rhyme scheme, so poets are especially deliberate in their choice of words. Because poems are usually short, every word counts. Pay attention to every detail.

Here are some more specific tips for dealing with poems:

1. Read the poems aloud in your head so you can "hear" how they sound. Read each poem at least twice: first to get a general sense of the poem and its sound, second to get a better understanding of its meaning.

2. Poems don't have a narrator, but there is still a specific voice speaking to the reader, telling the story, painting the picture, or capturing the emotion. Use tone and word choice to determine as much as you can about the speaker of the poem. Who is this person? How does he or she feel about the subject of the poem? Does he or she seem to be talking to someone in particular or to a general audience?

3. Look at the overall structure of the poem. Is there a rhyme scheme or meter? Does the structure fit a particular pattern or design? Think about how the structure might reflect the subject or meaning of the poem.

4. Look at the line breaks and stanzas, if any. Where are the line breaks? Do any of the end words seem significant? Are the lines separated into stanzas? If so, what holds the lines in the stanzas together? Are any words separated to stand out for readers?

5. Try to determine the purpose of the poem. Is the speaker telling a story? Explaining an idea or emotion? Making an argument? Capturing a moment? Celebrating or mourning a person, place, or thing? Determining the type of poem is central to determining the poem's theme.

6. Pay attention to repetition. If a word or line is repeated, especially if it is repeated at the end of a line or stanza, it is significant and may be symbolic.

7. Look carefully at word choice. Because poems are so compact, each word must be chosen with special care, and some words may be chosen because they have multiple meanings.

8. Remember that poems are about real people and real emotions. Think about how the poem makes you feel. Think about the emotions conjured up by the words and rhythm of the poem.

▶ Reading Essays

You can expect nonfiction texts, like essays, to be more straightforward than stories and poems. But the main idea may not always be stated in a topic sentence or thesis statement.

Here are some tips for handling essays:

1. Determine the author's purpose. Is the author describing a person? Making an argument? Telling a story? Exploring an idea?

2. Use questions to determine the main idea of the essay. How does the author seem to feel about the person he or she is describing? Why? What sort of relationship did they have? What position has the author taken on the issue he or she is discussing? Why? Look for a thesis statement that expresses the main idea.

3. Look for topic sentences in the paragraphs you have been given. What are the controlling ideas of each paragraph? What larger idea might these ideas be supporting?

4. Use clues in word choice and tone to determine how the author feels about the subject.

▶ Reading Commentary

Commentary on the arts aims to help readers better understand and appreciate a work of art.

Here are some specific tips for reading commentary:

1. When reading commentary, always be on the lookout for support. Whenever the author makes a claim, ask *why*? Look for the specific reasons the author has come to that conclusion.

2. A thoughtful commentary will look for both the good and the bad in its subject. It is rare that a review is entirely positive or that someone finds a work of art utterly worthless, without one redeeming quality. Look for both the positive and negative in the review.

▶ Business Documents

All GED Language Arts, Reading Exams include at least one business document. This may be a memorandum, report, e-mail, or other business text. Here are some tips for dealing with questions about business documents:

1. Remember that business documents are written for specific audiences and for specific purposes. Determine the specific audience and the reason for the communication.

2. Business documents are often written so that specific actions will be taken. Are there any specific instructions or steps to follow? Look for lists and other clues regarding things to do or understand.

3. If a business document is making an argument, look for support. What facts or ideas are used to support the main idea?

V ▶ The GED Science Exam

I N THIS SECTION, you will learn about the GED Science Exam. The first chapter explains how the exam is structured—what the questions are like and what topics they cover. Knowing what to expect will make you more confident and comfortable on the day of the exam; there will be no surprises. Chapters 25–32 review the basic information you need to know about science and scientific inquiry for the GED Science Exam. Chapter 33 offers specific tips for the test.

Before you begin Chapter 25, take the pretest that follows. The questions are similar to the questions you will find on the GED Science Exam. When you are finished, check the answer key carefully to evaluate your results. Your performance on the pretest will help you determine how much preparation you need and what subjects you will need to review and practice most.

▶ Pretest: GED Science

Directions: Read the following multiple-choice questions carefully and determine the best answer. To practice the timing of the GED Science Exam, you should take approximately 15 minutes to answer these questions. Record your answers on the answer sheet provided.

Note: On the GED, you are not permitted to write in the test booklet. Make any notes or calculations on a separate piece of paper.

ANSWER SHEET

1. ⓐ ⓑ ⓒ ⓓ ⓔ
2. ⓐ ⓑ ⓒ ⓓ ⓔ
3. ⓐ ⓑ ⓒ ⓓ ⓔ
4. ⓐ ⓑ ⓒ ⓓ ⓔ
5. ⓐ ⓑ ⓒ ⓓ ⓔ
6. ⓐ ⓑ ⓒ ⓓ ⓔ
7. ⓐ ⓑ ⓒ ⓓ ⓔ
8. ⓐ ⓑ ⓒ ⓓ ⓔ
9. ⓐ ⓑ ⓒ ⓓ ⓔ
10. ⓐ ⓑ ⓒ ⓓ ⓔ

1. Which of the following is unlikely to influence climate?
   a. latitude (distance from the equator)
   b. longitude (time zone)
   c. altitude (elevation from sea level)
   d. ocean currents
   e. presence of nearby mountain ranges

2. Metabolic rate per gram of body weight is higher in smaller animals. Which animal would you expect to burn the least amount of metabolic fuel per gram of its body weight?
   a. harvest mouse
   b. dog
   c. rabbit
   d. elephant
   e. shrew

Questions 3 and 4 are based on the following data table, which represents the population of both wolves and deer during the years 1955–1980 in a given area.

	1955	1960	1965	1970	1975	1980
Wolves	52	68	75	60	45	49
Deer	325	270	220	210	120	80

3. Which of the following statements is true about the years 1955–1980?
   a. The population of the wolves increased over time.
   b. The population of the deer decreased at a constant rate over time.
   c. The population of the wolves increased initially but decreased after 1965.
   d. The population of the deer increased over time.
   e. The population of deer in 1975 in the area was 45.

4. Which of the following statements is true of the wolf population from 1955–1980?
   a. The wolf population increased at a constant rate until 1975.
   b. The wolf population decreased at a constant rate after 1970.
   c. The increase in the wolf population was a result of the decrease in the deer population.
   d. The wolf population increased from 1955 to 1965, decreased from 1965 to 1975, and increased again in 1980.
   e. The wolf population was at a maximum in 1960.

5. Isomers are molecules that have the same number of the same elements, but in a different arrangement. Which one of the following is an isomer of 2-propanol (shown here), which contains Carbon (C), Hydrogen (H), and Oxygen (O)?

```
    H  OH  H
    |  |   |
H — C — C — C — H
    |  |   |
    H  H   H
```

a.
```
    H  OH  H   H
    |  |   |   |
H — C — C — C — C — H
    |  |   |   |
    H  H   H   H
```

b.
```
    H   H   H
    |   |   |
H — C — C — C — OH
    |   |   |
    H   H   H
```

c.
```
    H   H
    |   |
H — C — C — OH
    |   |
    H   H
```

d.
```
    H   OH
    |   |
H — C — C — H
    |   |
    H   H
```

e.
```
    H   H   H
    |   |   |
H — C — C — C — H
    |   |   |
    H   H   H
```

Questions 6 and 7 are based on the following passage.

The rectilinear propagation of light and the law of reflection had been observed long before the development of modern theories that correctly explain these observations. Rectilinear propagation of light refers to the fact that light travels in straight lines. Hero of Alexandria, who lived around the first century, explained these observations by stating that light travels along the shortest allowed path. It wasn't until 1657 that Pierre de Fermat rejected Hero's shortest-path theory and showed that light propagates along the path taking the least time. From his principle of least time, Fermat re-derived the law of reflection, as well as the law of refraction. This principle played an important role in the development of quantum mechanics.

6. The passage shows that
   a. reflection and refraction can't be explained by the same theory.
   b. the term *reflection* means that light travels in straight lines.
   c. Hero of Alexandria had insight into quantum mechanics.
   d. scientists develop theories to explain the phenomena they observe in nature.
   e. light travels along the shortest allowed path.

7. Which general statement about science is NOT supported by the passage?
   a. A scientific finding sometimes plays a role in other scientific findings.
   b. Centuries can pass before an observation is correctly explained by science.
   c. Theory should not be based on experimental evidence.
   d. Different scientists do not always come up with the same explanation for an observation.
   e. A scientific theory should be in agreement with observations.

8. Lung cancer accounts for over 30% of all cancers. 90% of lung cancer victims are smokers. Lung cancer is rare in societies that don't smoke. Which is NOT a likely consequence of these statistics?
   a. Most smokers don't quit because they experience withdrawal symptoms.
   b. Congress passed a bill requiring tobacco companies to label their product as harmful.
   c. The percentage of smokers dropped after these figures were made public.
   d. The U.S. military developed a program to eliminate all tobacco use from the armed forces.
   e. The Surgeon General issued a report stating that smoking is a health hazard.

9. Paola is an engineer at an environmental consulting firm. Her job is to analyze air quality and the amount of toxic emissions due to highway traffic. The amount of emissions depends on the number of lanes and on the average speed of the traffic. The greater the number of lanes, and the slower the cars move, the higher the amount of toxic emissions. Which of these choices corresponds to the highest amount of toxic emissions into the atmosphere?
a. a two-lane highway at 2 A.M. on Monday
b. a four-lane highway at 2 A.M. on Tuesday
c. a two-lane highway at 5:30 P.M. on Wednesday
d. a four-lane highway at 5:30 P.M. on Thursday
e. a two-lane highway at 5:30 P.M. on Sunday

10. Many types of learning occur only at particular times called *sensitive periods*. (For example, children born blinded by cataracts can learn to see if the cataracts are removed by age 10. If the cataracts are removed later in life, these people can see random shapes and colors, but are unable to interpret them.) A scientist is interested in knowing whether there is a sensitive period for chaffinch birds to learn to sing the species song, and if so, how long this period lasts. Which of the following experiments would be most suitable for his purpose?
a. Take 20 just-hatched chaffinch birds from their environment. Bring them up in isolation, so that they are not exposed to their species song. Every week, return one bird to its environment and keep a record of the number of weeks it spent in isolation and whether it learned to sing.
b. Take 20 just-hatched chaffinch birds from their environment. Bring them up with birds of a different species, so that they are exposed to songs that do not resemble their own. Every week, return one bird to its environment and keep a record of the number of weeks it spent with birds of a different species and which song it learned to sing.
c. Take 20 just-hatched chaffinch birds from their environment. Every day play them a recording of the song of their species. Reward with food the birds that try to imitate the recorded sound, and note the number of weeks it took each one to learn to sing.

d. Take 20 chaffinch birds, of any age. Every day, play a recording of the song of another bird species. Record the age of every bird that was able to learn the song of the other bird species.
e. Bring up 20 just-hatched chaffinch birds among both adult chaffinch birds and adult birds of another species. Record the amount of time it took just-hatched birds to sing and determine whether the presence of the other species improved or deterred their ability to learn to sing their species song.

▶ **Answers**

1. b. Longitude is the only factor on the list that does NOT influence climate. In places on Earth that have the same longitude, noon occurs at the same time, but those places don't necessarily have the same climate. For example, Maine and Florida are at approximately the same longitude, but the climate in Maine is much colder than Florida, because Florida is closer to the Equator (latitude), choice **a**. Altitude can influence climate, choice **c**. There is often snow at a top of a mountain when there isn't any at its base. Ocean currents can also influence climate, choice **d**. The Gulf stream is a warm Atlantic ocean current that provides countries in Northern Europe with a climate that is warmer than places at the same latitude in Canada. The presence of mountain ranges can influence climate, choice **e**. For example, it doesn't rain much in Nevada's Great Basin due to its proximity to the Sierra Nevada Mountains.

2. d. Metabolic rate per gram of body weight is higher in small animals. You can infer that a large animal has the lowest metabolic rate per gram of its body weight. The largest animal on the list is the elephant.

3. c. Choice **a** is incorrect because the population of wolves decreased during some periods, resulting in a net decrease from 1955 to 1980. Choice **b** is incorrect because although the population of deer decreased during every period, the decrease was sometimes more dramatic than during other times, i.e., the rate of decrease was not constant. Choice **d** is incorrect because the population of deer did not increase over time. Choice **e** is incorrect because the population of deer in 1975 was 120, not 45.

4. d. The information presented in the chart contradicts statements in choices **a**, **b**, and **e**. There is no discussion or direct evidence that can support statement **c**.

5. b. According to the molecular structure provided in the question, 2-propanol has three carbon atoms, eight hydrogen atoms, and one oxygen atom. Only the structure in choice **b** has the same number of each of those atoms, but in a different arrangement (oxygen is attached to a different carbon), making the structure in choice **b**, an isomer of 2-propanol.

6. d. Hero and Fermat both worked to develop theories to explain reflection and rectilinear propagation of light, phenomena they observed in nature. Choice **a** is incorrect: According to the text, Fermat explained both reflection and refraction with his principle of least time. Choice **b** is incorrect; the term *rectilinear propagation*, not *reflection*, means that light travels in straight lines. The statement in choice **c** is not supported by the passage. Although quantum mechanics had roots in the study of the propagation of light, which Hero pursued, there is no evidence that Hero, who lived centuries before quantum mechanics was formulated, had insight into quantum mechanics. Choice **e** is incorrect because Fermat rejected the shortest-path theory and showed that light travels along the path that takes the least time.

7. c. It is the only statement that is NOT supported by the passage. Both of the scientists mentioned tried to formulate theories that were based on observations and experimental evidence.

8. a. The data and information show a strong indication that there is a link between smoking and lung cancer. The possible effects of making these figures public are laws and social programs that aim to increase the awareness of the hazards of smoking, and limit smoking—choices **b**, **d**, and **e**. Another potential effect is a decrease in the number of smokers, choice **c**. The statement in choice **a** may be true, but is not connected to the figures that show a link between smoking and cancer.

9. d. You are told that the emissions are greater when there are more lanes of traffic. Therefore, a four-lane highway results in more emissions than a two-lane highway. This eliminates choices **a**, **c**, and **e**. Since emissions are greater when the cars move slowly, the emissions are likely to be higher during rush hour traffic jams, choice **d**, than at 2:00 A.M., choice **b**.

10. a. The experiments described in choices **b**, **d**, and **e**, which involve introducing the chaffinch birds to other bird species, contain too many variables and do not directly test what is required. Experiment **c** is faulty because the birds, although they are brought up in isolation, are exposed to the recording of the song. The effect of the lack of exposure can therefore not be tested. The fact that a reward for learning is included additionally complicates the experiment described in choice **c**, as it adds extra variables.

▶ Pretest Assessment

How did you do on the science pretest? If you answered seven or more questions correctly, you have earned the equivalent of a passing score on the GED Science Exam. But remember that this pretest only covers a fraction of the material you might face on the GED Science Exam. It is *not* designed to give you an accurate measure of how you would do on the actual test. Rather, it is designed to help you determine where to focus your study efforts. For success on the GED Science Exam, review all of the chapters in this section thoroughly. Focus on the sections that correspond to the pretest questions you answered incorrectly.

25 ▶ About the GED Science Exam

To prepare effectively for the GED Science Exam, you need to know exactly what the test is like. This chapter explains the structure of the exam, including the types of questions you will be asked and the topics that will be tested.

▶ What to Expect on the GED Science Exam

The science portion of the GED consists of 50 multiple-choice questions designed to evaluate your understanding of general science concepts. Each question is followed by five answer choices labeled **a** to **e**. You will be instructed to select the best answers to the question. There is no penalty for guessing. You will have 80 minutes (one hour 20 minutes) to answer the questions on this part of the exam. There will be some question sets—i.e., more than one question will be asked about a particular graphic or passage.

Types of Questions

On the test, you will encounter *conceptual understanding* and *problem-solving* questions that are based either on information provided on the test, or on information learned through life experience.

A question that tests your conceptual understanding requires you to *show* your understanding of the material presented as a part of the question. In this type of question, you could be asked to:

- read a graphic
- summarize the results of an experiment
- rephrase a fact or an idea described in a passage
- find supporting detail in a passage

- make a generalization about information presented in the question
- understand cause and effect

Problem-solving questions will ask you to *apply* your understanding of information presented as part of the question. Questions of this type could require you to:

- interpret results
- draw conclusions based on results
- analyze experimental flaws or logical fallacies in arguments
- make a prediction based on information provided in the question
- select the best procedure or method to accomplish a scientific goal
- select a diagram that best illustrates a principle
- apply scientific knowledge to everyday life
- use the work of renowned scientists to explain everyday global issues

Some questions will require you to draw on knowledge you have acquired through your daily life and prior schooling. In other questions, all the necessary information will be included in the passage or graphic provided as part of the question. In either case, reviewing basic science concepts presented in the following chapters, and answering as many practice questions as you can, will improve your performance.

Up to 60% of the problems on the GED Science Exam will require you to understand, interpret, or apply information presented in graphical form. Graphical information includes diagrams, charts, and graphs. Graphics are a concise and organized way of presenting information. Once you realize that all graphics have some common basic elements, it will not matter whether the information presented in them is in the area of biology, chemistry, physics, or Earth science.

Test Topics

The topics covered on the GED Science Exam are:

- **physical science**—35% of the questions
- **life science**—45% of the questions
- **Earth and space science**—20% of the questions

On the GED Science Exam, physical science includes high school physics and chemistry and covers the structure of atoms, the structure of matter, the properties of matter, chemical reactions, conservation of mass and energy, increase in disorder, the laws of motion, forces, and the interactions of energy and matter.

Life science deals with subjects covered in high school biology classes, including cell structure, heredity, biological evolution, behavior, and interdependence of organisms.

Earth and space science GED questions will test your knowledge of the Earth and solar system, the geochemical cycles, the origin and evolution of the Earth and the universe, and energy in the Earth system.

National Standards and the GED

In accordance with Education Standards set forth by the National Academy of Sciences, the GED Science Exam has been modified to include more interdisciplinary questions. These questions also fall into one of the three major categories (physical science, life science, and Earth and space science) but focus on themes common to all sciences. Common themes include the scientific method, the organization of knowledge, applications in technology and everyday situations, and the development of scientific ideas through history. Since many of the GED Science questions will be interdisciplinary, a chapter will cover each of the following themes:

- unifying concepts and processes
- science as inquiry
- science and technology
- science and personal and social perspectives
- history and nature of science

Unifying concepts and processes in science questions test your knowledge of the organization of scientific knowledge, development of scientific models based on experimental evidence, equilibrium, evolution, change, conservation, measurement, and relationship between form and function.

Science as inquiry questions require you to summarize and interpret experimental results, select relevant information, select the best plan for an investigation, understand and apply the scientific method, make a prediction or draw a conclusion based on given facts, and evaluate the source of experimental flaws and error.

Science and technology questions require you to understand: the function of an instrument, instructions for operating an instrument, technological processes, the elements of technological design, how technology uses scientific knowledge to improve products and processes, and the impact of technology on science, human life, and on the environment.

Science and personal and social perspectives questions cover human health (nutrition, exercise, disease prevention, genetics), climate, pollution, population growth, natural resources, social impact of natural disasters, human-induced environmental hazards, public policy, application of scientific knowledge to everyday situations, and application of scientific knowledge to explain global phenomena. These questions are quite common.

History and nature of science questions could include a passage on the development of an idea or theory through time, or the work of an important scientist. You can also expect to see general questions about the development of science as a field and its principles.

The chart below summarizes the approximate breakdown of question types and subjects covered in the questions on the GED Science Exam:

GED SCIENCE EXAM
50 QUESTIONS, 80 MINUTES

Type:	*conceptual understanding* questions and *problem-solving* questions
Format:	questions based on *text passages* and questions based on *visual text* (graphs, charts, tables, or diagrams)
Subject:	45% life science questions, 35% physical science questions, 20% Earth and space science questions
Content:	up to 60% of the questions are based on visual text; about 25% of the questions are grouped into question sets based on shared material, such as a passage or a diagram

In addition to the interdisciplinary questions, other recent changes to the GED Science Exam include:

- increased focus on environmental and health topics (recycling, heredity, prevention of disease, pollution, and climate)
- increased focus on science as found in daily life
- increased number of single item questions
- decreased number of questions based on the same passage/graphic

Now that you have a better idea of the kind of questions that may appear on the GED Science Exam, you can start reviewing the basic science concepts described in the next chapters.

26▶ Unifying Concepts and Processes

This chapter will review some of the unifying concepts and processes in science. You will learn the questions and themes that are common to each of the scientific disciplines and how scientists seek to answer those questions.

WHETHER THEY ARE chemists, biologists, physicists, or geologists, all scientists seek to organize the knowledge and observations they collect. They look for evidence and develop models to provide explanations for their observations. Scientists depend heavily on measurement and developed devices and instruments for measuring different properties of matter and energy. Scientists also use units to make the quantities they measure understandable to other scientists. Questions that come up in every science are:

- What causes change?
- What causes stability?
- How does something evolve?
- How does something reach equilibrium?
- How is form related to function?

▶ Systems, Order, and Organization

What happens when an Internet search produces too many results? Clearly, having some results is better than having none, but having too many can make it difficult to find the necessary information quickly. If scientists didn't systematically organize and order information, looking for or finding a piece of data or making a comparison would be as difficult as looking for one specific book in a huge library in which the books are randomly shelved. In every science knowledge is grouped into an orderly manner.

In biology, an organism is classified into a domain, kingdom, phylum, class, order, family, genus, and species. Members of the same species are the most similar. All people belong to the same species. People and monkeys belong to the same order. People and fish belong to the same kingdom, and people and plants share the same domain. This is an example of **hierarchical classification**—each level is included in the levels previously listed. Each species is part of an order, and each order is part of a kingdom, which is a part of a domain.

Another example of hierarchical classification is your address in the galaxy. It would include your house number, street, city, state, country, continent, planet, star system, and galaxy.

Here is another example of organization in biology. Each organism is made of cells. Many cells make up a tissue. Several tissues make up an organ. Several organs make up an organ system.

In chemistry, atoms are sorted by atomic number in the periodic table. Atoms that have similar properties are grouped.

Scientists also classify periods of time since Earth's formation 4.6 billion years ago, based on the major events in those eras. Time on Earth is divided into the following eras: Precambrian, Paleozoic, Mesozoic, and Cenozoic. The eras are further divided into periods, and the periods into epochs.

▶ Evidence, Models, and Explanation

Scientists look for evidence. The job of a scientist is to observe and explain the observations using factual evidence, and develop models that can predict unobserved behavior.

Scientific evidence should:
- be carefully documented and organized
- be quantified as much as possible
- be reproducible by other scientists

Scientific explanations should:
- be consistent with observations and evidence
- be able to predict unobserved behavior
- be internally consistent (two statements in the same explanation should not contradict each other)

Scientific models should:
- be consistent with observations
- be consistent with explanations
- be able to predict unobserved behavior
- cover a wide range of observations or behaviors

▶ Equilibrium and Change

A favorite pastime of scientists is figuring out why things change and why they stay the same. On one hand, many systems seek to establish equilibrium. In organisms, this equilibrium is called **homeostasis**. It is the tendency of organisms to maintain a stable inner environment, even when the outside environment changes. When people sweat, they are trying to cool off and maintain their equilibrium temperature.

Contrary to a common misconception, equilibrium is not a state of rest at which nothing happens. At chemical equilibrium, reactants continue to form products, and products continue to form reactants. However, the rate of formation of reactants is the same as the rate of formation of products, so that no net change is observed.

Equilibria are fragile states, and a little change, a tiny force, is often enough to disturb them. Think of a seesaw in balance. A little puff of wind, and the balance is gone. The same is true of chemical equilibrium—increase the pressure or temperature, and the equilibrium will shift. Your body is pretty good at keeping a steady temperature, but when you get sick, you are thrown out of balance; up goes your temperature, and out the window goes your homeostasis.

A change is often a response to a gradient or a difference in a property in two parts of a system. Here are some examples of common gradients and the changes they drive.

- Difference in **temperature**—causes heat to flow from hotter object (region) to colder object (region).

- Difference in **pressure**—causes liquid (water) or gas (air) to flow from region of high pressure to region of low pressure.
- Difference in **electric potential**—causes electrons to flow from high potential to low potential.
- Difference in **concentration**—causes matter to flow until concentrations in two regions are equalized.

▶ Measurement

An established principle in science is that observations should be quantified as much as possible. This means that rather than reporting that it's a nice day out, a scientist needs to define this statement with numbers. By *nice,* two different people can mean two different things. Some like hot weather. Some like lots of snow. But giving the specifics on the temperature, humidity, pressure, wind speed and direction, clouds, and rainfall allows everyone to picture *exactly what kind* of a nice day we are having.

For the same reason, a scientist studying the response of dogs to loud noise wouldn't state that the dog hates it when it's loud. A scientist would quantify the amount of noise in decibels (units of sound intensity) and carefully note the behavior and actions of the dog in response to the sound, without making judgment about the dog's deep feelings. Now that you are convinced that quantifying observations is a healthy practice in science, you will probably agree that instruments and units are also useful.

In the following table are the most common properties scientists measure and common units these properties are measured in. You don't need to memorize these, but you can read them to become acquainted with the ones you don't already know.

You should also be familiar with the following devices and instruments used by scientists:

- **balance:** for measuring mass
- **graduated cylinder:** for measuring volume (the bottom of the curved surface of water should always be read)
- **thermometer:** for measuring temperature
- **voltmeter:** for measuring potential
- **microscope:** for observing very small objects, such as cells
- **telescope:** for observing very distant objects, such as other planets

COMMON UNITS OF MEASURE

Length or distance	meter (about a yard)
	centimeter (about half an inch)
	micrometer (about the size of a cell)
	nanometer (often used for wavelengths of light)
	angstrom (about the size of an atom)
	kilometer (about half a mile)
	light-year (used for astronomical distances)
Time	second, hour, year, century
Volume	milliliter (about a teaspoon), liter (about $\frac{1}{4}$ of a gallon)
Temperature	degree Celsius, degree Fahrenheit, or Kelvin
Charge	coulomb
Electric potential	volt
Pressure	atmosphere, mm of Hg, bar
Force	newton

► Evolution

Most students tend to associate evolution with the biological evolution of species. However, **evolution** is a series of changes, either gradual, or abrupt in any type of system. Even theories and technological designs can evolve.

Ancient cultures classified matter into fire, water, earth, and air. This may sound naive and funny now, but it was a start. The important thing was to ask what is matter, and to start grouping different forms of matter in some way. As more observations were collected, our understanding of matter evolved. We started out with air, fire, earth, and water, and got to the periodic table, the structure of the atom, and the interaction of energy and matter.

Consider how the design of cars and airplanes has changed over time. Think of a little carriage with crooked wheels pulled by a horse and a plane with propellers. The car and the plane have evolved as well.

So did our planet. According to theory, 200 million years ago all the present continents formed one supercontinent. Twenty million years later, the supercontinent began to break apart. The Earth is still evolving, changing through time, as its plates are still moving and the core of the Earth is still cooling.

► Form and Function

There is a reason why a feather is light as a feather. In both nature and technology, form is often related to function. A bird's feathers are light, enabling it to fly more easily. Arteries spread into tiny capillaries, increasing the surface area for gas exchange. Surface area and surface to volume ratio are key issues in biology and chemistry. A cell has a relatively large surface to volume ratio. If it were larger, this ratio would increase. Through the surface, the cell regulates the transport of matter in and out of the cell. If the cell had a bigger volume, it would require more nutrients and produce more waste, and the area for exchange would be insufficient. Notice the difference between the leaves of plants that grow in hot dry climates and the leaves of plants in cooler, wetter climates. What function do the differences in form serve? Did you realize that a flock of birds tends to fly forming the shape much like the tip of an arrow? Several years ago, curved skis were brought onto the market and have almost replaced traditional straight-edge skis. There are countless examples of how form develops to serve a useful function. Your job is to open your eyes to these relationships and be prepared to make the connections on the GED Science Exam.

This chapter has shown you that there are common threads in all areas of science and that scientists in different disciplines use similar techniques to observe the patterns and changes in nature. Try to keep these key principles in mind, since they are bound to reappear—not only on the GED, but in your daily life as well.

27 ▶ Science as Inquiry

Whatever their discipline, all scientists use similar methods to study the natural world. In this chapter, you will learn what abilities are necessary for scientific inquiry and what lies at the root of all science.

ALL SCIENCES ARE the same in the sense that they involve the deliberate and systematic observation of nature. Each science is not a loose branch. The branches of science connect to the same root of objective observation, experiments based on the scientific method, and theories and conclusions based on experimental evidence. An advance in one branch of science often contributes to advances in other sciences, and sometimes to entirely new branches. For example, the development of optics led to the design of a microscope, which led to the development of cellular biology.

▶ Abilities Necessary to Do Scientific Inquiry

A good scientist is patient, curious, objective, systematic, ethical, a detailed record keeper, skeptical yet open-minded, and an effective communicator. While there are certainly many scientists who don't posses all these qualities, most strive to obtain or develop them.

Patience
Patience is a virtue for any person, but it is essential for a person who wants to be a scientist. Much of science involves repetition. Repetition to confirm or reproduce previous results, repetition under slightly different conditions, and

repetition to eliminate an unwanted variable. It also involves waiting—waiting for a liquid to boil to determine its boiling point, waiting for an animal to fall asleep in order to study its sleep pattern, waiting for weather conditions or a season to be right, etc. Both the repetition and the waiting require a great deal of patience. Results are not guaranteed, and a scientist often goes through countless failed attempts before achieving success. Patience and the pursuit of results in spite of difficulties are traits of a good scientist.

Curiosity

Every child asks questions about nature and life. In some people, this curiosity continues throughout adulthood, when it becomes possible to systematically work to satisfy that curiosity with answers. Curiosity is a major drive for scientific research, and it is what enables a scientist to work and concentrate on the same problem over long periods of time. It's the knowing of the how and the why, or at least a part of the answer to these questions, that keeps a scientist in the lab, on the field, in the library, or at the computer for hours.

Objectivity

Objectivity is an essential trait of a true scientist. By objectivity, we mean unbiased observation. A good scientist can distinguish fact from opinion and does not let personal views, hopes, beliefs, or societal norms interfere with the observation of facts or reporting of experimental results. An **opinion** is a statement not necessarily supported by scientific data. Opinions are often based on personal feelings or beliefs and are usually difficult, if not impossible to measure and test. On the GED Science Exam, answer choices that are opinions will almost always be incorrect answer choices. A **fact** is a statement based on scientific data or objective observations. Facts can be measured or observed, tested and reproduced. A well-trained scientist recognizes the importance of reporting all results, even if they are unexpected, undesirable, or inconsistent with personal views, prior hypothesis, theories, or experimental results.

Systematic Study

Scientists who are effective experimentalists tend to work systematically. They observe each variable independently, and develop and adhere to rigorous experimental routines or procedures. They keep consistent track of all variables and systematically look for changes in those variables. The tools and methods by which changes in variables are measured or observed are kept constant. All experiments have a clear objective. Good scientists never lose track of what the purpose of the experiment is and design experiments in such a way that the amount of results is not overwhelming and that the results obtained are not ambiguous. The scientific method, which will be described later in this chapter, forms a good basis for systematic research.

Record Keeping

Good record keeping can save scientists a lot of trouble. Most scientists find keeping a science log or journal helpful. The journal should describe in detail the basic assumptions, goals, experimental techniques, equipment, and procedures. It can also include results, analysis of results, literature references, thoughts and ideas, and conclusions. Any problem encountered in the laboratory should also be noted in the journal, even if it is not directly related to the experimental goals. For example, if there is an equipment failure, it should be noted. Conditions that brought about the failure and the method used to fix it should also be described. It may not seem immediately useful, but three years down the road, the same failure could occur. Even if the scientist recollected the previous occurrence of the problem, the details of the solution would likely be forgotten and more time would be needed to fix it. But looking back to the journal could potentially pin down the problem and provide a solution much more quickly. Scientific records should be clear and readable, so that another scientist could follow the thoughts and repeat the procedure described. Records can also prove useful if there is a question about intellectual property or ethics of the researcher.

Effective Communication

Reading scientific journals, collaborating with other scientists, going to conferences, and publishing scientific papers and books are basic elements of communication in the science community. Scientists benefit from exploring science literature because they can often use techniques, results, or methods published by other scientists. In addition, new results need to be compared or connected to related results published in the past, so that someone reading or hearing about the new result can understand its impact and context.

As many scientific branches have become interdisciplinary, collaboration among scientists of different backgrounds is essential. For example, a chemist may be able to synthesize and crystallize a protein, but analyzing the effect of that protein on a living system requires the training of a biologist. Rather than viewing each other as competition, good scientists understand that they have a lot to gain by collaborating with scientists who have different strengths, training, and resources. Presenting results at scientific conferences and in science journals is often a fruitful and rewarding process. It opens up a scientific theory or experiment to discussion, criticism, and suggestions. It is a ground for idea inception and exchange in the science community.

Scientists also often need to communicate with those outside the scientific community—students of science, public figures who make decisions about funding science projects, and journalists who report essential scientific results to the general audience.

Skepticism and Open-Mindedness

Scientists are trained to be skeptical about what they hear, read, or observe. Rather than automatically accept the first explanation that is proposed, they search for different explanations and look for holes in reasoning or experimental inconsistencies. They come up with tests that a theory should pass if it is valid. They think of ways in which an experiment can be improved. This is not done maliciously. The goal is not to discredit other researchers, but to come up with good models and understanding of nature.

Unreasonable skepticism, however, is not very useful. There is a lot of room in science for open-mindedness. If a new theory is in conflict with intuition or belief or previously established theories, but is supported by rigorously developed experiments, and can be used to make accurate predictions, refusal to accept its validity is stubbornness, rather than skepticism.

Ethics

Consider a chemist in the pharmaceutical company who, after much effort, designs a chemical that can cure brain tumors without affecting healthy brain cells. No doubt the scientist is excited about this result and its potential positive impact on humanity. Once in a while, however, experimental rats given this drug die from heart failure within minutes after the drug is administered. But since it happens only occasionally, the scientist assumes that it's only a coincidence, and that those rats that died had heart problems and would have died anyway. The scien-

tist doesn't report these few cases to the supervisor, and assumes that if it's a serious problem, the FDA (Food and Drug Administration) would discover it, and nobody would get hurt. While the scientist has good intentions, such as making the benefits of the new drug available to people who need it, failing to report and further investigate the potential adverse effects of the drug constitutes negligent and unethical behavior.

Scientists are expected to report data without making up, adjusting, downplaying, or exaggerating results. Scientist are also expected to not take credit for work they didn't do, to obey environmental laws, and to consider and understand the implications of the use of scientific knowledge they bring about.

▶ Understandings about Scientific Inquiry

Why study science? A scientist seeks to observe, understand, or control the processes and laws of nature. Scientists assume that nature is governed by orderly principles. They search for these principles by making observations. The job of a scientist is to figure out how something works, or to explain why it works the way it does. Looking for a pattern, for cause and effect, explanation, improvement, developing theories based on experimental results are all jobs of a scientist.

▶ The Scientific Method

There are many ways to obtain knowledge. Modern scientists tend to obtain knowledge about the world by making systematic observations. This principle is called **empiricism** and is the basis of the **scientific method**. The scientific method is a set of rules for asking and answering questions about science. Most scientists use the scientific method loosely and often unconsciously. However, the key concepts of the scientific method are the groundwork for scientific study, and we will review those concepts in this section.

The scientific method involves:

- asking a specific question about a process or phenomenon that can be answered by performing experiments

- formulating a testable hypothesis based on observations and previous results (i.e., making a guess)
- designing an experiment, with a control, to test the hypothesis
- collecting and analyzing the results of the experiment
- developing a model or theory that explains the phenomenon and is consistent with experimental results
- making predictions based on the model or theory in order to test it and designing experiments that could disprove the proposed theory

The Question

In order to understand something, a scientist must first focus on a specific question or aspect of a problem. In order to do that, the scientist has to clearly formulate the question. The answer to such a question has to exist and the possibility of obtaining it through experiment must exist. For example, the question "Does the presence of the moon shorten the life span of ducks on Earth?" is not valid because it cannot be answered through experiment. There is no way to measure the life span of ducks on Earth in the absence of the moon, since we have no way of removing the moon from its orbit. Similarly, asking a general question, such as "How do animals obtain food?" is not very useful for gaining knowledge. This question is too general and broad for one person to answer.

Better questions are more specific—for example, "Does each member of a wolf pack have a set responsibility or job when hunting for food?" A question that is too general and not very useful is "Why do some people have better memories than others?" A better, more specific question, along the same lines, is "What parts of the brain and which brain chemicals are involved in recollection of childhood memories?"

> A good science question is very specific and can be answered by performing experiments.

The Hypothesis

After formulating a question, a scientist gathers the information on the topic that is already available or published, and then comes up with an educated guess or a tentative explanation about the answer to the question. Such an educated guess about a natural process or phenomenon is called a **hypothesis**.

A hypothesis doesn't have to be correct, but it should be testable. In other words, a testable hypothesis can be disproved through experiment, in a reasonable amount of time, with the resources available. For example, the statement "Everyone has a soul mate somewhere in the world" is not a valid hypothesis. First of all, the term *soul mate* is not well defined, so formulating an experiment to determine whether two people are soul mates would be difficult. More important, even if we were to agree on what *soul mate* means and how to experimentally determine whether two people are soul mates, this hypothesis could never be proved wrong. Any experiment conceived would require testing every possible pair of human beings around the world, which, considering the population and the population growth per second, is just not feasible.

> A hypothesis can be a suggested explanation or an educated guess. Keep in mind that it doesn't need to be correct—it only has to be testable.

Disproving a hypothesis is not a failure. It casts away illusions about what was previously thought to be true, and can cause a great advance—a thought in another direction that can bring about new ideas. Most likely, in the process of showing that one hypothesis is wrong, a scientist may gain an understanding of what a better hypothesis may be. Disproving a hypothesis serves a purpose. Science and our understanding of nature often advance through tiny incremental pieces of information. Eliminating a potential hypothesis narrows down the choices, and eliminating the wrong answers sometimes leads to finding the correct one.

The Experiment

In an experiment, researchers manipulate one or more variables and examine their effect on another variable or variables. An experiment is carefully designed to test the hypothesis. The number of variables in an experiment should be manageable and carefully controlled. All variables and procedures are carefully defined and described, as is the method of observation and measurement.

Results of a valid experiment are reproducible, meaning that another researcher, following the same procedure should be able to obtain the same result.

A good experiment also includes one or more controls. Experimental controls are designed to get an understanding of the observed variables in the absence of the manipulated variables. For example, in pharmaceutical studies, three groups of patients are examined. One is given the drug, one is given a placebo (a pill containing no active ingredient), and one is not given anything. This is a good way to test whether the improvement in patient condition (observed variable) is due to the active ingredient in the pill (manipulated variable). If the patients in the group that was given the placebo recover sooner or at the same time as those who were given the drug, the effect of pill taking can be attributed to patient belief that a pill makes one feel better, or to other ingredients in the pill. If the group that was not given any pill recovers faster or just as fast as the group that was given the drug, the improvement in patient condition could be a result of the natural healing processes.

> An experimental control is a version of the experiment in which all conditions and variables are the same as in other versions of the experiment, but the variable being tested is eliminated or changed. A good experiment should include carefully designed controls.

The Analysis

Analysis of experimental results involves looking for trends in the data and correlation among variables. It also involves making generalizations about the results, quantifying experimental error, and correlation of the variable being manipulated to the variable being tested. A scientist who analyzes results unifies them, interprets them, and gives them a meaning. The goal is to find a pattern or sense of order in the observations and to understand the reason for this order.

Models and Theories

After collecting a sufficient amount of consistently reproducible results under a range of conditions or in different kinds of samples, scientists often seek to formulate a theory or a model. A **model** is a hypothesis that is sufficiently general and is continually effective in predicting facts yet to be observed. A **theory** is an explanation of the general principles of certain observations with extensive experimental evidence or facts to support it.

Scientific models and theories, like hypotheses, should be testable using available resources. Scientists make predictions based on their models and theories. A good theory or model should be able to accurately predict an event or behavior. Many scientists go a step beyond and try to test their theories by designing experiments that could prove them wrong. The theories that fail to make accurate predictions are revised or discarded, and those that survive the test of a series of experiments aimed to prove them wrong become more convincing. Theories and models therefore lead to new experiments; if they don't adequately predict behavior, they are revised through development of new hypotheses and experiments. The cycle of experiment-theory-experiment continues until a satisfactory understanding that is consistent with observations and predictions is obtained.

CHAPTER

28 ▶ Physical Science

Physical science includes the disciplines of chemistry (the study of matter) and physics (the study of energy and how energy affects matter). The questions on the physical science section of the GED will cover topics taught in high school chemistry and physics courses. This chapter reviews the basic concepts of physical science—the structure of atoms, the structure and properties of matter, chemical reactions, motions and forces, conservation of energy, increase in disorder, and interactions of energy and matter.

▶ The Structure of Atoms

You and everything around you are composed of tiny particles called atoms. The book you are reading from, the neurons in your brain, and the air that you are breathing can all be described as a collection of various atoms.

History of the Atom

The term **atom**, which means *indivisible*, was coined by Greek philosopher Democritus (460–370 B.C.). He disagreed with Plato and Aristotle—who believed that matter could infinitely be divided into smaller and smaller pieces—and postulated that matter is composed of tiny indivisible particles. In spite of Democritus, the belief that matter could be infinitely divided lingered until the early 1800s, when John Dalton formulated a meaningful atomic theory. It stated:

- Matter is composed of atoms.
- All atoms of a given element are identical.
- Atoms of different elements are different and have different properties.
- Atoms are neither created nor destroyed in a chemical reaction.

- Compounds are formed when atoms of more than one element combine.
- A given compound always has the same relative number and kind of atoms.

These postulates remain at the core of physical science today, and we will explore them in more detail in the following sections.

Protons, Neutrons, and Electrons

An atom is the smallest unit of matter that has a property of a chemical element. It consists of a nucleus surrounded by electrons. The nucleus contains positively charged particles called protons, and uncharged neutrons. Each neutron and each proton have a mass of about 1 atomic mass unit, abbreviated **amu**. An amu is equivalent to about 1.66×10^{-24} g. The number of protons in an element is called the atomic number. Electrons are negatively charged and orbit the nucleus in what are called electron shells.

Electrons in the outermost shell are called valence electrons. Valence electrons are most responsible for the properties and reaction patterns of an element. The mass of an electron is more than 1,800 times smaller than the mass of a proton or a neutron. When calculating atomic mass, the mass of electrons can safely be neglected. In a neutral atom, the number of protons and electrons is equal. The negatively charged electrons are attracted to the positively charged nucleus. This attractive force holds an atom together. The nucleus is held together by strong nuclear forces.

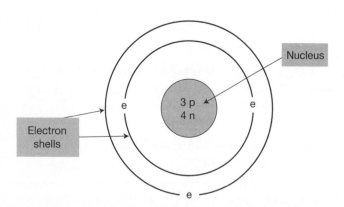

A representation of a lithium atom (Li). It has 3 protons (p) and 4 neutrons (n) in the nucleus, and 3 electrons (e) in the two electron shells. Its atomic number is 3 (p). Its atomic mass is 7 amu (p + n). The atom has no net charge because the number of positively charged protons equals the number of negatively charged electrons.

Charges and Masses of Atomic Particles

	Proton	Neutron	Electron
Charge	+1	0	-1
Mass	1 amu	1 amu	$\frac{1}{1,800}$ amu

Isotopes

The number of protons in an element is always the same. In fact, the number of protons is what defines an element. However, the number of neutrons in the atomic nucleus, and thus the atomic weight, can vary. Atoms that contain the same number of protons and electrons, but a different number of neutrons are called **isotopes**. The atomic masses of elements in the periodic table are weighted averages for different isotopes. This explains why the atomic mass (the number of protons plus the number of neutrons) is not a whole number. For example, most carbon atoms have 6 protons and 6 neutrons, giving it a mass of 12 amu. This isotope of carbon is called "carbon twelve" (carbon-12). But the atomic mass of carbon in the periodic table is listed as 12.011. The mass is not simply 12, because other isotopes of carbon have 5, 7, or 8 neutrons, and all of the isotopes and their abundance are considered when the average atomic mass is reported.

Ions

An atom can lose or gain electrons and become charged. An atom that has lost or gained one or more electrons is called an **ion**. If an atom loses an electron, it becomes a positively charged ion. If it gains an electron, it becomes a negatively charged ion. For example, calcium (Ca), a biologically important element, can lose two electrons to become an ion with a positive charge of +2 (Ca^{2+}). Chlorine (Cl) can gain an electron to become an ion with a negative charge of -1 (Cl^-).

The Periodic Table

The periodic table is an organized list of all known elements, arranged in order of increasing atomic number, such that elements with the same number of valence electrons, and therefore similar chemical properties, are found in the same column, called **group**. For example, the last column in the periodic table lists the inert (noble) gases, such as helium and neon—highly unreactive elements. A row in the periodic table is called a period. Elements that share the same row all have the same number of electron shells.

Common Elements

Some elements are frequently encountered in biologically important molecules and everyday life. Here, you will find a list of common elements, their symbols, and common uses.

H—Hydrogen: involved in the nuclear process that produces energy in the Sun, found in many organic molecules within our bodies (like fats and carbohydrates) and in gases (like methane)

He—Helium: used to make balloons fly

C—Carbon: found in all living organisms; pure carbon exists as graphite and diamonds

N—Nitrogen: used as a coolant to rapidly freeze food, found in many biologically important molecules, such as proteins

O—Oxygen: essential for respiration (breathing) and combustion (burning)

Si—Silicon: used in making transistors and solar cells

Cl—Chlorine: used as a disinfectant in pools and as a cleaning agent in bleach, and is also important physiologically as well, for example within the nervous system

Ca—Calcium: necessary for bone formation and muscle contraction

Fe—Iron: used as a building material; carries oxygen in the blood

Cu—Copper: a U.S. penny is made of copper; good conductor of electricity

I—Iodine: lack in the diet results in an enlarged thyroid gland, or goiter

Hg—Mercury: used in thermometers; ingestion can cause brain damage and poisoning

Pb—Lead: used for X-ray shielding in a dentist office

Na—Sodium: Found in table salt (NaCl), also important biologically within the nervous system and is a key player in the active transport process that occurs across cell membranes

Some elements exist in diatomic form (two atoms of such an element are bonded), and technically, they are molecules. These elements include hydrogen (H_2), nitrogen (N_2), oxygen (O_2), fluorine (F_2), chlorine (Cl_2), bromine (Br_2), and iodine (I_2).

▶ Structure and Properties of Matter

Matter has mass and takes up space. The building blocks of matter are atoms and molecules. Matter can interact with other matter and with energy. These interactions form the basis of chemical and physical reactions.

Molecules

Molecules are composed of two or more atoms. Atoms are held together in molecules by chemical bonds. Chemical bonds can be ionic or covalent. Ionic bonds form when one atom donates one or more electrons to another. Covalent bonds form when the electrons are shared between atoms. The mass of a molecule can be calculated by adding the masses of the atoms that it is composed of. The number of atoms of a given element in a molecule is designated in a chemical formula by a subscript after the symbol for that element. For example, the glucose (blood sugar) molecule is represented as $C_6H_{12}O_6$. This formula tells you that the glucose molecule contains six carbon atoms (C), twelve hydrogen atoms (H), and six oxygen atoms (O).

Organic and Inorganic Molecules

Molecules are often classified as organic or inorganic. Organic chemistry is technically defined as the study of carbon compounds. However, traditionally, certain compounds that contain carbon were considered inorganic (such as CO, carbon monoxide and CO_2, carbon dioxide). In fact, a lot of chemists still consider these compounds to be inorganic. Many modern chemists consider organic molecules to be those that contain carbon and one or more other elements (such as hydrogen, nitrogen, and oxygen). Examples of organic compounds are methane (natural gas, CH_4), glycine (an amino acid, NH_2CH_2COOH), and ethanol (an alcohol, C_2H_5OH). Inorganic compounds include sodium chloride (table salt, NaCl), ammonia (NH_3), and water (H_2O).

States of Matter

Matter is held together by intermolecular forces—forces between different molecules. Three common states of matter are solid, liquid, and gas. Matter is an atom, a molecule (compound), or a mixture. Examples of matter in solid form are diamonds (carbon atoms), ice (water molecules), and metal alloys (mixtures of different metals). A solid has a fixed shape and a fixed volume. The molecules in a solid have a regular, ordered arrangement and vibrate in place, but are unable to move far.

Examples of matter in liquid form are mercury (mercury atoms), vinegar (molecules of acetic acid), and perfume (a mixture of liquids made of different molecules). Liquids have a fixed volume, but take the shape of the container they are in. Liquids flow and their density (mass per unit volume) is usually lower than the density of solids. The molecules in a liquid are not ordered and can move from one region to another, through a process called **diffusion**.

Examples of matter in gaseous form include helium gas used in balloons (helium atoms), water vapor (molecules of water), and air (mixture of different molecules including nitrogen, oxygen, carbon dioxide, and water vapor). Gases take the shape and volume of the container they are in. They can be compressed when pressure is applied. The molecules in gases are completely disordered and move very quickly. Gas density is much lower than the density of a liquid.

Phase Changes

Change of phase involves the transition from one state of matter into another. Freezing water to make ice for cooling your drink, condensation of water vapor as morning dew, and sublimation of dry ice (CO_2) are examples of phase changes. A phase change is a physical process. No chemical bonds are being formed or broken. Only the intermolecular (physical) forces are affected.

Freezing is the process of changing a liquid into a solid by removing heat. The opposite process whereby heat energy is added to the solid until it changes into a liquid is called **melting**. **Boiling** is the change of phase from a liquid to a gas and also requires the input of energy. **Condensation** is the change from gas to liquid. Some substances **sublime**—change directly from the solid phase to the gas phase, without forming the liquid state first. Carbon dioxide is such a substance. Solid carbon dioxide, called dry ice, evaporates into the gas phase when heated. When gas changes directly into a solid, the process is called **deposition**.

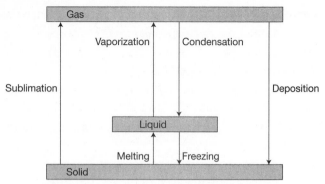

Phase changes between the three states of matter

The stronger the intermolecular forces are, the easier it is for the molecule to exist in one of the condensed states (liquid or gas) because these interactions among the molecules hold the solid or liquid together. For example, some neutral molecules have a positive end and a negative end even though, overall, the molecules have no net charge. Molecules such as these are considered **polar** and are attracted to each other by **dipole-dipole forces**. Molecules in which intermolecular forces are strong tend to have high boiling points, since these forces need to be overcome in order to turn the molecules into the gaseous state. This necessitates the input of more energy (heat).

Compounds and Mixtures

When two or more elements combine chemically, the result is a **compound**. Examples of compounds include carbon dioxide (a product of respiration), sucrose (table sugar), seratonin (a human brain chemical), and acetic acid (a component of vinegar). In each of these compounds, there is more than one type of atom, chemically bonded to other atoms in a definite proportion. The combination of these atoms also result in a fixed, definite structure.

When two or more elements combine physically, the result is a **mixture**. In a homogeneous mixture, the components can't be visually separated. Homogeneous mixtures also have the same composition (ratio of components) throughout their volume. An example is a mixture of a small amount of salt in water. A uniform mixture is often called a **solution**. In a solution, one substance (solute) is dissolved in another (solvent). In the salt and water mixture, the salt is the solute, and the water is the solvent. In a heterogeneous mixture, the components can often be visually identified, and the composition may vary from one point of the mixture to another. A collection of dimes and pennies is a heterogeneous mixture. A mixture of sugar and flour is also heterogeneous.

While both components (sugar and flour) are white, the sugar crystals are larger and can be identified.

Miscibility is the term used to describe the ability of two substances to form a homogeneous mixture. Water and alcohol are miscible. They can be mixed in such a way that the mixture will be uniform throughout the sample. At each point, it will look, smell, and taste the same. Oil and water are not miscible. A mixture of these two substances is not homogeneous, since the oil floats on water. In a mixture of oil and water, two layers containing the two components are clearly visible. Each layer looks, smells, tastes, and behaves differently.

▶ Chemical Reactions

Removing stains from clothes, digesting food, and burning wood in a fireplace are all examples of chemical reactions. Chemical reactions involve changes in the chemical arrangement of atoms. In a chemical reaction, the atoms of reactants combine, recombine or dissociate to form products. The number of atoms of a particular element remains the same before and after a chemical reaction. The total mass is also preserved. Similarly, energy is never created or destroyed by a chemical reaction. If chemical bonds are broken, energy from those bonds can be liberated into the surroundings as heat. However, this liberation of energy does not constitute creation, since the energy only changes form—from chemical to heat.

Writing Chemical Reactions

A chemical reaction can be represented by a chemical equation, where the reactants are written on the left side and the products on the right side of an arrow that indicates the direction in which the reaction proceeds. The following chemical equation represents the reaction of glucose ($C_6H_{12}O_6$) with oxygen (O_2) to form carbon dioxide (CO_2) and water (H_2O). Your body runs this reaction all the time to obtain energy.

$$(C_6H_{12}O_6) + 6\,(O_2) \rightarrow 6\,(CO_2) + 6\,(H_2O)$$

The numbers in front of the molecular formulas indicate the proportion in which the molecules react. No number in front of the molecule means that one molecule of that substance is reacting. In the previous reaction, one molecule of glucose is reacting with six molecules of oxygen to form six molecules of carbon

dioxide and six molecules of water. In reality, there are many molecules of each of the substances and the reaction tells you in what proportion the molecules react. So if you had ten molecules of glucose react with 60 molecules of oxygen, you would obtain 60 molecules of carbon dioxide and 60 molecules of water. In many ways, chemical equations are like food recipes.

$$2\ \text{Bread} + 1\ \text{Cheese} + 2\ \text{Tomato} \rightarrow \text{Sandwich}$$

With two slices of bread, one slice of cheese, and two slices of tomato, you can make one sandwich. If you had six slices of bread, three slices of cheese, and six slices of tomato, you could make three sandwiches. The same principles of proportion apply in chemical reactions.

Types of Chemical Reactions

Similar reactions can be classified and categorized into specific types of reactions. For example, chemical reactions can be classified as synthesis reactions, decomposition reactions, single-replacement reactions, and double-replacement reactions. Each of these reactions proceeds as you may expect by its name.

Synthesis Reaction

$A + B \rightarrow AB$

Decomposition Reaction

$AB \rightarrow A + B$

Single-Replacement Reaction

$C + AB \rightarrow CB + A$

Double-Replacement Reaction

$AB + CD \rightarrow AD + CB$

Just as in the sandwich equation previously described, the reactants will always combine in specific ratios to form the product. If two slices of bread are on the left side of the equation, then the sandwich formed on the right side will always have two slices, never one or three. If fours slices are on the left side, then you will end up with four slices on the right.

Look at the following synthesis reaction:

$$N2 + 3H2 \rightarrow 2NH3$$
$$\text{heat}$$

There are two nitrogen atoms on both sides of the equation. Also, there are six hydrogen atoms on each side of the equation. Matter is conserved.

Now look at this synthesis reaction involving ions:

$$2F^- + Ca^{2+} \rightarrow CaF^2$$

In addition to showing the conservation of matter, this example shows the conservation of charge. The two fluoride ions, each with a charge of –1 combine with a calcium ion which has a charge of +2. The product formed is neutral—the two –1 charges and the one +2 charge cancel each other out—charge is conserved.

In fact, all chemical reactions must conserve:

- matter (mass)
- energy
- electric charge

Heat of Reaction (Enthalpy)

The breaking of molecular bonds releases energy stored in those bonds. The energy is released in the form of heat. Similarly, the formation of new bonds requires an input of energy. Therefore, a chemical reaction will either absorb or give off heat, depending on how many and what kind of bonds are broken and made as a result of that reaction. A reaction that absorbs energy is called **endothermic**. A container in which an endothermic reaction takes place gets cold, because the heat of the container is absorbed by the reaction. A reaction that gives off energy is called **exothermic**. Burning gasoline is a reaction that is exothermic—it gives off energy.

Increase in Disorder (Entropy)

Disorder, or **entropy**, is the lack of regularity in a system. The more disordered a system, the larger its entropy. Disorder is much easier to come by than order. Imagine that you have 100 blue beads in one hand and 100 red beads in the other. Now place all of them in a cup and shake. What are the chances that you can pick out 100 beads in each hand so that they are separated by color, without looking? Not very likely! Entropy and chaos win. There is only one arrangement that leads to the ordered separation of beads (100 blue in one hand, 100 red in the other), and many arrangements that lead to mixed-up beads (33 blue, 67 red in one hand, 33 red and 67 blue in the other; 40 blue, 60 red in one hand, 60 blue, 40 red in the other . . .). The same is true of atoms. Sometimes

arrangement and order can be achieved. Atoms and molecules in solids, such as snowflakes, have very regular, ordered arrangements. But given enough time (and temperature), the snow melts, forming less ordered liquid water. So, although reactions that lead to a more ordered state are possible, the reactions that lead to disorder are more likely. The overall effect is that the disorder in the universe keeps increasing.

Catalysts

Often, a reaction needs help getting started. Such help can come from a **catalyst**. A catalyst is a substance or form of energy that gets a reaction going, without itself being changed or used up in the reaction. A catalyst acts by lowering what is called the **activation energy** of a reaction. The activation energy is often illustrated as a hill separating two valleys that needs to be crossed in order to get from one valley to the other (one valley representing the reactants, and the other the products). The catalyst acts by making the hill lower.

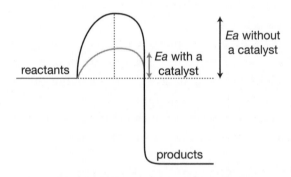

A catalyst acts by lowering the activation energy barrier (*Ea*) to product formation. In the diagram, the top hill represents a high activation energy. The catalyst acts to make the hill smaller, so that the bottom hill represents the activation energy in the presence of a catalyst.

Light is a catalyst for the photosynthesis reaction. In living systems reactions are catalyzed by special protein molecules called **enzymes**.

Reversible and Irreversible Reactions

Some reactions can proceed in both directions—reactants can form products, which can turn back into reactants. These reactions are called **reversible**. Other reactions are **irreversible**, meaning that reactants can form products, but once the products form, they cannot be turned back into reactants. While wood can burn (react with oxygen) to produce heat, water, and carbon dioxide, these products are unable to react to form wood. You can understand reversibility better if you look at the activation energy diagram in the previous section. The hill that needs to be crossed by reactants to form products is much lower than the hill that needs to be crossed by products to form reactants. Most likely, such a reaction will be irreversible. Now look at the following diagram. The hill that needs to be crossed is almost the same for reactants and for products, so the crossing could take place from both sides—the reaction would be reversible.

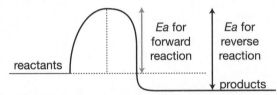

The activation energies *(Ea)* for the forward reaction (reactants forming products) and for the reverse reaction (products forming reactants) are about the same. Such a reaction is reversible.

▶ Motions, Forces, and Conservation of Energy

A **force** is a push or a pull. Objects move in response to forces acting on them. When you kick a ball it rolls. A force is also required to stop motion. The ball stops rolling because of the frictional force. What happens here? First your body breaks the chemical bonds in the food you have eaten. This supplies your body with energy. You use up some of that energy to kick the ball. You apply a force, and as a result the ball moves, carrying the energy your foot supplied it with. But some of that energy is transferred from the ball to the ground it rolls on in the form of heat, due to the frictional force it encounters on the surface of the ground. As energy is lost this way, the ball slows down. When all of the energy is used up through friction, the ball stops moving. This example illustrates the concept of conservation of energy, as well as Newton's first law—the Law of Inertia.

Law of Inertia

The velocity of an object does not change unless a force is applied.

What is the difference between speed and velocity? A speed, such as "30 miles per hour," has **magnitude**. A velocity has **magnitude and direction** (30 miles per hour, north). A similar distinction can be made in considering the difference in the terms **distance** and **displacement**. If you walk 20 feet to your mailbox and 20 feet back, the distance you traveled is 40 feet. Your **displacement** is zero, because displacement compares your ending point to the starting point.

Velocity is defined as the displacement divided by elapsed time. When you look at the change in velocity divided by the elapsed time, you are looking at **acceleration**. An acceleration that is negative (due to an ending velocity that is less than the starting velocity) is called a **deceleration**. For velocity of motion to change, either the speed and/or the direction must change and a net or unbalanced force must be applied. To summarize, an object at rest (whose speed is zero) remains at rest, unless some force acts on it—a person pushes it, the wind blows it away, gravity pulls it down . . . An object that is moving continues to move at the same speed in the same direction, unless some force is applied to it to slow it down, to speed it up, or to change its direction. The amount of acceleration or deceleration is directly proportional to the force applied. The harder you kick the ball, the faster it will move. The mass of the ball will also determine how much it will accelerate. Kick a soccer ball. Now kick a giant ball made of lead with the same force (watch your foot!). Which ball moves faster as a result of an equal kick? These observations constitute Newton's second law—the Law of Acceleration.

Law of Acceleration

The acceleration of an object depends on its mass and on the force applied to it. The greater the force, the greater the acceleration. The greater the mass, the lower the acceleration. Or, mathematically, *force = mass × acceleration* $(F = ma)$.

A good way to learn about the laws of motion is to shoot pool. What happens to billiard balls if you miss and fail to hit any of them? Nothing. They stay at rest. What happens when you hit the cue ball with the cue? It moves in the direction you hit it in. The harder you hit it, the faster it moves. Now, what happens when the cue ball collides with another ball? The other ball starts moving. The cue ball slows down. The energy is transferred from the cue ball to the ball it collided with. When an object exerts a force on a second object, the second object exerts an equal force in the opposite direction on the first object. This is Newton's third law—the Law of Interaction.

Law of Interaction

For every action, there is an equal and opposite reaction.

Types of Forces

Newton's laws do not depend on the type of force that is applied. Some types of forces include gravitational, electromagnetic, contact, and nuclear.

Gravitational Force

Gravitation is an attractive force that each object with mass exerts on any other object with mass. The strength of the gravitational force depends on the masses of the objects and on the distance between them. When we think of gravity, we usually think of Earth's gravity, which prevents us from jumping infinitely high, keeps our homes stuck to the ground, and makes things thrown upward fall down. We, too, exert a gravitational force on the Earth, and we exert forces on one another, but this is not very noticeable because our masses are very small in comparison with the mass of our planet. The greater the masses involved, the greater the gravitational force between them. The Sun exerts a force on the Earth, and the Earth exerts a force on the Sun. The moon exerts a force on the Earth, and the Earth on the moon. The gravitational force of the moon is the reason there are tides. The moon's gravity pulls the water on Earth. The Sun also exerts a force on our water, but this is not as apparent because the Sun, although more massive than the moon, is very far away. As the distance between two objects doubles, the gravitational force between them decreases four times.

Gravitation

Gravitation is an attractive force that exists among all objects. It is proportional to the masses of the objects and inversely proportional to the square of the distance between them.

What is the difference between weight and mass?

On Earth, the acceleration due to gravity, g, is -9.8 m/s^2. Your weight (w) is really a force. The formula $F = ma$ becomes $w = mg$. Since the acceleration, g, is -9.8 m/s^2, the overall force (w) is negative, which just means that its pull is in the downward direction: The Earth is pulling you towards its center. You have probably heard somebody say: "You weigh less on the moon!" This is true because the gravitational force on the moon is less than the Earth's gravitational force. Your mass, however, would still be the same, because mass is just a measure of how dense you are and the volume you take up.

Electromagnetic Force

Electricity and magnetism are two aspects of a single electromagnetic force. Moving electric charges produce magnetic forces, and moving magnets produce electric forces. The electromagnetic force exists between any two charged or magnetic objects, for example, a proton and an electron or two electrons. Opposite charges attract (an electron and a proton) while like charges repel (two protons or two electrons). The strength of the force depends on the charges and on the distance between them. The greater the charges, the greater the force. The closer the charges are to each other, the greater the force between them.

Contact Force

Contact forces are forces that exist as a result of an interaction between objects, physically in contact with one another. They include frictional forces, tensional forces, and normal forces.

The **friction force** opposes the motion of an object across a surface. For example, if a glass moves across the surface of the dinner table, there exists a friction force in the direction opposite to the motion of the glass. Friction is the result of attractive intermolecular forces between the molecules of the surface of the glass and the surface of the table. Friction depends on the nature of the two surfaces. For example, there would be less friction between the table and the glass if the table was moistened or lubricated with water. The glass would glide across the table more easily. Friction also depends on the degree to which the glass and the table are pressed together. Air resistance is a type of frictional force.

Tension is the force that is transmitted through a rope or wire when it is pulled tight by forces acting at each end. The tensional force is directed along the rope or wire and pulls on the objects on either end of the wire.

The **normal force** is exerted on an object in contact with another stable object. For example, the dinner table exerts an upward force on a glass at rest on the surface of the table.

Nuclear Force

Nuclear forces are very strong forces that hold the nucleus of an atom together. If nuclei of different atoms come close enough together, they can interact with one another and reactions between the nuclei can occur.

Forms of Energy

Energy is defined as the ability to do work. In addition, energy can't be created or destroyed. Energy can only change form. Forms of energy include potential energy and kinetic energy.

Potential energy is energy that is stored. **Kinetic energy** is the energy associated with motion. Look at the following illustration. As the pendulum swings, the energy is converted from potential to kinetic, and back to potential. When the hanging weight is at one of the high points, the gravitational potential energy is at a maximum, and kinetic energy is at the minimum. At the low point, the kinetic energy is maximized, and gravitational potential energy is minimized.

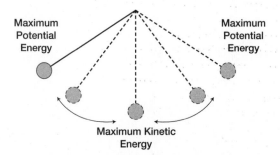

Maximum
Potential
Energy

Maximum
Potential
Energy

Maximum Kinetic
Energy

The change of potential energy into kinetic energy, and kinetic energy into potential energy, in a pendulum.

Examples of potential energy include nuclear energy and chemical energy—energy is stored in the bonds that hold atoms and molecules together. Heat, hydrodynamic energy, and electromagnetic waves are examples of kinetic energy—energy associated with the movement of molecules, water, and electrons or photons (increments of light).

▶ Interactions of Energy and Matter

Energy in all its forms can interact with matter. For example, when heat energy interacts with molecules of water, it makes them move faster and boil. Waves—including sound and seismic waves, waves on water, and light waves—have energy and can transfer that energy when they interact with matter. Consider what happens if you are standing by the ocean and a big wave rolls in. Sometimes the energy carried by the wave is large enough to knock you down.

Waves

Energy is also carried by electromagnetic waves or light waves. The energy of electromagnetic waves is related to their wavelengths. Electromagnetic waves include radio waves (the longest wavelength), microwaves, infrared radiation (radiant heat), visible light, ultraviolet radiation, X-rays, and gamma rays. The wavelength depends on the amount of energy the wave is carrying. Shorter wavelengths carry more energy.

When a wave hits a smooth surface, such as a mirror, it is reflected. Sound waves are reflected as echoes. Matter can also refract or bend waves. This is what happens when a ray of light traveling through air hits a water surface. A part of the wave is reflected, and a part is refracted into the water.

Each kind of atom or molecule can gain or lose energy only in particular discrete amounts. When an atom gains energy, light at the wavelength associated with that energy is absorbed. When an atom loses energy, light at the wavelength associated with that energy is emitted. These wavelengths can be used to identify elements.

Nuclear Reactions

In a nuclear reaction, energy can be converted to matter and matter can be converted to energy. In such processes, energy and matter are conserved, according to Einstein's formula $E = mc^2$, where E is the energy, m is the mass, and c is the speed of light. A nuclear reaction is different from a chemical reaction because in a nuclear reaction the particles in nuclei (protons and neutrons) interact, whereas in a chemical reaction, electrons are lost or gained by an atom. Two types of nuclear reactions are fusion and fission.

Fusion is a nuclear process in which two light nuclei combine to form one heavier nucleus. A fusion reaction releases an amount of energy more than a million times greater than the energy released in a typical chemical reaction. This gain in energy is accompanied by a loss of mass. The sum of the masses of the two light nuclei is lower than the mass of the heavier nucleus produced. This **mass defect** (the difference between the expected mass and the actual mass) is the m in Einstein's formula, and depending on how big m is, a proportional amount of energy will be released. Nuclear fusion reactions are responsible for the energy output of the Sun.

Fission is a nuclear process in which a heavy nucleus splits into two lighter nuclei. Fission was used in the first atomic bomb and is still used in nuclear power plants. Fission, like fusion, liberates a great amount of energy. The price for this energy is a loss in mass. A heavy nucleus that splits is heavier than the sum of the masses of the lighter nuclei that result.

Key Concepts

This chapter gave you a crash course in the basics of physical science. Here are the most important concepts to remember:

- All matter is composed of tiny particles called atoms.
- Matter cannot be created or destroyed, although it may change form.
- Atoms combine with other atoms to form molecules.
- In a chemical reaction, atoms in molecules rearrange to form other molecules.
- The three common states of matter are solid, liquid, and gas.
- The disorder in the universe is always increasing.
- Mass and energy can't be created or destroyed, although they may change forms
- Energy can change form and can be transferred in interactions with matter.

29 ▶ Life Science

Life science questions on the GED Science Exam cover the topics studied in high school biology classes. In this chapter, you will review the basics of biology and learn the answers to some of the key questions scientists ask about the nature of life and living beings.

LIFE SCIENCE EXPLORES the nature of living things, from the smallest building blocks of life to the larger principles that unify all living beings. Fundamental questions of life science include:

- What constitutes life?
- What are its building blocks and requirements?
- How are the characteristics of life passed on from generation to generation?
- How did life and different forms of life evolve?
- How do organisms depend on their environment and on one another?
- What kinds of behavior are common to living organisms?

Before Anthony van Leeuwenhoek looked through his homemade microscope more than 300 years ago, people didn't know that there were cells in our bodies and that there were microorganisms. Another common misconception was that fleas, ants, and other pests came from dust or wheat. Leeuwenhoek saw blood cells in blood, microorganisms in ponds, and showed that pests come from larvae that hatch from eggs laid by adult pests. However, it took more than 200 years for Leeuwenhoek's observations to gain wide acceptance and find application in medicine.

► The Cell

Today we know that a cell is the building block of life. Every living organism is composed of one or more cells. All cells come from other cells. Cells are alive. If blood cells, for example, are removed from the body, given the right conditions, they can continue to live independently of the body. They are made up of organized parts, perform chemical reactions, obtain energy from their surroundings, respond to their environments, change over time, reproduce, and share an evolutionary history.

All cells contain a membrane, cytoplasm, and genetic material. More complex cells also contain cell organelles. Here is a description of cell components and the functions they serve. Also, refer to the figures on the next page.

- **The cell wall** is made of cellulose, which surrounds, protects, and supports plant cells. Animal cells do not have a cell wall.
- **The plasma membrane** is the outer membrane of the cell. It carefully regulates the transport of materials in and out of the cell and defines the cell's boundaries. Membranes have selective permeability —meaning that they allow the passage of certain molecules, but not others. A membrane is like a border crossing. Molecules need the molecular equivalent of a valid passport and a visa to get through.
- **The nucleus** is a spherical structure, often found near the center of a cell. It is surrounded by a nuclear membrane and it contains genetic information inscribed along one or more molecules of DNA. The DNA acts as a library of information and a set of instructions for making new cells and cell components. In order to reproduce, every cell must be able to copy its genes to future generations. This is done by exact duplication of the DNA.
- **Cytoplasm** is a fluid found within the cell membrane, but outside of the nucleus.
- **Ribosomes** are the sites of protein synthesis. They are essential in cell maintenance and cell reproduction.
- **Mitochondria** are the powerhouses of the cell. They are the site of cellular respiration (breakdown of chemical bonds to obtain energy) and production of ATP (a molecule that provides energy for many essential processes in all organisms). Cells

that use a lot of energy, such as the cells of a human heart, have a large number of mitochondria. Mitochondria are unusual because unlike other cell organelles, they contain their own DNA and make some of their own proteins.

- **The endoplasmic reticulum** is a series of interconnecting membranes associated with the storage, synthesis, and transport of proteins and other materials within the cell.
- **The Golgi complex** is a series of small sacs that synthesizes, packages, and secretes cellular products to the plasma membrane. Its function is directing the transport of material within the cell and exporting material out of the cell.
- **Lysosomes** contain enzymes that help with intracellular digestion. Lysosomes have a large presence in cells that actively engage in phagocytosis—the process by which cells consume large particles of food. White blood cells that often engulf and digest bacteria and cellular debris are abundant in lysosomes.
- **Vacuoles** are found mainly in plants. They participate in digestion and the maintenance of water balance in the cell.
- **Centrioles** are cylindrical structures found in the cytoplasm of animal cells. They participate in cell division.
- **Chloroplasts** exist in the cells of plant leaves and in algae. They contain the green pigment chlorophyll and are the site of photosynthesis—the process of using sunlight to make high energy sugar molecules. Ultimately, the food supply of most organisms depends on photosynthesis carried out by plants in the chloroplasts.
- **The nucleolus** is located inside the nucleus. It is involved in the synthesis of ribosomes, which manufacture proteins.

In a multicellular organism, individual cells specialize in different tasks. For example, red blood cells carry oxygen, white blood cells fight pathogens, and cells in plant leaves collect the energy from sunlight. This cellular organization enables an organism to lose and replace individual cells, and outlive the cells that it is composed of. For example, you can lose dead skin cells and give blood and still go on living. This differentiation or division of labor in multicellular organisms is accomplished by expression of different genes.

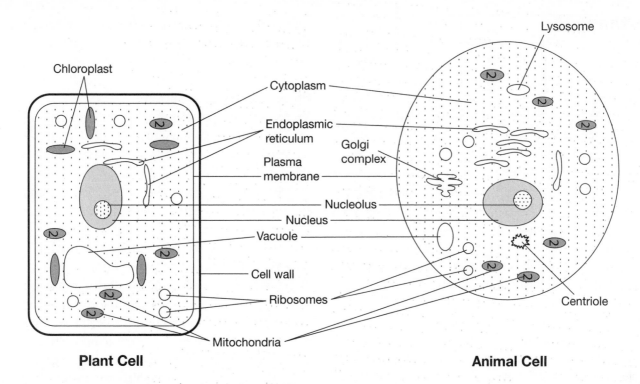

Plant Cell   **Animal Cell**

▶ Molecular Basis of Heredity

What an organism looks like and how it functions is largely determined by its genetic material. The basic principles of heredity were developed by Gregor Mendel, who experimented with pea plants in the nineteenth century. He mathematically analyzed the inherited traits (such as color and size) of a large number of plants over many generations. The units of heredity are genes carried on chromosomes. Genetics can explain why children look like their parents, and why they are, at the same time, not identical to the parents.

Phenotype and Genotype

The collection of physical and behavioral characteristics of an organism is called a **phenotype**. For example, your eye color, foot size, and ear shape are components of your phenotype. The genetic makeup of a cell or organism is called the **genotype**. The genotype is like a cookbook for protein synthesis and use. Phenotype (what an organism looks like or how it acts) is determined by the genotype (its genes) and its environment. By environment we don't mean the Earth, but the environment surrounding the cell. For example, hormones in the mother's body can influence the gene expression.

Reproduction

Asexual reproduction on the cellular level is called mitosis. It requires only one parent cell, which, after exactly multiplying its genetic material, splits in two. The resulting cells are genetically identical to each other and are clones of the original cell before it split.

Sexual reproduction requires two parents. Most cells in an organism that reproduces sexually have two copies of each chromosome, called **homologous pairs**—one from each parent. These cells reproduce through **mitosis**. Gamete cells (sperm and egg cells) are exceptions. They carry only one copy of each chromosome, so that there are only half as many chromosomes as in the other cells. For example, human cells normally contain 46 chromosomes, but human sperm and egg cells have 23 chromosomes. At fertilization, male and female gametes (sperm and egg) come together to form a zygote, and the number of chromosomes is restored by this union. The genetic information of a zygote is a mixture of genetic information from both parents. Gamete cells are manufactured through a process called **meiosis** whereby a cell multiplies its genetic material once, but divides twice, producing four new cells, each of which contains half the number of chromosomes that were present in the original cell before division. In humans, gametes are produced in testes and ovaries. Meiosis causes genetic diversity within a species by generating combinations of genes that are different from those present in the parents.

Alleles

Alleles are alternative versions of the same gene. An organism with two copies of the same allele is **homozygous**, and one with two different alleles is **heterozygous**. For example, a human with one gene for blue eyes and one gene for brown eyes is heterozygous, while a human with two genes for blue eyes or two genes for brown eyes is homozygous. Which of the two genes is expressed is determined by the dominance of the gene.

An allele is **dominant** if it alone determines the phenotype of a heterozygote. In other words, if a plant has a gene for making yellow flowers and a gene for making red flowers, the color of the flower will be determined by the dominant gene. So if the gene for red flowers is dominant, a plant that has both the gene for red and the gene for yellow will look red. The gene for yellow flowers in this case is called **recessive**, as it doesn't contribute to the phenotype (appearance) of a heterozygote (a plant containing two different alleles). The only way this plant would make yellow flowers is if it had two recessive genes—two genes both coding for yellow flowers.

For some genes, dominance is only partial and two different alleles can be expressed. In the case of partial dominance, a plant that has a gene that codes for red flowers and a gene that codes for white flowers would produce pink flowers.

A Punnett square can be used to represent the possible phenotypes that offspring of parents with known genotypes could have. Take the example with the yellow and red flower. Let's label the gene for the dominant red gene as **R** and the gene for yellow flowers as **r**. Cross a plant with yellow flowers (genotype must be **rr**) with a plant with red flowers and genotype **Rr**. What possible genotypes and phenotypes can the offspring have? In a Punnett square, the genes of one parent are listed on one side of the square and the genes of the other parent on the other side of the square. They are then combined in the offspring as illustrated here:

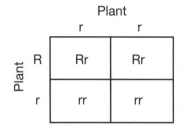

The possible genotypes of the offspring are listed inside the square. Their genotype will be either **Rr** or **rr**, causing them to be either red or yellow, respectively.

Sex Determination

In many organisms, one of the sexes can have a pair of unmatched chromosomes. In humans, the male has an X chromosome and a much smaller Y chromosome, while the female has two X chromosomes. The combination XX (female) or XY (male) determines the sex of humans. In birds, the males have a matched pair of sex chromosomes (WW), while females have an unmatched pair (WZ). In humans, the sex chromosome supplied by the male determines the sex of the offspring. In birds, the sex chromosome supplied by the female determines the sex.

Plants, as well as many animals, lack sex chromosomes. The sex in these organisms is determined by other factors, such as plant hormones or temperature.

Identical twins result when a fertilized egg splits in two. Identical twins have identical chromosomes and can be either two girls or two boys. Two children of different sex born at the same time can't possibly be identical twins. Such twins are fraternal. Fraternal twins can also be of the same sex. They are genetically not any more alike than siblings born at different times. Fraternal twins result when two different eggs are fertilized by two different sperm cells.

When meiosis goes wrong, the usual number of chromosomes can be altered. An example of this is Down syndrome, a genetic disease caused by an extra chromosome.

Changes in DNA (mutations) occur randomly and spontaneously at low rates. Mutations occur more frequently when DNA is exposed to mutagens, including ultraviolet light, X-rays, and certain chemicals. Most mutations are either harmful to or don't affect the organism. In rare cases, however, a mutation can be beneficial to an organism and can help it survive or reproduce. Ultimately, genetic diversity depends on mutations, as mutations are the only source of completely new genetic material. Only mutations in germ cells can create the variation that changes an organism's offspring.

▶ Biological Evolution

Mutations cause change over time. The result of a series of such changes is evolution, or as Darwin put it, "descent with modification." The great diversity on our planet is the result of more than 3.5 billion years of evolution. The theory of evolution argues that all species on Earth originated from common ancestors.

Evidence for Evolution

Several factors have led scientists to accept the theory of evolution. The main factors are described here.

- **Fossil record.** One of the most convincing forms of evidence is the fossil record. Fossils are the remains of past life. Fossils are often located in sedimentary rocks, which form during compression of settling mud, debris, and sand. The order of layers of sedimentary rock is consistent with the proposed sequence in which life on Earth evolved. The simplest organisms are located at the bottom layer, while top layers contain increasingly complex and modern organisms, a pattern that suggests evolution. The process of carbon dating has been used to confirm how old the fossils are and that fossils found in the lower layers of sedimentary rock are indeed older than the ones found in the higher layers. This helps scientists to chart evolutionary history based on time. And new fossils are turning up all the time; for example, the fossil called Tiktaalik, which was found in 2006, is believed to mark the transition from fish to land animals.
- **Biogeography.** Another form of evidence comes from the fact that species tend to resemble neighboring species in different habitats more than they resemble species that are in similar habitats but far away.
- **Comparative anatomy.** Comparative anatomy provides us with another line of evidence. It refers to the fact that the limb bones of different species, for example, are similar. Species that closely resemble one another are considered to be more closely related than species that do not resemble one another. For example, a horse and a donkey are considered to be more closely related than are a horse and a frog. Biological classifications (kingdom, phylum, class, order, family, genus, and species) are based on how organisms are related. Organisms are classified into a hierarchy of groups and subgroups based on similarities that reflect their evolutionary relationships. The same underlying anatomical structures of groups of bones, nerves, muscles, and organs are found in all animals, even when the function of these underlying structures differ.
- **Embryology.** Embryology provides another form of evidence for evolution. Embryos go through the developmental stages of their ancestors to some degree. The early embryos of fish, amphibians, reptiles, birds, and mammals all have common features, such as tails.
- **Comparative molecular biology.** Comparative molecular biology confirms the lines of descent suggested by comparative anatomy and fossil record. The *relatedness* of two different species can be found by comparing their DNA.

Darwin also proposed that evolution occurs gradually, through mutations and **natural selection**. He argued that some genes or combinations of genes give an individual a survival or reproductive advantage, increasing the chance that these useful combinations of genes will make it to future generations. Whether a given trait is advantageous depends on the environment of the organism. We can witness the changes in populations of living organisms: antibiotic-resistant bacteria, super lice that are resistant to chemical treatments, and the increased frequency of dark-colored moths versus the lightly colored variety (Biston betularia) after the industrial revolution in Britain. These are all examples of evidence of natural selection.

Natural selection is only one of several mechanisms by which gene frequency in a population changes. Other factors include mating patterns and breeding between populations.

▶ Interdependence of Organisms

The species in communities interact in many ways. They compete for space and resources, they can be related as predator and prey, or as host and parasite.

Plants and other photosynthetic organisms harness and convert solar energy and supply the rest of the food chain. Herbivores (plant eaters) obtain energy directly from plants. Carnivores are meat eaters and obtain energy by eating other animals. Omnivores eat both meat and plants. Decomposers feed on dead organisms. The flow of energy can then be represented as follows:

Sun → Photosynthetic organisms →
Herbivores → Carnivores or Omnivores→
Decomposers

The food chain is not the only example of the inter-dependence of organisms. Species often have to compete for food and space, so that the increase in population of one can cause the decrease in population of the other.

Organisms also may have a symbiotic relationship (live in close association), which could be classified as parasitism, mutualism, or commensalism. In a **parasitic** relationship, one organism benefits at the expense of the other. **Commensalism** is symbiosis in which one organism benefits and the other is neither harmed nor rewarded. In **mutualism**, both organisms benefit.

Under ideal conditions, with ample food and space and no predators, all living organisms have the capacity to reproduce infinitely. However, resources are limited, limiting the population of a species.

Humans probably come closest to being a species with seemingly infinite reproductive capacity. Our population keeps increasing. Our only danger seems to come from viruses and bacteria, which at this point we more or less have under control. When we need more food, we grow more, and when we need more space, we clear some by killing off other biomes. By doing this, humans modify ecosystems and destroy habitats through direct harvesting, pollution, atmospheric changes, and other factors. This attitude is threatening current global stability, and has the potential to cause irreparable damage.

▶ Behavior of Organisms

Even the most primitive unicellular organisms can act to maintain homeostasis. More complex organisms have nervous systems. The simplest organism found to have learning capability is a worm, suggesting a more complex nervous system. The function of the nervous system is the collection and interpretation of sensory signals, messages from the center of the nervous system (brain in humans) to other parts of the body. The nervous system is made of nerve cells, or neurons, which conduct signals, in the form of electrical impulses. Nerve cells communicate by secreting excitatory or inhibitory molecules called **neurotransmitters**. Many legal and illegal drugs act on the brain by disrupting the secretion or absorption of neurotransmitters, or by initiating a response by activating the receptors that neurotransmitters would normally bind to. Behavior can also be affected by hormonal control. Hormones are produced in one part of the body and are transported by the circulatory system to another part of the body where they ultimately act.

Many animals have sense organs that enable them to detect light, sound, and specific chemicals. These organs provide the animals with information about the outside world. Animals engage in innate and learned social behavior. These behaviors include hunting or searching for food, nesting, migrating, playing, taking care of their young, fighting for mates, and fighting for territory.

Plants also respond to stimuli. They turn toward the Sun and let their roots run deeper when they need water.

30▶ Earth and Space Science

Humans have always wondered about the origin of the Earth and the universe that surrounds it. What kinds of matter and energy are in the universe? How did the universe begin? How has the Earth evolved? This chapter will answer these fundamental questions and review the key concepts of Earth and space science.

EARTH AND SPACE science are concerned with the formation of the Earth, the solar system and the universe, the history of Earth (its mountains, continents, and ocean floors), the weather and seasons on Earth, the energy in the Earth system, and the chemical cycles on Earth.

▶ Energy in the Earth Systems

Energy and matter can't be created or destroyed. But energy can change form and can travel great distances.

Solar Energy
The Sun's energy reaches our planet in the form of light radiation. Plants use this light to synthesize sugar molecules, which we consume when we eat the plants. We obtain energy from the sugar molecules and our bodies use it. Ultimately our energy comes from the Sun. The Sun also drives the Earth's geochemical cycles, which will be discussed in the next section.

The Sun heats the Earth's surface and drives convection within the atmosphere and oceans, producing winds and ocean currents. The winds cause waves on the surface of oceans and lakes. The wind transfers some of its energy to the water, through friction between the air molecules and the water molecules. Strong winds cause large waves. Tsunamis, or tidal waves, are different. They result from underwater earthquakes, volcanic eruptions, or landslides, not wind.

Energy from the Core

Another source of Earth's energy comes from Earth's core. We distinguish four main layers of Earth: the inner core, the outer core, the rocky mantle, and the crust. The **inner core** is a solid mass of iron with a temperature of about 7,000°F. Most likely, the high temperature is caused by radioactive decay of uranium and other radioactive elements. The inner core is approximately 1,500 miles in diameter. The **outer core** is a mass of molten iron that surrounds the solid inner core. Electrical currents generated from this area produce the Earth's magnetic field. The **rocky mantle** is composed of silicon, oxygen, magnesium, iron, aluminum, and calcium and is about 1,750 miles thick. This mantle accounts for most of the Earth's mass. When parts of this layer become hot enough, they turn to slow moving molten rock or magma. The **Earth's crust** is a layer from four to 25 miles thick consisting of sand and rock.

The upper mantle is rigid and is part of the lithosphere (together with the crust). The lower mantle flows slowly, at a rate of a few centimeters per year. The crust is divided into plates that drift slowly (only a few centimeters each year) on the less rigid mantle. Oceanic crust is thinner than continental crust.

This motion of the plates is caused by convection (heat) currents, which carry heat from the hot inner mantle to the cooler outer mantle. The motion results in earthquakes and volcanic eruptions. This process is called **plate tectonics**.

Tectonics

Evidence suggests that about 200 million years ago, all continents were a part of one landmass, named Pangaea. Over the years, the continents slowly separated through the movement of plates in a process called **continental drift**. The movement of the plates is attributed to convection currents in the mantle. The theory of plate tectonics says that there are now 12 large plates that slowly move on the mantle. According to this theory, earthquakes and volcanic eruptions occur along the lines where plates collide. Dramatic changes on Earth's landscape and ocean floor are caused by collision of plates. These changes include the formation of mountains and valleys.

▶ Geochemical Cycles

Water, carbon, and nitrogen are recycled in the biosphere. A water molecule in the cell of your eye could have been at some point in the ocean, in the atmosphere, in a leaf of a tree, or in the cell of a bear's foot. The circulation of elements in the biosphere is called a **geochemical cycle**.

Water

Oceans cover 70% of the Earth's surface and contain more than 97% of all water on Earth. Sunlight evaporates the water from the oceans, rivers, and lakes.

Living beings need water for both the outside and the inside of their cells. In fact, vertebrates (you included) are about 70% water. Plants contain even more water. Most of the water passes through a plant unaltered. Plants draw on water from the soil and release it as vapor through pores in their leaves; this process is called **transpiration**.

Our atmosphere can't hold a lot of water. Evaporated water condenses to form clouds that produce rain or snow onto the Earth's surface. Overall, water moves from the oceans to the land because more rainfall reaches the land than is evaporated from the land.

Carbon

Carbon is found in the oceans in the form of bicarbonate ions (HCO_3-), the atmosphere, in the form of carbon dioxide, in living organisms, and in fossil fuels (such as coal, oil, and natural gas). Plants remove carbon dioxide in the atmosphere and convert it to sugars through photosynthesis. The sugar in plants enters the food chain first reaching herbivores, then carnivores, and finally scavengers and decomposers. All of these organisms release carbon dioxide back into the atmosphere when they breathe. The oceans contain 500 times more carbon than the atmosphere. Bicarbonate ions (HCO_3-) settle to the bottoms of oceans and form sedimentary rocks. Fossil fuels represent the largest reserve of carbon on Earth. Fossil fuels come from the carbon of organisms that had lived millions of years ago. Burning fossil fuels releases energy, which is why these fuels are used to power human

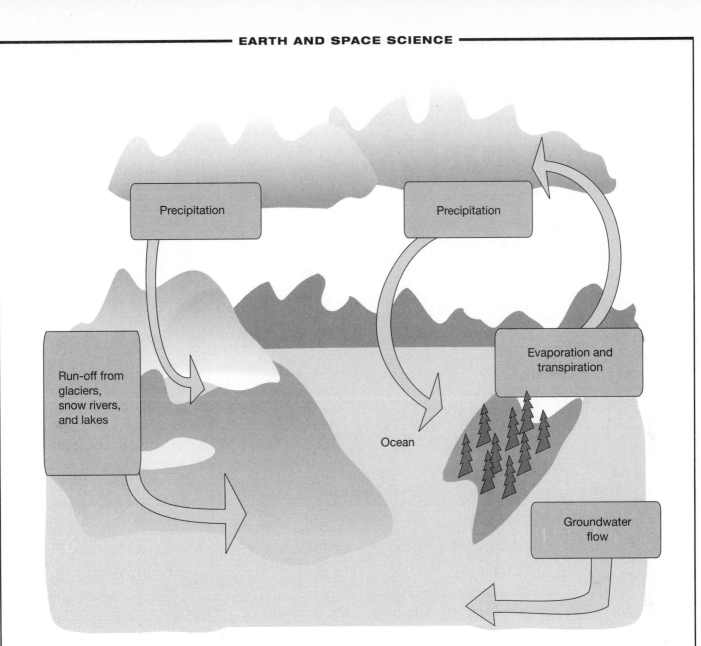

contraptions. When fossil fuels burn, carbon dioxide is released into the atmosphere.

Since the Industrial Revolution, people have increased the concentration of carbon dioxide in the atmosphere by 30% by burning fossil fuels and cutting down forests, which reduce the concentration of carbon dioxide. Carbon dioxide in the atmosphere can trap solar energy—a process known as the **greenhouse effect**. By trapping solar energy, carbon dioxide and other green house gases can cause **global warming**—an increase of temperatures on Earth. In the last 100 years, the temperatures have increased by 1°C. This doesn't seem like much, but the temperature increase is already creating noticeable climate changes and problems.

Many species are migrating to colder areas, and regions that normally have ample rainfall have experienced droughts. Perhaps the most dangerous consequence of global warming is the melting of polar ice. Glaciers all over the world are already melting, and the polar ice caps have begun to break up at the edges. If enough of this ice melts, coastal cities could experience severe flooding.

Reducing carbon dioxide concentrations in the atmosphere, either by finding new energy sources or by actively removing the carbon dioxide that forms, is a challenge to today's scientists.

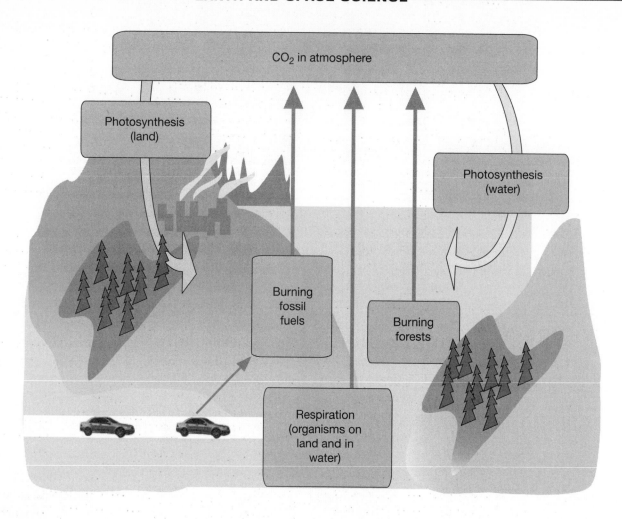

Nitrogen

The main component of air in the atmosphere is nitrogen gas (N_2). Nitrogen accounts for about 78% of the atmosphere. However, very few organisms can use the form of nitrogen obtained directly from the atmosphere. The reason for this is that the bond between two atoms in the nitrogen gas molecule is tough to break, and only a few bacteria have enzymes that can make it happen. These bacteria can convert the nitrogen gas into ammonium ions (NH_4+). Bacteria that do this are called **nitrifying** or **nitrogen-fixing bacteria**.

Another source of nitrogen for the non-nitrogen-fixing organisms is lightning. Lightning carries tremendous energy, which is able to cause nitrogen gas to convert to ammonium ions (NH_4+) and nitrate ions ($NO_3–$)—fixed nitrogen.

Plants, animals, and most other organisms can use only fixed nitrogen. Plants obtain fixed nitrogen from soil and use it to synthesize amino acids and proteins. Animals obtain fixed nitrogen by eating plants or other animals. When they break up proteins, animals lose nitrogen

in the form of ammonia (fish), urea (mammals), or uric acid (birds, reptiles, and insects). Decomposers obtain energy from urea and uric acid by converting them back into ammonia, which can be used again by plants.

The amount of fixed nitrogen in the soil is low, because bacteria break down most of the ammonium ion into another set of molecules (nitrite and nitrate), through a process called **nitrification**. Other bacteria convert the nitrite and nitrate back into nitrogen gas, which is released into the atmosphere. This process is called **denitrification**.

This limited amount of nitrogen has kept organisms in balance for millions of years. However, the growing human population presents a threat to this stability. In order to increase the growth rate of crops, humans manufacture and use huge amounts of fertilizer, increasing the amount of nitrogen in the soil. This has disrupted whole ecosystems, since, with extra nitrogen present, some organisms thrive and displace others. In the long run, too much nitrogen decreases the fertility of soil by depriving it of essential minerals, such as calcium.

Burning fossil fuels and forests also releases nitrogen. All forms of fixed nitrogen are greenhouse gases that are causing global warming. In addition, nitric oxide, a gas released when fossil fuels are burned, can convert into nitric acid, a main component of acid rain. Acid rain destroys habitats.

People are already suffering the consequences of the pollution they have caused. Preventing further damage to the ecosystems and fixing the damage that has been done is another challenge for today's scientists.

▶ Origin and Evolution of the Earth System

Earth Basics

Most people know that the Earth is round and revolves around its axis in about 24 hours. It is a part of the solar system, with the Sun in its center. Other planets and their moons orbit the Sun as well. Among the planets are Mercury and Venus, which are closer to the Sun than the Earth is, and Mars, Jupiter, Saturn, Uranus, and Neptune, which are farther away from the Sun. And even farther from the Sun is the **dwarf planet** Pluto.

It takes about one year for the Earth to complete its orbit around the Sun. The rotation of the Earth around its axis causes the change between day and night. The tilt in the Earth's axis gives rise to seasons.

Rocks and Rock Cycles

Rocks are made up of one or more minerals, homogeneous inorganic materials. Three types of rocks are igneous, sedimentary, and metamorphic. **Igneous** rocks result from cooling of molten rock. If the cooling from molten rock occurred quickly on or near the Earth's surface, it is called **volcanic igneous** rock. If the cooling took place slowly, deep beneath the surface, it is called **plutonic igneous** rock. **Sedimentary** rocks are formed in layers in response to pressure on accumulated sediments. **Metamorphic** rocks are formed when either igneous or sedimentary rocks are under intense heat and pressure deep beneath the Earth's surface.

The rock cycle is the transformation of one rock type into another. Molten rock material cools and solidifies either at or below the surface of the Earth to form igneous rocks. Weathering and erosion break the rocks down into smaller grains, producing soil. The soil is carried by wind, water, and gravity and is eventually deposited as sediment. The sediments are deposited in layers and become pressed firmly together and cemented or lithified, forming sedimentary rocks. Variations in temperature and pressure can cause chemical and physical changes in igneous and sedimentary rocks to form metamorphic rocks. When exposed to higher temperatures, metamorphic rocks may be partially melted, resulting in the creation once again of igneous rocks, starting the cycle all over again.

Molten material from inside the Earth often breaks through the floor of the ocean and flows from fissures where it is cooled by the water, resulting in the formation of igneous rocks. As the molten material flows from the fissure, it forms ridges adjacent to it.

Origin of the Earth and the Solar System

The Sun, the Earth, and the rest of the solar system formed 4.6 billion years ago, according to the **solar nebula theory**. This theory states that the solar system was initially a large cloud of gas and dust, which most likely originated from the explosions of nearby stars. This cloud is named the solar nebula. The Sun formed at the central, densest point of the nebula. One argument that supports this hypothesis is that planets closer to the Sun are composed of heavier elements, while light, gaseous planets are farthest from the Sun. The solar nebula theory also states that planets formed in conjunction with stars. This component of the theory is supported by the fact that other stars have planets and that the age of moon rocks is comparable to the age of the Earth.

▶ Origin and Evolution of the Universe

Nobody knows for sure how the universe originated. According to the **Big Bang theory**, the universe started off in a hot dense state under high pressure between ten and 20 billion years ago. The Big Bang theory also postulates that the universe has been expanding since its origination. The universe is still expanding and cooling. Some data suggest that the rate of expansion of the universe is increasing.

Whether the universe will continue to expand forever, eventually reach an equilibrium size, or shrink back into a small, dense, hot mass is unknown.

Stars are formed by the gravitational attraction of countless hydrogen and helium molecules. The stars became gravitationally bound to other stars, forming galaxies. The solar system is part of the Milky Way galaxy, which in addition to the Sun, contains about 200 billion other stars.

The energy of stars stems from nuclear reactions, mainly the fusion of hydrogen atoms to form helium. Nuclear processes in stars lead to the formation of elements.

31 ▶ Science and Technology

This chapter discusses the aims of technology, the relationship between science and technology, and the way in which needs and advances in one lead to needs and progress in the other. You will also learn what drives technological progress and what is involved in technological design.

WHILE SCIENCE IS the systematic study of the natural world, **technology** is the application of scientific knowledge to create tools, equipment, and procedures that often simplify and improve our lives. For every scientific discovery, there are dozens of potential applications of that knowledge. Technological advances often lead to further advances in the sciences. Thus, science and technology are highly interdependent.

▶ Abilities of Technological Design

Students tend to have a positive image of science. They associate science with medicine and nature. At the same time, students realize that technology plays multiple roles in our lives. There are positive applications, including the use of technology for medical diagnosing, communication, transportation, and everyday chores. However, technology often leads to pollution and problems. While pollution and problems may unfortunately be a by-product of certain technological processes, they are also the by-products of science. In reality, science and technology are extremely interrelated and similar in many ways.

One of the goals of technology is to apply the principles of science to make life more comfortable and work easier. The aim of technology is not to create problems, but to solve them. Technology is responsible for delivering the electricity we use every day, for the refrigerator that prevents our food from spoiling, for the ability to cross an ocean on a plane within hours, for the calculator, the ATM, and our connection to the Internet. Need we go on? The printing press, toothpaste . . .

Science-Technology-Science Relationship

Technology is applied science—science put to use. While science is driven by a desire to understand the world, technology is often driven by the desire to make the world safer, more convenient, and more fun for people. Scientific research that has immediate and wide applications tends to receive funding from the government and private companies more easily than research that is very abstract. Therefore, science that has technological importance or potential is encouraged and driven by a desire to produce and make a profit.

Technology is also science on a large scale. Running a chemical reaction in a beaker in the lab is usually classified as science. Running the same reaction in a huge reactor in a chemical plant is classified as technology. Science and technology have a profound influence on each other, and progress in one creates progress in the other.

Consider this example: Scientists figured out how optical lenses work. The science was used to make a microscope (technology). The microscope was used to observe a cell (science). In order to isolate the genetic material from this cell, an instrument had to be used (technology). But that instrument operates according to the laws of science.

Take another example: Scientists figured out the laws of fluid mechanics. Engineers used these laws to design airplanes. And now both scientists and engineers can fly to science conferences around the world.

Optimization of Existing Products and Processes

Technological inventions are often tools, instruments, machines, or processes. Engineers recognize a need for an invention and see it as a design opportunity. For example, an engineer realizes that people are carrying too many electronic devices—a telephone, a digital planner, a watch, a calculator, a laptop—why not create one device

that can be used to accomplish what all of the limited electronic devices do?

Consider how the need for computers arose. Scientists were tired of performing slow, repetitive calculations. It took too long, and progress was limited. So, computers were designed to perform these long, repetitive calculations. The first computers were massive and required the use of special punch cards. But with the advancement of technology, they became small enough to be portable. Improving existing designs or processes is another goal of technology.

Alternative Solutions, Models, and Computer Design

Just as there are many ways to get from one place to another, there are sometimes many solutions to an engineering problem. Because of that, engineers need to carefully evaluate several different designs and choose between alternative solutions. In addition to performing calculations, engineers build models of their design or simulate a process using specialized computer programs.

For example, a program called CAD (Computer Aided Design) can be used to analyze harmful emissions into the atmosphere from vehicles (cars, trucks, and buses). Based on computer simulations, engineers are able to predict whether adding a lane of traffic would increase emissions above levels determined to be safe by environmental protection agencies.

Chemical processes can also be simulated using computer programs. Chemists discover new reactions or chemicals, but it is the job of chemical engineers to design a chemical plant that will run that reaction. The design of chemical plants involves sizing reactors and figuring out the amount of reactants needed, how quickly the reaction will proceed, how the product should be stored, how the waste should be managed, at what temperature the reaction should be run, and how to control different aspects of the process. It would be very time-consuming, expensive, and tedious to make a physical model for hundreds of different conditions. With computers, processes can be simulated, and physical models can be built based on the computer simulations that work best.

Design Considerations

Each technological design has to meet a number of design criteria. The product or process should operate smoothly, without breaking down. The demand for such a product or process should be evaluated. The product or process should be an improvement over other similar products and processes. Improvement can be functional (working better), economic (more profitable), or aesthetic (better looking, or taking up less space). Products and processes can also be made safer for people to use or run, and safer for the environment. All of these design criteria need to be taken into account. Economics often limit the implementation of an otherwise best design. For example, the collection of solar energy is technologically possible and is good for the environment, but it is not widely used because it is not economical yet. Cars that run solely on electric power had been designed and built many years ago, but again economics prevented their production. Oil companies would lose profit if the use of electric cars became widespread, and designs were bought with the purpose of preventing their manufacture. We are finally seeing the arrival of hybrid cars on the market, as consumers react to the increasing oil prices. We may see other alternatives arise, such as incorporation of biofuels, or entirely electric cars, now that the demand for new technical designs has been demonstrated. Similarly, economical varieties of solar and wind energy may be developed, now that the need for alternative energy sources has become apparent.

Evaluating the Consequences

The consequences of a technology product or process need to be evaluated by scientists and engineers, but also by public policy makers and consumers. What kind of short-term and long-term effects does a technological advance have on individuals, on the population, and on the environment? You should be aware that technological advances can have a variety of beneficial or harmful consequences on the living standard, health, environment, and economy. You should also be able to state the tradeoffs often involved in choosing a particular design

or adopting a particular public policy. For example, you should be aware of the reasons for and consequences of the one-child policies in China, and the different positions in current debates such as the use of fetal tissue in stem cell research, genetic engineering, recycling policies, and other issues.

Communication

Communication is another component of technological development. Engineers often need to convince their superiors or the public of the advantages of their designs. The communication involves stating the problem, describing the process or design, and presenting the solution. This is done through publishing or presenting reports, models, and diagrams and showing that a particular design has advantages over alternative designs.

▶ Understandings about Science and Technology

Scientists in different disciplines ask different questions, and sometimes use different methods of investigation. Many science projects require the contributions of individuals from different disciplines, including engineering. The Human Genome Project, designed to map the human genome, involved thousands of researchers around the world and was the largest, most expensive project in the history of biology. New disciplines of science, such as geophysics and biochemistry, often emerge at the interface of two older disciplines.

Technological knowledge is often not made public because of patents and the financial potential of the idea or invention. Similarly, it takes a while for a new drug to reach the public because extensive testing and legal issues are often involved.

32▶ Personal and Social Perspectives in Science

Science does not happen in a vacuum. Scientific advances directly affect technology, which impacts politics and economics around the world. This chapter will discuss current personal and social concerns in the sciences, including health, population growth, use of natural resources, and environmental protection.

SOME PEOPLE MAY think that science is best left to the scientists. But science is really every citizen's concern. Individuals and society must decide which new research proposals to fund and which new technologies to let into society. These decisions involve understanding the alternatives, risks, costs, and benefits. By being informed and educated regarding these issues, we can better decide what kind of advances and projects are beneficial. Students should understand the importance of asking:

- What can happen?
- What are the odds?
- How do scientists and engineers know what will happen?

▶ Personal and Community Health

As human beings, we function better when we are healthy and well. Malnutrition and poor hygiene are factors that can affect health and the body's ability to function properly. An unhealthy body is prone to diseases and other hazards found in the environment. There are two kinds of diseases: **infectious** and **noninfectious**.

Infectious Disease

Diseases are caused by **pathogens** that invade a host body. Pathogens need a host in order to survive and multiply. Some examples of pathogens are bacteria, viruses, and fungi. They can spread through direct body contact, body fluids, and through contact with an object that an infected person has touched (since some viruses, like the common cold virus, can exist outside the body for a brief period before they get passed on to another host). Tuberculosis is also an infectious disease. Victims of tuberculosis cough up blood from their lungs. Treatment and vaccines for tuberculosis exist and this disease has been almost eliminated in some parts of the world. However, the total number of people in the world infected with tuberculosis keeps growing.

Noninfectious Disease

If the disease cannot spread from person to person, then it is considered noninfectious. Two examples of noninfectious diseases are cancer and heart disease. Here are some characteristics of noninfectious diseases:

- They do not transfer from person to person.
- They are not caused by viruses, bacteria, or fungi.
- They are sometimes **hereditary**—meaning that they are associated with genes and run in families.

Noninfectious diseases can be classified further:

- **Hereditary diseases.** Hereditary diseases are caused by genetic disorders that are passed down from previous generations. Since they are inherited, they are more difficult to treat because they are a part of the body's **genetic makeup**.
- **Age-related diseases.** Some diseases will start to develop as the body gets older. As the body grows old, it does not work as efficiently to battle routine diseases and **degenerative diseases** such as Alzheimer's disease—which causes mild to severe memory loss or distortion, forgetfulness, anxiety, and aggressive behavior.
- **Environmentally induced diseases.** An environment that has been polluted with toxins and hazardous waste can affect the population living in or around it. Radiation from toxic waste can cause cancer. Exposure to asbestos can lead to serious lung problems.

Staying healthy by taking care of the body is important in fighting and preventing disease. Poor hygiene and unhealthy living conditions are invitations for disease. Here are a few tips on staying healthy:

- Eat a nutritious diet.
- Keep your hands and body clean.
- Exercise regularly.
- Reduce stress.
- Don't smoke.
- Don't drink excessively.

It is also important to feel good about yourself. A positive view of who you are and what you look like can help reduce stress considerably.

Looking for Symptoms

Before diagnosing a patient with a disease, a doctor looks for the telltale symptoms. Every disease has specific symptoms that cause different reactions in the body. Some of the more common symptoms are fever, nausea, and pain. A doctor is trained to look for these symptoms to give a correct diagnosis and issue proper treatment. Blood tests and X-rays are special methods that are used to diagnose some diseases.

Epidemics

An epidemic is a disease that has infected a considerable portion of the population and that continues to spread rapidly. Epidemics can occur when there is no medicine for the disease, when diseases develop a resistance to medicine and drugs, or when environmental conditions are favorable for a specific type of disease. For example, cancer is rampant in areas with toxic chemicals and high levels of radiation. Autoimmune deficiency syndrome, or AIDS, which is caused by the HIV virus, is an epidemic that is killing millions of people worldwide. HIV is spread through sexual contact and through contact with the blood of an infected person.

Natural and Medical Defenses

Humans and most other living beings have a natural built-in disease-fighting mechanism known as the **immune system**. The immune system is composed of cells, molecules, and organs that defend the body against pathogens. The immune system is responsible for finding the pathogen in the body, and killing it, rendering it harmless, or expelling it from the body.

The development and use of vaccines and antibiotics have added to our defenses against diseases. Not only have advances in medicine found ways to fight disease from inside the body, but methods have also been developed to prevent the onset of disease.

Vaccines

Vaccines are usually made from either a dead version of an actual organism known to cause an immune response (such as a virus) or from a weakened or inactive form of the organism. By presenting the body with a weaker or deactivated form of an organism that would normally make a person very ill, the strategy is to stimulate an immune response without causing any illness. Then if the body ever comes in contact with the strong form, antibodies that were formed during the immune response to the weaker version, will be able to fight off this strong version.

Antibiotics

Antibiotics are chemicals that kill bacteria without harming our own cells. Some antibiotics, such as penicillin, kill bacteria by preventing it from synthesizing a cell wall. Other antibiotics interfere with bacterial growth by disrupting their genes or protein production. Bacteria can become resistant to antibiotics—there are strands of bacteria that are resistant to every known antibiotic.

Resistance

In every population, a small number of bacteria naturally have genes that make them resistant to antibiotics. With increased exposure to antibiotics, a normal population of bacteria, having a few resistant individuals, becomes resistant on average. This is a result of natural selection. The bacteria that survive are the ones that are resistant. Their offspring is also resistant, and as a result, the whole population becomes resistant. Some resistance enables bacteria to survive in the presence of an antibiotic. Another kind of resistance enables the bacteria to actually destroy the antibiotic. This kind of resistance is most dangerous. For example, someone who took antibiotics for treating acne could accumulate bacteria that are capable of destroying the antibiotic. If that same person became infected with a serious disease that is treated with the same antibiotic, the resistant bacteria could destroy the antibiotic before it was able to act on the disease.

Community and Public Health

People are dying from diseases in many parts of the world where clean water is scarce and living conditions are poor. Educating people on the importance of personal hygiene, cleanliness, and sanitation is key to preventing disease in populations. A clean, healthy environment will ensure better health and safety.

▶ Population Growth and Control

The human population growth rate was increasing relatively slowly up until 1,000 years ago. Before the invention of vaccines and antibiotics that prevented deadly infectious diseases, and before humans developed plumbing and sewage treatment plants to ensure safe, clean drinking water, factors such as the spread of diseases increased death rate. Lack of food supply and intolerance for living in extremely hot or extremely cold environments are also examples of **limiting factors** that control population growth.

By the early 1800s, the world population reached 1 billion. It took approximately 2.5 million years for humans to reach this mark. But now, only 200 years later, the world population has reached 6 billion.

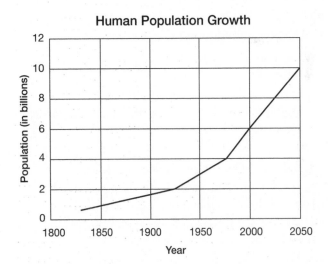

Human Population Growth

From 1850 to 1930, a period of less than 100 years, the estimated world population doubled. In 1975, less than 50 years later, the world population doubled again to reach 4 billion. Then only 12 years later, it reached 5 billion. It is estimated that by 2050, the world population will reach 10 billion.

When a couple has two children, each child replaces one of the parents, and, in theory, the population should stay the same. However, due to increased life expectancy, several generations of people are alive at the same time. It is estimated that even if everyone from now on had only one or two children, the population would continue to grow for about 50 years. The reason for this is that most of the world population is young and has yet to reproduce. In a way, the population has a momentum and its growth cannot stop immediately, in much the same way that you can't instantaneously stop a car that is running at 70 miles per hour. Coming to a stop takes time.

> Even if everyone in the world from this moment on started having no more than two children, the population would continue to grow for about another 50 years.

How Did This Happen?

So how did the human population grow so much and so rapidly? One of the main reasons is that many limiting factors to human population growth have been eliminated. Here are some explanations:

Advances in medicine and health care enabled the development of:
- vaccines to prevent the spread of infectious diseases
- antibiotics to cure common illnesses
- therapies to treat patients with noninfectious diseases such as cancer

Advances in technology enabled humans to:
- expand into new habitats
- live in places with extreme climate conditions
- develop sanitation and sewage-disposal systems

Advances in science enabled humans to:
- increase food supply and improve living conditions
- reduce deaths from natural disasters and other hazards
- use Earth's natural resources such as fossil fuels

Since people have learned to overcome some of the limiting factors that prevented human growth and survival, the death rate has steadily decreased, and because of the increase in production of food supply and other resources, the infant death rate has also decreased.

What Does This Mean for Our Future?

So what will happen if the human population continues to grow at this rate? The result is **overpopulation**. Overpopulation occurs when there are too many individuals in a given area, so that the resources are depleted faster than they can be replaced.

Overpopulation is not the same as **overcrowding**, which is another consequence of steady population growth. Overcrowding occurs when there are too many individuals living in an area—to the point where most of the individuals in the population live in substandard or poor conditions because of lack of work and lack of living space. Mexico City, Istanbul, China, and India are some examples of places in the world that are experiencing overcrowding.

How Will Overpopulation Affect Us?

Overpopulation can cause serious damage to our way of life as well as our environment. Here are just some effects of overpopulation.

- **Hunger and starvation.** Technology has enabled us to develop ways to improve food production and agriculture. However, the rate of food production increase at this moment is not keeping up with the rate of population growth. In other words, the amount of mouths to feed is increasing faster than our ability to feed them. The uneven distribution of food, rather than the lack of food, however, is causing most of the hunger problems. While huge amounts of food are being thrown away in some parts of the world, people in other parts of the world are starving to death.
- **Depletion of our natural resources.** Some resources are depleted faster than they are replenished. Our oil and coal supplies, for example, take millions of years to replenish and, given the consumption rate, they will eventually run out.
- **Ozone layer and global warming.** Ozone is a very reactive molecule, made of three oxygen atoms. At about ten to thirty miles above the Earth, a layer of ozone molecules absorbs ultraviolet light (UV) emitted by the Sun and shields living things from potentially dangerous amounts of this radiation.

UV light can increase the amount of mutations in DNA. Some biologists believe that too much UV light has driven some species of frogs to extinction. In humans, excess UV light is a major cause of higher rates of skin cancer. About 20 years ago, scientists began to document a thinning of the ozone layer, especially over Antarctica, where the ozone hole is larger than the size of North America. The depletion of the ozone layer is due largely to deforestation (to make room for houses, roads, and buildings) and chemicals such as chlorofluorocarbons (CFCs), that are being released into the atmosphere. CFCs are small molecules used as coolant in refrigerators and air conditioners and as propellants in some spray cans. The evidence that CFCs are destroying the ozone layer has become so clear that CFC producers have agreed to replace these compounds with others.

- **Effect on Biodiversity.** Overpopulation has a profound effect on biodiversity. In order to make room for ourselves, our houses, factories, and shopping centers, and to come by food and energy sources, we have disrupted natural animal and plant habitats. One way in which humans contribute to the extinction of species is by fragmenting their habitats—splitting them into several smaller habitats. This decreases the genetic diversity and structure of a habitat, which leads to inbreeding, reduced reproduction, and small population size. A small, inbred population is more likely to become extinct. Extinction of one species can lead to extinction of another that depends on the first for food.
- **Pollution.** Waste is produced faster than it can be dispersed or biodegraded. This causes the buildup of contaminants that can affect our water, soil, and air. Noise can also contaminate environments, especially in cities. This phenomenon is called noise pollution. Light pollution is another problem. Very few stars are visible from most cities, even on a clear night, because there is too much artificial light around. Images taken of North America at night show a series of bright spots throughout the continent. Traveling by plane at night makes the overwhelming amount of artificial light produced by humans very noticeable. Research suggests that light at night can affect the production of certain hormones, and in return

increase some health risks. In addition, excess light may be harmful to animals as well. Much of the problem can be solved by turning on only the lights that are absolutely necessary for safety reasons; making them only as bright as they need to be; pointing them toward the ground, not the sky; and shielding them to prevent scattering. Implementing these kinds of solutions will also help conserve resources by saving electricity.

▶ Natural Resources

Humans depend on resources to sustain life. A good part of the resources we use every day come directly from the environment. These are called **natural resources**—resources provided by nature. Air, water, sunlight, topsoil, and the various plant and animal life known as **biodiversity** are examples of Earth's natural resources. There are two kinds of natural resources: **renewable** and **nonrenewable**.

1. **Renewable resources** are resources that can be replaced or replenished over a short period of time. Plants and crops are examples of resources that, with proper agriculture, are replenishable.
2. **Nonrenewable resources** are resources that cannot be replaced or that take many years to replenish. Fossil fuels such as oil and coal are examples of nonrenewable resources.

Depletion of Natural Resources

Currently, many of our nonrenewable resources are in danger of being depleted. Water, topsoil, and energy are some of the essential resources that are in short supply.

- **Water.** Water is necessary for agriculture, but it is currently the resource in shortest supply. Some parts of Africa and the Middle East are experiencing mass starvation as a result of **drought** or water shortage. Availability of drinking water, free of chemical waste, is also decreasing.
- **Topsoil.** Fertile topsoil takes hundreds, maybe even thousands of years to replace. Human activities have already caused degradation of some of Earth's fertile topsoil, and as a result, the degraded topsoil is no longer able to sustain agriculture.

- **Energy.** Most of our energy resources come from fossil fuels such as oil and coal. They are used for heat, electricity, and gasoline. Fossil fuels are decreasing worldwide because they are being used faster than they are being produced.

Reuse, Reduce, and Recycle: Preserving Our Natural Resources

So how do we prevent our natural resources from depleting? There are several ways to help protect our natural resources.

Conserve

It is important that we all learn to **conserve** our natural resources. To conserve is to limit or control the use of natural resources, especially nonrenewable resources. While big industries are most responsible for energy use and pollution, small consumers (like you) in the company of six billion other small consumers can have a notable effect on the use and preservation of natural resources. So:

- If you are the last one to walk out of a room, turn off the lights. This will save electricity. Using energy-efficient bulbs will help too.
- When you brush your teeth, do you leave the water running? If you shut the water off while you brush, you are conserving water.
- Walking short distances instead of taking the car out will save fuel and limit air pollution.
- Cut back on hot water—use cold water in the washing machine.
- Eat less meat; animal agriculture is more taxing on our natural resources and environment that eating vegetables, fruits, grains, and legumes.
- Buy energy-efficient appliances.

Recycle

One way to protect our environment is by **recycling**—reusing solid waste as is or breaking it down to make new products.

- Old newspaper and cardboard can be shredded up and recycled to make new paper.
- Glass bottles can be melted down and used to make new bottles.
- Be sure to recycle old batteries properly; don't just throw them away.

These are examples of resource recovery, where the raw materials are extracted to make new ones.

Another form of recycling is reuse. If you have an old car, sell or donate it rather than discarding it. In this way, the car is recycled.

Much of our solid waste can be recycled. By recycling, we are decreasing the demand for use of more natural resources and decreasing the amount of space needed for waste disposal. Glass, paper, metal, and plastics are a few examples. If we recycled all our paper garbage, it would save thousands of trees every year from being chopped down to make paper. Recycling aluminum and other metals is more energy efficient than creating them from metal ores.

Protect Biodiversity

Protecting **biodiversity**—the various plant and animal life on Earth—means protecting our source of food, water, clean air, and fertile topsoil. **Extinction**, or the dying off of species of plants and animals, damages biodiversity. Humans play a big part in causing the extinction of essential plant and animal life by:

- interfering with and destroying natural habitats
- polluting the air and water that plants and animals feed off of
- using illegal methods (e.g., explosives) for fishing
- killing already endangered species

Come Up with Better Solutions

Another option is to come up with better solutions—new ways of using or obtaining energy, developing more efficient processes, and better designs.

For example, electric cars are beginning to show up in major cities like San Francisco and Los Angeles. Usually available for rent to cruise the city in style, these little innovations are starting to make it to the consumer market. If you have an AC power outlet in your garage, you are all set to own an electric car. The benefits of owning an electric car are easy to guess. They are quiet and they don't emit toxic chemicals that deplete the ozone layer. They also conserve natural resources needed to make gasoline.

More and more architectural designs are eco-friendly. Architects are designing buildings that can use the Sun's energy for warmth and the runoff of rainwater for cooling purposes.

▶ Science and Technology in Local, National, and Global Challenges

Science affects the way we live, work, act, and play. Our technological abilities have also given us the ability to confront certain global challenges. But we need to consider where our technological abilities lead us and make sure that our power doesn't destroy us. By having a basic science education, we are taking the first step in preventing this from happening.

War

Along with advances in technology came a different kind of warfare—mass destruction and complete disregard for the environment. To end World War II and test a new weapon, the United States dropped two atomic bombs on Japan, instantly ending countless lives. Chemical and biological weapons, and cluster bombs containing depleted uranium present another danger. All of these weapons affect not only the humans involved in wars now, but future generations, and plant and animal life as well.

Solar Power

Solar power refers to the conversion of solar energy to another, more useful form. Sunlight can be harnessed and collected in special greenhouses. Photosensitive cells can produce electricity when sunlight hits them. The Sun produces about ten times the energy fossil fuels create each year. Many scientists are convinced that this form of energy will one day replace ordinary fossil fuels. Currently, one reason that we still do not see solar-powered cars and houses is because fossil fuels are cheaper to collect and use. But technology is slowly catching up—solar plants are now being constructed in some parts of the United States. Scientists are hopeful that these new plants will be able to produce enough energy to power our cities in the future.

Genetic Engineering

One of the fastest growing fields in science, and also possibly the most controversial, genetic engineering, has been making headline news. The first thing that comes to mind is cloning. But there is more to genetic engineering than that. Genetic engineering is used to produce everyday products such as fruits, grains, plants, and even animals like fish. This might be a bit pointless, you might say. Certainly, we have had fruits, plants, and animals

before. Why do we have to genetically engineer these products?

We do not make these products from scratch. What genetic engineering allows us to do is modify the product to bring out certain qualities or to embed qualities that the product would not normally have. For example, Florida oranges grow best in Florida because oranges prefer lots of sun and warm temperatures. What genetic engineering can do is modify the trees so that the orange trees can grow in colder climates.

While making an orange tree that can grow anywhere seems like a good idea, we must look at the flip side and examine other projects. What effect would an orange tree in Alaska have on other plant and animal life in Alaska? In China, scientists concerned with overpopulation and hunger developed a strain of rice that will grow twice as fast as normal rice. This means that more food can be produced faster. Unfortunately, the faster-growing rice has half the nutrients of normal rice. Is this a step up? Now there is more rice available for the population, but it is less nutritious than natural rice.

Genetic engineering can also bring about serious social concerns. Consider the following two social perspectives regarding BT cotton. BT cotton grows from genetically modified cotton seeds and will resist certain pests and yield higher crops when modern irrigation systems are used. In the United States, where farmers do irrigate their crops, this product may pay off, and many farmers support this product. In India, however, farmers are sold on the idea of a superior product, but without using irrigation, output is a gamble—it depends on the weather. Many people in India, and worldwide, are concerned that products like these contribute to the debt that Indian cotton farmers face—a debt that is so severe that, statistically, every day three farmers commit suicide in India. Others grow concerned as pests evolve too, and are no longer hindered by these "pest-proof" plants.

▶ Environmental Quality

Many factors contribute to environmental quality. **Pollution**, the introduction of substances that affect or harm the environment, is one of the biggest environmental concerns scientists are faced with today.

There are many different forms of pollution. Some are natural, like volcanic eruptions. Humans, however, cause most other forms of pollution.

Air Pollution

Air is polluted by the introduction of harmful contaminants into the atmosphere. In and around big cities, smoke produced from factories and car emissions is called **smog**. Smog in the atmosphere can cause acid rain. Recently, people with allergic reactions to smog have found the need to catch the smog alerts commonly read with the weather reports. In addition to causing allergies, smog has been known to cause numerous health problems, damage habitats, and disrupt ecosystems.

Water Pollution

Many companies dispose of their waste by pumping it into rivers, causing pollution in our water systems. Sewage and pesticides are also factors that contribute to water pollution. About one in three rivers in the United States is polluted. This presents serious problems to all life that depends on clean water for survival.

Oceans also get polluted. Garbage dumping, oil spills, and contaminated rivers are the biggest contributing polluters for our oceans. This can be devastating for countries that depend heavily on fishing for food. In 1989, the oil tanker *Exxon Valdez* smashed into some rocks and spilled 260,000 barrels of oil in Alaska. The consequences of this ocean contamination were felt by land mammals and shore life in and around the area.

Because the Earth is a closed system, all the pollution we create eventually makes it back to our body or backfires in some other way. It seems easier to dump mercury waste, used in the extraction of gold from its ores, into the ocean. But the mercury waste can kill fish. The fish that survive contain the mercury we just spilled. If we eat the fish that survived or a fish that had eaten a fish that survived, the mercury makes it into our bodies. Mercury causes brain damage.

Soil Pollution

Soil pollution occurs when chemicals such as pesticides, fertilizers, toxic chemicals, or radioactive wastes are introduced into the soil. Considering that we all eat produce, this form of pollution is directly affecting us.

Hazardous Waste

This type of waste refers to all kinds of substances that are harmful to life, the environment, or are difficult to break down. Hazardous waste can cause cancer, genetic disorders, and death.

▶ Natural and Human-Induced Hazards

Floods, earthquakes, hurricanes, and drought are all examples of natural hazards. All these conditions produce stresses on the environment.

- **Floods** can erode the topsoil, destroy trees, grass, and crops, and even tear down homes. Floods can also contribute to the spread of disease by damaging sewage and waste disposal mechanisms. The results of a flood can take years to undo.
- **Earthquakes** can tear up the land and produce rock slides. They can even cause flooding if a river is redirected. The effects of an earthquake in a big city can be devastating.
- **Hurricanes** can wreak havoc along the coasts, destroying plants, trees, and even highways.

Human-induced hazards include global warming, forest depletion, pollution, and nuclear waste. Global warming is directly affected by the air pollution that humans create. It results from increased levels of carbon dioxide and other gases (greenhouse gases), which produce a **greenhouse effect**. The greenhouse effect occurs when the Sun's rays, after hitting the Earth's crust and bouncing back into space, get trapped in the atmosphere because of the greenhouse gases. The trapped heat causes a rise in global temperature.

33 ▶ History and Nature of Science

In this chapter, you will read about what drives science, the nature of scientific knowledge, and how the body of scientific knowledge grows and changes over time. You will also find a brief description of some foundation-shaking advances in science.

THE WORLD'S MOST renowned scientists once believed that the Earth was flat, that the Sun revolved around the Earth, and that human beings were already fully formed within a woman's body and simply had to grow to full size in the womb. Science has a rich and often tumultuous history. Driven by curiosity and desire to help humanity, scientists have made great progress in understanding nature. This knowledge was in most cases accumulated incrementally, with one small discovery leading to another. Theories were developed to unify and explain available facts. Different interpretation of facts by different scientists has lead to controversies in the past. Some major scientific discoveries created dramatic paradigm shifts—revolutions in our understanding of nature.

▶ Science as a Human Endeavor

What can possibly get someone to study for years, read science journals, repeat experiments countless times, write applications for funding, and present results? Just like a child reaches for a new object, touches it, looks at it, takes it apart, and tries to make it work again, so the scientist looks at nature and tries to understand it. The curiosity almost seems to be innate, and the thrill that comes from understanding nature, or making a new experiment work is well expressed in the following quote.

"I do not think there is any thrill that can go through the human heart like that felt by the inventor as he sees some creation of the brain unfolding to success . . . Such emotions make a man forget food, sleep, friends, love, everything."
—Nikola Tesla, physicist and inventor

Scientists are driven by curiosity and the thrill that comes from understanding or creating something. At the same time, they are motivated by the desire to improve the quality of life—making everyday chores easier, curing diseases, and solving global and environmental problems. Scientists also seek to use, predict, and control nature—to use sunlight and water for electrical power generation, to forecast the weather and earthquakes, to prevent floods, and to prevent infection of crops and cattle.

The result is that over the years, our understanding of science has greatly improved. Humanity has gone from attributing disease to supernatural beings to developing vaccines, antibiotics, and gene therapy to prevent and cure disease. Since Thales of Miletus proposed in 625 B.C. that the Earth is a disc that floats on water, humans have discovered the true nature of their planet, have observed other galaxies, and have landed on the moon. The immense progress people have made in science is well expressed in this quote:

"The simplest schoolboy is now familiar with truths for which Archimedes would have sacrificed his life."
—Ernest Renan, philosopher

▶ The Nature of Scientific Knowledge

Scientific knowledge is rooted in factual information that is compiled and interpreted to develop theories. While scientists can't help believing and hoping—that their experiments or inventions will work; that they will solve a problem; that their theories are correct—experiments are designed to eliminate, as much as possible, the effect of the beliefs and hopes of the scientist performing them. Different scientists often get conflicting data. Even the same scientist's data is not always consistent. Differences in experimental procedure, that the scientists may or may not be aware of, can all lead different scientists to different conclusions, or even the same scientist to different conclusions, at two different times. Occasionally, this leads to controversy. In the following sections we will briefly describe the nature of scientific knowledge and how beliefs and controversies play a part.

Facts

Scientific knowledge is dependent and inseparable from facts. The principles of the scientific method guide scientists to observe facts and to propose hypotheses that can be tested by observing other facts. A hypothesis that can't be verified by collecting scientific facts is not considered part of the domain of science.

Theories

As much as a collection of bricks does not equal a house, a collection of facts does not equal science. Scientific facts, like bricks, need to be sorted and stacked properly. Their relationships to each other matter, and need to be established. Scientists need to be able to envision the end result, the way an architect needs to have an idea of what a house should look like. For scientists, the house is the theory—something that unites the facts and makes them meaningful and useful. Theories are formed when a connection between facts is first observed. The theories are then developed by looking for more facts that fit into the theory, and by modifying the theory to include or explain the facts that do not fit.

Beliefs

One of the most difficult tasks of a scientist is to remain objective and to prevent beliefs from affecting observations. This is not to say that scientists purposely hide facts that don't support their hypotheses or that are in conflict with their beliefs. Most scientists are well trained to report everything they observe, even if it's inconsistent with what was previously observed and even if it seems unimportant. However, it is in human nature to notice and remember more the things that we believe in and that we expect.

This is a form of intellectual prejudice. If Bob believes that Julie hates him, he will tend to notice only Julie's negative behavior toward him such as not saying hello and making a joke about him. He will also tend to interpret Julie's actions in a negative way. For example, if Julie says that she can't go to the movies, Bob will take that as evidence for his hypothesis that Julie hates him. However, this is not necessarily true—Julie may have too much homework. Bob could also disregard or misinterpret the nice things that Julie does—it could be a coincidence that Julie sat next to him, and that she called him up just because she needed something. Scientists can't help but to occasionally do the same thing. For example, a scientist who is a smoker may note the great number of people who smoke and don't get cancer, and attribute the fact that some people who smoke and do get cancer to pollution sensitivity or lack of proper nutrition.

Marie Curie, a two-time Nobel Prize winner, refused to note overwhelming data that suggested that radium, an element she had discovered, was a health hazard. This inability to see was not caused by lack of training, as Curie was a well enough trained scientist for her doctoral thesis to be considered the greatest single contribution to science by a doctoral student. The inability to see is caused by a blindfold made of hopes and beliefs which scientists, like all other people, can't help having once in a while.

"Man can't help hoping even if he's a scientist. He can only hope more accurately."

—Karl Menninger, psychiatrist

Controversies

Conflicting data, or facts that seemingly can't be incorporated into the same theory, often cause controversies among scientists. The controversies can polarize the scientific community, as well as the general population, especially in matters of public or social importance. In the past, controversies also sprang up between scientists and religious establishments. Copernicus shook up the Church when he proposed that planets revolved around the Sun. Similarly, Darwin caused a lot of controversy when he presented his theory of evolution. There is still some debate on whether evolution theory should be taught in public schools.

The nature of light was not very well understood for a long time. There were observations that suggested that light is a stream of particles, as well as that light is a wave. Newton's belief that light was a series of particles prevailed from the 1700s until 1873, when James Clerk Maxwell showed that light is an electromagnetic phenomenon. Although many scientists before Maxwell found evidence for the wave nature of light, Newton's great reputation and social class allowed his ideas to prevail until there was enough evidence for the contrary. Max Planck's theory about the resolution of controversies is slightly more cynical:

"A new scientific truth does not triumph by convincing its opponents and making them see the light, but rather because its opponents eventually die, and a new generation grows up that is familiar with it."

—Max Planck, physicist

▶ Historical Perspectives

All sciences are rooted in philosophy, which they stemmed from, as knowledge in different sciences accumulated and became more specialized. Areas of science today include very specific subjects, such as oceanography, crystallography, and genetic engineering, as well as interdisciplinary subjects, such as biochemistry and biophysics.

Progress in science usually occurs in small incremental steps. For example, nucleic acids (building blocks of DNA) were discovered in the nuclei of cells in 1869. After that, progress was made. Different scientists made contributions to the study of DNA. However, scientists did not solve the structure of DNA until 1953, when Rosalind Franklin, James Watson, and Francis Crick obtained their results. About 20 years later, the first genome sequencing was presented—for a virus, having a relatively small amount of genetic material. More recently, the Human Genome Project was completed. Hundreds of scientists worked on this largest single federally funded project to date with the goal of identifying all human genes and mapping out the human DNA. Scientific advances usually depend on other scientific advances and progress is usually gradual. Many scientists put in a lot of time before a new concept becomes completely understood, and before a new area of science develops.

Occasionally, however, there are leaps in scientific progress. Such leaps represent major discoveries that shake the foundations of understanding and lead to new modes of thinking. Thomas Kuhn, philosopher of science, called such discoveries paradigm shifts.

Here are some major advances in science.

- 420 B.C.: Hippocrates begins the scientific study of medicine by maintaining that diseases have common causes.
- 260 B.C.: Archimedes discovers the principle of buoyancy.

- 180 A.D.: Galen studies the connection between paralysis and severance of the spinal cord.
- 1473: Copernicus proposes a heliocentric system.
- 1581: Galileo finds that objects fall with the same acceleration.
- 1611: Kepler discovers total internal reflection and thin lens optics.
- 1620: Francis Bacon discusses the principles of the scientific method.
- 1687: Newton formulates the laws of gravity.
- 1789: Lavoisier states the law of conservation of energy.
- 1837: Darwin uses natural selection to explain evolution.
- 1864: James Clerk Maxwell shows that light is an electromagnetic phenomenon.
- 1866: Mendel discovers the laws of heredity.
- 1869: Mendeleyev designs the periodic table of elements.

- 1870: Louis Pasteur and Robert Koch establish the germ theory of disease.
- 1895: Wilhelm Röntgen discovers X-rays.
- 1907: Pavlov demonstrates behavioral conditioning with salivating dogs.
- 1912: Alfred Wegener proposes that all continents once formed a single landmass that separated by continental drift.
- 1915: Einstein publishes his theory of relativity.
- 1928: Alexander Fleming discovers penicillin.
- 1953: Rosalind Franklin, James Watson, and Francis Crick solve the structure of DNA.
- 1969: Neil Armstrong and Buzz Aldrin walk on the moon.
- 2000: A network of scientists completes the Human Genome Project.

"There is a single light in science, and to brighten it anywhere is to brighten it everywhere."

—Isaac Asimov

34 ▶ Tips and Strategies for the GED Science Exam

In this chapter, you will briefly review some tips you can use on the GED Science Exam. Several tips apply to other sections of the GED as well.

NOW THAT YOU have reviewed the information you need to know, it's time to think about strategies you can use at test time. Throughout this chapter, you will review the structure of the GED Science Exam and learn specific tips you can use to improve your score. Read this chapter carefully, and then review your notes from the science section.

▶ Multiple-Choice Questions

The good thing about multiple-choice questions is that the answer is right in front of you. All you need to do is find it, or at least eliminate some of the choices that are clearly wrong.

At times you may not be able to eliminate all four of the incorrect choices. But there is no penalty for guessing on the GED. If you can eliminate one of the wrong choices, you will have a 20% chance of guessing correctly, and that is still better than leaving it blank. The more choices you eliminate, the better chance you have of getting the question right.

When answering multiple-choice questions, make sure you have read the question carefully. Sometimes the question will ask you to choose a statement that is NOT true or find an exception to the rule.

Even when you think you have found the correct choice, quickly glance at the other choices to make sure that no other choice is better or more specific. Also check whether one of the choices is "All of the above." You may well have picked out a correct statement, but if the rest of the statements are also correct, the answer needs to be, "All of the above."

▶ Types of Questions

Two types of questions appear on the GED Science Exam—conceptual understanding and problem-solving.

Conceptual understanding questions require you to read and understand the information provided or to recall basic knowledge you have acquired through prior schooling or everyday life. Read the question and information provided along with it carefully. Often, a question will ask you to restate what was already said or to make a generalization about the facts presented in a passage. By reading carefully, and making notes on a piece of scratch paper as you go along, you increase your chances of understanding the provided information correctly.

Problem-solving questions require you to apply what you have read or learned. As you are studying for the exam, when presented with a scientific fact, such as "energy can be converted from one form to another," think about the situations in which that fact is apparent. Think about a car—using the chemical energy in the fuel to cause the car to move and the engine to heat. Think about how the fuel level decreases as the car moves. Where is the fuel going? What is happening to the exhaust gases? The principles of science are all around you. By paying attention to them in your everyday life, you will be better prepared to answer problem-solving questions on the GED Science Exam.

▶ Reading and Understanding Graphics

Up to 60% of all GED Science Exam questions include graphics. By becoming familiar with different types of graphics and learning about their essential components, you will be better prepared to answer GED Science Exam questions that contain graphical information.

When looking at a chart or a graph, look at the title or caption first. This will give you an overview of what the graphic is showing. Next, look at any legends or axis labels provided. This will give you an idea of what variables are shown. Make a list of the variables. Once you have done that, you can try to interpret the chart or graph by noting any trends you may see. How is one variable changing in response to the other? Next, you can read the question and attempt to answer it. Here is more specific information about graphics.

Charts

CHART TITLE

	Title of Column 1	Title of Column 2
Title of Row 1		
Title of Row 2		
Title of Row 3		

All charts are composed of rows (horizontal) and columns (vertical). Entries in a single row of a chart usually have something in common, and so do entries in a single column. Determine what the common elements are when you try to answer the questions on the GED Science Exam.

Graphs

Three common types of graphs are scatter plots, bar graphs, and pie graphs. Here you will find a brief description of each.

Whenever a variable depends continuously on another variable, this dependence can be visually represented in a scatter plot. Examples include a change in a property (such as human population) as a function of time. A scatter plot consists of the horizontal (x) axis, the vertical (y) axis, and collected data points for variable y, measured at variable x. The variable points are often connected with a line or a curve. A graph often contains a legend, especially if there is more than one data set or more than one variable. A legend is a key for interpreting the graph.

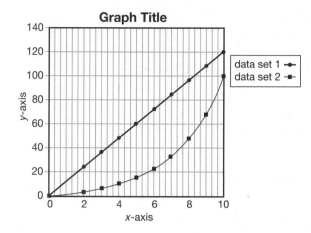

Look at the sample graph. The essential elements of the graph—the *x*- and *y*-axes—are labeled. The legend to the right of the graph shows that dots are used to represent the variable points in data set 1, while squares are used to represent the variable points in data set 2. If only one data set exists, the use of a legend is not essential.

Bar graphs are similar to scatter plots. Both have a variable *y* plotted against a variable *x*. However, in bar graphs data is represented by bars, rather than by points connected with a line. Bar graphs are often used to indicate an amount or level, as opposed to a continuous change. Pie graphs are often used to show what percentage of a total is taken up by different components of that whole.

Diagrams

Diagrams could be used to show a sequence of events, a chemical or biological process, the setup of a science experiment, a phenomenon, the relationship between different events or beings, and so forth. When you see a diagram, first ask yourself what its purpose is. What is it trying to illustrate? Then look at the different labeled parts of the diagram. What is their function? How are they interrelated?

▶ Reading and Understanding Scientific Passages

When you read a scientific passage, the most important thing is to focus on the big picture, or on what the passage is about. In many ways, the reading passages in the science part of the GED are the same as the reading passages in other areas. One important difference is that science passages may expose you to science jargon, specialized vocabulary you may not be familiar with. Try

not to let new words throw you off. You may be able to guess their meaning from the context. Even if you can't, keep reading. The questions following the passage may not require you to understand that particular word.

▶ Series of Questions Based on a Passage or Graphic

On the GED Science Exam, you will sometimes be asked more than one question based on the same graphic or passage. When this is the case, it is worth your while to invest a little more time to understand the graphic or passage. Even if you are unsure about the first one, try answering the rest of the questions—they may be easier for you.

▶ Experiment Skills

Experiments should be designed and conducted in accordance with the principles of the scientific method. This means that the goal of the experiment should be carefully formulated and the experiment should be set up to yield factual results. Review the concepts of the scientific method in the Science as Inquiry chapter if the tips included in this section are unfamiliar to you.

Setting Up an Experiment

Experiments should be set up to test one clearly formulated and testable hypothesis. The number of variables (things changing) in the experiment should be limited and carefully controlled. If possible, experiments should contain a control group. For example, if you were to study the effect of a new soil supplement on house plants, the soil supplement should not be used on a few plants, which will comprise the control group. If there is improvement in the growth of only the plants on which the supplement was used, then there is strong indication that the supplement increases the plant growth. If, however, the plants in the control group grow as much as the plants on which the supplement was used, then the causes of growth most likely are not linked to the supplement. In this example, there would be two variables— 1) the use of the supplement and 2) the plant growth.

How the supplement is administered and how plant growth is measured would need to be carefully described and controlled. For example, the scientist conducting the experiment would need to decide whether the supplement would be administered once, several times, or every day throughout the experiment. The scientist would also need to define what constitutes plant growth—the vertical increase, the number of new leaves, the growth of new branches and leaves, or some combination of these factors. One choice is not necessarily better than the others. Measuring the vertical growth wouldn't necessarily be worse than counting the number of new leaves. The important issue is to be consistent. If the number of leaves per plant is recorded on the first day, the number of leaves per plant should be recorded every day.

On the GED Science Exam, you may be asked to pick out the best design for an experiment. Before you look at the choices, determine what the important variables are, and think what would make a good control. Select the choice that contains the variables you thought of, that has the most logical experimental control, and in which the variables not studied are held constant.

Interpreting Others' Results

In some GED Science Exam questions, you will be asked to interpret others' results. You will need to make a generalization about the results or to draw a conclusion. Don't base your answer on what you believe is right. Base your answers on the results provided. Look at the choices given. Some could be inaccurate—if one part of the result doesn't fit the description in the choice, the choice is wrong (unless words such as *generally* or *in most cases* make room for exceptions). Make sure you don't jump to conclusions. A trend doesn't always indicate a cause and effect relationship. For example, every morning your alarm clock goes off and every morning you get hungry. However, the alarm clock is not what is making you hungry. The two events just happen to occur at the same time. Before you conclude that there is a cause and effect relationship, consider other conclusions, and then pick the most logical one.

Analyzing Experimental Flaws

A common GED Science Exam question requires you to analyze the flaws of an experiment. Experiments should be based on the scientific method. Common experimental flaws include:

- not testing the hypothesis
- having too many variables
- unforeseen variables

- lack of experimental control
- jumping to conclusions

Applying Scientific Conclusions

What good is science if we don't benefit from it? How would the finding that keeping a laptop on your lap for too long can damage your pelvic organs influence you? You would not keep the laptop on your lap for too long, right? Many questions on the GED Science Exam require you to apply a scientific conclusion, either to your personal life or to global phenomena. These are almost always questions from the problem-solving category. You are presented with a fact in one context and asked to apply it in another context. For example, if you read in a passage about different methods of determining the poles of the Earth in nature without a compass, you could be asked which of the methods would best work if you were in a particular situation—lost on a cloudy night in a forest, on the ocean on a clear day, etc. If necessary, as you are reading information provided in the question, make quick diagrams and summarize the important concepts on a piece of scrap paper. These strategies may help you visualize the concepts or the situation given and could help you make sense of the question.

▶ Other Useful Skills

The more material you are exposed to, the easier it will become to understand it. Reading about science and applying science takes practice, just like riding a bike. At first you may be a bit clumsy with it, but if you stick with it, you improve rapidly and it begins to click. To comprehend science better, read as much about science as you can—in newspapers, magazines, and online. Make sure you look at graphics as well. As you are reading, think about what the passage or graphic is communicating to you. What are the possible applications of the science concepts discussed? What can you conclude based on the information given? What methods were used to arrive at the facts presented? Is anything that is presented an opinion or belief rather than a fact? Try to make up questions about the passage or graphic you read. Imagine that you are making up the GED Science Exam: What could you ask the students? By anticipating the move of your opponent, you are better prepared to respond to it.

▶ Science Glossary

A good working science vocabulary is a very important asset when taking the GED Science Exam. Remember that the best way to learn vocabulary is also the easiest: make long lists of words you don't know and then break them down into short lists. Learn a short list every day.

You should also try and write sentences using the new scientific words. When you learn a new word, use it in conversation as soon as possible. Repetition is key—use a word three times, and it's yours!

Another alternative is to work with flash cards. Flash cards are pieces of paper or index cards that are used as a learning aid. Write the science word on one side and the definition on the other. Or, try writing a sentence that uses the word on one side of the flash card and the definition of the word on the other. Flash cards are easy to handle, they're portable, and they're friend-friendly, so you can study with a buddy. You and your friends can drill each other. If you can make games out of learning new science terms, studying will be more fun and you will learn more as well!

Now, review the following glossary.

acceleration: the rate that velocity changes per unit of time and the direction it changes in, computed from the change in velocity divided by the change in time. Common units are meters per second squared ($\frac{m}{s^2}$).

acceleration due to gravity: the acceleration of an object that is only acted on by the force of the Earth's gravity. This value is given the symbol *g*, and near the surface of the Earth it has a value of approximately $9.8 \frac{m}{s^2}$. The direction of acceleration due to gravity is downward.

accuracy: the closeness of an experimental measurement to the accepted or theoretical value

acid: a substance that is a proton donor. The pH of an acid is less than 7.

analysis: a stage in the scientific method where patterns of the observations are made

aqueous solution: a solution in which the solvent is water

arteries: the vascular tissues that carry blood away from the heart

astronomy: the study of the planets, stars, and space

atom: the smallest structure that has the properties of an element. Atoms contain positively charged protons and uncharged neutrons in the nucleus. Negatively charged electrons orbit around the nucleus.

ATP (Adenosine Triphosphate): a chemical that is considered to be the "fuel" or energy source for an organism

atria: the chambers of the heart that receive blood

base: a substance that is a proton acceptor. The pH of a base is greater than 7.

calibration: the examination of the performance of an instrument in an experiment whose outcomes are known, for the purpose of accounting for the inaccuracies inherent in the instrument in future experiments whose outcomes are not known

capillaries: vascular tissues that receive blood from the arterioles and release the blood to the venuoles

catalyst: an agent that changes the rate of a reaction, without itself being altered by the reaction

celestial equator: the extension of the Earth's equator out onto the celestial sphere

celestial poles: the extension of the Earth's north and south poles onto the celestial sphere

celestial sphere: the imaginary sphere which all the stars are viewed as being on for the purposes of locating them

cell membrane: an organelle found in all cells that acts as the passageway through which materials can pass in and out. This organelle is selectively permeable, only allowing materials to pass through that it "chooses" chemically.

cell wall: an organelle found primarily in plant cells and fungi cells, and also some bacteria. The cell wall is a strong structure that provides protection, support, and allows materials to pass in and out without being selectively permeable.

centripetal force: the net force that acts to result in the centripetal acceleration. It is not an individual force, but the sum of the forces in the radial direction. It is directed toward the center of the circular motion.

chemical change: a process that involves the formation or breaking of chemical bonds *chromosome*: an organelle that contains the entire DNA of the organism

component: the part of a vector that lies in the horizontal or vertical direction

compound: a substance composed of more than one element that has a definite composition and distinct physical and chemical properties

concentration: a measure of the amount of solute that is present in a solution. A solution that contains very little solute is called dilute. A solution that contains a relatively large amount of solute is said to be concentrated.

conclusion: the last stage of the scientific method, where explanations are made about why the patterns identified in the analysis section occurred

constellation: an apparent grouping of stars in the sky that is used for identification purposes. These stars are not necessarily near each other in space, since they are not necessarily the same distance from the Earth.

continental rift: the region on a continent where new crust is being created, and the plates on either side of the rift are moving apart

convergent boundary: a boundary between two of the Earth's plates that are moving toward each other

cosmology: the study of the formation of the universe

crystal: a solid in which atoms or molecules have a regular repeated arrangement

current: the flow of charge past a point per unit time; current is measured in amperes (A)

cuticle: the top layer on a leaf. It is a nonliving layer consisting primarily of wax that is produced by the epithelium, a cell layer directly underneath.

cytoplasm: a jellylike substance located in the cell where all of the internal organelles can be found. The cytoplasm consists primarily of water and supports the cell and its organelles.

cytoskeleton: organelles that are the internal "bones" of the cell. They exist in thick and thin tubules.

decibel: a unit of measure for the relative intensity of sounds

declination: measures how many degrees, minutes, and seconds north or south of the celestial equator an object is

delta: a fan-shaped deposit of material at the mouth of a river

density: the mass of a substance for a given unit volume. A common unit of density is grams per milliliter (g/ml).

displacement: the change in position of an object, computed by calculating the final position minus the initial position. Common units of measure are meters (m).

divergent boundary: a boundary between two of the Earth's plates that are moving away from each other

DNA: contains all genetic material for an organism. The smallest units of DNA are called nucleotides.

ecliptic: the apparent path of the Sun across the sky over the course of a year

electric potential energy: the energy due to an object's position within an electric field

electromagnetic wave: a light wave that has an electric field component and a magnetic field component. An electromagnetic wave does not require a medium to travel through.

electrostatic force: the force that exists between particles due to their charge. Particles of like charge repel, particles of unlike charge attract.

element: the smallest entity that has distinct chemical properties. It cannot be decomposed by ordinary chemical reactions.

ellipse: a geometric shape that is formed when a plane intersects with a cone. In this case, the plane intersects the cone at an angle, so that a shape similar to a circle but stretched in one direction is formed. The orbits of the planets around the Sun represent ellipses.

endoplasmic reticulum: an organelle that is used to transport proteins throughout the cell

energy: the ability to do work or undergo change. Kinetic energy is the energy of motion, while potential energy is stored energy.

epicycle: smaller circles on which the planets traveled around the Earth in the geocentric model of the solar system. Epicycles were used to explain the retrograde motion of planets and helped make the predicted positions of the planets match the observed positions.

equilibrium: a state at which the forward and reverse reactions proceed at the same rate

focal length: the distance from a focal point to a mirror or lens

force: that which acts on an object to change its motion; a push or pull exerted on one object by another. Common units are newtons (N).

freefall: an object in one-dimensional motion that is only acted on by the force of the Earth's gravity. In this case, its acceleration will be *–g* or *g* downward.

frequency: the number of cycles or repetitions per second. Frequency is also often measured as the number of revolutions per second. The common units of frequency are hertz (Hz), where one hertz equals 1 cycle/second.

frictional force: the force that acts parallel to surfaces in contact opposite the direction of motion or tendency of motion

functional group: a group of atoms that give a molecule a certain characteristic or property

gel electrophoresis: a process used in laboratories to determine the genetic makeup of DNA strands. This process involves the movement of chromosomes through a gel from one pole to the other. Magnetism is used to pull the chromosomes through the gel.

geocentric model: the model of the solar system that places the Earth at the center with the planets and the Sun orbiting around it

geology: the study of rocks and minerals

glacier: a large mass of snow-covered ice

Golgi apparatus: an organelle that packages proteins so that they can be sent out of the cell

gravitational force: the attractive force that exists between all particles with mass

heliocentric model: the model of the solar system that places the Sun at the center with the planets orbiting around it

heterogeneous: a mixture that is not uniform in composition

homogeneous: a mixture in which the components are uniformly distributed

hydrate: a crystal of a molecule that also contains water in the crystal structure. If the water evaporates, the crystal becomes anhydrous.

hydrology: the study of the Earth's water and water systems

hypothesis: a step in the scientific method where a prediction is made about the end result of an experiment. A hypothesis is generally based on research of related data.

igneous rock: a rock formed through the cooling of magma

image distance: the distance from an image to a mirror or lens

inertia: the tendency of an object to follow Newton's First Law, the law of inertia. That is the tendency of an object to remain at rest or in motion with constant velocity unless acted on by a force.

inorganic: a material that is neither plant nor animal in origin

intensity: the power per unit area of a wave; measured in Watts/m^2

ion: an atom that has either lost electrons to become a positively charged cation, or has gained electrons to become a negatively charged anion

isomers: substances that have the same molecular formula (same number of elements) in different arrangements

isotopes: atoms of the same element, with different numbers of neutrons, and hence a different atomic mass

Jovian planet: one of the outer planets of the solar system that have characteristics similar to that of Jupiter. They are also called gas planets. They are large, have high mass, have many moons, may have rings, are far from the Sun and each other, have thick atmospheres, are gaseous and have low density, have a composition similar to that of the Sun, have short rotation rates, and have long revolution periods around the Sun. The Jovian planets are Jupiter, Saturn, Uranus, and Neptune.

kinetic energy: the energy due to an object's motion or velocity

land breeze: the breeze that develops on the shoreline due to unequal heating of the air above the land and ocean. Land breeze occurs at night when the air above the land is cooler and the air above the ocean is warmer. The breeze blows from the land to the sea.

latitude: the coordinate used to measure positions on the Earth north or south of the Earth's equator. Latitude is measured in degrees, minutes, and seconds. Zero degrees latitude is the Earth's equator.

longitude: the coordinate used to measure positions on the Earth east or west of the prime meridian, which goes through Greenwich, England. Longitude is measured in degrees, minutes, and seconds.

longitudinal wave: a wave that has the direction of motion of the particles in the medium parallel to the direction of motion of the wave. Sound is an example of a longitudinal wave.

mass: the amount of matter in an object; also a measure of the amount of inertia of an object. Common units are kilograms (kg).

meander: a broad curve in a river

meiosis: a process of cellular reproduction where the daughter cells have half the amount of chromosomes. This is used for purposes of sexual reproduction to produce sex cells that will be able to form an offspring with a complete set of chromosomes with different DNA than the parents.

meniscus: the curved surface of a liquid in a container, caused by surface tension

metamorphic rock: a rock whose crystal structure has been changed through heat and/or pressure

meteorology: the study of the Earth's atmosphere and weather

mid-oceanic ridge: a region under the ocean where new crust is being created, and the plates on either side of the ridge are moving apart

mineral: a naturally occurring element or compound found in the Earth's crust

mitochondria: an organelle that produces ATP

mitosis: a process in which cells produce genetically identical offspring

mixture: a physical combination of different substances

mole: the amount of substance that contains as many particles as there are atoms in 12 grams of the carbon 12 isotope (6.022×10^{23} particles)

molecular mass: the sum of the atomic masses in a molecule

molecule: a substance formed by a chemical bond between two or more atoms

net force: the vector sum of all the forces acting on an object

newton: the metric and System International unit of force. One newton equals one kg/s^2.

non-renewable resource: a resource that is not replaced in nature as quickly as it is used. In many cases it is not replaced or re-formed at all.

normal force: this force acts between any two surfaces in contact. It is the part of the contact force that acts normally or perpendicular to the surfaces in contact.

nucleolus: an organelle found inside a nucleus that is responsible for the production of ribosomes

nucleotide: the smallest unit of DNA. There are five different types of nucleotides: adenine, guanine, thymine, cytosine, and uracil. The arrangement of genes is based directly on the specific arrangement of nucleotides.

nucleus: an organelle in a cell that contains all of the DNA and controls the functions of the cell

object distance: the distance from an object to a mirror or lens

oceanography: the study of the Earth's oceans

orbit: the path an object takes as it travels around another in space

organic: a material that is plant or animal in origin

oxbow lake: a crescent-shaped lake formed when a meander is cut off from the river it was part of

oxidation: the loss of electrons by a substance in a chemical reaction *parallel circuit*: a circuit with more than one path for the current to follow

period: the time, often measured in seconds, for one complete repetition or rotation

phloem: vascular tissue found in plants that transports mostly sugar and water; can travel either "shoot to root" or "root to shoot."

photon: a particle of light. A discreet amount of light energy where a single photon of light is the smallest unit of light energy possible.

photosynthesis: a process by which the sunlight's energy, water, and carbon dioxide are transformed into sugar and oxygen

physical property: a property that can be observed without performing a chemical transformation of that substance

plate tectonics: the theory in which Earth's crust is made up of many plates that float on the mantle. This theory explains the movement of the continents, the formation of mountains and volcanoes, and the existence of mid-oceanic ridges and earthquakes.

polymer: a large molecule made up of repeating units of one or more small molecules (monomers)

position: the location of an object in a coordinate system. Common units of measure are meters (m).

potential difference: the difference in electric potential energy per unit charge between two points. This is commonly called voltage. The common unit of measure for potential difference is called volts.

potential energy: the energy due to an object's position or state

precession: the process by which the Earth's axis traces out a circle on the celestial sphere

precision: the closeness of measurements obtained from two or more experimental runs

pressure: force per unit area. Units used to measure pressure are torr, atmosphere (atm), and pascal (pa).

procedure: a logical list of steps that explain the exact actions taken to perform an experiment

projectile: an object in two-dimensional motion that has a vertical acceleration equal to $-g$ (or g downward) and a horizontal acceleration of zero

protein synthesis: a process by which DNA will transport its information by way of RNA to the ribosomes where proteins will be assembled

qualitative observation: an observation that includes characteristics other than amounts or measurements; may include shapes, colors, actions, and odors

quantitative observation: an observation that includes characteristics of measurements or amounts

radiation: the emission of energy

reactant: a substance that is consumed in a chemical reaction to form products

reduction: the gain of electrons by a substance in a chemical reaction

renewable resource: a renewable resource is replaced in nature as quickly as it is used

resistance: the resistance to the flow of electrons through a circuit. The resistance is dependant on the current flowing through the circuit element and the voltage across the circuit element; resistance is measured in ohms.

respiration: a process by which sugar is converted into ATP and carbon dioxide; may include oxygen, which is called aerobic respiration

retrograde motion: the apparent westward motion of objects in the sky from one night to another

reversible reaction: a reaction in which products can revert back into reactants

ribosome: an organelle where protein synthesis occurs; can be found floating freely in the cytoplasm or attached to the outside of endoplasmic reticulum

right ascension: the celestial coordinate similar to that of longitude on the Earth. Right ascension is measured in hours, minutes, and seconds with 24 hours making up 360° around the celestial sphere.

river system: a river and its associated tributaries and drainage basin

RNA: ribonucleic acid; responsible for transmitting genetic information from the DNA to the ribosomes for protein synthesis

rock cycle: the rock cycle summarizes how rocks of different types are formed and how they can be transformed from one type into another

scalar: a quantity that has a magnitude or amount only

scientific method: a process by which data is collected to answer an integral question. The major steps are problem, hypothesis, research, procedure, observations and data collection, analysis of data, and conclusion.

sedimentary rock: a rock made up of sediments that have been deposited and compacted and cemented over time

sea breeze: the breeze that develops on the shoreline due to unequal heating of the air above the land and ocean. Sea breeze occurs during the day when the air above the ocean is cooler and the air above the land is warmer. The breeze blows from the sea to the land.

series circuit: a circuit with only one path for the current to follow. The current in each element in a series circuit is the same.

solubility: the amount of solute that can be dissolved completely in a solvent at a given temperature

solution: a homogeneous mixture of a solute (usually solid, but sometimes liquid or gas) in a solvent (usually a liquid, but sometimes a solid or gas)

speed: the magnitude of velocity. It measures the rate position changes with time without regard to the direction of motion; common units are meters per second (m/s).

speed of light: The speed of light in a vacuum is the fastest speed possible. As light travels in other materials, it will change speed. The speed of light in any material is still the fastest speed possible in that material; commonly denoted by the symbol *c*.

spindle fiber: an organelle used during mitosis and meiosis that separates and "pulls" chromosomes toward the opposite poles of the cell

spontaneous reaction: a reaction that does not require an external source of energy to proceed

star: a body composed mostly of hydrogen and helium that radiates energy and that has fusion actively occurring in the core

states of matter: solid, liquid, and gas. In solids, atoms or molecules are held in place. The shape and volume of a solid usually do not vary much. In liquids atoms or molecules can move, but their motion is constrained by other molecules. Liquids assume the shape of their container. In gases the motion of atoms or molecules is unrestricted. Gases assume both the volume and the shape of their containers and they are easily compressible.

temperature: the measure of the average kinetic energy of the molecules of a substance

tension: the force that acts and is transferred along ropes, strings, and chains

terminal moraine: a ridge of material deposited by a glacier at its farthest point of advance

terrestrial planet: one of the inner planets of the solar system that have characteristics similar to that of the Earth. They are small, have low mass, have few or no moons, have no rings, are close to the Sun and are close to each other, have thin or no atmosphere, are rocky and have high density, have long rotation rates, and have short revolution periods around the Sun. The terrestrial planets are Mercury, Venus, Earth, and Mars.

topography: the study of the surface features of the planet primarily through mapping

transverse wave: a wave that has the direction of motion of the particles in the medium perpendicular to the direction of motion of the wave.

uniform circular motion: motion with constant speed in a circle. Since the direction of the velocity changes in this case, there is acceleration even though the speed is constant.

valence electrons: electrons that are in the outer atomic shell and can participate in a chemical reaction

vector: a quantity that has both a magnitude (an amount) and a direction. In one-dimensional motion, the direction can be represented by a positive or negative sign. In two-dimensional motion, the direction is represented as an angle in the coordinate system.

veins: in plants, found in the leaves; sometimes called the vascular bundle that contains the xylem and phloem. In animals, tubelike tissue that usually transports blood.

velocity: the rate that a position changes per unit time and the direction it changes in. Common units are meters per second (m/s).

ventricles: chambers found in animal hearts that pump blood away from the heart

voltage: another name for potential difference

voltmeter: a device used to measure voltage in a circuit

water cycle: the movement of water between the land, oceans, and atmosphere

weight: the force of the Earth's gravity on an object. Near the surface of the Earth the weight is equal to the object's mass times the acceleration due to gravity ($W = mg$).

xylem: vascular tissue found in plants that transports water in one direction: "root to shoot." This is the water that will be sent to the photosynthetic cells in order to perform photosynthesis.

VI ▶ The GED Social Studies Exam

IN THIS SECTION, you will learn about the GED Social Studies Exam: what the exam is like, the types of questions to expect, and tips and strategies for answering those questions. Review chapters will also provide you with an overview of basic social studies topics and key terms.

Before you begin Chapter 35, take the pretest that follows. The pretest is a sample of the kinds of questions you will find on the GED Social Studies Exam. After you complete the pretest, compare your answers with the answer key. Your pretest results will show you which areas you need to review and how much preparation you need.

▶ **Pretest: GED Social Studies**

Directions: Read each question carefully. The questions are multiple choice and may be based on a passage, table, or illustration. Select the one best answer for each question. Record your answers on the answer sheet that follows. To practice the timing of the exam, take approximately 15 minutes to complete the pretest.

Note: On the GED, you are not permitted to write in the test booklet. Make any notes or calculations on a separate piece of paper.

ANSWER SHEET

1. ⓐ ⓑ ⓒ ⓓ ⓔ
2. ⓐ ⓑ ⓒ ⓓ ⓔ
3. ⓐ ⓑ ⓒ ⓓ ⓔ
4. ⓐ ⓑ ⓒ ⓓ ⓔ
5. ⓐ ⓑ ⓒ ⓓ ⓔ
6. ⓐ ⓑ ⓒ ⓓ ⓔ
7. ⓐ ⓑ ⓒ ⓓ ⓔ
8. ⓐ ⓑ ⓒ ⓓ ⓔ
9. ⓐ ⓑ ⓒ ⓓ ⓔ
10. ⓐ ⓑ ⓒ ⓓ ⓔ

Questions 1–2 are based on the following passage.

An **oligarchy** is a form of government in which power is shared by a select, often elite, group of people. The theory behind this type of government is that some people are better equipped to rule than others. The ancient Greek city-state of Sparta is a famous example of an oligarchy. In Sparta, two kings served as heads of the city-state. The government also included a council of elders and an assembly of citizens called "equals." However, the most powerful rulers were those who sat on a board of five **ephors**—Spartan citizens who were elected each year. They fulfilled most of the executive, legislative, and judicial functions of the city-state.

1. What is the main idea of the paragraph?
   a. The Spartan dual kingship was not as powerful as the board of ephors.
   b. Finding capable leaders was a problem in ancient Greece.
   c. The government of Sparta is a good example of an oligarchy.
   d. People today discount the effectiveness of an oligarchy.
   e. Oligarchy is based on the idea that having one ruler is best.

2. According to this passage, what is the central idea behind an oligarchy?
   a. All citizens should participate equally in government.
   b. Government should be controlled by those most fit to govern.
   c. Government by a single, all-powerful ruler is best.
   d. A system of checks and balances is necessary to prevent any individual or branch of government from gaining too much power.
   e. Effective government requires that a nation have two kings.

Questions 3–4 are based on the following chart.

Educational Level and Income

EDUCATIONAL LEVEL	AVERAGE TOTAL EARNINGS, 2005 (IN DOLLARS)	
	MEN, AGE 25 AND OLDER	**WOMEN, AGE 25 AND OLDER**
Less than 9th grade	16,321	9,496
9th to 12th grade (no diploma)	22,934	11,136
High school graduate (includes GED)	30,134	16,695
Some college, no degree	36,930	21,545
Associate's degree	41,903	26,074
Bachelor's degree	51,700	32,668
Master's degree	64,468	44,385
Professional degree	90,878	59,934
Doctorate degree	76,937	56,820

Source: U.S. Census Bureau.

3. Of workers age 25 and older, who earned the most money on average in 2005?
- a. men with a professional degree
- b. men with a doctorate degree
- c. women with a professional degree
- d. women with a college degree of any level
- e. men with a master's degree

4. Based on the chart, what conclusion can you draw?
- a. Women receive equal pay for equal work.
- b. Earning a high school equivalency does not pay.
- c. Men earn more than women at every educational level.
- d. Men and women with doctorate degrees earn the most.
- e. Attending college does not affect earning power.

▶ Answers

1. **c.** Choice **c** best describes the main idea. Choice **a** is a detail from the passage. Choices **b** and **d** are not supported by the paragraph, and choice **e** is incorrect.

2. **b.** The paragraph states, "The theory behind this type of government is that some people are better equipped to rule than others." Choice **b** is a good paraphrase of this statement.

3. **a.** Men, age 25 and older, with professional degrees earned on average $90,878 in 2005—more than women and any other educational level.

4. **c.** The chart shows that men earn more on average than women at every level of education.

▶ Pretest Assessment

How did you do on the social studies pretest? Remember that this pretest covers only a fraction of the material you might find on the actual GED. The pretest is *not* designed to give you an accurate measure of how you would do on the official GED. Rather, it is designed to help you determine where to focus your study efforts. For success on the GED, review all of the chapters in this section thoroughly. Focus on the topics that correspond to the pretest questions you answered incorrectly.

35 ▶ About the GED Social Studies Exam

To prepare effectively for the GED Social Studies Exam, you need to know exactly what the exam is like. This chapter explains the structure of the exam, including the types of questions and stimuli you will see on the exam.

▶ What to Expect on the GED Social Studies Exam

The GED Social Studies Exam covers basic social studies concepts and includes questions from four main content areas:

1. U.S. and world history
2. geography
3. civics and government
4. economics

The exam applies these four topics to your daily life and looks at how they affect your role as an individual, a member of a community, a family member, a worker or student, and a consumer. You will not be asked to memorize facts. Instead, the exam will measure your critical thinking skills. These skills include your ability to understand, analyze, and evaluate social studies material.

The exam includes 50 multiple-choice questions (items) for which you will have 70 minutes to complete. Each multiple-choice question has five answer choices. The exam will include some question sets, meaning that several questions may address a single graphic or reading passage. Question sets usually have from two to five items.

The exam may require you to use your understanding of different social studies concepts within the same question set.

Kinds of Stimuli

Exam questions are based on three kinds of stimuli materials: reading passages, visuals, and combined stimuli that use both reading passages and visuals. Here is what you can expect on the GED Social Studies Exam:

- **Reading passages** from articles, speeches, textbooks, laws, or other documents. Reading passages range in length from 50 to 60 words for single-item questions to no more than 200 words for question sets. Forty percent of the questions on the GED Social Studies Exam will be based on reading passages. The exam will include one or more excerpts from the U.S. Declaration of Independence, U.S. Constitution, Federalist Papers, and Supreme Court landmark cases. Review these documents before taking the exam to familiarize yourself with their fundamental concepts.
- **Visuals** including maps, graphs, charts, tables, diagrams, photographs, and political cartoons. Forty percent of the questions in the exam are based on some form of graphic. The exam will also use one practical document such as a voter's registration form, consumer guide, tax form, budget tool, survey, workplace contract, bank statement, insurance form, or other document.
- **Combined stimuli** using both text and visuals. Combined materials make up 20% of the exam's questions.

GED Components

Here is a quick breakdown of how material will be presented on the GED Social Studies Exam:

Reading Passages	40%
Visuals	40%
Combined Text and Visuals	20%

Kinds of Questions

The questions on the GED Social Studies Exam measure four major thinking skills: *comprehension* (your ability to understand), *application* (apply information to new sit-

uations), *analysis* (break down information and analyze it), and *evaluation* (make judgments about information). Here is the breakdown of the types of questions on the GED Social Studies Exam:

Comprehension questions	20%
Application questions	20%
Analysis questions	40%
Evaluation questions	20%

Each question type looks at a different thinking skill.

- **Comprehension.** For these questions, you will read passages or review visuals and demonstrate that you understand the meaning of the text or graphic. To answer these questions, you may need to restate information that you have read, summarize ideas from a passage, or draw conclusions. When answering these types of questions, **do not use any prior or additional knowledge of a subject that you might have**. These exam questions measure your ability to find the best answer based only on the information that is provided. Comprehension questions are typically worded as in the following examples:

  - Which of the following best describes the passage?
  - What is the purpose of this paragraph?
  - According to the map, which of the following is true?
  - What conclusion can you make based on the information in the chart?

- **Application.** These questions ask you to take information or ideas from one situation and apply them to a different situation. Here are some examples of application questions:

  - Who might use the information in this graph to support their position?
  - Which of the following is the most similar to the situation described?

- **Analysis.** For these questions, you need to break down ideas and show relationships between ideas. You might be asked to differentiate between fact and opinion, identify an assumption that the author has made but has not stated explicitly, identify cause-and-effect relationships, or compare and contrast information or ideas. Typical analysis questions may be worded as in the following examples:

- Based on the quotation, what can we infer about the speaker?
- The writer's position depends on which of the following assumptions?

■ **Evaluation.** These questions ask you to synthesize information and make your own hypothesis or theory. Some questions will require that you evaluate information or ideas and make a judgment about whether the information is accurate. You will need to look at data to back up conclusions, identify how values and beliefs shape decisions, and uncover arguments that might be illogical. Here are some examples of typical evaluation questions:

- Which of the following is supported by the information given in the passage?
- Which of the following is an unlikely explanation of the information presented in the graph?
- Which of the following expresses an opinion rather than a fact?

Exam Topics

The exam covers four main subjects:

1. history
2. geography
3. civics and government
4. economics

Although you will not need to memorize facts from these four categories, you will need to use your knowledge of social studies concepts and apply your critical thinking skills. This will help you review key social studies terms and offer basic information in each content area.

Four Main Subjects

The GED Social Studies Exam covers these four topics:

History	United States, 25%; World, 15%
Geography	15%
Civics and Government	25%
Economics	20%

Questions also indirectly address the following interdisciplinary themes:

- Culture
- Time, Continuity, and Change
- People, Places, and Environments
- Individual Development and Identity
- Individuals, Groups, and Institutions
- Power, Authority, and Governance
- Production, Distribution, and Consumption
- Science, Technology, and Society
- Global Connections
- Civic Ideals and Practice

Although it is obvious how certain themes relate to the specific content standards in history (i.e., Production, Distribution, and Consumption to Economics), the majority of these themes are interwoven throughout the history content areas.

Sixty percent of the items or passages in the exam have a global or international context. Forty percent concerns specific developments in U.S. history. In some cases, the United States factors into the international setting, while in others, questions focus on different parts of the world.

The GED Social Studies Exam has an emphasis on the way material is presented, with graphic or visual source materials making up the majority of the exam's stimuli. In addition, a great percentage of questions measure your ability to analyze.

36▶ History

On the GED, questions about *history* will include both world and U.S. history. Many history questions will ask you to interpret and analyze a photograph, map, chart, or graph.

▶Defining "Social Studies"

Social studies is the study of how people live every day. It explores many aspects of life: the physical environment in which people live, the beliefs and traditions they follow, and the societies they form and inhabit. Social studies include many different fields, broadly described as history, civics and government, economics, and geography. Each of these four categories is related. To understand an event or a complex issue, you would examine all four branches of social sciences. For example, if you were studying the stock market crash of 1929, you would explore what was happening in the country at the time (history); how the free enterprise system works (economics); what programs and policies were implemented to safeguard against another crash (civics and government); and how this event affected people in different areas of the country and why (geography).

This chapter introduces you to key terms and time periods from the history branch of social studies. The exercises in this chapter will help you review the information you learn and are similar to those on the GED Social Studies Exam.

▶World History

The Beginnings of Civilization

Early humans lived in nomadic groups that followed the animal herds they hunted. Over time, these nomads settled in areas with a fresh water source, fertile soil, a hospitable climate, and plentiful animal life. From cave drawings, artifacts, fossils, and skeletal remains, scientists have learned about early humans and their communities. Artifacts of stone tools like hammers or axes are some of the earliest evidence of human culture. As communities grew, a system of **bartering**—trading goods or services—developed. Forms of government—systems that organized societies—also evolved. Through trade routes and wars, human cultural achievements spread between places and some civilizations became empires with large land holdings. For example, the area of Mesopotamia (see map below) gave rise to several ancient civilizations—Babylonian, Sumerian, Phoenician, and Greek.

Religion

Religion, or belief in a spiritual reality, is an influential part of human culture. Early belief systems, including those of the Egyptians, Greeks, and the early Roman Empire, were **polytheistic**, meaning they revered more than one god. The Jewish tribes of Israel were **monotheistic**, believing in one all-powerful god. See the table on page 301. In the Far East, there were religious practices that were polytheistic and others that were monotheistic.

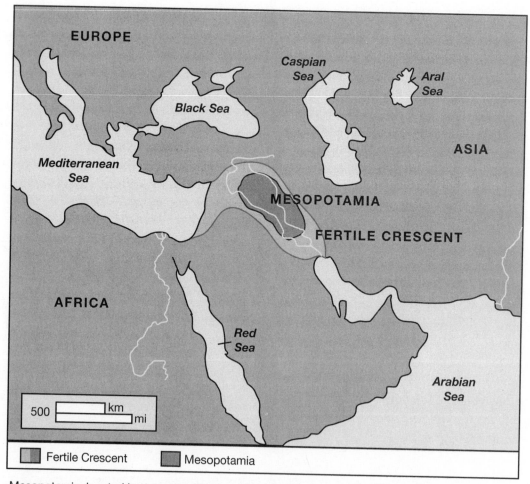

Mesopotamia, located between the Tigris and Euphrates rivers in what is now Iraq, is called the "cradle of civilization." Many ancient civilizations thrived in this fertile area.

RELIGION	ORIGIN	CHARACTERISTICS
Hinduism	India in 1500 B.C.	■ Hinduism has no single founder; it developed over a period of 4,000 years. ■ One of its main features is a caste system, in which people are born into a prescribed class and follow the ways of that class. ■ Hindus are polytheistic.
Buddhism	India in 525 B.C.	■ It was founded by Siddhartha Gautama, called the Buddha. ■ Buddhists believe in a cycle of rebirth. ■ The ultimate goal of the Buddhist path is to achieve *nirvana,* an enlightened state free from suffering.
Judaism	Middle East, now Israel—the Jewish calendar begins with the biblical time of the Creation	■ The belief in a single, all-powerful God is central to Judaism. ■ The Torah—the instructions believed to be handed down from God to Moses—encompasses Jewish law and custom.
Christianity	Jerusalem, now in Israel—Christian calendar begins with the birth of Jesus	■ Early followers believed that Jesus fulfilled the Jewish prophesy of the Messiah. ■ The Gospels in the Bible's New Testament describe the teachings and life of Jesus. ■ Beliefs include that Jesus is the son of God and that after crucifixion, he rose from the dead.
Islam	Arabia in 622 A.D.	■ Its followers, called Muslims, believe in one all-powerful God. ■ Muslims adhere to the codes of living set forth in the holy book of Islam, the Qur'an (Koran). ■ The founder of Islam was Muhammed, a prophet who lived in Mecca in the sixth century, A.D.

Exercise 1

Choose the best answer to the question based on the information you learned in the chart.

1. What conclusion can you make based on the information in the chart?
   a. All major religions believe in a single, all-powerful God.
   b. Most religions developed in the last millennium.
   c. Religion is not a force in today's world culture.
   d. Many of the world's major religions have influenced human culture for more than a thousand years.
   e. All of today's major religions had their beginnings in the Middle East.

The answer is on page 340.

The Middle Ages

As the Roman Empire began to fracture in the fourth and fifth centuries, a period that historians refer to as the **Middle Ages** began in Western Europe. During this time, Western culture centered on Christianity as the Roman Catholic Church gained authority and missionaries spread Christian ideas. A new social organization called **feudalism** developed. Based on an agricultural society, this system divided people into classes. The ruling class consisted of **nobles**, while the majority of people were in the **peasant** or **serf** class. Between the eleventh and fourteenth centuries, European Christians led a series of wars called the **Crusades** to recover the Holy Land from the Muslims. Although they did not achieve this goal, the wars brought Europe in contact with Arab culture, stimulated commerce between regions, and increased geographical knowledge. By the fourteenth century, wars, famine, and the spread of the **bubonic plague**, or **Black**

Death—an infectious disease that killed up to one-third of all Europeans—weakened the feudal economy.

The Renaissance

In the 1400s, a rediscovery of Greek and Roman literature led to the **humanist** movement in Europe, which called for a return to classical ideals. As Western Europe regained stability, a period of intellectual development began. The **Renaissance**, meaning "rebirth," led to advances in the sciences, music, literature, art, and architecture. During its height in the fifteenth and early sixteenth centuries, artists like Piero della Francesca, Leonardo da Vinci, Michelangelo, and Rafael contributed works praised for their grandeur and sense of harmony.

The New World

European exploration of North America began in the tenth century when Viking explorers landed in Greenland and Newfoundland. However, Christopher Columbus's landing in the Bahamas in 1492 had a greater impact on the history of the world because he brought news of his exploration back to Europe. Under the service of Spain, Columbus sailed west, hoping to discover a quicker trade route to Asia. He landed in the Caribbean instead. His historic journey marked the start of European exploration and colonization in the New World. (See the table on this page.)

Age of Enlightenment

The Enlightenment describes a period in Europe and America during the eighteenth century in which philoso-phers celebrated rational thought, science, and technological progress. The scientific developments of the sixteenth and seventeenth centuries acted as a precursor to the Enlightenment. Galileo Galilei, Nicolaus Copernicus, and Isaac Newton contributed new ideas about astronomy and physics that challenged the conventional understanding of the physical world. Later, the philosophy of John Locke influenced attitudes about the role of the individual in society and challenged the notion that knowledge is inborn. The works of the French philosopher Jean Jacques Rousseau shaped political and educational theory, as did the ideas of Immanuel Kant in Germany, David Hume in England, and Benjamin Franklin and Thomas Jefferson in the American colonies.

Exercise 2

Select the best answer based on the paragraph about the Age of Enlightenment.

1. Which of the following statements about the Enlightenment is an opinion?
   a. The proponents of the Enlightenment believed in rationality.
   b. The Enlightenment philosophers challenged formerly held beliefs.
   c. The Enlightenment was an international movement.
   d. John Locke contributed the most to the Enlightenment philosophy.
   e. Hume, Kant, Jefferson, and Franklin shared a faith in human reason.

Early European Explorers

DATE (A.D.)	EXPLORER	ORIGIN	LANDING SITE
986	Eric the Red	Iceland	Greenland
1000	Leif Ericsson	Norway	North America, possibly Newfoundland
1492	Christopher Columbus	Spain	Bahamas, Cuba, and Hispaniola
1497	John Cabot	England	Cape Breton Island
1499	Amerigo Vespucci	Italy, later Spain	North coast of South America
1500	Gasper Corte-Real	Portugal	Between Labrador and Newfoundland
1513	Juan Ponce de Leon	Spain, later governor of Puerto Rico	Florida and Mexico

2. Which of the following was the most likely factor that contributed to the beginning of the Enlightenment?
   a. scientific discoveries in the previous century
   b. feudalism
   c. the French Revolution
   d. the Crusades
   e. missionaries of the Roman Catholic Church in Europe

The answers are on page 340.

French Revolution

The French Revolution (1789–1799) ranks as one of the most important events in European history. Increased criticism of the monarchy by Enlightenment thinkers, unequal taxation, and persecution of religious minorities all helped encourage political upheaval. Food shortages and economic depression were an even more immediate cause. Parisians revolted in 1789 by violently overtaking the **Bastille**, a prison in Paris. Aristocrats, including the king and queen, were beheaded. Political unrest followed until Napoleon Bonaparte emerged as a leader in 1799 and declared himself emperor in 1804. Although it appeared to be a failure at the time, the Revolution created a precedent for representative governments around the world. It also introduced revolution as a means of seeking different kinds of freedom.

The Industrial Era

By the mid-nineteenth century, changes in technology began to transform Europe and the United States from societies with an agricultural base to ones with an industrial base. This period is called the **Industrial Revolution**. The introduction of steam-powered engines, the invention of machines that increased the output of cotton textiles, and the advent of the railroad are some of the technological changes that increased the speed of production and transportation of goods.

The doctrine of *laissez-faire* appealed to factory owners of the Industrial Revolution. Supported by economists like Adam Smith and John Stuart Mill, this doctrine stated that economic systems work better without intervention by government, and that markets were guided by an "unseen hand" that saw to it that everyone's best interests were served. *The Communist Manifesto*, a document of communist principles, presented quite a different viewpoint on industrialization and free market economies. Authored by German writer Karl Marx in 1848, the *Manifesto* described the history of society as a history of class struggles between the ruling class and the exploited working class. Marx believed that free-market economies widened the divide between the wealthy and the poor, and that ultimately the poor working class would overthrow the powerful capitalist class of the Industrial Revolution, resulting in a new, classless society. His ideas later influenced Vladimir Ilyich Lenin and the formation of a Communist state in Russia.

World War I

World War I (1914–1918) involved 32 countries, including many European nations, the United States, and other nations around the world. By the war's end, 10 million soldiers were killed and 20 million wounded. The assassination of the heir to the Austro-Hungarian throne by a Serbian nationalist was the immediate cause of the war, but conflicts between European nations over territory and economic power were also factors. Two coalitions of European nations formed. The Central Powers included Austria-Hungary, Germany, Bulgaria, and Turkey. The Allied Powers included Great Britain, France, Serbia, Russia, Belgium, and Italy. The fighting ended in 1918 when the Allies defeated German forces. With the *Treaty of Versailles* in 1919, the war officially ended. One of the most destructive wars in European history, World War I left European powers in enormous financial debt and greatly weakened.

The Russian Revolutions of 1917

Peasant and worker uprisings led to two revolutions in Russia during 1917. The first overthrew Tsar Nicholas II, an absolute monarch. A provisional government took control but could not solve the problems that led to the uprising, mainly the devastating effect of the country's involvement in World War I. Vladimir Lenin and a group of revolutionary socialists called the *Bolsheviks* took power. The Bolsheviks hoped to transform Russia into a classless society called the **Union of Soviet Socialist Republics (USSR)**. However, the Communist regime that they created became increasingly authoritarian and eventually controlled the economic, social, and political life of the nation. After Lenin's death, Bolshevik Joseph Stalin became the dictator of the Soviet Union. He ruled with total and often brutal control. The Communist regime continued to hold power until its collapse in 1991.

World War II

World War II (1939–1945), the deadliest and most destructive war in history, began between Germany and the English and French, but later included all of the major powers of the world. The rise of **fascism**—an Italian term for a military-based totalitarian government—as well as the effects of economic depression fueled the conflict. Also, the peace settlements of World War I had left three powers—Germany, Italy, and Japan—dissatisfied, and each wanted to increase its territory. In Germany, Adolf Hitler of the **German National Socialist (Nazi) Party** promoted national pride and offered scapegoats for the country's economic problems: the Jews, Roma peoples (or gypsies), various Slavic groups, and homosexuals. His racist policies led to the persecution and murder of millions of Jewish people and other groups, an atrocity now known as **the Holocaust**.

Germany, with Hitler in power, began an aggressive campaign in Europe, invading Czechoslovakia. Hitler then created an alliance with Italy and Japan to form **the Axis Powers**. When Germany invaded Poland, Great Britain and France entered the war. By 1940, the only Allied force to resist German occupation was Great Britain. However, Great Britain gained an ally when Germany invaded the Soviet Union in 1941.

Although the United States at first sought to be neutral in the conflict, events forced it to enter the war. On December 7, 1941, Japan attacked **Pearl Harbor**, a U.S. military base in the Pacific. On December 11, Germany and Italy declared war on the United States. The United States joined the Allied forces and helped turn the war in its favor. In May 1945, Germany surrendered. In August 1945, the United States dropped the first atomic bomb on **Hiroshima**, Japan, and soon after dropped another on **Nagasaki**. Five days later, Japan surrendered.

World War II devastated entire cities, and both civilians and soldiers suffered. Tens of millions of people were killed. The war revolutionized warfare by introducing nuclear weapons. Politically, power shifted away from Great Britain and France, and the United States and the Soviet Union emerged as world powers. After the war, the Soviet Union kept control of its occupation zones and took power in Eastern Europe. This expansion threatened the West and started the **Cold War**, a struggle for power between the capitalist West and the Communist bloc that lasted until 1989.

Exercise 3

Use the information from the passage about World War II to answer the questions.

1. Which of the following was NOT a likely consequence of World War II?
   a. death of millions
   b. the end of racism
   c. destruction of cities
   d. shift in world power
   e. threat of nuclear war

2. Based on the information about World War II, which of the following is a likely assumption as to why Hitler rose to power?
   a. Hitler's totalitarian government exercised absolute power.
   b. Many citizens resisted the rise of the Nazi Party.
   c. Germans wanted a powerful leader who would lift them out of financial chaos.
   d. Germans needed a leader to fend off British and French aggression.
   e. Nazi propaganda techniques were not successful.

The answers are on page 340.

▶ U.S. History

A New Nation

After Columbus landed in the Bahamas in 1492, Western Europe began colonization of the Americas. Spain, Portugal, France, the Netherlands, and England had vast holdings in the New World. A group of English migrants called **Puritans**—people seeking to purify the Church of England—started settlements in New England. One group, known as the **Pilgrims**, landed in Plymouth, Massachusetts, in 1620. These settlers established the Plymouth Colony and created the *Mayflower Compact*, an agreement that said the colonists would make decisions by the will of the majority. This became the first instance of self-government in America. Throughout the British colonies, forms of self-government developed.

The Declaration of Independence

In the mid-eighteenth century, England and France fought over land in the upper valley of Ohio in the **French and Indian War**. England gained control of all territory east of the Mississippi, but the war left the country deeply in debt. To pay off the debt, **King George III** and **British Parliament** established ways to tax the colonists. **The Stamp Act of 1765** required that all printed material—newspapers, legal documents, and other papers—bear a British stamp and that colonists pay for these seals. **The Townshend Acts of 1767** placed new taxes on glass, lead, paints, paper, and tea. Boston merchants began boycotting English goods. When three shipments of tea arrived in Boston Harbor in 1773, angry citizens threw the cargo overboard in an incident that came to be known as the **Boston Tea Party**.

In punishment for this protest, England closed the port of Boston and passed the **Intolerable Acts**, which limited the political freedom of the colonists. This led to further protest; in 1775, fighting between the colonists and the British marked the start of the **Revolutionary War**. Thomas Jefferson drafted the **Declaration of Independence**, a document that describes the American ideal of government and lists the injustices of the king. The **Second Continental Congress**, a meeting of representatives from the 13 colonies, approved the declaration on July 4, 1776.

The U.S. Constitution

The colonies won their independence after seven years of the Revolutionary War. The new states created a system of government under the **Articles of Confederation**. This framework limited the power of the central government and allowed the states to act as separate nations. It was a flawed system incapable of addressing issues such as national defense, trade between states, and the creation of a common currency. In 1787, leaders met and created a new system of government, which it defined in the **United States Constitution**. The states approved the Constitution in 1788.

The Constitution outlines the fundamental principles of the American republic. It defines the powers of Congress, the president, and the federal judicial system, and divides authority in a system of **checks and balances** so that no branch of government can dominate the others. To calm the fears of those who believed a central government would interfere with individual freedoms, the framers of the Constitution added the **Bill of Rights**.

These ten amendments to the Constitution safeguard citizens' rights, such as freedom of speech, freedom of the press, and freedom of religion. Learn more about the Constitution in the Civics and Government review section of this book.

Exercise 4

Read the following question and select the best answer.

1. Which of the following was a consideration in creating the Bill of Rights?
   a. dividing power between the three branches of government
   b. creating a judicial system
   c. forming a strong central government
   d. ratifying the Articles of Confederation
   e. securing the liberties of individuals

The answer is on page 340.

Sectionalism

During the late 1700s and early 1800s, the United States expanded its territory. In 1803, President Thomas Jefferson doubled the size of the country by buying land from France through the **Louisiana Purchase**. Under President James Monroe, westward expansion continued. Despite this growth and the country's increased wealth, economic and cultural differences between regions developed. **Sectionalism**—each section of the country supporting its own self-interests instead of the nation's interests—took root. The Northeast relied on an industrial economy while the South had an agricultural economy supported by slave labor. One major issue concerned whether new states in the Union would become free states or allow slavery. A group called the **abolitionists** believed slavery was wrong and wanted it banned throughout the nation. In 1857, the **Dred Scott decision** by the Supreme Court increased the hostility between the North and South. In the case, Dred Scott, a slave, argued that because his owner moved to a free territory, he should be free. The Court ruled that slaves were not citizens and, therefore, could not sue. It also ruled that it could not ban people from bringing slaves to free territories.

The Civil War

Abraham Lincoln, whom the South considered a threat to slavery and to the rights of states to govern themselves, was elected president in 1860. Eleven southern states withdrew from the Union. They formed a separate government called the **Confederate States of America**. Here is the division between free and slave states in 1861:

Free States

California	New Hampshire
Connecticut	New Jersey
Illinois	New York
Indiana	Ohio
Iowa	Oregon
Kansas	Pennsylvania
Maine	Rhode Island
Massachusetts	Vermont
Michigan	Wisconsin
Minnesota	

Slave States

Alabama*	Mississippi*
Arkansas*	Missouri
Delaware	North Carolina*
Florida*	South Carolina*
Georgia*	Tennessee*
Kentucky	Texas*
Louisiana*	Virginia*
Maryland	

Territories

Colorado	Nevada
Dakota	New Mexico
Indian	Utah
Nebraska	Washington

Confederate States

In 1861, Confederate soldiers opened fire on Fort Sumter in Charleston, South Carolina, and the Civil War began. The "War Between the States" lasted four years and eventually killed more than 600,000 people. It also destroyed an estimated $5 billion in property. The war ended in 1865 after the surrender of Robert E. Lee, the most important general of the Confederacy. Four million slaves were freed during the period of **Reconstruction** that followed the war. Five days after the Northern victory, a Confederate sympathizer assassinated President Lincoln. Resentment and division between the South and North continued for decades after the war's end.

Big Business

From 1860 into the next century, the United States experienced an explosion of industrialization. Just as the **Industrial Revolution** changed Europe, it altered life in the new nation. Abundant natural resources, technological advances, railroad expansion, and a new wave of immigrants in the workforce made industrial growth possible. Businesses began to operate over broad geographic areas and grew into large corporations. Tycoons of the steel and oil industry, such as Andrew Carnegie and John D. Rockefeller, controlled much of the marketplace. The powerful industrialists supported the policy of *laissez-faire*: They believed government should not interfere with business.

Large-scale production changed the workplace. Laborers were more likely to work in large factories than in small workshops. Machines and unskilled workers replaced skilled workers to keep costs down. Many worked long hours doing monotonous work in dangerous conditions. As a result, **national labor unions** began to form to protect the rights of workers. The first national labor union was the **Knights of Labor**, which organized in 1869. In 1886, the **American Federation of Labor (AFL)** formed, joining together a network of local unions. Led by Samuel Gompers, an immigrant cigar maker, the union rallied for improved hours, wages, and working conditions. Reformers, called the **Progressives**, wanted to curb the power of big business and protect working people. Among other goals, progressive reformers wanted to end child labor and introduce a minimum wage. Through their efforts, government at the local, state, and national level began to regulate business. Learn more about labor unions in the Economics review section of this book.

Exercise 5

Use the information about big business to select the best answer for each question.

1. Which of the following slogans would industrialist John D. Rockefeller most likely support?
   a. Live Free or Die
   b. Our Union, Our Voice
   c. Equal Pay for Equal Work
   d. That Government Is Best Which Governs Least
   e. Big Government

2. Which of the following was NOT a goal of the Progressives?
   a. improve workers' safety
   b. stop antitrust legislation
   c. increase government regulation
   d. prohibit child labor
   e. establish a minimum wage

The answers are on page 340.

The Great Depression

In the 1920s, the country enjoyed a prosperous period. Business expanded and investors speculated in the stock market, often borrowing money on easy credit to buy shares of a company. Money flowed into the stock market until October 24, 1929, when the market collapsed. Investors lost fortunes overnight, businesses started to close, workers were laid off, and banks closed. The **stock market crash of 1929** marked the onset of the **Great Depression**, which lasted through the 1930s. By 1933, unemployment reached 25%, more than 5,000 banks were closed, and over 85,000 businesses had failed.

Elected in 1932, President Franklin D. Roosevelt started a relief effort to revive the economy and bring aid to people who were suffering the effects of the depression. He called his program the **New Deal**. In what is now called the **First Hundred Days**, Roosevelt and Congress passed major legislation that saved banks from closing and regained public confidence. The sidebar lists some of the important measures passed in 1933, the first year of Roosevelt's presidency.

The New Deal

Agricultural Adjustment Act—paid farmers to slow their production in order to stabilize food prices

National Industrial Recovery Act—outlined codes for fair competition in industry

Securities and Exchange Commission—established to regulate stock market

Federal Deposit Insurance Corporation—insured bank deposits in the case that banks fail

Public Works Administration—built roads, public buildings, dams

Tennessee Valley Authority—brought electric power to parts of the Southeast

---

The New Deal brought relief, but did not end the depression. The economy did not revive until the nation entered World War II in the 1940s. However, the New Deal had long-lasting effects: It expanded the powers of the central government to regulate the economy, and it created "safety-net" programs that would assist citizens.

An Era of Expanding Rights

The twentieth century brought about expanded civil rights and civil liberties for a wide range of American citizens, a trend that accelerated as the century progressed. Early in the century, the **Progressive movement** gave voters more power over their government through the introduction of the **ballot initiative**, which allowed voters to propose new laws; the **referendum**, which gave the public the power to vote on new laws; and the **recall**, which allowed voters to remove elected officials from office before their terms ended. They also campaigned for, and won, a Constitutional amendment to allow for the direct election of U.S. senators (previously, senators were chosen by state governments). Women received **suffrage**, or the right to vote, in 1920 through an amendment to the Constitution. During the 1930s, Franklin D. Roosevelt took several actions that increased workers' right to organize, most notably through the creation of the federal **National Labor Relations Board** (NLRB).

African Americans waged a long fight for equal rights throughout the twentieth century, often in the face of violent opposition. Advances were slow in coming.

President Truman integrated the military in 1948, partly in response to African-American soldiers' bravery during World War II. Progress quickened during the 1950s, first as the Supreme Court ruled in ***Brown v. Board of Education*** that segregated schools violated the Constitution, and then with the **Montgomery bus boycott**, during which African Americans in Birmingham, Alabama, boycotted the bus system to protest segregation in public transportation. The boycott was sparked by the arrest of **Rosa Parks**; the boycott, which lasted for one year, helped elevate one of its leaders, **Martin Luther King, Jr.**, to a position of national leadership in the civil rights movement. The success of the boycott spurred civil rights activists to other acts of **civil disobedience**, the peaceful violation of laws in an effort to sway public opinion to one's cause. The civil rights movement resulted in some dramatic victories, including the passage of major civil rights legislation in the 1960s that addressed discrimination in voting, housing, and employment.

American Indians also sought to redress past wrongs during the 1960s. Throughout much of the twentieth century, the federal policy toward American Indians was to encourage assimilation into the U.S. mainstream. The American Indian Movement (AIM), founded in 1968, sought to counter that policy by reinforcing American Indian autonomy and pride. It campaigned to compel the federal government to honor past treaties with American Indian tribes, provide relief for Indians harmed by previous government policies, and respect the autonomy of tribal governments. The movement received national attention as a result of its connection to the siege at Wounded Knee, a 71-day standoff between Oglaga Sioux and federal troops. Throughout its history, AIM has continued to use sometimes-violent confrontation to achieve its goals. Other advocacy groups have emerged to protect American Indian legal and economic rights, with some success.

The 1960s was also a time of expanding rights for American women. The **feminist movement** called attention to discrimination against women in education, the workplace, the financial world, and in the legal system; it also fought widely held beliefs that women were in some ways less capable than men. The movement enjoyed many successes in changing societal attitudes toward women, although it failed in its efforts to get a Constitutional amendment (called **the Equal Rights Amendment**) that would guarantee equal rights to all women.

37 ▶ Civics and Government

The civics and government questions on the GED Social Studies Exam will come from both national (American) and global contexts, so you should be prepared to answer a wide variety of questions.

I N THIS CHAPTER, you will learn about the basic ideas of civics (the rights and responsibilities of citizens) and government (the way that political power is organized and distributed). After an overview of the different types of political systems that exist in other countries, you will review the American system of government: its structure at the federal, state, and local levels; political parties; voting and election procedures; the ways individuals and groups influence the government apart from voting; and the process of becoming an American citizen.

▶Political Systems

Varying types of political systems can be found around the world. These types differ in how power is attained and how it is used. See chart on the next page.

TYPE OF GOVERNMENT	CHARACTERISTICS	EXAMPLES
Monarchy	■ One person from a royal family is ruler. ■ Power is inherited from generation to generation. ■ *Absolute monarchs* have complete authority. ■ *Constitutional monarchs* have limited authority; a representative democracy governs.	■ Saudi Arabia ■ Morocco *Absolute monarchy:* ■ Swaziland *Constitutional monarchies:* ■ Great Britain ■ Japan ■ Sweden
Dictatorship	■ It is ruled by one leader who has absolute power over many aspects of life, including social, economic, and political. ■ Leader is not elected by the people.	■ Nazi (National Socialist) government of Adolf Hitler ■ General Augusto Pinochet in Chile from 1973–1990
Oligarchy	■ It is governed by a small upper-class group. ■ Leaders are not elected by the people.	■ City-state of Sparta in ancient Greece
Democracy	■ In *direct democracy,* decisions are made by the people. ■ In *representative democracy,* people elect officials to represent their views.	*Representative democracies:* ■ United States ■ Canada ■ Most European nations

Exercise 6

Use the information from the chart to answer the following questions.

1. A military leader uses his power to overthrow a country's government and seizes absolute control. He takes over all of the nation's television stations and newspapers. What kind of government has he set up?
  a. absolute monarchy
  b. dictatorship
  c. oligarchy
  d. direct democracy
  e. representative democracy

2. In which of the following political systems would citizens have the most influence over lawmaking?
  a. absolute monarchy
  b. dictatorship
  c. oligarchy
  d. direct democracy
  e. representative democracy

The answers are on page 340.

The American System of Government

The United States is a **federal republic**—a representative democracy in which power is split between a central government and the states. Under the federal system, certain powers are the exclusive domain of the federal government, including declaring war, conducting foreign policy, printing money, and regulating interstate and international trade. Other powers belong exclusively to the states, including regulating intrastate business and issuing licenses. Certain powers are shared. For example, both the federal government and state governments may collect taxes, build roads, and conduct trials. Occasionally, this results in conflicts between the national government and state governments.

The rules explaining powers and the limits on power of the U.S. government are explained in the **United States Constitution**, which is the highest law of the land. So that power is not concentrated in one authority, the central, or federal, government is divided into three branches: **legislative**, **executive**, and **judicial**. Each branch has an important function:

- The legislative branch **makes laws.**
- The executive branch **carries out laws.**
- The judicial branch **interprets laws.**

The powers of each branch are protected by the principle of **separation of powers**, which is laid out in the U.S. Constitution.

The U.S. Constitution also allows each branch to place controls or limits on the power of the other two branches, so that no one branch dominates. This framework is called the **system of checks and balances**. For example, the legislature (U.S. Congress) may pass a bill, but before it can become law, the executive (the president) must sign it. The president can refuse it by vetoing it. However, Congress can still pass the bill into law—in an action called **overriding the veto**—if two-thirds of its members vote for it. Likewise, the judicial branch has the power to overturn a law by declaring it unconstitutional; the legislature may respond by passing a new law that adheres to the court's judgment, or it may seek to initiate an **amendment,** or change, to the Constitution. (See the following table.)

STRUCTURE OF FEDERAL GOVERNMENT

Executive Branch	President Vice President Agencies Departments	■ A president is elected by the voters for four-year term. ■ A president cannot serve more than two terms. ■ Vice president becomes head of state if the president becomes disabled or dies in office. ■ Agencies carry out a president's policies and provide special services. ■ Department heads advise a president and carry out policies.
Legislative Branch	U.S. Congress: House of Representatives Senate	■ Number of representatives for each state is based on the population of that state. ■ Representatives serve two-year terms. ■ Each state has two senators. ■ Senators serve six-year terms.
Judicial Branch	U.S. Supreme Court Circuit Courts of Appeals Federal District Courts	■ U.S. Supreme Court is the highest court in the nation. ■ The president appoints the nine justices of the Supreme Court. ■ Term is for life.

The Constitution is often described as a "living document," meaning that it is open to interpretation. The Constitution lays out broad principles but does not contain much in the way of specifics; thus, the exact powers reserved to each branch of government and the rights of the people and states as described in the Constitution are often open to debate. Throughout American history, the power of each branch of government relative to the others has ebbed and flowed, depending on historical circumstances and the individuals leading each branch. During times of war and other national crises, **executive power** has tended to expand. Following periods in which the executive overreaches—for example, as Richard Nixon did—the executive branch is subsequently weakened, and the legislative branch gains power. The power of the judiciary depends largely on how judges themselves interpret their powers.

The fact that the Constitution can be changed by amendment is another reason that it is described as a living document. The Constitution has been amended 27 times over the course of American history. The first ten amendments were added soon after the Constitution was ratified; together, they are known as the **Bill of Rights**. These amendments protect the rights of individuals against the federal government. Those protections include the following:

- the right to practice one's religion freely
- the right to free speech
- the right to a free press
- the right to bear firearms
- the right to meet and to petition the government
- the right to a fair and speedy trial
- the right to representation by a lawyer
- the right to know the crime with which one is being charged
- protection from being tried twice for the same crime
- protection from excessive bail and/or cruel and unusual punishment

The final two amendments to the Bill of Rights reinforce the notion that the U.S. national government is a limited government. The Ninth Amendment states that U.S. citizens have rights above and beyond those described in the first eight amendments; in other words,

the government may not deny an individual right simply because it is not mentioned in the Bill of Rights. The Tenth Amendment states that any power not specifically granted the federal government by the Constitution belongs to the states or to the people, rather than to the federal government.

It's a good thing the Constitution can be changed, because the original document included some serious flaws. It allowed for slavery, for one thing. It also allowed states to deny the right to vote on the basis of race and gender. Amendments to the Constitution corrected these imperfections and others, abolishing slavery (1865), prohibiting racial discrimination in voting rights (1870), granting women the right to vote (1920), limiting the number of terms a president may serve (1951), banning poll taxes as a means of preventing citizens from voting (1964), and lowering the voting age from 21 to 18 (1971). Amendments to the Constitution generally have limited federal power and/or expanded the rights of individual citizens.

State and Local Governments

State governments resemble the federal government in the way that they are structured. The governor acts as the chief executive and can veto legislation. Most states have legislatures made of two houses, and each state has its own court system, constitution, and a system of checks and balances.

Local governments vary from the state and federal model. There are three basic forms of local government:

1. **Mayor-council**—in this form, voters elect a mayor as city or town executive and they elect a council member from each specific ward.
2. **Council-manager**—in this form, voters elect council members, who, in turn, hire a manager to run the day-to-day operations of the city or town.
3. **Commission**—in this form, voters elect commissioners to head a city or county department, such as the fire, police, or public works department.

State governments must approve and grant power to, or **charter**, all town and city governments.

Political Parties

Although the U.S. Constitution does not mention the existence of political parties, they have played an influential role throughout most of the country's history. A political party is an organization that presents its positions on public issues and promotes candidates that support its point of view. Political parties serve several functions:

- recruit candidates and run election campaigns
- formulate positions on issues that affect the public and propose solutions
- educate the public on issues
- mobilize their members to vote
- create voting blocs in Congress

Since the mid-nineteenth century, two political parties have dominated in American politics: the Republican and Democratic parties. The two parties differ on social, economic, and domestic policies. They also hold different beliefs as to the role of government. The **Republican Party** supports relatively powerful state governments with less involvement on the federal level, while the **Democratic Party** supports a strong centralized government with less power on the state level. Other current political organizations include the **Green**, **Libertarian**, **Reform**, and **Socialist** parties.

Exercise 7

Choose the best answer based on the information provided about political parties.

1. Which of the following conclusions about political parties is best supported by the passage?
   a. They should be outlawed because they are not mentioned in the Constitution.
   b. The Know-Nothings and the Whigs are still influential political parties today.
   c. Political parties have an influential role in the political process today.
   d. It's hard to tell the Democratic and Republican Parties apart these days.
   e. Third-party candidates can alter the outcome of an election.

The answer is on page 341.

Voting and Elections

To vote in the United States, a person must be 18 years old and a U.S. citizen. Presidential elections occur every four years, and Congressional elections are held every two years. Most national elections in the United States use a **plurality system**, which means that a candidate need only receive more votes than his or her opponent to win. In contrast, some European nations have **proportional representation**. In this system, if a political party earns 15% of the vote, it would be awarded 15% of the parliamentary seats.

In the United States, **primary elections** are held before general elections. In primaries, voters give their preference for a political party's candidate. **General elections** then decide the ultimate winner. In the United States, the presidential election is unique in that the popular vote does not necessarily determine the outcome of the general election. That is because the president is actually elected by the **Electoral College**, a constitutionally mandated representative body to which the states send delegates. States are free to allocate their electoral votes in any way they see fit; currently, all but two states use a "winner take all" system, meaning that a presidential candidate who wins the statewide election for president receives all of the state's electoral votes. Under this system, it is possible for a candidate to win the presidency even if he or she loses the nationwide popular vote. In fact, this has happened three times in U.S. history—in 1876, 1888, and 2000.

Exercise 8

Questions 1 and 2 are based on the following map.

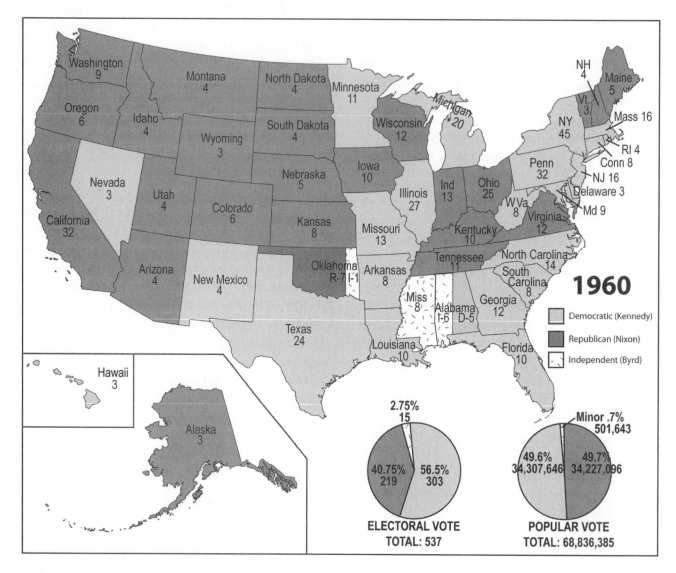

1960

Democratic (Kennedy)
Republican (Nixon)
Independent (Byrd)

ELECTORAL VOTE
TOTAL: 537

2.75%
15
40.75%
219
56.5%
303

POPULAR VOTE
TOTAL: 68,836,385

Minor .7%
501,643
49.6%
34,307,646
49.7%
34,227,096

1. This map shows the results of the popular and electoral vote in the presidential election of 1960. Which of the following conclusions does the map support?

   a. The winner of the popular vote always wins the electoral vote.

   b. The electoral vote is a more accurate reflection of the people's will than is the popular vote.

   c. If Richard Nixon had won Louisiana's ten electoral votes instead of Kennedy, Nixon would have won the election.

   d. All Southern states supported Kennedy in the 1960 election.

   e. The electoral vote results can distort the results of the popular vote.

2. According to the map, which state did NOT use a "winner take all" system to allocate its electoral votes in 1960?

   a. New York

   b. Oklahoma

   c. Tennessee

   d. Virginia

   e. Wyoming

   The answers are on page 341.

Interest Groups, Lobbyists, and PACs

Voting and elections are not the only way to influence the American political system. Citizens often band together around common causes and goals to form **interest groups**. These groups work to influence the government on a particular issue or set of related issues. Interest groups include the National Rifle Association, which promotes firearms rights; the National Association of Advancement for Colored People (NAACP), which promotes a slate of issues that affect the African-American community; the United Auto Workers (UAW), a union championing the interests of employees of automobile manufacturing plants; the National Right to Life Committee (NRLC), which opposes abortion rights; and many, many others. Groups representing businesses, workers, religious groups, racial and ethnic groups, and even the interests of foreign governments all attempt to influence how American government operates.

One of the main ways in which interest groups influence the government is through **lobbyists**. Lobbyists are professional representatives of interest groups. Their job is to convince legislators to write, endorse, and pass bills; to channel political donations to candidates who support their causes; to file court actions that protect and represent their group's goals; and to operate public relations campaigns to sway the American public to their side of an issue.

Because political campaigns are extremely expensive, candidates for office must spend a lot of time fund-raising. **Political action committees (PACs)** are groups of people united around a special interest or a set of issues. They raise money and donate to the campaigns of those candidates who champion their goals. PACs operate under certain restrictions designed to keep them from exerting too much influence over elections, but they are quite powerful all the same. So too are **527 groups**, named after the clause in the federal tax code that allows them to operate under tax-free status. These groups have fewer spending restrictions but may spend only on campaigns to promote specific issues; they may not run advertisements for or against a particular candidate. Some 527 groups have found loopholes in these regulations that allow them to play a significant role in election campaigns.

Becoming an American Citizen

Immigrants come the United States for many reasons: Some seek economic opportunity, while others wish to escape political persecution in their native countries. Benefits of U.S. citizenship include enjoying the freedoms and rights guaranteed by the Constitution. To become a citizen, a person must apply, pass an exam, and appear for a court hearing. The process of becoming a citizen, also called **naturalization**, is conducted by the **United States Citizenship and Immigration Service** (**USCIS**, formerly known as the Immigration and Naturalization Service, or INS for short). The following are some of the requirements for citizenship. Candidates must:

- be at least 18 years old
- reside legally in the United States for five years
- be a person of good moral character
- understand and be able to communicate in basic English
- demonstrate a basic knowledge of U.S. history, government, and the Constitution
- be willing to take an oath of allegiance to the United States

38 ▶ Economics

On the GED Social Studies Exam, questions about economics will include the areas of supply and demand, inflation and deflation, and economic systems. Many economics questions will ask you to interpret and analyze a chart or graph, so practice in working with visual aids will be helpful in your preparation.

ECONOMICS IS DEFINED as the study of the ways that goods (and services) are bought, sold, distributed, and used. The economics questions on the GED Social Studies Exam will require that you have a good grasp of the relationship of supply and demand, recession and depression, how economic growth is measured, and how the U.S. government is involved in the nation's economy.

▶ Scarcity

Scarcity is the central concept of economics. We do not have unlimited time and resources, unfortunately; it is impossible to study for the GED and play basketball at the same time. For that same reason, it is impossible to buy all available consumer goods and services. There are limits to our time and money, and so we must make choices. Economics studies the factors that determine how individuals and businesses make these choices (this field of economics is called **microeconomics**). It also studies the way the economy as a whole behaves in response to individual choices, business choices, government intervention, international trade, and other large-scale influences (this field of economics is called **macroeconomics**).

TYPE	CHARACTERISTICS	EXAMPLES
Capitalism	■ Individuals and private organizations own and operate businesses. ■ Free market determines production and distribution of goods and services. ■ Prices set by supply and demand.	■ United States
Socialism	■ State owns and operates many businesses and services. ■ Private ownership is allowed. ■ Citizens pay high taxes to fund state-run social services, including healthcare, food, and housing.	■ Sweden
Communism	■ State, or the community, owns *all* businesses. ■ State controls distribution of goods and services. ■ State provides social services.	■ People's Republic of China ■ Cuba ■ Former Soviet Union

▶ Types of Economic Systems

In political terms, there are three basic economic systems operating in the modernized nations of the world: **capitalism**, **socialism**, and **communism**. The table lists defining characteristics of each. None of these systems exists in pure form; modern capitalist states typically also allow for some times of government planning and intervention, while communist states have grown more open to free trade and allowing citizens to profit from their businesses in recent years.

The terms *capitalism, socialism,* and *communism* describe economic systems, but they are not the terms economists favor. Economists prefer the terms **market economy**, which describes an economic system in which prices, wages, and production are set by markets; **command economy**, which describes an economic system in which the government plans production; and **traditional economy**, which describes an economic system in which certain jobs are reserved to certain classes of society (feudalism is one historic example of a traditional economy). Nearly all the world's economies are **mixed economies**, combining in different degrees elements of market, command, and traditional economies.

Consider the United States. In many areas, the United States allows markets to determine the amount of goods produced, the price at which goods are sold, and the wages paid to workers. However, the government imposes a **minimum wage** that prevents employers from paying workers an unfair, unlivable wage. The government also intervenes to provide goods and services that the market will not provide because they are not profitable enough. Health insurance and housing for the poor are two areas in which the government intervenes. Thus, the U.S. economy is a mixed economy in which markets usually, but don't always, drive economic activity.

Command economies have been disappearing from the world since the demise of the Soviet Union. North Korea is one of the world's few remaining command economies. Because all economic decisions, from the development of raw materials to production to shipping to retail sales, are made centrally by the government, command economies lack efficiency. They are characterized by frequent shortages of goods, underemployment, and poor economic growth.

▶ Microeconomics

The Marketplace

In predominantly market economies like the United States, prices are determined by the principle of **supply and demand. Supply** is the amount of goods and services available for purchase. **Demand** is determined by how many people want to buy those goods and services. Generally, when demand increases, supply increases, because more producers want to get into the market. Similarly, when demand decreases, supply decreases, because producers stop producing the unpopular product and instead start producing something they believe will sell better.

Producers and consumers both act out of self-interest. Businesses attempt to earn a **profit**—money in excess of the amount it costs to manufacture a product or deliver a service. Thus, they will charge the highest price they believe they can get for their goods or services. Consumers, on the other hand, look for the lowest price they can find. This, along with competition among producers for consumer dollars, is what drives prices down. (When there is no competition, there is no force to drive prices down. Businesses that control a market—called **monopolies**—may essentially set prices at whatever level they wish.)

When companies make the exact amount of a product or service at a price that customers are willing to buy, they have reached a point of **equilibrium**. If the price is greater than this point, demand drops and there may be a **surplus**, which is when there are more goods produced than customers are willing to buy. If the price falls below the point of equilibrium, demand may increase and create a **shortage** in supply.

For example, Company X is introducing a new cell phone model, the XLZ. (See graph on this page.) The business wants to find out the equilibrium point so that it will not have a surplus or shortage of the product. To cover its costs and make a profit, Company X can supply 10 phones for $1,100. As the price increases, the company can offer more phones for sale. However, few customers are willing to pay high prices for the phones. As the price drops, demand increases.

Exercise 9

Refer to the graph "Supply and Demand Curves for Cell Phone XLZ" to answer the following questions.

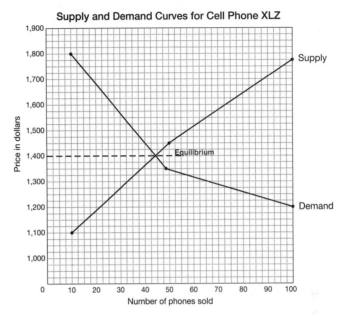

1. At what price does the supply of cell phone model XLZ equal that of demand?
   a. $1,400
   b. $1,300
   c. $1,250
   d. $1,500
   e. $1,550

2. If the market price for cell phone model XLZ increased to $1,600, what would be the likely result?
   a. Stores would quickly run out of product.
   b. Demand would decrease.
   c. The manufacturer would not be able to keep up with demand.
   d. The manufacturer would produce the cell phone model at the same rate.
   e. The manufacturer would go out of business.

The answers are on page 341.

Labor

Businesses are not just sellers in the marketplace; they are also buyers. Manufacturers must buy raw goods and machinery to produce their products. Retailers must buy goods at wholesale to sell in their stores. All businesses need to hire workers to make their businesses run. We use the term **labor market** to describe the competition for workers.

As in other markets, the labor market is driven by supply and demand. Jobs for which there are many more potential employees than there are positions—low-end service jobs in fast-food restaurants, for example—pay poorly and typically offer few or no **benefits** such as paid vacation, health insurance, and professional development training. Jobs that require highly specialized skills typically have fewer suitable candidates, and thus offer high pay and attractive benefits. In each case, the employer looks to pay the worker enough so that the worker will be satisfied (and thus will stay in the job and do it well) while still running the business profitably.

Workers must bargain with employers for their pay and benefits. In order to strengthen their bargaining position, some workers form **labor unions** that negotiate contracts for all members in a process called **collective bargaining**. When the employer and the union cannot come to an agreement, the union may call a **strike**, which means that the workers stop coming to work. They usually picket the site of their employment, shutting down the business in an effort to force an agreement. In some cases, the employer decides to shut down production in an effort to force the union to come to an agreement; this action is called a **lockout**.

▶ Macroeconomics

Business Cycles

Capitalist economies experience **business cycles**, periods of growth followed by a period of low productivity and income, called a **recession**. A **depression** occurs when recession lasts for a long period and is severe. During the Great Depression in the 1930s, the United States experienced its worst depression. At that time, large numbers of people suffered unemployment and homelessness.

Economic growth is the goal of capitalism. During a boom period, companies are able to produce more goods and services, and consumers are able to buy more goods and services. **Inflation** occurs when the amount of money in circulation increases and the amount of con-sumer goods (supply) decreases. The dollar drops in value and prices increase. **Deflation** happens when the money supply decreases and the amount of consumer goods increases. Prices are lower, but companies lose profit and lay off employees, which results in higher rates of **unemployment**.

Role of the Government

The government plays many important roles in the functioning of the economy. Free markets cannot exist without some form of government regulation. For example, if the government did not protect patent and property rights, inventors would not have as much incentive to develop new technologies, nor would investors have much incentive to invest in their development; why would they, if they knew the idea could be easily stolen, thus depriving them of any reward for their efforts and investments? The government must also enforce contracts, without which modern commerce is impossible. And, of course, the government must provide a reliable currency with which trade can be conducted.

The government regulates the markets in other ways as well. To avoid inflation and unemployment, the U.S. Federal Reserve System ("the Fed") takes measures to keep the economy in balance by controlling the supply of money in the country. One way it does this is by setting the **reserve ratio**. Every bank that is a member of the Fed must keep a reserve—a ratio of its deposits—that is not used to make loans. To fight inflation, the Fed might set a high reserve ratio, so that less money is available in the economy. During recession or high unemployment, the Fed might set a low reserve ratio, so there is more money available within the economy.

The Federal Reserve Board can also affect the nation's economy by altering the **discount rate**, which is the interest rate that the Fed charges banks to borrow money. To make a profit, banks charge their customers a higher interest rate than the rate they pay to the Fed. When the Fed sets a high discount rate, banks charge more interest on loans, which makes it more difficult for people and businesses to borrow. When the Fed sets a low discount rate, banks charge less, and more people and businesses can afford loans.

Other government actions impact the economy. Government **regulations** increase the cost of producing goods and thus increase prices. While people argue about the need for specific regulations, most agree that some regulations are worthwhile even though they drive prices up. For example, government regulations ensure that the food and drugs we use are safe (through the Food and Drug Administration), protect the environment (through the Environmental Protection Agency), protect workers from unsafe work conditions (through the Occupational Safety and Health Administration), and protect consumers from false advertising (through the Federal Trade Commission).

Finally, there is the impact of government taxation on the economy. The rate at which individuals and businesses are taxed, for example, has a direct influence on how much money is available for investment and consumer spending. The effect of taxes on the economy is a complex one. The government spends the money it collects in taxes, which helps drive certain sectors of the economy (military contractors, for example). Also, when the government does not collect enough taxes to pay for federal spending, it must borrow money, either by selling bonds or by borrowing the money from foreign governments. When that debt grows too high, it can have a negative impact on the economy.

Measuring Economic Growth

Economists use different data to study the health of the economy. They look at stock market trading, the cost of living, unemployment rates, and the **gross domestic product (GDP)**. The GDP measures the total value of goods and services produced within the United States over the course of a year. The **gross national product (GNP)** takes into account both the GDP and foreign investments. If the GNP decreases for two consecutive quarters during a year, the economy is considered to be in recession.

Consumer Price Index—All Urban Consumers 1990–2007

Source: U.S. Department of Labor, Bureau of Labor Statistics.

The **Consumer Price Index (CPI)** measures changes in the cost of living. To calculate the CPI, the U.S. Bureau of Labor Statistics tracks changes in prices in common goods and services—food, clothing, rent, fuel, and others—each year. The graph shows the CPI in all U.S. cities between 1990 and 2007. To make comparisons between years, the graph uses the years 1982–1984 as a base period (1982–1984 = $100). For instance, if the average urban consumer spent $100 on living expenses in 1982–1984, he or she spent more than $150 on the same expenses in 1995.

Exercise 10

Using the graph and passage about the Consumer Price Index, answer the following questions.

1. How much would an urban consumer expect to pay in 2001 for an item that cost $50 in 1982–1984?
  a. $88
  b. $100
  c. $176
  d. $43
  e. $131

2. What conclusion can you make based on the graph?
  a. The CPI tracks price changes for common household expenses.
  b. The cost of living has decreased in recent years.
  c. The rate of increase in the cost of living slowed between 1999 and 2000.
  d. If the cost of living continues to rise, people will move out of the cities.
  e. The cost of living for city residents steadily increased between 1990 and 2001.

The answers are on page 341.

Foreign Trade

Foreign trade—trade that crosses national borders—involves both microeconomic and macroeconomic issues. In terms of microeconomics, the law of supply and demand once again holds sway. Countries typically are not self-sufficient; in fact, even if they could provide all the goods and services they need, it would not necessarily be in their interests to do so, because doing so may require them to spend resources that could be spent more productively elsewhere. For example, it is possible that the United States could grow enough coconuts to meet domestic consumption. However, it is probably more efficient for the United States simply to buy coconuts from a country where they can be produced cheaply; that allows the United States to spend the resources it might use to grow coconuts in a more profitable way (in software development, for example). This is a process known as **specialization**, and it's a good thing. Economists believe that it is more advantageous for an economy to do some things very well than to do all things poorly.

When one country buys goods from another county, it **imports** those goods. When it sells goods to another country, it **exports** those goods. The ratio of exports to imports is called the **balance of trade**. When a country imports more than it exports, it has a **trade deficit**. When it exports more than it imports, it has a **trade surplus**.

Macroeconomic issues in foreign trade include government policies. Governments may enact **tariffs**, which are taxes on imported goods. Some such tariffs are enacted to counter unfair trade policies by foreign nations. Others are enacted simply to protect domestic producers; these tariffs are often described as **protectionist**. Foreign trade is also influenced by the value of each trading nation's **currency**, or money. The more valuable one currency is relative to another, the more goods it can buy. A strong currency is good for importers but bad for exporters, because it makes goods more expensive overseas. Thus, a strong dollar means that imported electronics are relatively cheap, but it also means that American automobiles are more expensive overseas, making them more difficult to sell outside the United States.

Exercise 11

Use the following table and the text of the preceding section on foreign trade to answer question 1.

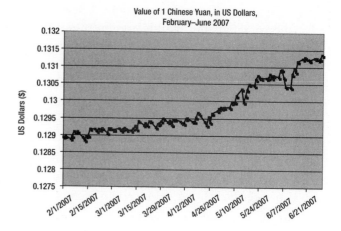

1. What happened to the value of one Chinese Yuan between February and June 2007?
   a. It increased by approximately $0.25.
   b. It increased by approximately $0.0025.
   c. Its value in U.S. dollars did not change.
   d. It decreased by approximately $0.0025.
   e. It decreased by approximately $0.25.

2. Based only on the data in the graph, which MOST likely occurred between February and June 2007?
   a. Chinese exports to the United States decreased.
   b. The United States enacted protectionist tariffs against China.
   c. China had a trade deficit with the United States.
   d. The United States increased exports to Japan.
   e. Chinese exports to the United States increased.

The answers are on page 341.

39 ▶ Geography

In the geography section of the GED Social Studies Exam, you will be asked to answer questions relating to both physical geography (the features of the Earth's surface) and cultural geography (the way humans relate to their physical environment).

THE GEOGRAPHY SECTION of the GED Social Studies Exam will cover many areas, including topography (landforms), climate, culture, and population distribution. This section will also test your ability to use and understand maps. Many questions will use a photograph, map, chart, table, or other source to present material.

▶ Physical Geography

Physical geography studies the features of the earth's surface. This branch of geography looks at climate, plant and animal life, bodies of water, and landforms. Maps are the most important tool of geography. **Topographical maps** give details about land. They show different elevations above and below sea level. **Globes** and **world maps** show oceans, seas, and the seven continents of the planet. **Political maps** show countries' borders, capitals, and major cities. Other common types of maps include **road maps**, **climate maps**, **population maps**, and **contour maps** (which show changes in elevation).

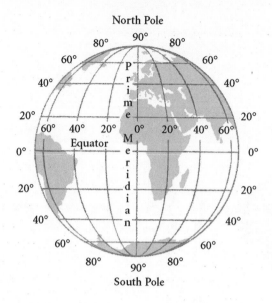

North Pole

South Pole

Reading and Understanding Maps

Intersecting lines that form a grid help locate specific areas on a world map. Lines of **latitude** run parallel to the equator, an imaginary line that runs east and west. The equator is at 0° latitude. It divides the globe into two halves, called the **northern** and **southern hemispheres**. Lines of **longitude** run parallel to the **prime meridian**, an imaginary line that runs north and south through Greenwich, England. The prime meridian is at 0° longitude. It divides the globe into two halves, called the **eastern** and **western hemispheres**. To find a specific location on the globe, look for the point where its latitude and longitude intersect. For example, you can find the western portion of Brazil if you are given its coordinates as 45° west longitude and 10° south latitude.

Landforms

Landform is the name we give to a specific feature of the Earth's surface. Landforms are defined by their shape, their location, and type of terrain of which they are constituted. The table on page 325 lists landforms with which you should be familiar.

Climate

Climate describes the atmosphere of a region over a long period of time. It includes rainfall, humidity, wind, and other elements. A region's climate is most affected by its latitude. Broad areas, called **climatic zones**, lie along latitudinal lines between the equator and the North and South poles. The **tropical zone** includes all land and water that falls between two imaginary lines called the **Tropic of Cancer** (23.5° north latitude) and the **Tropic of Capricorn** (23.5° south latitude). The tropics—hot, wet, with little seasonal change—contain the world's largest rain forests. It also contains savanna and desert climates. Much of Africa, Central America, the Caribbean, South America, Southeast Asia, and India are part of the tropical zone.

The **temperate zones** lie between the tropics and the polar circles. They are characterized by four seasons, usually a hot summer, cold winter, and intermediate spring and fall. Much of North America, Europe, Russia, China, and the Middle East are found in the northern temperate zone. Australia and the southern part of South America fall within the southern temperate zone. The **polar** or **arctic zones** are the areas near the North and South poles. This zone is characterized by long, cold winters and short, cool summers. The **Arctic Circle** marks the region near the North Pole and the **Antarctic Circle** marks the area surrounding the South Pole.

Landforms

Landform	Definition
archipelago	a chain of islands
bay	a body of water that is mostly enclosed by land
butte	a hill with a flat top and steep sides
canyon	a deep valley with steep sides, typically formed by erosion
continent	a major landmass; there are seven continents (Africa, Antarctica, Asia, Australia, Europe, North America, South America)
delta	a triangular landmass found at the mouth of a river, formed by sediment deposits
desert	a region with little rainfall or water
gulf	a body of water that is mostly enclosed by land and is larger than a bay
isthmus	a narrow strip of land bordered by water connecting two larger landmasses
marsh	a lowland that floods as a result of rain, tides, and other events that bring additional water to the area
mountain	an elevated landmass, usually more than 2,000 feet above sea level, rising to a peak
peninsula	a landmass surrounded by water on all but one side, connected to a larger landmass
plateau	an elevated landform with a relatively flat top; larger than a butte
prairie	an extensive grassland, typically with little or no change in elevation throughout
swamp	a low-lying expanse of spongy terrain upon which water collects
valley	a lowland between two hills, mountains, or cliffs
volcano	a mountain or hill topped by a crater through which lava, vapor, gas, and/or rocks may erupt
wetland	an expanse consisting of swamps and marshes

Resources

One of the most important traits of a region—at least from the point of view of humans and other living beings—is the availability of **resources** that can sustain life and civilization. Water is the most important resource, because it is both essential to life and not universally available. Populations settle around bodies of water, which serve not only as sources of drinking water but also as transportation routes and sources of power. Given its importance, it is not surprising that many wars have been fought over the control of waterways.

The resources available to an area play a major role in how that area develops. In the nineteenth century, the American south relied on its climate, its fertile soil, and the availability of land to develop into a major agricultural producer. The northeast, on the other hand, utilized its large population and easy access to trade routes with Europe to develop into an industrial power. Each region developed in the direction to which its geographic characteristics were better suited. In this way, geographic characteristics such as climate and natural resources are major factors in the development of a region's, and country's, economy. Areas with abundant natural resources can become very wealthy, while areas with relatively few natural resources will have a hard time developing beyond a subsistence level. Much of the Arabian Peninsula consists of desert land, where water is scarce and growing crops is difficult. This would be a major impediment to economic growth if not for the fact that the region is home to vast supplies of oil, which the world's rich industrial nations need in great quantities. As a result, countries on the Arabian Peninsula have a means to accrue wealth despite a shortage of some essential natural resources.

Resources are not limitless. Improperly managed, resources can be depleted. **Conservationists** are people who work to persuade others to use resources wisely. They champion **recycling**, the reuse of materials, and **sustainable resource use**, which means using resources in a way that they won't run out. For example, sustainable resource use might call for planting trees whenever trees are harvested for lumber. Conservationists also campaign for protection of endangered plants and species, arguing that as stewards of the planet it is our responsibility to maintain biodiversity. Conservationists also note that all plants and creatures serve a purpose in the **biosphere**, the portion of the Earth inhabited by living creatures. Because we cannot predict how the elimination of one plant or species might impact others that depend on it, we must be careful about our impact.

▶Cultural Geography

Cultural geography explores the relationship between humans and their natural environment. It looks at how people both adapt to and transform their physical surroundings to suit their needs. Many aspects of **culture**—a shared way of living among a group of people that develops over time—are influenced by environment. Geographers study the belief systems, language, food, architecture, and clothing of particular regions.

They also study **population**—the size, makeup, and distribution of people in a given area over a period of time. This field, called **demography**, looks at changes in population through birth rate, death rate, and migration from one place to another. One major factor affecting where people live is a region's type of economy. In areas that depend on agriculture for their economy, people generally live in rural areas. In places with an industrial economy, urban areas become major population centers. In 1950, 29% of the world's population lived in urban areas. In 1990, this figure increased to 43%.

Today, more than half of the world's population—an estimated 6.7 billion—lives in Asia, with China and India as major contributors. North America makes up less than 5% of the global total.

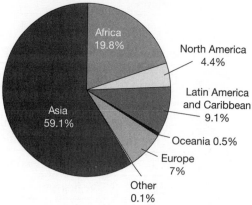

Predicted Distribution of World Population 2050

Africa 19.8%
North America 4.4%
Latin America and Caribbean 9.1%
Oceania 0.5%
Europe 7%
Other 0.1%
Asia 59.1%

Source: Data from United Nations Population Division.

The U.S. Census Bureau predicts that the world population will reach more than nine billion people by 2050, with most of the population increase occurring in less developed countries.

Exercise 12

Use the pie graph and paragraph about world population distribution to answer the following question.

1. Which of the following is a statement of fact rather than opinion?
   a. The Chinese government should continue its "one child–one family" policy to curtail its population growth.
   b. The world population will exceed nine billion people by 2050.
   c. Three out of five persons on Earth today live in Asia.
   d. The U.S. population will decline in the next century because it is too expensive to live here.
   e. Population growth should be a top concern for all nations.

The answer is on page 341.

40 ▶ Tips and Strategies for the GED Social Studies Exam

You have reviewed what you need to know for the GED Social Studies Exam. Now you will learn some specific tips and strategies to use on the exam.

O N THE GED Social Studies Exam, you will read short passages, varying in length from 50 to 200 words, and then answer a multiple-choice question or set of questions concerning the passage. Reading passages may be taken from a number of sources, often drawn from a workplace or academic context. The exam uses both primary sources, such as firsthand historical or practical documents, and secondary sources, such as excerpts from editorials, news articles, or news magazines.

▶ Be an Active Reader

When you read social studies material, you use a similar set of skills as you do when you read other kinds of text. Reading is an active exercise in which you interact with the text, paying close to attention to the key thoughts and details of a passage. Try skimming a passage first so that you can discern its organization and get clues about its main ideas. If you read at a slow pace initially, you may lose the overall idea in too many details. Look to see if a reading excerpt is broken into sections, if there are any helpful topic headings, and what key terms are boldfaced or highlighted. After you finish skimming, go back and read more closely. This time, ask yourself questions as you read to help you better understand and recall the passage: What is the main point of the text? How did the author support his or her point? As you read, consider making quick notes on a separate piece of paper to help you highlight important words or ideas.

Where Is the Main Idea?

To show that you understand the concepts presented in social studies material, the exam will sometimes ask you to find the main idea of a passage. A **main idea** is a general statement that contains all of the ideas within a passage. It is an author's main point.

To locate a main idea, carefully read the topic sentence of the passage. The first sentence may contain the overall idea that an author wishes to express. However, sometimes an author may build up to his or her point, in which case you may find the main idea in the last sentence of the introductory paragraph or even the last sentence of the entire passage. Students often confuse the topic or subject of a passage—that is, what the passage is about—with the main idea. The main idea is what the author intends to say *about* the subject. For example, read the following paragraph:

> The fertile black soil of the Nile River Valley in northeastern Africa gave rise to the agriculture-based society of ancient Egypt. For more than 3,000 years beginning as early as 5,000 B.C., this civilization flourished. Its cultural contributions include basic concepts of arithmetic and geometry, a calendar, jewelry, pottery, statues, the pyramids at Giza, underground burial chambers, and the mummification process. The Egyptian script, called hieroglyphics, is a form of writing based on pictures. The Rosetta Stone, a granite slab inscribed in 196 B.C. with three identical texts, aided scholars in deciphering hieroglyphics.

Note that a statement might be too general to best describe the main idea of a passage. For example, look at the following choices. Which best describes the main idea of the selection?

a. Early civilizations often developed near a water source.
b. Before deciphering the Rosetta Stone, scholars could not read Egyptian hieroglyphics.
c. Ancient Egypt was a sophisticated civilization that made many contributions to human culture.
d. The most important of Egyptian contributions was a written script called hieroglyphics.
e. Scholars have found similarities between heiroglyphics and ancient Greek.

Although choice **a** is a true statement, it is too general to express the main idea of the paragraph. Choice **b** is also a true statement but is too specific to describe the passage's main idea. Choice **d** is an opinion that is not supported by the details of the passage. Choice **e** is not supported by the passage. Choice **c** best describes the paragraph's main idea.

To practice finding the main idea, ask yourself some of the following questions when you read:

- What is this passage about?
- What is the author's purpose?
- If you were asked to choose a headline or title for the passage, what would you choose?
- Which sentence contains all of the ideas expressed in the passage?

Finding Supporting Ideas

After you have determined the main idea of a passage, the next step is to find the details or facts that an author has provided to support his or her main position. While a main idea is a general statement, a supporting idea is a statement that provides specific information. For example, read the next paragraph from a U.S. Census Bureau report:

> The growth of human population has been, is now, and in the future will be almost entirely determined in the world's less-developed countries (LDCs). Ninety-nine percent of global natural increase—the difference between numbers of births and numbers of deaths—now occurs in the developing regions of Africa, Asia, and Latin America.

The topic of this paragraph is world population. The main idea of the passage is what the writer is saying about world population. In this case, the first sentence expresses the main idea: *The growth of human population has been, is now, and in the future will be almost entirely determined in the world's less-developed countries (LDCs)*. The next sentence offers specific information that supports the main idea. It offers a specific fact in the form of a statistic (*99% of global natural increase*) and gives details about which areas of the world the passage is talking about (*developing regions of Africa, Asia, and Latin America*).

These words and phrases are often used to introduce a detail or idea that supports an author's position:

for example   *for instance*
one reason is   *in one case*
in particular   *specifically*

To practice locating supporting ideas while you read, skim the text and look for the following:

- examples that bolster the main idea
- contrasting arguments that clarify the author's point
- arguments for the author's position
- details that answer what, when, where, why, or how

Restating Information

The GED Social Studies Exam will ask you to answer questions based on details supplied in a passage. However, the answer choices will not present the details in the same words—they may paraphrase the information, which means to restate it in different terms. To strengthen your critical thinking skills, when you are reading, pause and think about what the material is stating. Then try putting it in your own words. This will help you better understand reading material and increase your ability to recognize the same material even if it is written in new terms. For example, read the following passage.

> The North American Free Trade Agreement (NAFTA) is an agreement between Canada, Mexico, and the United States to remove tariffs and trade barriers from goods made and sold on the continent. Before the pact was approved in 1993, lawmakers and special-interest groups fiercely debated the issue. Labor groups believed that NAFTA would make it easier for U.S. businesses to move their production plants to Mexico to take advantage of cheap labor. Environmental groups opposed NAFTA because they felt that pollution regulations would be more difficult to enforce.

Think about how you would rephrase this information in your own words. Now answer the practice question.

According to the information in the paragraph, which of the following is true?

a. Supporters of NAFTA were not challenged.
b. Opponents of NAFTA wanted to keep duties and other tariffs on U.S. goods shipped to Mexico.
c. Labor groups were afraid that U.S. jobs would be lost.
d. Canada and the United States never approved NAFTA.
e. Labor groups believe it is cheaper to produce goods in the United States.

Choice **c** is correct. It restates the following sentence from the passage: *Labor groups believed that NAFTA would make it easier for U.S. businesses to move their plants to Mexico to take advantage of cheap labor.* Choices **a** and **d** are incorrect statements. Choice **b** may be true, but is not mentioned in the paragraph.

Making Inferences

While restating information tests your ability to know what a text says, making inferences about a passage demonstrates your ability to know what a text means. Sometimes an author may not explicitly state his or her main idea or offer a conclusion. You must infer the author's meaning. Being able to make inferences is an important critical thinking skill. To figure out an unstated idea or conclusion, look at what the author has stated. Ask yourself these questions:

- What can I conclude based on the information provided?
- What is the author suggesting?
- What will be the outcome?
- Would the same outcome occur in another setting?

Read the following excerpt from Elizabeth Cady Stanton's paper, "Self-Government the Best Means of Self-Development," which she presented to the United States Senate Committee on Woman Suffrage at a March 7, 1884 hearing. Then answer the practice question.

> "They who say that women do not desire the right of suffrage, that they prefer masculine domination to self-government, falsify every page of history, every fact in human experience. It has taken the whole power of the civil and canon law to hold woman in the subordinate position which it is said she willingly accepts."

What is the author of this passage suggesting?

a. Women do not want the right to vote.

b. Women need to have access to education before they are allowed the right to vote.

c. Lawmakers and religious leaders have been coercive in maintaining women's status as "second-class" citizens.

d. Women can still be influential citizens without the right to vote.

e. Women willingly accept their subordinate position.

Statements **a**, **d**, and **e** are incorrect. Elizabeth Cady Stanton is making a counterargument against the position that women do not want the right to vote. Statement **b** is not supported by the details given in the passage. Statement **c** is the best answer. Stanton uses strong language to make her argument for women's suffrage. She says that "canon law," which refers to the laws of the Christian Church, and "civil law," which refers to the laws of the United States, have been used to keep women in a "subordinate position."

Looking for Proof

Just because something is in print does not mean that the reader must believe it or take it as fact. Most written material has some bias. Sometimes a writer's beliefs may unknowingly affect how he or she writes about an event. In other instances, a writer purposefully tries to shape your reaction and opinion. For example, a writer may present only one perspective of an event or include only facts that support his or her position. One crucial thinking skill that the GED Social Studies Exam will measure is your ability to make judgments about what you read. As you read, you will need to challenge the author's assumptions and positions, tell the difference between fact and opinion, and look for complete and accurate information.

Fact versus Opinion

A **fact** is a statement that can be verified by a reliable source. Because all sources have some bias, you must decide whether you think a source presents accurate, researched information. Examples of reliable sources of information may include official government documents, encyclopedias, or well-documented studies. Here is an example of a factual statement:

The U.S. population is growing older—in fact, adults over age 65 are the fastest-growing segment of today's population.

This sentence could be supported by the recent national census.

An **opinion** is a statement of the beliefs or feelings of a person or group. It cannot be proven by a reliable source. An opinion is a judgment that may or may not be true. It includes predictions of the future because they cannot be proven at the current time. The following sentence represents an opinion:

The population boom among elderly Americans will create a future healthcare crisis.

This statement represents a belief or speculation about the future. Others may disagree with this prediction. Regardless, it cannot be proven, so it is a statement of opinion, not a statement of fact.

Be alert to the common words that may introduce a statement of opinion:

likely	*should/could*	*say*
possibly	*think*	*charge*
probably	*believe*	*attest*

Emotional Language

Propaganda refers to techniques that try to influence your opinion, emotions, and attitudes to benefit an organization or individual. Propaganda uses language that targets your emotions—your fears, beliefs, values, prejudices—instead of appealing to reason or critical thinking. Advertising, media, and political campaigns use propaganda techniques to influence you. To detect propaganda, ask yourself the following questions about written material:

- Who does it benefit?
- What are its sources?
- What is the purpose of the text?

Here are six common propaganda techniques:

1. **Bandwagon.** The basic message of bandwagon propaganda is "everyone else is doing something, so you should be, too." It appeals to the desire to join the crowd or be on the winning team. Phrases

like "Americans buy more of our brand than any other brand" or "the brand that picky parents choose" are examples of the bandwagon technique. To evaluate a message, ask these questions:

- Does this program or policy serve my particular interests?
- What is the evidence for or against it?

2. **Common Man.** This approach tries to convince you that its message is "just plain old common sense." Politicians and advertisers often speak in an everyday language and use common jokes and phrases to present themselves as one "of the people," thereby appealing to their audience. For example, a presidential candidate campaigning in New Hampshire may dress in a plaid shirt and chop wood or visit a mill in order to look like an ordinary citizen. To avoid the common-man technique, ask yourself these questions:

- What ideas is the person presenting—separate from the person's image or language?
- What are the facts?

3. **Euphemisms.** Instead of emotionally loaded language that rouses its audience, these terms "soften" an unpleasant reality and make it less emotional. Terms that soften the nature of war are an example. A historical instance of euphemism is when in the 1940s, the U.S. government renamed the War Department to the Department of Defense. Stay alert to euphemisms. What facts are being softened or hidden?

4. **Generalities.** This approach uses words and phrases that evoke deep emotions. Examples of generalities are *honor, peace, freedom,* or *home.* These words carry strong associations for most people. By using these terms, a writer can appeal to your emotions so that you will accept his or her message without evaluating it. Generalities are vague so that you will supply your own interpretations and not ask further questions. An example might be, "The United States must further restrict immigration in order to preserve freedom and liberty."

Try to challenge what you read or hear. Ask yourself:

- What does the generality really mean?
- Has the author used the generality to sway my emotions?
- If I take the generality out of the sentence, what are the merits of the idea?

5. **Labeling or name-calling.** This method links a negative label, name, or phrase to a person, group, belief, or nation. It appeals to hates and fears. Name-calling can be a direct attack or indirect (using ridicule). Labels can evoke deep emotions, such as Commie, Nazi, or Terrorist. Others can be negatively charged, depending on the situation: Yuppie, Slacker, Liberal, or Reactionary. When a written text or speech uses labeling, ask yourself these questions:

- Does the label have any real connection to the idea being presented?
- If I take away the label, what are the merits of the idea?

6. **Testimonials.** In advertising, athletes promote a range of products, from cereal to wristwatches. In politics, celebrities endorse presidential candidates. Both are examples of testimonials. A testimonial uses a public figure, expert, or other respected person to endorse a policy, organization, or product. Because you may respect or admire a person, you may be less critical and accept a product, candidate, or idea more readily. Ask yourself these questions:

- Does the public figure have any expert knowledge about this subject?
- Without the testimonial, what are the merits of the message?

Only Half the Story

Another way that a writer may slant information is to omit evidence. A writer may try to convince you to accept his or her interpretation of an event or issue by giving you only one side of the story and by leaving out contrasting facts or perspectives. When this is done deliberately, it is a propaganda technique called **card stacking**. When you read, evaluate whether the author has presented different points of view and offered balanced evidence. For instance, a campaign ad will certainly highlight a candidate's positive qualities while leaving out unfavorable characteristics. Campaign ads might also target an opponent, presenting negative qualities and omitting positive ones, thereby creating a distorted perspective.

Cause-and-Effect Relationships

The GED Social Studies Exam will ask you to identify the relationships between events. Often, historical events are connected to situations that came before them. When you are considering the causes of an event, be aware that multiple causes can create one effect, just as one cause can have many effects. Sometimes what is considered a cause can be controversial. In the following passage, legislators and criminologists argue over the causes that might have contributed to a drop in the youth crime rate.

> **Juvenile crime** has reached its lowest national level since 1988. The number of arrests for juvenile murder has also dropped. It is now at the lowest level since 1966. Backers of "adult time" legislation—"get-tough" laws that send violent teenagers to adult prison—believe that fear of imprisonment is stopping juveniles from committing crimes. However, the decrease in crime often started before these laws took effect. Some criminologists believe a drop in crack cocaine use and gun carrying is the more likely cause. These experts argue that as the crack market dropped off in the mid-1990s, fewer teens were dealing drugs and fewer were carrying guns to protect themselves. Police also increased their efforts to enforce gun laws. With fewer young people carrying weapons, the teen murder rate dropped.

According to the criminologists mentioned in the passage, which of the following is NOT a cause of the drop in juvenile crime?
  a. fewer gun-carrying juveniles
  b. enforced gun laws
  c. fear of jail time
  d. fewer drug dealers on the street
  e. police presence

The correct choice is **c**. In the passage, criminologists argue that "adult time" laws have not had an effect on the decrease in youth crime. They believe that choices **a**, **b**, **d**, and **e** are multiple causes of the drop in crime.

▶ Social Studies Key Words

As with any type of study, the social sciences use specific terms and vocabulary. While you are studying for the exam, use a dictionary to look up unfamiliar terms. However, even if you do not recognize a word, you might be able to figure out its meaning. The parts of a word—**prefix**, **root**, and **suffix**—can offer clues to its meaning. A number of terms used in social studies derive from Latin or Greek. Knowing some useful word parts can help you make an educated guess about the meaning of a word. Review these common Latin and Greek word parts:

ante	before	**cracy**	rule	**inter**	between	**super**	over
anthrop	human	**co, con**	with	**mis**	wrong	**theo**	god
arche	beginning, government	**demo**	people	**mono**	one	**topos**	place
auto	self	**dis**	not, opposite	**ology**	study	**tri**	three
bi	two	**femina**	woman	**poly**	many	**uni**	one
bio	life	**geo**	earth	**proto**	first		
bene	good	**genos**	race	**sub**	under, below		

Using the chart, isolate the word parts of the following words:

monotheism _____

autocrat _____

democracy _____

Now you can guess what they mean. **Monotheism** is the belief that there is only one God. **Autocrat** means someone who rules by him- or herself: a ruler with unlimited power. **Democracy** is a government in which the people rule either directly or indirectly through representatives.

Context—the words and sentences surrounding a term—can also offer clues to its meaning. Sometimes a word will be followed by a phrase that restates and explains its meaning.

Example: President Truman instituted a set of domestic programs that were later labeled the Fair Deal; these policies continued and developed Roosevelt's New Deal programs.

In this sentence, you can determine what the term *Fair Deal* means from the text that surrounds it. The Fair Deal is both "a set of domestic programs" and a continuation of "Roosevelt's New Deal programs."

A **contrast** or opposing point of view can also offer clues to the meaning of a term. The following sentence uses the term *bipartisanship:*

Example: Despite the president's plea for bipartisanship, Republican senators accused Democratic leaders of petty politics.

The sentence tells you that the Republicans are making accusations about the actions of the Democrats. The two groups are not in agreement. In the sentence, the term *bipartisanship* refers to the opposite. So, you can guess that it refers to the two groups when they are in agreement.

▶ Tools and Methods in Social Science

Social scientists use **polls** in order to learn the attitudes and opinions of a population. Polls are surveys that ask people about the way they live and what they believe. One method of polling is called **sampling**, in which a polltaker questions a small part of a group so that he or she can speculate about the opinions of the whole group. In this way, polltakers can make accurate predictions. However, sometimes polls are inaccurate. A historic polling failure occurred in 1948, when polling groups predicted that presidential candidate Harry S. Truman would lose the election. In the 2000 presidential election, the narrow margin in some states between candidates George W. Bush and Al Gore made it difficult for polling organizations to make predictions.

In addition to forecasting voting patterns in elections, polls can determine the opinions of groups on a whole range of issues from consumer trends to healthcare and education. Polltakers may use personal interviews, telephone interviews, or mail-in questionnaires. The data from these methods are then tabulated and evaluated.

After social scientists gather information from surveys or studies, they can organize the information into the form of numbers, or **statistics**. Statistics can help social scientists interpret information. They use statistics to follow trends in global or national rates of population, education level, housing status, crime, or another category. They can also use statistics to make comparisons between groups.

Example: The U.S. Census Bureau found that 47% of U.S. citizens between the ages of 18 and 24 voted in the November 2004 election, while 72% of citizens 55 and older voted.

From this information, a social scientist can hypothesize about the causes and effects of this age difference in people who vote.

Primary Sources

To gather information about the past, social scientists and historians use a wide range of sources. **Primary sources** are firsthand records of the past that include letters, legal records, business records, diaries, oral histories, photographs, posters, maps, or artifacts. **Secondary sources** are accounts of an event made some time after the event took place. These include newspaper articles, pamphlets, books, or interviews. Together, these clues about the past make up the historical record.

When reading historical sources, you need to use the same analysis skills that you would apply to a present-day source. Here are some basic questions to ask when you are evaluating the reliability of a historical source:

- Consider the purpose of the author. Was the source intended for a private or public audience?
- Did the author witness the event or rely on others' accounts?
- Did the author express an opinion? What was his or her point of view?
- Can you verify the source with other evidence?
- How much time elapsed after the event before the author made his or her account? (The sooner an account is made, the more reliable a source tends to be. Also, the nearer the witness is in proximity to the event, the more reliable. Social scientists and historians call this the time and place rule.)

▶ Presenting Facts

Social scientists often use tables, charts, and graphs to arrange information. Charts and tables divide figures into columns. They organize information so that you can see the relationships between facts. **Graphs** visually display information so that you can interpret facts more easily. Graphs include **tables**, **bar graphs**, **line graphs**, and **circle graphs**.

Tables

Tables arrange figures (numbers) into columns in order to show a relationship between them. To read a table, begin by noting the title of the table (the title runs across the top of the table). Next, read each column heading. Now you can locate facts and begin to discern the relationships between them.

World Energy Consumption, 1970–2020

Year	Quadrillion Btu Consumed
1970	207
1975	243
1980	285
1985	311
1990	346
1995	366
2000	382
2005	439
2010	493
2015	552
2020	612

Sources: History—Energy Information Administration (EIA), Office of Energy Markets and End Use, International Statistics Database and International Energy Annual 1999, DOE/EIA-0119(99), Washington, DC, February 2001. Projections—EIA, World Energy Projection System (2002).

Exercise 13
Look at the table, "World Energy Consumption, 1970–2020," and then answer the following questions on a separate sheet of paper.

1. How much energy did the world consume in 1980?

2. What is the table's estimate of world energy consumption for the year 2015?

3. What is the trend of the world's energy consumption?

4. In which five-year period in the past was the increase in the world's energy consumption the greatest?

5. Between 1970 and 2020, how many times will the world's consumption rate grow, according to the table's estimate?

The answers are on page 341.

Bar Graphs

A **bar graph** is one way to present facts visually. A bar graph features a vertical axis (running up and down on the left-hand side of the graph) and a horizontal axis (running along the bottom of the graph). The graph represents quantities in strips or bars. To construct a bar graph from the table, "World Energy Consumption, 1970–2020," mark the five-year increments on the bottom horizontal axis and the units of energy consumed (by increments of 100 quadrillion Btu) on the vertical axis. By representing the table's data in a bar graph, you can visualize the world's energy consumption trend more easily.

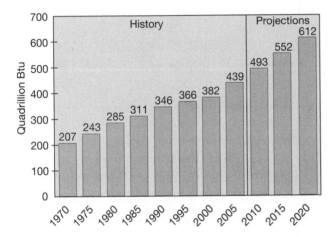

Line Graphs

Line graphs compare two or more things and help you visualize trends at a glance. Like the bar graph, a line graph features a horizontal and vertical axis. Look at the graph, "Immigrants Admitted: Fiscal Years 1900–2000." The vertical axis marks the number of immigrants (in thousands). The horizontal axis measures each decade between 1900 and 2000. A point for each year is plotted on the coordinate plane and a line connects each point. By using a line graph, you can readily see immigration trends over the century.

IMMIGRANTS ADMITTED TO THE UNITED STATES: FISCAL YEARS 1900–2000

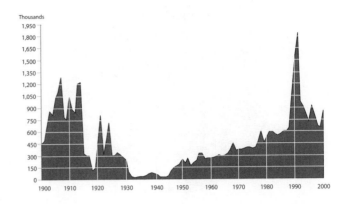

Source: 2000 Statistical Yearbook of the Immigration and Naturalization Service.

Exercise 14

Look at the line graph, "Immigrants Admitted to the United States," and then answer the following questions.

1. What was the general trend of U.S. immigration between 1950 and 1990?

2. In which decades was the lowest point of U.S. immigration in the last century?

3. When did the highest point occur?

The answers are on page 341.

Circle Graphs

Circle graphs, also called **pie charts**, display information so that you can see relationships between parts and a whole. The entire circle in the graph represents 100% of something. The graph divides the whole into parts, or pie slices. To understand a circle graph, read the title of the graph. What does the graph represent? Read all other headings and labels. What does each portion of the circle represent? Now you are ready to see how the parts of information relate. Review the following circle graph and then answer the practice questions.

The Federal Government Dollar

Where It Comes From

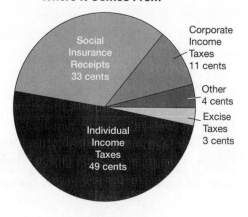

Social Insurance Receipts 33 cents

Corporate Income Taxes 11 cents

Other 4 cents

Excise Taxes 3 cents

Individual Income Taxes 49 cents

Where It Goes

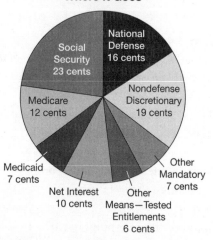

National Defense 16 cents

Social Security 23 cents

Nondefense Discretionary 19 cents

Medicare 12 cents

Medicaid 7 cents

Net Interest 10 cents

Other Means—Tested Entitlements 6 cents

Other Mandatory 7 cents

Source: U.S. Office of Management and Budget, the Executive Office of the President.

Reading and Interpreting Graphs

▶ Note the title of the graph.

▶ Look at the labels of the axes (or pie slices in a circle graph).

▶ Carefully read the information in the legend or key if there is one.

▶ Look for relationships between the facts presented.

Exercise 15

Use the circle graph "The Federal Government Dollar" to answer the following questions.

1. What percentage of the federal budget comes from social insurance receipts and corporate income taxes?

2. What is the biggest source of income for the federal government?

3. Which program receives the largest share of the national budget?

4. What proportion of the budget goes to paying off debt?

The answers are on page 342.

▶ Maps

Maps are printed or drawn representations of a geographic area. Social scientists use different types of maps to understand the natural or cultural facts about an area. Maps can visually display many kinds of information, such as the physical features of the land, political boundaries between nations, or population densities.

Topographic maps show the physical features of land, including land elevations and depressions, water depth, rivers, forests, mountains, or human-made cities and roads.

Political maps display political divisions and borders.

Special-purpose maps can depict a wide range of information about an area, from average rainfall, crop distribution, or population density, to migration patterns of people.

To read a map, carefully review each of the following:

■ **Title**—describes what the map represents

■ **Legend, or key**—a table or list that explains the symbols used in a map

■ **Latitude and longitude**—latitude refers to the lines on a map that are parallel to the equator; longitude refers to lines parallel to the prime meridian that run north to south through Greenwich, England. These lines help locate specific areas on a map.

- **Scale**—shows the map's proportion in relation to the area it represents. For example, on a topographic map, the scale might show the distance on the map that equals a mile or kilometer on land.

Exercise 16

Review the special-purpose map below, paying careful attention to its details, and then answer the practice questions.

1. What is the title of the map?

2. What do the four shades of gray indicate in the legend?

3. How much did the population change in this decade in the state of California?

4. Which states experienced the largest population change in this decade?

5. Which areas experienced a loss?

The answers are on page 342.

▶ Political Cartoons

A regular feature in American newspapers since the early nineteenth century, political cartoons use satirical humor to comment on a current event. Their purpose is to express an opinion—the political point of view of the cartoonist or the newspaper or magazine in which they appear. A cartoon will often focus and simplify a single issue or event so that readers can easily grasp its message. Cartoons employ few words, often just enough to make their point clear. They sometimes use **caricature**, a technique in which the cartoonist deliberately exaggerates the features of well-known people (often politicians) to make fun of them.

Because of their emotional appeal, political cartoons can be effective tools in swaying public opinion. The power of political cartoons was demonstrated in 1869 when *Harper's Weekly* cartoonist Thomas Nast used his art to help end the corrupt Boss Tweed Ring in New York City. Nast first introduced symbols that we still use today: the elephant for the Republican Party and the donkey for the Democratic Party.

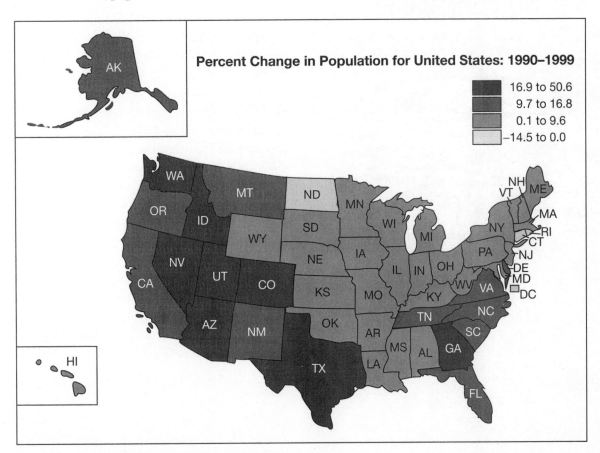

Percent Change in Population for United States: 1990–1999

	16.9 to 50.6
	9.7 to 16.8
	0.1 to 9.6
	−14.5 to 0.0

Source: Population Estimates Program, U.S. Census Bureau.

Interpreting Political Cartoons

To understand and interpret a cartoon, you can use the same critical thinking skills that you employ when finding meaning in a written text. This political cartoon is from December 9, 2002. It refers to the United States's demand for weapons inspections in Iraq. Review the cartoon and ask yourself these basic questions:

- What are the details or symbols used in the cartoon? Did the cartoonist use a caricature?
- What is happening in the cartoon?
- What comparisons or contrasts are depicted in the cartoon?
- Political cartoons express an opinion. What is the point of view of the cartoonist?
- What is the historical context of the cartoon? Historical cartoons may be more difficult for today's readers to interpret. You will need to consider the conditions of the time period in which the cartoon was created.

Copyright © 2002 by Mike Lane. Reprinted by permission of caglecartoons.com.

Exercise 17

Now use the political cartoon to select the best answer to the following question.

Which statement best describes the main idea of the cartoon?

a. The U.S. government believed in 2002 that Iraq was developing weapons of mass destruction.

b. The United States believes in a pacifist approach.

c. In 2002, the U.S. government was hypocritical in its demand that Iraq disarm its weapons of mass destruction.

d. Saddam Hussein was a leader who could be trusted.

e. George Bush personally inspected Iraq for weapons of mass destruction.

The answer is on page 342.

▶ Photographs

Photographs are powerful visual documents of personal or public life. In addition to recording a specific time period or event, they are effective tools of persuasion. In the nineteenth century, William H. Jackson's photographs of the Yellowstone region were influential in persuading the U.S. Congress to designate the area a national park, journalist Jacob Riis's photographs of New York City slums led to needed social reform, and Lewis Hine's shocking images of children working in factories resulted in the passage of child-protection legislation in 1916. Photographs are also an important part of the historic record. Photographers like James Van Der Zee, who chronicled life in Harlem for 60 years, contribute information about a past culture.

When you look at a photograph, use the same critical thinking skills you would when reading a written passage or other type of graphic. Does the photograph express a main idea or theme? What is the supporting evidence? Ask yourself the following questions:

- What is happening in the photo?
- What details can I learn from the image?
- What do I think is the message that the photographer is trying to express?
- Is there a caption or title to the photo?
- What is the historical context of the image?

Look at the following photograph of working children in an Indiana factory at the beginning of the twentieth century.

Child Laborers in Indiana Glass Works, Midnight, Indiana, 1908.
Source: The National Archives and Records Administration.

Exercise 18

Which of the following conclusions can you draw from the photo?

a. Laws in the early 1900s protected children from long working hours.

b. The photographer believed that children could make significant contributions to the economy.

c. Children in 1908 worked in occupations where they would not be permitted today.

d. The Progressives fought to create labor laws that would protect children.

e. Children should work to contribute to their families.

The answer is on page 342.

▶ Web Resources

The following resources can help you expand your knowledge of the kinds of material covered on the GED Social Studies Exam. At the time of publication, these sites were accurate.

www.bls.gov
Website of the U.S. Bureau of Labor Statistics with information about U.S. employment and unemployment rates, consumer spending, productivity, and other statistics.

www.census.gov
Official U.S. Census Bureau website—provides statistics from the 2000 census.

www.congresslink.org
Educational website operated by the Dirksen Congressional Center—offers a guide to Congress and posts historical materials.

www.constitutioncenter.org
Website of the National Constitution Center (NCC), a nonpartisan, nonprofit organization established by Congress in 1988—gives information about fundamental principles of the Constitution and offers basic research tools.

www.federalreserve.gov
Official website of the United States Federal Reserve—includes consumer information about personal finances.

www.fedstats.gov
Offers statistics and maps from more than 100 federal agencies.

www.usa.gov
Official Internet portal to all U.S. government information with links to agencies of federal, state, local, and tribal governments—provides frequently requested federal forms and information for citizens, businesses, and government employees.

www.geographyiq.com
Online world atlas with geographic, political, and cultural information.

www.HistoryCentral.com
Covers American and world history topics and includes links to primary historical documents.

www.ilo.org
Website of the International Labour Organization with information about working conditions around the globe.

www.memory.loc.gov
Historic collections from the U.S. Library of Congress—includes primary resources about the history and culture of the United States.

www.socialstudies.org
Website of National Council for the Social Studies—includes links to teaching resources on a wide range of social studies themes.

www.supremecourtus.gov
Offers an overview of the Supreme Court—its history, procedures, and traditions—and transcripts from Supreme Court cases.

www.un.org
Website of the United Nations—includes information and maps about economic and social development, human rights, and peace and security issues around the world.

▶ Answers

Exercise 1 (page 301)

1. **d.** Based on the information in the column marked "Origin," you can conclude that each of the major religions has existed for more than a thousand years. The column with the heading "Characteristics" describes some of the influences each religion has had on human culture.

Exercise 2 (page 302)

1. **d.** *John Locke contributed the most to the Enlightenment philosophy* is a statement of opinion. Scholars could, and do, argue about who contributed the most to the Age of Reason or who is considered the most influential writer or thinker of the time.
2. **a.** Although the proponents of the Enlightenment were reacting against the influences of the Middle Ages—feudalism, the Crusades, and the Roman Catholic Church—the most likely factors that contributed positively to the Age of Enlightenment were the scientific discoveries of the sixteenth and seventeenth centuries.

Exercise 3 (page 304)

1. **b.** Because racism takes many forms and exists in places throughout the world, it is not likely that even a powerful event like World War II could stop it from occurring.
2. **c.** Choice **c** is the most likely assumption. You can theorize that Hitler's focus on national pride and strength appealed to a population in a dire economic situation (described in the passage about World War II).

Exercise 4 (page 305)

1. **e.** The passage states that the Bill of Rights was added to the Constitution to protect the rights of individual citizens.

Exercise 5 (page 307)

1. **d.** Rockefeller believed that the government should not interfere with business, so he would most likely support the motto, "That Government Is Best Which Governs Least."
2. **b.** The progressives wanted to curb big business, so they would support antitrust legislation that restricted business practices.

Exercise 6 (page 310)

1. **b.** Complete government control of the media and rule by one individual are characteristics of a dictatorship.
2. **d.** Citizens in a direct democracy vote on every law. They would have the most influence over lawmaking decisions.

Exercise 7 (page 313)

1. **c.** Choices **a** and **d** are statements of opinion. Choice **b** is incorrect and choice **e** is not discussed in the passage. Only choice **c** is supported by the information in the passage.

Exercise 8 (page 314)

1. **e.** The popular vote in 1960 was extremely close; fewer than 200,000 votes out of nearly 69 million separated Kennedy and Nixon. The electoral vote was not as close, due to the "winner take all" rule that gave each candidate *all* the electoral votes in states where the popular vote was extremely close. Thus, it is accurate to conclude that the map shows how the electoral vote results can distort the results of the popular vote

2. **b.** The map shows that both Alabama and Oklahoma split their electoral votes in the 1960 election.

Exercise 9 (page 319)

1. **a.** The point where the lines connect is at $1,400. That is the point of equilibrium.

2. **b.** As the price increases, the demand decreases.

Exercise 10 (page 321)

1. **a.** The graph's baseline is an item that cost $100 in the time period 1982–1984. The graph shows that an item that cost $100 in the base period cost about $176 in 2001. Thus, something that cost $50—half of $100—in the base period would cost about $88 (half of $176) in 2001.

2. **e.** Choice **a** is not a conclusion based on the graph. Choices **b** and **c** are not true, and choice **d** is speculation not supported by the information of the graph. Only choice **e** is a valid conclusion.

Exercise 11 (page 322)

1. **b.** The table shows that the value of the Yuan increased against the dollar; therefore, choice **a** or **b** must be correct. The Yuan increased in value from just under $0.13 to just over $0.13. The increase was less than one penny, so **b** must be the correct answer.

2. **a.** The value of the Yuan increased against the dollar. According to the passage, that would make Chinese goods more expensive to United States consumers. Therefore, it is most likely that Chinese exports to the United States would decrease as a result of the change shown in the graph.

Exercise 12 (page 326)

1. **c.** Today more than 60% of the world's population, or about three in five people, live in Asia. This fact is supported by the information in the graph. The word *should* in choices **a** and **e** alerts the reader that they are opinions. Choices **b** and **d** are predictions—they are based on current factors that may change in the future.

Exercise 13 (page 334)

1. 285 quadrillion Btu
2. 552 quadrillion Btu
3. The trend of world energy consumption is increasing. You can answer this question by simply observing that the numbers in the right-hand column are increasing.
4. The period between 2000 and 2005—consumption increased by 57 quadrillion Btu. The years in the left-hand column are divided by five-year increments (except one). To answer this question, find the greatest difference between each of the first eight rows in the right-hand column.
5. About three times, from 207 to 612 quadrillion Btu. Divide the quantity predicted for the year 2020 by the quantity consumed in 1970.

Exercise 14 (page 335)

1. The trend was increasing. Even though the graph plots small rises and falls in immigration, between 1950 and 1990 the plotted line increases overall.
2. Between the years 1930 and 1950—the line graph shows a "valley" where immigration rates decreased in these decades.
3. The year 1991 is the highest "peak" on the graph.

Exercise 15 (page 336)

1. 44%
2. individual income taxes
3. Social Security
4. 19% to the Medicare and Medicaid programs

Exercise 16 (page 337)

1. Percent Change in Population for U.S. States: 1990 to 1999
2. black—highest gain; dark gray—average gain; medium gray—smallest gain; and light gray—loss
3. between 9.7% and 16.8%
4. Washington, Idaho, Nevada, Utah, Colorado, New Mexico, Texas, Georgia
5. North Dakota, Rhode Island, Connecticut, Washington, D.C.

Exercise 17 (page 338)

1. The correct choice is **c**. By exaggerating the power and force of the U.S. aircraft, the cartoonist suggests that the United States is developing its military force while at the same time demanding that other nations (Iraq, in this case) halt any efforts to do the same. The cartoonist uses the symbol of the American flag to show that the fighter plane belongs to the United States, and he uses the initial "W" to convey that its pilot is President George W. Bush.

Exercise 18 (page 339)

1. The correct answer is **c**. This is the only choice supported by the caption and photo. The photo contradicts choice **a**—clearly, laws did not protect children from working as late as midnight. The photo does not support choice **b**—the image does not express a positive opinion about child labor. Choice **d** is true—the Progressives did seek to heighten awareness about working children, but the photo does not supply evidence of their involvement. Choice **e** represents an opinion.

The GED Mathematics Exam

In this section, you will learn all about the GED Mathematics Exam, what the test is like, what kinds of questions to expect, and how to tackle those questions. You will also learn guidelines for using calculators.

Before you begin with Chapter 41, take a few minutes to do the pretest that follows. The questions are the same type you will find on the GED. When you are finished, check the answer key carefully to assess your results. Your pretest score will help you determine how much preparation you need and the areas in which you need the most careful review and practice.

▶ Pretest: GED Mathematics

Before you review math topics common to the GED, take a few minutes to do the pretest that follows.

To practice the timing of the GED Mathematics Exam, please allow 18 minutes for this pretest. Record your answers on the answer sheet provided here and the answer grids for questions 9 and 10.

Directions: Read each question carefully and determine the best answer.

Note: On the GED, you are not permitted to write in the test booklet. Make any notes or calculations on a separate piece of paper.

ANSWER SHEET

1. ⓐ ⓑ ⓒ ⓓ ⓔ
2. ⓐ ⓑ ⓒ ⓓ ⓔ
3. ⓐ ⓑ ⓒ ⓓ ⓔ
4. ⓐ ⓑ ⓒ ⓓ ⓔ
5. ⓐ ⓑ ⓒ ⓓ ⓔ
6. ⓐ ⓑ ⓒ ⓓ ⓔ
7. ⓐ ⓑ ⓒ ⓓ ⓔ
8. ⓐ ⓑ ⓒ ⓓ ⓔ
9. ⓐ ⓑ ⓒ ⓓ ⓔ
10. ⓐ ⓑ ⓒ ⓓ ⓔ

1. On 5 successive days, a motorcyclist listed his mileage as follows: 135, 162, 98, 117, 216.

   If his motorcycle averages 14 miles for each gallon of gas used, how many gallons of gas did he use during these 5 days?
   a. 42
   b. 52
   c. 115
   d. 147
   e. 153

2. Bugsy has a piece of wood 9 feet 8 inches long. He wishes to cut it into 4 equal lengths. How far from the edge should he make the first cut?
   a. 2.5 feet
   b. 2 feet 5 inches
   c. 2.9 feet
   d. 29 feet
   e. 116 inches

Question 3 is based on the following figure.

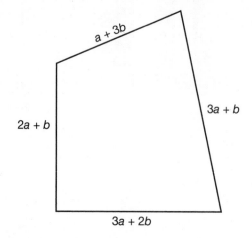

3. What is the perimeter of the figure?
   a. $8a + 5b$
   b. $9a + 7b$
   c. $7a + 5b$
   d. $6a + 6b$
   e. $8a + 6b$

4. Jossie has $5 more than Siobhan, and Siobhan has $3 less than Michael. If Michael has $30, how much money does Jossie have?
   a. $30
   b. $27
   c. $32
   d. $36
   e. Not enough information is given.

Questions 5 and 6 are based on the following graph.

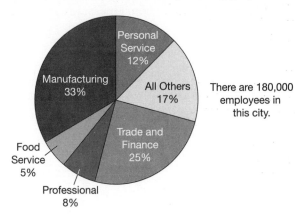

5. The number of persons engaged in food service in the city during this period was
   a. 3,600
   b. 9,000
   c. 10,000
   d. 18,000
   e. 36,000

6. If the number of persons in trade and finance is represented by *M*, then the number in manufacturing is represented as
   a. $\frac{M}{5}$
   b. $M + 3$
   c. $30M$
   d. $\frac{4M}{3}$
   e. Not enough information is given.

Question 7 is based on the following figure.

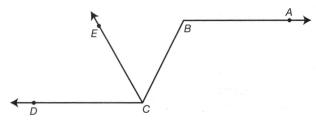

7. In the figure $\overline{AB} \parallel \overline{CD}$, $\overline{CE}$ bisects $\angle BCD$, and $m\angle ABC = 112°$. Find $m\angle ECD$.
   a. 45°
   b. 50°
   c. 56°
   d. 60°
   e. Not enough information is given.

8. Mr. DeLandro earns \$12 per hour. One week, Mr. DeLandro worked 42 hours; the following week, he worked 37 hours. Which of the following indicates the number of dollars Mr. DeLandro earned for 2 weeks?
   a. $12 \cdot 2 + 37$
   b. $12 \cdot 42 + 42 \cdot 37$
   c. $12 \cdot 37 + 42$
   d. $12 + 42 \cdot 37$
   e. $12(42 + 37)$

9. What is the slope of the line that passes through points *A* and *B* on the following coordinate graph? Mark your answer in the circles in the grid that follows.

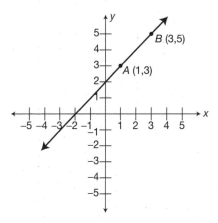

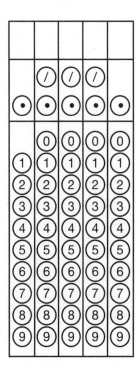

10. What is the value of the expression $3(2x - y) + (3 + x)^2$, when $x = 4$ and $y = 5$? Mark your answer in the circles on the following grid.

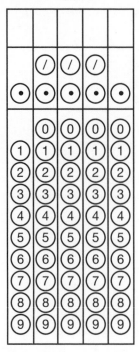

▶ **Answers**

1. b. First, find the total mileage: $135 + 162 + 98 + 117 + 216 = 728$ miles. Divide the total mileage (728) by the number of miles covered for each gallon of gas used (14) to find the number of gallons of gas needed: $728 \div 14 = 52$ gallons.

2. b. 1 ft. = 12 in.; 9 ft. 8 in. = $9 \cdot 12 + 8 = 116$ in.; $116 \div 4 = 29$ in. = 2 ft. 5 in.

3. b. To find the perimeter of the figure, find the sum of the lengths of the four sides: $2a + b + a + 3b + 3a + b + 3a + 2b = 9a + 7b$.

4. c. Michael has \$30. Siobhan has \$30 − \$3 = \$27. Jossie has \$27 + \$5 = \$32.

5. b. Five percent of the pie chart represents food service professionals, and 180,000 employees are represented in total on the chart: 5% of 180,000, or $.05 \times 180,000$, is equal to 9,000.

6. d. M = number of persons in trade and finance. Because M = 25% of the total, $4M$ = total number of city workers. Number of persons in manufacturing = $\frac{\text{total number of workers}}{3} = \frac{4M}{3}$.

7. c. Because pairs of alternate interior angles of parallel lines have equal measures, m∠BCD = m∠ABC. Thus, m∠BCD = 112°. m∠ECD = $\frac{1}{2}$m∠BCD = $\frac{1}{2}$(112) = 56°

8. e. In 2 weeks, Mr. Delandro worked a total of (42 + 37) hours and earned \$12 for each hour. Therefore, the total number of dollars he earned was $12(42 + 37)$.

9. 1.

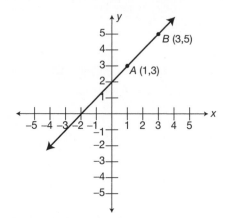

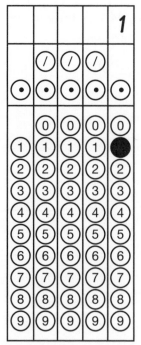

The coordinates of point A are (1,3). The coordinates of point B are (3,5). Use the slope formula:

$$\frac{(y_2 - y_1)}{(x_2 - x_1)}$$

Substitute and solve:

$$\frac{(5 - 3)}{(3 - 1)} = \frac{2}{2}, \text{ or } \frac{1}{1} = 1$$

10. 58.

$3(2x - y) + (3 + x)^2, x = 4$ and $y = 5$

$3(2 \times 4 - 5) + (3 + 4)^2 =$

$3(8 - 5) + (7)^2 =$

$3(3) + 49 =$

$9 + 49 =$

58

▶ **Pretest Assessment**

How did you do on the math pretest? If you answered seven or more questions correctly, you have earned the equivalent of a passing score on the GED Mathematics Exam. But remember that this pretest covers only a fraction of the material you might face on the GED Mathematics Exam. It is not designed to give you an accurate measure of how you would do on the actual exam. Rather, it is designed to help you determine where to focus your study efforts. For success on the GED, review all of the chapters in this section thoroughly. Focus on the sections that correspond to the pretest questions you answered incorrectly.

41 ▶ About the GED Mathematics Exam

In this chapter, you will learn all about the GED Mathematics Exam, including the number and types of questions, the topics and skills that will be tested, and guidelines for the use of calculators.

▶ What to Expect on the GED Mathematics Exam

The GED Mathematics Exam is a test used to measure your understanding of the mathematical knowledge needed in everyday life. The questions are based on information presented in words, diagrams, charts, graphs, and pictures. In addition to testing your math skills, you will also be asked to demonstrate your problem-solving skills. Examples of some of the skills needed for the mathematical portion of the GED are:

- understanding the question
- organizing data and identifying important information
- selecting problem-solving strategies
- knowing when to use appropriate mathematical operations
- setting up problems and estimating
- computing the exact, correct answer
- reflecting on the problem to ensure the answer you choose is reasonable

This section will give you lots of practice in the basic math skills that you use every day, as well as crucial problem-solving strategies.

The GED Mathematics Exam is given in two separate sections. The first section permits the use of a calculator; the second does not. The time limit for the GED is 90 minutes, meaning that you have 45 minutes to complete each section. The sections are timed separately but weighted equally. This means you must complete both sections in one testing session to receive a passing grade. If only one section is completed, the entire exam must be retaken.

The test contains 40 multiple-choice questions and 10 gridded-response questions for a total of 50 questions overall. Multiple-choice questions give you several answers to choose from and gridded-response questions ask you to come up with the answer yourself. Each multiple-choice question has five answer choices, **a** through **e**. Gridded response questions use a standard grid or a coordinate plane grid. (The guidelines for entering a gridded-response question will be covered later in this section.)

Exam Topics

The math section of the GED tests you on the following subjects:

- measurement
- algebra
- geometry
- number relations
- data analysis

Each of these subjects is detailed in this section along with tips and strategies for solving them.

Using Calculators

The GED Mathematics Exam is given in two separate booklets; Part I and Part II. The use of calculators is permitted on Part I only. You will not be allowed to use your own. The testing facility will provide a calculator for you. The calculator that will be used is the Casio fx-260 SOLAR. It is important for you to become familiar with this calculator as well as how to use it. Use a calculator only when it will save you time or improve your accuracy.

Formula Page

A page with a list of common formulas is provided with all test forms. You are allowed to use this page when you are taking the exam. It is necessary for you to become familiar with the formula page and to understand when and how to use each formula. An example of the formula page is on page 352 of this book.

Gridded-Response and Set-Up Questions

There are ten non–multiple-choice questions in the math portion of the GED. These questions require you to find an answer and to fill in circles on a grid or on a coordinate axis.

Standard Grid-in Questions

When you are given a question with a grid like the one that follows, keep these guidelines in mind:

- First, write your answer in the blank boxes at the top of the grid. This will help keep you organized as you "grid in" the bubbles and ensure that you fill them out correctly.
- You can start in any column, but leave enough columns for your whole answer.
- You do not have to use all of the columns. If your answer takes up only two or three columns, leave the others blank.
- You can write your answer by using either fractions or decimals. For example, if your answer is $\frac{1}{4}$, you can enter it as a fraction, 1/4, or as a decimal, .25.

The slash (/) is used to signify the fraction bar of the fraction. The numerator should be bubbled to the left of the fraction bar and the denominator should be bubbled in to the right. See the example that follows.

- When your answer is a mixed number, it must be represented on the standard grid in the form of an improper fraction. For example, for the answer $1\frac{1}{4}$, grid in 5/4.
- When you are asked to plot a point on a coordinate grid like this one, simply fill in the bubble where the point should appear.

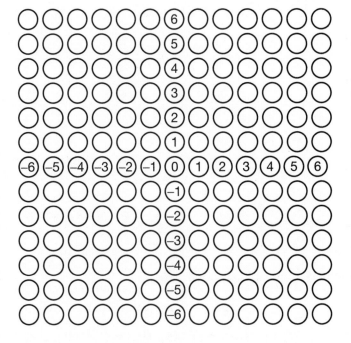

Set-Up Questions

These questions measure your ability to recognize the correct procedure for solving a problem. These questions ask you to choose an expression that represents how to "set up" the problem.

> Example: Samantha makes $24,000 per year at a new job. Which expression shows how much she earns per month?
> **a.** $24,000 + 12
> **b.** $24,000 − 12
> **c.** $24,000 × 12
> **d.** $24,000 ÷ 12
> **e.** 12 ÷ $24,000

The answer is choice **d.** You know there are 12 months in a year. To find Samantha's monthly income, you would divide the total ($24,000) by the number of months (12). Choice **e** is incorrect because it means 12 is divided by $24,000.

Graphics

At least 25 out of the 50 questions on the GED Mathematics Exam use diagrams, pie charts, graphs, tables, and other visual stimuli as references. Sometimes, more than one of these questions will be grouped under a single graphic. Do not let this confuse you. Learn to recognize question sets by reading both the questions and the directions carefully.

▶ What's Specific for the GED?

The structure of the GED Mathematics Exam, revised in 2002, ensures that no more than two questions should include "not enough information is given" as a correct answer choice. Given this fact, it is important for you to pay attention to how many times you select this answer choice. If you find yourself selecting the "not enough information is given" for the third time, be sure to check the other questions for which you have selected this choice because one of them must be incorrect.

Additionally, the current GED has an increased focus on "math in everyday life." This is emphasized by allowing the use of a calculator on Part I as well as by an increased emphasis on data analysis and statistics. As a result, gridded-response questions and item sets are more common. The number of item sets varies.

Formulas

Area of a:

square	$A = \text{side}^2$
rectangle	$A = \text{length} \times \text{width}$
parallelogram	$A = \text{base} \times \text{height}$
triangle	$A = \frac{1}{2} \times \text{base} \times \text{height}$
trapezoid	$A = \frac{1}{2}(\text{base}_1 + \text{base}_2) \times \text{height}$
circle	$A = \pi \times \text{radius}^2$; π is approximately equal to 3.14

Perimeter of a:

square	$P = 4 \times \text{side}$
rectangle	$P = 2 \times \text{length} + 2 \times \text{width}$
triangle	$P = \text{side}_1 + \text{side}_2 + \text{side}_3$

Circumference of a circle $= \pi \times \text{diameter}$; π is approximately equal to 3.14

Volume of a:

cube	$V = \text{edge}^3$
rectangular solid	$V = \text{length} \times \text{width} \times \text{height}$
square pyramid	$V = \frac{1}{3} \times (\text{base edge})^2 \times \text{height}$
cone	$V = \frac{1}{3} \times \pi \times \text{radius}^2 \times \text{height}$; π is approximately equal to 3.14

Coordinate Geometry

distance between points $= \sqrt{(x_2 - x_1)^2 + (y_2 - y_1)^2}$; (x_1, y_1) and (x_2, y_2) are two points on the line

slope of a line $= \frac{(y_2 - y_1)}{(x_2 - x_1)}$; (x_1, y_1) and (x_2, y_2) are two points on the line

Pythagorean relationship $a^2 + b^2 = c^2$; a and b are legs and c is the hypotenuse of a right triangle

Measures of Central Tendency

mean $= \frac{x_1 + x_2 + \ldots + x_n}{n}$, where the x's are the values for which a mean is desired, and n is the total number of values for x

median = the middle value of an odd number of ordered data, and halfway between the two middle values of an even number of ordered scores

Simple Interest   principal $\times$ rate $\times$ time

Distance   rate $\times$ time

Total Cost   (number of units) $\times$ (price per unit)

Adapted from official GED materials.

42 ▶ Measurement

The GED Mathematics Exam emphasizes real-life applications of math concepts, and this is especially true of questions about measurement. This chapter will review the basics of measurement systems used in the United States and other countries, performing mathematical operations with units of measurement, and the process of converting between different units.

THE USE OF measurement enables you to form a connection between mathematics and the real world. To measure any object, assign a number and a unit of measure. For instance, when a fish is caught, it is often weighed in ounces and its length measured in inches. The following lesson will familiarize you with the types, conversions, and units of measurement.

▶ Types of Measurements

Following are the types of measurements used most frequently in the United States.

Units of Length
12 inches (in.) = 1 foot (ft.)
3 feet = 36 inches = 1 yard (yd.)
5,280 feet = 1,760 yards = 1 mile (mi.)

Units of Volume
8 ounces* (oz.) = 1 cup (c.)
2 cups = 16 ounces = 1 pint (pt.)

2 pints = 4 cups = 32 ounces = 1 quart (qt.)
4 quarts = 8 pints = 16 cups = 128 ounces =
   1 gallon (gal.)

Units of Weight
16 ounces* (oz.) = 1 pound (lb.)
2,000 pounds = 1 ton (T)

Units of Time
60 seconds (sec.) = 1 minute (min.)
60 minutes = 1 hour (hr.)
24 hours = 1 day
7 days = 1 week
52 weeks = 1 year (yr.)
12 months = 1 year
365 days = 1 year

Notice that ounces are used to measure both the dimensions of volume and weight.

▶ Converting Units

When you perform mathematical operations, it is necessary to convert units of measure to simplify a problem. Units of measure are converted by using either multiplication or division:

- To change a larger unit to a smaller unit, simply multiply the specific number of larger units by the number of smaller units in only one of the larger units.

  For example, to find the number of inches in 5 feet, simply multiply 5, *the number of larger units*, by 12, *the number of inches in one foot*:

  5 feet = how many inches?
  5 feet × 12 inches (the number of inches in a single foot) = 60 inches

Therefore, there are 60 inches in 5 feet.

Try another:

  Change 3.5 tons to pounds.
  3.5 tons = how many pounds?
  3.5 tons × 2,000 pounds (*the number of pounds in a single ton*) = 6,500 pounds

Therefore, there are 6,500 pounds in 3.5 tons.

- To change a smaller unit to a larger unit, simply divide the specific number of smaller units by the number of smaller units in only one of the larger units.

  For example, to find the number of pints in 64 ounces, simply divide 64, *the smaller unit*, by 16, *the number of ounces in one pint*.

  $$\frac{64 \text{ ounces}}{16 \text{ ounces}} = 4 \text{ pints}$$

Therefore, 64 ounces are equal to 4 pints.

Here is one more:

  Change 32 ounces to pounds.

  $$\frac{32 \text{ ounces}}{16 \text{ ounces}} = 2 \text{ pounds}$$

Therefore, 32 ounces are equal to 2 pounds.

▶ Basic Operations with Measurement

It will be necessary for you to review how to add, subtract, multiply, and divide with measurement. The mathematical rules needed for each of these operations with measurement follow.

Addition with Measurements
To add measurements, follow these two steps:

1. Add like units.
2. Simplify the answer.

Example: Add 4 pounds 5 ounces to 20 ounces.
4 lbs. 5 oz. Be sure to add ounces to ounces.
+   20 oz.
4 lbs. 25 oz. Because 25 ounces is more than 16 ounces (1 pound), simplify by dividing by 16. Then, add the 1 pound to the 4 pounds.

↓

4 lbs. + 25 oz.

↓

$$4 \text{ lbs.} + 16\overline{)25} \quad \begin{array}{r} 1\text{lb.} \\ \hline \end{array}$$
$$\begin{array}{r} -16 \\ \hline 9 \text{ oz.} \end{array}$$

4 pounds 25 ounces =
4 pounds + 1 pound 9 ounces =
5 pounds 9 ounces

Subtraction with Measurements

To subtract measurements, follow these three steps:

1. Subtract like units.
2. Regroup units when necessary.
3. Write the answer in simplest form.

For example, 6 pounds 2 ounces subtracted from 9 pounds 10 ounces.

$$\begin{array}{r} 9 \text{ lbs. } 10 \text{ oz.} \\ -\ 6 \text{ lbs. } 2 \text{ oz.} \\ \hline 3 \text{ lbs. } 8 \text{ oz.} \end{array}$$ Subtract ounces from ounces. Then, subtract pounds from pounds.

Sometimes, it is necessary to regroup units when subtracting.

Example: Subtract 3 yards 2 feet from 5 yards 1 foot.

$$\begin{array}{r} \overset{4}{\cancel{5}} \text{ yds. } \overset{4}{\cancel{1}} \text{ ft.} \\ -3 \text{ yds. } 2 \text{ ft.} \\ \hline 1 \text{ yd. } 2 \text{ ft.} \end{array}$$

From 5 yards, regroup 1 yard to 3 feet. Add 3 feet to 1 foot. Then, subtract feet from feet and yards from yards.

Multiplication with Measurements

To multiply measurements, follow these two steps:

1. Multiply like units if units are involved.
2. Simplify the answer.

Example: Multiply 5 feet 7 inches by 3.

$$\begin{array}{r} 5 \text{ ft. } 7 \text{ in.} \\ \times\ 3 \\ \hline 15 \text{ ft. } 21 \text{ in.} \end{array}$$ Multiply 7 inches by 3, and then multiply 5 feet by 3. Keep the units separate. Because 12 inches = 1 foot, simplify 21 inches.

15 ft. 21 in. = 15 ft. + 1 ft. + 9 in. = 16 feet 9 inches

Example: Multiply 9 feet by 4 yards.

First, change yards to feet by multiplying the number of feet in a yard (3) by the number of yards in this problem (4).

3 feet in a yard × 4 yards = 12 feet

Then, multiply 9 feet by 12 feet = 108 square feet.

(**Note:** feet × feet = square feet)

Division with Measurements

For division with measurements, follow these steps:

1. Divide into the larger units first.
2. Convert the remainder to the smaller unit.
3. Add the converted remainder to the existing smaller unit if any.
4. Divide into smaller units.
5. Write the answer in simplest form.

Example

Divide 5 quarts 4 ounces by 4.

Step 1: $$\begin{array}{r} 1 \text{ qt. } \text{R1} \\ 4\overline{)5} \\ -4 \\ \hline 1 \end{array}$$

Step 2: R1 = 32 oz.

Step 3: 32 oz. + 4 oz. = 36 oz.

Step 4: $$\begin{array}{r} 9 \text{ oz.} \\ 4\overline{)36} \end{array}$$

Step 5: 1 qt. 9 oz.

▶ Metric Measurements

The metric system is an international system of measurement also called the **decimal system.** Converting units in the metric system is much easier than converting units in the English system of measurement. However, making conversions between the two systems is much more difficult. Luckily, the GED will provide you with the appropriate conversion factor when needed.

The basic units of the metric system are the meter, gram, and liter. Here is a general idea of how the two systems compare:

Metric System	English System
1 meter	A meter is a little more than a yard; it is equal to about 39 inches.
1 gram	A gram is a very small unit of weight; there are about 30 grams in 1 ounce.
1 liter	A liter is a little more than a quart.

Prefixes are attached to these basic metric units to indicate the amount of each unit.

For example, the prefix *deci-* means one-tenth ($\frac{1}{10}$); therefore, one decigram is one-tenth of a gram, and one decimeter is one-tenth of a meter. The following six prefixes can be used with every metric unit:

Kilo	Hecto	Deka	Deci	Centi	Milli
(k)	(h)	(dk)	(d)	(c)	(m)
1,000	100	10	$\frac{1}{10}$	$\frac{1}{100}$	$\frac{1}{1,000}$

Examples

- 1 hectometer = 1 hm = 100 meters
- 1 millimeter = 1 mm = $\frac{1}{1,000}$ meter = .001 meter
- 1 dekagram = 1 dkg = 10 grams
- 1 centiliter = 1 cL* = $\frac{1}{100}$ liter = .01 liter
- 1 kilogram = 1 kg = 1,000 grams
- 1 deciliter = 1 dL* = $\frac{1}{10}$ liter = .1 liter

Notice that liter is abbreviated with a capital letter—L.

The following chart illustrates some common relationships used in the metric system:

Length	Weight	Volume
1 km = 1,000 m	1 kg = 1,000 g	1 kL = 1,000 L
1 m = .001 km	1 g = .001 kg	1 L = .001 kL
1 m = 100 cm	1 g = 100 cg	1 L = 100 cL
1 cm = .01 m	1 cg = .01 g	1 cL = .01 L
1 m = 1,000 mm	1 g = 1,000 mg	1 L = 1,000 mL
1 mm = .001 m	1 mg = .001 g	1 mL = .001 L

Conversions within the Metric System

An easy way to do conversions with the metric system is to move the decimal point either to the right or left because the conversion factor is always ten or a power of ten. As you learned previously, when you change from a large unit to a smaller unit you multiply, and when you change from a small unit to a larger unit you divide.

Making Easy Conversions within the Metric System

When you multiply by a power of ten, you move the decimal point to the right. When you divide by a power of ten, you move the decimal point to the left.

To change from a large unit to a smaller unit, move the decimal point to the right.

kilo   hecto   deka   UNIT   deci   centi   milli

To change from a small unit to a larger unit, move the decimal point to the left.

Example

Change 520 grams to kilograms.

Step 1: Be aware that changing meters to kilometers is going from small units to larger units; therefore, you will move the decimal point three places to the left.

Step 2: Beginning at the UNIT (for grams), you need to move three prefixes to the left.

k   h   dk   unit   d   c   m

Step 3: Move the decimal point from the end of 520 to the left three places: 520.

Place the decimal point before the 5.   .520

Your answer is 520 grams = .520 kilograms.

Example

You are packing your bicycle for a trip from New York City to Detroit. The rack on the back of your bike can hold 20 kilograms. If you exceed that limit, you must buy stabilizers for the rack that cost $2.80 each. Each stabilizer can hold an additional kilogram. If you want to pack 23,000 grams of supplies, how much money will you have to spend on the stabilizers?

Step 1: First, change 23,000 grams to kilograms.

kg   hg   dkg   g   dg   cg   mg

Step 2: Move the decimal point three places to the left:

$$23,000 \text{ g} = 23.000 \text{ kg} = 23 \text{ kg}$$

Step 3: Subtract to find the amount over the limit:

$$23 \text{ kg} - 20 \text{ kg} = 3 \text{ kg}$$

Step 4: Because each stabilizer holds 1 kilogram and your supplies exceed the weight limit of the rack by 3 kilograms, you must purchase 3 stabilizers from the bike store.

Step 5: Each stabilizer costs $2.80, so multiply $2.80 by 3:

$$\$2.80 \times 3 = \$8.40$$

43 ▶ Number Relations

A good grasp of the building blocks of math will be essential for your success on the GED Mathematics Exam. This chapter covers the basics of mathematical operations and their sequence, variables, integers, fractions, decimals, and square and cube roots.

BASIC PROBLEM SOLVING in mathematics is rooted in whole number math facts—mainly addition facts and multiplication tables. If you are unsure of any of these facts, now is the time to review. Make sure to memorize any parts of this review that you find troublesome. Your ability to work with numbers depends on how quickly and accurately you can do simple mathematical computations.

▶ Addition and Subtraction

Addition is used to combine amounts. The answer in an addition problem is called the **sum**, or the **total**. It is helpful to stack the numbers in a column when adding. Be sure to line up the place-value columns and work from right to left, starting with the ones column.

Example
Add 40 + 129 + 24.

1. Align the numbers you want to add on the ones column. Because it is necessary to work from right to left, begin to add starting with the ones column. The ones column equals 13, so write the 3 in the ones column and regroup or "carry" the 1 to the tens column:

```
    1
   40
  129
+  24
    3
```

2. Add the tens column, including the regrouped 1.

```
    1
   40
  129
+  24
   93
```

3. Then add the hundreds column. Because there is only one value, write the 1 in the answer.

```
    1
   40
  129
+  24
  193
```

Subtraction is used to find the difference between amounts. Write the greater number on top, and align the amounts on the ones column. You may also need to regroup as you subtract.

Example

If Kasima is 45 and Deja is 36, how many years older is Kasima?

1. Find the difference in their ages by subtracting. Start with the ones column. Because 5 is less than the number being subtracted (6), regroup or "borrow" a ten from the tens column. Add the regrouped amount to the ones column. Now subtract 15 – 6 in the ones column.

```
   1
  4̸5
- 36
   9
```

2. Regrouping 1 ten from the tens column left 3 tens. Subtract 3 – 3, and write the result in the tens column of your answer. Kasima is 9 years older than Deja. Check: 9 + 36 = 45.

```
  3 1
  4̸5
- 36
  09
```

▶ Multiplication and Division

In multiplication, you combine the same amount multiple times. For example, instead of adding 30 three times, 30 + 30 + 30, you could simply multiply 30 by 3. If a problem asks you to find the product of two or more numbers, you should multiply.

Example

Find the product of 34 and 54.

1. Line up the place values as you write the problem in columns. Multiply the ones place of the top number by the ones place of the bottom number: $4 \times 4 = 16$. Write the 6 in the ones place in the first partial product. Regroup the 10.

```
    1
   34
×  54
    6
```

2. Multiply the tens place in the top number by 4: $4 \times 3 = 12$. Then, add the regrouped amount 12 + 1 = 13. Write the 3 in the tens column and the 1 in the hundreds column of the partial product.

```
    1
   34
×  54
  136
```

3. Now multiply by the tens place of 54. Write a placeholder 0 in the ones place in the second partial product, because you're really multiplying the top number by 50. Then multiply the top number by 5: $5 \times 4 = 20$. Write 0 in the partial product and regroup the 2. Multiply $5 \times 3 = 15$. Add the regrouped 2: 15 + 2 = 17.

```
    34
×   54
   136
  170̲0̲—placeholder
```

4. Add the partial products to find the total product: 136 + 1,700 = 1,836.

```
    34
×   54
   136
  1700
  1,836
```

In division, the answer is called the **quotient**. The number you are dividing by is called the **divisor** and the number being divided is the **dividend**. The operation of division is finding how many equal parts an amount can be divided into.

Example

At a bake sale, 3 children sold their baked goods for a total of $54. If they share the money equally, how much money should each child receive?

1. Divide the total amount ($54) by the number of ways the money is to be split (3). Work from left to right. How many times does 3 go into 5? Write the answer, 1, directly above the 5 in the dividend. Because $3 \times 1 = 3$, write 3 under the 5 and subtract $5 - 3 = 2$.

$$
\begin{array}{r}
18 \\
3\overline{)54} \\
-3 \\
\hline
24 \\
-24 \\
\hline
0
\end{array}
$$

2. Continue dividing. Bring down the 4 from the ones place in the dividend. How many times does 3 go into 24? Write the answer, 8, directly above the 4 in the dividend. Because $3 \times 8 = 24$, write 24 below the other 24 and subtract $24 - 24 = 0$.

3. If you get a number other than 0 after your last subtraction, this number is your remainder.

Example

9 divided by 4.

$$
\begin{array}{r}
2 \\
4\overline{)9} \\
-8 \\
\hline
1\text{—remainder}
\end{array}
$$

The answer is 2 R1.

► Sequence of Mathematical Operations

There is an order for doing a sequence of mathematical operations, which is illustrated by the acronym **PEMDAS**, which can be remembered by using the first letter of each of the words in the phrase: **P**lease **E**xcuse **M**y **D**ear **A**unt **S**ally. Here is what it means mathematically:

P: Parentheses. Perform all operations within parentheses first.

E: Exponents. Evaluate exponents.

M/D: Multiply/Divide. Work from left to right in your expression.

A/S: Add/Subtract. Work from left to right in your expression.

Example

$\frac{(5+3)^2}{4} + 27 =$

$\frac{(8)^2}{4} + 27 =$

$\frac{64}{4} + 27 =$

$16 + 27 = \mathbf{43}$

► Squares and Cube Roots

The square of a number is the product of a number and itself. For example, in the expression $3^2 = 3 \times 3 = 9$, the number 9 is the **square** of the number 3. If we reverse the process, we can say that the number 3 is the **square root** of the number 9. The symbol for square root is $\sqrt{}$ and it is called the **radical**. The number inside of the radical is called the **radicand**.

Example

$5^2 = 25$; therefore, $\sqrt{25} = 5$

Because 25 is the square of 5, it is also true that 5 is the square root of 25.

▶ Perfect Squares

The square root of a number might not be a whole number. For example, the square root of 7 is 2.645751311 . . . It is not possible to find a whole number that can be multiplied by itself to equal 7. A whole number is a **perfect square** if its square root is also a whole number.

Examples of perfect squares:
1, 4, 9, 16, 25, 36, 49, 64, 81, 100 . . .

▶ Odd and Even Numbers

An **even number** is a number that can be divided by the number 2: 2, 4, 6, 8, 10, 12, 14 . . . An **odd number** cannot be divided by the number 2: 1, 3, 5, 7, 9, 11, 13 . . . The even and odd numbers listed are also examples of **consecutive even numbers** and **consecutive odd numbers** because they differ by two.

Here are some helpful rules for how even and odd numbers behave when added or multiplied:

even + even = even	and	even × even = even
odd + odd = even	and	odd × odd = odd
odd + even = odd	and	even × odd = even

▶ Prime and Composite Numbers

A positive integer greater than the number 1 is either prime or composite, but not both. A **factor** is an integer that divides evenly into a number.

- A **prime number** has only itself and the number 1 as factors.
  Examples: 2, 3, 5, 7, 11, 13, 17, 19, 23 . . .

- A **composite number** is a number that has more than two factors.
  Examples: 4, 6, 8, 9, 10, 12, 14, 15, 16 . . .

- The number 1 is neither prime nor composite.

▶ Number Lines and Signed Numbers

You have probably dealt with number lines before. The concept of the number line is simple: Less than is to the left and greater than is to the right.

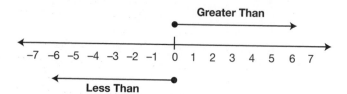

▶ Absolute Value

The absolute value of a number or expression is always positive because it is the distance of a number from zero on a number line.

Example
$|-1| = 1$
$|2 - 4| = |-2| = 2$

▶ Working with Integers

An **integer** is a positive or negative whole number. Here are some rules for working with integers:

Multiplying and Dividing
$(+) \times (+) = +$ $(+) \div (+) = +$
$(+) \times (-) = -$ $(+) \div (-) = -$
$(-) \times (-) = +$ $(-) \div (-) = +$

A simple way to remember these rules: If the signs are the same when multiplying or dividing, the answer will be positive, and if the signs are different, the answer will be negative.

Adding
Adding the same sign results in a sum of the same sign:

$(+) + (+) = +$
$(-) + (-) = -$

When adding numbers of different signs, follow this two-step process:

1. Subtract the absolute values of the numbers.
2. Keep the sign of the larger number.

Example

$-2 + 3 =$

1. Subtract the absolute values of the numbers:
$3 - 2 = 1$
2. The sign of the larger number (3) was originally positive, so the answer is positive 1.

Example

$8 + -11 =$

1. Subtract the absolute values of the numbers:
$11 - 8 = 3$
2. The sign of the larger number (11) was originally negative, so the answer is -3.

Subtracting

When subtracting integers, change all subtraction to addition and change the sign of the number being subtracted to its opposite. Then, follow the rules for addition.

Examples

$(+10) - (+12) = (+10) + (-12) = -2$
$(-5) - (-7) = (-5) + (+7) = +2$

▶ Decimals

The most important thing to remember about decimals is that the first place value to the right begins with tenths. The place values are as follows:

1	2	6	8	•	3	4	5	7
THOUSANDS	HUNDREDS	TENS	ONES	DECIMAL POINT	TENTHS	HUNDREDTHS	THOUSANDTHS	TEN THOUSANDTHS

In expanded form, this number can also be expressed as:

$1,268.3457 = (1 \times 1,000) + (2 \times 100) + (6 \times 10)$
$+ (8 \times 1) + (3 \times .1) + (4 \times .01) + (5 \times .001)$
$+ (7 \times .0001)$

Comparing Decimals

Comparing decimals is actually quite simple. Just line up the decimal points and fill in any zeros needed to have an equal number of digits.

Example

Compare .5 and .005

Line up decimal points	.500
and add zeros	.005

Then, ignore the decimal point and ask, which is bigger: 500 or 5? 500 is definitely bigger than 5, so .5 is larger than .005.

▶ Variables

In a mathematical sentence, a **variable** is a letter that represents a number. Consider this sentence: $x + 4 = 10$. It's easy to figure out that x represents 6. However, problems with variables on the GED will become much more complex than that, so you must learn the rules and procedures. Before you learn to solve equations with variables, you need to learn how they operate in formulas. The next section on fractions will give you some examples.

▶ Fractions

To do well when working with fractions, it is necessary to understand some basic concepts. Here are some math rules for fractions using variables:

$$\frac{a}{b} \times \frac{c}{d} = \frac{(a \times c)}{(b \times d)}$$
$$\frac{a}{b} \div \frac{c}{d} = \frac{a}{b} \times \frac{d}{c} = \frac{(a \times d)}{(b \times c)}$$
$$\frac{a}{b} + \frac{c}{d} = \frac{(ad + bc)}{bd}$$

Multiplying Fractions

Multiplying fractions is one of the easiest operations to perform. To multiply fractions, simply multiply the numerators and the denominators, writing each product in the respective place over or under the fraction bar.

Example
$$\frac{4}{5} \times \frac{6}{7} = \frac{24}{35}$$

Dividing Fractions

Dividing fractions is the same thing as multiplying fractions by their reciprocals. To find the reciprocal of any number, switch its numerator and denominator.

For example, the reciprocals of the following numbers are:

$$\frac{1}{3} = \frac{3}{1} = 3$$
$$x = \frac{1}{x}$$
$$\frac{4}{5} = \frac{5}{4}$$
$$5 = \frac{1}{5}$$

When dividing fractions, simply multiply the dividend by the divisor's reciprocal to get the answer.

Example
$$\frac{12}{21} \div \frac{3}{4} = \frac{12}{21} \times \frac{4}{3} = \frac{48}{63} = \frac{16}{21}$$

Adding and Subtracting Fractions

To add or subtract fractions with like denominators, just add or subtract the numerators and leave the denominator as it is.

Example
$$\frac{1}{7} + \frac{5}{7} = \frac{6}{7}$$
$$\frac{5}{8} - \frac{2}{8} = \frac{3}{8}$$

To add or subtract fractions with unlike denominators, you must find the **least common denominator**, or **LCD**.

For example, for the denominators 8 and 12, the LCD is 24 because $8 \times 3 = 24$, and $12 \times 2 = 24$. In other words, the LCD is the smallest number divisible by each of the denominators.

Once you know the LCD, convert each fraction to its new form by multiplying both the numerator and denominator by the necessary number to get the LCD, and then add or subtract the new numerators.

Example
$$\frac{1}{3} + \frac{2}{5} = \frac{5(1)}{5(3)} + \frac{3(2)}{3(5)} = \frac{5}{15} + \frac{6}{15} = \frac{11}{15}$$

43 ▶ Algebra

When you take the GED Mathematics Exam, you will be asked to solve problems using basic algebra. This chapter will help you master algebraic equations by familiarizing you with polynomials, the FOIL method, factoring, quadratic equations, inequalities, and exponents.

▶ What Is Algebra?

Algebra is an organized system of rules that help solve problems for "unknowns." This organized system of rules is similar to rules for a board game. Like any game, to be successful at algebra, you must learn the appropriate terms of play. As you work through the following section, be sure to pay special attention to any new words you may encounter. Once you understand what is being asked of you, it will be much easier to grasp algebraic concepts.

Equations
An equation is solved by finding a number that is equal to an unknown variable.

Simple Rules for Working with Equations
1. The equal sign separates an equation into two sides.
2. Whenever an operation is performed on one side, the same operation must be performed on the other side.
3. Your first goal is to get all of the variables on one side and all of the numbers on the other side.
4. The final step often will be to divide each side by the coefficient, the number in front of the variable, leaving the variable alone and equal to a number.

Example

$$5m + 8 = 48$$
$$-8 = -8$$
$$\frac{5m}{5} = \frac{40}{5}$$
$$m = 8$$

Checking Equations

To check an equation, substitute the number equal to the variable in the original equation.

Example

To check the equation you just solved, substitute the number 8 for the variable m.

$$5m + 8 = 48$$
$$5(8) + 8 = 48$$
$$40 + 8 = 48$$
$$48 = 48$$

Because this statement is true, you know the answer $m = 8$ must be correct.

Special Tips for Checking Equations

1. If time permits, be sure to check all equations.
2. If you get stuck on a problem with an equation, check each answer, beginning with choice **c**. If choice **c** is not correct, pick an answer choice that is either larger or smaller, whichever would be more reasonable.
3. Be careful to answer the question that is being asked. Sometimes, this involves solving for a variable and then performing an additional operation. Example: If the question asks the value of $x - 2$, and you find $x = 2$, the answer is not 2, but $2 - 2$. Thus, the answer is 0.

Cross Multiplying

To learn how to work with percentages or proportions, it is first necessary for you to learn how to cross multiply. You can solve an equation that sets one fraction equal to another by cross multiplication. Cross multiplication involves setting the products of opposite pairs of terms equal.

Example

$$\frac{x}{10} = \frac{70}{100}$$
$$100x = 700$$
$$\frac{100x}{100} = \frac{700}{100}$$
$$x = 7$$

Percent

There is one formula that is useful for solving the three types of percentage problems:

$$\frac{x}{\#} = \frac{\%}{100}$$

When reading a percentage problem, substitute the necessary information into the previous formula based on the following:

- Always write 100 in the denominator of the percentage sign column.
- If given a percentage, write it in the numerator position of the percentage sign column. If you are not given a percentage, the variable should be placed there.
- The denominator of the number column represents the number that is equal to the whole, or 100%. This number always follows the word *of* in a word problem.
- The numerator of the number column represents the number that is the percent, or the part.
- In the formula, the equal sign can be interchanged with the word *is*.

Examples

Finding a percentage of a given number:
What number is equal to 40% of 50?

$$\frac{x}{50} = \frac{40}{100}$$

Solve by cross multiplying.
$$100(x) = (40)(50)$$
$$100x = 2{,}000$$
$$\frac{100x}{100} = \frac{2{,}000}{100}$$
$$x = 20$$

Therefore, 20 is 40% of 50.

Finding a number when a percentage is given:
40% of what number is 24?

$$\frac{24}{x} = \frac{40}{100}$$

Cross multiply.
$$(24)(100) = (40)(x)$$
$$2{,}400 = 40x$$
$$\frac{2{,}400}{40} = \frac{40x}{40}$$
$$60 = x$$

Therefore, 40% of 60 is 24.

Finding what percentage one number is of another:
What percentage of 75 is 15?

$\frac{15}{75} = \frac{x}{100}$

Cross multiply.

$15(100) = (75)(x)$

$1,500 = 75x$

$\frac{1,500}{75} = \frac{75x}{75}$

$20 = x$

Therefore, 20% of 75 is 15.

Like Terms

A **variable** is a letter that represents an unknown number. Variables are frequently used in equations, formulas, and in mathematical rules to help you understand how numbers behave.

When a number is placed next to a variable, indicating multiplication, the number is said to be the coefficient of the variable.

Example

$8c$ 8 is the coefficient to the variable c.

$6ab$ 6 is the coefficient to both variables a and b.

If two or more terms have exactly the same variable(s), they are said to be like terms.

Example

$7x + 3x = 10x$

The process of grouping like terms together performing mathematical operations is called **combining like terms**.

It is important to combine like terms carefully, making sure that the variables are exactly the same. This is especially important when working with exponents.

Example

$7x^3y + 8xy^3$

These are not like terms because x^3y is not the same as xy^3. In the first term, the x is cubed, and in the second term, the y is cubed. Because the two terms differ in more than just their coefficients, they cannot be combined as like terms. This expression remains in its simplest form as it was originally written.

Polynomials

A **polynomial** is the sum or difference of two or more unlike terms.

Example

$2x + 3y - z$

This expression represents the sum of three unlike terms $2x$, $3y$, and $-z$.

Three Kinds of Polynominals

- A **monomial** is a polynomial with one term, as in $2b^3$.
- A **binomial** is a polynomial with two unlike terms, as in $5x + 3y$.
- A **trinomial** is a polynomial with three unlike terms, as in $y^2 + 2z - 6$.

Operations with Polynominals

- To add polynomials, be sure to change all subtraction to addition and the sign of the number that was being subtracted to its opposite. Then, simply combine like terms.

Example

$(3y^3 - 5y + 10) + (y^3 + 10y - 9)$

Change all subtraction to addition and the sign of the number being subtracted:

$3y^3 + -5y + 10 + y^3 + 10y + -9$

Combine like terms:

$3y^3 + y^3 + -5y + 10y + 10 + -9 = 4y^3 + 5y + 1$

If an entire polynomial is being subtracted, change all of the subtraction to addition within the parentheses and then add the opposite of each term in the polynomial.

Example

$(8x - 7y + 9z) - (15x + 10y - 8z)$

Change all subtraction within the parentheses first:

$(8x + -7y + 9z) - (15x + 10y + -8z)$

Then, change the subtraction sign outside of the parentheses to addition and the sign of each term in the polynomial being subtracted:

$(8x + -7y + 9z) + (-15x + -10y + 8z)$

Note that the sign of the term $8z$ changes twice because it is being subtracted twice. All that is left to do is combine like terms:

$8x + -15x + -7y + -10y + 9z + 8z = -7x + -17y + 17z$

is your answer.

To multiply monomials, multiply their coefficients and multiply like variables by adding their exponents.

Example

$(-5x^3y)(2x^2y^3) = (-5)(2)(x^3)(x^2)(y)(y^3) = -10x^5y^4$

To multiply a polynomial by a monomial, multiply each term of the polynomial by the monomial and add the products.

Example

$6x(10x - 5y + 7)$
Change subtraction to addition:
$6x(10x + -5y + 7)$
Multiply:
$(6x)(10x) + (6x)(-5y) + (6x)(7)$
$60x^2 + -30xy + 42x$

FOIL

The FOIL method can be used when multiplying binomials. FOIL stands for the order used to multiply the terms: First, Outer, Inner, and Last. To multiply binomials, you multiply according to the FOIL order and then add the like terms of the products.

Example

$(3x + 1)(7x + 10)$
$3x$ and $7x$ are the first pair of terms.
$3x$ and 10 are the outermost pair of terms.
1 and $7x$ are the innermost pair of terms.
1 and 10 are the last pair of terms.
Therefore, $(3x)(7x) + (3x)(10) + (1)(7x) + (1)(10)$
$= 21x^2 + 30x + 7x + 10$.
After we combine like terms, we are left with the answer: $21x^2 + 37x + 10$.

Factoring

Factoring is the reverse of multiplication:

Multiplication: $2(x + y) = 2x + 2y$
Factoring: $2x + 2y = 2(x + y)$

Three Basic Types of Factoring

- Factoring out a common monomial.
  $10x^2 - 5x = 5x(2x - 1)$ and $xy - zy = y(x - z)$
- Factoring a quadratic trinomial using the reverse of FOIL:
  $y^2 - y - 12 = (y - 4)(y + 3)$ and
  $z^2 - 2z + 1 = (z - 1)(z - 1) = (z - 1)^2$

- Factoring the difference between two perfect squares using the rule:
  $a^2 - b^2 = (a + b)(a - b)$ and $x^2 - 25 = (x + 5)(x - 5)$

Removing a Common Factor

If a polynomial contains terms that have common factors, the polynomial can be factored by using the reverse of the distributive law.

Example

In the binomial $49x^3 + 21x$, $7x$ is the greatest common factor of both terms.
Therefore, you can divide $49x^3 + 21x$ by $7x$ to get the other factor.
$\frac{49x^3 + 21x}{7x} = \frac{49x^3}{7x} + \frac{21x}{7x} = 7x^2 + 3$

Thus, factoring $49x^3 + 21x$ results in $7x(7x^2 + 3)$.

Quadratic Equations

A quadratic equation is an equation in which the greatest exponent of the variable is 2, as in $x^2 + 2x - 15 = 0$. A quadratic equation has two roots, which can be found by breaking down the quadratic equation into two simple equations.

Example

Solve $x^2 + 5x + 2x + 10 = 0$.
Combine like terms: $x^2 + 7x + 10 = 0$
Factor: $(x + 5)(x + 2) = 0$
$x + 5 = 0$ or $x + 2 = 0$
$\frac{-5 -5}{x = -5}$ $\qquad$ $\frac{-2 -2}{x = -2}$
Now check the answers.
$-5 + 5 = 0$ and $-2 + 2 = 0$
Therefore, x is equal to both -5 and -2.

Inequalities

Linear inequalities are solved in much the same way as simple equations. The most important difference is that when an inequality is multiplied or divided by a negative number, the inequality symbol changes direction.

Example

$10 > 5$, but if you multiply by -3, $(10)(-3) < (5)(-3)$
$-30 < -15$

Solving Linear Inequalities

To solve a linear inequality, isolate the letter and solve the same as you would in an equation. Remember to reverse the direction of the inequality sign if you divide or multiply both sides of the equation by a negative number.

Example

If $7 - 2x > 21$, find x.

Isolate the variable.

$7 - 2x > 21$

$7 - 2x - 7 > 21 - 7$

$-2x > 14$

Because you are dividing by a negative number, the direction of the inequality symbol changes direction.

$\frac{-2x}{-2} > \frac{14}{-2}$

$x < -7$

The answer consists of all real numbers less than -7.

Exponents

An **exponent** tells you how many times the number, called the **base**, is a factor in the product.

Example

$2^5 \leftarrow$ exponent $= 2 \times 2 \times 2 \times 2 \times 2 = 32$

 base

Sometimes you will see an exponent with a variable:

b^n

The b represents a number that will be a factor to itself n times.

Example

b^n where $b = 5$ and $n = 3$

Don't let the variables fool you. Most expressions are very easy once you substitute in numbers.

$b^n = 5^3 = 5 \times 5 \times 5 = 125$

Laws of Exponents

- Any base to the zero power is always 1.
  $5^0 = 1 \quad 70^0 = 1 \quad 29{,}874^0 = 1$
- When you multiply identical bases, add the exponents.
  $2^2 \times 2^4 \times 2^6 = 2^{12} \quad a^2 \times a^3 \times a^5 = a^{10}$
- When you divide identical bases, subtract the exponents.

  $\frac{2^5}{2^3} = 2^2$

  $\frac{a^7}{a^4} = a^3$

- Here is another method of illustrating multiplication and division of exponents:
  $b^m \times b^n = b^{m+n}$
  $b^m b^n = b^{m-n}$
- If an exponent appears outside of parentheses, you multiply the exponents together.
  $(3^3)^7 = 3^{21}$
  $(g^4)^3 = g^{12}$

45 ▶ Geometry

Chapter 45 reviews the geometry concepts you will need to know for the GED Mathematics Exam. You should become familiar with the properties of angles, lines, polygons, triangles, and circles, as well as the formulas for area, volume, and perimeter. A grasp of coordinate geometry will also be important when you take the GED.

GEOMETRY IS THE study of shapes and the relationships among them. The geometry you are required to know for the GED Mathematics Exam is fundamental and practical. Basic concepts in geometry will be detailed and applied in this section. The study of geometry always begins with a look at basic vocabulary and concepts. Therefore, here is a list of definitions of important terms.

area—the space inside a two-dimensional figure

bisect—cut in two equal parts

circumference—the distance around a circle

diameter—a line segment that goes directly through the center of a circle (the longest line you can draw in a circle)

equidistant—exactly in the middle of

hypotenuse—the longest leg of a right triangle, always opposite the right angle

line—an infinite collection of points in a straight path

point—a location in space

parallel—lines in the same plane that will never intersect

perimeter—the distance around a figure

perpendicular—two lines that intersect to form 90-degree angles

quadrilateral—any four-sided closed figure

radius—a line from the center of a circle to a point on the circle (half of the diameter)

volume—the space inside a three-dimensional figure

▶ Angles

An **angle** is formed by an endpoint, or vertex, and two rays.

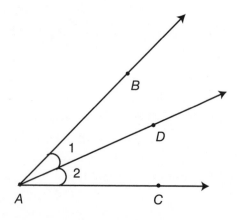

Naming Angles

There are three ways to name an angle.

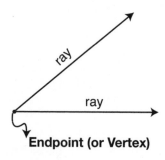

1. An angle can be named by the vertex when no other angles share the same vertex: ∠A.
2. An angle can be represented by a number written across from the vertex: ∠1.
3. When more than one angle has the same vertex, three letters are used, with the vertex always being the middle letter: ∠1 can be written as ∠*BAD* or as ∠*DAB*; ∠2 can be written as ∠*DAC* or as ∠*CAD*.

Classifying Angles

Angles can be classified into the following categories: acute, right, obtuse, and straight.

- An **acute** angle is an angle that measures less than 90 degrees.

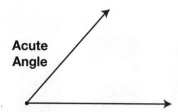

Acute Angle

- A **right** angle is an angle that measures exactly 90 degrees. A right angle is represented by a square at the vertex.

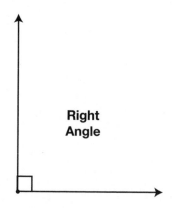

Right Angle

- An **obtuse** angle is an angle that measures more than 90 degrees, but less than 180 degrees.

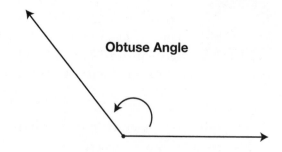

Obtuse Angle

- A **straight** angle is an angle that measures 180 degrees. Thus, both of its sides form a line.

Straight Angle

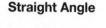

180°

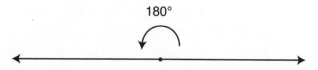

Complementary Angles

Two angles are **complementary** if the sum of their measures is equal to 90 degrees.

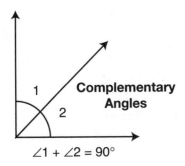

Complementary Angles

∠1 + ∠2 = 90°

Supplementary Angles

Two angles are **supplementary** if the sum of their measures is equal to 180 degrees.

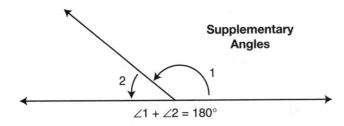

Supplementary Angles

∠1 + ∠2 = 180°

Adjacent Angles

Adjacent angles have the same vertex, share a side, and do not overlap.

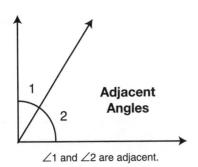

Adjacent Angles

∠1 and ∠2 are adjacent.

The sum of all of the measures of adjacent angles around the same vertex is equal to 360 degrees.

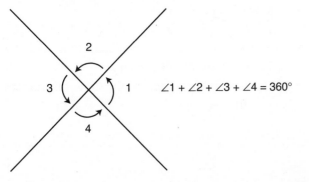

∠1 + ∠2 + ∠3 + ∠4 = 360°

Angles of Intersecting Lines

When two lines intersect, two sets of nonadjacent angles called **vertical** angles are formed. Vertical angles have equal measures and are supplementary to adjacent angles.

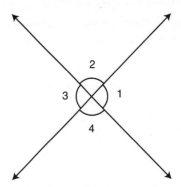

- m∠1 = m∠3 and m∠2 = m∠4
- m∠1 = m∠4 and m∠3 = m∠2
- m∠1 + m∠2 = 180 and m∠2 + m∠3 = 180
- m∠3 + m∠4 = 180 and m∠1 + m∠4 = 180

Bisecting Angles and Line Segments

Both angles and lines are said to be bisected when divided into two parts with equal measures.

Example

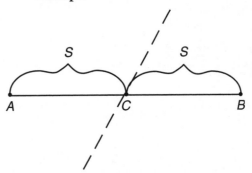

Line segment *AB* is bisected at point *C*.

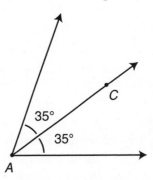

According to the figure, ∠A is bisected by ray *AC*.

Angles Formed by Parallel Lines

When two parallel lines are intersected by a third line, vertical angles are formed.

- Of these vertical angles, four will be equal and acute, and four will be equal and obtuse.
- Any combination of an acute and an obtuse angle will be supplementary.

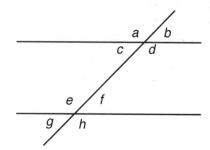

In the previous figure:

- $\angle b$, $\angle c$, $\angle f$, and $\angle g$ are all acute and equal.
- $\angle a$, $\angle d$, $\angle e$, and $\angle h$ are all obtuse and equal.
- Also, any acute angle added to any obtuse angle will be supplementary.

Examples

$m\angle b + m\angle d = 180°$
$m\angle c + m\angle e = 180°$
$m\angle f + m\angle h = 180°$
$m\angle g + m\angle a = 180°$

Example

In the following figure, if $m \parallel n$ and $a \parallel b$, what is the value of x?

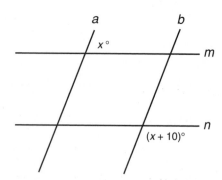

Solution

Because both sets of lines are parallel, you know that $x°$ can be added to $x + 10$ to equal 180. The equation is thus $x + x + 10 = 180$.

Example

Solve for x:

$$2x + 10 = 180$$
$$\underline{-10 \quad -10}$$
$$\frac{2x}{2} = \frac{170}{2}$$
$$x = 85$$

Therefore, $m\angle x = 85$ and the obtuse angle is equal to $180 - 85 = 95$.

Angles of a Triangle

The measures of the three angles in a triangle always equal 180 degrees.

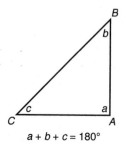

$$a + b + c = 180°$$

Exterior Angles

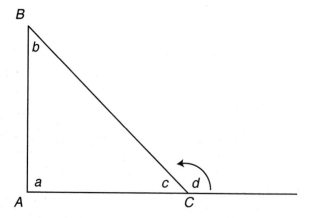

$$d + c = 180° \text{ and } d = b + a$$

An **exterior** angle can be formed by extending a side from any of the three vertices of a triangle. Here are some rules for working with exterior angles:

- An exterior angle and interior angle that share the same vertex are supplementary.
- An exterior angle is equal to the sum of the nonadjacent interior angles.

Example

$m\angle 1 = m\angle 3 + m\angle 5$

$m\angle 4 = m\angle 2 + m\angle 5$

$m\angle 6 = m\angle 3 + m\angle 2$

The sum of the exterior angles of a triangle equal 360 degrees.

▶ Triangles

It is possible to classify triangles into three categories based on the number of equal sides:

Scalene	Isosceles	Equilateral
(no equal sides)	(two equal sides)	(all sides equal)

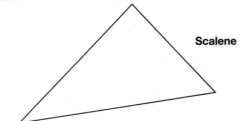

Scalene

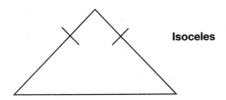

Isoceles

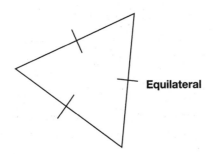

Equilateral

It is also possible to classify triangles into three categories based on the measure of the greatest angle:

Acute	Right	Obtuse
greatest angle is acute	greatest angle is 90°	greatest angle is obtuse

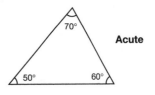

Acute

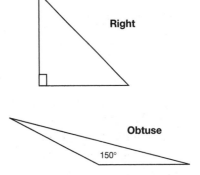

Right

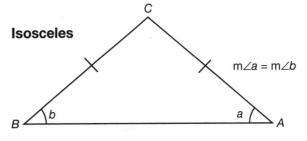

Obtuse

Angle-Side Relationships

Knowing the angle-side relationships in isosceles, equilateral, and right triangles will be useful in taking the GED Exam.

- In isosceles triangles, equal angles are opposite equal sides.

Isosceles

$m\angle a = m\angle b$

- In equilateral triangles, all sides are equal and all angles are equal.

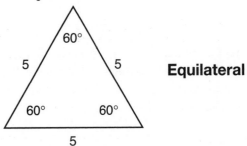

Equilateral

- In a right triangle, the side opposite the right angle is called the **hypotenuse**. This will be the largest side of the right triangle.

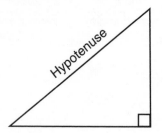

Right

Pythagorean Theorem

The **Pythagorean theorem** is an important tool for working with right triangles. It states $a^2 + b^2 = c^2$, where a and b represent the legs and c represents the hypotenuse.

This theorem allows you to find the length of any side as long as you know the measure of the other two.

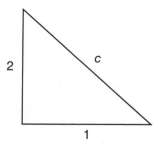

$$a^2 + b^2 = c^2$$
$$1^2 + 2^2 = c^2$$
$$1 + 4 = c^2$$
$$5 = c^2$$
$$\sqrt{5} = c$$

45-45-90 Right Triangles

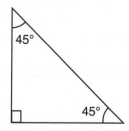

A right triangle with two angles each measuring 45 degrees is called an **isosceles** right triangle. In an isosceles right triangle:

- The length of the hypotenuse is $\sqrt{2}$ multiplied by the length of one of the legs of the triangle.

- The length of each leg is $\frac{(\sqrt{2})}{2}$ multiplied by the length of the hypotenuse.

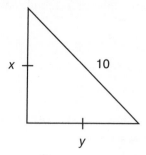

$$x = y = \frac{(\sqrt{2})}{2} \times \frac{10}{1} = 10\,\frac{(\sqrt{2})}{2} = 5\sqrt{2}$$

30-60-90 Triangles

In a right triangle with the other angles measuring 30 and 60 degrees:

- The leg opposite the 30-degree angle is half of the length of the hypotenuse. (And, therefore, the hypotenuse is two times the length of the leg opposite the 30-degree angle.)
- The leg opposite the 60-degree angle is $\sqrt{3}$ times the length of the other leg.

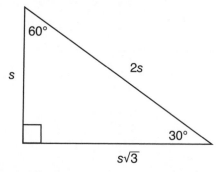

Example

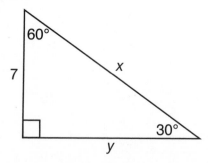

$$x = 2 \times 7 = 14 \text{ and } y = 7\sqrt{3}$$

Comparing Triangles

Triangles are said to be **congruent** (indicated by the symbol ≅) when they have exactly the same size and shape. Two triangles are congruent if their corresponding parts (their angles and sides) are congruent. Sometimes, it is easy to tell if two triangles are congruent by looking. However, in geometry, you must be able to prove that the triangles are congruent.

If two triangles are congruent, one of the following three criteria must be satisfied.

Side-Side-Side (SSS)—The side measures for both triangles are the same.

Side-Angle-Side (SAS)—The sides and the angle between them are the same.

Angle-Side-Angle (ASA)—Two angles and the side between them are the same.

Example: Are △*ABC* and △*BCD* congruent? Given: ∠*ABD* is congruent to ∠*CBD* and ∠*ADB* is congruent to ∠*CDB*. Both triangles share side *BD*.

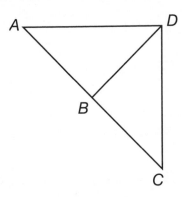

Step 1: Mark the given congruencies on the drawing.

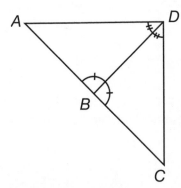

Step 2: Determine whether this is enough information to prove the triangles are congruent.

Yes, two angles and the side between them are equal. Using the ASA rule, you can determine that triangle *ABD* is congruent to triangle *CBD*.

▶ Polygons and Parallelograms

A **polygon** is a closed figure with three or more sides.

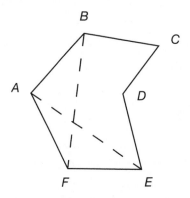

Terms Related to Polygons

- Vertices are corner points, also called **endpoints**, of a polygon. The vertices in this polygon are *A*, *B*, *C*, *D*, *E*, and *F*.
- A **diagonal** of a polygon is a line segment between two nonadjacent vertices. The two diagonals in this polygon are line segments *BF* and *AE*.
- A **regular** polygon has sides and angles that are all equal.
- An **equiangular** polygon has angles that are all equal.

Angles of a Quadrilateral

A **quadrilateral** is a four-sided polygon. Because a quadrilateral can be divided by a diagonal into two triangles, the sum of its interior angles will equal 180 + 180 = 360 degrees.

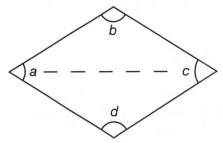

m∠*a* + m∠*b* + m∠*c* + m∠*d* = 360°

Interior Angles

To find the sum of the interior angles of any polygon, use this formula:

$S = 180(x - 2)°$, with x being the number of polygon sides

Example

Find the sum of the angles in the following polygon:

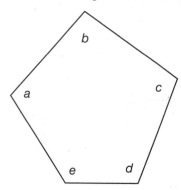

$S = (5 - 2) \times 180°$
$S = 3 \times 180°$
$S = 540°$

Exterior Angles

Similar to the exterior angles of a triangle, the sum of the exterior angles of any polygon equals 360 degrees.

Similar Polygons

If two polygons are similar, their corresponding angles are equal and the ratios of the corresponding sides are in proportion.

Example

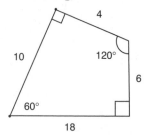 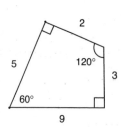

These two polygons are similar because their angles are equal and the ratios of the corresponding sides are in proportion.

Parallelograms

A **parallelogram** is a quadrilateral with two pairs of parallel sides.

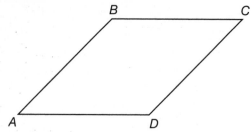

In this figure, line $AB \parallel CD$ and $BC \parallel AD$.
A parallelogram has:

- opposite sides that are equal ($AB = CD$ and $BC = AD$)
- opposite angles that are equal (m$\angle a$ = m$\angle c$ and m$\angle b$ = m$\angle d$)
- and consecutive angles that are supplementary (m$\angle a$ + m$\angle b$ = 180°, m$\angle b$ + m$\angle c$ = 180°, m$\angle c$ + m$\angle d$ = 180°, m$\angle d$ + m$\angle a$ = 180°)

Special Types of Parallelograms

- A **rectangle** is a parallelogram that has four right angles.

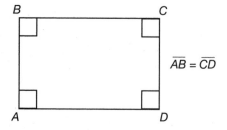

$\overline{AB} = \overline{CD}$

- A **rhombus** is a parallelogram that has four equal sides.

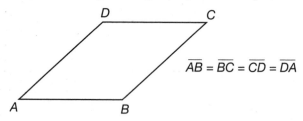

$\overline{AB} = \overline{BC} = \overline{CD} = \overline{DA}$

- A **square** is a parallelogram in which all angles are equal to 90 degrees and all sides are equal to each other.

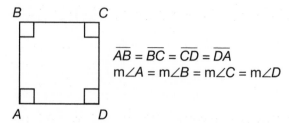

$\overline{AB} = \overline{BC} = \overline{CD} = \overline{DA}$
m$\angle A$ = m$\angle B$ = m$\angle C$ = m$\angle D$

Diagonals

In all parallelograms, **diagonals** cut each other into two equal halves.

- In a rectangle, diagonals are the same length.

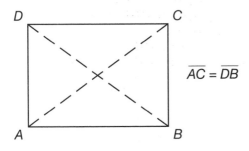

$$\overline{AC} = \overline{DB}$$

- In a rhombus, diagonals intersect to form 90-degree angles.

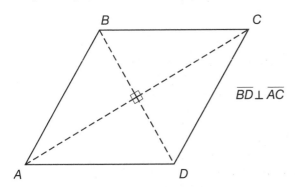

$$\overline{BD} \perp \overline{AC}$$

- In a square, diagonals have both the same length and intersect at 90-degree angles.

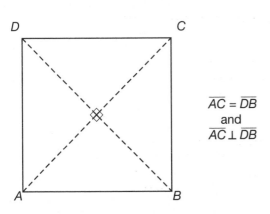

$$\overline{AC} = \overline{DB}$$
and
$$\overline{AC} \perp \overline{DB}$$

▶ Solid Figures, Perimeter, and Area

The GED provides you with several geometrical formulas. These formulas will be listed and explained in this section. It is important that you be able to recognize the figures by their names and to understand when to use which formulas. Don't worry. You do not have to memorize these formulas. They will be provided for you on the exam.

To begin, it is necessary to explain five kinds of measurement:

1. **Perimeter**
   The perimeter of an object is simply the sum of all of its sides.

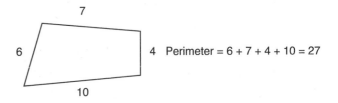

Perimeter = 6 + 7 + 4 + 10 = 27

2. **Area**
   Area is the space inside of the lines defining the shape.

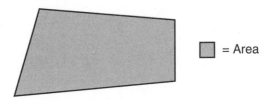

= Area

3. **Volume**
   Volume is a measurement of a three-dimensional object such as a cube or a rectangular solid. An easy way to envision volume is to think about filling an object with water. The volume measures how much water can fit inside.

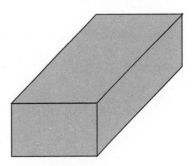

4. Surface Area

The surface area of an object measures the area of each of its faces. The total surface area of a rectangular solid is double the sum of the areas of the three faces. For a cube, simply multiply the surface area of one of its sides by six.

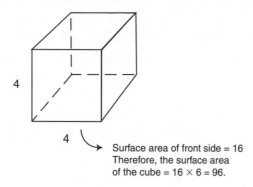

Surface area of front side = 16
Therefore, the surface area
of the cube = 16 × 6 = 96.

5. Circumference

Circumference is the measure of the distance around the outside of a circle.

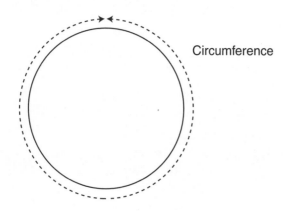

Circumference

▶ Coordinate Geometry

Coordinate geometry is a form of geometrical operations in relation to a coordinate plane. A **coordinate plane** is a grid of square boxes divided into four **quadrants** by both a **horizontal** (x) axis and a **vertical** (y) axis. These two axes intersect at one coordinate point, (0,0), the **origin**. A **coordinate point**, also called an **ordered pair**, is a specific point on the coordinate plane with the first number, or coordinate, representing the horizontal placement and the second number, or coordinate, representing the vertical. Coordinate points are given in the form of (x,y).

Graphing Ordered Pairs

The x-coordinate:

- The x-coordinate is listed first in the ordered pair and tells you how many units to move to either the left or to the right. If the x-coordinate is positive, move to the right. If the x-coordinate is negative, move to the left.

The y-coordinate:

- The y-coordinate is listed second and tells you how many units to move up or down. If the y-coordinate is positive, move up. If the y-coordinate is negative, move down.

Example

Graph the following points: (2,3), (3,–2), (–2,3), and (–3,–2).

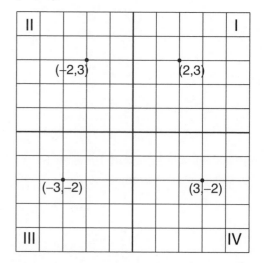

Notice that the graph is broken up into four quadrants with one point plotted in each one.

Here is a chart to indicate which quadrants contain which ordered pairs based on their signs:

POINTS	SIGN OF COORDINATES	QUADRANTS
(2,3)	(+,+)	I
(–2,3)	(–,+)	II
(–3,–2)	(–,–)	III
(3,–2)	(+,–)	IV

Lengths of Horizontal and Vertical Segments

Two points with the same y-coordinate lie on the same horizontal line and two points with the same x-coordinate lie on the same vertical line. The length of a horizontal or vertical segment can be found by taking the absolute value of the difference of the two points, or by counting the spaces on the graph between them.

Example

Find the length of line AB and line BC.

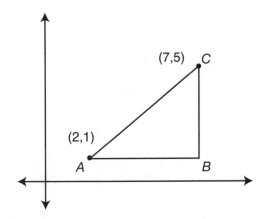

Solution

$| 2 - 7 | = 5 = \overline{AB}$
$| 1 - 5 | = 4 = \overline{BC}$

Midpoint

To find the midpoint of a segment, use the following formula:

$$\text{Midpoint } x = \frac{(x_1 + x_2)}{2}$$

$$\text{Midpoint } y = \frac{(y_1 + y_2)}{2}$$

Example

Find the midpoint of line segment AB.

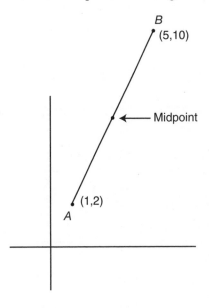

Solution

$$\text{Midpoint } x = \frac{(1 + 5)}{2} = \frac{6}{2} = 3$$

$$\text{Midpoint } y = 2 + \frac{(10)}{2} = \frac{12}{2} = 6$$

Therefore, the midpoint of $\overline{AB}$ is (3,6).

Slope

The slope of a line measures its steepness. It is found by writing the change in the *y*-coordinates of any two points on the line, over the change of the corresponding *x*-coordinates. (This is also known as the rise over the run.) The last step is to simplify the fraction that results.

Example

Find the slope of a line containing the points (3,2) and (8,9).

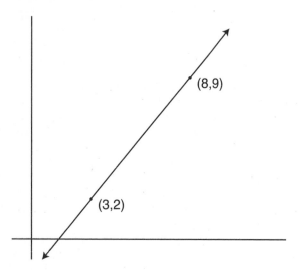

Solution

$$\frac{(9-2)}{(8-3)} = \frac{7}{5}$$

Therefore, the slope of the line is $\frac{7}{5}$.

Note: If you know the slope and at least one point on a line, you can find the coordinates of other points on the line. Simply move the required units determined by the slope. In the previous example, from (8,9), given the slope $\frac{7}{5}$, move up seven units and to the right five units. Another point on the line, thus, is (16,13).

Important Information about Slope

- A line that rises from left to right has a positive slope and a line that falls from left to right has a negative slope.
- A horizontal line has a slope of 0, and a vertical line does not have a slope at all—it is undefined.
- Parallel lines have equal slopes.
- Perpendicular lines have slopes that are negative reciprocals.

46 ▶ Word Problems and Data Analysis

Many students struggle with word problems. In this chapter, you will learn how to solve word problems with confidence by translating the words into a mathematical equation. Because the GED Mathematics Exam focuses on real-life situations, it's especially important for you to know how to make the transition from sentences to a math problem.

THIS SECTION WILL help you become familiar with the word problems on the GED and to analyze data using specific techniques.

▶ Translating Words into Numbers

The most important skill needed for word problems is the ability to translate words into mathematical operations. This list provides some common examples of English phrases and their mathematical equivalents.

- *Increase* means add.
  A number *increased* by five = $x + 5$.
- *Less than* means subtract.
  10 *less than* a number = $x - 10$.
- *Times* or *product* means multiply.
  Three *times* a number = $3x$.
- *Times the sum* means to multiply a number by a quantity.
  Five *times the sum* of a number and three = $5(x + 3)$.

- Two variables are sometimes used together.
  A number y exceeds five times a number x by ten.
  $y = 5x + 10$
- Inequality signs are used for at least and at most, as well as less than and more than.

  The product of x and 6 is greater than 2.
  $x \times 6 > 2$

  When 14 is added to a number x, the sum is less than 21.
  $x + 14 < 21$

  The sum of a number x and 4 is at least 9.
  $x + 4 \geq 9$

  When seven is subtracted from a number x, the difference is at most 4.
  $x - 7 \leq 4$

▶ Assigning Variables in Word Problems

It may be necessary to create and assign variables in a word problem. To do this, first identify an unknown and a known. You may not actually know the exact value of the "known," but you will know at least something about its value.

Examples
Max is three years older than Ricky.
Unknown = Ricky's age = x.
Known = Max's age is three years older.
Therefore,
Ricky's age = x and Max's age = $x + 3$.

Lisa made twice as many cookies as Rebecca.
Unknown = number of cookies Rebecca made = x.
Known = number of cookies Lisa made = $2x$.

Cordelia has five more than three times the number of books that Becky has.
Unknown = the number of books Becky has = x.
Known = the number of books Cordelia has = $3x + 5$.

▶ Ratio

A **ratio** is a comparison of two quantities measured in the same units. It can be symbolized by the use of a colon—$x{:}y$ or $\frac{x}{y}$ or x to y. Ratio problems can be solved using the concept of multiples.

Example
A bag containing some red and some green candies has a total of 60 candies in it. The ratio of the number of green to red candies is 7:8. How many of each color are there in the bag?

From the problem, it is known that 7 and 8 share a multiple and that the sum of their product is 60. Therefore, you can write and solve the following equation:
$7x + 8x = 60$
$15x = 60$
$\frac{15x}{15} = \frac{60}{15}$
$x = 4$
Therefore, there are $7x = (7)(4) = 28$ green candies and $8x = (8)(4) = 32$ red candies.

▶ Mean, Median, and Mode

To find the **average**, or **mean**, of a set of numbers, add all of the numbers together and divide by the quantity of numbers in the set.

$$\text{Average} = \frac{\text{sum of the number set}}{\text{quantity of set}}$$

Example
Find the average of 9, 4, 7, 6, and 4.
$\frac{9+4+7+6+4}{5} = \frac{30}{5} = 6$ The average is 6.
(Divide by 5 because there are 5 numbers in the set.)

To find the median of a set of numbers, arrange the numbers in ascending order and find the middle value.

- If the set contains an odd number of elements, then simply choose the middle value.

Example
Find the median of the number set: 1, 3, 5, 7, 2.
First arrange the set in ascending order: 1, 2, 3, 5, 7, and then choose the middle value: 3. The answer is 3.

- If the set contains an even number of elements, simply average the two middle values.

Example

Find the median of the number set: 1, 5, 3, 7, 2, 8. First arrange the set in ascending order: 1, 2, 3, 5, 7, 8, and then choose the middle values, 3 and 5. Find the average of the numbers 3 and 5: $\frac{(3+5)}{2} = 4$. The median is 4.

▶ Mode

The mode of a set of numbers is the number that occurs the greatest number of times.

Example

For the number set 1, 2, 5, 3, 4, 2, 3, 6, 3, 7, the number 3 is the mode because it occurs the most often.

▶ Percent

A percent is a measure of a part to a whole, with the whole being equal to 100.

- To change a decimal to a percentage, move the decimal point two units to the right and add a percentage symbol.

Example

.45 = 45%

.07 = 7%

.9 = 90%

- To change a fraction to a percentage, first change the fraction to a decimal. To do this, divide the numerator by the denominator. Then change the decimal to a percentage.

Example

$\frac{4}{5} = .80 = 80\%$

$\frac{2}{5} = .4 = 40\%$

$\frac{1}{8} = .125 = 12.5\%$

- To change a percentage to a decimal, simply move the decimal point two places to the left and eliminate the percentage symbol.

Example

64% = .64

87% = .87

7% = .07

- To change a percentage to a fraction, put the percent over 100 and reduce.

Example

$64\% = \frac{64}{100} = \frac{16}{25}$

$75\% = \frac{75}{100} = \frac{3}{4}$

$82\% = \frac{82}{100} = \frac{41}{50}$

- Keep in mind that any percentage that is 100 or greater will need to reflect a whole number or mixed number when converted.

Example

$125\% = 1.25$ or $1\frac{1}{4}$

$350\% = 3.5$ or $3\frac{1}{2}$

Here are some conversions you should be familiar with. The order is from most common to less common.

Fraction	Decimal	Percentage
$\frac{1}{2}$	.5	50%
$\frac{1}{4}$	.25	25%
$\frac{1}{3}$	.333 . . .	$33.\overline{3}\%$
$\frac{2}{3}$	.666 . . .	$66.\overline{6}\%$
$\frac{1}{10}$	.1	10%
$\frac{1}{8}$	.125	12.5%
$\frac{1}{6}$	.1666 . . .	$16.\overline{6}\%$
$\frac{1}{5}$	.2	20%

► Calculating Interest

Interest is a fee paid for the use of someone else's money. If you put money in a savings account, you receive interest from the bank. If you take out a loan, you pay interest to the lender. The amount of money you invest or borrow is called the principal. The amount you repay is the amount of the principal plus the interest.

The formula for simple interest is found on the formula sheet in the GED. Simple interest is a percent of the principal multiplied by the length of the loan:

$$Interest = principal \times rate \times time$$

Sometimes it may be easier to use the letters of each as variables:

$$I = prt$$

Example
Michelle borrows $2,500 from her uncle for three years at 6% simple interest. How much interest will she pay on the loan?

Step 1: Write the interest as a decimal. $\qquad$ $6\% = 0.06$

Step 2: Substitute the known values in the formula $\qquad$ $I = prt$
and multiply. $\qquad$ $= \$2,500 \times 0.06 \times 3$
$\qquad = \$450$

Michelle will pay $450 in interest.

Some problems will ask you to find the amount that will be paid back from a loan. This adds an additional step to problems of interest. In the previous example, Michelle will owe $450 in interest at the end of three years. However, it is important to remember that she will pay back the $450 in interest as well as the principal, $2,500. Therefore, she will pay her uncle $2,500 + $450 = $2,950.

In a simple interest problem, the rate is an annual, or yearly, rate. Therefore, the time must also be expressed in years.

Example
Kai invests $4,000 for nine months. Her investment will pay 8%. How much money will she have at the end of nine months?

Step 1: Write the rate as a decimal. $\qquad$ $8\% = 0.08$

Step 2: Express the time as a fraction by writing the length of time in months over 12 (the number of months in a year).
$$9 \text{ months} = \tfrac{9}{12} = \tfrac{3}{4} \text{ year}$$

Step 3: Multiply. $\qquad\qquad\qquad I = prt$
$$= \$4,000 \times 0.08 \times \tfrac{3}{4}$$
$$= \$180$$

Kai will earn $180 in interest.

► Probability

Probability is expressed as a fraction and measures the likelihood that a specific event will occur. To find the probability of a specific outcome, use this formula:

$$\text{Probability of an event} = \frac{\text{Number of specific outcomes}}{\text{Total number of possible outcomes}}$$

Example
If a bag contains 5 blue marbles, 3 red marbles, and 6 green marbles, find the probability of selecting a red marble:

Probability of an event =

$$\frac{\text{Number of specific outcomes}}{\text{Total number of possible outcomes}}$$

$$= \frac{3}{(5 + 3 + 6)}$$

Therefore, the probability of selecting a red marble is $\tfrac{3}{14}$.

Helpful Hints about Probability
- If an event is certain to occur, the probability is 1.
- If an event is certain not to occur (impossible), the probability is 0.
- If you know the probability of all other events occurring, you can find the probability of the remaining event by adding the known probabilities together and subtracting their total from 1.

▶ Graphs and Tables

The GED Mathematics Exam will test your ability to analyze graphs and tables. It is important to read each graph or table very carefully before reading the question. This will help you to process the information that is presented. It is extremely important to read all of the information presented, paying special attention to headings and units of measure. Here is an overview of the types of graphs you will encounter:

- Circle graphs or pie charts
  This type of graph is representative of a whole and is usually divided into percentages. Each section of the chart represents a portion of the whole, and all of these sections added together will equal 100% of the whole.

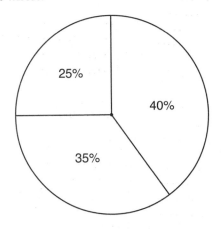

- Bar graphs
  Bar graphs compare similar things with different length bars representing different values. Be sure to read all labels and legends, looking carefully at the base and sides of the graph to see what the bars are measuring and how much they are increasing or decreasing.

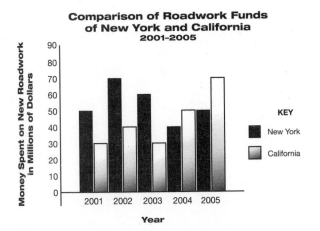

- Broken line graphs
  Broken line graphs illustrate a measurable change over time. If a line is slanted up, it represents an increase whereas a line sloping down represents a decrease. A flat line indicates no change as time elapses.

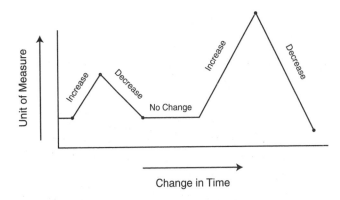

▶ Scientific Notation

Scientific notation is a method used by scientists to convert very large or very small numbers to more manageable ones. You will have to make a few conversions to scientific notation on the GED Mathematics Exam. Expressing answers in scientific notation involves moving the decimal point and multiplying by a power of ten.

Example
A space satellite travels 46,000,000 miles from the earth. What is the number in scientific notation?

Step 1: Starting at the decimal point to the right of the last zero, move the decimal point until only one digit remains to its left:

    46,000,000 becomes 4.6.

Step 2: Count the number of places the decimal was moved left. In this example, the decimal point was moved 7 places, and express it as a power of 10:

    10^7

Step 3: Express the full answer in scientific notation by multiplying the reduced answer from step 1 by 10^7:

    4.6×10^7

Example

An amoeba is .000056 inch long. What is its length in scientific notation?

Step 1: Move the decimal point to the right until there is one digit other than zero to the left of the decimal.

.000056 becomes 5.6

Step 2: Count the number of places moved to the right—5. However, because the value of the number is being increased as it is expressed in scientific notation, it is written as a negative exponent.

10^{-5}

Step 3: Express the full answer in scientific notation:

.0000056 becomes 5.6×10^{-5}

▶ General Strategies for Math Questions

- Skipping and returning.

  If you are unsure of what you are being asked to find, if you don't know how to solve a problem, or if you will take a long time to find the correct answer, skip the question and come back to it later. Do the easy problems first. The GED Mathematics Exam is not arranged with increasingly difficult questions. The difficult questions appear alongside of the easier questions. Therefore, it is important to skip difficult problems and come back to them.

- Plugging in.

  There will be times when you should use the answer choices to find the correct answer. This can be done when you have a problem that gives you a formula or equation. Plug in answers when you feel it will be quicker than solving the problem another way, and when you have enough information to do so.

- Eliminating.

  Eliminate choices you know are wrong so that you can spend more time considering choices that might be right. It may sound like a simple strategy but it can make a big difference.

- Making educated guesses.

  It's important to remember you are not penalized for a wrong answer. If you don't know the answer to a question and you are approaching the time limit, simply use the last few minutes to make an educated guess to the remaining questions. You can surely eliminate some of the answer choices and improve your odds of getting it right.

VIII ▶ The Practice Exams

Are you ready for the GED? The practice exams in Part VIII will show you how much you know and what you might still need to study. And because the questions are just like those on the GED, these practice exams will show you exactly what you can expect on the official exams.

Now it's time to put all that you have learned and reviewed into practice. In this section, you will find two sets of practice exams. Each set includes a full-length practice exam in each subject area—writing, reading, science, math, and social studies.

Take Practice Exam 1 in each subject area first. You should find a quiet place to complete these exams and try timing yourself to mimic the official GED time constraints for each subject. Have a blank sheet of scratch paper and pencils available. For one part of the math exam, you will also need your calculator. Be sure to answer every question; you will not be penalized for incorrect answers. Do not spend too much time on any one question so you can be sure to complete the questions in the allotted time. After you are done with each exam, check your answers. This will allow you to see what concepts and skills you still need to review.

Follow up any review sessions by taking Practice Exam 2 in each subject area. Again, compare your answers and study the explanations. Good luck!

47 ▶ Practice Exam 1, GED Language Arts, Writing

▶ Part I

Directions: In each of the following passages, the paragraphs are lettered and the sentences are numbered. Read each passage carefully and then answer the questions that follow.

Questions 1–10 refer to the following meeting minutes.

Employee Advocate Committee
Minutes of Meeting Held: July 21, 2008

In Attendance:
Dakota Mills, vice president
Rebecca Styles, committee chairperson
Oliver Perez, committee secretary
Brenda Oslowski
Michael Wen
Jamal Roberts

Absent:
Anthony Wilkins

A

1. Employee Lounge. (1) Brenda reported an increase in complaints about the employee lounge. (2) The complaints include:

- insufficient locker space
- insufficient and uncomfortable seating
- a refrigerator that is dirty
- malfunctioning microwave

B

(3) Jamal suggested creating a survey to determine how to best redesign the lounge. (4) Rebecca suggested putting a suggestion box in the lounge. (5) The committee agreed that a survey would be more systematic and getting more input from employees. (6) Michael volunteered to create the survey that he will bring a draft of to the next meeting. (7) Oliver volunteers to research the cost of a new microwave and refrigerator. (8) The need for more telephones was another complaint about the lounge that was discussed.

C

2. Employee Appreciation Day. (9) Rebecca reminded the committee that it was time to plan the annual Employee Appreciation Day, we brainstormed several ideas for Appreciation Day activities, including:

- buffet lunch
- employee appreciation awards, such as "most reliable" or "most enthusiastic"
- raffle with prizes such as gift certificates for dinner.

D

(10) Brenda noted that the company could best show its appreciation by moving quickly improving the lounge. (11) The committee have agreed that the survey should be completed before Employee Appreciation Day.

E

(12) The committee will reconvene next Monday July 28 at 10 A.M.

1. Sentence 2: The complaints include:

- insufficient locker space
- insufficient and uncomfortable seating
- a refrigerator that is dirty
- malfunctioning microwave

Which revision should be made to this sentence?
   a. Change the bulleted list to regular text.
   b. Replace <u>malfunctioning</u> with <u>malfunction</u>.
   c. Put the bulleted list items in alphabetical order.
   d. Change <u>a refrigerator that is dirty</u> to <u>a dirty refrigerator</u>.
   e. Replace <u>insufficient locker space</u> with <u>not having enough locker space</u>.

2. Sentence 5: The committee agreed that a survey would be more systematic and getting more input from employees.
   Which correction should be made to this sentence?
   a. Change <u>agreed</u> to <u>agreeing</u>.
   b. Insert a comma after <u>survey</u>.
   c. Replace <u>getting</u> with <u>get</u>.
   d. Delete <u>and</u>.
   e. No correction is necessary.

3. Sentence 6: Michael volunteered to create the survey <u>that he will bring a draft of</u> to the next meeting.
   Which is the best way to write the underlined portion of this sentence? If the original is the best way, choose option **a**.
   a. that he will bring a draft of
   b. and will bring a draft
   c. bringing a draft of it
   d. therefore, he will bring a draft of it
   e. that he is going to bring a draft of

4. Sentence 7: Oliver volunteers to research the cost of a new microwave and refrigerator.
   Which correction should be made to sentence 7?
   a. Change <u>volunteers</u> to <u>volunteered</u>.
   b. Replace <u>cost of</u> with <u>costing</u>.
   c. Change <u>new</u> to <u>knew</u>.
   d. Insert a hyphen between <u>new</u> and <u>microwave</u>.
   e. No correction is necessary.

5. Sentence 8: The need for more telephones was another complaint about the lounge that was discussed.

What revision should be made to sentence 8?
a. Move sentence 8 to follow sentence 4.
b. Revise for parallel structure.
c. Delete the sentence from the memo.
d. Turn sentence 8 into a bullet point for sentence 2.
e. Start a new paragraph with sentence 8.

6. Sentence 9: Rebecca reminded the committee that it was time to plan the annual Employee Appreciation <u>Day, we</u> brainstormed several ideas for Appreciation Day activities, including:

Which is the best way to write the underlined portion of this sentence? If the original is the best way, choose option **a**.
a. Day, we
b. Day, therefore we
c. Day. We
d. Day; and we
e. Day we

7. Sentence 9: Rebecca reminded the committee that it was time to plan the annual Employee Appreciation Day, we brainstormed several ideas for Appreciation Day activities, including:

Which correction should be made to sentence 9?
a. Insert commas after <u>committee</u> and <u>time</u>.
b. Change the colon after <u>including</u> to a semicolon.
c. Replace <u>that</u> with <u>which</u>.
d. Change <u>we</u> to <u>the committee</u>.
e. No correction is necessary.

8. Sentence 10: Brenda noted that the company could best show its appreciation by moving quickly improving the lounge.

Which correction should be made to sentence 10?
a. Change <u>noted</u> to <u>had noted</u>.
b. Replace <u>improving</u> with <u>to improve</u>.
c. Change <u>the company</u> to <u>The Company</u>.
d. Move <u>quickly</u> to follow <u>by</u>.
e. No correction is necessary.

9. Sentence 11: The committee have agreed that the survey should be completed before Employee Appreciation Day.

Which correction should be made to sentence 11?
a. Change <u>agreed</u> to <u>agrees</u>.
b. Replace <u>before</u> with <u>preceding</u>.
c. Put <u>should</u> in parentheses.
d. Delete <u>have</u>.
e. No correction is necessary.

10. Sentence 12: The committee will reconvene next Monday July 28 at 10 A.M.

Which correction should be made to sentence 12?
a. Change <u>will reconvene</u> to <u>is reconvening</u>.
b. Replace <u>will</u> with <u>we'll</u>.
c. Insert commas after <u>Monday</u> and <u>28</u>.
d. Place <u>July 28</u> in parentheses.
e. No correction is necessary.

Questions 11–20 refer to the following passage.

Yoga

A

(1) One of today's hottest fads is also one of the world's oldest practices the ancient art of yoga. (2) Yoga is different from other fitness activities because it is not only physical. (3) In the correct form, yoga is a practice of unification: an emotional, spiritual, *and* physical exercise.

B

(4) A simple sitting pose such as *staff pose,* for example, requiring that you to tighten and lengthen stomach, back, and arm muscles as you stretch your legs out in front of you and place your hands by your side. (5) More difficult poses, such as *brave warrior,* require you to balance on one leg and hold a pose that strengthens leg, back, and stomach muscles. (6) Though it may seem easy to those who have never practiced, yoga poses require great concentration, and they are surprisingly effective in stretching and strengthening muscles.

C

(7) While yoga tones and strengthens the body, it also tones and strengthens the mind. (8) Many poses can only be held if you are completely focused on the task, and full benefit of the poses

are coming only through proper breathing. (9) Concentrated, deep breathing during yoga helps you extend more fully into the poses. (10) Thereby gaining greater benefit from the stretch. (11) And the steady circulation of breath through you're body both calms and energizes.

D

(12) I am still relatively new to the practice of yoga. (13) I have been practicing yoga for only one year. (14) I am addicted to yoga unlike any other physical activity because it is also a spiritual practice. (15) Through yoga, I am able to release tensions that lodge in various parts of my body: the tight shoulders, the cramped legs, the belly that is in knots. (16) The physical release is also a spiritual release. (17) I feel calm after doing yoga, reconnected to my body, and reconnected to my inner self.

11. Sentence 1: One of today's hottest fads is also one of the world's oldest practices the ancient art of yoga.

Which correction should be made to sentence 1?
a. Delete the apostrophe in today's.
b. Change oldest to most old.
c. Insert a comma after fads.
d. Insert a colon after practices.
e. No correction is necessary.

12. Sentence 3: In the correct form, yoga is a practice of unification: an emotional, spiritual, *and* physical exercise.

Which is the best way to write the underlined portion of sentence 3? If the original is the best way, choose option **a**.
a. In the correct form
b. Formed in the correct manner
c. Done correctly
d. Being done correctly
e. Doing it in the correct way

13. Sentence 4: A simple sitting pose such as *staff pose*, for example, requiring that you tighten and lengthen stomach, back, and arm muscles as you stretch your legs out in front of you and place your hands by your side.

Which is the best way to write the underlined portion of sentence 4? If the original is the best way, choose option **a**.
a. requiring that you tighten
b. requires you to tighten
c. it requires you to tighten
d. requires tightening
e. in which you are required to tighten

14. Sentence 6: Though it may seem easy to those who have never practiced, yoga poses require great concentration, and they are surprisingly effective in stretching and strengthening muscles.

Which revision should be made to the placement of sentence 6?
a. Remove sentence 6.
b. Move sentence 6 to follow sentence 3.
c. Move sentence 6 to begin paragraph B.
d. Move sentence 6 to follow sentence 4.
e. Move sentence 6 to follow sentence 7.

15. Sentence 8: Many poses can only be held if you are completely focused on the task, and full benefit of the poses are coming only through proper breathing.

Which correction should be made to sentence 8?
a. Change breathing to breath.
b. Remove the comma after task.
c. Replace full benefit with benefiting fully.
d. Change are coming to comes.
e. No correction is necessary.

16. Sentences 9 and 10: Concentrated, deep breathing during yoga helps you extend more fully into the poses. Thereby gaining greater benefit from the stretch.

Which correction should be made to the underlined portion of sentence 9? If the original is the best way, choose option **a**.
a. poses. Thereby
b. poses; thereby
c. poses, so thereby
d. poses thereby
e. poses, thereby

17. Sentence 11: And the steady circulation of breath through you're body both calms and energizes.

  Which correction should be made to sentence 11?
  a. Delete <u>both</u>.
  b. Change <u>you're</u> to <u>your</u>.
  c. Insert a comma after <u>breath</u> and <u>body</u>.
  d. Move <u>of breath</u> to follow <u>body</u>.
  e. No correction is necessary.

18. Sentences 12 and 13: I am still relatively new to the practice of yoga. I have been practicing yoga for only one year.

  Which is the most effective way to combine sentences 12 and 13?
  a. I am still relatively new to yoga, the practice of which I have been doing for only one year.
  b. I am still relatively new to the practice of yoga, of which I have only been practicing for one year.
  c. I am still relatively new to yoga, which I have been practicing for only one year.
  d. I have only been practicing yoga for one year, which means I am still relatively new to the practice.
  e. Because I am still relatively new to yoga, I have only been practicing for one year.

19. Sentence 14: I am addicted to yoga unlike any other physical activity because it is also a spiritual practice.

  The most effective revision of sentence 14 would begin with which word or phrase?
  a. Since
  b. Surprisingly,
  c. In the end,
  d. Similarly,
  e. However,

20. Sentence 15: Through yoga, I am able to release tensions that lodge in various parts of my body: the tight shoulders, the cramped legs, <u>the belly that is in knots</u>.

  Which is the best way to write the underlined portion of sentence 15? If the original is the best way, chose option **a**.
  a. the belly that is in knots
  b. the belly with knots
  c. the knots in the belly
  d. the knotted belly
  e. the belly having knots

Questions 21–30 refer to the following passage.

How to Be an Active Listener

A

(1) Effective face to face communication depends upon the ability to listen well. (2) Many of us hear what others say without really listening to the message they are sending. (3) We must listen actively to correctly understand what is being said.

B

(4) The first step to active listening is to pay attention. (5) Don't fidget, doodle, or look off at something else. (6) Daydreaming is something that you shouldn't do, or look at your watch, or worry about what you're going to make for dinner.

C

(7) You should actively respond to what you hear. (8) Use nonverbal responses, nod or shake your head, laugh or smile, and make other appropriate gestures. (9) Lean forward and look the speaker in the eye to be shown that you are paying attention.

D

(10) As you listen, respond verbally as well. (11) Offer affirmations such as "yes" "uh-huh" and "I understand." (12) Ask questions to get details or examples or to clarify matters. (13) Paraphrasing what you hear to be sure you are understanding things correctly.

E

(14) The third step is that distractions should be avoided. (15) If you are going to listen to someone; turn off the television or radio. (16) Don't look at your computer screen or pick up the phone. (17) Close the door if possible to avoid interruptions or outside distractions, and you will be a more effective listener.

21. Sentence 1: Effective face to face communication depends upon the ability to listen well.

Which correction should be made to sentence 1?

a. Insert a comma after <u>depends</u>.

b. Change <u>face to face</u> to <u>face-to-face</u>.

c. Replace <u>well</u> with <u>good</u>.

d. Change <u>to listen</u> to <u>of listening</u>.

e. No correction is necessary.

22. Sentence 6: <u>Daydreaming is something that you shouldn't do, or</u> look at your watch, or worry about what you're going to make for dinner.

Which is the most effective revision to the underlined portion of sentence 6? If the original is the best way, choose option **a.**

a. Daydreaming is something that you shouldn't do, or

b. Don't daydream,

c. Never daydream while you

d. If you want to daydream, don't, and don't

e. One thing not to do is daydream, or

23. Sentence 7: You should actively respond to what you hear.

What revision should be made to sentence 7?

a. Move sentence 7 to the end of paragraph C.

b. Change <u>You should</u> to <u>The second step is to</u>.

c. Insert the number <u>2</u> at the beginning of the paragraph.

d. Change the <u>you</u>'s in the sentence to <u>we</u>'s.

e. Delete sentence 7.

24. Sentence 8: Use nonverbal <u>responses, nod or shake</u> your head, laugh or smile, and make other appropriate gestures.

Which is the best way to write the underlined portion of sentence 8? If the original is the best way, choose option **a.**

a. responses, nod or shake

b. responses, including nodding or shaking

c. responses. To nod or shake

d. responses; for example, nod or shake

e. responses that include the nodding or shaking

25. Sentence 9: Lean forward and look the speaker in the eye to be shown that you are paying attention.

Which correction should be made to sentence 9?

a. Change <u>be shown</u> to <u>show</u>.

b. Replace <u>paying</u> with <u>pay</u>.

c. Change <u>in the eye</u> to <u>in-the-eye</u>.

d. Start a new sentence after <u>eye</u>.

e. No correction is necessary.

26. Sentence 11: Offer affirmations such as "yes" "uh-huh" and "I understand."

Which correction should be made to sentence 11?

a. Delete the quotation marks around <u>yes</u>.

b. Start a new sentence after <u>affirmations</u>.

c. Insert commas after <u>yes</u> and <u>uh-huh</u>.

d. Delete <u>uh-huh</u>.

e. No correction is necessary.

27. Sentence 13: Paraphrasing what you hear to be sure you are understanding things correctly.

Which correction should be made to sentence 13?

a. Change <u>to be sure</u> to <u>being sure that</u>.

b. Move <u>correctly</u> to follow <u>paraphrasing</u>.

c. Replace <u>are</u> with <u>do</u>.

d. Change <u>paraphrasing</u> to <u>paraphrase</u>.

e. No correction is necessary.

28. Sentence 14: The third step is that distractions should be avoided.

Which is the most effective way to write sentence 14? If the original is the most effective, choose option **a.**

a. The third step is that distractions should be avoided.

b. The third step being to avoid distractions.

c. Distractions should be avoided as the third step.

d. Avoid distractions.

e. The third step is to avoid distractions.

29. Sentence 15: If you are going to listen to someone; turn off the television or radio.

Which correction should be made to sentence 15?

a. Change the semicolon to a period.

b. Delete <u>if</u>.

c. Replace the semicolon with a comma.

d. Move the semicolon to after <u>going</u>.

e. No correction is necessary.

30. Sentence 17: Close the door if possible to avoid interruptions or outside distractions, and you will be a more effective listener.

Which revision should be made to sentence 17?

a. Move sentence 17 to the beginning of paragraph E.
b. Delete <u>and you will be a more effective listener</u>.
c. Insert <u>. Follow these steps,</u> after <u>distractions</u>.
d. Insert <u>To avoid distractions</u> at the beginning of the sentence.
e. Change <u>outside distractions</u> to <u>distractions that are coming from outside</u>.

Questions 31–35 refer to the following passage.

A

(1) Charles Darwin was born in 1809 at Shewsbury England. (2) He was a biologist whose famous theory of evolution is important to philosophy for the effects it has had about the nature of man. (3) After many years of careful study, Darwin attempted to showed that higher species come into existence as a result of the gradual transformation of lower species; and that the process of transformation could be explained through the selective effect of the natural environment upon organisms.

B

(4) Darwin concluded that the principles of natural selection and survival of the fittest govern all life. (5) Darwin's explanation of these principles is that because of the food supply problem, the young born to any species compete for survival. (6) Favorable natural changes, which are then passed on through heredity, tend to be embodied by those young that survive to produce the next generation. (7) His major book that contained these theories is On the Origin of Species written in 1859. (8) Many religious opponents condemned this work.

31. Sentence 1: Charles Darwin was born in 1809 at Shewsbury England.

Which correction should be made to sentence 1?

a. Change <u>was</u> to <u>is</u>.
b. Insert a comma after <u>Shewsbury</u>.
c. Delete <u>at</u>.
d. Insert a comma after <u>Darwin</u>.
e. No correction is necessary.

32. Sentence 2: He was a <u>biologist whose famous theory of evolution is important to philosophy for the effects it</u> has had about the nature of man.

Which is the best way to write the underlined portion of sentence 2? If the original is the best way, choose option **a**.

a. biologist whose famous theory of evolution is important to philosophy for the effects it
b. biologist who's famous theory of evolution is important to philosophy for the effects it
c. biologist whose famous theory of evolution is important to philosophy for the affects it
d. biologist whose famous theory of evolution is important to philosophy for the effects he
e. biologist, whose famous theory of evolution, is important to philosophy for the effects it

33. Sentence 3: After many years of careful study, Darwin attempted to showed that higher species come into existence as a result of the gradual transformation of lower species; and that the process of transformation could be explained through the selective effect of the natural environment upon organisms.

What revision should be made to sentence 3?

a. Move sentence 3 to the end of paragraph B.
b. Change <u>to showed</u> to <u>to show</u>.
c. Change the <u>as a result of</u> to <u>as of result from</u>.
d. Change <u>upon organisms</u> to <u>because organisms</u>.
e. Delete sentence 3.

34. Sentence 6: <u>Favorable natural changes, which are then passed on through heredity, tend to be embodied by those young that survive to produce the next generation.</u>

Which is the best way to write the underlined portion of sentence 6? If the original is the best way, choose option **a**.

a. Favorable natural changes, which are then passed on through heredity, tend to be embodied by those young that survive to produce the next generation.

b. Favorable natural changes that are then passed on through heredity tend to be embodied by those young that survive to produce the next generation.

c. Then passed on through heredity, favorable natural changes tend to be embodied by those young that survive to produce the next generation.

d. Those young that survive to produce the next generation, which are then passed on through heredity, tend to embody favorable natural changes.

e. Those young that survive to produce the next generation tend to embody favorable natural changes, which are then passed on through heredity.

35. Sentence 7: His major work that contained these theories is On the Origin of Species written in 1859.

What revision should be made to sentence 7?

a. Change <u>that</u> to <u>which</u>.

b. Change <u>is</u> to <u>are</u>.

c. Italicize <u>On the Origin of Species</u>.

d. Place quotation marks before and after <u>On the Origin of Species</u>.

e. No revision is necessary.

Please use the following to answer questions 36–40.

A

(1) Every spring, hundreds of movie actors and actresses put on their finest clothes and walk down a red carpet to an opulent theater. (2) Interviewers and reporters clamor for their attention. (3) Inside, songs and films are shown, but what everyone wants to see is the opening of a small envelope. (4) And millions of people at home are watching on TV. (5) What is this elegant ritual? (6) It's the Academy Awards!

B

(7) The Academy Awards are prizes given for excellence in motion pictures, or movies. (8) Most people know them by the nickname the Oscars. (9) The awards come in the form of a small gold statuette. (10) They are given in many categories, including best picture, Best Actor, Best Actress, Best Director, Best Original Song, and many, many more. (11) There are 25 categories in all, including other prizes like Best Sound Editing, Best Animated Feature Film, and Best Costume Design. (12) Most people are interested in only a few!

C

(13) The nominees and award winners are chosen by a group called the Academy of Motion Picture Arts and Sciences. (14) It is composed of many people who work on movies, including actors, directors, writers, producers, and technicians. (15) This group began the tradition of the Academy Awards in 1928. (16) The number of awards has grown over the years. (17) New categories have been added. (18) In 1953, the awards ceremony was first shown on TV, and many more people were able to watch the stylish show.

D

(19) During the ceremony, there is a host to introduce different categories and provide entertainment between the awards. (20) The people or movies which have been nominated for awards are announced one by one. (21) Then, an actor or actress is assigned to present the different nominees, and sometimes a part of the nominated movie is shown. (22) Then, the presenter will open an envelope which contains the name of the winner. (23) Then, the winner receives the gold Oscar statuette and sometimes gives a speech.

E

(24) These are the traditions of the Academy Awards. (25) They have developed over its long history. (26) Now they are enjoyed by millions of movie fans every spring!

36. Sentence 12: Most people are interested in only a few!

The most effective revision to this sentence would begin with which of the following?
a. Additionally
b. However
c. On the other hand
d. Therefore
e. As a result

37. Sentences 16 and 17: The number of awards has grown over the years. New categories have been added.

Which is the most effective combination of sentences 16 and 17?
a. The number of awards has grown over the years, new categories have been added.
b. Many new categories have been added over the years.
c. The number of awards has grown over the years new categories have been added.
d. The number of awards has grown over the years, as new categories have been added.
e. The number of awards has grown over the years, but new categories have been added.

38. Sentences 24 and 25: These are the traditions of the Academy Awards. They have developed over its long history.

Which is the most effective combination of sentences 24 and 25?
a. These are the traditions of the Academy Awards which have developed over its long history.
b. These are the traditions of the Academy Awards, they have developed over its long history.
c. These are the traditions of the Academy Awards' history.
d. Over its long history, these are the traditions of the Academy Awards.
e. Developed, these are the traditions of the Academy Awards.

39. Sentence 1: Every spring, <u>hundreds of movie actors and actresses put on their finest clothes and walk down a red carpet</u> to an opulent theater.

Which of the following is the best way to write the underlined portion of this sentence? If you think the original is the best way, choose answer choice **a.**
a. hundreds of movie actors and actresses put on their finest clothes and walk down a red carpet
b. hundreds of movies, actors, and actresses put on their finest clothes and walk down a red carpet
c. hundreds of movie actors—and actresses—put on their finest clothes and walk down a red carpet
d. hundreds of movie actors and actresses put on their finest clothes, and walk down a red carpet
e. hundreds of movie actors and actresses, put on their finest clothes, and walk down a red carpet

40. Paragraph B, sentences 7 through 12: The Academy Awards are prizes . . . in only a few!

Which sentence would be the best addition to this paragraph?
a. I am interested in only two categories.
b. The official name of the gold statuette is the *Academy Award of Merit.*
c. All members must be invited to join and invitation comes from the Board of Governors, on behalf of Academy Branch Executive Committees.
d. Membership eligibility may be achieved by a competitive nomination or a member may submit a name based on other significant contribution to the field of motion pictures.
e. Though winning an Academy Award usually results in an invitation to join, membership is not automatic.

Please use the following to answer questions 41–45.

A

(1) Have you ever wondered why gourmet coffee shops are so popular, or why cola is almost everyone's favorite drink? (2) The success of these "pick-me-up" beverages could be due to the fact that Americans are largely sleep-deprived. (3) Although most sleep experts recommend that adults get seven to nine hours per night, and adolescents the full nine, many of us do not get the restful sleep we require. (4) One common cause of this lack of sleep is obstructive sleep apnea, or OSA.

B

(5) OSA actually causes people to stop breathing throughout the night, disrupting their sleep. (6) This temporary stoppage of breathing can last for over a minute and, in severe cases, happen up to 500 times per night. (7) OSA is fairly common. OSA affects about one in five in adults. (8) It affects 1–3% of all children. (9) A common cause of OSA is the sleeping person's tongue becoming too relaxed and blocking the throat. (10) This disorder is also called "Snoring Disease," because many people with sleep apnea snore. (11) Living with a snorer is really difficult.

C

(12) Sleep apnea can have several negative effects. (13) It can result in excessive daytime drowsiness, poor intellectual functioning, depression and memory problems. (14) These can lead to bigger problems like poor grades, job loss, car accidents and serious stuff like heart attacks, strokes, and high blood pressure.

D

(15) Fortunately, there is a highly effective treatment for sleep apnea. (16) It is a special face mask worn during sleep, which is connected to an air supply generator by a hose. (17) Wearing the mask takes some getting used to. (18) Most people are greatly helped by the mask. (19) They are relieved to wake up feeling rested.

41. Sentences 17, 18, and 19: Wearing the mask takes some getting used to. Most people are greatly helped by the mask. They are relieved to wake up feeling rested.

Which is the most effective combination of these sentences?

a. Wearing the mask takes some getting used to, most people are greatly helped by the mask, they are relieved to wake up feeling rested.

b. People are greatly helped by the mask and they are relieved to wake up feeling rested, however though wearing the mask takes some getting used to.

c. Although wearing the mask takes some getting used to, most people are greatly helped by the mask and relieved to wake up feeling rested.

d. But wearing the mask takes some getting used to. Most people are greatly helped by the mask. They are relieved to wake up feeling rested.

e. Wearing the mask takes some getting used to by most people are greatly helped by the mask. They are relieved to wake up. Feeling rested.

42. Sentences 7, 8, and 9: OSA is fairly common. OSA affects about one in five adults. It affects 1–3% of all children.

Which is the most effective combination of sentences 7, 8, and 9?

a. OSA is fairly common, affecting about one in five adults and 1–3% of all children.

b. OSA is fairly common, it affects about one in five adults and 1–3% of all children.

c. OSA is fairly common. However, it affects about one in five adults and 1–3% of all children.

d. OSA is fairly common; affects about one in five adults and 1–3% of all children.

e. Affecting 1–3% of all children, fairly common OSA affects about one in five adults.

43. Paragraph D, sentences 15 through 19: Fortunately, there is a highly effective treatment . . . wake up feeling rested.

Which sentence would be the best addition to this paragraph?

a. The air helps the person sleep.

b. The air pressure keeps the person asleep.

c. The air pressure keeps the airway open, eliminates snoring and breathing pauses, and allows the person to get uninterrupted sleep.

d. The air pressure is like a miracle cure.

e. It takes its name from the Greek word *apnea*, which means "without breath."

44. Sentence 14: These can lead to bigger problems like poor grades, job loss, car accidents and <u>serious stuff like heart attacks</u>, strokes, and high blood pressure.

Which of the following is the best way to write the underlined portion of this sentence? If you think the original is the best way, choose answer choice **a**.

a. serious stuff like heart attacks

b. serious stuff, heart attacks

c. serious problems like heart attacks

d. serious dilemmas like heart attacks

e. serious ailments like heart attacks

45. Sentence 10: This disorder is also called "Snoring Disease," because many people with sleep apnea snore.

Which of the following is the best way to write the underlined portion of this sentence? If you think the original is the best way, choose answer choice **a**.

a. This disorder is also called "Snoring Disease," because many people with sleep apnea snore.

b. This disorder is also called "Snoring Disease." Because many people with sleep apnea snore.

c. This disorder is also called "Snoring Disease"; however, many people with sleep apnea snore.

d. This disorder is also called "Snoring Disease," because snoring creates many people with sleep apnea.

e. "Snoring Disease" is also called the disorder, because many people with sleep apnea snore.

Please use the following to answer questions 46–50.

A

(1) Athletes and sports lovers around the world look forward to the Olympic Games. (2) In addition to being given the chance to be recognized as the best in their sport, athletes competing in the Games have the chance to be noted in history as part of a long line of Olympians, dating back to Ancient Greece.

B

(3) The first ancient Olympic Games occurred in 776 B.C. (4) The Olympics were named after the open plains of Olympia. (5) They were played in honor of Zeus. (6) They were played in honor of other ancient Greek gods, too. (7) These ancient Games continued for almost 1,200 years. (8) In 393 A.D., the Christian Emperor Theodosius declared that all pagan cults were forbidden, which meant the end of the ancient Olympic Games.

C

(9) A concept that represents the overriding spirit of the early games is the truce. (10) As they played against each other, their dedication and athleticism did much to unite them and served to minimize their differences.

D

(11) As they squared off against each other in the stadium and hippodrome, the athletes became famous and were immortalized by their wins. (12) The events in the ancient Games consisted of running, long jump, shot put, javelin, boxing, equestrian events, and pankration (a brutal combination of boxing and wrestling). (13) Plato was a famous Greek philosopher. (14) He was a two-time winner of the pankration event. (15) Other famous Greeks who participated in or viewed the games were fellow philosophers Socrates, Aristotle, and Pythagoras. (16) One group not represented in the games, or even allowed to watch, was women. (17) However, some women disguised themselves as men to sneak into the Games. (18) Their desire to be there must have been very strong, since they risked being thrown off Mt. Typiaon as a punishment if they were discovered. (19) Now that's what I call Olympic fever!

46. Sentences 4, 5, and 6: The Olympics were named after the open plains of Olympia. They were played in honor of Zeus. They were played in honor of other ancient Greek gods, too.

Which is the most effective combination of sentences 4, 5, and 6?

a. The Olympics were named that way because they were played in honor of Zeus and the other ancient Greek gods. They were played on the open plains of Olympia in their honor.

b. The Olympics got its name from Olympia, where they were played, and where Zeus and the other ancient Greek gods were honored by the Olympics.

c. The Olympics were so named because they were played on the open plains of Olympia in honor of Zeus and other ancient Greek gods.

d. Zeus and the other ancient Greek gods were the ones who were honored by the Olympics that were played in the open plains of Olympia in their honor.

e. The Olympics, played in honor of Zeus, were named after the open plains of Olympia and other ancient gods.

47. Paragraph C, sentences 9 and 10: A concept that represents the overriding spirit of the early games is the truce. As they played against each other, their dedication and athleticism did much to unite them and served to minimize their differences.

Which sentence would be the best addition to this paragraph?

a. When rival Greek cities came together in Olympia to compete, they realized they were not so different from their enemies.

b. When they met each other at the Olympics, they had a lot in common, so it was good.

c. All the athletes played against each other, but they didn't have to like each other.

d. When rival Greek cities used to come together in Olympia to play against each other at the Olympics, they would realize after a while that they were really not all that different from their enemies who were the other people they were playing against.

e. In fact, the Greek calendar was based on the Olympiad, the four-year period between games.

48. Sentences 13 and 14: Plato was a famous Greek philosopher. He was a two-time winner of the pankration event.

Which is the most effective combination of sentences 13 and 14?

a. Plato, a famous Greek philosopher, he was a two-time winner of the pankration event.

b. Plato, was a famous Greek philosopher, who was a two-time winner of the pankration event.

c. Plato, a famous Greek philosopher, was a two-time winner of the pankration event.

d. A two-time winner of the pankration event was Plato.

e. Plato was a famous Greek philosopher, two-time winner, and pankration event.

49. Sentence 11: As they squared off against each other in the stadium and hippodrome, the athletes became famous and were immortalized by their <u>wins</u>.

Which of the following is the best way to write the underlined portion of this sentence? If you think the original is the best way, choose answer choice **a.**

a. wins

b. attitudes

c. achievements

d. mortality

e. winningness

50. Sentence 8: In 393 A.D., the Christian Emperor Theodosius declared that all pagan cults were forbidden, which meant the end of the ancient Olympic Games.

The most effective revision to this sentence would begin with which of the following?

a. In addition,

b. Although,

c. Meanwhile,

d. Eventually,

e. Also,

▶ Part II

Answer the following writing prompt. Spend only 45 minutes on your response. Be sure you have a piece of scrap paper to brainstorm ideas and outline your essay. On the GED, you will not be allowed to write in the test booklet.

Follow these guidelines for Part II:
1. Write only on the assigned topic.
2. Write legibly on the lined pages provided.

3. Plan your essay carefully. Use a piece of scrap paper to brainstorm your essay and develop an outline.
4. After you have finished writing, review what you have written and make any changes that will improve your essay.

Prompt:
We all have things that we are afraid of. Many of our most memorable experiences are times when we faced something that scared us. Tell about a time when you faced a great fear. Use supporting details throughout your essay.

_____

_____

_____

_____

_____

_____

_____

_____

_____

_____

_____

_____

_____

_____

_____

_____

_____

_____

▶ Answers

Part I

1. **d.** The items in the list should use the same grammatical pattern (parallel structure), so a refrigerator that is dirty should be a dirty refrigerator to match the adjective, noun pattern of the other items in the list. Choice **a** is incorrect because the list is more effective as a bulleted list, especially for a business document. Choice **b** is incorrect because malfunctioning is an adjective and the phrase requires an adjective. Choice **c** is incorrect because the list does not need to be in alphabetical order (it is probably most effective in order of importance, for example, from the biggest problem to the smallest problem). Choice **e** is incorrect because the change would destroy parallel structure and add unnecessary words.

2. **c.** This choice creates parallel structure in the sentence, with both verbs (*be* and *get*) in the same form to work with the helping verb *would*. Choice **a** is incorrect because the memorandum is in past tense. Choice **b** is incorrect because commas should not be inserted between a subject and verb. Choice **d** is incorrect because *and* is necessary to show that there are two benefits from the survey (it is more systematic *and* it would get more input). Choice **e** is incorrect because the correction in choice **c** is necessary.

3. **b.** This version correctly states the second action Michael will take in this compound verb: Michael volunteered and will bring a draft to the next meeting. Choice **a** is incorrect because it is wordy and awkward, especially with the placement of *of* after draft. Choice **c** is incorrect because it is also awkward and does not have the helping verb *will* to indicate the future tense of the verb. Choice **d** is incorrect because it creates a run-on sentence. Choice **e** is grammatically correct but bulky and awkward because it uses *is going to bring* instead of *will bring* and because, like choice **a**, it places *of* after *draft*.

4. **a.** The memorandum is in the past tense, so the verb *volunteers* should be changed to *volunteered* to be consistent. Choice **b** is incorrect because the regular noun form *cost* is required

here, not the present participle *costing*. Choice **c** is incorrect because *knew* is the past tense of *know*, and the adjective *new* is what is needed here. Choice **d** is incorrect because *new* modifies *microwave*, so there should not be a hyphen between them. Choice **e** is incorrect because the verb tense correction should be made.

5. **d.** This sentence should be turned into a bullet point since it is a complaint about the lounge, and the other complaints are listed as bullets in sentence 2. Choice **a** is incorrect because the complaints are discussed in paragraph A, not paragraph B. Choice **b** is incorrect because there is no opportunity to use parallel structure in this sentence (however, when the sentence is moved to the bulleted list, it should be revised to fit the parallel structure of the list: insufficient telephones or not enough telephones). Choice **c** is incorrect because the sentence is important to the memo and should not be deleted. Choice **e** is incorrect because this sentence belongs in paragraph A; it should not be after paragraph B and should not be its own paragraph.

6. **c.** Sentence 9 contains two complete thoughts and should be separated into two sentences, which makes choice **a** incorrect. The sentences can be combined with a semicolon (choice **d**), but both sentences are rather long (especially with the list), so two separate sentences is the best choice. Choice **b** is incorrect because it is a run-on sentence; the comma should be a semicolon or a period. Choice **e** is incorrect because it also creates a run-on sentence.

7. **d.** The memo refers to the committee in the third person throughout. In sentence 9, the point of view shifts to the first person *we*. *We* should be changed to *the committee* to maintain consistency. Choice **a** is incorrect because *that it was time* is not a nonessential phrase that should be set off by commas; it is necessary to the meaning of the sentence. Choice **b** is incorrect because colons are used to introduce lists. The sentence requires *that*, not *which*, since it is not selecting among choices, so choice **c** is incorrect. Choice **e** is incorrect because the pronoun shift should be corrected.

8. b. The sentence is describing an action, so it requires the verb *to improve* rather than the gerund (noun) *improving*. Choice **a** is incorrect because the memorandum is using the simple past tense; the verb should be *noted,* not *had noted,* with a past tense helping verb. Choice **c** is incorrect because *the company* is not a specific noun and should not be capitalized. Choice **d** is incorrect because the best placement for the adverb *quickly* is immediately following the verb it describes (*moving*). Choice **e** is incorrect because the verb error needs to be corrected.

9. d. The present tense helping verb *have* is incorrect and should be deleted. Choice **a** is incorrect because it changes the past tense verb to the present, making the verb tense inconsistent. Choice **b** changes *before* to *preceding,* which is slightly pretentious and not as direct. Choice **c** puts parentheses around necessary information, so it is incorrect. Choice **e** is incorrect because the verb *have* must be deleted.

10. c. Commas are required in dates: Monday, July 28, at 10 A.M. Choice **a** is incorrect because the helping verb should indicate the future (*will*) rather than the present (*is*). Choice **b** is incorrect because *we'll* is a contraction of *we will*; this change would double the subject (*committee* and *we*) and shift the pronoun; also, an *and* would be required between the two subjects. Choice **d** is incorrect because the date should be set off by commas, not parentheses; it is not irrelevant or unimportant, since members need to know the date of the next meeting. Choice **e** is incorrect because the comma error needs to be corrected.

11. d. Colons are used to introduce lists, quotations, and explanations. In this sentence, *the ancient art of yoga* "explains" what one of the *world's oldest practices* is. Choice **a** is incorrect because the apostrophe is necessary to show possession (a fad belonging to today). Choice **b** is incorrect because the superlative of one-syllable words is formed by adding -*est*. Choice **c** is incorrect because commas should not be placed between subjects and verbs. Choice **e** is incorrect because the colon needs to be inserted.

12. c. This is the most concise and correct choice. The phrase should have a verb, because the action is what must be performed correctly, so choice **a** is incorrect. Choice **b** is incorrect because it is wordy and awkward. Choice **d** is incorrect because *being* is unnecessary and ungrammatical. Choice **e** is awkward and wordy, adding the pronoun *it* to confuse the sentence.

13. b. *Pose* is the subject, so the verb must be *requires* to agree. Choice **c** is incorrect because it adds a second subject, *it.* Choice **d** has the correct form of the verb, but it disrupts the parallel structure of the sentence; *lengthen* would also have to be changed to *lengthening.* Choice **e** is incorrect because it creates a sentence fragment. Choice **e** is a prepositional phrase, and this change would take away the main verb of the sentence.

14. c. Sentence 6 introduces the idea of how yoga poses stretch and strengthen muscles. It is therefore best placed at the beginning of paragraph B before sentence 4, which provides a specific example of a pose that stretches and strengthens muscles. Removing the sentence (choice **a**) would remove the transition needed between paragraphs A and B and would make sentence 4, which has the phrase *for example,* awkward. Choice **b** is incorrect because sentence 6 introduces the ideas discussed in paragraph B, not paragraph A. Choice **d** is incorrect because the sentence states the general idea that sentence 4 provides a specific example of; therefore, it must precede sentence 4. Choice **e** is incorrect because sentence 7 is in paragraph C, which discusses a different idea (the mental aspect of yoga).

15. d. The sentence requires the simple present tense *comes,* not the present participle *are coming.* Choice **a** is incorrect because it is *breathing* that is required, not simply *breath.* Choice **b** is incorrect because the sentence is a complex sentence with two independent clauses connected with the coordinating conjunction *and*; because the sentences are long, they should have a comma between them. Choice **c** is incorrect because *benefit* needs to be a noun with its adjective *full,* not a verb (*benefiting*) with an adverb (*fully*). Choice **e** is incorrect because the verb error needs to be addressed.

16. e. Sentence 10 is an incomplete thought (sentence fragment) and must be connected to sentence 9, so choice **a** is incorrect. A semicolon can only be placed between two independent clauses (complete thoughts), so choice **b** is incorrect. Choice **c** is incorrect because *so* and *thereby* together creates an awkward transition between sentences, and *so* does not convey the correct relationship between sentences. Choice **d** is incorrect because sentence 10 is "unnecessary" information and should be set off by commas. Choice **e** is correct because the sentence fragment is corrected.

17. b. *You're* is a contraction of *you are*; the sentence requires the possessive *your*. *Both* could be deleted, but keeping it in the sentence is not an error, so choice **a** is incorrect. Choice **c** is incorrect because *through your body* is a prepositional phrase necessary for the meaning of the sentence, so it should not be set off by commas. Choice **d** creates an awkward word order by moving *breath* farther away from *circulation,* so it is incorrect. Choice **e** is incorrect because *you're* must be corrected.

18. c. This is the most concise and correct choice. Choice **a** contains an awkward and wordy phrase: *the practice of which I have been doing.* Choice **b** is also awkward and wordy, repeating *practice* and using an unnecessary *of* before *which.* Choice **d** is grammatically correct but turns the idea order around and is also wordy with the repetition of *practice.* Choice **e** is incorrect because it is a run-on sentence; *because* makes the first clause dependent.

19. e. Sentence 14 offers a contrast to the information in sentence 13, so *however* is the best transition between the sentences. Choice **a** is incorrect because *since* is a subordinating conjunction and makes sentence 14 a fragment. Choice **b** is incorrect because it does not fit the context of the paragraph or passage. Choice **c** is incorrect for the same reason. Choice **d** is incorrect because sentence 14 does not offer an idea similar to the one in sentence 13.

20. d. Choice **d** gives the sentence parallel structure; the other items in the list follow the adjective, noun pattern of the knotted belly. Choices **a**, **b**, **c**, and **e** are all incorrect because they do not correct the lack of parallel structure.

21. b. The words *face-to-face* work together as one adjective to describe a kind of communication, so they must be hyphenated. Choice **a** is incorrect because no comma is necessary between *depends* and *upon.* Choice **c** is incorrect because *listen* is a verb, and *well* modifies verbs; *good* should only modify a noun. Choice **d** is incorrect because *ability* should be followed by an infinitive. Choice **e** is incorrect because the hyphens must be added to the sentence.

22. b. This is the most concise choice; it is also the only one that creates parallel structure by using the grammatical pattern established in sentence 5. Choice **c** changes the meaning; it does not list daydreaming as a separate item to be avoided but rather something that you might do while looking at your watch. It also does not establish parallel structure. Choices **d** and **e** are incorrect.

23. b. This revision creates a smooth transition between paragraphs B and C by clearly introducing the second step. Choice **a** is incorrect because sentence 7 is the topic sentence of paragraph C and should be placed before the specific examples of active listening. Choice **c** is incorrect because none of the other paragraphs use numbers for the steps. Choice **d** is incorrect because changing the *you*'s to *we*'s would make the point of view inconsistent throughout the passage. Choice **e** is also incorrect because the topic sentence is necessary and should not be deleted.

24. d. Choice **a** is a run-on sentence. Choice **b** is awkward because it does not have parallel structure (*nodding and shaking* vs. *laugh, smile, and make*). Choice **c** creates a sentence fragment. Choice **d** effectively separates the two complete thoughts and adds a transition that clearly shows the relationship between the two sentences. Choice **e** is incorrect for the same reason as choice **b**.

25. a. The infinitive is formed by using *to + the base form of the verb,* so *be shown* should be changed to *show.* Choice **b** is incorrect because the participle form *paying* should follow the helping verb *are.* Choice **c** is incorrect because the words *in the eye* are not working together as one modifier or noun, so they should not be hyphenated. Choice **d** would create a sentence fragment, so it is incorrect. Choice **e** is incorrect because the verb error must be corrected.

26. c. Commas should be inserted after the items in a list. Choice **a** is incorrect because the responses should have quotation marks around them. Choice **b** is incorrect because it would create a sentence fragment. Choice **d** is incorrect because it would delete one of the examples. Choice **e** is incorrect because commas need to be added to the sentence.

27. d. The sentence needs to begin with a command to create parallel structure (match the grammatical pattern of the other sentences in the paragraph) and to make the sentence a complete thought (as it stands, the sentence is a fragment). Choice **a** is incorrect because an infinitive should follow *hear*. Choice **b** is incorrect because it changes the meaning of the sentence and makes the idea illogical. Choice **c** is incorrect because *understanding* cannot follow *do*. Choice **e** is incorrect because the sentence fragment must be corrected.

28. e. This choice is concise and fits the grammatical pattern of the other two sentences that state the steps, creating parallel structure. Choice **a** is wordy and does not continue the parallel structure of steps one and two. Choice **b** is a sentence fragment. Choice **c** is wordy and uses the passive voice; it also does not continue the parallel structure. Choice **d** is the most concise, but it does not offer the transitional phrase *the third step*.

29. c. Semicolons can be used between two independent clauses but not between an independent and dependent clause. *If you are going to listen to someone* is a dependent clause and should be followed by a comma. Choice **a** creates a sentence fragment. Choice **b** is grammatically correct, but *if* is necessary for the sentence to be logical (to show the relationship between the two clauses). Choice **d** is incorrect because there would still be an incomplete thought on one side of the semicolon. Choice **e** is incorrect because the semicolon must be replaced by a comma.

30. c. This choice separates a specific step from a summary of the whole passage and adds a transitional phrase to introduce the concluding idea. Choice **a** is incorrect because this sentence includes a conclusion, so it does not belong at the beginning of the paragraph. Choice **b** is incorrect because it deletes the concluding idea. Choice **d** is incorrect because it is repetitive. Choice **e** is incorrect because it is wordy and slightly awkward.

31. b. Shewsbury is a town in England. The rules specify to use a comma to set off all geographical names and addresses (except the street number and name).

32. a. This sentence is correct as is. Inserting the contraction *who's* (*who is*) would introduce a mistake; Darwin is not a famous theory. Choice **c** is incorrect; the majority of the time you use *affect* with an *a* as a verb and *effect* with an *e* as a noun. *Affect* means "to influence" or "to act in a way that you don't feel." *Effect* has a lot of subtle meanings as a noun, but the meaning "a result" seems to be at the core of all the definitions. Changing *it* to *he* is an error (choice **d**); *it* is referring to a theory, which should not have a personal pronoun. Choice **e** is an improper use of commas.

33. b. This sentence requires an infinitive, which is formed with *to* plus the root of a verb. Choices **a**, moving the sentence, and **e**, deleting the sentence would not benefit the support in this passage, nor the organization structure. Choice **c** is incorrect; *of* is the correct preposition to use, not *from*. Changing *upon* for *because*, is not a logical choice; this word would be incorrect word usage.

34. e. This choice rewrites this sentence to avoid the passive voice. All the other choices are grammatically incorrect or wordy.

35. c. Titles of books should be in italics. Choices **a** and **b** would insert errors into this sentence. Choice **d** would be accurate if this was a short story, not a book.

36. b. This transition shows the contrast between how many awards are given and how many awards most people are interested in. *However* is the best transition word to show the relationship between these two sentences. In choice **a**, the transition *Additionally* implies that this sentences contains more similar information. In choice **c**, while *On the other hand* is a transition that shows two different things, it also implies that the two things are equal and opposite. Choices **d** and **e** are transition words, which show that one sentence follows logically from the sentence before. This is not the case with sentence 12, which shows something that goes against the previous sentence.

37. d. This new sentence uses a comma and the word *as* to show how the two phrases are now connected into one sentence. This sentence correctly uses a subordinate phrase and creates a new sentence, which is grammatically correct and contains all of the information from the two original sentences.

38. a. This sentence combines the two original sentences through the use of the preposition *which*. This links the sentences together in a new, grammatically correct sentence. Choice **b** uses only a comma to connect the two sentences. Because the second half of the new sentence is not a subordinate phrase or clause, the sentence is now a run-on sentence and grammatically incorrect. Choices **c**, **d**, and **e** are grammatically correct, but delete too many of the words of the original sentences. Therefore, they do not fully contain the ideas of both sentences.

39. a. This sentence is best written as is. Choice **b** personifies *movies* and claims that they can put on clothes, which is obviously not true. Choice **c** is not grammatically incorrect; however, it draws special, unnecessary attention to *actresses* away from their male counterparts. Choices **d** and **e** demonstrate an improper use of commas.

40. b. This sentence would provide an interesting detail to support sentence 9 and enhance paragraph B. Choice **a** is a vague sentence. Choices **c**, **d**, and **e** would all support paragraph C, not paragraph B.

41. c. By using the transition *although* to introduce the first idea, the writer signals that despite the inconvenience, the benefit of wearing the mask is valuable. This choice also eliminates the choppiness of the last two sentences. Choice **a** is incorrect because using commas is not the correct way to combine complete sentences. The result is an ungrammatical run-on sentence. Choice **b** is incorrect because *however* and *though* cannot be used together. The result does not make sense. Choices **d** and **e** do nothing to improve the short, choppy nature of the sentences. The result in choice **e** also does not make sense.

42. a. This choice effectively combines the three closely related, shorter sentences into one more complex sentence by eliminating redundant subjects. Choice **b** is incorrect because merely inserting a comma between two complete sentences is not sufficient to grammatically separate them; the result is a run-on sentence. Choice **c** is incorrect because it erroneously uses the transition *however*, which does not fit when the context of the sentence is considered. Choice **d** is incorrect because the use of a semicolon requires that the clause that follows it be an independent clause (a complete sentence) and the writer has eliminated the subject in the second half of the sentence. Choice **e** is not an effective combination; separating the groups affected by OSA creates a convoluted sentence.

43. c. This sentence details the specific way that the mask is used to eliminate OSA. Choice **a** is too general and does not provide an adequate description of how the mask works. Similarly, choice **b** does nothing to inform the reader about how the mask operates. Choice **d** comments on the great effectiveness of the mask, but also does not provide concrete details of how it works. Choice **e** would better serve paragraph A or B.

44. e. Because heart attacks, strokes, and high blood pressure are all ailments, or things that cause illness, this is the most precise word choice. Choices **a** and **b** are not the best choice because they join the vague *serious stuff* with specific ailments. Choice **c** is not the best choice because the word *problems* is found earlier in the sentence. It would be better to vary that word to differentiate the latter, health-related problems from the former (poor grades, job loss, and car accidents). Choice **d** is incorrect because a dilemma is a puzzling problem that can be solved by arriving at a solution. The health-related problems cannot be solved this way.

45. a. This sentence is best as written. Choice **b** creates a sentence fragment. In choice **c**, *however*, loses the intended meaning of this sentence. Choice **d** introduces a passive clause (*snoring creates . . .*). Choice **e** is inaccurate. "Snoring Disease" is not called the disorder.

46. c. This choice best combines the short, rather redundant sentences. Choice **a** is incorrect because the use of *named that way* is awkward. Choice **b** is incorrect because the phrase *were honored by the Olympics* at the end of the sentence is awkward and detracts from the flow of the writing. Choice **d** is incorrect because the word order (syntax) is poor, which detracts from the sentence. In addition, the repetition of the idea *in their honor* is redundant. Choice **e** loses the meaning of the sentence; it implies that the Olympics were named after the plains of Olympia and other ancient Gods, which is not true.

47. a. Because the third paragraph is about truce, it is wise to include an explanation of how the concept operated at the Olympics. This sentence is the most specific, clear explanation of how this concept operated. Choice **b** is incorrect because *it was good* is too general to lend solid support. Choice **c** is incorrect because it makes a point that does not really make sense in light of the rest of the paragraph. Choice **d** is wordy and confusing. Choice **e** would be better placed in paragraph B.

48. c. This choice correctly subordinates the phrase *a famous Greek philosopher* while preserving the focus, which is that he won the pankration event twice. Choice **a** is incorrect because the writer erroneously repeats the subject *he*. Choice **b** is incorrect because it incorrectly subordinates the idea of *a famous Greek philosopher* by beginning the clause with *was*. Choice **d** is incorrect because the word order is awkward, placing the subject at the end of the sentence. Choice **e** has an erroneous list—Plato *was* a philosopher and two-time winner, but *not* an event.

49. c. *Achievements* connotes the victories but also the overall importance of their athletic pursuits. Choice **b** is incorrect because it is not closely related to the underlined word at all and would totally change the meaning of the sentence. Choice **d** is incorrect because it does not make sense; *mortality* means subject to death. Choice **e** is incorrect because *winningness* is not a word. It is an attempt to create a noun that doesn't exist.

50. d. This transition signals that after a time (the passage states 1,200 years) the games were stopped by Emperor Theodosius. Choices **a** and **e** are incorrect, because *in addition* and *also* are used to introduce another idea or example. Choice **b** is incorrect because it would cause the second sentence to be ungrammatical. Choice **c** is incorrect because it is clear from the passage that these two events did not occur simultaneously, which is what *meanwhile* would demand.

Part II

For the essay prompt, you will find a sample score 6, 4, and 1 essay.

Sample Score 6 Essay

When I was young, I was shy—really shy. There was nothing more terrifying to me than having to speak in front of others. In school, I never raised my hand, even though I usually knew the right answer. I was an excellent speller, but during spelling bees, I would be so nervous when my name was called that I couldn't even think about the word I was supposed to spell. I was so shy that I was even nervous during roll call, dreading the moment when the teacher called my name and I had to say "Here."

My teachers knew I was painfully shy, and they usually avoided calling on me in class. When they did, I would blush with embarrassment and whisper the answer. They would have to ask me to repeat myself, which would only make me even more embarrassed.

I conquered this shyness, though, in sixth grade, thanks to my big sister and an assignment from Mr. Attenborough's social studies class. Our project was to research a historical figure, dress up as that figure, and give a speech about that person's life to the class. I chose William Shakespeare as my subject. My oldest sister was acting in Romeo and Juliet for her college theater club, and she couldn't stop talking about Shakespeare and reciting lines from the play. The more I heard about him, and the more I read about him, the more fascinated I became, both with his life and times and with the whole phenomenon of the stage. I became increasingly interested in the theater, and I began reading parts of plays out loud in front of the mirror and with my sister. I didn't always understand what I was saying, but that didn't matter. What mattered was that I realized I could step into a role and pretend to be someone else, and I didn't have to be afraid.

When it was time for my presentation, I wore a puffy shirt, a vest, tight pants, and a fake moustache. I pretended I was Shakespeare, and for the first time in front of my classmates, I spoke loudly and clearly. I was no longer terrified. In fact, I was happy.

Sample Score 4 Essay

I was always a shy kid. In school I was afraid of everything, I never raised my hand to answer questions in case I was wrong. I was so shy it hurt. I'm not so shy anymore, thanks to a project in sixth grade.

I had to research someone famous and pretend to be that person for a day, including giving a speech about my life. Because my sister was practicing for her play in "Romeo and Juliet," she was always talking about Shakespear. I started learning about him and it was really interesting. So, that's who I dressed

up as. The best thing was that I started reading from his plays, and practicing in front of a mirror. We (my sister and me) together did a lot of acting. It was really fun to pretend to be someone else, and I wasn't shy when I did it. It was all of a sudden easy for me to talk in front of others.

When I did my presentation, I wasn't even a little bit afraid. Thanks to this project, I wasn't so shy anymore, and it felt wonderful.

Sample Score 1 Essay

There are many things we afraid off, like the darkness or monsters. I always fearing talking in front of others, being I was so shy all the time. It was always the hard thing for me.

The problem is it is not good for being so shy. I feel often angry at myself for it, but what to do? Learning about Shakespeer is one thing to do. It fixed me for being afraid. Who is not so shy any more? I am so glad.

48 ▶ Practice Exam 1, GED Language Arts, Reading

Directions: Read each passage carefully and answer the multiple-choice questions that follow. Choose the one best answer to each question.

Questions 1–5 refer to the following passage.

What Has Happened to Gregor?

(1) As Gregor Samsa awoke one morning from uneasy dreams he found himself transformed in his bed into a gigantic insect. He was lying on his hard, as it were armor-plated, back and when he lifted his head a little he could see his domelike brown belly divided into stiff arched segments on top of which the bed quilt could hardly keep in position and was about to slide off completely. His numerous legs,

(5) which were pitifully thin compared to the rest of his bulk, waved helplessly before his eyes.
What has happened to me? he thought. It was no dream. His room, a regular human bedroom, only rather too small, lay quiet between the four familiar walls. Above the table on which a collection of cloth samples was unpacked and spread out—Samsa was a commercial traveler—hung the picture which he had recently cut out of an illustrated magazine and put into a pretty gilt frame. It showed a lady, with a fur cap on and a

(10) fur stole, sitting upright and holding out to the spectator a huge fur muff into which the whole of her fore-arm had vanished!
[. . . .]

He slid down again into his former position.
This getting up early, he thought, makes one
(15) quite stupid. A man needs his sleep. Other commercials live like harem women. For instance,
when I come back to the *hotel in the morning to
write* up the orders I've got, these others are only
sitting down to breakfast. Let me just try that
(20) with my chief; I'd be sacked on the spot. Anyhow, that might be quite a good thing for me,
who can tell? If I didn't have to hold my hand
because of my parents I'd have given notice long
ago, I'd have gone to the chief and told him
(25) exactly what I think of him. That would knock
him endways from his desk! It's a queer way of
doing, too, this sitting on high at a desk and talking down to employees, especially when they
have to come quite near because the chief is hard
(30) of hearing. Well, there's still hope; once I've
saved enough money to pay back my parents'
debts to him—that should take another five or
six years—I'll do it without fail. I'll cut myself
completely loose then. For the moment, though,
(35) I'd better get up, since my train goes at five.
                    —Franz Kafka, from *The Metamorphosis* (1912)

1. When Gregor Samsa wakes up, he realizes that he
  a. has been having a nightmare.
  b. is late for work.
  c. has turned into a giant bug.
  d. dislikes his job.
  e. needs to make a change in his life.

2. Which of the following best describes Gregor's job?
  a. magician
  b. traveling clothing salesman
  c. advertisement copywriter
  d. clothing designer
  e. magazine editor

3. Why must Gregor keep his current job for several more years?
  a. His parents owe his boss money.
  b. Gregor is an apprentice and must complete his program.
  c. Gregor wants to take over the chief's job.
  d. His parents own the company he works for.
  e. He needs to earn enough money to buy a bigger house for his family.

4. Based on the passage, which is the most logical conclusion to draw about Gregor's personality?
  a. Gregor is lazy and stupid.
  b. Gregor is a very successful salesman.
  c. Gregor resents being told what to do by people in authority.
  d. Gregor is hardworking and reliable.
  e. Gregor is very close to his family.

5. In line 35, Gregor tells himself, "I'd better get up, since my train goes at five." This suggests that
  a. Gregor has woken up as a bug before and is used to it.
  b. the other characters in the story are also bugs.
  c. Gregor is still dreaming.
  d. Gregor is going to be late.
  e. Gregor does not yet realize how serious his condition is.

Questions 6–10 refer to the following poem.

What Did the Speaker Learn from Alfonso?

Alfonso
(1) I am not the first poet born to my family.
We have painters and singers, actors and
    carpenters.

I inherited my trade from my zio, Alfonso.
Zio maybe was the tallest man
(5) in the village, he certainly was
the widest. He lost
his voice to cigarettes before I was born, but still

he roared
with his hands, his eyes,
(10) with his brow, and his deafening smile.

He worked the sea with my nonno
fishing in silence among the grottoes
so my father could learn to write and read
and not speak like the guaglione,
(15) filled with curses and empty pockets.

He would watch me write with wonder,
I could hear him on the couch, he looked at
the lines over my shoulder, tried to teach himself to
        read

late in the soft Adriatic darkness.
(20)   Wine-stained pages gave him away.

But I learned to write from Zio—
He didn't need words, still he taught me the language
of silence, the way

the sun can describe a shadow, a
(25)   gesture can paint a moment,
a scent could fill an entire village with words and
color and sound,

a perfect little grape tomato can be the most
beautiful thing in the world, seen through the
(30)   right eyes.

—Marco A. Annunziata,
Reprinted by permission of the author (2008)

6. In line 3, the speaker says, "I inherited my trade from my zio, Alfonso." What trade did the speaker inherit?
   a. painting
   b. fishing
   c. writing poetry
   d. singing
   e. carpentry

7. Which word best describes the speaker's feelings toward Alfonso?
   a. shame
   b. admiration
   c. frustration
   d. superiority
   e. anger

8. Which of the following statements about Alfonso is TRUE?
   a. He was a writer.
   b. He could not speak with his voice.
   c. He could speak many languages.
   d. He was a farmer.
   e. He was a painter.

9. In lines 8–10, the speaker says that Alfonso "roared / with his hands, his eyes, / with his brow, and his deafening smile." These lines suggest that Alfonso
   a. was a very loud person.
   b. was always angry.
   c. was like a lion.
   d. was always yelling.
   e. was very expressive with his body.

10. Which of the following best sums up what the speaker has learned from Alfonso?
   a. how to appreciate the beauty of the world
   b. how to listen to others
   c. how to appreciate his family
   d. how to understand himself
   e. how to read poetry

Questions 11–15 refer to the following passage.

How Are Robots Different from Humans?

[Helena is talking to Domain, the general manager of Rossum's Universal Robots factory.]

(1)   DOMAIN: Well, anyone who's looked into anatomy will have seen at once that man is too complicated, and that a good engineer could make him more simply. So young Rossum
(5)   began to overhaul anatomy and tried to see what could be left out or simplified. In short— but this isn't boring you, Miss Glory?

HELENA: No; on the contrary, it's awfully interesting.

(10)   DOMAIN: So young Rossum said to himself: A man is something that, for instance, feels happy, plays the fiddle, likes going for walks, and, in fact, wants to do a whole lot of things that are really unnecessary.

(15)   HELENA: Oh!

DOMAIN: Wait a bit. That are unnecessary when he's wanted, let us say, to weave or to count. Do you play the fiddle?

HELENA: No.

(20) DOMAIN: That's a pity. But a working machine must not want to play the fiddle, must not feel happy, must not do a whole lot of other things. A petrol motor must not have tassels or ornaments, Miss Glory. And to manufacture artificial
(25) workers is the same thing as to manufacture motors. The process must be of the simplest, and the product of the best from a practical point of view. What sort of worker do you think is the best from a practical point of view?

(30) HELENA: The best? Perhaps the one who is most honest and hard-working.

DOMAIN: No, the cheapest. The one whose needs are the smallest. Young Rossum invented a worker with the minimum amount of require-
(35) ments. He had to simplify him. He rejected everything that did not contribute directly to the progress of work. In this way he rejected everything that made man more expensive. In fact, he rejected man and made the Robot. My
(40) dear Miss Glory, the Robots are not people. Mechanically they are more perfect than we are, they have an enormously developed intelligence, but they have no soul. Have you ever seen what a Robot looks like inside?

(45) HELENA: Good gracious, no!

DOMAIN: Very neat, very simple. Really a beautiful piece of work. Not much in it, but everything in flawless order. The product of an engineer is technically at a higher pitch of per-
(50) fection than a product of nature.

HELENA: Man is supposed to be the product of nature.

DOMAIN: So much the worse.

—Karel Čapek,
from *R.U.R.* (1923, translated by P. Selver)

11. According to the passage, why are robots better workers than humans?
   a. Robots have a very simple anatomy.
   b. Robots are more intelligent.
   c. Robots are more honest and hardworking.
   d. Robots do not have a soul.
   e. Robots want things that are unnecessary.

12. Rossum created robots because
   a. humans are complicated and inefficient.
   b. humans are not honest enough.
   c. robots are always happy.
   d. he wanted to see if he could.
   e. there weren't enough people to do the work.

13. Which of the following best expresses Rossum's view of nature?
   a. Nature is beautiful.
   b. It is dangerous to try to improve upon nature.
   c. Nature is imperfect and unnecessarily complicated.
   d. Mother Nature is the greatest engineer of all.
   e. Machines are also a part of nature.

14. Based on the passage, Rossum is most likely
   a. a robot.
   b. a part-time inventor.
   c. a retired doctor.
   d. a foreman in the factory.
   e. a very intelligent engineer.

15. Based on the passage, we can tell that Domain
   a. admires Rossum's work.
   b. fears Rossum will take over the world.
   c. is romantically interested in Helena.
   d. wants to replace the robots with human workers.
   e. is jealous of Rossum.

Questions 16–19 refer to the following passage.

What's Wrong with Commercial Television?

(1) Kids who watch much commercial television ought to develop into whizzes at the dialect; you have to keep so much in your mind at once because a series of artificially short attention

(5) spans has been created. But this in itself means that the experience of watching the commercial channels is a more informal one, curiously more "homely" than watching BBC [British Broad-casting Corporation].

(10) This is because the commercial breaks are constant reminders that the medium itself is artificial, isn't, in fact, "real," even if the gesticu-lating heads, unlike the giants of the movie screen, are life-size. There is a kind of built-in

(15) alienation effect. Everything you see is false, as Tristan Tzara gnomically opined. And the young lady in the St. Bruno tobacco ads who currently concludes her spiel by stating categorically: "And if you believe that, you'll believe anything," is

(20) saying no more than the truth. The long-term effect of habitually watching commercial televi-sion is probably an erosion of trust in the televi-sion medium itself.

 Since joy is the message of all commercials, it

(25) is as well they breed skepticism. Every story has a happy ending, gratification is guaranteed by the conventions of the commercial form, which contributes no end to the pervasive unreality of it all. Indeed, it is the chronic bliss of everybody

(30) in the commercials that creates their final divorce from effective life as we know it. Grumpy mum, frowning dad, are soon all smiles again after the ingestion of some pill or potion; minimal concessions are made to mild frustra-

(35) tion (as they are, occasionally, to lust), but none at all to despair or consummation. In fact, if the form is reminiscent of the limerick and the presentation of the music-hall, the overall mood—in its absolute and unruffled

(40) decorum—is that of the uplifting fables in the Sunday school picture books of my childhood.

 —Angela Carter, from *Shaking a Leg* (1997)

16. According to the author, what is the main differ-ence between commercial channels and public tel-evision stations like the BBC?
   a. Commercial television is very artificial.
   b. Public television is more informal and uplifting.
   c. Commercial television teaches viewers not to believe what they see on television.
   d. Commercial television is more like the movies than public television.
   e. Commercial television portrays people in a more realistic manner.

17. Which of the following would the author most likely recommend?
   a. Don't watch any television at all; read instead.
   b. Watch only the BBC.
   c. Watch only commercial television.
   d. Watch what you like, but don't believe what commercials claim.
   e. Watch what you like, but don't watch more than an hour a day.

18. According to the author, what is the main thing that makes commercials unrealistic?
   a. Everyone in commercials always ends up happy.
   b. The background music is distracting.
   c. Commercials are so short.
   d. The people in commercials are always sick.
   e. The claims commercials make are unrealistic.

19. According to the author, what might happen as a result of watching a lot of commercial television?
   a. Viewers will become zombie-like.
   b. Viewers will increasingly distrust the messages they see and hear on television.
   c. Viewers will become frustrated with commercials and buy cable.
   d. Viewers will choose to watch more movies at the theater.
   e. Viewers will stop watching television altogether.

Questions 20–24 refer to the following passage.

What Happened When he Came to America?

(1) My parents lost friends, lost family ties and patterns of mutual assistance, lost rituals and habits and favorite foods, lost any link to an ongoing social milieu, lost a good part of the
(5) sense they had of themselves. We lost a house, several towns, various landscapes. We lost documents and pictures and heirlooms, as well as most of our breakable belongings, smashed in the nine packing cases that we took with us to
(10) America. We lost connection to a thing larger than ourselves, and as a family failed to make any significant new connection in exchange, so that we were left aground on a sandbar barely big enough for our feet. I lost friends and rela-
(15) tives and stories and familiar comforts and a sense of continuity between home and outside and any sense that I was normal. I lost half a language through want of use and eventually, in my late teens, even lost French as the language
(20) of my internal monologue. And I lost a whole network of routes through life that I had just barely glimpsed.

Hastening on toward some idea of a future, I only half-realized these losses, and when I did
(25) realize I didn't disapprove, and sometimes I actively colluded. At some point, though, I was bound to notice that there was a gulf inside me, with a blanketed form on the other side that hadn't been uncovered in decades. My project of
(30) self-invention had been successful, so much so that I had become a sort of hydroponic vegetable, growing soil-free. But I had been formed in another world; everything in me that was essential was owed to immersion in that place,
(35) and that time, that I had so effectively renounced. [. . . .]

Like it or not, each of us is made, less by blood or genes than by a process that is largely accidental, the impact of things seen and heard
(40) and smelled and tasted and endured in those few years before our clay hardens. Offhand remarks, things glimpsed in passing, jokes and commonplaces, shop displays and climate and flickering light and textures of walls are all

(45) consumed by us and become part of our fiber, just as much as the more obvious effects of upbringing and socialization and intimacy and learning. Every human being is an archeological site.

—Luc Sante, from *The Factory of Facts* (1998)

20. The narrator came to the United States when he was
   a. an infant.
   b. a toddler.
   c. in his early teens.
   d. in his late teens.
   e. a young adult.

21. In the first paragraph, the narrator lists more than a dozen things that he and his family lost when they immigrated to the United States. He does this in order to
   a. convince others not to immigrate.
   b. show how careless his family was when packing.
   c. show how much he missed his homeland.
   d. show how many intangible and important things were left behind.
   e. prove that you are never too old to change.

22. According to the narrator, our personalities are formed mostly by
   a. our genes.
   b. our education.
   c. our environment.
   d. our parents and caregivers.
   e. our peers.

23. When the narrator came to the United States, he
   a. embraced American culture.
   b. rejected his roots.
   c. made sure to keep his heritage alive.
   d. became withdrawn.
   e. became very possessive about things he owned.

24. In the last sentence of the passage, the author writes that "Every human being is an archeological site." What does he mean by this?

   a. The environment that formed us is a permanent, if buried, part of us.

   b. We must dig deep within ourselves to discover our past.

   c. We all have a piece of our past that we would prefer to keep buried.

   d. Only archaeologists understand the impact of our environment.

   e. The past is always with us, no matter where we go.

Questions 25–27 refer to the following passage.

What Is the Work-Study Program?

(1) **Overview of the Work-Study Program**

The Federal Work-Study (FWS) Program is a student employment program subsidized by the federal government and designed to help students finance their

(5) post-secondary education. The program provides funds to colleges, universities, and affiliated organizations which then provide employment to work-study students. Students receive their work-study financial awards in the form of paychecks from their

(10) work-study positions.

Applying for Work-Study

Both undergraduate and graduate students are eligible to apply. Work-Study grants are awarded based upon demonstrated financial need. To apply,

(15) students must complete the Free Application for Federal Student Aid. This application must be submitted each year Work-Study employment is desired.

What Are the Advantages of Work-Study?

A work-study job is essentially just like any other

(20) job—you go to work, do your job, and get paid. But Work-Study positions have several distinct advantages over "regular" jobs:

   ■Students can work in an environment suited to their skills, preferences, and possible career goals.

(25)   ■Employers are committed to the students' education and will help students work around their class schedules.

   ■Work-study wages are not counted toward the next year's student contribution for financial aid.

(30) **What Types of Work-Study Jobs Are Available?**

The work-study positions at Madison Community College are as diverse as the functions of the college.

Work-study students are employed as clerical assistants, data entry clerks, computer technicians, labo-

(35) ratory monitors, research assistants, language tutors, and more.

In addition, Madison Community College has long-standing relationships with a number of employers and agencies that provide services

(40) for the community and have been approved to participate in the Federal Work-Study Program, including the Madison County Children's Museum, the Madison County Library, Children First Day Care, and Right Start Tutoring Agency.

(45) Students may be employed as museum guides, library aides, child caregivers, research assistants, tutors, and more.

25. Who is eligible for the Work-Study Program?

   a. first-year students only

   b. undergraduate students only

   c. graduate students only

   d. undergraduate and graduate students

   e. unemployed students only

26. According to the passage, what is one way Work-Study employers are different from "regular" employers?

   a. Work-Study employers offer higher wages.

   b. Students work fewer hours with Work-Study employers.

   c. Work-Study employers offer more flexible scheduling for students.

   d. Work-Study employers offer a wide range of positions.

   e. Students earn academic credit for positions with Work-Study employers.

27. Based on the information in the passage, you should apply for Work-Study if

   a. you live on campus.

   b. you can't get a "regular" job.

   c. you didn't get any scholarships.

   d. you need financial aid and are willing to work.

   e. you enjoy working with community service organizations.

Questions 28–31 refer to the following passage.

Why Are the Characters Arguing?

[Sophie, the narrator, is talking with Tante Atie. The first line is spoken by Tante Atie. "Tante" means "aunt."]

(1)   "Do you know why I always wished I could read?" Her teary eyes gazed directly into mine.

   "I don't know why." I tried to answer as politely as I could.

(5)   "It was always my dream to read," she said, "so I could read that old Bible under my pillow and find the answers to everything right there between those pages. What do you think that old Bible would have us do right now, about this moment?"

(10)   "I don't know," I said.

   "How can you not know?" she asked. "You try to tell me there is all wisdom in reading but at a time like this you disappoint me."

   "You lied!" I shouted.

(15)   She grabbed both my ears and twisted them until they burned.

   I stomped my feet and walked away. As I rushed to bed, I began to take off my clothes so quickly that I almost tore them off my body.

(20)   The smell of lemon perfume stung my nose as I pulled the sheet over my head.

   "I did not lie," she said, "I kept a secret, which is different. I wanted to tell you. I needed time to reconcile myself, to accept it. It was very sudden,

(25) just a cassette from Martine saying, 'I want my daughter,' and then as fast as you can put two fingers together to snap, she sends me a plane ticket with a date on it. I am not even certain that she is doing this properly. All she tells me is that she

(30) arranged it with a woman who works on the airplane."

   "Was I ever going to know?" I asked.

   "I was going to put you to sleep, put you in a suitcase, and send you to her. One day you would

(35) wake up there and you would feel like your whole life here with me was a dream." She tried to force out a laugh, but it didn't make it past her throat.

—Edwidge Danticat,
from *Breath, Eyes, Memory* (1998)

28. What is the relationship between the narrator and Tante Atie?
- **a.** They are sisters.
- **b.** They are friends.
- **c.** Tante Atie is the narrator's guardian.
- **d.** Tante Atie is the narrator's mother.
- **e.** Tante Atie is the narrator's teacher.

29. What is happening to the narrator?
- **a.** She just found out she must leave to live with her mother.
- **b.** She just found out she must leave to go to boarding school.
- **c.** She just found out Tante Atie is ill.
- **d.** She is being transferred to a new foster home.
- **e.** She is being punished.

30. Why is the narrator so upset?
- **a.** She misses her mother.
- **b.** She doesn't want to leave.
- **c.** She doesn't like Tante Atie.
- **d.** She is afraid of flying.
- **e.** She never learned to read.

31. How will Tante Atie feel when the narrator is gone?
- **a.** happy
- **b.** relieved
- **c.** angry
- **d.** sad
- **e.** afraid

Questions 32–35 refer to the following passage.

What Is the Author Asking For?

(1)   The President in Washington sends word that he wishes to buy our land. But how can you buy or sell the sky? The land? The idea is strange to us. If we do not own the freshness of the air and the

(5) sparkle of the water, how can you buy them?

   Every part of this earth is sacred to my people. Every shining pine needle, every sandy shore, every mist in dark woods, every meadow, every humming insect. All are holy in the memory and

(10) experience of my people.

   We know the sap which courses through the trees as we know the blood that courses through our veins. We are part of the earth and it is part of us. The perfumed flowers are our sisters. The bear,

(15) the deer, the great eagle, these are our brothers.
The rocky crests, the juices in the meadow, the
body heat of the pony, and man, all belong to the
same family.

The shining water that moves in the streams
(20) and rivers is not just water, but the blood of our
ancestors. If we sell you our land, you must
remember that it is sacred. Each ghostly reflection
in the clear water of the lakes tells of events and
memories in the life of my people. The water's
(25) murmur is the voice of my father's father.

The rivers are our brothers. They quench our
thirst. They carry out canoes and feed our children. So you must give to the rivers the kindness
you would give any brother.
(30)   If we sell you our land, remember that the air
is precious to us, that the air shares its spirit with
all the life it supports. The wind that gave our
grandfather his first breath also receives his last
sigh. The wind also gives our children the spirit of
(35) life. So, if we sell you our land, you must keep it
apart and sacred, as a place where man can go to
taste the wind that is sweetened by the meadow
flowers.

Will you teach your children what we have
(40) taught our children? That the earth is our mother?
What befalls the earth, befalls all sons of the earth.

This we know: The earth does not belong to
man, man belongs to the earth. All things are connected like the blood which unites us all.

—Chief Seattle, from
"This We Know" (1854)

32. According to the author, what sort of relationship
do his people have with the land?
   a. They own it and do whatever they want
   with it.
   b. They respect it and do not understand how
   anyone can own it.
   c. They are indifferent and can live anywhere.
   d. They live there only because they have to and
   would be glad to sell it.
   e. They believe it is haunted and full of spirits
   and ghosts.

33. The intended audience of this essay is most
likely
   a. President George Washington only.
   b. American Indians only.
   c. all new Americans.
   d. all Americans, native and new.
   e. Chief Seattle himself.

34. What is the author's main goal in this essay?
   a. to convince the American government not to
   buy the land
   b. to convince American Indians to fight the
   new Americans
   c. to persuade Americans that the land is not
   worth buying
   d. to convince the new Americans that the land
   is sacred
   e. to show how much power he has over his
   people

35. Former President Ronald Reagan is recorded as
having said, "If you've seen one tree, you've seen
them all." How does this idea compare with the
ideas of Chief Seattle?
   a. They express essentially the same attitude
   toward the land.
   b. They express essentially opposite attitudes
   toward the land.
   c. Reagan seems to care more about the land
   than Chief Seattle.
   d. We cannot compare them, because Chief
   Seattle does not talk about trees.
   e. Chief Seattle would agree that trees are all
   alike, but he would not want them cut down.

Questions 36–40 refer to the following passage.

What Has Mrs. Mallard Realized?
[Mrs. Mallard, having just learned of the death of
her husband, has locked herself in a room.]

(1)   She sat with her head thrown back upon the cush-
ion of the chair, quite motionless, except when a
sob came up into her throat and shook her, as a
child who has cried itself to sleep continues to sob
(5)   in its dreams.

She was young, with a fair, calm face, whose lines bespoke repression and even a certain strength. But now there was a dull stare in her eyes, whose gaze was fixed away off yonder on one (10) of those patches of blue sky. It was not a glance of reflection, but rather indicated a suspension of intelligent thought.

There was something coming to her and she was waiting for it, fearfully. What was it? She did (15) not know; it was too subtle and elusive to name. But she felt it, creeping out of the sky, reaching toward her through the sounds, the scents, the color that filled the air.

Now her bosom rose and fell tumultuously. She (20) was beginning to recognize this thing that was approaching to possess her, and she was striving to beat it back with her will—as powerless as her two white slender hands would have been.

When she abandoned herself, a little whispered (25) word escaped her slightly parted lips. She said it over and over under her breath: "free, free, free!" The vacant stare and the look of terror that had followed it went from her eyes. They stayed keen and bright. Her pulses beat fast, and the coursing (30) blood warmed and relaxed every inch of her body.

She did not stop to ask if it were or were not a monstrous joy that held her. A clear and exalted perception enabled her to dismiss the suggestion as trivial.

(35) She knew that she would weep again when she saw the kind, tender hands folded in death; the face that had never looked save with love upon her, fixed and gray and dead. But she saw beyond that bitter moment a long procession of years to (40) come that would belong to her absolutely. And she opened and spread her arms out to them in welcome.

There would be no one to live for during those coming years; she would live for herself. There (45) would be no powerful will bending hers in that blind persistence with which men and women believe they have a right to impose a private will upon a fellow-creature. A kind intention or a cruel intention made the act seem no less a crime as she (50) looked upon it in that brief moment of illumination.

—Kate Chopin,
from "The Story of an Hour" (1894)

36. What is Mrs. Mallard doing at the beginning of the passage?
   a. comforting her child
   b. sleeping
   c. crying
   d. laughing
   e. feeling ill

37. Why does Mrs. Mallard stop crying and feel joy?
   a. She learns her husband is not dead after all.
   b. She realizes she will inherit a lot of money.
   c. She often has drastic mood swings.
   d. She realizes she can now live for herself and do what she wants.
   e. She can marry someone else now.

38. Mrs. Mallard repeats the word "free" several times. What is it that she will be free from?
   a. debt
   b. fear
   c. criticism from others
   d. having to do what someone else wants
   e. problems with family members who can't mind their own business

39. The last sentence of the passage states, "A kind intention or a cruel intention made the act seem no less a crime as she looked upon it in that brief moment of illumination." What does Mrs. Mallard believe is a crime?
   a. imposing your will on someone else
   b. getting married
   c. being happy when someone you love has died
   d. selfishly wanting to do everything your way
   e. welcoming death

40. Given the evidence in the passage, which most accurately describes Mrs. Mallard's feelings toward her husband?
   a. bitter hatred
   b. unyielding contempt
   c. deep love
   d. gentle resignation
   e. aggressive rebelliousness

▶ Answers

1. c. The first sentence states that when Gregor awoke, "he found himself transformed in his bed into a gigantic insect." The sentence clearly states that he "awoke," so he is not dreaming, and choice **a** is incorrect. The last sentence reveals that he has to catch a train at five, and he plans on getting up to catch that train, so he is not late, and choice **b** is incorrect. There is no evidence in the passage that Gregor dislikes his job (choice **d**). He does wish he could get more sleep and tell his boss what he thinks of him, but there's no evidence in the passage that Gregor realizes he needs to make a change in his life (choice **e**).

2. b. We learn that on Gregor's table, "a collection of cloth samples was unpacked and spread out" and that Gregor "was a commercial traveler." Thus, we can conclude that he is a traveling clothing salesman. There is no evidence that he is a magician (choice **a**), and though he has an advertisement hanging on his wall, it is just a decoration, not something from his work (choice **c**). Because the passage specifically states he is a commercial traveler, we can also eliminate choices **d** and **e**.

3. a. In lines 30–32, Gregor reveals that he must keep his job because his parents are indebted to his boss: "once I've saved enough money to pay back my parents' debts to him." There is no evidence that he is an apprentice (choice **b**); in fact, an apprentice is not likely to be traveling about on his own. He wants to tell his boss what he thinks of him and quit, not take his boss's job, so choice **c** is incorrect. The quote rules out his parents owning the company (choice **d**), and there is no evidence that he needs the money to buy a bigger house (choice **e**). The passage does mention that his room is small, but the only reason given for Gregor keeping his job is to pay off those debts.

4. d. Gregor clearly works hard—he comes to breakfast only after he's already gotten some orders (line 18), and he gets up early to travel to his destinations. He is also reliable; he plans on getting up and catching the train even though he is an insect. This evidence rules out choice **a**; he

is not lazy. While we learn that Gregor does get orders, we do not know the level of his success as a salesman, so choice **b** is incorrect. Gregor does resent his boss (see lines 20–34), but that could very well be personal, not a matter of general resentment of authority, so choice **c** is not the best answer. We do know that Gregor is working to pay off his parents' debts, but there is no indication in the passage of how close Gregor is to his family, so choice **e** is incorrect.

5. e. Gregor is so preoccupied with work and his routine that he seems to think he can just get up and go to work, even if he appears to be a bug. The tone and word choice in the opening sentence of the passage (which is also the opening sentence of this short story) suggest that this is the first time this happened to Gregor. He also asks, "What has happened to me?" If this had happened before, he would not likely ask that question, and his internal dialogue would be quite different. Thus, choice **a** is incorrect. There is no evidence in the story that the other characters are also bugs. The woman in the picture, at any rate, is a real woman, not a bug. Choice **b** is therefore incorrect. The first sentence clearly states that he awoke, so choice **c** is incorrect. Gregor says "I'd better get up, since my train goes at five," suggesting that he still has time to catch that 5:00 train. Choice **d** is therefore incorrect.

6. c. Line 1 states, "I am not the first poet in my family, and line 21 states, "But I learned to write from Zio." Thus, he learned to write poetry from Zio. There is no evidence that either of them paints, except through words and gestures (see line 25), so choice **a** is incorrect. Zio's trade was fishing, but the speaker is not a fisherman, so **b** is incorrect. There is no evidence that he is a singer or carpenter, so choices **d** and **e** are incorrect.

7. b. The speaker clearly admires Alfonso's way of seeing beauty in simple things (see lines 28–30), and is impressed by how Alfonso can communicate without a voice. The speaker is not ashamed of Alfonso (choice **a**) even though Alfonso cannot read or write (lines 16–18). The speaker seems to be able to understand Alfonso very well, so he is not frustrated with Alfonso's inability to speak with his voice (choice **c**). The speaker makes much of how he learned to write and see beauty from Alfonso. The speaker does not feel superior to Alfonso; rather he feels indebted to Alfonso (choice **d**). Finally, there is no evidence in the poem to suggest the speaker was ever angry with Alfonso (choice **e**).

8. b. The speaker states in lines 6–7 that Alfonso "lost his voice to cigarettes before [the speaker] was born." Therefore, Alfonso cannot speak with his voice, although he does communicate well with gestures and expressions. The speaker states in line 16 that Alfonso watched him "write with wonder" and that Alfonso tried to teach himself to read, so clearly Alfonso could not write (choice **a**). Choice **c** is incorrect since Alfonso could not speak at all. Choices **d** and **e** are incorrect because the speaker states Alfonso fished for a living in lines 11–12. The reference to painting in line 25 is symbolic, not literal.

9. e. Alfonso could not speak, so he could not be loud (choice **a**) or always yelling (choice **d**). There is no evidence that he was always angry (choice **b**) or that he was like a lion (choice **c**). Rather, the poem suggests that he was fun-loving and kind.

10. a. Lines 28–30 show that the speaker has learned how to appreciate, and express, the beauty of the world. Alfonso does not talk, so he does not teach the speaker how to listen (choice **b**). There is no evidence that the speaker learns how to appreciate his family or understand himself (choices **c** and **d**). Line 18 reveals that Alfonso couldn't read, so choice **e** is incorrect.

11. d. Domain states that the best workers are those who are "the cheapest" and "whose needs are the smallest" (lines 32–33). To create a creature with minimal needs, Rossum created machines with no soul, because the soul "did not contribute directly to the progress of work"—it made people want to play the fiddle, for example. Robots do have a more simple anatomy (choice **a**), but anatomy does not have to do with the needs that might distract a robot from work. Robots are more intelligent (choice **b**), but Domain clearly states that

price, not intelligence, is the key factor. Helena suggests that honesty and work ethic are most important, but Domain's statement contradicts this, so choice **c** is incorrect. Robots were designed so that they did not want anything that was not necessary, so choice **e** is also incorrect.

12. a. Domain tells us that Rossum "began to overhaul anatomy and tried to see what could be left out or simplified" (lines 5–6) because he thought "man is too complicated" (lines 2–3). He also states that the things humans like to do (e.g., play the fiddle) are "unnecessary" (lines 12–14), and that "a working machine must not want to play the fiddle" (lines 20–21) if it is to be efficient. He does not question the honesty of humans (choice **b**) or mention anything about the robot's level of happiness (choice **c**); in fact, the passage suggests that the robots aren't able to feel any emotions at all. Choice **d** is incorrect because Rossum had a specific reason for creating the robots. There is no evidence that there weren't enough people to do the work (nor is there any indication of what sort of work it is), so choice **e** is incorrect.

13. c. Rossum wanted to simplify nature, and Domain states that "the product of an engineer is technically at a higher pitch of perfection than a product of nature" (lines 48–50), showing that Rossum felt nature was imperfect and unnecessarily complicated. Rossum seems to think that machines are more beautiful (more perfect) than nature, so choice **a** is incorrect. Rossum clearly tries to improve upon nature and seems to think he's a better engineer, so choices **b** and **d** can be ruled out. There is a clear distinction in the passage between products of humans (engineers) and products of nature, so choice **e** is incorrect.

14. e. Domain tells Helena in lines 1–5 that "anyone who's looked into anatomy will have seen at once that man is too complicated, and that a good engineer could make him more simply. So young Rossum began to overhaul anatomy." This makes **e** clearly the best choice. Rossum created robots, so choice **a** is incorrect. Rossum was clearly an inventor (choice **b**), but the emphasis in the passage is on his engineering skills. Domain mentions engineers again in lines 48–50: "The product of an engineer is technically at a higher pitch of perfection than a product of nature." There is no evidence that Rossum was a doctor (choice **c**) or that he was a foreman in the factory (choice **d**).

15. a. Clearly Domain admires Rossum as Domain calls Rossum a "good engineer" and describes the robots as "beautiful pieces of work" and "flawless." There is no evidence that Domain fears Rossum in any way (choice **b**). Domain gives no indication of a romantic interest in Helena (choice **c**); he is simply explaining the robots to her. Domain repeatedly indicates that he feels robots are superior workers to humans so choice **d** is incorrect. Finally, Domain's continued praise of Rossum and his work indicates admiration, not jealousy (choice **e**).

16. c. The author states in lines 10–12 that "commercial breaks are constant reminders that the medium itself is artificial" and that "the long-term effect of habitually watching commercial television is probably an erosion of trust in the television medium itself" (lines 20–23). Thus, commercial television teaches viewers not to believe what they see or hear on television. Commercial television is very artificial (choice **a**), but we do not get a sense from the passage about the level of artificiality of public television stations. Choice **b** is incorrect because line 7 states that watching commercial channels is a "more informal" experience than watching public television. The only comparison to the movies is in lines 10–14, which simply state that the people on television are more "realistic" because they are life-size, so choice **d** is incorrect. The entire third paragraph discusses how commercials portray people in a very unrealistic manner (they are always happy), so choice **e** is incorrect.

17. d. The author doesn't seem to think watching television—whether it is commercial or public—is inherently a bad thing, so choice **a** is incorrect. She doesn't state that we shouldn't watch commercial television and only watch the BBC (choice **b**); rather, she is emphasizing that we should not (indeed, can't) believe

everything we see on commercial television (choice **d**). She does not suggest that we do not watch public television, so choice **c** is incorrect. There is no indication of how much time in front of the television the author would recommend, so choice **e** is incorrect.

18. a. The author writes that "Every story has a happy ending . . . which contributes no end to the pervasive unreality of it all" (lines 25–29) and "it is the chronic bliss of everybody in the commercials that creates their final divorce from effective life as we know it" (lines 29–31). There is no mention of background music, so choice **b** is incorrect. She does not discuss the length of commercials, so choice **c** can be eliminated. The author notes that anyone who is ill in a commercial ends up feeling better by the end, so choice **d** is incorrect. She does not discuss specific claims or the merits of those claims, so choice **e** is also incorrect.

19. b. The author states, "The long-term effect of habitually watching commercial television is probably an erosion of trust in the television medium itself." There is no evidence in the passage to suggest that the author believes viewers will become zombies (choice **a**), purchase cable (choice **c**), watch more theater movies (choice **d**), or stop watching television (choice **e**).

20. c. The narrator was most likely in his early teens when he came to America. The author writes that "I lost half a language through want of use and eventually, in my late teens, even lost French as the language of my internal monologue" (lines 17–20). This makes it clear that he must have been in the United States several years before he was in his "late teens," making choices **d** and **e** incorrect. He was also old enough to have friends "and stories and familiar comforts and a sense of continuity between home and outside" and "a whole network of routes through life that I had just barely glimpsed" (lines 15–16 and 20–22), so choices **a** and **b** are incorrect.

21. d. While some of the things the narrator's family lost were tangible (the house, the heirlooms), most of the list includes intangible things that are very important in establishing our identity and sense of self. He is not trying to convince others not to immigrate (choice **a**); he is not criticizing the United States or his experience since he arrived. There is no evidence that the crates were smashed because his family packed carelessly (choice **b**). In the second paragraph, the author writes that he did not consciously miss his homeland; he "actively colluded" in the losses they suffered and tried to re-invent himself. Thus, choice **c** is incorrect. The focus of this passage is how important place is to one's sense of self; it is not trying to show that you are never too old to change (choice **e**).

22. c. The author writes, "Like it or not, each of us is made, less by blood or genes than by a process that is largely accidental, the impact of things seen and heard and smelled and tasted and endured . . ." The entire third paragraph lists things in our environment that contribute to who we are. The first sentence in the paragraph contradicts choices **a** and **d**. There is no mention of education (choice **b**) or peers (choice **e**).

23. b. The author states that he lost his native language through lack of use and that he not only didn't disapprove of losing his heritage—he often "actively colluded." In addition, he states that he "had so effectively renounced" the part of him that "had been formed in another world" (lines 32–36). This directly contradicts choice **c**. We do not know if he embraced American culture (choice **a**) or became withdrawn (choice **d**). There is no evidence that he became possessive about the things he owned, as there is no mention of what he owned in the United States.

24. a. In the third paragraph, the author lists all of the aspects of our environment that have an impact on our identity and sense of self. Even if we don't consciously think of these things, or even notice them, they are a part of who we are. We do not necessarily have to dig deep within ourselves to discover our past, so choice **b** is incorrect. We may all have a part of our past that we want to keep buried (choice **c**), but the author doesn't state that anywhere in the passage. The author does not appear to be an archaeologist, and he does not claim that only archaeologists understand the impact of our environment, so choice **d** is incorrect. Choice **e** may be true, and

the author seems to convey this in the passage, but that is not what he means by this sentence.

25. d. The second paragraph clearly states that "both undergraduate and graduate students are eligible to apply." This eliminates choices **a**, **b**, and **c**. There are no employment criteria mentioned, so choice **e** is incorrect.

26. c. The second of the three bulleted points under "Advantages" states that "employers are committed to the students' education and will help students work around their class schedules." There is no mention of wages or number of hours of employment, so choices **a** and **b** are incorrect. Work-Study employers may offer a wide range of positions, but so do "regular" employers, so choice **d** is incorrect. There is no mention of earning academic credit for Work-Study positions, so choice **e** is also incorrect.

27. d. The first paragraph states that the Work-Study Program is "designed to help students finance their post-secondary education" and that students in the program receive their "financial awards in the form of paychecks from their work-study positions." Thus, it is reasonable to conclude that students should only apply for Work-Study if they (1) need money to finance their education and (2) are willing to work (choice **d**). These students may or may not live on campus (choice **a**) and may or may not have tried and failed to get "regular" jobs (choice **b**). They may or may not have scholarships (choice **c**); students who did receive scholarships may not have received enough to cover their expenses, so they may still need Work-Study. It would be good if students who applied for Work-Study liked working with community service organizations (choice **e**), but that is not one of the reasons to apply for Work-Study. Those students could volunteer or apply for a regular position with a community service organization.

28. c. Tante Atie is the narrator's guardian, possibly her aunt (*tante* means "aunt" in French, but it is also used as a title of respect). She is clearly in a position of authority over the narrator (she grabs Sophie's ears, for example), they seem to live together, and Tante Atie seems to be in charge of where Sophie goes and when; she will put Sophie on the plane to go to her mother. They are not sisters (choice **a**), because they would have the same mother. They are not friends (choice **b**) because Tante Atie is older than Sophie and again is in a position of authority. Tante Atie is not her mother, because the "secret" is that she must send Sophie back to her mother, so choice **d** is incorrect. Sophie goes to bed (lines 17–18), so they are not in school but rather living together, so choice **e** is incorrect.

29. a. She has just learned the secret that Tante Atie was keeping from her: that she must leave Tante Atie and live with her mother. Tante Atie tells her, "I kept a secret. [. . .] It was very sudden, just a cassette from Martine saying, 'I want my daughter,' and then as fast as you can put two fingers together to snap, she sends me a plane ticket with a date on it" (lines 22–28). There is no indication that Sophie will be going to boarding school (choice **b**) or that she just learned Tante Atie is ill (choice **c**). We know from the lines that she is going to her mother's, not a new foster home (choice **d**). There is no evidence that she is being punished, so choice **e** is also incorrect.

30. b. The narrator doesn't want to go. She may be upset that she didn't know the secret, but it is the content of the secret that is so upsetting. The last lines of the passage are the strongest clues. That Tante Atie would even joke about putting her on a plane while she was asleep to imagine that their time together was a dream suggests that they are happy together and that she didn't tell Sophie because she knew Sophie would not want to go. There is no evidence that Sophie misses her mother (choice **a**), that she doesn't like Tante Atie (choice **c**), or that she is afraid of flying (choice **d**). Tante Atie tells us that Sophie can read ("You try to tell me there is all wisdom in reading"), so choice **e** is incorrect.

31. d. Tante Atie can't even laugh at her own joke because she is so upset about the circumstances. She says she didn't tell Sophie because "I needed time to reconcile myself, to accept it" (lines 23–24). She doesn't want Sophie to go, so choices **a** and **b** are incorrect. She may feel angry (choice **c**), but sadness is more likely to be the dominant emotion. There is no evidence that she will be afraid (choice **e**).

32. b. Throughout the essay, the author expresses his people's respect for the land. "Every part of the earth is sacred to my people," he states (line 6), for example, and "The earth does not belong to man, man belongs to the earth" (lines 42–43). They clearly do not think they own the land (choice **a**); the author states in lines 2–4, "how can you buy or sell the sky? The land? The idea is strange to us. If we do not own the freshness of the air. . . ." Their reverence for the land contradicts choices **c** and **d**. There is no evidence that they believe the land is haunted (choice **e**).

33. c. The author is addressing all new Americans—the people to whom he would be selling the land. There is a clear distinction between the "you" of the new Americans and the "we" of the American Indians, so choices **b**, **d**, and **e** are incorrect. Choice **a** is incorrect because he speaks of President Washington in the third person.

34. d. The questions the author asks and the statements he makes are aimed at convincing the new Americans to treat the land with respect: "you must give to the rivers the kindness you would give any brother" (lines 28–29); "if we sell you our land, you must keep it apart and sacred" (lines 35–36). He does not offer any reasons for the new Americans not to buy the land, so choice **a** is incorrect. He does not address the American Indians nor suggest that they fight, so choice **b** is incorrect. He does not state any reasons not to buy the land, and he praises the land rather than pointing out any flaws, so choice **c** is incorrect. There is no evidence of the power he has over his people, so choice **e** is also incorrect.

35. b. For Chief Seattle, every part of nature was sacred. "We know the sap which courses through the trees as we know the blood that courses through our veins," he writes in lines 11–13, suggesting that each tree is important and valuable. This directly contrasts the indifference of Reagan's statement, so choice **a** is incorrect, and so is choice **e**. Reagan does not seem to care about the land, so choice **c** is also incorrect. Chief Seattle does talk about trees, as previously noted, so choice **d** is incorrect.

36. c. The introduction to the passage states that Mrs. Mallard has just learned of her husband's death; this alone would indicate that she is crying, but the text makes reference to "sobs" and compares Mrs. Mallard to a "child who has cried itself to sleep." The text mentions a child, but it is for comparison purposes; there is no literal child in the text (choice **a**). Again, the text refers to a sleeping child but this is a comparison so choice **b** is incorrect. Choice **d** has no textual support at all, and it would be highly unlikely that Mrs. Mallard would be laughing at such a time. Later in the passage, the author states that Mrs. Mallard feels joy, but there is no indication that she is laughing. Choice **e** also has no textual support. Although she is motionless and has a "dull stare," it is due to her emotional state, not illness.

37. d. Mrs. Mallard "saw beyond that bitter moment"—her husband's funeral—"a long procession of years to come that would belong to her absolutely" (lines 38–40). "There would be no one to live for during those coming years; she would live for herself" (lines 43–44) reveals the root of her joy. There is no suggestion in the story that she learned her husband was not dead, so choice **a** is incorrect. There is no evidence that she realizes she will inherit a lot of money—in fact, there is no mention of money at all in the passage—so choice **b** is incorrect. We do not know if she has drastic mood swings—there is no evidence of it in the passage—so choice **c** is incorrect. She does not mention any desire to marry someone else, so choice **e** is also incorrect.

38. d. The freedom, again, will be from a "powerful will bending hers in that blind persistence with which men and women believe they have a right to impose a private will upon a fellow-creature" (lines 45–48). There is no evidence that she lives in debt (choice **a**) or fear (choice **b**) or that she is often criticized by others (choice **c**). We do not know anything about any other family members, so choice **e** is also incorrect.

39. a. The freedom she embraces is the freedom from another's will. In her mind, it is criminal to try to "bend someone's will." The sacredness of the individual—the freedom to do as one pleases—is the ultimate right of a person, and to violate that is a crime. There is no evidence that she thinks getting married is in and of itself a crime (choice **b**). She "did not stop to ask if it were or were not a monstrous joy that held her," so she does not consider her joy a crime (choice **c**), nor does she seem to consider wanting to do things your way a crime (choice **d**); rather, she thinks having someone try to make you do it any other way is a crime. She does not welcome death, and that is not the focus of her joy, so choice **e** is also incorrect.

40. d. The passage makes it clear that although Mrs. Mallard's husband was kind and loved her, Mrs. Mallard feels a great sense of freedom at his death. There is no indication that their marriage was stormy or violent, but rather that Mrs. Mallard submitted to her husband's will quietly even though she did not like doing it. Choice **a** is incorrect because Mrs. Mallard does feel sadness at her husband's death; there is no indication that she hates him. Although Mrs. Mallard appears to have resented the fact that her husband imposed his will upon her, she does not appear to feel superior to him in any way (choice **b**). Choice **c** is incorrect because although the passage states that Mr. Mallard "never looked save with love upon her," there is no indication that Mrs. Mallard deeply loved her husband. She appreciated his kindness and love, but does not seem to have fully reciprocated it. Choice **e** is incorrect because there is no evidence that Mrs. Mallard ever rebelled against her husband; in fact, part of why she feels such freedom is because she has always acquiesced to his will.

49 ▶ Practice Exam 1, GED Science

Directions: Read the following questions carefully and choose the best answer for each question. Some questions may refer to a passage, illustration, or graph.

1. The boiling point in hydrocarbons (molecules containing H and C) increases with increasing molecular weight due to larger intermolecular forces. Which of these hydrocarbons would you expect to have the highest boiling point?

   a.

$$H - \overset{\displaystyle H}{\underset{\displaystyle H}{\overset{|}{\underset{|}{C}}}} - H$$

   b.

$$H - \overset{\displaystyle H}{\underset{\displaystyle H}{\overset{|}{\underset{|}{C}}}} - \overset{\displaystyle H}{\underset{\displaystyle H}{\overset{|}{\underset{|}{C}}}} - H$$

c.

H−C−C−C−H (with H atoms above and below each carbon)

d.

H−C−C=C (with H atoms as shown)

e.

H−C−C−C−C−H (with H atoms above and below each carbon)

2. Determine how much water there is in the graduated cylinder, by reading the bottom of the meniscus (surface of water).

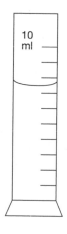

10
ml

a. 3.0 ml
b. 5.5 ml
c. 6.5 ml
d. 7.5 ml
e. 10.0 ml

3. The following graph shows how the concentration (amount per unit volume) changes with time. What information can be obtained from the data?

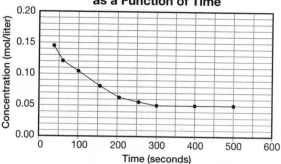

Concentration of a Reactant as a Function of Time

Concentration (mol/liter) vs Time (seconds)

a. The amount of reactant does not change with time.
b. The amount of product is decreasing.
c. The amount of reactant first decreases and then stays constant.
d. After 500 seconds, all of the reactant is used up.
e. At 300 seconds, the concentration of the reactant is at maximum.

4. The following pie chart illustrates the relative productivity (new plant material produced in one year) of different biomes. Based on the chart, which biome has the largest effect on the overall productivity?

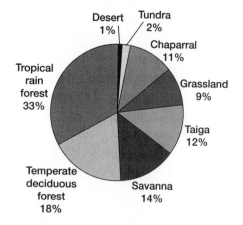

Relative Productivity of Biomes

Desert 1%, Tundra 2%, Chaparral 11%, Grassland 9%, Taiga 12%, Savanna 14%, Temperate deciduous forest 18%, Tropical rain forest 33%

a. chaparral
b. savanna
c. tropical rain forest
d. desert
e. temperate deciduous forest

5. In 1969, two scientists devised an experiment to test a hypothesis that the number of species in an ecosystem depends on the area of the ecosystem. They counted all the arthropod species on a few very tiny islands. They then exterminated all the arthropods (mostly insects) with a pesticide. Over six months, they monitored the gradual repopulation of the island and noticed that by the end of the observation period, each island had almost the same number of species as it had before pesticide was used. However, the kinds of species that arrived were often different than the species that were on the island prior to pesticide use. Following is a chart that illustrates the results.

Number of Species

Trophic Level	Before Pesticide Use	After Pesticide Use
Herbivores	55	55
Scavengers	7	5
Detrivores	13	8
Wood borers	8	6
Ants	32	23
Predator	36	31
Parasite	12	9

Based on the chart, which trophic level suffered the greatest net loss (number of species) in diversity?
a. herbivores
b. scavengers
c. detrivores
d. wood borers
e. ants

Questions 6–7 are based on the following diagram.

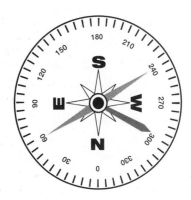

6. This instrument is used to
   a. determine the direction of the wind.
   b. determine the directions of the world.
   c. find the nearest piece of land when navigating the seas.
   d. find underground waters.
   e. determine the direction of water flow.

7. This instrument works because
   a. it has an internal clock.
   b. the needle points to the direction of minimum pressure.
   c. the needle changes position depending on the position of the Sun.
   d. the Earth has two magnetic poles.
   e. the temperatures on Earth's poles are very low.

Questions 8–10 are based on the following passage and table.

Minerals are an important component of the human diet. Some minerals are needed in relatively large amounts. These include calcium, phosphorus, potassium, sulfur, chlorine, and magnesium. Others, including iron, manganese, and iodine, are needed in smaller amounts. Humans need 26 minerals altogether, but some of them are only required in tiny amounts. Some minerals, such as lead and selenium, are harmful in large quantities. Dietary supplements can decrease the chance of mineral deficiencies listed in the following table, but should be taken with great care since overdose can lead to poisoning.

MINERAL	GOOD SOURCES	SYMPTOMS OF DEFICIENCY	FUNCTIONS
Sodium	Table salt, normal diet	Muscle cramps	Water balance, muscle and nerve operation
Potassium	Fruits, vegetables, grains	Irregular heartbeat, fatigue, muscle cramps	Muscle and nerve operation, acid-base balance
Calcium	Dairy, bony fish, leafy green vegetables	Osteoporosis	Formation of bone and teeth, clotting, nerve signaling
Phosphorous	Dairy, meat, cereals	Bone loss, weakness, lack of appetite	Formation of bone and teeth, energy metabolism
Magnesium	Nuts, greens, whole grains	Nausea, vomiting, weakness	Enzyme action, nerve signaling

8. The directions on a bottle of iron supplements list the dosage as one pill per day. Taking several of these iron pills per day may
   a. decrease the chance of bone loss.
   b. make you stronger.
   c. help relieve the symptoms of PMS.
   d. cause poisoning.
   e. make up for an unbalanced diet.

9. Which of the minerals listed in the table are you most likely lacking if you experience an irregular heartbeat?
   a. sodium
   b. potassium
   c. calcium
   d. phosphorous
   e. magnesium

10. Which two minerals are necessary for formation of healthy bones and teeth?
   a. calcium and magnesium
   b. calcium and phosphorous
   c. calcium and potassium
   d. calcium and sodium
   e. sodium and magnesium

11. A woman is most likely to get pregnant if she has unprotected sex a few days before and on the day of ovulation, when the egg is released from the ovaries. The release of the egg is hormonally stimulated, meaning that a hormone in the woman's body triggers ovulation. On average, women ovulate around the 14th day of their menstrual cycle. What follows is a graph showing the levels of three hormones throughout the menstrual cycle of an average woman.

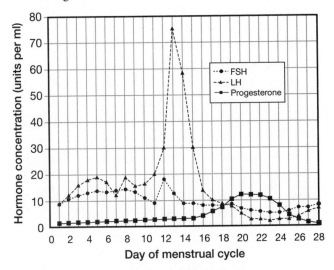

Based on the graph, which hormone is most directly responsible for triggering ovulation?

a. FSH
b. LH
c. progesterone
d. testosterone
e. cholesterol

12. The amount of solute that can be dissolved in a solvent at a given temperature is called solubility. For most substances, solubility increases with temperature. Rock candy can be made from sugar solutions that have an excess of sugar dissolved. The amount of sugar per 100 grams of water at a given temperature has to be higher than the amount that is normally soluble in order to make rock candy. Based on the solubility of sugar in water as a function of temperature, plotted in the graph, how much sugar would you need to dissolve in 100 grams of water to make rock candy at 40 degrees Celsius?

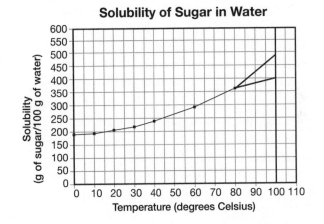

a. less than 50 grams
b. between 50 and 100 grams
c. between 100 and 150 grams
d. between 150 and 200 grams
e. more than 250 grams

13. Which of the following energy sources causes the least pollution to the environment?

a. coal
b. nuclear
c. gasoline
d. solar
e. oil

Questions 14–15 are based on the following passage.

In 1628, the English physician William Harvey established that the blood circulates throughout the body. He recognized that the heart acts as a pump, and does not work by using up blood as earlier anatomists thought. To carefully observe the beating of the heart and the direction of blood flow, Harvey needed to see the works of the blood in slow motion. Since there was no way for him to observe a human heart in slow motion, he studied the hearts of toads and snakes, rather than the rapidly beating hearts of "warm blooded" mammals and birds. By keeping these animals cool, he could slow their hearts down. The main argument for his conclusion that the blood circulates stemmed from his measurement of the amount of blood pumped with each heartbeat. He calculated that the amount of blood pumped each hour by far exceeds the total amount of blood in the body and proved that the same blood passes through the heart over and over again.

14. What misconception did scientists harbor before Harvey's study?
   a. The heart circulates blood.
   b. The heart pumps blood.
   c. The heart uses up blood.
   d. The heart contains no blood.
   e. The heart of birds beats faster than the heart of frogs.

15. Which of the following did Harvey do?
   I. observe the heartbeat and blood flow in snakes and frogs
   II. determine that the heart acts as a pump
   III. count the number of blood cells that pass through the heart every hour
   IV. show that the blood circulates

   a. He did only I.
   b. He did I and II.
   c. He did I, II, and IV.
   d. He did I, III, and IV.
   e. He did II, III, and IV.

Questions 16–17 are based on the following passage.

Radiation from radioisotopes can be used to kill cancer cells. The chemist Marie Curie received two Nobel Prizes for her work with radioisotopes. Her work led to the discovery of the neutron and synthesis of artificial radioactive elements. She died of leukemia at 67, caused by extensive exposure to radiation. Curie never believed that radium and other materials she worked with were a health hazard. In World War I, glowing radium was used on watch dials to help soldiers read their watches in the dark and to synchronize their attacks. Unfortunately, women who worked in factories were drawing their radium stained brushes to fine points by putting them between their lips. As a result, their teeth would glow in the dark. But this was an amusement for children more than a cause of worry. About ten years later, the women developed cancer in their jaws and mouths and had problems making blood cells. This exposed the dangers of radiation.

16. Based on the information in the passage, which statement about radioisotopes is FALSE?
   a. Radioisotopes can kill cancer cells.
   b. Radioisotopes can cause cancer.
   c. A radioisotope can glow in the dark.
   d. Einstein received the Nobel Prize for working with isotopes.
   e. A radioisotope was used in watch dials.

17. Which dangers of radiation were mentioned in the passage?
   I. Radiation can cause genetic mutations.
   II. Radiation can lead to leukemia.
   III. Radiation can cause chemotherapy.

   a. I only
   b. II only
   c. III only
   d. I and II
   e. II and III

Questions 18–19 are based on the following passage.

In the past, people thought that the Earth was flat and that a ship that sailed too far would fall off the edge of the world. The Earth appears flat because the Earth is too large for humans to see its curvature. Several events helped shed this misconception. For one, during a lunar eclipse, the Earth is positioned between the Sun and the moon. It eclipses the moon by casting a shadow on it. The shadow the Earth casts is round. Second, when Magellan circumnavigated the Earth, he proved that one could not fall off the edge of the Earth, because the Earth was round and had no edges. Finally, space missions provided us with images of our round Earth from far away and showed us how beautiful our planet looks, even from a distance.

18. In the passage, what was cited as proof that the Earth is round?
  I. Earth casts a round shadow on the moon during a lunar eclipse.
  II. Earth revolves around the Sun.
  III. Magellan circumnavigated the Earth.
  IV. Images from space.

  a. I and II
  b. I, II, and III
  c. I, II, and IV
  d. I, III, and IV
  e. II, III, and IV

19. With which misconception about the Earth is the passage concerned?
  a. that the Earth turned
  b. that the Earth was in the center of the solar system
  c. that the Earth was flat
  d. that the Earth was created at the same time as the Sun
  e. that the Earth could be eclipsed by the Sun

Questions 20–22 are based on the following passage.

In chemical reactions, atoms react and combine with other atoms to form molecules, or molecules are separated into different atoms, but the elements involved do not themselves change. Nuclear reactions actually involve the formation of different elements from the starting elements. Fission and fusion reactions are nuclear reactions. Fission reactions involve the splitting of the nucleus of an atom into nuclei of lighter atoms. This process releases energy. Fusion reactions occur when light nuclei combine to form a heavier nucleus. The energy that powers the Sun comes from combining 4 hydrogen atoms into 1 helium atom. The helium atom that results weighs less than the sum of the 4 hydrogen atoms that combined to produce it.

20. The reaction that occurs in the Sun can best be described as
  a. a fission reaction because energy is released.
  b. a fusion reaction because nuclei are combining to form a heavier nucleus.
  c. a chemical reaction because the atoms involved in the reaction do not change.
  d. both a fission reaction because energy is released and a fusion reaction because the hydrogen atom fuses into a new element.
  e. a non-nuclear fusion reaction.

21. Based on the passage, which of the following can be assumed?
  a. The helium atom that is produced does not actually weigh less; it just appears that way because helium is light.
  b. A similar reaction occurs on the surface of the Earth.
  c. The helium is subsequently split apart into lighter nuclei.
  d. This reaction occurs without any release net of energy.
  e. The energy that is released corresponds to the decrease mass that is observed.

22. Due to the reaction described in the passage, every second, the Sun releases energy equivalent to 1 million hydrogen bombs. This reaction causes an expansion of the Sun. Which of the following would explain why the Sun has not exploded?
  a. Both a fission reaction and a fusion reaction are occurring and they counterbalance each other.
  b. The gravitational force of the Sun counters the expansion.
  c. Meteors bombard the Sun and cause it to compress.
  d. The fission reaction place absorbs energy from its surroundings.
  e. The net gravitational pull from all the orbiting planets counteracts the force of the reaction.

Questions 23 is based on the following passage.

Arteriosclerosis, a disease, is produced by modern diets and lifestyles and results in the thickening and hardening of arteries as people age. Cholesterol, calcium, and other substances form deposits that build up on the inner lining of arteries. Plaque blockages may lead to a heart attack or even stroke. There is, however, a town in Italy whose residents are resistant to arteriosclerosis. The resistance can be traced back all the way to the original host of the mutation. Natural selection had kept this resistance present even in the most recent generations.

23. Based on the passage, which of the following inferences can be made?
  a. Italians who carried a gene for resistance passed this gene onto their children.
  b. Arteriosclerosis will eventually threaten human existence, as the radius of those affected grows outward from Italy.
  c. Plaque blockages are caused by lack of exercise.
  d. There is no cure for genetic mutation.
  e. People should avoid fat in their diets.

Questions 24–25 are based on the following passage.

The air we inhale is approximately 78% nitrogen, 21% oxygen, 0.96% argon and 0.04% carbon dioxide, helium, water, and other gases (% by volume). The gases present in the air we exhale consist of about 78% nitrogen, 15% to 18% oxygen, 4% to 5% carbon dioxide, and 0.96% argon (% by volume). Additionally vapors and trace gases are present: 5% water vapor, as well as small amounts of hydrogen and carbon monoxide, ammonia, acetone, methanol, ethanol, and other volatile organic compounds. Not all of the oxygen breathed in is replaced by carbon dioxide; around 16% of what we breathe out is still oxygen. The exact amount of exhaled oxygen and carbon dioxide varies according to the fitness, energy expenditure, and diet of a particular person.

24. According to the passage, in every breath exhaled from human lungs, approximately what percentage is oxygen?
  a. 78%
  b. 21%
  c. 16%
  d. 5%
  e. trace amounts

25. The human body absorbs how much nitrogen gas?
  a. 50%
  b. 42%
  c. 7%
  d. none
  e. trace amounts

26. Which part of the human lung passes oxygen to the blood stream?
  a. bronchi
  b. larynx
  c. diaphragm
  d. stamen
  e. alveoli

27. Which of the following is NOT an organelle?
a. cell membrane
b. nucleus
c. golgi apparatus
d. endoplasmic reticulum
e. lysosome

28. Aerobic cellular respiration occurs in the presence of oxygen. Anaerobic cellular respiration occurs in the absence of oxygen. Which organelle provides fuel for the cell in the presence of oxygen?
a. cell wall
b. vacuole
c. mitochondria
d. ribosome
e. chitin

29. What is the function of the nucleus of a cell?
a. acting as a protective wall
b. packing proteins for export to other cells
c. digesting organic material
d. housing the DNA of the cell
e. secreting hormones

30. There are four blood types in humans: A, B, AB, and O. A person with blood type A has antibodies for B, so that he or she can't receive type B blood. Similarly, a person with blood type B has antibodies for type A, and can't receive type A blood. A person with AB blood type has no antibodies, and can receive blood from anyone. A person with type O blood has both A and B antibodies and can receive blood only from someone else with type O blood. Based on this information, someone with type B blood can donate to
a. blood groups B and O.
b. blood groups B and AB.
c. only blood group B.
d. only blood group AB.
e. only blood group O.

31. Two main chemicals are responsible for the communication of the brain with the organs you have no conscious control over (heart, digestive system, endocrine system). The chemical norepinephrine helps your body get ready for a fight-or-flight action by stirring up energy stores. In contrast, the chemical acetylcholine helps conserve energy by slowing the heart and increasing intestinal absorption. Which of the following situations is LEAST likely to lead to increased levels of norepinephrine?
a. being chased by a flesh-eating animal
b. running away from someone holding a knife
c. petting a rabbit
d. taking an important exam
e. going on a first date with someone

32. Most bacteria cannot grow in high concentrations of salt. As a result,
a. salt acts as a preservative in ham, beef jerky, and other salty foods.
b. people who don't eat enough salt become anemic.
c. Utah's Great Salt Lake is filled with bacteria.
d. most antibiotics are sweet.
e. there are no bacteria in fresh water.

33. The following diagram represents which of the following?

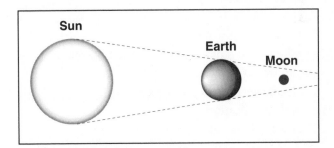

a. solar eclipse
b. lunar eclipse
c. new moon
d. conjunction
e. a solar flare

Questions 34–36 are based on the following passage.

When humans first arrived on Madagascar, there were at least 50 lemur species living on the island, the largest of which rivaled the body mass of a male gorilla or orangutan. Presently only 33 species of lemurs remain on Madagascar. Not one of the 33 lemur species that survive on the island presently is as large as even the smallest species that inhabited Madagascar when humans first arrived. The many species of gorilla-sized lemurs disappeared from Madagascar during the past several millennia. Along with the giant lemurs, Madagascar was populated by other megafauna—giant plants, which have also since vanished. Over the past two thousand years, all of Madagascar's large endemic animals became extinct, and it is estimated that less than only 3 percent of what was once a huge expanse of western deciduous forest remains in existence today.

34. Based on the passage, what percentage of deciduous forest in Madagascar was lost over time?
a. 100%
b. 3%
c. 50%
d. 97%
e. a negligible amount

35. Using the information in the passage, which of the following is a plausible reason that the giant lemurs are becoming extinct?
a. Lemurs became cannibals.
b. desertification
c. They were eaten by dinosaurs.
d. Humans have captured them to keep in zoos.
e. deforestation

36. Madagascar is an island several miles off the coast of southeastern Africa. Many land-dwelling animal species on the island are similar to the land dwelling species on the main continent, and, in some cases, the fossils' common ancestors have been found. What answer choice best offers an explanation of the genetic differences between the somewhat similar modern-day species described here?
a. competition of all species for a limited food source
b. geographic isolation resulting from continental drift
c. human intervention
d. convergence
e. inbreeding

Questions 37–38 are based on the following passage.

Europa is a moon of the planet Jupiter. Some scientists hypothesize that under its icy surface, there exists an ocean very similar to Earth's. These scientists also theorize that this celestial object has an iron core, as well as a magnetic field, and an oxygen rich atmosphere.

Earth's moon has an atmosphere that is so thin, it barely exists. The atmosphere on Earth's moon consists of released gases, such as radon, that originate from radioactive decay processes within the crust and mantle. The elements sodium (Na) and potassium (K) have been detected in this atmosphere using Earth-based spectroscopic methods, whereas the element radon-222 and polonium were detected using instruments left by the Apollo missions.

37. According to the passage, which of the statements is a fact?
    I. Oceans exist under the ice on Europa.
    II. Scientists detected elements, such as potassium, in Earth's moon's atmosphere.
    III. There is no life on Earth's moon.
    IV. Humans have traveled to Europa.

a. I and II
b. II and III
c. II only
d. IV only
e. I only

38. Which of the statements are hypotheses?
  a. I, II, and III
  b. I, III and IV
  c. II and III
  d. IV
  e. I and III

39. A student attempts to illuminate a lightbulb using a battery, a set of wires, and a switch. Which of the following must be true in order for the lightbulb to work?
  a. The wire must be connected to the battery.
  b. The battery must hold a charge.
  c. The wire must be connected, negative to negative, positive to positive.
  d. **a**, **b**, and **c**
  e. **b** and **c** only

40. A ball is pushed while laying at rest on a flat surface. What enables the ball to continue in one direction once pushed, barring the effect of friction and air resistance?
  a. inertia
  b. centripetal force
  c. perpetual motion
  d. friction
  e. centripetal acceleration

41. Which of the following produce(s) energy through the process of photosynthesis?

Figure I   Figure II   Figure III

  a. I
  b. II
  c. I and II
  d. II and III
  e. I, II, and III

42. As the pressure of a gas increases at constant temperature, the volume of the gas decreases.
  If you were a diver and you wanted to take an oxygen tank with you, what would you do?
  a. Pressurize the oxygen, so that more of it can fit in a tank of a manageable size.
  b. Decrease the pressure of oxygen in the tank, so that the tank doesn't explode.
  c. Increase the temperature of oxygen in the tank, so that the cold oxygen doesn't damage the lungs.
  d. Decrease the temperature of oxygen, so that it doesn't escape from the tank.
  e. Increase the temperature of the oxygen and decrease the pressure, so that the volume stays the same.

43. Which of the following best describes an electromagnet?
  a. rubbing iron wire and a magnet together
  b. passing electric current through a wire wrapped around an iron core
  c. passing electric current through a copper wire
  d. positioning lodestones in a small confined area
  e. using the Earth's magnetic field with a thin copper wire

44. Vaccinations prepare the body to fight certain diseases. When you are vaccinated, you are injected
  a. when you contract the disease.
  b. with antibiotics.
  c. with a variation of the disease before exposure.
  d. with white blood cells.
  e. with saline.

45. Which of the following is NOT an amphibian?
  a. a frog
  b. a newt
  c. a toad
  d. a salamander
  e. a beaver

46. Which of the following is NOT true of neurons?
a. They release neurotransmitters into a synapse.
b. They can communicate with skeletal muscle to bring about contraction.
c. They function by transmitting electric current down a long axon.
d. They can communicate with smooth muscle to bring about contraction.
e. They are only found in the central nervous system.

47. An accelerating mass produces a net force according to the equation *Force = mass × acceleration*, or *F = ma*. Which of the following statements is true?
a. If the net acceleration is zero, there is a negative, or downward, force.
b. For a given force, doubling the value of *m* will also double the value of *a*.
c. The value for *a* cannot be negative.
d. For a given acceleration, doubling the value of *m* will also double the value of *F*.
e. When considering the force of gravity due to Earth, *F* is always greater than zero.

48. The fossilized organisms found in the lowest rock layers are
a. more complex species.
b. mostly mammalian.
c. younger than those found in the above layers.
d. usually less complex and older than species in layers above.
e. from various eras.

49. For many years a farmer treated his land with large amounts of fertilizer. Upon having the soil analyzed it was found to have decreased fertility and to be low in calcium. Which of the following explanations can account for these findings?
a. The carbon cycle was disrupted, so extra carbon dioxide was reacting with the calcium in the soil.
b. The rock cycle was disrupted so rocks were not reacting with calcium to produce fertile soil.
c. The nitrogen cycle was disrupted, and excess nitrogen depleted the fertility of the soil.
d. The water cycle was disrupted, and excess water was reacting with the calcium and reducing the fertility of the soil.
e. The soil cycle was disrupted and cycle rejuvenation of soil did not occur, so the soil became less fertile.

50. The Earth's magnetic poles are not permanent. In fact, they can migrate as much as 15 km a year. It has been proposed that there were times in history when the poles were actually reversed. Scientists are studying iron-rich rocks that were formed by lava long ago. How may studying these rocks enable scientists to learn more?
a. If they dig through the layers of rock formed by the lava they will reach the actual poles of the Earth.
b. The rocks can be used as magnets to determine the strength of the Earth's magnetic field.
c. The rocks can protect the Earth from solar flares.
d. At the time when the lava cooled and the rocks were formed, a record of the Earth's magnetic field was locked into place.
e. If the scientists can understand the concepts of magnetism by first examining rocks, then they can explore larger magnets and ultimately study the Earth.

▶ Answers

1. e. The molecule in choice **e** has the most atoms, and the largest molecular weight. It therefore has the highest boiling point.

2. d. The top division on the graduated cylinder is the 10 ml mark. There are 10 divisions, so each one is 1 ml. The bottom of the meniscus (the lowest point of the curve at the surface of the water) is between 7 ml and 8 ml, so 7.5 ml is the best answer.

3. c. The amount of reactant starts at almost .15, then decreases, and then stays steady at .01. Thus, choice **c** is correct. Choice **a** is incorrect because initially the concentration is almost .15 and then it decreases. The chart provides no information about the product that is formed, so choice **b** is incorrect. (Also, if the amount of reactant is decreasing, we would expect to see the amount of product increasing.) Choice **d** is incorrect because at 500 seconds the concentration in not equal to zero, it is equal to .05. Choice **e** is incorrect because at 300 seconds, the concentration is lower than at other times shown.

4. c. The largest slice of the pie corresponds to the section labeled: Tropical rain forest 33%. Thus, tropical rain forests are the most productive.

5. e. The number of species lost was greatest for ants, because prior there were 32 species and this dropped to 23. The number of species lost was $32 - 23 = 9$. Looking at the *before* and *after* columns for all tropic levels, 9 represents the largest decrease.

6. b. The instrument is a compass, used to find direction because the needle points north due to the magnetism of the Earth, so choice **b** is the best answer.

7. d. The needle on the compass responds to the Earth's magnetic poles, so the correct choice is **d.**

8. d. Taking too many minerals can lead to poisoning. The last sentence of the passage notes that minerals should be taken with great care because an overdose can lead to poisoning, so choice **d** is correct. None of the statements in the other choices were discussed in the passage or listed in the table.

9. b. Looking at the column titled Symptoms of Deficiency, irregular heartbeat results from a deficiency in potassium, so choice **b** is correct. No other listed mineral deficiency has this symptom.

10. b. The table shows that both calcium and phosphorous are involved in the formation of healthy bones and teeth. This information is listed in the column titled Functions. Thus choice **b** is correct.

11. b. The graph shows that the level of LH rapidly rises right before the 14th day of the cycle, and then falls. It is logical to assume that this spike in LH triggers ovulation, so choice **b** is correct.

12. e. According to the graph, at 40 degrees Celsius, about 250 grams of sugar can be normally dissolved in 100 grams of water. In order to make rock candy, this amount has to be exceeded, so choice **e** is correct.

13. d. Unlike the other choices, there is no pollution or waste associated with solar energy; thus, choice **d** is correct.

14. c. The passage explained that other scientists at the time mistakenly thought that the heart used up blood, so choice **c** is correct. Choices **a, b,** and **e** are not misconceptions. Choice **d** was not mentioned in the passage.

15. c. The passage explained that Harvey did I, II, and IV, so choice **c** is correct. Although he also calculated the amount of blood that passes through the heart every hour, he did not count the blood cells one by one (III), nor did he have the technology to do that. All answer choices that include III can be eliminated by the process of elimination, so we know choices **d** and **e** are incorrect. Only choice **c** includes the three correct statements.

16. d. There was no mention of Einstein in the passage, so choice **d** is the correct answer. All of the other statements were made in the passage.

17. b. Statement II was mentioned in the passage: Curie died of leukemia because of lifelong exposure to radiation (**b** is correct). Statement I is true, but was not discussed in the passage (choices **a** and **d** can be eliminated). Statement III is false; radiation does not cause chemotherapy. (Radiation is applied in chemotherapy.) Choices **c** and **e** can be eliminated by recognizing that III is false.

18. d. Statements I, III, and IV were made in the passage, so choice **d** is correct. Statement II is true, but does not prove that the Earth is round and was not discussed in the passage.

19. c. The whole passage is focused on listing evidence that the Earth is round, not flat, so choice **c** is the correct answer. Choice **a** is not a misconception. Choices **b, d,** and **e** were not discussed in the passage.

20. b. The passage states that fusion occurs when light nuclei combine to form a heavier nucleus. It also describes how four hydrogen atoms combine to form a helium atom, making **b** the correct answer. Choice **a** is incorrect because fission involves the splitting of a nucleus. This is not a chemical reaction (choice **c**) because the starting element (hydrogen) is changing into a different element (helium). This reaction is only a fusion reaction, which is a type of nuclear reaction (both **d** and **e** are incorrect).

21. e. The helium atom that is produced does, indeed, have a lower mass (and weight) than the hydrogen atoms that reacted (choice **a** is incorrect) and the mass defect that is observed corresponds to the amount of energy released by this reaction (choice **e** is correct). The other answer choices are incorrect, and nothing in the passage would indicate that any of them would be plausible.

22. b. The fusion reaction described powers the Sun by releasing enormous amounts of energy and causes the Sun to expand. This question requires you to think logically about what could possibly counter the expansion. The only choice that is reasonable is that the gravitational pull of the Sun keeps the Sun from expanding or exploding. There is no fission reaction to counter the fusion reaction (choice **a**), and fission reactions also release energy. The other choices would not balance out the expansion.

23. a. Although arteriosclerosis is a disease affecting the quality life of others, it seems at this point that it will not threaten human existence (choice **b** is incorrect). With this disease, lifestyle can contribute to its onset. Certain humans with genetic differences were capable of developing a resistance to this disease because they carried a particular trait in their DNA. The passage suggests their traits were naturally selected because they were advantageous in the given environment. These traits were passed on to subsequent generations (choice **a** is correct). No reference was made as to whether exercise was a factor, nor did the passage suggest that people should eat less fat (choices **c** and **e** are incorrect). Nothing was stated regarding any evidence supporting a lack of a cure for genetic mutation (choice **d** is incorrect).

24. c. According the passage, between 15% and 18% of each exhaled breath is oxygen, so choice **c** is the correct answer.

25. d. According to the passage, the same percentage of nitrogen is exhaled as is inhaled, and that percentage is 78%. We can assume, then, that humans do not absorb nitrogen gas through the lungs (choice **d**).

26. e. The bronchi (choice **a**) are highly branched tubules ringed with cartilage which subdivide and grow progressively smaller as they go deeper into the lungs. The larynx (choice **b**) is the voice box in which air passes to allow us to make noise when we speak. The diaphragm (choice **c**) is the muscle that allows us to control the inhalation and exhalation of air. Choice **d**, stamen, is not part of the respiratory system in humans. Alveoli (choice **e**) are the tiny air sacks that actually absorb oxygen into the bloodstream.

27. a. The definition of an organelle is "a subcomponent within the cell that performs a specific task." Each choice aside from choice **a**, cell membrane, is located within the cell wall and performs various duties crucial to the cell's function.

28. c. The cell membrane or cell wall (choice **a**) protects the interior of the cell from the outside world as well as provides structure and support. The vacuole (choice **b**) attaches to the cell membrane and performs secretory, excretory, and storage functions. The mitochondria (choice **c**) is the powerhouse of the cell, and is where energy is generated (ATP gets made) in the presence of oxygen. The ribosome (choice **d**) is the organelle responsible for the manufacture of proteins. Chitin (choice **e**) is not an organelle.

29. d. The function of the nucleus is to store the genetic information (DNA) of the cell.

30. b. Someone who has blood type B can donate blood to those who don't have antibodies for B. These include other people with type B blood (they have antibodies for A only) and those with type AB blood (they don't have any antibodies), so choice **b** is correct.

31. c. Levels of norepinephrine rise when there is a potential for danger, stress, or excitement. Choice **c**, petting a rabbit, is the only choice that would tend to calm, rather than stress out or excite, a person.

32. a. Salty foods are less prone to bacterial attack because most bacteria can't grow in environments that are too salty. Being anemic (choice **b**) is not related to bacteria. Choice **c** is inconsistent with the question. Choices **d** and **e** are not true and are inconsistent with the question.

33. b. Since the Earth is blocking the sunlight from reaching the moon, this diagram best displays a lunar eclipse.

34. d. In the passage, it is stated that the percentage of forest that remains in Madagascar is less than 3% of the original forest. This implies that approximately 97% of the forest has been lost over time.

35. e. With the information provided, there is no evidence supporting choice **a**, **c**, or **d**. Although Madagascar is said to be losing forest, the passage does not mention if desertification is the cause. Choice **e** is the most logical reason for the giant lemurs' extinction.

36. b. Madagascar is an isolated island off the coast of Africa. If the fossil record turned up some common ancestors to different species, we can assume that there was a point of divergence. The only choice that explains this divergence is choice **b**, because if the original members of a single species were isolated due to continental drift, over time two different species could evolve.

37. c. Statement II, choice **c**, is the only fact. Using the passage as a reference, all of the other choices are not facts, but merely hypotheses based on scientific study.

38. e. Statement II is a fact (measured by scientific instruments). Humans did not travel to Europa, so IV is a false statement. The passage states that some scientists hypothesized that there is an ocean under the icy surface, so statement I is a hypothesis. Life on the moon is yet to be unproven until the entire moon is explored. A hypothesis has to be testable, so III is a hypothesis as well.

39. d. In order for the lightbulb to work, the student must complete the electrical circuit by making sure the battery is connected, the battery is charged, and the wires are connected to the correct terminals. Choice **d** includes all of these criteria.

40. a. The ball, while at rest on a flat surface, must be pushed (by a force) to start moving. Once the ball is in motion, it will stay in motion unless a force acts to stop it. An object in motion will stay in motion, and an object at rest will stay at rest unless a force is applied. Thus choice **a** is the correct answer.

41. d. Of the pictures shown, only the tree and the flower are able to produce energy by way of photosynthesis.

42. a. A diver would want to take a lot of oxygen, without letting the tank get too bulky. The other choices are either false (choices **d** and **e**) or not a major concern (choices **b** and **c**).

43. b. An electromagnet is just a coil of wire wound around a metallic (usually iron) core and connected to a current source. The electromagnet becomes energized and creates a magnetic field just like a regular magnet.

44. c. The statement that best describes a vaccine is choice **c**. When being administered a vaccination, the subject receives a (mild) variation of a disease. In response, the body produces the necessary defenses but does not contract the disease. If ever exposed to the disease, the person will have antibodies in his or her system.

45. e. Each of the animals listed are amphibious with the exception of the beaver. Although the beaver swims and spends a lot of time in the water, it is a mammal and is not a member of the amphibian family. The other three creatures have the ability to breathe on both land and in water.

46. e. Neurons do release neurotransmitters into a synapse, they can communicate with skeletal muscle to bring about contraction, they do function by transmitting electric current down a long axon, and they can communicate with smooth muscle to bring about contraction. Neurons are found in the central nervous system and the peripheral nervous system; thus, choice **e** is not true.

47. d. Given that accelerating mass produces a net force according to the equation *Force = mass × acceleration,* or $F = ma$, if a equals zero, the whole equation equals zero, so **a** is incorrect. If F is constant, doubling the value of m will also halve the value of a, so **b** is incorrect. An acceleration can be negative, as is the case for decelerating masses, so **c** is incorrect. For a given acceleration, doubling the value of m will also double the value of F because these variables are on opposite sides of the equation. Thus **d** is correct. The force of gravity due to Earth, produces a negative a, so F is definitely not always greater than zero, so **e** is incorrect.

48. d. Fossilized organisms in the lowest rock layer are generally older and less complex than those found in the above layers, so choice **d** is correct.

49. c. Fertilizers tend to be high in nitrogen, so it is likely that the nitrogen cycle was disrupted, with the excess nitrogen depleting the fertility of the soil. Thus choice **c** is correct. Humans typically have an adverse effect on the carbon cycle (choice **a**) by contributing to the greenhouse effect through the use of fossil fuels, for example. There is no such thing as a soil cycle (choice **e**). The rock cycle is about one type of rock transforming into another, so choice **b** is incorrect. Similarly, it is unlikely that a change in the water cycle is the cause of his fertility problems, as it mostly deals with precipitation and evaporation.

50. d. If the poles were reversed while the lava was cooling, the magnetic particles inside would be aligned in the way we know magnets align themselves: with the south pole of the magnetic particles being attracted to the (then) North Pole of the Earth. So, at the time when the lava cooled and the rocks were formed, a record of the Earth's magnetic field would have been recorded; thus, choice **d** is correct.

50 ▶ Practice Exam 1, GED Mathematics

▶ Part I

You are about to begin Part I of this exam. You may use your calculator for these questions.

1. Evaluate $(6 \times 10^5) \div (4 \times 10^3)$.
   a. 20
   b. 100
   c. 150
   d. 1,500
   e. 2,000

2. A box in the form of a rectangle solid has a square base 5 feet in length, a width of 5 feet, and a height of h feet. If the volume of the rectangular solid is 200 cubic feet, which of the following equations may be used to find h?
   a. $5h = 200$
   b. $5h^2 = 200$
   c. $25h = 200$
   d. $h = 200 \div 5$
   e. $h = 5(200)$

Questions 3–5 are based on the following information.

Question 6 refers to the following figure.

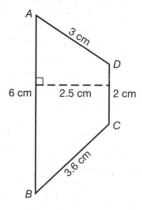

3. A 3-foot-wide walkway is built around a swimming pool that is 20 feet by 30 feet, as shown in the figure. In order to determine how much flagstone to buy, the homeowner needs to know the total area, in square feet, of the walkway. Which of the following expressions represents this area?
   a. (23)(33)
   b. (26)(36)
   c. (23)(33) − (20)(30)
   d. (26)(36) − (20)(30)
   e. (26)(36) − (23)(33)

6. In quadrilateral *ABCD*, side *AB* is parallel to side *CD*. Sides *AD* and *BC* are not parallel. What is the area of the figure to the nearest square centimeter? Mark your answer in the following grid.

4. If the depth of the pool is 6 feet, what volume of water, in cubic feet, is needed to fill the pool?
   a. 56
   b. 300
   c. 600
   d. 3,000
   e. 3,600

5. What is the total area, in square feet, of the pool and the walkway?
   a. 50
   b. 62
   c. 759
   d. 936
   e. Not enough information is given.

7. A parallelogram is drawn on a coordinate grid so that three vertices are located at (3,4), (−2,4), and (−4,1). At what coordinates should the fourth vertex be located? Mark your answer in the following coordinate grid.

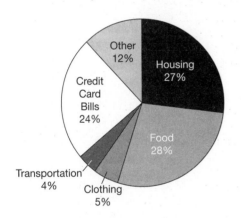

Questions 8 and 9 refer to the following graph.

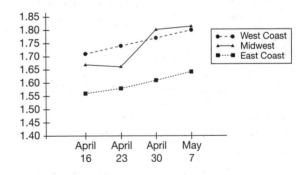

The Kleins are trying to pay off their credit card debt, so they developed this budget based on their monthly take-home pay.

8. If the Kleins' monthly take-home pay is $2,500, about how much do they plan to pay each month on their credit card bills?
   a. $600
   b. $450
   c. $300
   d. $240
   e. Not enough information is given.

9. What fraction of the Kleins' monthly take-home pay goes toward clothing? Mark your answer in the following grid.

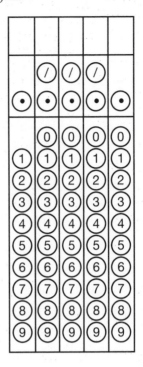

Questions 10 and 11 refer to the following information.

10. On what date and in what location was there the greatest jump in the price of gasoline from one week to the next?
   a. April 23 on the West Coast
   b. April 30 in the Midwest
   c. April 30 on the West Coast
   d. May 7 on the East Coast
   e. May 7 in the Midwest

11. Based on the information in the graph, which of the following is the best prediction of the price per gallon of gasoline on the West Coast for the week following May 7?
a. $1.64
b. $1.71
c. $1.76
d. $1.82
e. $1.86

12. The Northridge Quakers have won 20 games and lost 15. What is the ratio of games won to games played?
a. 3:4
b. 3:7
c. 4:3
d. 4:7
e. 4:10

13. There are 35 marbles in a jar. There are 5 equal amounts of differently colored marbles. What is the theoretical probability of picking any one random color?
a. 1 out of 5
b. 5 out of 35
c. 5 out of 7
d. 1 out of 7
e. 7 out of 7

14. Eight athletes ran a 1-mile race. The winner's time was 4 minutes 8 seconds. If the median time was 4 minutes 48 seconds, what was the time of the athlete who finished last?
a. 5 min. 28 sec.
b. 5 min. 4 sec.
c. 4 min. 46 sec.
d. 4 min. 28 sec.
e. Not enough information is provided.

15. Evaluate $y^2(4x - y)$ if $y = -2$ and $x = 8$.
a. −18
b. 18
c. 86
d. 96
e. 136

16. Ken earned x dollars at his part-time job on Friday. His wife earned $12 more than twice Ken's pay $(2x + 12)$. Together, they earned $174. How much did Ken earn on Friday?
a. $54
b. $87
c. $108
d. $120
e. $162

17. Two adults and four children pay $48 to get into the fair. A child's ticket is $6 less than an adult's ticket. What is the cost of an adult's ticket?
a. $18
b. $15
c. $12
d. $9
e. $6

18. Charlie borrowed $1,500 from his aunt. He plans to pay his aunt back in 9 months. If he pays 4% interest on the loan, what is the total amount he will pay back in 9 months?
a. $540
b. $1,455
c. $1,545
d. $1,560
e. $2,040

19. Patricia wants to order business cards. A printing company determines the cost (C) to the customer using the following function, where b = the number of boxes of cards and n = number of ink colors.

$$C = \$25.60b + \$14.00b(n - 1)$$

If Patricia orders 4 boxes of cards printed in 3 colors, how much will the cards cost?
a. $214.40
b. $168.00
c. $144.40
d. $102.40
e. $56.00

20. Nick scored 7 more points than Josh in a basketball game. Paul scored 2 points less than Josh in the same game. If the three boys scored a total of 38 points, how many points did Josh score?

a. 5

b. 9

c. 11

d. 14

e. 15

21. Maggie and Christian decided to share the cost of buying their friends a wedding gift. Maggie put in $20 less than twice the amount that Christian contributed. Together, they spent $94. How many dollars did Maggie contribute toward the gift? Mark your answer in the following grid.

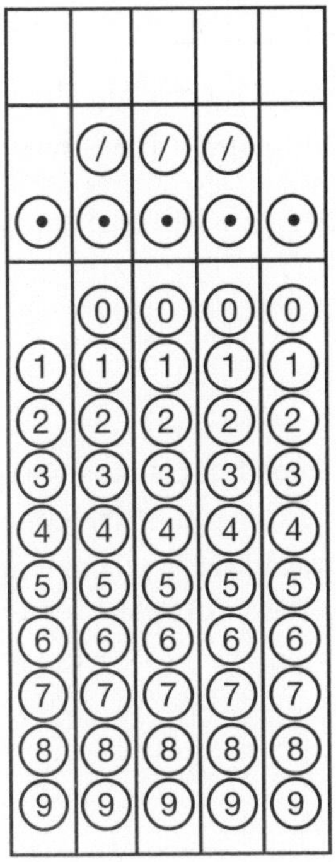

22. David is 56 and Debra is half his age plus the square root of 16. How old is Debra?

a. 28

b. 44

c. 60

d. 32

e. 24

23. Find the product of 42 and 68. Mark your answer in the following grid.

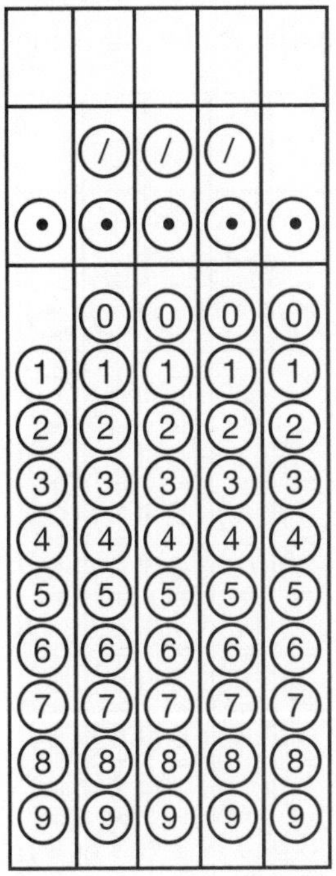

24. Which has the greater value, the absolute value of −28 or the absolute value of 15? Mark your answer in the following grid.

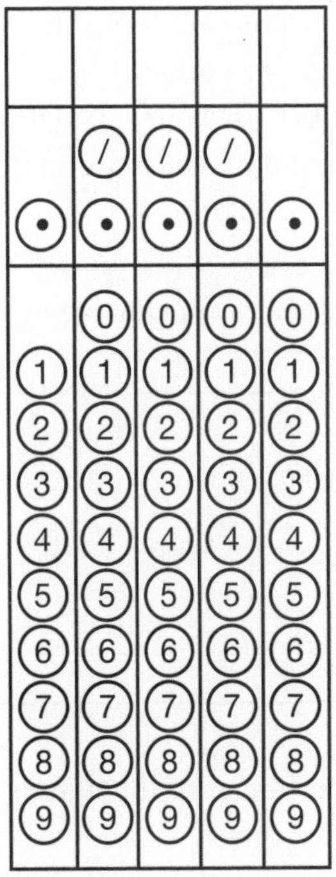

25. A school raised $372 during a carwash fundraiser. If the earnings are to be split equally among 4 classes, how much money will each class receive? Mark your answer in the following grid.

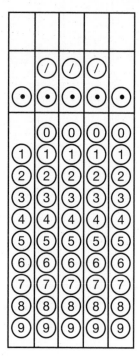

▶ **Part II**

You are about to begin Part II of this exam. In this section, you must answer an additional 25 questions. Unlike Part I, you may NOT use your calculator for these questions, so be sure to put it away to simulate the actual GED testing experience.

Question 26 is based on the following figure.

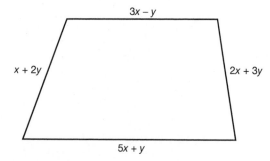

26. What is the perimeter of the figure?
  a. $11x + 5y$
  b. $10x + 5y$
  c. $11x + 4y$
  d. $9x - y$
  e. $8x + 3y$

27. The lengths of the sides of $\triangle ABC$ are 6 inches, 8 inches, and 10 inches. Which of the following conclusions must be true?
  a. $\angle C$ is a right angle.
  b. $\triangle ABC$ is an acute triangle.
  c. $\triangle ABC$ contains one obtuse angle.
  d. $\angle A$ is an acute angle.
  e. $m\angle A + m\angle B + m\angle C = 180°$

Question 28 is based on the following figure.

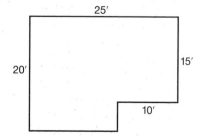

28. The diagram represents a large living room. What is the area, in square yards, of the room?
  a. 16.6
  b. 33.3
  c. 45
  d. 50
  e. 450

29. At a certain time of day, a man 6 feet tall casts a shadow 4 feet in length. At the same time, a church steeple casts a shadow 28 feet in length. How high, in feet, is the church steeple?
  a. 30
  b. 32
  c. 42
  d. 48
  e. 56

30. A bookcase has 3 large shelves and 4 small shelves. Each large shelf contains 8 more books than each small shelf. If the bookcase contains 297 books, how many books does each small shelf hold? Mark your answer in the following grid.

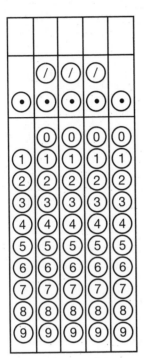

31. Which of the following is a graph of the inequality $-2 \le x < 4$?

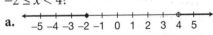

a. −5 −4 −3 −2 −1 0 1 2 3 4 5

b. −5 −4 −3 −2 −1 0 1 2 3 4 5

c. −5 −4 −3 −2 −1 0 1 2 3 4 5

d. −5 −4 −3 −2 −1 0 1 2 3 4 5

e. −5 −4 −3 −2 −1 0 1 2 3 4 5

32. One number is 12 more than 3 times another number. The sum of the 2 numbers is −20. What are the numbers?
a. −2 and −18
b. −4 and −16
c. −5 and −15
d. −6 and −14
e. −8 and −12

33. What is the value of the expression $-3 \times 5^2 + 2(4 - 18) + 33$?
a. −130
b. −76
c. −20
d. 74
e. 130

34. If the square of a number is added to the number increased by 4, the result is 60. If n represents the number, which equation can be used to find n?
a. $n^2 + 4 = 60$
b. $n^2 + 4n = 60$
c. $n^2 + n + 4 = 60$
d. $n^2 + 60 = 4n + 4$
e. $n^2 + n = 64$

35. On a road map, $\frac{1}{4}$ inch represents 8 miles of actual road distance. The towns of Alton and Waverly are represented by points $2\frac{1}{8}$ inches apart on the map. What is the actual distance, in miles, between Alton and Waverly?
a. 17
b. 32
c. 40
d. 60
e. 68

Question 36 is based on the following figure.

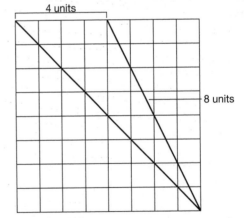

36. What is the area, in square graph units, of the triangle?
a. 8
b. 10
c. 16
d. 32
e. 48

37. 1 kilometer =
   a. 10 meters
   b. 100 meters
   c. 1,000 centimeters
   d. 10,000 centimeters
   e. 1,000,000 millimeters

Question 38 is based on the following figure.

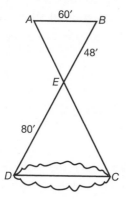

38. To measure the distance (DC) across a pond, a surveyor takes points A and B so that $\overrightarrow{AB}$ is parallel to $\overrightarrow{DC}$. If $\overrightarrow{AB} = 60$ feet, $\overrightarrow{EB} = 48$ feet, and $\overrightarrow{ED} = 80$ feet, find $\overrightarrow{DC}$.
   a. 72 ft.
   b. 84 ft.
   c. 96 ft.
   d. 100 ft.
   e. Not enough information is given.

39. Jason is rolling a 6-sided number cube. What will the probability be of him rolling a prime number? Mark your answer in the following grid.

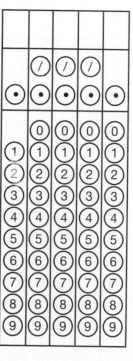

40. The Southside Rebels have lost 15 games out of 45. What is the ratio of games won to lost? (Show your answer as a fraction.) Mark your answer in the following grid.

41. Andrea is flipping a coin. What is the probability that the coin will land on heads twice in a row?

a. $\frac{1}{2}$

b. $\frac{1}{3}$

c. $\frac{1}{4}$

d. $\frac{2}{6}$

e. 0

42. How many combinations of outfits can David make if he has 9 shirts, 7 pants, 11 pairs of shoes, and 3 hats?

a. 2,079

b. 1,045

c. 124

d. 77

e. 30

43. If two coins are dropped on the floor, what is the probability that both coins will land on heads?

a. 1 out of 4

b. 2 out of 4

c. 1 out of 2

d. 2 out of 2

e. 4 out of 2

44. Which is more likely, rolling an even number or a prime number on a six-sided die?

a. even

b. odd

c. equally likely

d. prime

e. Not enough information is provided.

45. Evaluate: $7\sqrt{16} \div |-14| + \sqrt{25}$

a. 5

b. 7

c. 9

d. 11

e. 13

46. Find the difference between the first prime number and the fifth prime number.

a. 1

b. 5

c. 7

d. 9

e. 11

47. James is thinking of a two-digit number. The sum of the two digits is 7. The product of the two digits is zero. Which number is Jason thinking of?

a. 81

b. 70

c. 61

d. 25

e. 16

48. Which of the following has the smallest numerical value?

a. 5^2

b. 2^5

c. 3^3

d. 8^2

e. 9^2

49. Which of the following values are in order from greatest to least?

a. $2^4, 3^3, 5^2$

b. $5^2, 3^3, 2^4$

c. $5^2, 2^4, 3^3$

d. $3^3, 5^2, 2^4$

e. 3, 2, 5

50. Which of the following sets of numbers has 4 as a greatest common factor?

a. 6, 8, 16

b. 4, 12, 20

c. 4, 6, 8

d. 8, 30, 36

e. 2, 4, 6

▶ Answers

1. c. $6 \times 10^5 = 600,000$
$4 \times 10^3 = 4,000$
$600,000 \div 4,000 = 600 \div 4 = 150$

2. c. Use the formula $V = lwh$. In this case, $l = 5$, $w = 5$, and $h = h$. Therefore, $V = 5 \times 5 \times h = 25h$ and $25h = 200$.

3. d. As you can see from the figure, to find the area of the walkway, you need to subtract the area of the inner rectangle, $(20)(30)$ sq. ft., from the area of the outer rectangle, $(26)(36)$ sq. ft.:
$(26)(36) - (20)(30)$ sq. ft.

4. e. Since the average depth of the pool is 6 ft., the water forms a rectangular solid with dimensions 30 by 20 by 6. The volume of water is the product of these three numbers: $(30)(20)(6) = 3{,}600$ ft.^{3}.

5. d. Taken together, the pool and the walkway form a rectangle with dimensions 36 by 26. The total area is the product of these numbers: $(36)(26) = 936$ sq. ft.

6. 10.

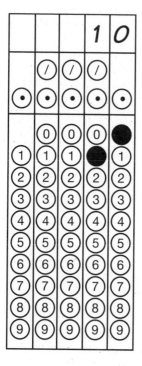

Quadrilateral *ABCD* is a trapezoid because it has one pair of parallel sides. The bases are the parallel sides, *AB* and *CD*. The height is the length 2.5 cm. Use the formula for the area of a trapezoid.

$$A = \frac{1}{2} \times (b_1 + b_2) \times h$$
$$= \frac{1}{2} \times (6 + 2) \times 2.5$$
$$= \frac{1}{2} \times 8 \times 2.5$$
$$= 4 \times 2.5$$
$$= 10 \text{ cm}^2$$

7. (1,1).

Plot the points given in the problem and complete the parallelogram. Remember that in a parallelogram, both pairs of opposite sides are equal and parallel.

8. a. Find 24% of $2,500.

$$\frac{x}{2{,}500} = \frac{24}{100}$$
$$\frac{100x}{100} = \frac{60{,}000}{100}$$
$$x = 600$$

9. $\frac{1}{20}$ or $\frac{5}{100}$.

Clothing expenses take 5% of the Kleins' pay. Change 5% to a fraction to get $\frac{5}{100}$, which can also be reduced to $\frac{1}{20}$.

10. b. The steepest rise on the graph was from April 23 to April 30. The symbol indicates that it was in the Midwest.

11. d. The prices for the West Coast have been rising steadily by 2 or 3 cents each week. On May 7, the price on the West Coast is a little beneath $1.80. If it rises 2 or 3 cents, it should be at about $1.82 by the following week. The question gives no reason to expect a sudden decline in price or a sharp increase.

12. d. The number of games played is the total of the wins and losses, (20 + 15 = 35). Write the ratio and simplify. $\frac{20}{35} = \frac{4}{7}$.

13. $\frac{1}{5}$.

If there are 35 marbles and 5 different colors, there must be 7 of each color marbles; thus, the probability of picking any one color would be $\frac{7}{35}$ or $\frac{1}{5}$.

14. e. The median time is the middle time when all times are arranged in order. There is no way of knowing how far behind the median the slowest runner was.

15. e. Replace the variables with their given values. $(-2)^2 (32 - (-2)) = 4(34) = 136$.

16. a. Solve:

$x + (2x + 12) = \$174$

$3x + 12 = \$174$

$3x = \$162$

$x = \$54$

17. c. Let x = the price of an adult's ticket and $x - \$6$ = the price of a child's ticket. In the problem, the cost of 2 adults' tickets and 4 children's tickets is $48. Write and solve an equation:

$2x + 4(x - 6) = \$48$

$2x + 4x - \$24 = \$48$

$6x - \$24 = \$48$

$6x = \$72$

$x = \$12$

18. c. Find the amount of interest. For the time period, use $\frac{9}{12}$, which equals $\frac{3}{4}$ or .75. Multiply. $\$1,500 \times 0.04 \times 0.75 = \$45$. Add to find the amount paid back. $\$1,500 + \$45 = \$1,545$.

19. a. Substitute 4 for b and 3 for n into the function. Then solve the equation.

$C = \$25.60(4) + \$14(4)(3 - 1)$

$= \$102.40 + \$112.00$

$= \$214.40$

20. c. Let x = number of points scored by Josh, $x + 7$ = number of points scored by Nick, and $x - 2$ = number of points scored by Paul.

$x + x + 7 + x - 2 = 38$

$3x + 5 = 38$

$3x = 33$

$x = 11$

21. 56.

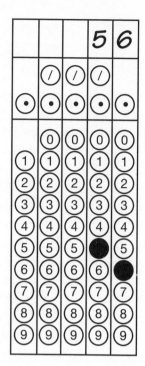

Let *x* represent the amount that Christian put in and $2x - 20$ represent Maggie's contribution. Solve the equation.

$x + 2x - 20 = 94$

$3x = 114$

$x = 38$

Christian put in \$38 and Maggie put in $94 - 38 = \$56$.

22. d. First, find half of 56 ($56 \div 2 = 28$). Then, find $\sqrt{16} = 4$ ($4 \times 4 = 16$). Add $28 + 4 = 32$. Debra is 32 years old.

23. 2856.

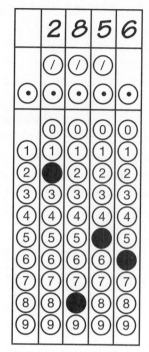

$42 \times 68 = 2,856$.

24. 28.

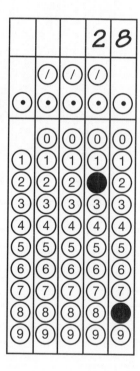

$|-28| = 28$

$|15| = 15$

$28 > 15$

25. 93.

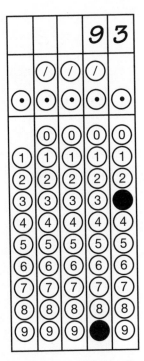

$372 ÷ 4 classrooms = $93 per classroom

26. a. The perimeter of the figure is $x + 2y + 3x - y + 2x + 3y + 5x + y = 11x + 5y$.

27. e. $\triangle ABC$ is a right triangle, but you have no way of knowing which angle is a right angle, so eliminate choice **a.** Regardless of the type of triangle, the sum of the measures of the interior angles of a triangle must be 180°.

28. d. Divide the floor space into two rectangles by drawing a line segment. The area of the large rectangle = $20 \times 15 = 300$ sq. ft. The area of the small rectangle = $10 \times 15 = 150$ sq. ft. The total area of floor space = $150 + 300 = 450$ sq. ft. Since 9 sq. ft. = 1 sq. yd., 450 sq. ft. ÷ 9 = 50 sq. yds.

29. c. Let x = height of steeple. Set up a proportion:

$$\frac{\text{height of object}}{\text{length of shadow}} : \frac{x}{28} = \frac{6}{4}$$
$$4x = 6(28) = 168$$
$$x = 168 ÷ 4 = 42 \text{ ft.}$$

30. 39.

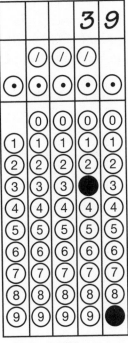

Let x = number of books on the small shelf, and $x + 8$ = number of books on the large shelf. Then $4x$ = number of books on 4 small shelves, and $3(x + 8)$ = number of books on 3 large shelves.

$$4x + 3(x + 8) = 297$$
$$4x + 3x + 24 = 297$$
$$7x + 24 = 297$$
$$7x = 297 - 24$$
$$7x = 273 ÷ 7 = 39$$

31. d. Separate the inequality into two inequalities, $x < 4$ and $-2 \leq x$. Choice **d** is the only graph that represents the inequalities. There must be an open circle to represent that the 4 is not included and a shaded circle to represent that the -2 is included.

32. e. x = one number and $3x + 12$ = the other number, for the equation:

$$x + 3x + 12 = -20$$
$$4x + 12 = -20$$
$$4x = -32$$
$$x = -8$$
$$3(-8) + 12 = -12$$

33. b. Use the order of operations.

$$-3 \times 5^2 + 2(4 - 18) + 33$$
$$-3 \times 25 + 2(-14) + 27$$
$$-75 + (-28) + 27$$
$$-76$$

34. c. Let n = number. Then n^2 = square of a number, and $n^2 + n + 4 = 60$.

35. e. Since $\frac{1}{4}$ in. represents 8 mi., 1 in. represents $4 \times 8 = 32$ mi., and 2 in. represents $2 \times 32 = 64$ mi., $\frac{1}{8}$ in. represents 4 mi. Then $2\frac{1}{8}$ in. represent $64 + 4 = 68$ mi.

36. c. Use the formula for the area of a triangle.
$A = (\frac{1}{2})bh$
$(\frac{1}{2})(4)(8) = 16$

37. e. 1 km = 1,000 m and 1 m = 100 cm. So 1 km = 100,000 cm and 1 km = 1,000,000 mm.

38. d. Let $x = \overrightarrow{DC}$. Since $\triangle ABE$ is similar to $\triangle CED$, the lengths of their corresponding sides are in proportion.
$\frac{x}{60} = \frac{80}{48}$
$48x = 80(60) = 4,800$
$x = 4,800 \div 48 = 100$
100 feet is the answer.

39. $\frac{1}{2}$.

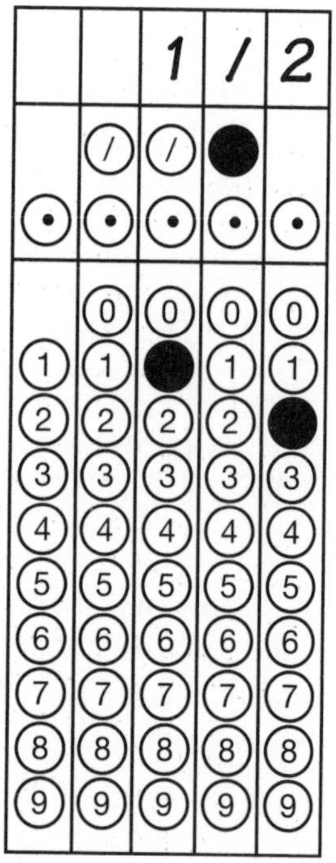

In a six-sided number cube, there are three prime numbers (2, 3, 5). The probability of landing on a prime number the first time would be $\frac{1}{2}$.

40. 2/1.

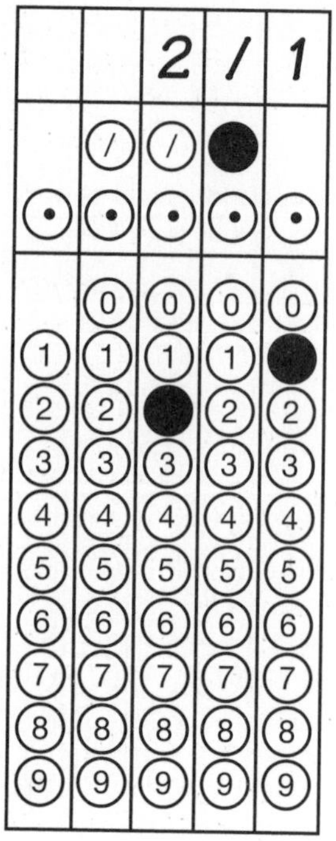

The number of total games played minus games lost will result in the number of games won ($45 - 15 = 30$). Write the ratio and simplify: 30/15 = 2/1.

41. c. When you flip a coin, the probability it will land on heads is $\frac{1}{2}$ (heads or tails). Flip that coin again and the possibilities you have would be HH, HT, TH, TT. You now have 4 combinations of which only one would give you HH (heads-heads); hence, the probability of that coin landing on heads twice in a row would be 1 out of 4 or $\frac{1}{4}$.

42. a. This is a simple combinations problem where order is not important. $9 \times 7 \times 11 \times 3 = 2,079$

43. a.

Possible Outcomes

Coin 1	heads	heads	tails	tails
Coin 2	tails	heads	tails	heads

The table lists the possible outcomes for the event of two coins being dropped on the floor. There are 4 possible outcomes. In 1 out of 4 occasions, both coins will land on heads.

44. **c.** The possible outcomes when rolling a six-sided die are: 1, 2, 3, 4, 5, 6. The even integers are 2, 4, and 6. The prime integers are 2, 3, and 5. Therefore, the likelihood of rolling a prime or even number are equal.

45. **b.** Evaluate using rules for order of operations:

$7(4) \div 14 + 5$

$(28 \div 14) + 5$

$2 + 5$

7

46. **d.** The first prime number is 2 and the fifth is 11; $11 - 2 = 9$

47. **b.** The product of any number and zero is zero. The only possible choice is 70 (**b**), because it has zero as one of its digits: $7 \times 0 = 0$.

48. **a.** Evaluate each choice:

$5^2 = 5 \times 5 = 25$

$2^5 = 2 \times 2 \times 2 \times 2 \times 2 = 32$

$3^3 = 3 \times 3 \times 3 = 27$

$8^2 = 8 \times 8 = 64$

$9^2 = 9 \times 9 = 81$

25 is the least numerical value; therefore, choice **a** is correct.

49. **d.** Each choice has the same three values arranged in different orders. First, evaluate the three values:

$2^4 = 2 \times 2 \times 2 \times 2 = 16$

$3^3 = 3 \times 3 \times 3 = 27$

$5^2 = 5 \times 5 = 25$

$5^2, 3^3, 2^4$ are in order from greatest to least.

50. **b.** Choices **a** and **c** are not correct because 4 is not a factor of 6. Choice **d** is also not correct, because 4 is not a factor of 30. That leaves only choice **b**.

Directions: Read each question carefully. The questions are multiple choice and may be based on a passage, table, or illustration. Select the one best answer for each question. Note: On the GED, you are not permitted to write in the test booklet. Make any notes on a separate piece of paper.

Questions 1–2 refer to following photograph and passage.

Source: National Archives and Record Administration.

After 72 years of campaigning and protest, women were granted the right to vote in 1920. Passed by Congress and ratified by 36 of the then 48 states, the Nineteenth Amendment of the U.S. Constitution states, "The right of citizens of the United States to vote shall not be denied or abridged by the United States or by any State on account of sex."

1. Who are the women in this photograph addressing?
   a. other women who say they don't want the right to vote
   b. President Woodrow Wilson
   c. abolitionists
   d. suffragettes
   e. isolationists

2. With which of the following statements would the photographer most likely agree?
   a. Women should behave in a dignified and orderly manner even if they are protesting.
   b. Women stand outside the gates of governmental power.
   c. The suffragettes would be more effective if they had more powerful slogans.
   d. Demonstrations are the most effective ways to influence lawmaking.
   e. Demonstrations are always ineffective.

Questions 3–5 refer to the following graphs.

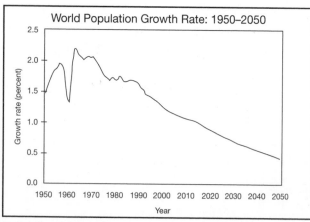

Rate of population growth = birth rate – death rate
Source: U.S. Census Bureau, International Data Base 10-2002.

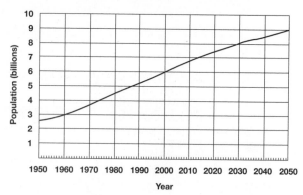

Source: U.S. Census Bureau, International Data Base 10-2002.

3. The greatest increase in the population growth rate between 1950 and 2000 occurred in
   a. 2001–2002
   b. 2000–2001
   c. 1990–2000
   d. 1962–1963
   e. 1956–1957

4. The world population growth rate dropped one percentage point between the mid-1950s and 1960. Which of the following best explains this occurrence?
   a. The ratio of births to deaths was higher in the mid-1950s than it was in 1960.
   b. A baby boom in the decade after World War II caused a spike in the birth rate.
   c. The introduction of the birth control pill in 1960 in the United States helped to slow the birth rate.
   d. There were more births in 1960 than there were in the mid-1950s.
   e. There were more deaths in 1960 than there were in the mid-1950s.

5. Which of the following statements is proved by the information in the two graphs?
   a. The population will reach its limit by 2050.
   b. When the rate of population growth decreases, so does the population.
   c. When the rate of population growth increases, so does the population.
   d. The rate of population growth will reach an all-time low in 2050.
   e. Even though the rate of population growth is decreasing, the population is increasing.

Question 6 is based on the following graph.

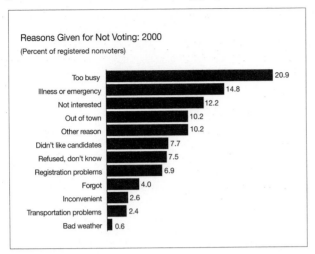

Reasons Given for Not Voting: 2000
(Percent of registered nonvoters)

Reason	Percent
Too busy	20.9
Illness or emergency	14.8
Not interested	12.2
Out of town	10.2
Other reason	10.2
Didn't like candidates	7.7
Refused, don't know	7.5
Registration problems	6.9
Forgot	4.0
Inconvenient	2.6
Transportation problems	2.4
Bad weather	0.6

Source: U.S. Census Bureau, Current Population Survey, November 2000.

6. Based on the information in the graph, which of the following proposals might best improve the voting rate?

  a. Distribute umbrellas to all households to encourage people to vote on rainy election days.

  b. Organize buses to help people get to voting places.

  c. Send reminders to registered voters so they do not forget to vote.

  d. Reschedule Election Day to a weekend so that people who are busy at work and at school can be available to vote.

  e. Provide more interesting candidates who inspire people to vote.

Questions 7–8 refer to the following passage.

The U.S. Constitution gives the president the power to veto, or reject, a bill passed by Congress. The president typically states his objections to the bill when he announces the veto. Because it takes a two-thirds vote from both the House of Representatives and the Senate to override a veto, Congress often changes the bill to make it more acceptable to the president. Sometimes Congress adds provisions to a bill that the president strongly favors. The president does not have the power of line-item veto, in which lines or parts of a bill can be rejected individually. The president must accept or reject the bill as Congress has written it.

7. Which of the following statements can you infer from the passage?

  a. Congress is more powerful than the president.

  b. Congress tries to get the president to accept its provisions by attaching provisions to a bill that the president supports.

  c. A president is more effective when members of the same political party are the majority in Congress.

  d. If a president vetoes a bill, there is no way to get it passed into law.

  e. Bills that the president vetoes are unconstitutional.

8. Which of the following conclusions can you make based on the passage?

  a. It is easier to rewrite and make a bill more acceptable to the president than it is to override a veto.

  b. It is easier to override a veto than it is to rewrite and make a bill more acceptable to the president.

  c. The U.S. Constitution gives the president the power to edit the bills he receives from Congress.

  d. The system of checks and balances insures that the president has no influence over the lawmaking branch of government.

  e. Presidents rarely use their power to veto.

Questions 9–10 are based on the following map.

World War I European Powers

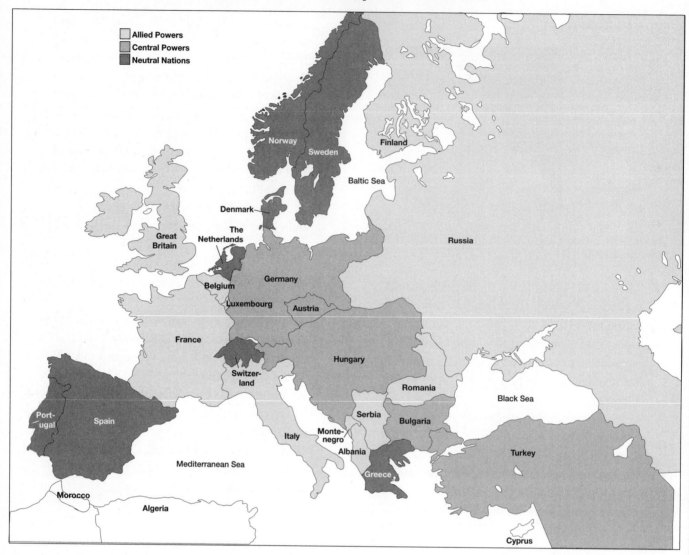

9. The United States maintained its neutrality in the war until Germany announced its intention to use unrestricted submarine warfare in the seas. The U.S. Congress declared war on Germany on April 6, 1917. By doing so, with what other nations was it siding?

  a. Bulgaria and Turkey

  b. Greece and Sweden

  c. Denmark and Sweden

  d. Morocco and Algeria

  e. Russia and Italy

10. U.S. President Woodrow Wilson called the war one "to make the world safe for democracy." Based on the map and this quotation, what conclusion can be drawn?

  a. Communist Russia was a threat to democracy in 1917.

  b. In 1917, Italy had become a fascist state that threatened democracy.

  c. Spain did not have a representative government in 1917.

  d. Germany and Austria-Hungary were not democracies in 1917.

  e. Great Britain was a constitutional monarchy in 1917.

Question 11 refers to the following map.

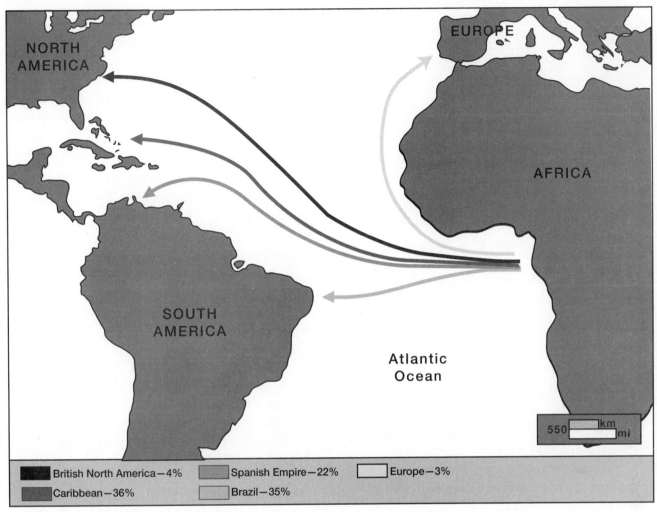

NORTH AMERICA

EUROPE

AFRICA

SOUTH AMERICA

Atlantic Ocean

550 km / mi

| | British North America—4% | | Spanish Empire—22% | | Europe—3% |
| | Caribbean—36% | | Brazil—35% | | |

Source: Data derived from Hugh Thomas, *The Slave Trade.* Simon and Schuster, 1997.

11. According to the information given in the map, which of the following conclusions can be drawn?

  a. The British colonies were the main destination of African slaves.

  b. South America did not allow the importation of slaves.

  c. Most slaves were sent to work on sugar plantations in Brazil and in the Caribbean.

  d. South America has a large population of African origin today.

  e. The main slave-trading region in Africa stretched 550 miles long.

Questions 12–13 are based on the following passage.

Mohandas Gandhi, also known as Mahatma Gandhi, developed a policy of passive resistance in his civil rights struggle for Indian immigrants in South Africa, and later in the campaign for Indian independence from British rule. The writings of the Russian author Leo Tolstoy and the essay, "Civil Disobedience," by nineteenth-century American Henry David Thoreau inspired Gandhi. Gandhi called acts of nonviolent resistance *satyagraha,* a Sanskrit term meaning "truth and firmness." The Salt Satyagraha of 1930 exemplified his policy. In protest to the British government's salt tax, Gandhi led tens of thousands of Indians on a 200-mile march to the Arabian Sea, where they made salt from evaporated sea water. Thousands, including Gandhi, were arrested. When the British conceded to his demands, Gandhi stopped the campaign. When he was released from prison in 1931, he traveled to London as a representative of the Indian National Congress to negotiate reform measures.

12. Which of the following would be the best title for this passage?
   a. The Salt March of 1930
   b. How to Lead an Effective Protest
   c. Gandhi's Acts of Nonviolent Resistance
   d. Free India
   e. Mahatma Gandhi and Henry David Thoreau

13. Which of the following conclusions can be drawn from the passage?
   a. Gandhi's nonviolent protests were effective political tools.
   b. The British did not respond to the Salt Satyagraha.
   c. *Satyagraha* means "truth and firmness" in Sanskrit.
   d. Gandhi refused to support the British government in World War II until it granted India its independence.
   e. India could not win its independence without resorting to violent revolution.

Questions 14–16 refer to the following passage.

In January 1863, during the Civil War, President Abraham Lincoln's *Emancipation Proclamation* freed more than three million slaves who lived in the Confederate states. Lincoln stated:

   "And by virtue of the power and for the purpose aforesaid, I do order and declare that all persons held as slaves within said designated states and parts of states are, and henceforward shall be, free; and that the Executive Government of the United States, including the military and naval authorities thereof, will recognize and maintain the freedom of said persons.

   "And I hereby enjoin upon the people so declared to be free and abstain from all violence,

unless in necessary self-defense; and I recommend to them that, in all cases when allowed, they labor faithfully for reasonable wages.

   "And I further declare and make known that such persons, of suitable condition, will be received into the armed service of the United States to garrison forts, positions, stations, and other places, and to man vessels of all sorts in said service."

Source: HistoryCentral.com.

14. According to the passage, which of the following was NOT one of Lincoln's expectations for the former slaves?
   a. to fight for the Union army
   b. to become free citizens
   c. to join the paid workforce
   d. to defend themselves if necessary
   e. to incite a rebellion among slaves in states that were loyal to the Union

15. Based on the values expressed in the *Emancipation Proclamation,* which of the following groups would have DISAPPROVED of it?
   a. nations like Great Britain and France where there was strong anti-slavery sentiment
   b. Confederate leaders
   c. abolitionists
   d. Union armed forces
   e. humanitarians

16. Which of the following is the most likely reason that Lincoln did not emancipate all slaves?
   a. Lincoln did not want to appease radical abolitionist groups.
   b. He believed slavery was an economic necessity.
   c. He did not want to upset the slaveholding states that were loyal to the Union—Delaware, Maryland, Kentucky, and Missouri.
   d. Lincoln did not believe that the complete abolition of slavery was possible.
   e. He wanted to uphold the Supreme Court decision in the Dred Scott case, which said that Congress could not regulate slavery in new territories.

Questions 17–19 are based on the following map.

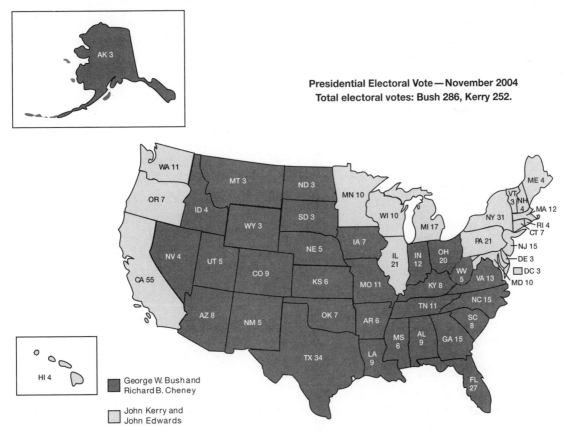

Presidential Electoral Vote—November 2004
Total electoral votes: Bush 286, Kerry 252.

George W. Bush and Richard B. Cheney

John Kerry and John Edwards

The electoral college is a group of electors who choose the president and vice president. Each state is allowed the same number of electors as its total number of U.S. senators and representatives—so each state has at least three electors. In most states, the candidate who wins the most popular votes earns that state's electoral votes.
Source: National Archives and Records Administration.

17. Based on the information in the map, which of the following might be true of Kerry's campaign strategy?
   a. It focused on winning the states in the Southeast.
   b. Kerry targeted his campaign efforts in his home state of Massachusetts.
   c. It targeted states that have large populations and a large number of electoral votes.
   d. It focused on winning most of the states with small populations.
   e. Kerry campaigned vigorously in George W. Bush's home state of Texas.

18. Which of the following is NOT a true statement?
   a. George W. Bush won a larger number of states.
   b. John Kerry was popular in New England.
   c. If Kerry had won Florida's electoral votes, he would have become president.

   d. If Kerry had won South Dakota's electoral votes, he would have become President.
   e. Bush did not appeal to the majority of voters on the west coast.

19. Which of the following conclusions can you make from the information in the map?
   a. Women are more likely than men to vote for the democratic party.
   b. Increasing numbers of Americans consider themselves political independents.
   c. The Sunbelt—the southern and southwestern states—was once a stronghold of the democratic party.
   d. There were distinct regional differences in voting patterns.
   e. You cannot make any predictions about voting patterns based on region.

Questions 20–21 refer to the following chart.

United States Foreign Trade Partners

COUNTRY	TOTAL TRADE	EXPORTS TO UNITED STATES (IN MILLIONS)	IMPORTS FROM UNITED STATES (IN MILLIONS)
Canada	407,995	178,786	229,209
Mexico	246,837	110,926	135,911
Japan	211,831	65,254	146,577
China	116,316	16,253	100,063
Germany	87,981	29,244	58,737
United Kingdom	85,038	41,579	43,459
Korea (South)	68,202	27,902	40,300

Source: U.S. Census Bureau.

20. Which of the following conclusions can you draw from the information in the chart?
   a. The United States trades the most with the countries that are geographically closest to it.
   b. Geographic location does not influence international trade.
   c. There is a relationship between the size of a country and its economic status.
   d. There is a relationship between the population density of a country and its economic status.
   e. Of all the U.S. trade partners, Canada has the highest gross national product (GNP).

21. Which of the following statements is best supported by the chart?
   a. The level of goods and services imported to the United States has increased in the last decade.
   b. Policies that restrict international trade do not have any effect on the U.S. economy.
   c. Japan imports and exports more than any other country in the world.
   d. The most important U.S. trade partners are industrialized, developed nations.
   e. Some products that are now imported were once manufactured in the United States.

Questions 22–25 refer to the following definitions of political beliefs and policies.

Isolationism: a national policy of avoiding political alliances with other nations

Nationalism: a sense of allegiance to the interests and culture of a nation

Socialism: the belief that essential property and services should be owned and managed by the government

Pacifism: the belief that nations should settle their disputes peacefully

Regionalism: a political division between two regions within an area

22. Read the quotation and identify which term best describes it.

"This whole nation of one hundred and thirty million free men, women, and children is becoming one great fighting force. Some of us are soldiers or sailors, some of us are civilians . . . A few of us are decorated with medals for heroic achievement, but all of us can have that deep and permanent inner satisfaction that comes from doing the best we know how—each of us playing an honorable part in the great struggle to save our democratic civilization."

—*Radio address of Franklin D. Roosevelt, October 12, 1942*

a. isolationism
b. nationalism
c. socialism
d. pacifism
e. regionalism

23. Read the quotation and identify which term best describes it.

"The . . . parties solemnly declare in the names of their respective peoples that they condemn recourse to war for the solution of international controversies, and renounce it as an instrument of national policy in their relations with one another."

—*Kellogg-Briand Pact, Article I, 1928*

a. isolationism
b. nationalism
c. socialism
d. pacifism
e. regionalism

24. Read the quotation and identify which term best describes it.

"The great rule of conduct for us in regard to foreign nations is, in extending our commercial relations, to have with them as little political connection as possible. So far as we have already formed engagements let them be fulfilled with perfect good faith."

—*President George Washington, Farewell Address, 1796*

a. isolationism
b. nationalism
c. socialism
d. pacifism
e. regionalism

25. Read the quotation and identify which term best describes it.

"The free States alone, if we must go on alone, will make a glorious nation. Twenty millions in the temperate zone, stretching from the Atlantic to the Pacific, full of vigor, industry, inventive genius, educated, and moral; increasing by immigration rapidly, and, above all, free—all free—will form a confederacy of twenty States scarcely inferior in real power to the unfortunate Union of thirty-three States which we had on the first of November."

—*Rutherford Birchard Hayes, January 4, 1861*

a. isolationism
b. nationalism
c. socialism
d. pacifism
e. regionalism

Questions 26–29 refer to the following map.

Time Zones across the Continental United States

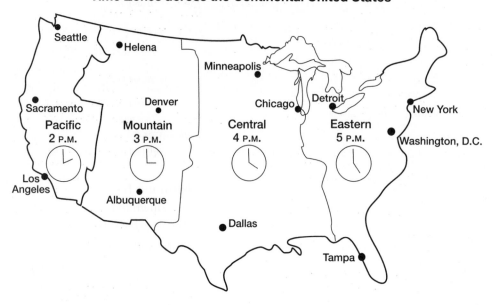

The Earth is divided into 24 time zones. The Earth rotates 15 degrees in one hour, so each time zone equals 15 degrees of longitude. The map illustrates the four time zones across the continental United States.

26. According to the map, what time is it in Dallas when it is noon in Sacramento?
- **a.** 2:00 P.M.
- **b.** 3:00 P.M.
- **c.** 2:00 A.M.
- **d.** 1:00 A.M.
- **e.** 11:00 P.M.

27. What time is it in Sacramento, CA, when it is midnight in Tampa, FL?
- **a.** 1:00 A.M.
- **b.** 12:00 P.M.
- **c.** 9:00 A.M.
- **d.** 9:00 P.M.
- **e.** 10:00 P.M.

28. As a traveler moves west, she can expect to
- **a.** change time zones.
- **b.** move into an earlier time zone for every 15 degrees of latitude she travels.
- **c.** experience jet lag.
- **d.** move into an earlier time zone for every 15 degrees of longitude she travels.
- **e.** move into a later time zone for every 15 degrees of latitude she travels.

29. In presidential elections, polling places typically close at 8 P.M. local time. In past elections, television networks have made predictions about which candidate is likely to win as soon as polls closed on the East Coast. Which of the following statements explains why this would anger some voters?
- **a.** The polls close later in New York than in Chicago.
- **b.** Voters in the Central time zone want to know who won in the eastern states before they cast their ballots.
- **c.** Polls in the Pacific time zone should open earlier if voters want their votes to matter.
- **d.** Even if the presidential election is decided early, people should still turn out to vote in their local elections.
- **e.** Predictions based on voting in the Eastern time zone may influence those who have not yet voted in the Pacific time zone.

Questions 30–31 refer to the following.

Voter Registration Application
For U.S. Citizens

	You can use this form to: ■ register to vote ■ report that your name or address has changed ■ register with a party **Please print in blue or black ink**	This space for office use only.		

1	Mr. Mrs. Miss Ms.	Last Name	First Name	Middle Name(s)	(Circle one) Jr Sr II III IV

2	Address (see instructions)— Street (or route and box number)	Apt. or Lot #	City/Town	State	Zip Code

3	Address Where You Get Your Mail If Different From Above (see instructions)	City/Town	State	Zip Code

4	Date of Birth ___/___/___ Month Day Year	5	Telephone Number (optional)	6	ID Number (see item 6 in the instructions for your State)

7	Choice of Party (see item 7 in the instructions for your State)	8	Race or Ethnic Group (see item 8 in the instructions for your State)

9	I swear/affirm that: ■ I am a United States citizen ■ I meet the eligibility requirements of my state and subscribe to any oath required. (See item 9 in the instructions for your state before you sign.) ■ The information I have provided is true to the best of my knowledge under penalty of perjury. If I have provided false information, I may be fined, imprisoned, or (if not a U.S. citizen) deported from or refused entry to the United States.	Please sign full name (or put mark) ↓ Date: ___/___/___ Month Day Year

10	If the applicant is unable to sign, who helped the applicant fill out this application? Give name, address and phone number (phone number optional).

Fold here

Please fill out the sections below if they apply to you.

If this application is for a **change of name,** what was your name before you changed it?

A	Mr. Mrs. Miss Ms.	Last Name	First Name	Middle Name(s)	(Circle one) Jr Sr II III IV

If you were **registered before but this is the first time you are registering from the address in Box 2**, what was your address where you were registered before?

B	Street (or route and box number)	Apt. or Lot #	City/Town	State	Zip Code

If you live in a rural area but do not have a street number, or if you have no address, please show on the map where you live.

C	■ Write in the names of the crossroads (or streets) nearest to where you live. ■ Draw an **X** to show where you live. ■ Use a dot to show any schools, churches, stores, or other landmarks near where you live, and write the name of the landmark.	NORTH ↑

Example — Route #2 — ● Grocery Store — Woodchuck Road — Public School ● — X

To Mail: 1. Address the back of this application (see address under your state).   3. Fold form at middle and seal at top.
2. Remove plastic strip below.   4. Put on a first-class stamp and mail.

Questions 30–31 refer to the form on page 469.

30. Which of the following is NOT a purpose of this form?
   a. notifying the government that you have changed your name
   b. registering with a political party
   c. applying for U.S. citizenship
   d. registering to vote in an upcoming local election
   e. indicating that you have moved and will be voting in another district

31. Which of the following expresses a FACT rather than an opinion?
   a. States have different requirements about who is eligible to vote.
   b. The voting age should be changed from 18 to 21 years of age.
   c. Every state should institute a "voter-motor" program in which people can register to vote at the same time that they are registering their motor vehicle.
   d. The government should allow non-citizens to vote.
   e. Voting should be considered a privilege, not a right.

Questions 32–33 are based on the following chart.

Consumer Price Index (CPI)—All Urban Consumers
1982–1984 = 100

YEAR	ANNUAL CPI	ANNUAL INFLATION RATE %
1920	20.0	15.6
1930	17.5	–2.3
1940	14.0	0.7
1950	24.1	1.3
1960	29.6	1.7
1970	38.8	5.7
1980	82.4	13.5
1990	130.7	5.4
2000	172.2	3.4

The Consumer Price Index (CPI) measures changes in the cost of living by comparing the prices in common goods and services like food, clothing, rent, fuel, and others. This chart uses the years 1982–1984 as a base period (1982–1984 = 100). An item that costs $100 in the base period would cost the amount listed in the CPI column for that year.
Source: U.S. Department of Labor, Bureau of Labor Statistics.

32. The inflation rate peaked in 1920 following World War I. What other time period was marked by a high inflation rate?
   a. the years immediately following the stock market crash of 1929
   b. the year following the oil crisis of 1979
   c. the recession of 1990
   d. the years preceding the U.S. entry into World War II
   e. the post-World War II period

33. Based on the information given, which decade experienced a decrease in the cost of living?
   a. 1930–1940
   b. 1940–1950
   c. 1950–1960
   d. 1970–1980
   e. 1990–2000

Question 34 is based on the following passage.

The First Amendment to the U.S. Constitution states the following: "Congress shall make no law respecting an establishment of religion, or prohibiting the free exercise thereof; or abridging the freedom of speech, or of the press; or the right of the people peaceably to assemble, and to petition the Government for a redress of grievances."

34. Which of the following situations is NOT protected by the First Amendment?
  a. a *New York Times* editorial criticizes the government's foreign policy
  b. a neo-Nazi group applies for a permit and stages a rally in a public square
  c. a criminal threatens to kill his victim if the victim does not forfeit his wallet
  d. a group meets in a chapel to worship
  e. students protest federal budget cuts in education

Questions 35–36 refer to the following paragraph.

From 2000 B.C. until the twentieth century, a succession of dynasties ruled China. The word China comes from the Ch'in Dynasty (221–206 B.C.), which first unified the country by conquering warring land-owning feudal lords. King Cheng named himself Shih Huang-ti, or first emperor, and consolidated his empire by abolishing feudal rule, creating a centralized monarchy, establishing a system of laws and a common written language, and building roads and canals to the capital. Scholars speculate that construction of the Great Wall or *chang cheng,* meaning "long wall," began during the Ch'in Dynasty in order to protect China's northern border from invaders. Shih Huang-ti ruled with absolute power, imposing strict laws and heavy taxes and doling out harsh punishments. He also is reputed to have burned books on topics that he did not consider useful. Shih Huang-ti died in 210 B.C. His son succeeded him but soon peasants and former nobles revolted and overthrew the dynasty. The Han Dynasty replaced it, ruling China until A.D. 220.

35. Which of the following is NOT a contribution of the Ch'in Dynasty?
  a. unification of territory
  b. feudal aristocracy
  c. road construction
  d. standardized written script
  e. regulations and penalties

36. Which of the following conclusions can you make based on the passage?
  a. The Ch'in Dynasty enjoyed a stable and long-lasting rule.
  b. By abolishing feudalism, Ch'in Shih Huang-ti promoted democracy in China.
  c. The Ch'in Dynasty was popular among peasants and displaced nobles.
  d. Disunity and disorder marked the Ch'in Dynasty.
  e. The Ch'in Dynasty had long-lasting influence.

37. Which of the following is the most reasonable explanation for a shortage of a product?
  a. Customers found the product overpriced.
  b. The producers overestimated the demand for the product.
  c. The producers underestimated the demand for the product.
  d. A rival company produced a cheaper version of the product.
  e. The product has very few uses.

Questions 38–39 are based on the following excerpt.

Beginning in 1958 . . . local NAACP [National Association for the Advancement of Colored People] chapters organized sit-ins, where African Americans, many of whom were college students, took seats and demanded service at segregated all-white lunch counters. It was, however, the sit-in demonstrations at Woolworth's store in Greensboro, North Carolina, beginning on February 1, 1960, that caught national attention and sparked other sit-ins and demonstrations in the South. One of the four students in the first Greensboro sit-in, Joe McNeil, later recounted his experience: ". . . we sat at a lunch counter where blacks never sat before. And people started to look at us. The help, many of whom were black, looked at us in disbelief too. They were concerned about our safety. We asked for service, and we were denied, and we expected to be denied. We asked why we couldn't be served, and obviously we weren't given a reasonable answer and it was our intent to sit there until they decided to serve us."

Source: www.congresslink.org and Henry Hampton and Steve Fayer (eds.), *Voices of Freedom: An Oral History of the Civil Rights Movement from the 1950s through the 1980s.* Vintage Paperback, 1995.

38. The writer has not directly stated, but would support, which of the following statements?
   a. Without the sit-in in Greensboro, NC, the civil rights movement would never have started.
   b. Woolworth's served affordable lunches.
   c. Local NAACP chapters were causing trouble and upsetting citizens.
   d. Nobody was surprised when black college students took a seat at the all-white lunch counter.
   e. The college students showed courage when they participated in the Greensboro sit-in.

39. What is the author's purpose in including Joe McNeil's quotation?
   a. to show that young people are the most likely to push for societal change
   b. to demonstrate that everyone has a different point of view
   c. to give a firsthand account of what has become a historic event
   d. to discount the importance of the civil rights movement
   e. to show that the college students had not intended to create a stir

Questions 40–41 are based on the following graph and passage.

The World's Child Laborers

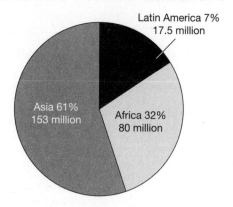

Of the world's 250 million child laborers, 186 million are under age five, and 170 million perform hazardous work. Most working children in rural areas labor in agriculture, while urban children work in trade and services, with a smaller percentage working in manufacturing, construction, and domestic service.

Source: Data from the International Labor Organization (ILO), www.ilo.org.

40. Based on the graph and passage, where would child-labor reform measures be the most effective?
   a. in Europe
   b. in rural areas
   c. in the developing world
   d. in areas where children are employed to work in mines
   e. in Latin America

41. Which conclusion can be made using the details provided in the chart?
   a. Eighty million African children work.
   b. Child labor is a worldwide problem.
   c. The problem of child labor has grown substantially in recent decades.
   d. If children work, they are most likely not attending school.
   e. The majority of working children reside in Asia.

Question 42 refers to the following chart.

Ten Fastest Growing Occupations, 2000–2010

OCCUPATION	PROJECTED GROWTH %	INCOME RANK	EDUCATION AND TRAINING
Computer software engineers, applications	100	1	Bachelor's degree
Computer support specialists	97	2	Associate's degree
Computer software engineers, systems software	90	1	Bachelor's degree
Network and computer systems administrators	82	1	Bachelor's degree
Network systems and data communications analysts	77	1	Bachelor's degree
Desktop publishers	67	2	Post-secondary vocational certificate
Database administrators	66	1	Bachelor's degree
Personal and home care aides	62	4	Short-term on-the-job training
Computer systems analysts	60	1	Bachelor's degree
Medical assistants	57	3	Moderate on-the-job training

Income rank categories
1 = very high ($39,700 and over)
2 = high ($25,760 to $39,660)
3 = low ($18,500 to $25,760)
4 = very low (up to $18,490)
Source: U.S. Department of Labor, Bureau of Labor Statistics.

42. Which of the following statements is supported by the information presented?

a. The largest number of jobs in the United States will be computer-related in the decade 2000–2010.

b. Computer-related jobs are the best paying in the nation.

c. Of the ten fastest growing jobs, the lowest paying is medical assistant.

d. Computer software engineers will have the most jobs of any field from which to choose.

e. Of the ten fastest growing jobs, the best paying require the most education.

Questions 43–44 are based on the following engraving.

Paul Revere made and sold this engraving depicting the "Boston Massacre," a pre-Revolutionary encounter between British troops and American colonists, in which five colonists were killed.

Source: HistoryCentral.com.

43. Which of the following messages did Paul Revere most likely want to convey in his engraving?
   a. American colonists should not protest the presence of British troops in Boston.
   b. The British troops were defending themselves against rowdy gangs of colonists.
   c. British troops savagely killed unarmed citizens.
   d. Americans should willingly pay the British taxes on imports of glass, paper, paint, and tea.
   e. British troops used only necessary force in dealing with the rioting crowd.

44. What can you infer was Revere's purpose in creating and selling the engraving?
   a. to make a large profit for himself
   b. to calm the rebellious spirit of Boston citizens
   c. to create support for the British empire
   d. to represent both sides of the event
   e. to fuel the revolutionary cause

Questions 45–46 are based on the following quotations.

"We might as easily reprove the east wind, or the frost, as a political party, whose members, for the most part, could give no account of their position, but stand for the defence [sic] of those interests in which they find themselves."
   —Ralph Waldo Emerson (1803–1882),
   American essayist

"A party of order or stability, and a party of progress or reform, are both necessary elements of a healthy state of political life."
   —John Stuart Mill (1806–1873),
   British philosopher

45. Which of the following party systems would Emerson most likely support?
   a. one in which citizens are loyal to a political party at all costs
   b. a single-party system
   c. a system with a liberal party that advocates for change and a conservative party that maintains tradition
   d. one in which citizens are independent and think for themselves
   e. a multi-party system

46. Which of the following party systems would Mill most likely support?
   a. one in which citizens are loyal to a political party at all costs
   b. a single-party system
   c. a system with a liberal party that advocates for change and a conservative party that maintains tradition
   d. one in which citizens are independent and think for themselves
   e. a multi-party system

Question 47 is based on the following passage.

German printer Johannes Gutenberg is often credited with the invention of the first printing press to use movable type. He used hand-set type to print the *Gutenberg Bible* in 1455. Although his invention greatly influenced printing in Europe, similar technologies were used earlier in China and Korea. Chinese printers used movable block prints and type made of clay as early as 1040, and Korean printers invented movable copper type about 1392.

47. What is the purpose of the paragraph?
a. to praise the advances of printing technology
b. to connect the early advances in printing with today's technological advances
c. to show that technological advances can develop in different geographical areas over periods of time
d. to give credit to Gutenberg for the first movable-type printing press
e. to show how Gutenberg's invention made printed materials more widely available

48. Cyclical unemployment is job loss that is caused by a recession or by fluctuations in the economy. Which of the following is an example of cyclical unemployment?
a. construction workers in the Northeast who are out of work during cold months
b. agricultural workers who are unemployed during non-growing seasons
c. employees who quit their jobs because they are dissatisfied
d. airline employees who are laid off because slow economic times have discouraged people from traveling
e. tradespeople who lose work because machines can perform a task faster and for less money

49. By 1878, the Standard Oil Company, owned by John D. Rockefeller, had bought out most of its business rivals and controlled 90% of the petroleum refineries in the United States. Which of the following was a likely effect of Standard Oil's business practices?
a. The company set limits on its prices.
b. The company increased oil prices.
c. Competition in the oil market flourished.
d. Standard Oil increased its efforts to attract needed customers.
e. The federal government offered a subsidy to make the company more competitive abroad.

Question 50 is based on the following graph.

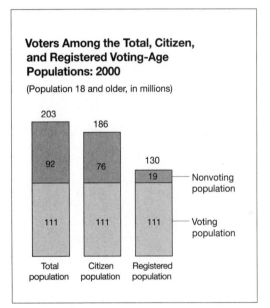

Source: U.S. Census Bureau, Current Population Survey, November 2000.

50. According to the graph, how many eligible U.S. citizens are NOT registered to vote?
a. 19 million
b. 56 million
c. 76 million
d. 92 million
e. 130 million

▶ Answers

1. b. The women in the photograph hold posters that ask, "MR. PRESIDENT HOW LONG MUST WOMEN WAIT FOR LIBERTY." Their protest is directed at President Wilson.

2. b. By portraying the women picketing outside the tall gates of the White House, the photographer is making a visual statement that concurs with choice **b**. The photograph provides no information to support any of the other answer choices.

3. d. The first graph shows the highest point in population growth rate between 1962 and 1963.

4. a. The population growth rate increases when the ratio of births to deaths increases.

5. e. Using the two graphs, you can compare the rate of population growth with the growth of the population. The growth rate is decreasing, while the population is increasing. None of the other statements are supported by the graphs. Choice **d** may seem correct; however, the graph only provides information for the years 1950 to 2050, making it impossible to draw conclusions about the "all-time low" of the world population growth rate.

6. d. Because the most common reason for not voting is "too busy," it is reasonable to conclude that rescheduling Election Day to a day when many people are not at work may improve the voting rate. Choices **b** and **c** may also help increase voter turnout slightly, but fewer people cite forgetfulness and transportation problems as a reason for not voting, so these answers would not be as effective as choice **d** would be.

7. b. Choice **b** is suggested in the passage. Because the president cannot reject single items within a bill, he must accept them if he wants the provisions he favors to become law.

8. a. Because Congress would rather rewrite a bill than try to override a veto, you can conclude that it is easier to do so. Choices **c** and **d** are not true and choice **e** is not discussed in the passage.

9. e. By declaring war on Germany, the United States joined forces against the Central Powers and thus with the Allied Powers, which included Russia and Italy.

10. d. Because Wilson allied the United States against the Central Powers, you can infer that the Central Powers were not democracies. Only choice **d** names Central Powers.

11. c. According to the map, 36% of slaves went to the Caribbean and 35% went to Brazil, far more than other destinations in the Americas.

12. c. Choice **c** is general enough to encompass the main ideas of the passage. Each of the incorrect answers is either too general (choices **b** and **d**) or too specific (choices **a** and **e**).

13. a. The British concession to Gandhi's demands shows that his use of nonviolent protest was an effective political tool. Choice **c** is a detail from the passage, not a conclusion that can be drawn from the passage; choices **b** and **e** are untrue; and choice **d** is not supported by the passage.

14. e. Lincoln stated that freed slaves should "abstain (withhold) from all violence, unless in necessary self-defense." He most likely did not want freed slaves to begin rebellions in areas where states loyal to the Union still held slaves.

15. b. The basic value expressed by the proclamation is liberty for enslaved people. Although it had limitations—it freed only slaves in states that had seceded—the proclamation marked a shift in Lincoln's policy. Slavery was completely abolished in 1865 with the Thirteenth Amendment. Pro-slavery Confederate leaders had the most reason to dislike the proclamation. They feared it would cause rebellion.

16. c. Lincoln was reluctant to issue an order that abolished slavery throughout the nation out of loyalty to the four slaveholding border states that stayed with the Union.

17. c. You can infer from the map that Kerry's campaign strategy focused on winning states with large populations and a large number of electoral votes, like California, Illinois, New York, Pennsylvania, and Michigan.

18. d. Had Kerry won South Dakota's three electoral votes, the final electoral vote total would have been Bush 283, Kerry 255. Therefore, Kerry's winning in South Dakota would not have been enough to change the results of the election. In contrast, had Kerry won in Florida (choice **c**), the final electoral vote would have been Kerry 279, Bush 259 (you must remember to add Florida's 27 votes to Kerry's total AND subtract Florida's 27 votes from Bush's total).

19. d. The map highlights the regional differences in the 2000 presidential election. Bush was clearly more popular in the southern and mountain states; Kerry was clearly more popular in the Northeast and on the Pacific coast. The map does not provide any information to support any of the other statements.

20. a. The countries that the United States trades the most with—Canada and Mexico—are also its geographic neighbors. The chart does not provide information to support conclusions about the size of U.S. trading partners (choice **c**), population density (choice **d**), or the GNP of trading partners (choice **e**).

21. d. Most of the countries listed as the United States' top trade partners are industrialized, developed nations. The chart does not provide information about the change in imports and exports over time, so choice **a** cannot be correct. Choices **b** and **e** are also unsupported by information in the chart; choice **c** is untrue.

22. b. The purpose of Roosevelt's address was to inspire a spirit of nationalism during World War II.

23. d. Signed by the United States and 15 other nations, the *Kellogg-Briand Pact of 1928* tried to promote pacifism. However, because there was no way to enforce the pact, it was not effective.

24. a. Washington advocates avoiding political attachments with other nations, which is an isolationist view.

25. e. This comment demonstrates the political division between the North and South before the outbreak of the Civil War.

26. a. Dallas falls in the central time zone, which is two hours ahead of Sacramento, which is located in the Pacific time zone.

27. d. Sacramento falls in the Pacific time zone, which is three hours behind Tampa, located in the Eastern time zone.

28. d. As illustrated on the map, a traveler would enter an earlier time zone as he or she moves west. According to the caption, each time zone "equals 15 degrees of longitude."

29. e. Some voters in the Pacific time zone have not yet cast their votes when the polls close in the East. Critics feel that early predictions can affect elections in this time zone.

30. c. You cannot use this form to apply for U.S. citizenship. The uses of the form appear in its upper left-hand corner.

31. a. The information on the voter registration form provides proof that choice **a** is a statement of fact. The inclusion of the word *should* in each of the incorrect answer choices is a strong indicator that these choices represent opinions rather than facts.

32. b. The second highest inflation rate listed on the chart is 13.5% in 1980, the year following the oil crisis of 1979.

33. a. The CPI decreased from 17.5 in 1930 to 14 in 1940.

34. c. The First Amendment protects political and religious speech. It does not give someone the right to threaten another person.

35. b. Ch'in Shih Huang-ti abolished the aristocracy of feudalism, instead appointing officials to carry out his rules in all of China's provinces.

36. e. The Ch'in Dynasty introduced a centralized government ruled by a monarchy—a form of government that lasted in China until 1911, when revolutionaries overthrew the last dynasty. The Ch'in Dynasty itself lasted for only 16 years however, so it could not be described as "stable and long-lasting" (choice **a**).

37. c. If the product were overpriced, overproduced, or had few uses, there would likely be a surplus of the product rather than a shortage.

38. e. Although the author does not state that the college students were brave, the firsthand account notes that the African-American Woolworth's employees "were concerned" about the students' safety. This implies that the students could not be sure of what consequences they would face.

39. c. The author uses Joe McNeil's account to give a firsthand description of what it was like to be a part of a significant event in the civil rights movement.

40. c. The majority of child labor takes place in the developing world, of which Africa, Asia, and Latin America are a part. You can theorize that the most effective reform measures would target the areas where most working children live.

41. b. Choices **a** and **e** are facts directly stated in the graph; they are not conclusions drawn based on analysis of the facts. Choices **c** and **d** are not supported by the information given. Choice **b** is a valid conclusion.

42. e. Choice **e** is the only one supported by the details of the chart. Although the chart offers the rate of growth of occupations, it does not give the overall number of jobs available.

43. c. By depicting the British troops firing into an unprotected crowd, Revere most likely wanted to show them as savage killers.

44. e. Revere most likely made and distributed this powerful image to further incite American colonists against the British.

45. d. Emerson portrays loyal party members as followers who cannot defend the positions of their own party. Emerson would most likely choose a system that encourages individual thought.

46. c. Mill believes that a healthy system needs political parties with the opposing goals of change and order.

47. c. Although Gutenberg is given credit for the invention of movable type, others in different parts of the world at different time periods had used a similar technique. This does not lessen the great effect that Gutenberg's invention had on European culture.

48. d. Employees who are laid off because of the effects of a recession are an example of cyclical unemployment.

49. b. Choice **b** is the most likely effect. By eliminating its competitors, Standard Oil controlled most of the production of oil and could artificially drive up prices.

50. b. Subtract the registered population (130 million) from the citizen population (186 million). Fifty-six million citizens are not registered to vote.

52▶ Practice Exam 2, GED Language Arts, Writing

▶ Part I

Directions: In each of the following passages, the paragraphs are lettered and the sentences are numbered. Read each passage carefully and then answer the questions that follow.

Questions 1–10 refer to the following memorandum.

Memorandum

To: All Jubilee Products Employees

From: Blair Borowski, Facilities Manager

Date: March 3, 2008

Re: New Carpet

ATTENTION

A

(1) This Saturday and Sunday, March 8 and 9, under your feet carpet company will be installing new carpets throughout the building. (2) All office areas being currently carpeted will get new carpeting. (3) All office areas that are not currently carpeted will also be carpeted.

B

(4) To prepare for the carpet installation, Under Your Feet have requested the following:
1. (5) Remove ALL non-furniture items from the carpet or floor in your work area.
2. (6) ALL items except computers and telephones from the top of your furniture should be removed.
(7) If for your office items you need boxes or storage space, please contact me at extension 425. (8) The new carpet will be dark blue.

C

(9) Your compliance is very important, I will circulate a reminder on Thursday and again on Friday mourning.

D

(10) Thank you in advance for your cooperation. (11) If you have any questions, please don't hesitate to contacting me.

1. Sentence 1: This Saturday and Sunday, March 8 and 9, under your feet carpet company will be installing new carpets throughout the building.
   Which correction should be made to sentence 1?
   a. Delete the commas after <u>Sunday</u> and <u>9</u>.
   b. Change <u>under your feet carpet company</u> to <u>Under Your Feet Carpet Company</u>.
   c. Replace <u>your</u> with <u>you're</u>.
   d. Change <u>new carpets</u> to <u>new-carpets</u>.
   e. No correction is necessary.

2. Sentence 2: All office areas being currently carpeted will get new carpeting.
   Which correction should be made to sentence 2?
   a. Change <u>being</u> to <u>that are</u>.
   b. Replace <u>office</u> with <u>Office</u>.
   c. Change <u>will get</u> to <u>is getting</u>.
   d. Move <u>all</u> to follow <u>areas</u>.
   e. No correction is necessary.

3. Sentence 3: All office areas that are not currently carpeted will also be carpeted.
   Which correction should be made to sentence 3?
   a. Change <u>that are</u> to <u>being</u>.
   b. Replace <u>carpeted</u> with <u>being carpeted</u>.
   c. Change <u>will</u> to <u>would</u>.
   d. Insert commas after <u>areas</u> and <u>carpeted</u>.
   e. No correction is necessary.

4. Sentence 4: To prepare for the carpet installation, Under Your Feet have requested the following:
   Which correction should be made to sentence 4?
   a. Change to <u>prepare</u> to <u>preparing</u>.
   b. Delete the comma after <u>installation</u>.
   c. Replace <u>have</u> with <u>has</u>.
   d. Change <u>Your</u> to <u>You're</u>.
   e. No correction is necessary.

5. Sentence 6: ALL items except computers and telephones from the top of your furniture should be removed.
   Which is the most effective version of sentence 6? If the original is the most effective, choose option **a**.
   a. ALL items except computers and telephones from the top of your furniture should be removed.
   b. Except computers and telephones, remove ALL items from the top of your furniture.
   c. ALL items should be removed, except computers and telephones, from the top of your furniture.
   d. Remove ALL items except computers and telephones from the top of your furniture.
   e. From the top of your furniture, you should remove ALL items except computers and telephones.

6. Sentence 7: If <u>for your office items</u> you need boxes or storage space, please contact me at extension 425.
   Which is the best location for the underlined portion of sentence 7? If the original is the best location, choose option **a**.
   a. following <u>If</u>
   b. following <u>boxes</u>
   c. following <u>space</u>
   d. following <u>please</u>
   e. following <u>425</u>

7. Sentence 8: The new carpet will be dark blue.
   Which revision should be made to the placement of sentence 8?
   a. Delete sentence 8.
   b. Move sentence 8 to follow sentence 3.
   c. Begin a new paragraph with sentence 8.
   d. Move sentence 8 to the end of paragraph C.
   e. Move sentence 8 to follow sentence 10.

8. Sentence 9: <u>Your compliance is very important, I will</u> circulate a reminder on Thursday and again on Friday mourning.

Which is the best way to write the underlined portion of sentence 9? If the original is the best way, choose option **a**.

a. Your compliance is very important, I will

b. Since your compliance is very important. I will

c. Being that your compliance is very important, I will therefore

d. Your compliance, being very important, I will

e. Your compliance is very important. I will

9. Sentence 9: Your compliance is very important, I will circulate a reminder on Thursday and again on Friday mourning.

Which correction should be made to sentence 9?

a. Change <u>will</u> to <u>should</u>.

b. Insert a comma after <u>again</u>.

c. capitalize <u>reminder</u>.

d. Replace <u>mourning</u> with <u>morning</u>.

e. No correction is necessary.

10. Sentence 11: If you have any questions, please don't hesitate to contacting me.

Which correction should be made to sentence 11?

a. Delete <u>if</u>.

b. Change <u>contacting</u> to <u>contact</u>.

c. Insert <u>not</u> after <u>don't</u>.

d. Change the period to a question mark.

e. No correction is necessary.

Questions 11–20 refer to the following passage.

How to Buy a Gift

A

(1) We by gifts all throughout the year for many different occasions. (2) Including birthdays, weddings, and anniversaries. (3) A few simple strategies can help you pick a good gift every time.

B

(4) First, decide how much money you will spend on the gift. (5) This depend upon two things: how much you can afford to spend and how much you want to spend. (6) You may be able to afford $100. (7) You may only want to spend $25. (8) A maximum limit should be set so that you do not go over budget.

C

(9) Second, decide what sort of gift you want to give. (10) Do you want your gift to be something practical, or would you rather give something whimsical. (11) Do you want a gift that is unique, or would the receiver prefer something ordinary? (12) Do you need something that's top of the line, or would the receiver appreciate a bargain brand? (13) Even if you don't know exactly what you want to get, having an idea of the kind of gift you want can help you make the most of your time while you are shopping.

D

(14) Determine where you can purchase the kind of gift you want within your budget. (15) For example, don't go to an upscale department store if your budget is only $25. (16) A little research can help you find the right place for your purchase. (17) That is making you, your wallet, and your gift recipient happy.

11. Sentence 1: We by gifts all throughout the year for many different occasions.

Which correction should be made to sentence 1?

a. Change <u>by</u> to <u>buy</u>.

b. Insert a semicolon after <u>year</u>.

c. Replace <u>occasions</u> with <u>occasion</u>.

d. Delete <u>throughout</u>.

e. No correction is necessary.

12. Sentence 2: Including birthdays, weddings, and anniversaries.

Which revision should be made to sentence 2?

a. Delete sentence 2.

b. Add <u>for example</u> to the beginning of the sentence.

c. Connect sentence 2 to sentence 1.

d. Move sentence 2 to follow sentence 3.

e. No revision is necessary.

13. Sentence 5: This depend upon two things: how much you can afford to spend and how much you want to spend.

Which correction should be made to sentence 5?

a. Add <u>Second</u> to the beginning of the sentence.

b. Change <u>depend</u> to <u>depends</u>.

c. Replace <u>can</u> with <u>should</u>.

d. Change <u>want</u> to <u>wants</u>.

e. No correction is necessary.

14. Sentences 6 and 7: You may be able to afford $100. You may only want to spend $25.

Which is the most effective combination of sentences 6 and 7?

a. You may be able to afford $100, you may only want to spend $25.

b. Since you may be able to afford $100, you may only want to spend $25.

c. In the case that you may be able to afford $100, you may only want to spend $25.

d. You may be able to afford $100 while only wanting to spend $25.

e. You may be able to afford $100 but only want to spend $25.

15. Sentence 8: A maximum limit should be set so that you do not go over budget.

Which is the best way to write sentence 8? If the original is the best way, chose option **a.**

a. A maximum limit should be set so that you do not go over budget.

b. Set a maximum limit so that you do not go over budget.

c. Having a maximum limit should be so that you do not go over budget.

d. With setting a maximum limit, budgets should not be gone over.

e. Do not go over budget without a maximum limit.

16. Sentence 10: Do you want your gift to be something practical, or would you rather give something whimsical.

Which correction should be made to sentence 10?

a. Change to be to being.

b. Replace would with will.

c. Change the period to a question mark.

d. Replace something whimsical with a whimsical thing.

e. No correction is necessary.

17. Sentence 13: Even if you don't know exactly what you want to get, having an idea of the kind of gift you want can help you make the most of your time while you are shopping.

Which is the most effective way to write the underlined portion of sentence 13? If the original is most effective, chose option **a.**

a. of your time while you are shopping

b. of your shopping time

c. of your time that is spent shopping

d. while you are spending your time shopping

e. of shopping at the time

18. Sentence 14: Determine where you can purchase the kind of gift you want within your budget.

The most effective revision to the beginning of sentence 14 would be:

a. At last, determine where you can purchase

b. One of the things to determine is where you can purchase

c. After you determine where to purchase

d. Third, determine where you can purchase

e. Yet, determining where you can purchase

19. Sentence 15: For example, don't go to an upscale department store if your budget is only $25.

Which correction should be made to sentence 15?

a. Change go to going.

b. Replace your with you're.

c. Change is to were.

d. Move for example to the end of the sentence.

e. No correction is necessary.

20. Sentence 17: That is making you, your wallet, and your gift recipient happy.

Which is the most effective way to write the underlined portion of sentence 17? If the original is the most effective, choose option **a.**

a. That is making you

b. That will make you

c. You will be made

d. While it makes you

e. Having made, you

Questions 21–30 refer to the following passage.

The Gateway Arch

A

(1) The skyline of St. Louis, Missouri, is fairly unremarkable, with one huge exception, the Gateway Arch that stands on the banks of the Mississippi. (2) Part of the Jefferson National Expansion Memorial, the Arch is a remarkable monument builded to honor St. Louis' role as the gateway to the West.

B

(3) Construction on the 630-foot-high structure began in 1961. (4) The construction was completed four years later in 1965. (5) The monument includes an underground visitor center that explores westward expansion threw galleries and a theater. (6) Two passenger trams take visitors to the Observation Room and the Museum of Westward Expansion at the top.

C

(7) In 1947, a group of interested citizens held a nationwide competition to select a design for a new monument that will celebrate the growth of the United States. (8) Other U.S. monuments are spires, statues, or imposing buildings. (9) The winner of this contest was a plan for a completely unique structure. (10) The man who submitted the winning design Eero Saarinen later became a famous architect. (11) In designing the Arch, Saarinen wanted to "create a monument which would have lasting significance and would be a landmark of our time."

D

(12) The Gateway Arch is a masterpiece of engineering. (13) A monument even taller than the Great Pyramid in Egypt, and in it's own way, at least as majestic. (14) The Gateway is an inverted catenary curve, the same shape that a heavy chain will form if suspended between two points. (15) Covered with a sleek skin of stainless steel, dazzling bursts of sunlight are often reflected by the Arch. (16) In a beautiful display of symmetry, the height of the arch is the same as the distance between the legs at ground level.

21. Sentence 2: Part of the Jefferson National Expansion Memorial, the Arch is a remarkable monument builded to honor St. Louis' role as the gateway to the West.

Which correction should be made to sentence 2?

a. Change <u>role</u> to <u>roll</u>.
b. Replace <u>builded</u> with <u>built</u>.
c. Delete the comma after <u>Memorial</u>.
d. Change <u>monument</u> to <u>Monument</u>.
e. No correction is necessary.

22. Sentences 3 and 4: Construction on the 630-foot-high structure began in 1961. The construction was completed four years later in 1965.

Which is the most effective combination of sentences 3 and 4?

a. Construction on the 630-foot-high structure began in 1961, following four years later with the completion of the construction.
b. The construction on the 630-foot-high structure was completed four years later in 1965, after construction began in 1961.
c. Construction on the 630-foot-high structure began in 1961 and was completed four years later in 1965.
d. Construction on the 630-foot-high structure, which began in 1961, was completed in 1965, being four years later.
e. Construction on the 630-foot-high structure began in 1961, therefore, it was completed four years later in 1965.

23. Sentence 5: The monument includes an underground visitor center that explores westward expansion threw galleries and a theater.

Which correction should be made to sentence 5?

a. Change <u>includes</u> to <u>including</u>.
b. Replace <u>explores</u> with <u>explored</u>.
c. Change <u>westward</u> to <u>Westward</u>.
d. Replace <u>threw</u> with <u>through</u>.
e. No correction is necessary.

24. Sentence 7: In 1947, a group of interested citizens held a nationwide competition to select a design for a new monument that will celebrate the growth of the United States.

Which correction should be made to sentence 7?

a. Change <u>will</u> to <u>would</u>.
b. Replace <u>held</u> with <u>did hold</u>.
c. Insert a comma after <u>monument</u>.
d. Move <u>in 1947</u> to the end of the sentence.
e. No correction is necessary.

25. Sentence 9: The winner of this contest was a plan for a completely unique structure.

The most effective revision to this sentence would begin with which of the following?

a. Similarly,
b. However,
c. Later,
d. In conclusion,
e. Therefore,

26. Sentence 10: The man who submitted the winning design Eero Saarinen later became a famous architect.

Which correction should be made to sentence 10?

a. Change <u>who</u> to <u>that</u>.
b. Insert a comma after <u>later</u>.
c. Replace <u>became</u> with <u>would have become</u>.
d. Insert a comma after <u>design</u> and <u>Saarinen</u>.
e. No correction is necessary.

27. Paragraph C, sentences 7 through 11: In 1947, a group of interested citizens ". . . would be a landmark of our time."

Which revision should be made to the placement of this paragraph?

a. Move paragraph C to the first sentence of the passage.
b. Move paragraph C to follow paragraph A.
c. Move paragraph C to the last paragraph in the essay.
d. Delete paragraph C.
e. No revision to placement is necessary.

28. Sentences 12 and 13: The Gateway Arch is a masterpiece of <u>engineering. A monument even taller</u> than the Great Pyramid in Egypt, and in it's own way, at least as majestic.

Which is the best way to write the underlined portion of these sentences? If the original is the best way, choose option **a.**

a. engineering. A monument even taller
b. engineering. A monument that was even taller
c. engineering, a monument even taller
d. engineering; a monument more tall
e. engineering, being a monument even as tall

29. Sentence 13: A monument even taller than the Great Pyramid in Egypt, and in it's own way, at least as majestic.

Which correction should be made to sentence 13?

a. Change <u>it's</u> to <u>its</u>.
b. Delete the comma after <u>way</u>.
c. Replace <u>at least as</u> with <u>just as much as</u>.
d. Change <u>taller</u> to <u>more tall</u>.
e. No correction is necessary.

30. Sentence 15: Covered with a sleek skin of stainless steel, <u>dazzling bursts of sunlight are often reflected by the Arch</u>.

Which is the best way to write the underlined portion of sentence 15? If the original is the best way, choose option **a.**

a. dazzling bursts of sunlight are often reflected by the Arch.
b. bursts of sunlight that dazzle are often reflected by the Arch.
c. dazzling, bursting sunlight, reflected by the Arch, is often seen.
d. often reflected by the Arch are dazzling bursts of sunlight.
e. the Arch often reflects dazzling bursts of sunlight.

Questions 31–33 refer to the following passage.

Augustus Saint-Gaudens

A

(1) Augustus Saint-Gaudens was born March 1, 1848, in Dublin, Ireland, to Bernard Saint-Gaudens, a French shoemaker, and Mary McGuinness, his Irish wife. (2) Six months later, the family immigrated to New York City, where Augustus grew up. (3) Upon completion of school at age 13, he expressed a strong interest in art as a career so his father apprenticed him to a cameo cutter. (4) While working at his cameo lathe, Augustus also took art classes at the Cooper Union and the National Academy of Design.

B

(5) At 19, his apprenticeship completed, Augustus traveled to Paris, France, where he studied under Francois Jouffry at the renown Ecole des Beaux-Arts. (6) In 1870, he left Paris for Rome, where for the next five years he studies classical art and architecture and worked on his first commissions. (7) In 1876, he received his first major commission—a monument to Civil War Admiral David Glasgow Farragut. (8) Unveiled in New York's Madison Square in 1881, the monument was a tremendous success; its combination of realism and allegory was a departure from previous American sculpture. (9) Saint-Gaudens' fame grew, and other commissions were quickly forthcoming.

31. Sentence 3: Upon completion of school at age 13, he expressed a strong interest in art as a career so his father apprenticed him to a cameo cutter.

Which correction should be made to sentence 3?

a. Insert a comma before <u>so</u>.
b. Change <u>completion</u> to <u>completing</u>.
c. Remove this sentence from the passage.
d. Change <u>upon</u> to <u>when</u>.
e. No correction is necessary.

32. Sentence 5: At 19, his apprenticeship completed, Augustus traveled to Paris, France, where he studied under Francois Jouffry at the renown Ecole des Beaux-Arts.

Which correction should be made to sentence 5?

a. Delete the comma after <u>Paris</u>.
b. Delete the comma after <u>at 19</u>.
c. Move <u>his apprenticeship completed</u> to the end of the sentence.
d. Change <u>renown</u> to <u>renowned</u>.
e. No correction is necessary.

33. Sentence 6: In 1870, he left Paris for Rome, where for the next five years he studies classical art and architecture and worked on his first commissions.

Which correction should be made to sentence 6?

a. Change <u>studies</u> to <u>studied</u>.
b. Delete the comma after <u>in 1870</u>.
c. Replace <u>for the next five years</u> with <u>from the next five years</u>.
d. Change <u>architecture</u> to <u>architect</u>.
e. No correction is necessary.

Questions 34–35 refer to the following passage.

Arson Response

A

(1) Following a recent series of arson fires in public-housing buildings, the mayor of West New York has decided to expand the city's Community Patrol—made up of 18- to 21-year-olds—to about 400 people. (2) The Community Patrol has been an important part of the city's efforts to reduce the number of arson crimes.

B

(3) In addition to the expanded patrol, the city has also decided to reduce the seriousness of these fires, most often set in stairwells, by stripping the paint from the stairwell walls. (4) Fed by the thick layers of oil-based paint, these arson fires race up the stairwells at an alarming speed.

C

(5) Fire retardant failed to work in almost all cases. (6) When the city attempted to control the speed of these fires by covering walls with a flame retardant. (7) In the most recent fire, the flames raced up ten

stories after the old paint under the newly applied fire retardant ignited. (8) Because the retardant failed to stop the flames, the city has decided to stop applying it will now strip the stairwells down to the bare walls.

34. Sentence 3: In addition to the expanded patrol, the city has also decided to reduce the seriousness of these fires, most often set in stairwells, by stripping the paint from the stairwell walls.

Which correction should be made to sentence 3?

a. Remove the word <u>also</u>.
b. Change <u>patrol</u> to <u>patrols</u>.
c. Change <u>has also decided</u> to <u>decided</u>.
d. Remove the word <u>these</u>.
e. No correction is necessary.

35. Paragraph C, sentences 5 through 8: Fire retardant failed . . . down to the bare walls.

Which revision should be made to this paragraph?

a. Move sentence 8 before sentence 7.
b. Move sentence 5 to the end of paragraph C.
c. Correct the nonstandard sentence.
d. Delete paragraph C.
e. No revision is necessary.

Please use the following to answer questions 36–40.

A

(1) Do you want to help save the earth? (2) Then put down that hair spray, put on a sweater, and get ready to go shopping! (3) Despite the widespread belief that the harmful effects of global warming are solely the responsibility of large factories, the individual consumer can do many things to stop this dangerous trend.

B

(4) Global warming is the gradual increase in the earth's temperature due to the greenhouse effect. (5) Greenhouse gases surround the earth. (6) Greenhouse gases have increased since the Industrial Revolution. (7) They surround the earth in a kind of "thermal blanket." (8) In the past 100 years, the atmospheric temperature of the earth has increased 1.1 degree F. (9) Sea level went up a bit, too. (10) The results of these changes are serious, the potential for increased flooding, agricultural changes, tropical storms, and tropical diseases.

C

(11) Most people have heard that increased factory emissions and air pollution contribute to global warming. (12) This is true. (13) The individual can also do a great deal to help slow down the process. (14) As a consumer, the choices you make can help save the earth from these effects. (15) Avoid buying anything with chlorine compounds. (16) They are very harmful to the environment. (17) They are found in spray paint, fire extinguishers, bleach and other products. (18) Other harmful chemicals which should be avoided are butane, found in air fresheners and hair sprays, and phosphates in laundry detergents.

D

(19) You can even be an environmentalist without leaving your house. (20) Maintain your air conditioner and refrigerator so to be sure no harmful chemicals like Freon leak into the earth. (21) By lowering your thermostat and putting on a sweater, you reduce our reliance on fossil fuels. (22) Simply using recycled toilet paper could save 373,000 trees if every U.S. household did it. (23) These simple changes could have a great benefit on the future of our planet.

36. Sentences 12 and 13: This is true. The individual can also do a great deal to help slow down the process.

The most effective transition to combine these sentences would be which of the following?

a. Despite
b. Meanwhile
c. Eventually
d. While
e. Furthermore

37. Sentences 5, 6, and 7: Greenhouse gases surround the earth. (6) Greenhouse gases have increased since the Industrial Revolution. (7) They surround the earth in a kind of "thermal blanket."

Which is the most effective combination of sentences 5, 6, and 7?

a. Since the Industrial Revolution, greenhouse gases, which surround the earth in a kind of "thermal blanket," have increased.

b. Greenhouse gases, which surround the earth, since the Industrial Revolution have increased in a kind of "thermal blanket."

c. Since the Industrial Revolution, greenhouse gases have surrounded the earth and they are increasing, they are a kind of "thermal blanket."

d. Greenhouse gases, surrounding the earth, are gases; they surround the earth in a "thermal blanket" and have increased since the Industrial Revolution.

e. Greenhouse gases surround and have increased since the Industrial Revolution they surround the earth in a kind of "thermal blanket."

38. Sentence 20: Maintain your air conditioner and refrigerator so to be sure no harmful chemicals like Freon leak into the earth.

What is the most effective way to write sentence 20? If the original is the most effective, choose option **a**.

a. Maintain your air conditioner and refrigerator so to be sure no harmful chemicals like Freon leak into the earth.

b. Maintain your air conditioner, and refrigerator, so you can be sure nothing harmful, like Freon or other chemicals, are leaked into the earth.

c. If you maintain your air conditioner and refrigerator you can be sure nothing harmful like Freon or other chemicals leaked into the earth.

d. Maintaining your air conditioner and refrigerator will ensure that no harmful chemicals such as Freon are leaked into the earth.

e. When you maintain your air conditioner and refrigerator, you will be able to be resting assured that nothing, like Freon or any other chemicals, will ever be found to be leaking into the earth.

39. Sentences 14 and 15: As a consumer, the choices you make can help save the earth from these effects. Avoid buying anything with chlorine compounds.

The most effective transition to combine these sentences would be which of the following?

a. Consequently

b. On the other hand

c. However

d. For example

e. Therefore

40. Sentence 10: The results of these changes are serious, the potential for increased flooding, agricultural changes, tropical storms, and tropical diseases.

The most effective revision to sentence 10 is which of the following? If you think the original is the best way, choose answer choice **a**.

a. The results of these changes are serious, the potential for increased flooding, agricultural changes, tropical storms, and tropical diseases.

b. The results of these changes are serious: the potential for increased flooding, agricultural changes, tropical storms, and tropical diseases.

c. The results of these changes, like the potential for increased flooding and agricultural changes and tropical storms and tropical diseases are serious.

d. The results of these changes are serious; the potential for increased flooding, agricultural changes, tropical storms, and tropical diseases.

e. The results of these changes are serious. The potential for increased flooding, agricultural changes, tropical storms, and tropical diseases.

Please use the following to answer questions 41–43.

A

(1) What's one of the newest additions to the Winter Olympics that involves spinning head over heels above the crowd with no equipment but a board? (2) It's snowboarding, of course!

B

(3) Snowboarding is similar to skiing, but it is actually more like surfing and skateboarding. (4) Snowboarding began in 1965 in the Michigan backyard of Sherman Poppen, who invented an early board

called a "Snurfer." (5) Today, snowboarding has evolved into a popular winter sport, with devotees all over the world.

C

(6) There are four distinct styles of snowboarding, with a slightly different snowboard design for each. (7) Freeriding is the basic cruising down the mountain, with no focus on speed or "tricks." (8) Freeriding is closely connected to surfing, since it rides whatever topography approaches the board, as surfers ride the waves they encounter.

D

(9) Probably the most popular style of snowboarding is freestyle. (10) Freestyle is not as effortless as the name implies. (11) In freestyle, the snowboarder tries to do different tricks, either in the air or on the ground. (12) These include spins, turns, and other maneuvers. (13) Freestyle is the riskiest form of snowboarding, and often the most exciting to watch. (14) When I go snowboarding next month, I will be trying freestyle again. (15) Boards are shorter and softer. (16) The snowboarders' boots are also softer, which makes doing moves easier. (17) Freestyle is a close cousin of skateboarding.

E

(18) Alpine snowboarding is where turns are made by carving into the snow rather than skidding. (19) This variation is much less popular in the United States than the other types of snowboarding. (20) Alpine boarders use hard plastic boots and ride on longer, narrower, and stiffer boards.

F

(21) The final style, backcountry, has an interesting history. (22) In the early days, before snowboarding enjoyed its current popularity, people who wanted to enjoy fresh powder snow on snowboards were not permitted at ski resorts. (23) In order to get their thrills, the snowboarders would have to hike up the mountains at the outskirts of the ski resorts without the benefit of a ski lift. (24) This situation led to the evolution of backcountry boarding, where a "splitboard" is often used. (25) A splitboard is a snowboard cut down the middle and then worn like snowshoes, allowing the boarder to hike up the mountain. (26) Then, when the top of the mountain is reached, the two pieces fit back together and the snowboarder goes down the mountain on the single board. (27) Other people use actual snowshoes or snowmobiles to ascend the mountain. (28) Safety is an important issue when engaging in backcountry boarding. (29) Avalanches can occur because of the instability of the fresh powder. (30) Riders should carry avalanche equipment with them.

41. Paragraph F, sentences 21 through 30: The final style, backcountry, has an interesting history . . . carry avalanche equipment with them.

    What addition should be made to the conclusion of this paragraph?
    a. Whether it's freeriding, freestyle, alpine, or backcountry snowboarding, this exciting sport offers a fun and challenging way to enjoy winter's snowy days!
    b. Backcountry riders should never snowboard alone.
    c. The American team recently won medals at the 2006 Winter Olympics.
    d. Skiers and snowboarders often argue over which sport requires more skill.
    e. If they get injured during backcountry runs, snowboarders can be in trouble.

42. Paragraph D, sentences 9 through 17: Probably the most popular style of snowboarding . . . is a close cousin of skateboarding.

    What sentence is irrelevant and should be eliminated from this paragraph?
    a. Freestyle is not as effortless as the name implies.
    b. These include spins, turns, and other maneuvers.
    c. When I go snowboarding next month, I will be trying freestyle again.
    d. Boards are shorter and softer.
    e. The most common binding stance used in freestyle is called "duck foot."

43. Sentence 18: Alpine snowboarding is where turns are made by carving into the snow rather than skidding.

Which addition should be made after sentence 18?

a. Done at a high rate of speed, alpine boarders make high-speed slalom-type turns, which are very powerful and closely resemble skiing.

b. Alpine boards should not be used for freestyle tricks.

c. Alpine boarders use plate bindings not used by other types of snowboarders.

d. It is important to decide which kind of snowboarding you want to do before you spend money on a particular snowboard.

e. An avalanche is a flow of snow down a mountainside.

Please use the following to answer questions 44–46.

A

(1) Your alarm clock rings, rousing you from sleep. (2) You switch on the lamp beside your bed, grab your remote, and watch the weather forecast. (3) Before you get out of bed, you call a friend on your phone. (4) You make plans to see a movie together that night. (5) Have you ever thought about how indebted you are to a hyperactive first-grade failure, without whom none of these actions would be possible?

B

(6) Thomas Alva Edison was born in 1847 in Ohio. (7) Throughout his life as a scientist and inventor, he was awarded an astonishing 1,093 patents, a national record. (8) He is famous not only for his inventions, but for his belief in hard work and perseverance. (9) At times, Edison spent 20 hours a day working on his inventions. (10) He uttered the famous quote, "Genius is 1 percent inspiration and 99 percent perspiration." (11) Earlier in his life, however, his future did not look so promising.

C

(12) Edison did not speak until he was almost four years old, but once he started, he never stopped asking questions. (13) He demanded that adults explain to him how everything he saw worked. (14) I have a little brother like that, so I know how annoying that can be. (15) After attending only three months of school, his teacher became frustrated and made it known that he thought hyperactive Tom's brains were "scrambled." (16) His devoted mother withdrew him from school and began homeschooling him, focusing on the "three r's" and the Bible. (17) His father inspired him to read great classic literature, rewarding him with a dime for each book he read. (18) His resulting passion for literature made him briefly consider becoming a Shakespearean actor, but stage fright and his high-pitched voice made him abandon that idea.

D

(19) Tom's early life, however, was filled with more than just academics. By age 12 he was also working, selling newspapers, candy and other food to commuters on trains. (20) At age 14 he began self-publishing a newspaper, which became quite popular. (21) He dealt with his profound hearing loss, which eventually left him totally deaf in one ear and 80% deaf in the other. (22) Rather than view this as an obstacle, he chose to look at the bright side: it "allowed him to tune out an ever more noisy world."

E

(23) As a teenager during the Civil War, Tom became a telegraph operator, a job that eventually led him to connect with inventors like Alexander Graham Bell. (24) Through his hard work and refusal to give up, Edison contributed a great deal to our country as a whole, and to us as individuals. (25) Eventually, Tom's questions proved too hard for his parents to answer, so they hired a private tutor to work with him.

44. Sentence 25: Eventually, Tom's questions proved too hard for his parents to answer, so they hired a private tutor to work with him.

Where would this sentence be effectively placed in this passage?

a. after sentence 1

b. after sentence 9

c. after sentence 14

d. after sentence 11

e. before sentence 24

45. Paragraph E, sentences 23 and 24: As a teenager during the Civil War, Tom became a telegraph operator, a job that eventually led him to connect with inventors like Alexander Graham Bell. Through his hard work and refusal to give up, Edison contributed a great deal to our country as a whole, and to us as individuals.

What addition should be made to the conclusion of this paragraph?

a. Thomas Edison proved that hearing loss is not an insurmountable obstacle.

b. Today, Thomas Edison would probably be labeled as having Attention Deficit Disorder.

c. Our lives, from how we live in our homes to how we are entertained, would not have been the same without the tireless efforts of this first-grade failure.

d. Thomas Edison's life reveals that some of us are just more gifted with great ideas than others.

e. Thomas Edison is proof that being gifted is a rare instance.

46. Which elimination would improve the effectiveness of this passage?

a. sentence 5

b. sentence 14

c. sentence 16

d. sentence 22

e. sentence 25

Please use the following to answer questions 47–50.

A

(1) The Civil War was one of the bloodiest and most difficult times in our history. (2) Out of this painful time, however, came a wealth of inspiring, lasting music. (3) In fact, General Robert E. Lee went as far as saying, "Without music, there would have been no army."

B

(4) In the years leading up to the Civil War, Americans are enthralled by music and social dancing. (5) When the war began, they continued their obsession with music. (6) Music had a place on the battlefield, in the camps, and among the family members awaiting the soldiers' return. (7) Among the soldiers, the various instruments played specific roles. (8) For example, the field drum kept soldiers in step while they marched, and also gave commands to troops on the battlefield. (9) The fife also helped soldiers march and was used to issue commands on the battlefield. (10) The fife was especially useful because its high pitch could be heard over loud battlefield noises. (11) Buglers played a critical and practical role as well, since they also issued commands to troops.

C

(12) Beyond practical uses within actual battles, the music of the Civil War served other purposes as well. (13) Music uplifted the solders' spirits and entertained them with stories of home. (14) It helped the soldiers bond with each other, especially important among the Confederate soldiers who were trying to establish a new nation.

D

(15) By the end of the Civil War, more music had been written and sung than in all other wars combined. (16) Many of these songs have endured to this day and are still sung by young and old alike.

47. Which sentence would improve the effectiveness of this passage?

a. General Robert E. Lee was first asked to lead the Union army, but declined.

b. Two enduring songs from the Civil War era are "The Battle Hymn of the Republic" and "Dixie Land," which can still be heard today.

c. The Civil War lasted four years.

d. Today, soldiers are more likely to listen to their own individual preferences rather than patriotic songs known to all.

e. Lee became the great Southern hero of the war, and his popularity grew in the North as well after his death in 1870.

48. Paragraph D, sentences 15 and 16: By the end of the Civil War, more music had … by young and old alike.

What addition should be made to the conclusion of this paragraph?

a. We should all realize that the music we listen to today was actually born on the Civil War battlefield.

b. It is clear from the history of the Civil War that nobody would join the army without inspiring music.

c. In reflecting upon the Civil War, music is an important component that should not be ignored.

d. The Civil War should make everyone want to learn a musical instrument so that they too can live on in history.

e. The music of the Civil War made me learn an instrument.

49. Sentence 8: For example, the field drum kept soldiers in step while they marched, and also gave commands to troops on the battlefield.

Which point does this sentence support?

a. The Civil War was one of the bloodiest and most difficult times in our history.

b. Among the soldiers, the various instruments played specific roles.

c. Music uplifted the soldiers' spirits and entertained them with stories of home.

d. Many of these songs have endured to this day and are still sung by young and old alike.

e. The Civil War divided families and friends.

50. Sentence 4: In the years leading up to the Civil War, Americans are enthralled by music and social dancing.

Which of the following is the best way to write the underlined portion of this sentence? If you think the original is the best way, choose answer choice **a.**

a. In the years leading up to the Civil War, Americans are enthralled by music and social dancing.

b. In the years since the Civil War, Americans are enthralled by music and social dancing.

c. In the years, leading up to the Civil War, Americans are enthralled by music and social dancing.

d. In the years leading up to the Civil War, Americans are going to be enthralled by music and social dancing.

e. In the years leading up to the Civil War, Americans were enthralled by music and social dancing.

▶ Part II

Answer the following writing prompt. Spend only 45 minutes on your response. Be sure you have a piece of scrap paper to brainstorm ideas and outline your essay. On the GED, you will not be allowed to write in the test booklet.

Follow these guidelines for Part II:

1. Write only on the assigned topic.
2. Write legibly on the lined pages provided.
3. Plan your essay carefully. Use a piece of scrap paper to brainstorm your essay and develop an outline.
4. After you have finished writing, review what you have written and make any changes that will improve your essay.

Prompt:

Many public schools have vending machines that sell junk food such as chips and soda. Because these foods are not part of a well-balanced diet, some people believe these machines should be banned from public school grounds. Others feel that students should have the choice to purchase the foods that they like. In your essay, state what you believe should be done about this issue and why. Use your personal observations, experiences, and knowledge to support your essay.

▶ Part II

▶ Answers

1. b. Under Your Feet Carpet Company is a proper noun (a specific company) and should be capitalized. Choice **a** is incorrect because there should be commas around the month and dates of the month. Choice **c** is incorrect because *you're* is a contraction of *you are;* the sentence needs the possessive *your.* Choice **d** is incorrect because *new* modifies *carpets,* so there should not be a hyphen between them. Choice **e** is incorrect because the proper noun must be capitalized.

2. a. The clause *that are currently carpeted* is the correct clause to modify *all office areas.* Choice **b** is incorrect because *office* is not a proper noun and should not be capitalized. Choice **c** is incorrect because the helping verb *will* is necessary to indicate the future tense. Choice **d** creates an awkward word order and does not correct the problem with *being currently carpeted,* which is the present perfect tense and incorrect. Choice **e** is incorrect because *being currently carpeted* must be corrected.

3. e. No correction is necessary to this sentence. Choice **a** is incorrect because *being* is the wrong tense; the carpets are already carpeted, not being carpeted. Choice **b** is incorrect for the same reason. Choice **c** is incorrect because *would* is the past tense; the action will take place in the future. Choice **d** is incorrect because *that are not currently carpeted* is an essential clause and should not be set off by commas.

4. c. The subject of the sentence, Under Your Feet [Company], is singular, so the verb must also be singular (*has,* not *have*). Choice **a** is incorrect because the infinitive form is *to + verb base,* not *verb + -ing.* Choice **b** is incorrect because the comma after *installation* is necessary; commas should follow introductory phrases. Choice **d** is incorrect because *Your* should remain possessive, not *you're,* which is a contraction of *you* and *are.* Choice **e** is incorrect because the error in subject-verb agreement must be corrected.

5. d. This choice follows the grammatical pattern of sentence 5, creating parallel structure. It is also the most active and direct. Choice **a** is incorrect because the phrase *from the top of your furniture* should come after the verb *removed.* It also does not use the structure of sentence 5. Choice **b** is incorrect because the *except* phrase, which lists the items that should not be removed, should come after items. Choice **c** is incorrect for the same reason; it is also passive and does not create parallel structure. Choice **e** is incorrect for the same reasons as choice **a**.

6. c. The space in question is for office items, so the prepositional phrase should immediately follow the word *space.* All other choices are awkward and/or illogical.

7. b. The best place for this sentence is immediately after sentence 3 because paragraph A focuses on the new carpet. Paragraph B is about what to do to prepare for the installation; paragraph C is about the importance of complying; and paragraph D is a conclusion, so the sentence does not belong in any of these paragraphs. Choices **d** and **e** are therefore incorrect. The color of the carpet is not essential information, but it is something employees would like to know, and the sentence should not be deleted (choice **a**). Choice **c** is incorrect because there is not enough information in the sentence to stand alone as a paragraph.

8. e. Sentence 9 (choice **a**) is incorrect because it is a run-on, and a period (choice **e**) corrects the run-on. Choice **b** also inserts a period after *important,* but it is incorrect because adding *since* makes the first sentence a fragment. Choice **c** uses the awkward and grammatically incorrect phrase *being that* instead of *since* or *because.* Choice **d** incorrectly uses *being* instead of *is* and uses a superfluous comma after *compliance.*

9. d. *Mourning* is the act or state of grieving; it is a homonym of *morning.* Choice **a** is incorrect because the helping verb that expresses an action that will be taken in the future is *will.* Choice **b** is incorrect because no comma is needed after *again. Reminder* is not a proper noun, so it should not be capitalized; choice **c** is therefore incorrect. Choice **e** is incorrect because *mourning* must be corrected.

10. b. There should not be an *-ing* on the end of a verb in an infinitive phrase. Choice **a** is incorrect because the subordinating conjunction *if* is necessary for the logic of the sentence. Choice **c** is incorrect because inserting *not* would make a double negative. Choice **d** is incorrect because the sentence is a statement, not a question. Choice **e** is incorrect because the infinitive needs to be corrected.

11. a. The preposition *by* is a homonym of the verb *buy*, which means to purchase. The verb *buy* is what is needed in the context of this sentence. Choice **b** is incorrect because semicolons can be used between complete sentences but not between an independent and dependent clause. Choice **c** is incorrect because *occasions* must be plural to agree with *many*. Choice **d** is incorrect because *throughout* is necessary for the logic of the sentence. Choice **e** is incorrect because *by* must be changed.

12. c. Sentence 2 is a fragment and should be connected to sentence 1. Choice **a** is incorrect because sentence 2 provides useful examples; there is no reason to delete it. Choice **b** is incorrect because adding *for example* would not fix the sentence fragment. Choice **d** is incorrect because the examples of reasons to buy gifts should immediately follow sentence 1. Choice **e** is incorrect because the fragment needs to be corrected.

13. b. *Depend* needs to be changed to *depends* to correct the error in subject-verb agreement; *this* is singular and needs a singular verb. Choice **a** is incorrect because the sentence does not offer another reason but rather an explanation of the first reason. Choice **c** is incorrect because *can* is the proper helping verb in this context; it is a matter of ability, not expectation. Choice **d** is incorrect because the change would create another error in subject-verb agreement; *you* and *want* both need to be singular. Choice **e** is incorrect because the subject-verb agreement error needs to be corrected.

14. e. This is the most concise and effective combination of sentences. Choice **a** creates a run-on sentence. The use of *since* in choice **b** makes the sentence illogical. Choice **c** is unnecessarily wordy. Choice **d** lacks the parallel structure of choice **e** and is awkward with the shift to *wanting* instead of *want*.

15. b. This is the most concise and active sentence, and it is written in the style of the rest of the passage. Choice **a** is incorrect because it uses the passive voice in the first part of the sentence. Choice **c** is incorrect because it is wordy and awkward. Choice **d** is incorrect because it is passive in both parts of the sentence. Choice **e** is illogical.

16. c. The sentence asks a question, so the period should be a question mark. Choice **a** is incorrect because an infinitive should always follow *want*. Choice **b** is incorrect because *would* is correct for asking preference. Choice **d** is incorrect because it does not use parallel structure. Choice **e** is incorrect because the question mark must be added.

17. b. This is the most concise and clear version. Choices **a**, **c**, and **d** are incorrect because they are unnecessarily wordy. Choices **d** and **e** are also awkward, and **e** is illogical.

18. d. This is the third step, and it should follow steps one and two by using a number transition. Choice **a** is incorrect because while this is the third and last step in the passage, *at last* is not the most effective transition given the context. Choice **b** is wordy and does not indicate the number of the step. Choice **c** is incorrect because it would create an illogical sentence fragment. Choice **e** is incorrect because the sentence does not contrast with the ideas in sentence 13.

19. e. This sentence is correct. Choice **a** is incorrect because the verb base form, not the *-ing* form, should follow *don't*. Choice **b** is incorrect because the possessive *your* is correct in the sentence. Choice **c** is incorrect because the sentence should be in the present tense. Choice **d** is incorrect because *for example* does not need to be moved. It could go to the end of the sentence, but the change is not necessary, and the phrase is better as an introduction.

20. b. The helping verb needs to express that the action takes place in the future, so *will* is the best choice. Choice **a** is incorrect because it uses a helping verb that expresses present, not future, action. Choice **c** is incorrect because it is illogical. Choice **d** is incorrect because it creates a sentence fragment. Choice **e** is incorrect; it also creates a sentence fragment, and it is illogical.

21. b. The past tense of *build* is irregular and should be *built*. Choice **a** is incorrect because roll has a different meaning. Choice **c** is incorrect because the comma is necessary after the introductory phrase. Choice **d** is incorrect because *monument* is not a specific noun as it is used in this sentence. Choice **e** is incorrect because the verb needs to be corrected.

22. c. Choice **c** is the most concise and correct version. Choice **a** is wordy and awkward. Choice **b** is not in chronological order, stating when construction was completed before stating when construction began. In choice **d**, the *being* is incorrect and should be removed, and *four years later* should be moved to before *in 1965*. Choice **e** is a run-on sentence, and therefore is not appropriate in the context.

23. d. *Threw* is the past tense of *throw;* the sentence requires the preposition *through*. Choice **a** is incorrect because the verb should be the regular third person present tense. Choice **b** is incorrect because the verbs should be in the present tense. Choice **c** is incorrect because *westward* is a general adjective (not referring to a specific region) and should not be capitalized. Choice **e** is incorrect because *threw* must be changed.

24. a. The past tense of the helping verb *will* is required. Choice **b** is incorrect because the simple past tense is required. Choice **c** is incorrect because no comma is necessary between *monument* and the descriptive clause that follows. Choice **d** is incorrect because it changes the meaning of the sentence, indicating that the growth of the United States occurred in 1947. Choice **e** is incorrect because the verb tense needs to be changed.

25. b. This transition establishes the correct relationship between sentence 8, which describes what other monuments are like, and sentence 9, which states that this monument design was unique. Choice **a** is incorrect because sentence 9 does not state an idea similar to the one in sentence 8. Choice **c** is incorrect because sentence 9 does not follow sentence 8 chronologically. Choice **d** is incorrect because it does not offer a conclusion to the ideas that precede it. Choice **e** is incorrect because sentence 9 does not offer an "effect" of sentence 8.

26. d. The designer's name is parenthetical information that should be set off by commas. Choice **a** is incorrect because *who* should be used when referring to people, not *that*. Choice **b** is an unnecessary comma. Choice **c** is incorrect because the helping verbs *would have* change the meaning and suggest that Saarinen didn't become a famous architect. Choice **e** is incorrect because the commas are necessary.

27. b. It is most logical to switch the order of paragraphs B and C so that the passage is in chronological order. Choice **a** is incorrect because paragraph A introduces us to the Arch and should remain the first paragraph of the passage. Choice **c** is incorrect because it further disrupts the chronological order, and paragraph D is the logical conclusion to the passage. Choice **d** is incorrect because the paragraph offers important information and should not be deleted. Choice **e** is incorrect because the paragraph is best moved before paragraph B.

28. c. Choices **a**, **b**, and **d** are sentence fragments. Choice **e** uses *being* incorrectly. Only choice **c** is correct, setting the description off with a comma.

29. a. *It's* is a contraction of *it is;* the sentence requires the possessive *its*. Choice **b** is incorrect because the phrase *in its own way* needs to be set off by commas on both sides. Choice **c** is incorrect because the change is awkward and does not convey quite the same idea. Choice **d** is incorrect because the superlative of one-syllable words should be formed by adding *-er*. Choice **e** is incorrect because the contraction should be changed.

30. e. This choice uses the active voice and has the correct subject: It's *the Arch* that reflects the sunlight, not the bursts of sunlight (choices **a**, **c**, and **e**). Choices **b** and **c** use the passive voice, and **b** also uses a phrase (*that dazzle*) rather than an adjective (*dazzling*) to modify *bursts*.

31. a. This sentence requires a comma before the coordinate conjunction *so*. Choices **b** and **d** would introduce diction errors. Choice **c** is incorrect because it removes information that is vital to the passage.

32. d. The context requires that the noun *renown* be replaced by the adjective *renowned*. Choices **a** and **b** would remove necessary punctuation from this sentence. Choice **c** moves a clause too far from its antecedent.

33. a. This choice changes the verb to the simple past tense, which is the tense used throughout the passage. Choice **b** is unnecessary. Choice **c** introduces an error—an incorrect preposition. Choice **d** would insert the incorrect word; *architecture* is the object that is created and can be studied and an *architect* creates this object.

34. c. This question tests the ability to identify a sentence fragment, which is a nonstandard sentence. Choices **a** and **b** would not serve the organization structure of the passage and would also create confusion. Choice **d** is not a logical revision; this paragraph adds to the overall message of the passage.

35. a. This question assesses the ability to recognize redundancy in a sentence. Choice **a** removes the redundancy by taking out the word *also*, which repeats the meaning of the introductory phase *in addition to*. Choice **b** is incorrect because the passage only mentions one patrol, so making the word plural would not make sense. Choice **c** suggests an unnecessary correction in verb tense. Choice **d** is a change that suggests that the writer is talking about all fires, rather than specifically about the arson fires that are the subject of the passage.

36. d. Using the transition *While* before the clause of the new sentence will alert the reader that the clause will introduce a new idea. Choice **a** is incorrect because, although the meaning of *despite* is similar, placing it before *this is true* will result in an ungrammatical sentence. Choice **b** is incorrect because *meanwhile* is a transition used to show concurrent events. Choice **c** is incorrect because *eventually* is used when something occurs after a period of time, which is not what the writer is trying to express here. Choice **e** is incorrect because *furthermore* is used to indicate an addition, which is not what the writer is trying to express here.

37. a. This choice is the most succinct, clear and grammatical way to combine the sentences while preserving the meaning of the original writing. Choice **b** is incorrect because the mid-sentence placement of *since the Industrial Revolution* is awkward. Choice **c** is incorrect because the comma splice creates a run-on sentence. Choice **d** is incorrect because it is redundant (repeating the idea of *surrounding*) and the use of the semicolon is incorrect considering the meaning of the sentence. Choice **e** creates a run-on sentence.

38. d. This is the clearest, most grammatical expression of the idea. Choice **b** uses too many commas, distracting the reader from the main point of the sentence. Choice **c** is incorrect because the use of the past tense (*leaked*) is incorrect. Choice **d** is incorrect because it is wordy and confusing. The construction *you will be able to be resting assured* is also ungrammatical. Choice **e** is both illogical and grammatically incorrect.

39. d. This is the best choice because the second sentence introduces an example to support the first sentence. Choices **a** and **e** are incorrect because the second sentence is not a result of the first. Choices **b** and **c** are incorrect because they signal an idea that appears to contradict or go against the first sentence, and that is not the case here.

40. b. Inserting a colon before the three specified results is grammatical and helps keep the meaning clear to the reader. Choice **c** is incorrect because the repeated use of *and* results in a stringy sentence. Choice **d** is incorrect because a semicolon must be followed by an independent clause. Choice **e** is incorrect because using a period to separate the sentences makes the second dependent clause a fragment.

41. a. This choice sums up the main idea of the writing and provides closure for the article. Choices **b** and **e** are incorrect because they provide further support for the paragraph on backcountry skiing, but do not summarize or tie up the rest of the article. Choice **c** is also incorrect because it does not relate to the focus of the passage as a whole. This statement would fit in one of the two background information paragraphs rather than at the end of the essay. Choice **d** is incorrect because it is unrelated to the focus as a whole and is irrelevant.

42. c. This is a personal comment that does nothing to explain the topic of the paragraph and thus does not add to the strength of the essay. Choice **a** is incorrect because it tells the reader something about freestyle: that it is difficult. This supports the focus of the paragraph. Choices **b** and **e** are incorrect because they provide specific examples of freestyle moves and stance, so they are relevant. Choice **d** is incorrect because the essay as a whole does focus on the different types of boards that are used for each type of snowboarding.

43. a. This choice provides further information about the topic of the paragraph, Alpine snowboarding. Choice **b** is incorrect because sentence 18 does not deal with the type of boards used; this information is found later in the paragraph, in sentence 20. Similarly, choice **c** is incorrect because information on bindings would fit in after sentence 20. Choices **d** and **e** are incorrect because they do not focus on the main point of the paragraph at all and are irrelevant.

44. a. This statement would make the most sense in the paragraph dealing with Tom's homeschooling experience. Choice **b** is incorrect because this statement comments on Tom's schooling and would not make sense following a discussion of his inventions and hard work. Choice **c** is incorrect because the statement begins with the transition *eventually*, leading us to conclude that Tom's parents did not hire a tutor immediately after they withdrew him from school. Choice **d** is incorrect because it would detract from the chronological order used in discussing Tom's schooling. Choice **e** is not reasonable; this sentence does not belong in the final paragraph.

45. c. This choice expresses the main idea of the article and even echoes the introductory paragraph. Choice **a** is incorrect because, although the article mentions hearing loss as a problem Edison overcame, it is not the focus of the article and is just a supporting detail. Choice **b** is incorrect because it does not summarize or provide closure for the article. If it were to be used as a supporting detail, it would need to be placed in the paragraph on Edison's schooling, after sentence 14. Choices **d** and **e** are incorrect because they are actually in opposition to the main point of the article. Edison's quotation in line 10 showed that he believed, as does the writer, that genius is more attributable to hard work than natural ability.

46. b. This is a personal reflection that is off the main topic and focus of the passage. It also does not have the same tone as the rest of the essay. Choice **a** is incorrect because it is background information that piques the reader's interest and is connected to the main point of the writing. Choice **c** shows that even when Tom was ridiculed by his teacher and then withdrawn from school, he obtained a good education from his parents. Choice **d** is incorrect because Tom's attitude toward his hearing loss is a further example of his perseverance and refusal to give up. Choice **e** is not correct; this is a valid conclusion for this passage.

47. b. This provides two examples of the lasting songs mentioned but not clarified in the last sentence of the essay. By adding these song titles, the writer provides concrete support for her claim. Choices **a** and **e** are incorrect because the focus of the article is not Lee. Adding these details will not help develop any of the main points of the passage. Choice **c** also does not lend support to any assertions made in the article. Although the broad topic includes the Civil War, the specific focus is the music, so this point does not strengthen the piece. Choice **d** is incorrect because it strays far from the topic of Civil War music and focuses on today's music.

48. c. This choice best expresses the main idea, that music was an integral part of the war. Choice **a** is incorrect because it overgeneralizes. Clearly, not all of today's music has its roots in the Civil War. Choice **b** is incorrect because it also makes too broad an assertion; despite Lee's quote in the first paragraph, it is untrue that literally nobody would join the army without music. He made the quote to make a point, using hyperbole or exaggeration, but to sum up the entire article by restating the quote as literal truth is incorrect. Choice **d** is incorrect because the point of the article is not the importance of individual musicians in history, so encouraging people to study music does not logically follow the passage. Likewise, choice **e** is incorrect; this passage is not intended to share personal details of the writer's life.

49. b. This statement gives examples of the role the field drum played. Choices **a** and **e** are incorrect because the statement does not give any specific information to support the number of people killed during the Civil War. Choice **c** is incorrect because the commands and marching beat given by the drum did not entertain them with thoughts of home. Choice **d** is incorrect because it deals with songs that are still played today, and the statement does not attempt to give any specific details to back this up.

50. e. This choice corrects the verb tense error. Because the Civil War is over, the years leading up to Civil War must be discussed using the past tense, not the present. Choice **b** changes the meaning of the sentence and neglects the verb tense problem. Choice **c** also ignores the verb tense error. Choice **d** mistakenly uses a future tense.

▶ Part II

For the essay prompt, you will find a sample score 6, 4, and 1 essay.

SAMPLE SCORE 6 ESSAY

Cigarette machines are not permitted on school grounds, of course. Now there's talk of banning vending machines that sell junk food as well. This isn't as crazy as it might sound. Potato chips and the like are obviously not as lethal as cigarettes, but they are unhealthy. As much as I believe in freedom of choice, I do not believe that vending machines that sell junk food should be allowed on primary and secondary school campuses.

Think about the typical vending machine, if you will. What's inside? Greasy potato chips, nachos dusted with artificial flavorings and MSG, candy bars, and sodas. The typical vending machine offers nothing with any nutritional value. Most don't even offer water or fruit juice (in fact, most "fruit juices" in vending machines contain less than 10% real fruit juice—the rest is sugar).

These foods are not just devoid of nutritional value—in large quantities, they are downright hazardous to your health. Most vending machine offerings are full of processed sugar, artificial colors and flavors, and fat. Too much of these ingredients can cause obesity, hyperactivity, and gastrointestinal distress. They can also cause problems in the classroom. Students on a heavy junk food diet can be disorderly (from too much sugar) or lethargic (from "crashing" after too many empty calories or from eating too much fat). They can have difficulty concentrating on their work and participating in physical activities.

OK, so junk food is bad for you. But what about freedom of choice? Don't we have the right to determine what we put into our bodies? Yes, we do. But eleven year olds might not be the best judge of what they should put in their bodies. Schools have the responsibility to create a healthy environment for students. If students really want to eat junk food, they can bring it from home or purchase it at a deli or store near school. It doesn't need to be available as an alternative to healthy lunches or snacks from the cafeteria. All school food offerings should be designed with the students' health as the number one priority.

If schools want to have vending machines on their property, fine. Just make sure that those machines offer students healthy choices. Schools teach students that they should eat healthy, and they should help students practice what they preach.

SAMPLE SCORE 4 ESSAY

Some people believe that junk food vending machines should not be allowed in schools, anymore. Even though this might bother people's freedom of choice, I think it's a good idea. The reason for this is because junk food is unhealthy, and schools should not offer things to students that are unhealthy.

For example, potato chips and soda are the most popular things from vending machines. Potato chips have a lot of salt and fat, and they don't have any vitamins or protein, nothing that is good for you. Soda is full of sugar, and it doesn't have any vitamins or protein, either. These foods are just "empty calories."

Eating a lot of junk food can be a very bad thing. For example, you can get headaches from sugar crashes. Too much sugar can make you hyper in class, or have trouble in concentrating. Too much fat can also make you too heavy or slow.

It's the school's responsibility to make sure it always offers healthy food to students. Junk food vending machines just aren't responsible. Schools can have vending machines, just the food needs to be different.

SAMPLE SCORE 1 ESSAY

In school are many vending machine with food to chose from. Student have lunch in the school everyday, they have allot of thing to chose from. The lunch, should be well, balanced. With vegetebles, also milk. Do not to eat much fat and so many empty caloreys.

This question is a very important one for the school's to make, about vending. What foods are healthy to be eaten? This is, for deciding, a difficult question!

53 ▶ Practice Exam 2, GED Language Arts, Reading

Directions: Read each passage carefully and answer the multiple-choice questions that follow. Choose the one best answer to each question.

Questions 1–6 refer to the following poem.

How Does the Speaker Feel about War?
War Is Kind

(1)   Do not weep, maiden, for war is kind.
        Because your lover threw wild hands toward the sky
        And the affrighted steed ran on alone,
        Do not weep.
(5)   War is kind.
            Hoarse, booming drums of the regiment
            Little souls who thirst for fight,
            These men were born to drill and die
            The unexplained glory flies above them
(10)   Great is the battle-god, great, and his kingdom—
            A field where a thousand corpses lie.

Do not weep, babe, for war is kind.
Because your father tumbled in the yellow
 trenches,
(15) Raged at his breast, gulped and died,
Do not weep.
War is kind.
  Swift, blazing flag of the regiment
  Eagle with crest of red and gold,
(20) These men were born to drill and die
  Point for them the virtue of slaughter
  Make plain to them the excellence of killing
  And a field where a thousand corpses lie.
Mother whose heart hung humble as a button
(25) On the bright splendid shroud of your son,
Do not weep. War is kind.
        —Stephen Crane (1899)

1. Which of the following words best describes the tone of the poem?
- **a.** celebratory
- **b.** mournful
- **c.** sarcastic
- **d.** joyful
- **e.** tender

2. The speaker repeats the line "War is kind" five times in the poem. Why?
- **a.** He wants to emphasize the truth of this line.
- **b.** He is talking to five different people.
- **c.** He is talking about several different wars.
- **d.** It emphasizes the irony of the statement.
- **e.** It is the theme of the poem.

3. Which of the following best conveys the theme of the poem?
- **a.** War is unkind, but necessary.
- **b.** There is no virtue in war.
- **c.** We should not weep for soldiers, because they died in glory.
- **d.** Everyone must sacrifice in a war.
- **e.** There are many ways to die in a war.

4. The speaker addresses three people in the poem: a maiden (line 1), a babe (a child, line 12), and a mother (line 24). What feeling in these listeners is the speaker addressing?
- **a.** their grief
- **b.** their pride
- **c.** their anger
- **d.** their joy
- **e.** their fear

5. From what you know about the speaker in the poem, what do you think he would do if his country went to war?
- **a.** join the military right away
- **b.** travel around the country trying to rally support for the war
- **c.** protest against the war
- **d.** cover the war as a reporter
- **e.** hurt himself so he would not have to fight

6. The speaker calls the "kingdom" of the "battle-god" (line 10) a "field where a thousand corpses lie" (line 11) and repeats lines 4 and 5 again in lines 16, 17, and 26. What is the effect of this line and its repetition?
- **a.** It demonstrates the might of the battle god.
- **b.** It shows how many casualties you can expect in a war.
- **c.** It reminds us to expect many deaths in a battle.
- **d.** It makes us fear the anger of such a powerful god.
- **e.** It shows us that the battle-god is a terrible god who should not be worshipped.

Questions 7–11 refer to the following passage.

What's Wrong with Biff and Happy?
[Biff is talking with his brother, Happy. They are together with their parents in the home where they grew up.]

(1) BIFF: [*with rising agitation*] Hap, I've had twenty or thirty different kinds of jobs since I left home before the war, and it always turns out the same. I just realized it lately. In Nebraska, when I herded cattle, and

(5) the Dakotas, and Arizona, and now in Texas. It's why I came home now, I guess, because I realized it. This farm I work on, it's spring there now, see? And they've got about fifteen new colts. There's nothing more inspiring or—beautiful than the sight of a

(10) mare and a new colt. And it's cool there now, see? Texas is cool now, and it's spring. And whenever spring comes to where I am, I suddenly get the feeling, my God, I'm not gettin' anywhere! What the hell am I doing, playing around with horses, twenty-eight

(15) dollars a week! I'm thirty-four years old, I oughta be makin' my future. That's when I come running home. And now, I get here, and I don't know what to do with myself. [*After a pause.*] I've always made a point of not wasting my life, and ever time I come

(20) back here I know that all I've done is to waste my life.

HAPPY: You're a poet, you know that, Biff? You're a—you're an idealist!

BIFF: No, I'm mixed up very bad. Maybe I oughta get married. Maybe I oughta get stuck into something.

(25) Maybe that's my trouble. I'm like a boy. I'm not married, I'm not in business, I just—I'm like a boy. Are you content, Hap? You're a success, aren't you? Are you content?

HAPPY: Hell, no!

(30) BIFF: Why? You're making money, aren't you?

HAPPY: [*moving about with energy, expressiveness*] All I can do now is wait for the merchandise manager to die. And suppose I get to be merchandise manager? He's a good friend of mine, and he just built a

(35) terrific estate on Long Island. And he lived there about two months and sold it, and now he's building another one. He can't enjoy it once it's finished. And I know that's just what I would do. I don't know what the hell I'm workin' for. Sometimes I sit in my

(40) apartment—all alone. And I think of the rent I'm paying. And it's crazy. But then, it's what I always wanted. My own apartment, a car, and plenty of women. And still, goddammit, I'm lonely.

—Arthur Miller,
from *Death of a Salesman* (1949)

7. Biff has come home because
   a. he needs a vacation.
   b. he isn't earning enough money at his new job.
   c. he feels like he isn't getting anywhere in life.
   d. he likes to be home in springtime.
   e. he misses his family.

8. Which of the following sentences best describes what's wrong with Happy?
   a. You can't run away from yourself.
   b. Money can't buy happiness.
   c. What goes around, comes around.
   d. Good things come to those who wait.
   e. Money is the root of all evil.

9. Which of the following sentences best describes what's wrong with Biff?
   a. He needs to stop being selfish and find someone to love.
   b. He needs to grow up and stop acting like a baby.
   c. He needs to pick one career and work hard until he achieves success.
   d. He needs to stop moving around so much and just stay in one place.
   e. He needs to accept who he is and stop searching elsewhere for happiness.

10. Why isn't the merchandise manager happy?
   a. He doesn't have enough money.
   b. He knows Happy is after his job.
   c. The more he has, the more he wants.
   d. He is lonely.
   e. He didn't like the way his estate was built.

11. Based on this passage, which of the following can we conclude about Happy's name?
   a. It is ironic.
   b. It is appropriate.
   c. It is a nickname.
   d. It is not his real name.
   e. It is symbolic.

Questions 12–16 refer to the following passage.

Why Is the Man Screaming?

(1) Edvard Munch's 1893 painting *The Scream* is a powerful work of art that has true aesthetic value. In its raw depiction of the unavoidable human emotions of alienation, anxiety and fear, *The Scream* invites

(5) meaningful introspection as the viewer internalizes its message of the vulnerability of the human psyche.

  The Scream is a very dynamic and yet frightening painting. The blood-red sky and eerie water/air seem

(10) to be moving and twirling, even enveloping the screaming man's mind as he stands on a bridge completely disregarded by passers-by who do not share in his horror. Viewers of the painting cannot help but ask: Why is the man screaming? And why is he alone

(15) in his scream? What is he afraid of? Or, what has he realized or seen that is making him scream? Why aren't the others as affected as he? The threat must be internal, yet the brushstrokes, colors and perspective seem to indicate that the horror is also bound to

(20) something in nature, something outside of the man. In any case, the agony and alienation are inescapable. Something horrible has happened or been realized by the man who cannot contain his horror, but it has not affected the others on the bridge.

(25)   That the people in the background are calm and do not share this horror conveys a truth regarding the ownership of our own feelings. We are often alone in our feelings, as can be especially noticed when we are in pain. The horror is the man's own; he

(30) must carry it himself.

  In this expressionist piece, the black, red, and orange colors are both bold and dark, illuminating and haunting at the same time. Remarkably, the light from the blood-reds and vibrant oranges in the dis-

(35) tant sky seem to be somewhat detached from the figure in the forefront, failing to reach his persona, suggesting that there is little to illuminate his (and the viewer's) fears. The man's face is nondescript; in fact, it almost looks more like a skull than a living

(40) man's face, hollow with two simple dots to indicate the nostrils, no hair, no wrinkles of the skin. This could be any man or woman, left to deal with his or her own horrors.

12. Which of the following best describes what is depicted in the painting?
   a. a man screaming as he falls through the sky
   b. a man standing alone on a bridge and screaming
   c. several people on a bridge, with the man in the forefront screaming
   d. several people on a bridge, all of them screaming
   e. something horrible happening to people on a bridge

13. According to the author, all of the following may be causing the man to scream EXCEPT
   a. He has seen something horrible.
   b. He has realized something horrible about himself.
   c. He has realized that he is alone.
   d. He has committed a murder.
   e. Something in nature has frightened him.

14. According to the author, what is the main effect of viewing this painting?
   a. We feel sorry for the screamer.
   b. We feel haunted by his agony and horror.
   c. We feel relieved that we are not on the bridge.
   d. We feel a sense of calm and quiet.
   e. We feel like screaming.

15. Which statement best shows the author's attempt to help viewers of *The Scream* make a personal application of the painting to their lives?
   a. "Edvard Munch's 1893 painting *The Scream* is a powerful work of art that has true aesthetic value."
   b. "*The Scream* is a very dynamic and yet frightening painting."
   c. "We are often alone in our feelings, as can be especially noticed when we are in pain."
   d. "The threat must be internal, yet the brushstrokes, colors and perspective seem to indicate that the horror is also bound to something in nature, something outside of the man."
   e. "Viewers of the painting cannot help but ask: Why is the man screaming?"

16. Based on the review, we can infer that Munch left the face of the screamer "nondescript" because
   a. he wanted to show that we are all the screamer.
   b. he did not like to paint detailed portraits of people, especially their faces.
   c. he couldn't decide how to make the person look.
   d. he wanted the person to look childlike and innocent.
   e. he wanted the hollow face to contrast with the swirling sky.

Questions 17–21 refer to the following passage.

What Is the New Dress Code Policy?

(1) Memorandum
   TO: All Employees
   FROM: Helen Suskind, Director,
            Human Resources Department
(5) DATE: March 22, 2008
   RE: Implementation of New Dress Code

A new dress code for all employees will take effect on September 1. All employees will be required to wear professional business attire while in the office. In this
(10) context, professional business attire excludes T-shirts, sleeveless shirts, shorts, jeans, athletic attire, mini-skirts, sandals, flip flops, and sneakers. The attached sheet provides a complete list of attire that is inappropriate for the office. Please be sure to review this list carefully.
(15)   Violations of the new dress code will be handled as follows:

   • First offense: Verbal warning
   • Second offense: Written warning and 30-day probation period
(20) • Third offense: Dismissal

      If you have any questions about the parameters of the dress code, please contact Martin Lamb in Human Resources immediately to schedule an appointment.
(25)   It is important that all employees understand the seriousness of this policy. Management based its decision to implement this code upon evidence that casual dress codes lead to a decrease in productivity. Our new dress code will help to maintain the repu-
(30) tation and integrity of our company by keeping us aware of the need for professionalism.
      Thank you for your cooperation.

17. According to the new policy, employees
   a. can wear sandals but not flip-flops.
   b. can wear short-sleeved shirts but not T-shirts.
   c. must wear suits or dresses.
   d. can wear shorts on very hot days.
   e. cannot wear hats in the office.

18. An employee who violates the dress code for the third time will
   a. receive a verbal warning.
   b. receive a written warning.
   c. be put on probation.
   d. be dismissed.
   e. meet with Martin Lamb.

19. The new dress code policy will take effect in approximately
   a. six days.
   b. two weeks.
   c. six weeks.
   d. six months.
   e. one year.

20. According to the memorandum, management decided to implement a formal dress code because
   a. a formal dress code makes a good impression on customers.
   b. casual dress may ruin the company's reputation.
   c. casual dress makes people less productive.
   d. formal dress reflects management's personal taste.
   e. formal dress helps create an atmosphere of cooperation.

21. It is possible to conclude from this memorandum that
   a. the company does not currently have a dress code.
   b. the dress code has been a controversial issue at the company.
   c. the company used to have a formal dress code and it is simply being reinstated.
   d. the employees will be unhappy about the policy.
   e. there has been a recent change in management.

Questions 22–25 refer to the following passage.

What Inspires Thomas?

[Thomas Builds-the-Fire is a Spokane Indian living on the Spokane Indian Reservation.]

(1) So Thomas went home and tried to write their first song. He sat alone in his house with his bass guitar and waited for the song. He waited and waited. It's nearly impossible to write a song with a bass guitar,
(5) but Thomas didn't know that. He'd never written a song before.

"Please," Thomas prayed.

But the song would not come, so Thomas closed his eyes, tried to find a story with a soundtrack. He
(10) turned on the television and watched *The Sound of Music* on channel four. Julie Andrews put him to sleep for the sixty-seventh time, and neither story nor song came in his dreams. After he woke up, he paced around the room, stood on his porch, and lis-
(15) tened to those faint voices that echoed all over the reservation. Everybody heard those voices, but nobody liked to talk about them. They were loudest at night, when Thomas tried to sleep, and he always thought they sounded like horses.

(20) For hours, Thomas waited for the song. Then, hungry and tired, he opened his refrigerator for something to eat and discovered that he didn't have any food. So he closed the fridge and opened it again, but it was still empty. In a ceremony that he had
(25) practiced since his youth, he opened, closed, and opened the fridge again, expecting an immaculate conception of a jar of pickles. Thomas was hungry on a reservation where there are ninety-seven different ways to say fry bread.
(30)   [. . . .]

As his growling stomach provided the rhythm, Thomas sat again with his bass guitar, wrote the first song, and called it "Reservation Blues."
—Sherman Alexie, from *Reservation Blues* (1995)

22. Based on the passage, we can conclude that Thomas
   a. does not take good care of himself.
   b. is poor.
   c. has always wanted to be in a band.
   d. is waiting for someone to help him.
   e. watches too much television.

23. Thomas titles the song "Reservation Blues." Based on this passage, you can expect the song to be about
   a. the good times he's had on the reservation.
   b. how he and his friends started a band.
   c. fry bread.
   d. the sounds he hears at night on the reservation.
   e. the difficulties of living on a reservation.

24. Why does Thomas keep opening and closing the refrigerator?
   a. He keeps hoping food will magically appear.
   b. He can't believe that the refrigerator is empty.
   c. He is angry and wants the door to break off.
   d. He likes the noise the door makes.
   e. He is bored.

25. The narrator tells us that "Thomas was hungry on a reservation where there are ninety-seven ways to say fry bread." What is the purpose of this sentence?
   a. to show us how important fry bread is to the language
   b. to show us how hungry Thomas was
   c. to make us want to try fry bread
   d. to show us the irony of the situation
   e. to show us how Thomas was inspired

Questions 26–30 refer to the following passage.

What Is the Narrator's Father Like?

(1) It was an impressive place: old, solidly built, in the Tudor style, with leaded windows, a slate roof, and rooms of royal proportions. Buying it had been a big step for my parents, a sign of growing wealth. This
(5) was the best neighborhood in town, and although it was not a pleasant place to live (especially for children), its prestige outweighed its deadliness. Given the fact that he wound up spending the rest of his life in that house, it is ironic that my father at first resis-
(10) ted moving there. He complained about the price (a constant theme), and when at last he relented, it was with grudging bad humor. Even so, he paid in cash. All in one go. No mortgage, no monthly payments. It was 1959, and business was going well for him.

(15) Always a man of habit, he would leave for work early in the morning, work hard all day, and then, when he came home (on those days he did not work

late), take a short nap before dinner. Sometime during our first week in the new house, before we had (20) properly moved in, he made a curious kind of mistake. Instead of driving home to the new house after work, he went directly to the old one, as he had done for years, parked his car in the driveway, walked into the house through the back door, climbed the stairs, (25) entered the bedroom, lay down on the bed, and went to sleep. He slept for about an hour. Needless to say, when the new mistress of the house returned to find a strange man sleeping in her bed, she was a little surprised. But unlike Goldilocks, my father did not (30) jump up and run away. The confusion was eventually settled, and everyone had a good laugh. Even today, it still makes me laugh. And yet, for all that, I cannot help regarding it as a pathetic story. It is one thing for a man to drive to his old house by mistake, (35) but it is quite another, I think, for him not to notice that anything has changed inside it.

—Paul Auster, from *The Invention of Solitude* (1982)

26. Why did the narrator's family move into the new house?
   a. Their old house was falling apart.
   b. They needed a house with more room.
   c. The new house was in a prestigious neighborhood.
   d. The neighborhood was great for children.
   e. The price was affordable.

27. Why did the narrator's father pay for the house in cash?
   a. He could not obtain a mortgage.
   b. He had the money because his business was successful.
   c. He borrowed the money from a friend.
   d. He didn't like to be in debt.
   e. He knew he would sell the house soon anyway.

28. The passage suggests that the narrator's father
   a. did not like change.
   b. was a very calculating man.
   c. was unhappy with his life.
   d. was very proud of his house.
   e. had many bad habits.

29. Why does the narrator think the story of his father's mistake is pathetic?
   a. It shows how stubborn his father was.
   b. It shows how little he knew his father.
   c. It shows how blind his father was to his needs.
   d. It shows how little attention his father paid to things around him.
   e. It shows how attached he was to the old house.

30. Based on the passage, how does the narrator feel about his father's life?
   a. His father was a great businessman.
   b. His father lived a sad, lonely life.
   c. His father was a financial genius.
   d. His father was often cruel, but always had good intentions.
   e. His father was impressive and strong, like the house where they lived.

Questions 31–34 refer to the following passage.

What Is Akakiy's Life Like?

(1) The young officials laughed at and made fun of him, and told in his presence various stories concocted about him, and about his landlady, an old woman of seventy; declared that she beat him; asked when the (5) wedding was to be; and strewed bits of paper over his head, calling them snow. But Akakiy Akakievitch answered not a word, any more than if there had been no one there besides himself. It even had no effect upon his work: amid all these annoyances he (10) never made a single mistake in a letter. But if the joking became wholly unbearable, as when they jogged his hand and prevented his attending to his work, he would exclaim, "Leave me alone! Why do you insult me?" And there was something strange in (15) the words and the voice in which they were uttered. There was in it something which moved to pity; so much that one young man, a newcomer, who, taking pattern by the others, had permitted himself to make sport of Akakiy, suddenly stopped short, as (20) though all about him had undergone a transformation, and presented itself in a different aspect. Some unseen force repelled him from the comrades whose acquaintance he had made, on the supposition that they were well-bred and polite men. Long afterwards (25) there recurred to his mind the little official with the bald forehead, with his heart-rending words, "Leave

me alone! Why do you insult me?" In these moving words, other words resounded—"I am thy brother." And the young man covered his face with his hand;
(30) and many a time afterwards, in the course of his life, shuddered at seeing how much inhumanity there is in man. [. . . .]

It would be difficult to find another man who lived so entirely for his duties. It is not enough to say
(35) that Akakiy labored with zeal: no, he labored with love. In his copying, he found a varied and agreeable employment. Enjoyment was written on his face: some letters were even favorites with him; and when he encountered these, he smiled, winked, and
(40) worked with his lips, till it seemed as though each letter might be read in his face, as his pen traced it.

Moreover, it is impossible to say that no attention was paid to him. One director being a kindly man, and desirous of rewarding him for his long service,
(45) ordered him to be given something more important than mere copying. So he was ordered to make a report of an already concluded affair to another department: the duty consisting simply in changing the heading and altering a few words from the first
(50) to the third person. This caused him so much toil that he broke into a perspiration, rubbed his forehead, and finally said, "No, give me rather something to copy." After that they let him copy on forever.

—Nikolai Vasilievich Gogol,
from "The Cloak" (1835)

31. Most of the time Akakiy's colleagues treat him with
a. respect.
b. admiration.
c. contempt.
d. pity.
e. reverence.

32. What does the newcomer learn from his experience with Akakiy?
a. Teasing is a form of cruelty.
b. Some people cannot take a joke.
c. The other officials are nice people.
d. Akakiy and he are long-lost brothers.
e. Akakiy deserves poor treatment.

33. Which best describes Akakiy's attitude toward his work?
a. He resents being just a copier.
b. He is a risk-taker.
c. He starts trouble with other workers.
d. He loves his work.
e. He is bored with his work as a copier.

34. All of the following describe Akakiy EXCEPT
a. patient.
b. anxious.
c. diligent.
d. angry.
e. shy.

Questions 35–37 refer to the following passage.

How Do the Characters Feel about Each Other?

(1) Young George Willard, who had nothing to do, was glad about the snow because he did not feel like working that day. The weekly paper had been printed and taken to the post office Wednesday
(5) evening and the snow began to fall on Thursday. At eight o'clock, after the morning train had passed, he went up to Waterworks Pond. There he built a fire against the side of a log and sat down at the end of the log to think.

(10) The young reporter was thinking of Kate Swift, who had once been his school teacher. On the evening before he had gone to her house to get a book she wanted him to read and had been alone with her for an hour. For the fourth or fifth time the
(15) woman had talked to him with great earnestness and he could not make out what she meant by her talk. He began to believe she must be in love with him and the thought was both pleasing and annoying. Looking about to be sure he was alone he talked aloud,
(20) "Oh," he declared. "I am going to find out about you. You wait and see."

It was past ten o'clock when Kate Swift set out and the walk was unpremeditated. It was as though the boy, by thinking of her, had driven her forth into the
(25) wintry streets. Kate Swift's mind was ablaze with thoughts of George Willard. In something he had written as a school boy she thought she had recognized the spark of genius and wanted to blow on the spark. One day in the summer she had gone to the

(30) *Eagle* office and finding the boy unoccupied had taken him out Main Street to the Fair Ground, where the two sat on a grassy bank and talked. The school teacher tried to bring home to the mind of the boy some conception of the difficulties he would have to

(35) face as a writer. "You will have to know life," she declared, and her voice trembled with earnestness. She took hold of George Willard's shoulders and turned him about so that she could look into his eyes. A passer-by might have thought them about to

(40) embrace. "If you are to become a writer you'll have to stop fooling with words," she explained. "It would be better to give up the notion of writing until you are better prepared. Now it's time to be living. I don't want to frighten you, but I would like to make you

(45) understand the import of what you think of attempting. You must not become a mere peddler of words. The thing to learn is to know what people are thinking about, not what they say."

—Sherwood Anderson,
from "The Teacher" (1919)

35. Why does George suspect Kate loves him?
   a. She told him.
   b. She gave him good grades in school.
   c. She wrote him a letter.
   d. She embraced him once.
   e. She has spoken to him several times with great enthusiasm.

36. What is Kate's reason for pursuing George?
   a. She is, in fact, in love with him.
   b. She wants to encourage him in his writing.
   c. She wants him to teach her how to build a fire.
   d. She wants his advice about writing.
   e. She wants to frighten him.

37. Kate gives George the following advice: "It would be better to give up the notion of writing until you are better prepared. Now it's time to be living." What does she mean by this?
   a. George will never be a good writer.
   b. George should forget about writing because he's going to die soon.
   c. George should have experiences in life before he starts writing.
   d. George should go to college to learn how to write.
   e. George should make more time in his life for writing.

Questions 38–40 refer to the following passage.

What Advice Is the Speaker Giving?

(1)   If you can keep your head when all about you
         Are losing theirs and blaming it on you;
      If you can trust yourself when all men doubt you,
         But make allowance for their doubting too:
(5)   If you can wait and not be tired by waiting,
         Or, being lied about, don't deal in lies,
      Or being hated don't give way to hating,
         And yet don't look too good, nor talk too wise;

      If you can dream—and not make dreams your
         master;
(10)   If you can think—and not make thoughts
            your aim,
      If you can meet with Triumph and Disaster
         And treat those two impostors just the same:
      [. . .]

      If you can talk with crowds and keep your virtue,
(15)   Or walk with Kings—nor lose the common
            touch,
      If neither foes nor loving friends can hurt you,
         If all men count with you, but none too much:
      [. . .] then
      Yours is the Earth and everything that's in it,
(20)   And—which is more—you'll be a Man, my son!
                  —Rudyard Kipling, from "If"

38. The first stanza of this poem appears to give advice about
   a. not allowing other people to influence you.
   b. following what other people do.
   c. how it's okay to lie if someone has lied to you.
   d. how you should only hate people who hate you.
   e. not waiting for good things to happen to you.

39. What is the best paraphrase of the following line: "If you can dream—and not make dreams your master"?
   a. Pursue your goals no matter what happens.
   b. Dreaming too much can ruin your life.
   c. Don't allow the pursuit of your dreams to take over your life.
   d. Help others make their dreams come true.
   e. Mastering your dreams will make you successful.

40. Which would make a good title for this passage?
   a. Lying in Wait for Haters
   b. Master Your Dreams
   c. How to Be Rich and Famous
   d. Win Over Kings and Commoners
   e. Living Successfully

▶ Answers

1. c. The tone of the poem, especially of the line "war is kind," is sarcastic; the poem shows how war is cruel in taking the lives of the soldiers. The sarcasm is particularly clear in lines 21–22: "Point for them the virtue of slaughter / Make plain to them the excellence of killing." Choice **a** is incorrect; there is no celebration in the poem. The lover, child, and mother all mourn (choice **b**) but they are not joyful (choice **d**). The dominant tone is sarcasm. There is tenderness expressed in a few lines, such as: "Mother whose heart hung humble as a button / On the bright splendid shroud of your son," but these tender lines only serve to heighten the sarcasm of the final line, "Do not weep. / War is kind."

2. d. Throughout the poem, the speaker shows how war is not kind: it kills a lover, a father, and a son; it leaves fields littered with thousands of corpses. The line is meant to show how nonsensical that statement is given all the evidence in the poem about how horrible war is. That war is kind is therefore not the theme of the poem (choice **e**), and it is not the truth he wants to emphasize (choice **a**), rather it is the irony of this line that he wants to emphasize. He talks to three different people, not five, so choice **b** is incorrect. He is talking about war in general—no specific war is mentioned—so choice **c** is also incorrect.

3. b. The tone of the poem makes it clear that war is not kind and that there is no virtue in slaughter or excellence in killing. There is no suggestion in the poem that war is necessary, so choice **a** is incorrect. The poem shows that the soldiers did not die in glory (indeed, the glory is "unexplained"), so choice **c** is incorrect. Each of the people the speaker addresses has sacrificed, but the theme of the poem is that such sacrifice is unnecessary and wrong, so choice **d** is incorrect. The poem describes a few ways to die in a war (choice **e**), but this is not a central idea of the poem.

4. a. The speaker is telling the maiden, child, and mother not to weep, and they have all lost a loved one, so he is addressing their grief. They may also be proud (choice **b**), angry (choice **c**) or afraid (choice **e**), but their main emotion concerning the death of their loved one is grief. They are not weeping with joy, so choice **d** is also incorrect.

5. c. The speaker does not approve of war and would most likely protest against it. Because he does not believe war is kind, because he does not see any virtue in slaughter, he would not join the military (choice **a**). The speaker is clearly anti-war, so he would definitely not travel the country rallying support for the war (choice **b**). He probably would not want to fight, but there is no evidence that he would attempt to hurt himself so he would not have to fight (choice **e**). Rather, his aim seems to be to help prevent war, making choice **c** the most logical answer. There is no evidence to suggest that he would cover the war as a reporter (choice **d**).

6. e. If the kingdom of a god is only corpses, he must be a powerful god (he can create such death and destruction), but he is also a terrible god who lacks love and compassion. In addition, if his kingdom is only corpses, then he has no living worshippers to follow him, so his power is paradoxical and, essentially, useless. These lines do show that the battle-god is mighty (choice **a**), but the theme of the poem is the terrible nature of war, so **e** is a better choice. There are indeed many casualties in a war (choice **b**) and many deaths in a battle (choice **c**), but these ideas do not convey an attitude toward war, and repetition is usually used to help convey theme. The poem does not try to make us afraid of war; rather, it wants us to see the terrible nature of war, so choice **d** is incorrect.

7. c. Biff tells Happy, "And whenever spring comes to where I am, I suddenly get the feeling, my God, I'm not gettin' anywhere! [. . . .] I oughta be makin' my future. That's when I come running home" (lines 11–17). The answer is clearly stated in this passage, so choices **a**, **b**, **d**, and **e** are incorrect.

8. b. Happy seems to think that money can buy him happiness (Biff seems to think this, too). Happy tells the story of his manager, who built himself a wonderful house and can't enjoy it—and he says he'd do the same thing. He tells Biff: "I think of the rent I'm paying. And it's crazy. But then, it's what I always wanted. My own apartment, a car, and plenty of women. And still, goddammit, I'm lonely" (lines 40–43). Happy believed that these material things would bring him happiness. He doesn't try to run away from himself (that's what Biff does), so choice **a** is incorrect. There's no evidence that he's getting what's coming to him, or that he's done something that he will be retaliated for, so choice **c** is incorrect. The passage suggests that he doesn't have a lot of patience, so choice **d** is incorrect. Although money isn't making Happy happy, it has not made him evil, just lonely; choice **e** is therefore incorrect.

9. e. Biff seems to keep moving around as if he is trying to get away from something (himself, his past) and searching for something else (happiness). But as he tells Happy, every spring, wherever he is, he realizes he is still not happy and he doesn't know what he's doing with his life. There is no evidence that he is selfish, so choice **a** is incorrect. He does not appear to be very mature, but he does not act like a baby (he is independent enough to travel around and support himself through work), so choice **b** is incorrect. Settling on one career won't necessarily bring him happiness, and he can't pick the right career until he accepts who he is and what sort of work is best suited for him, so choice **c** is not correct. Moving around (choice **d**) and switching careers are further part of the root problem, which is Biff's attempt to run away from himself and his past.

10. c. Happy explains that the manager built a "terrific estate" but only lived there for two months because "He can't enjoy it once it's finished" (line 37). Happy says he would do the same thing, and Happy is also a character who always wants more. The manager clearly has a lot of money, so choice **a** is incorrect. There is no evidence that he knows Happy is after his job, so choice **b** is incorrect. Happy tells us that he is lonely, but we do not know if the manager is also lonely, so choice **d** is incorrect. Happy says that the estate was "terrific," and there is no evidence that the manager didn't like the way it was built, so choice **e** is incorrect.

11. a. Happy is clearly not happy. As he tells Biff, he is very lonely. Thus, his name contradicts his state of being. Choice **b** is therefore incorrect. We do not know if Happy is a nickname or not his real name, so choices **c** and **d** are incorrect. Because *happy* is an adjective, not a thing, it is difficult for it to be symbolic and represent something else, so choice **e** is incorrect.

12. c. The author states that the man "stands on a bridge" and is "completely disregarded by passers-by" (lines 11–12). Thus, he is not falling through the sky (choice **a**), nor is he alone on the bridge (choice **b**). The author asks why the man is "alone in his scream" (lines 14–15), so the others are not screaming, and choice **d** is incorrect. Because the passers-by are unaffected, we can also rule out choice **e**.

13. d. The author speculates about a number of reasons for the man's scream. In lines 14–17 the author poses questions about why the man might be screaming. The author concludes "Something horrible has happened or been realized by the man who cannot contain his horror, but it has not affected the others on the bridge." This conclusion indicates that choices **a, b, c** and **e** may be reasons for the scream. The only exception is **d** as there is no evidence at all that the man has committed murder—this idea is a bit too specific to be inferred from the text.

14. b. The author says that it is "a very dynamic and yet frightening painting" that causes the viewers to wonder about the man's horror. Because the painting does not offer any answers to those questions, the viewers are left carrying the image of a screaming man with them, wondering what is the root of his horror. The author also states that the colors of the painting are "haunting" (line 33) and points out that viewers can connect to the man's feelings ("We are often alone in our feelings"). Choice **a** is incorrect because the main feeling conveyed by the painting is loneliness and horror; we do not know why he is suffering, so it is difficult to feel pity. We may feel relieved that we are not on the bridge (choice **c**), but the impact of the scream is far more powerful. We certainly do not feel a sense of calm and quiet (the "blood-red sky and eerie water/air seem to be moving and twirling"), so choice **d** is incorrect. Because the horror belongs to the man, not to us (although the point is that we can relate to that horror), the viewer is not likely to feel like screaming, so choice **e** is also incorrect.

15. c. This is the only answer choice that demonstrates the author's attempt to personalize the painting for the reader. By using the pronoun *we,* the author includes the viewer in his analysis of the painting and the statement itself is true for many people. Choices **a, b,** and **d** are simply statements of analysis in general, not as it applies to viewers' experiences. Choice **e** mentions the viewer but the questions are directed at the man in the painting, not at the feelings or experiences of the viewer.

16. a. The last sentence states, "This could be any man or woman, left to deal with his or her own horrors," suggesting that the reason the face is nondescript is to enable us all to identify with the screamer. There is no evidence that Munch did not like to paint faces (choice **b**) or that he couldn't decide how to make the person look (choice **c**). He may have wanted the person to look innocent (choice **d**) or to have the face contrast with the sky (choice **e**), but there is no suggestion of this in the review.

17. b. The first paragraph lists several items that are expressly prohibited by the new dress code. These items include sandals, flip flops, and shorts, so choices **a** and **d** are incorrect. The memo does not specify that employees must wear suits or dresses (choice **c**), nor does it mention the suitability of hats (choice **e**). T-shirts are prohibited, but short-sleeved shirts are not on the list, so choice **b** is the only possible correct answer.

18. d. The second paragraph clearly states the penalties for each offense. Employees will be dismissed for their third offense.

19. d. The memo is dated March 22 and states that the policy will go into effect September 1. This means it will take effect in about six months.

20. c. The fourth paragraph clearly states management's reason for implementing the dress code: because casual dress codes lead to a decrease in productivity. Formal dress codes may make a better impression than casual clothes on customers (choice **a**), but this is not mentioned in the memorandum. Management feels that formal dress will help "maintain the reputation" of the company, but there is no suggestion that management worries that casual dress will ruin the company's reputation (choice **b**). There is nothing in the memorandum suggesting the personal tastes of the management (choice **d**), nor is there evidence that formal dress fosters cooperation (choice **e**).

21. a. The memo begins by stating that a "new" dress code was going into effect, suggesting that this is the first policy of its kind for employees. More important, if there were an existing dress code, the memorandum would make comparisons between the current and new dress codes throughout the memo (e.g., "Under the new policy, employees will no longer be permitted to wear jeans to the office"). If the company were reinstating a prior policy (choice **c**), the memorandum would likely say so, especially for the benefit of employees who may remember the former code. It may be true that the dress code has been controversial (choice **b**), that employees will be unhappy with the code (choice **d**), or that there has been a recent change in management (choice **e**), but there is no evidence of any of these choices in the memorandum.

22. b. We can conclude that Thomas is poor because he does not have any food; his refrigerator is empty. The passage suggests that Thomas takes care of himself—he attempts to feed himself when he is hungry—and there is no evidence that he doesn't take care of himself, so choice **a** is incorrect. We do not know if Thomas had always wanted to be in a band or not (choice **c**). Thomas is waiting for inspiration, but there is no indication that he is waiting for someone to help him, so choice **d** is incorrect. He watches television in this passage, but we have no way of judging whether this is "too much" television or not, so choice **e** is also incorrect.

23. e. Even if you don't know that "the blues" are typically songs about hard times, the fact that Thomas used "his growling stomach" to "provide the rhythm" (line 31) tells us that the song is about the hard times he has experienced on the reservation. We learn that this is not the first time he has been hungry and found his refrigerator empty; opening and closing the refrigerator was "a ceremony that he had practiced since his youth" (lines 24–25). The passage does not include any references to good times Thomas has had on the reservation, so choice **a** is incorrect. There is no information in the passage about how he and his friends started the band, so choice **b** is also incorrect. The passage does mention fry bread (choice **c**), but then the title of the song would logically have some reference to fry bread. Choice **d** is incorrect for the same reason.

24. a. Thomas refers to this opening and closing of the refrigerator as a "ceremony," and he was "expecting an immaculate conception of a jar of pickles" (lines 26–27)—a magical appearance of food. He is unlikely to feel disbelief that there is no food (choice **b**) because he has always had an empty refrigerator (he's performed this "ceremony [. . .] since his youth"). There is no evidence that Thomas is angry (choice **c**) or that he likes the noise of the door (choice **d**), if the door indeed makes any noise. Thomas may be bored (choice **e**), but lines 26–27 indicate that choice **a** is the best answer.

25. d. It is ironic that in a place where there are so many ways to describe one food (indicating that this food is a central part of the culture), Thomas is hungry. The passage does not mention the language of the reservation, so choice **a** is incorrect. The sentence does not show any measure of how hungry Thomas was, so choice **b** is incorrect. The sentence does not describe fry bread or make it sound in any way appealing, so choice **c** is also incorrect. The passage tells us that it was Thomas's hunger, not the number of ways to say fry bread, that provided his inspiration, so choice **e** is incorrect.

26. c. The narrator tells us that the new house was in "the best neighborhood in town," and the neighborhood's "prestige outweighed its deadliness" (lines 5–7). There is no indication that their old house was falling apart (choice **a**) or that they needed more room (choice **b**). The neighborhood is clearly not great for children ("it was not a pleasant place to live [especially for children]"), so choice **d** is incorrect. The narrator tells us that business was going well for his father—so well, in fact, that he could pay for the house in cash—but that does not mean the house was affordable (choice **e**). In fact, if it was in the most prestigious neighborhood, it was probably expensive.

27. b. Although most people need a mortgage to buy a house, the narrator's father's business was so successful he was able to pay cash. There is no evidence in the passage to indicate choices **a**, **c**, **d**, or **e**. In fact, the father lived in the house the rest of his life (choice **e**).

28. a. The narrator tells us that his father was "always a man of habit"—so much so that he forgot he'd moved and went to his old house, into his old room, and lay down for a nap, not even noticing that the furniture was different. This suggests that he has a difficult time accepting and adjusting to change. There is no evidence that he is a calculating man (choice **b**). He may be unhappy with his life (choice **c**), which could be why he chose not to notice things around him, but there is little to support this in the passage, while there is much to support choice **a**. We do not know if he was proud of the house (choice **d**). We do know that he was a man of habit, but we do not know if any of those habits were bad (choice **e**).

29. d. That his father would not realize that someone else was living in the house—that he would not notice, for example, different furniture arranged in a different way—suggests that his father did not pay any attention to things around him and just went through the motions of his life by habit. Being habitual is different from being stubborn, so choice **a** is incorrect. The narrator is talking about his father and seems to know him quite well, so choice **b** is incorrect. We do not know if the narrator's father was inattentive to his needs (choice **c**), though if he did not pay attention to things around him, he likely did not pay much attention to his children. Still, there is not enough evidence in this passage to draw this conclusion. His father may have been very attached to the old house (choice **e**), but the incident doesn't just show attachment; it shows a lack of awareness of the world around him.

30. b. The bulk of this passage is the story that the narrator finds "pathetic," so the most logical conclusion regarding his feelings for his father is that he lived a sad life. We know that his business was going well, but the narrator does not discuss his father's methods or approach to business, so choice **a** is incorrect. Choice **c** is likewise incorrect; there is no discussion of his father's handling of financial affairs. Choice **d** is

incorrect because there is no evidence that his father was ever cruel. His father may have been impressive and strong (choice **e**), but the dominant theme is his habitual nature and the sad fact that he did not notice things changing around him.

31. c. The opening lines of this passage show Akakiy's colleagues making jokes about him, throwing paper over his head, and disrupting his work. These are all signs of contempt. Nowhere is there evidence of his colleagues having respect (choice **a**), admiration (choice **b**), or reverence (choice **e**) for Akakiy. Although one colleague feels sorry after making fun of Akakiy, this is only one man, not most of his colleagues, most of the time, which is why choice **d** is incorrect.

32. a. The newcomer at first joins the other officials in teasing Akakiy, but when Akakiy finally objects, the newcomer realizes that people can be very cruel to one another. This lesson actually remains with him throughout his life. Although the officials are joking with Akakiy (choice **b**), the jokes are clearly at his expense, and in fact, he does ignore the jokes until they interfere with his work, so this choice is incorrect. Choice **c** is clearly not true as the other officials are portrayed as fairly mean. The passage states that Akakiy's hidden meaning in his objection to the teasing is "I am thy brother." This is not meant to be taken literally but to remind the newcomer (and the reader) that we are all human and deserve a certain amount of respect; therefore, choice **d** is incorrect. There is nothing to indicate that Akakiy deserves this poor treatment (choice **e**).

33. d. The passage states, "It is not enough to say that Akakiy labored with zeal: no, he labored with love." He does not resent being a copier (choice **a**), and actually becomes nervous when given a more responsible duty (choice **b**). He insists on going back to copying and remains doing that "forever," so it can be assumed that he is not bored with it (choice **e**). The other workers do tease Akakiy, but he himself does not start the trouble (choice **c**).

34. d. Despite all the teasing, there is no indication that Akakiy ever becomes angry. When he objects, the text states, "And there was something strange in the words and the voice in which they were uttered. There was in it something which moved to pity." All the other choices accurately describe Akakiy. He is patient in his work and with his colleagues (choice **a**); he becomes anxious when given additional responsibility (choice **b**); he is a hard worker (choice **c**); and he presents as rather shy (choice **e**).

35. e. The passage states, "For the fourth or fifth time the woman had talked to him with great earnestness and he could not make out what she meant by her talk. He began to believe she must be in love with him and the thought was both pleasing and annoying." Choice **a** is incorrect because Kate has not told George that she loves him; that is why he is confused about it. Choice **b** is incorrect because there is no indication that Kate gave him good grades; he was apparently intelligent and earned good grades. The passage makes no reference to Kate writing a letter (choice **c**). Although the passage states that a passer-by might have thought they were about to embrace, Kate and George do not embrace in this passage.

36. b. The passage states, "In something he had written as a school boy she thought she had recognized the spark of genius and wanted to blow on the spark," and then continues to show Kate discussing writing with George. There is no indication that Kate is in love with George (choice **a**). The reference to a spark is symbolic and has nothing to do with a real fire (choice **c**). Kate gives George advice about writing rather than George giving Kate advice (choice **d**). Kate explains that she is not trying to frighten George (choice **e**).

37. c. Apparently Kate believes that good writers draw from life experiences. Choice **a** is incorrect because Kate clearly sees George's writing talent. Choice **b** is incorrect because there is no indication that George is going to die. Choice **d** is incorrect because Kate mentions nothing about college. Choice **e** is incorrect because Kate actually encourages him to spend less time writing.

38. a. The first stanza states several examples of what NOT to do, even though others are doing that very thing: losing their heads, hating, and lying. The first stanza basically states NOT to do what others are doing so choice **b** is incorrect. The poem mentions lying, hating and waiting, but not in the contexts of choices **c**, **d**, and **e**.

39. c. This line advises that a person should have dreams but not allow the pursuit of them to take over (master) his life. Choice **a** states the complete opposite of the speaker's intention. Choice **b** is incorrect because the speaker encourages the person to dream. The speaker does not mention anything about helping others (choice **d**). Although choice **e** may be true, it is not what the speaker is stating in this line.

40. e. The poem offers advice to a young person about how to obtain true success in life. The speaker implies that true maturity and success have nothing to do with power and riches, but rather, are measured by integrity. Although choices **a**, **b**, **c**, and **d** are all items mentioned in the poem, they do not reflect the theme of the poem.

CHAPTER

54 ▶ Practice Exam 2, GED Science

Directions: Read the following questions carefully and choose the best answer for each question. Some questions may refer to a passage, illustration, or graph.

1. Birds need large amounts of food to meet their high energy needs. Since birds do not have teeth, they take in food using their beaks. The shape of a bird's beak is an adaptation to the kind of food it eats. Woodpeckers have long, tweezer-thin beaks to pull insects from cracks in the barks of trees. Which of the following is the most likely reason why hawks have sharp, hooked beaks?
   a. to eat small seeds
   b. to tear the flesh of their prey
   c. to crush soft berries
   d. to strain food from water
   e. to grind the bones of their prey

Question 2 is based on the following table.

MINERAL	FUNCTION	FOOD SOURCES
Calcium	builds healthy bones and teeth; helps nerves and muscles	milk; cheese; green, leafy vegetables; fish; eggs
Iodine	helps body use energy	iodized salt; fish; seafood
Iron	keeps red blood cells healthy	liver; meat; green, leafy vegetables; eggs
Magnesium	helps muscles and nerves	vegetables; cereals; meat; nuts; milk
Sodium	controls water balance; helps nerves	salt, most foods

2. Why might a person decide to eat more fish?
  a. to fight off infection
  b. to sleep better at night
  c. to have healthy red blood cells
  d. to perspire less
  e. to avoid having brittle bones

Question 3 is based on the following information.

Three pans of water are lined up as follows:

Very warm   Water at room   Ice water
water   temperature

Several students place their left hand in the warm water and right hand in the ice water. After waiting several minutes, the students transfer both hands into the center pan of room-temperature water. All the students report that their left hand feels cold while their right hand feels warm.

3. What does this experiment demonstrate?
  a. Receptors in the skin sense change in temperature rather than the actual temperature.
  b. A cold sensation travels faster to the brain than a warm sensation.
  c. There are more cold sensors in the left hand than in the right hand.
  d. It takes several minutes for water to warm the hands.
  e. The left hand is naturally colder than the right hand.

Questions 4–6 are based on the following passage.

Coal and petroleum products, such as gasoline, currently provide about 60% of the energy used each year in the United States. However, these fossil fuels are also a major source of air pollution. Burning them produces soot and gases that make the air hard to breathe. These by-products also create acid rain, which destroys forests and lakes. In addition, they trap heat in the atmosphere, creating dangerous global warming. So as demand for energy increases, we need to find ways to avoid burning more fossil fuels.

One way is to practice energy conservation. Motorists who drive less and who keep their car engines tuned and tires inflated use less energy and reduce the use of fossil fuels. Homeowners who buy energy-efficient appliances do the same. Business and industries can reduce the use of fossil fuels by saving energy. Recycling is also a great energy saver. For example, getting aluminum from used aluminum cans takes only one-twentieth the energy needed to get aluminum from ore.

Another way to reduce the use of fossil fuels is to switch to alternative energy sources such as solar, geothermal, and wind energy. Unlike fossil fuels, these sources do not pollute the atmosphere, and they are also renewable. Scientists are now working on ways to make these energy sources cheaper and more practical so that more people can take advantage of them.

4. Which energy source is conserved when people drive less and switch to public transportation such as trains and buses?
  a. coal
  b. solar energy
  c. petroleum
  d. electrical energy
  e. nuclear energy

5. Which is the best reason for switching from fossil fuels to alternative energy sources such as solar and wind energy?
  a. to reduce homeowners' energy bills
  b. to increase the supply of coal
  c. to increase the amount of energy available for transportation
  d. to reduce the amount of energy used in recycling
  e. to reduce the air pollution caused by burning fossil fuels

6. Which is a good way to reduce the energy needed to cool and warm a house?
  a. insulate the windows and floors
  b. recycle metal and glass containers
  c. run appliances early in the morning or late at night
  d. take shorter and fewer showers
  e. turn off the television when no one is watching

Question 7 is based on the following information.

The sounds you hear are caused by vibrations. A vibration is the back-and-forth movement of matter. A sound wave is produced by vibration.

The human ear can detect sounds with frequencies between 20 and 20,000 hertz. This means the human ear can hear sound waves that vibrate matter back and forth 20 to 20,000 times each second. The following diagram shows the range of audible frequencies for humans, dogs, cats, bats, and porpoises.

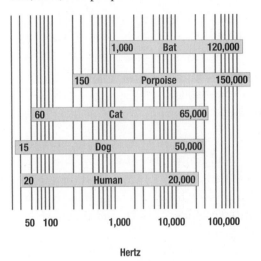

7. According to the diagram, which animal can hear the highest sound frequencies?
  a. bat
  b. porpoise
  c. cat
  d. dog
  e. human

Question 8 is based on the following information.

The law of conservation of mass states that matter cannot be created or destroyed in a chemical reaction. This law is reflected in the writing of chemical equations, in which the number of atoms of the starting substances that react with each other must balance the number of atoms of new substances, or products, that are created. For example, in the reaction between sodium metal and chlorine gas, which produces common table salt, NaCl, the number of atoms of Na and Cl are balanced by the number of atoms in the compound NaCl.

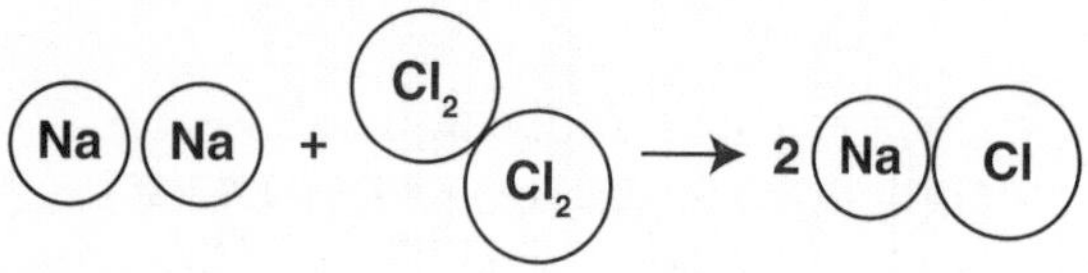

$$\text{Na} \; \text{Na} \; + \; \overset{\text{Cl}_2}{\underset{\text{Cl}_2}{}} \; \longrightarrow \; 2 \; \text{Na} \; \text{Cl}$$

$2\text{Na} + \text{Cl}_2 \rightarrow 2\text{NaCl}$
Reactants   Product

In this reaction, 2 sodium atoms and 2 chlorine atoms yield 2 molecules of sodium chloride.

Note that the unit of Cl_2 has been joined to each unit of Na—each Cl atom has joined to a Na atom. Thus, the coefficient is two, and the subscript is no longer present.

8. Which of the following is a balanced chemical equation for the formation of water (H_2O) from hydrogen and oxygen gas?
 a. $H_2 + O_2 \rightarrow H_2O$
 b. $H_2 + O_2 \rightarrow H_2O_2$
 c. $2H_2 + O_2 \rightarrow H_4O_2$
 d. $H_2 + 2O_2 \rightarrow 2H_2O$
 e. $2H_2 + O_2 \rightarrow 2H_2O$

Questions 9–10 are based on the following information.

Taxonomy is the science of classifying living things according to common characteristics. The largest groups that contain organisms with similar characteristics are called kingdoms. Within each kingdom are six levels of increasingly narrow subcategories. The following diagram shows the organization of these subcategories within a kingdom from the largest, the phylum, to the smallest, the species. The members of a species are more closely related to each other than to any other group of organisms.

Diagram 1

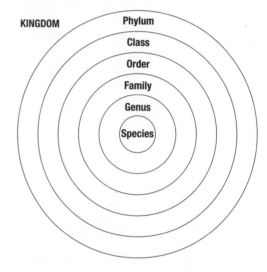

Taxonomy shows the evolutionary relationships of organisms. The smaller the subgroup two organisms share, the more recently the two organisms had a common ancestor.

Diagram 2 shows the subgroup relationships between four members of the animal kingdom.

Diagram 2

	Giant Clam	Leopard	Chimpanzee	Human
Kingdom	Animalia	Animalia	Animalia	Animalia
Phylum	Mollusca	Chordata	Chordata	Chordata
Class	Bivalvia	Mammalia	Mammalia	Mammalia
Order	Venroida	Carnivora	Primate	Primate
Family	Tridacnidae	Felidae	Pongidae	Hominidae

9. Based on the information in Diagram 1, which of the following is the correct organization of subcategories, from largest to smallest, within a kingdom?
   a. order, class, family, phylum, genus, species
   b. phylum, family, class, order, species, genus
   c. phylum, class, order, family, genus, species
   d. class, phylum, order, family, species, genus
   e. species, genus, order, family, class, phylum

10. Which of the following statements is TRUE?
   a. Giant clams and leopards have a more recent common ancestor than leopards and chimpanzees.
   b. Leopards and chimpanzees are members of the same order.
   c. Chimpanzees and humans have a more recent common ancestor than chimpanzees and leopards.
   d. Giant clams, leopards, and humans are members of the same phylum.
   e. Chimpanzees and humans are members of the same family.

11. Weathering is the natural breaking-down process of rocks and other natural and human-made materials on Earth's surface. There are several kinds of weathering. In abrasion, solid particles carried by wind or water wear away the solid surface. In root-pry, plant roots crack apart the solid rock. In frost-action weathering, water seeps into a crack and then freezes, breaking apart the solid surface. In carbonation, carbonic acid in water dissolves rocks on and beneath Earth's surface. In oxidation, oxygen combines with iron in rocks to form rust.

   A pothole opens in a road surface on a cold winter night. This is an example of which type of weathering?
   a. abrasion
   b. frost-action
   c. root-pry
   d. carbonation
   e. oxidation

Questions 12–13 are based on the following information.

Five types of chemical reactions are described here.

composition—a reaction in which two substances combine to form a new substance
decomposition—a reaction in which a compound is broken down into two or more simpler substances
single replacement—a reaction in which one element is replaced by another in another compound
double replacement—a reaction in which the elements of the reacting compounds change place
no reaction—the substance or substances involved remain chemically unchanged

12. In smelting, hematite (common iron ore; Fe_2O_3) is melted with charcoal (elemental carbon; C) and heated in a fired clay pot. In this reaction, carbon dioxide (CO_2) is released into the air leaving iron (Fe) in the ore. Which reaction type is this procedure?
   a. composition
   b. decomposition
   c. single replacement
   d. double replacement
   e. no reaction

13. When hydrochloric acid (HCl) is mixed with sodium hydroxide (NaOH), table salt (sodium chloride; NaCl) and water (H_2O) are formed. Which reaction type is this procedure?
   a. composition
   b. decomposition
   c. single replacement
   d. double replacement
   e. no reaction

Questions 14–15 are based on the following information.

Traits such as height, eye color, and even dimples are passed by parents to offspring. For each trait, the off-spring receives a pair of genes, one from each parent. Genes can be either dominant or recessive. A domi-nant gene will make the trait appear. If only recessive genes are present, the trait will not appear. However, if just one dominant gene is present, the offspring will have the trait, even if the other gene is recessive. An organism that has two identical genes for a trait is said to be purebred.

A Punnett square is a chart that shows all the pos-sible combinations of genes for a trait that are passed on from parents to offspring. Dominant genes are indicated with a capital letter, and recessive genes are indicated with a small letter. The mother's genes are shown at the top. The father's genes are shown at the left. The four boxes show the gene combinations that are possible in the offspring. Each combination has an equal likelihood of occurring. This Punnett square shows the cross between a father and mother who both have dimples.

	D	d
D	DD	Dd
d	Dd	dd

14. If the father and mother have four children, how many of the four children are likely to have dimples?
   a. 4
   b. 3
   c. 2
   d. 1
   e. 0

15. A different couple also produces four children. The father has dimples and is purebred for that trait. The mother does not have dimples. How many of the four children are likely to have dimples?
   a. 4
   b. 3
   c. 2
   d. 1
   e. 0

16. An electromagnet is a temporary magnet. It can be made by wrapping a coil of wire around a piece of iron and sending an electric current through the wire. When the current runs through the wire, the coil and iron become magnetic. When the current is shut off, the coil and iron are no longer magnetic.

A worker is using an electromagnet to lift and carry some scrap iron. What happens to the iron when the worker shuts off the electric current?
   a. It becomes magnetized.
   b. It overheats and melts the electromagnet.
   c. It produces an electric charge.
   d. It falls away from the electromagnet.
   e. It becomes brittle and shatters.

Question 17 is based on the following information.

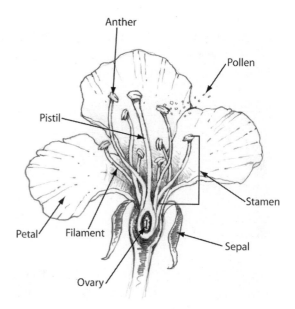

A flower is a complex structure with many parts. At its base is a ring of leaflike parts called sepals. They protect the flower bud while it is developing. Inside the sepals are other leaflike structures called petals. Petals protect the reproductive organs of the flower and also attract animals that assist in pollination.

The reproductive parts of the flower include the stamens, slender structures with knoblike ends called anthers. The anthers are male reproductive organs. Each anther is supported by a thin stalk called the filament. Pollen grains are produced by the anthers.

The stamens encircle one or more carpels, which are female reproductive organs. At the base of the carpel is the ovary, within which eggs develop. A narrow stalk called a style extends from the upper part of the ovary. At its tip is a sticky area called the stigma. The stigma traps pollen from the anthers. In this way pollination takes place.

17. According to the passage, which part(s) of the flower enclose the female reproductive organs?
a. the anther
b. the sepals
c. the filament
d. the stamen
e. the ovary

Question 18 is based on the following information.

Physical fitness is the condition of your body as a result of a regular exercise program. There are four kinds of exercises you can do to increase your physical fitness.

1. Isometric exercise is exercise in which you contract your muscles without moving them. These exercises give you muscular strength. Making a fist and holding it for five seconds is an example of an isometric exercise.
2. Isotonic exercise is exercise in which you contract your muscles and move them. These exercises give you muscular strength and some muscular endurance. Swimming is an example of isotonic exercise.
3. Anaerobic exercise is exercise done for a short time and gets the necessary energy without the utilization of inspired oxygen. These exercises develop speed, muscular strength, and some muscular endurance. Running a 100-yard dash is an example of an anaerobic exercise.
4. Aerobic exercise is exercise that uses a lot of oxygen over a period of time. Aerobic exercise helps your body be lean and trim. Your heart muscle becomes strong, which helps promote cardiovascular fitness. Riding a bike for 30 minutes is an example of an aerobic exercise.

18. Frank is about to begin a physical fitness program. He wants to increase his muscular endurance and his cardiovascular fitness. Which of the following activities would best achieve Frank's goals?
a. sprint up and down the stairs of his home
b. do five minutes of stretching exercises before doing 20 sit-ups
c. dribble a basketball for 10 minutes
d. sit in a chair, put his arms in front and with the palm of his hands touching, push the palms against each other for eight seconds
e. jog each day, increasing the distance jogged as time goes on

Questions 19–20 are based on the following passage.

Pathogens are germs that cause disease. Some pathogens are bacteria. Harmful bacteria can enter the body and cause diseases such as strep throat.

Other pathogens are viruses. Viruses are the smallest known pathogens. They cannot be seen under a common microscope. Viruses cause many kinds of diseases such as the common cold, measles, and chicken pox. Both viruses and bacteria multiply in the body and produce toxins, poisons that harm healthy body cells and cause disease. Medicines called antibiotics can kill bacteria. Medicines called antivirals can kill viruses.

Still other pathogens are fungi. Some fungi can cause diseases such as athlete's foot or ringworm.

There are many ways you may come into contact with pathogens. The most common way is by touch. You can get pathogens from another person through the air. Insects such as flies can spread pathogens. You can get pathogens from food not properly cooked, or from polluted water.

19. Which of the following is the most effective way for a person to avoid coming into contact with pathogens?
a. Visit a doctor regularly.
b. Dress properly before going outdoors.
c. Wash your hands properly before preparing or eating food.
d. Drink plenty of liquids that contain vitamin C.
e. Get plenty of sleep.

20. Suppose you are ill and see a doctor. After a thorough examination, the doctor writes a prescription for an antibiotic. You are told to take this antibiotic for five days. Which statement best describes the doctor's diagnosis?
   a. You are suffering from a virus.
   b. You have a bacterial infection.
   c. You caught a cold by not washing your hands properly.
   d. You have the chicken pox.
   e. The doctor feels that more tests are needed.

Question 21 is based on the following information.

Gaining or losing weight depends on whether you consume more or fewer calories than your body "burns" over a given period. If you consume more calories than you burn, you gain weight, which your body stores as body fat. If you consume fewer calories than you burn, you lose weight.

21. A realistic, healthy weight-loss goal is to lose 1 pound per week. If 1 pound = 3,500 calories, which of the following would be a good way to reach your goal?
   a. consume 100 more calories per day
   b. consume 250 fewer calories per day
   c. consume 300 more calories per day
   d. consume 500 fewer calories per day
   e. consume 700 more calories per day

Question 22 is based on the following information.

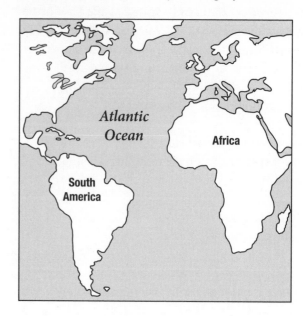

In the early 1900s, German geophysicist Alfred Wegener looked at a map like the one shown and decided that the Atlantic coastlines of South America and Africa looked like matching pieces of a giant puzzle. Wegener developed a thesis to explain what he saw. He believed that all of the continents had once made up one great land mass, which he called Pangaea ("all lands"). According to Wegener's hypothesis, Pangaea later split apart, and the separate land masses slid across the ocean floor to their present locations. Wegener tested his hypothesis by collecting more data and eventually developed the theory of continental drift.

22. Which of the following evidence supports Wegener's theory of continental drift?
   I.   Many geologic features on the east coast of South America match features on the facing coast of Africa.
   II. Mountains in Argentina have ice caps.
   III. Identical fossil remains of a small reptile called Mesosaurus were found in both Africa and South America.
   a. I only
   b. II only
   c. III only
   d. I and II
   e. I and III

Question 23 is based on the following information.

A solution is formed when one substance dissolves in another. The two components of a solution are called the solute and the solvent. The solute is the substance that is dissolved. The solvent is the substance in which the solute is dissolved. There is always more of the solvent than of the solute.

Solubility is the measure of how much solute will dissolve in a solvent. Solubility is affected by temperature. Heating usually increases the amount of a solute that can be dissolved in a solvent. However, for gas solutes in liquid, heating decreases solubility. The solubility of a gas solute is also affected by pressure. Decreasing the pressure decreases the solubility of a gas in liquid.

On a hot summer day you open a bottle of cold soda. You pour the soda into a glass as shown. Ten minutes later you notice that the soda has gone completely flat.

23. What happened to the soda that caused the gas to escape?
   a. Its temperature increased and the pressure on it decreased.
   b. Its temperature and the pressure on it both increased.
   c. Its temperature and the pressure on it both decreased.
   d. Its temperature decreased and the pressure on it increased.
   e. Its temperature increased, but the pressure on it remained the same.

24. Acoustics is the study of how materials influence the production and movement of sound. The aim of acoustic design is to fill each part of the room with desired sounds while reducing unwanted sounds. You can create good sound distribution by using reflective surfaces such as wood or tiles. You can use sound-absorbing materials such as fabrics to eliminate or reduce unwanted sounds.

   Which would be the most effective way to reduce disturbing echoes inside the auditorium during a school concert?
   a. Use electronic microphones.
   b. Hang draperies and carpet the floors of the auditorium.
   c. Close the doors of the auditorium.
   d. Have the musicians and audience stand rather than sit.
   e. Increase the lighting on stage.

25. The half-life of a radioactive element is the amount of time needed for half the nuclei in a sample of the element to decay, or change, into nuclei of a different element. The half-life of radium-226 is 1,600 years.

   About how old is an object in which $\frac{1}{64}$ of the original radium-226 is still present?
   a. 9,600 years
   b. 8,000 years
   c. 6,400 years
   d. 3,200 years
   e. 25 years

Questions 26–27 are based on the following passage.

The period of development before birth is called the gestation period. Each species of mammals has a different gestation period. For example, a human fetus develops inside its mother for an average of 266 days.

The group of offspring born to a mammal in a multiple birth is referred to as a litter. Litter size varies from species to species, just as the gestation period varies.

The table shows the length of gestation period, litter size, and average life span for 12 mammals.

ANIMAL	GESTATION PERIOD (DAYS)	LITTER SIZE*	LIFE SPAN (YEARS)
Deer Mouse	21	5–9	5
Cotton Tail Rabbit	30	4–7	8
Red Fox	52	4–7	12
Coyote	63	5–7	14
Wolf	63	3–8	15
Raccoon	68	1–6	13
Tiger	109	2–6	25
Black Bear	210	1–4	25
Chimpanzee	240	1	40
Moose	244	1–3	20
Human	266	1	75
Dolphin	300	1	25

* In humans, single births are the most common, although multiple births sometimes occur.

26. Based solely on the data, which of the following conclusions is valid?
   a. Small animals have long gestation periods.
   b. Large animals have larger litters than small animals.
   c. Animals with the shortest gestation periods have the longest life spans.
   d. Animals that have long gestation periods generally have fewer offspring at one time than do animals with short gestation periods.
   e. Animals that have short gestation periods generally have fewer offspring at one time than do animals with long gestation periods.

27. Which of the following statements most likely explains the advantage of having a large litter?
   a. The larger the litter, the healthier the offspring tend to be.
   b. The larger the litter, the easier it is for the parents to nourish the offspring.
   c. The larger the litter, the easier it is for the parents to protect the offspring.
   d. The larger the litter, the better the chance that some offspring will survive to adulthood.
   e. The larger the litter, the longer the offspring will stay with the parents.

Question 28 is based on the following information.

A food chain is the transfer of energy in the form of food from one organism to another. A producer is an organism that makes its own food. A consumer is an organism that eats other organisms. The food chain shown here shows the transfer of energy between organisms in a pond.

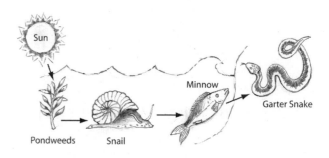

28. In the food chain, which organism or organisms are producers?
   a. only the snail
   b. only the minnow
   c. only the pond weeds
   d. the snail and the minnow
   e. the pond weeds and the garter snake

29. Isomers are compounds with the same molecular formula but different structural formulas. Butane is a compound with the molecular formula C_4H_{10}. Its structural formula is shown here.

$$H-\overset{\overset{\displaystyle H}{|}}{\underset{\underset{\displaystyle H}{|}}{C}}-\overset{\overset{\displaystyle H}{|}}{\underset{\underset{\displaystyle H}{|}}{C}}-\overset{\overset{\displaystyle H}{|}}{\underset{\underset{\displaystyle H}{|}}{C}}-\overset{\overset{\displaystyle H}{|}}{\underset{\underset{\displaystyle H}{|}}{C}}-H$$

Which of the following shows the structural formula of isobutane, an isomer of butane?

a.

$$H-\overset{\overset{\displaystyle C}{|}}{C}-\overset{\overset{\displaystyle C}{|}}{\underset{\underset{\displaystyle H}{|}}{C}}-\overset{}{\underset{\underset{\displaystyle H}{|}}{C}}-H$$

b.

$$H-\overset{\overset{\displaystyle H}{|}}{\underset{\underset{\displaystyle H}{|}}{C}}-\overset{\overset{\displaystyle H}{|}}{\underset{\underset{\displaystyle\;}{|}}{C}}-\overset{\overset{\displaystyle H}{|}}{\underset{\underset{\displaystyle H}{|}}{C}}-H$$
$$\underset{\underset{\displaystyle H}{|}}{H-C-H}$$

c.

$$H-\overset{\overset{\displaystyle H}{|}}{\underset{\underset{\displaystyle C}{|}}{C}}-\overset{\overset{\displaystyle H}{|}}{C}-\overset{\overset{\displaystyle H}{|}}{C}-\overset{\overset{\displaystyle H}{|}}{\underset{\underset{\displaystyle C}{|}}{C}}-H$$

d.

$$H-\overset{\overset{\displaystyle C}{|}}{C}-\overset{\overset{\displaystyle C}{|}}{\underset{\underset{\displaystyle H}{|}}{C}}-\overset{}{\underset{\underset{\displaystyle H}{|}}{C}}-H$$

e.

$$H-\overset{\overset{\displaystyle H}{|}}{\underset{\underset{\displaystyle H}{|}}{C}}-\overset{\overset{\displaystyle H}{|}}{\underset{\underset{\displaystyle C}{|}}{C}}-\overset{\overset{\displaystyle H}{|}}{C}-H$$

30. The portable rechargeable batteries used in cameras, cellular phones, and other devices may seem harmless, but they actually contain substances such as cadmium and lithium that are highly poisonous. These substances are particularly dangerous if they leak into the air, the ground, or water supplies when the batteries decompose.

You need to dispose of a battery from a cellular phone. Which of the following would be a safe way to get rid of it?
a. toss it into a nearby lake
b. take it to a recycling center for proper disposal
c. take it apart and burn the pieces
d. bury it in your backyard
e. dispose of it in an open landfill

31. Population growth in an ecosystem is controlled by limiting factors. Changes in the size of one population affect the sizes of other populations.

Sea otters feed on sea urchins, which in turn feed on undersea forests of kelp (a type of seaweed). Hunting by humans reduced the number of sea otters. Which of the following most likely resulted?
a. Declining sea urchin populations allowed the kelp forests to expand.
b. The sea urchin population grew but the kelp forest was unaffected.
c. The sea urchin population and the kelp forests both decreased in size.
d. Growing numbers of sea urchins seriously reduced the kelp forest.
e. Expanding kelp forests allowed the sea urchin population to grow.

32. When the weather gets cold, some animals survive by burrowing into soil or mud and beginning a resting period called hibernation. During hibernation, an animal's metabolism slows down. Its body temperature drops and it breathes only a few times a minute. The animal uses the fat stored in its body to get energy.

Which aspect of hibernation might decrease the animal's chances for survival?
a. the animal's inability to move around
b. the animal's lowered temperature
c. the animal's slowed breathing rate
d. the animal's use of stored body fat
e. the animal's lower body metabolism

Questions 33–35 are based on the following passage.

The moon's apparent shape changes from day to day. Sometimes you can see a full moon. At other times, only half a moon is visible. At other times, the moon is invisible.

What causes its appearance to change? The moon shines by reflecting sunlight from its surface. Half of the moon is lighted while the other half is dark. The moon rotates on its axis every 27.3 days, which is about the same amount of time the moon takes to revolve around Earth. Because these two motions take nearly the same amount of time, the same side of the moon always faces Earth. The other side is never turned toward us.

Moon phases are the changing appearances of the moon as seen from Earth. The phase you see depends on the relative positions of the moon, the Earth, and the Sun.

This diagram shows four positions of the moon as it revolves around Earth.

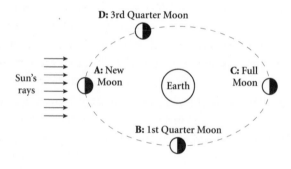

33. Why is one side of the moon always facing Earth?
  a. The moon's period of revolution around Earth equals Earth's period of revolution around the Sun.
  b. The moon's rotation period equals Earth's period of revolution around the Sun.
  c. The moon's rotation period equals its period of revolution around Earth.
  d. The moon's rotation period equals Earth's rotation period.
  e. The moon's rotation period is greater than its period of revolution around Earth.

34. Which statement accurately describes the far side of the moon?
  a. It is always in darkness.
  b. It is always in sunlight.
  c. It is always seen on Earth.
  d. It is seen only during a full moon.
  e. It is never seen from Earth.

35. At which point on the diagram is the greatest part of the moon visible on Earth?
  a. A
  b. B
  c. C
  d. D
  e. B and D

36. In dry weather, plants can easily dry out. Water passes out of the plant through openings called stomates on the surfaces of leaves. If too much water is lost, the plant may wilt or even die. Plants that live in dry climates have developed many ways to reduce water loss.

Which of the following traits helps conifers such as pine trees and spruces flourish in regions that are dry or where water is frozen most of the year?
  a. woody tissue that strengthens and supports the tree trunk
  b. seeds that are dispersed by wind
  c. the ability to produce both male and female cones
  d. needle-shaped leaves that have very little surface area
  e. the ability to make food through photosynthesis all year round

37. Why might the leaves at the top of a tree produce more food than the leaves at the bottom of a tree?
  a. The top leaves receive more nutrients from the soil.
  b. The top leaves need fewer minerals.
  c. The top leaves receive more sunlight.
  d. The top leaves are beyond the reach of caterpillars.
  e. The top leaves have more spores.

Question 38 is based on the following information.

Acceleration is the rate at which velocity changes. All falling objects accelerate at the same rate. This is true regardless of the mass of the objects. A falling object stops accelerating when it reaches its terminal, or maximum, velocity. The terminal velocity depends on the size and weight of the object and on the amount of resistance (frictional force) it meets from the medium (such as air) through which it is falling. At terminal velocity, the force of gravity on an object is balanced by the resistance of the medium. As a result, some objects reach their terminal velocity sooner than others. The lighter an object is, the sooner weight and resistance are balanced and terminal velocity is reached.

38. Based on this information, which of the following statements is true?
   a. As a feather and a brick fall, their rate of speed decreases.
   b. Because a brick has a greater mass, it will accelerate faster than a feather when both are falling.
   c. Because a feather has less mass, it will accelerate faster than a brick when both are falling.
   d. If you drop a feather and a brick in a vacuum, the feather will accelerate more slowly than the brick.
   e. A feather falling in air will reach terminal velocity sooner than a brick.

39. An organism is defined as any individual living creature, either one-celled or multicellular. You and a classmate view a clump of cells on a microscope slide. Your classmate says that the clump is a multicellular organism. You believe that the clump is made up of many one-celled organisms. Which of the following must be true if your belief is correct?
   a. Each cell in the clump carries out all life processes.
   b. Each cell performs a different life process.
   c. Each cell has an outer boundary.
   d. Groups of cells in the clump carry out different life processes.
   e. The cells lack chromosomes to control life processes.

40. Fish are the oldest living vertebrates. Fossil evidence indicates that fishlike animals existed over 520 million years ago. As ponds and swamps started to dry up between 360 and 370 million years ago, many fish had to compete for food and space.

Which of the following adaptations might a group of bony fish called lobe-finned fish have most likely made to survive in the changing environment?
   a. Develop short stubby fins to push their bodies across the muddy swamps and evolve lungs for breathing.
   b. Develop hair for trapping heat.
   c. Develop sharp pointed teeth for tearing the flesh of their prey.
   d. Develop paddle-shaped front limbs for swimming.
   e. Develop large brains to perform and remember complex tasks.

Questions 41–43 are based on the following passage.

Nuclear power plants produce energy through a process called nuclear fission. In this process, a free neutron collides with the nucleus of an atom of a fuel such as uranium-235. The nucleus then splits into smaller nuclei, releasing energy and more free neutrons. Some of the released neutrons then collide with other nuclei. The result is a chain reaction. The energy released is used to create steam, which turns a turbine to create electricity.

One drawback of nuclear fission is that some of the waste products are highly radioactive. That is, as they decay they release particles and gamma rays that can penetrate the human body and damage tissue. There is now no known safe way to dispose of these nuclear wastes. Another drawback is the possibility that the reactor, the device that contains and controls the reaction, may malfunction. A malfunction could release large amounts of hazardous radioactive material.

Another way to produce energy is through a reaction called nuclear fusion. In a fusion reaction, the nuclei of two or more atoms combine to form a new nucleus, releasing an enormous amount of energy. The fuels used in nuclear fusion are isotopes that are easily available from water. As a result, the fusion process may someday offer an almost unlimited energy supply. However, certain problems must first be solved before nuclear fusion becomes practical. One is that it is extremely difficult to create and maintain the very high temperatures needed for fusion to take place. Another problem is finding a container that can safely hold materials at such high temperatures.

41. Which of the following describes the difference between nuclear fission and nuclear fusion?
   a. Nuclear fusion is a physical reaction, while nuclear fission is a chemical reaction.
   b. Nuclear fission is an uncontrolled process, while nuclear fusion is a controlled process.
   c. In nuclear fission a heavier nucleus is formed, but in nuclear fusion a lighter nucleus is formed.
   d. Nuclear fission has no waste products, but nuclear fusion produces radioactive waste materials.
   e. In nuclear fission the nucleus of an atom is split, while in nuclear fusion, the nuclei of two atoms are combined.

42. Why might nuclear fusion eventually be a better energy source than nuclear fission?
   a. Nuclear fusion does not require very high temperatures.
   b. The fuels for nuclear fusion are plentiful and cheap.
   c. The waste products of nuclear fusion are easily disposable.
   d. Nuclear fusion produces gamma rays.
   e. Nuclear fusion uses fuels that are not isotopes.

43. What is the main reason why there are now no nuclear fusion plants generating electricity?
   a. A nuclear fusion reaction produces too little energy.
   b. Laws prohibit nuclear fusion plants.
   c. Nuclear fusion releases dangerous radioactivity.
   d. Scientists have not yet learned how to create and maintain the high temperatures for nuclear fusion.
   e. Scientists have not yet learned how to prevent the release of gamma rays during nuclear fusion.

Questions 44–46 are based on the following passage.

Products called sunscreens protect the skin against the damaging effects of ultraviolet (UV) radiation. They contain chemicals that prevent the radiation from entering the lower layer of the skin. The most widely used chemical is paraminobenzoic acid, or PABA.

All sunscreens protect against UV-B radiation, which is the more dangerous type of UV radiation. Exposure to UV-B radiation can cause sunburn, wrinkles, premature aging of the skin, and skin cancer. Some sunscreens also protect against UV-A, a less dangerous form of ultraviolet radiation. UV-A radiation may cause people taking certain medications to have allergic reactions.

The SPF factor, or "sun protection factor" tells you how long a sunscreen will allow you to stay out in the sun without burning. An SPF rating of 5, for example, tells a person who normally takes 12 minutes to burn that he or she can spend 5×12, or 60, minutes in the sun without burning. However, the SPF applies only if your skin stays dry after applying the sunscreen. Many sunscreens wash off if you go swimming, although some are water-resistant.

This table lists five sunscreen products and indicates some of their characteristics.

Sunscreen Product	SPF	Minutes in Water*	Contains PABA	Protects Against UV-A
A	25	20	yes	no
B	15	20	yes	yes
C	8	40	no	no
D	20	40	no	yes
E	20	80	yes	yes

*Number of minutes it takes for sunscreen to wash off if you go swimming.

44. Which sunscreen product should you use if you are allergic to PABA and you are currently taking a medication that makes your skin more sensitive to UV-A radiation?
   a. Sunscreen A
   b. Sunscreen B
   c. Sunscreen C
   d. Sunscreen D
   e. Sunscreen E

45. Suppose you normally burn in 15 minutes. How much longer could you sunbathe using sunscreen D compared to sunscreen B?
- **a.** 5 minutes longer
- **b.** 15 minutes longer
- **c.** 20 minutes longer
- **d.** 75 minutes longer
- **e.** 100 minutes longer

46. Which person would most likely use sunscreen E?
- **a.** someone who intends to stay in a pool most of the day
- **b.** someone who wants the best protection against UV-B
- **c.** someone who burns very quickly without using a sunscreen
- **d.** someone who doesn't burn easily
- **e.** someone who plans to sunbathe all afternoon

47. Soil is a mixture of rock particles and the remains of tiny dead and living organisms. Erosion is the wearing away of soil by wind or water. To prevent water from washing soil downhill, farmers contour plow their land. The grooves that run across the plowed land catch running water, allowing it to seep slowly into the soil. Which of the following actions would aid in preventing soil erosion by the wind?
- I. build underground wells
- II. plant rows of trees
- III. grow plants with thick fibrous roots
- **a.** I only
- **b.** II only
- **c.** III only
- **d.** I and II only
- **e.** II and III only

48. The sum of the charges in an ionic compound must always equal zero. Aluminum (Al) has a charge of 3+. Oxide (O) has a charge of 2−. Which of the following shows the formula for aluminum oxide?
- **a.** Al_3O_2
- **b.** Al_2O_3
- **c.** AlO_2
- **d.** AlO
- **e.** AlO_3

Question 49 is based on the following information.

Ordinary light waves vibrate up and down as well as left and right. A polarizing filter allows light to pass through only in one specific direction. It might allow only the vertical (up-and-down) wave vibrations to go through and absorb the horizontal (left-right) vibrations. Or it might do the opposite and let the horizontal vibrations pass through and absorb the vertical vibrations.

Filter A lets only vertical light waves through.

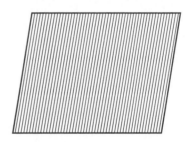

Filter B lets only horizontal light waves through.

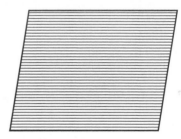

49. Suppose you enter a room that is completely dark and you shine a flashlight at a box that is behind filters A and B. Which of the following describes what you would see as you looked at the box?
- **a.** the top of the box
- **b.** the entire box
- **c.** vertical lines running up and down the box
- **d.** horizontal lines running across the box
- **e.** nothing

Question 50 is based on the following passage.

About half of the radiation that reaches Earth from the Sun is absorbed and converted into heat (thermal energy). This heat warms Earth's lands and oceans and is also radiated back into the atmosphere. Molecules of carbon dioxide, water vapor, and methane in the atmosphere absorb some of the heat. They then release the heat back into the atmosphere to keep it warm. This trapping and releasing of thermal energy in the atmosphere is called the greenhouse effect. The amount of carbon dioxide in the atmosphere is currently increasing, due mainly to the burning of fossil fuels such as oil, coal, and gasoline. With more carbon dioxide in the atmosphere, more heat is trapped and released. The result, scientists believe, is that the atmosphere will become steadily warmer.

50. Which of the following actions would be the most effective way to reduce the greenhouse effect?
   a. replace coal- and oil-burning power plants with solar-powered plants
   b. eat only organic foods that have not been sprayed with pesticides
   c. plant more flowers, shrubs, and trees
   d. build lower buildings
   e. take fewer showers and run appliances only at off-peak times

▶ Answers

1. b. The hawk is a carnivore. A sharp, hooked beak helps it tear the flesh from the animals it preys upon, making choice **b** is the best answer.

2. e. Fish is a source of calcium and iodine. Of the choices offered, choice **e** is the best answer since calcium helps promote healthy bones.

3. a. Choices **b**, **c**, and **e** are not demonstrated by the experiment. Choice **d**, while correct, is not demonstrated by the experiment. The experiment shows that the receptors located near the surface of the skin can sense relative temperature, rather than actual temperature. Less warm compared to warm feels cold. Similarly, slightly warm compared to cold feels warm, so choice **a** is the correct answer.

4. c. If more people take public transportation, fewer people are driving cars. This reduces gasoline usage, which means petroleum is conserved. Thus, choice **c** is the correct answer.

5. e. Alternative energy sources are not necessarily cheaper than fossil fuels, so switching to them may not reduce homeowners' energy bills. Thus choice **a** is incorrect. Since fossil fuels are nonrenewable, you cannot increase the amount, so choice **b** is incorrect. Choice **c** does not solve the problem of air pollution from using fossil fuels. Using alternative energy sources would not reduce the amount of energy used in recycling, so choice **d** is not correct. Only choice **e** states the real benefit of using alternative energy sources.

6. a. Choice **b** has nothing to do with reducing the energy needed to heat or cool a home. Choices **c** and **e** will reduce the use of electric energy, but not the energy used for heating or cooling a home. Choice **d** saves energy for heating water, not the home. Choice **a** is the best choice because insulation helps save energy for heating and cooling a home.

7. b. Humans (choice **e**) can hear sounds only up to 20,000 hertz. The cat and the dog (choices **c** and **d**) can hear sounds of up to 65,000 hertz and 50,000 hertz, respectively. The bat (choice **a**) can hear sounds of up to 120,000 hertz. However, only the porpoise (choice **b**) can hear sounds of up to 150,000 hertz. Choice **b** is the correct answer.

8. e. In choices **a** and **d** the numbers of atoms of hydrogen and oxygen in the product (right side) do not match the numbers of atoms in the reactants (left side). In choices **b** and **c**, the numbers of atoms of hydrogen and oxygen match but do not produce H_2O. Only in choice **e** are the numbers of hydrogen atoms (4) and oxygen atoms (2) the same on both sides of the reaction. So choice **e** is the correct answer.

9. c. According to Diagram 1, the correct order of subcategories of a kingdom, from largest to smallest, is phylum, class, order, family, genus, and species. Only choice **c** lists the subcategories in this order.

10. c. The leopard and chimpanzee are members of the same class, which is a smaller group than the same kingdom of which the giant clam and leopard are members. So, the leopard and chimpanzee have a more recent common ancestor, making choice **a** incorrect. While the leopard and chimpanzee are members of the same class, they are members of different orders, so choice **b** is incorrect. Choice **d** is incorrect because the giant clam is a member of a different phylum from leopards and humans. Since humans and chimpanzees are members of different families, choice **e** is not true. Since the human and chimpanzee are members of the same order, they have a more recent common ancestor than the chimpanzee and leopard, which are members of the same class. Thus, choice **c** is the correct answer.

11. b. A pothole is the result of water seeping into a crack in a roadway and expanding as it freezes in cold weather. This expansion causes the crack in the road surface to widen, creating a pothole. Choice **b** is the correct answer.

12. c. In the reaction, carbon replaces the iron in hematite to form the new compound, carbon dioxide. This is an example of single replacement, which is choice **c**. The reaction is: $Fe_2O_3 + 3C \rightarrow 4Fe + 3CO_2$.

13. d. In the reaction, the sodium and hydrogen exchange places:
$HCl + NaOH \rightarrow NaCl + HOH$ or (H_2O).
Thus, this is an example of double replacement. Thus, choice **d** is the correct answer.

14. b. According to the Punnett square, since having dimples is the dominant trait (D), $\frac{3}{4}$ of the combinations (DD, Dd, and Dd) will lead to the offspring having dimples. Therefore, $\frac{3}{4}$, or 3 out of 4, of this couple's children are likely to have dimples, so choice **b** is the correct answer.

15. a. All combinations of offspring would have dimples, since having dimples is the dominant trait (D). Therefore, choice **a** is the correct answer.

16. d. An electromagnet loses its magnetism when no electricity flows through it. So the scrap iron load will no longer be held to the electromagnet. So, choice **d** is the correct answer.

17. d. Choice **a**, the anther, is incorrect since it is the male reproductive organ. Choice **c**, the filament, is the stalk or stem that supports the anther. Choice **b**, the sepals, are outer, leaflike structures that protect the flower bud while it develops. Choice **e**, the ovary, is the female reproductive organ that is enclosed. Choice **d** is the correct answer. The stamen surrounds and encloses the carpels of the flower.

18. e. Choice **a**, sprinting up and down a staircase, is an example of an anaerobic exercise. It develops muscle strength and some muscular endurance. Choice **b** is a warm-up exercise that develops muscle flexibility. Choice **c**, dribbling a basketball, is an example of an isotonic exercise. It will not help develop cardiovascular fitness. Choice **d** is an example of an isometric exercise. It will increase muscular strength but will not increase muscular endurance or develop cardiovascular fitness. Choice **e**, jogging over increasing distances, is both an isotonic and aerobic exercise and is the best activity for developing both muscular endurance and cardiovascular fitness. Thus, choice **e** is the correct answer.

19. c. Washing your hands will prevent pathogens from your hands getting on the food that you eat. So choice **c** is the correct answer. Choices **a**, **b**, **d**, and **e** are healthful actions but have no effect on the number of pathogens you come in contact with.

20. b. Antibiotics kill bacteria. Since the doctor prescribed an antibiotic, you can conclude that the doctor must feel that you are suffering from a bacterial infection, choice **b**. None of the other choices is supported by the information in the passage or in the question.

21. d. To lose 3,500 calories in a week, you would need to consume, on average, $3,500 \div 7 = 500$ fewer calories per day. So choice **d** is the correct answer. Choices **a**, **c**, and **e** are incorrect because they would mean consuming more calories, not fewer, than the body burns per day. Choice **b** is incorrect because consuming 250 fewer calories per day would not achieve the goal of 3,500 fewer calories in seven days.

22. e. If plant and rock formations evolved on a single land mass, which then split into parts that drifted away from one another, you would expect to find similar fossils and rock formations on the now separated masses. Ice caps are formed on mountain tops as a result of climatic conditions in higher altitudes. This possibility is unrelated to the theory of continental drift. Statements I and III support the theory of continental drift. Choice **e** is the best answer.

23. a. When the bottle was opened, the pressure on the soda was immediately decreased. When the soda was poured into the glass, pressure was further decreased. In addition, the temperature of the soda increased because of the hot day. Thus, because of the decrease in pressure and the increase in temperature of the solvent, the solubility of the gas was decreased, and carbon dioxide was released from the soda in the glass. Choice **a** is the only correct answer. The other answer choices do not state both conditions that result from opening the bottle and pouring the soda.

24. b. The only option that discusses adding materials that absorb sound and reduce the possibility of echoes is choice **b**. Choices **a** and **c** would increase, not decrease, sound levels. The other choices, **d** and **e**, would have no effect on sound.

25. a. $\frac{1}{64}$ is equal to $(\frac{1}{2})^6$. This means that the original isotope has gone through six half-lives. Therefore, the age of the object is equal to $6 \times 1,600$, or 9,600 years. So choice **a** is the correct answer.

26. d. The conclusion stated in choice **a** is not supported by data in the table. Choices **b** and **c** are also not supported by data in the table. The conclusion stated in choice **e** is the opposite of what the data shows about animals with short gestation periods. The conclusion in choice **d** is valid and is the only conclusion supported by the given data.

27. d. The reasons given in choices **a, b, c,** and **e** have no scientific basis and do not offer a valid explanation of the advantage of having a large litter. Choice **d** states a valid inference about the advantages of a large litter, given the fact that disease, lack of parental care, and the presence of predators can cause the size of a litter to decrease. So choice **d** is the best answer.

28. c. In the food chain shown, only the pond weeds can produce their own food through photosynthesis. So choice **c** is the correct answer. The snail, the minnow, and the garter snake are all consumers, not producers.

29. b. Since isobutane is an isomer of butane, it must have the same molecular formula as butane, even though the elements are in a different structural arrangement. The only structural formula that has four molecules of carbon bonded with ten molecules of hydrogen is choice **b**.

30. b. Because the toxic substances in portable rechargeable batteries are dangerous when they leak into the air, the ground, or water supplies, it is not safe to dispose of a battery by tossing it in a lake (choice **a**), burning it (choice **c**), or burying it in soil (choices **d** and **e**). The only safe thing to do is to take it to a recycling center for proper disposal.

31. d. If the sea otter population is reduced, the sea urchin population will increase as a result of the decrease in the number of predators. More sea urchins means that more kelp will be eaten, which will reduce the kelp forest. Choice **d** is the only answer choice that states that inference. The other choices are not valid because they are not logical results of a decline in the sea otter population.

32. a. During hibernation, the animal is stationary. This inability to move around means that it could not escape from its predators, which would decrease its chances of survival. Therefore, choice **a** is the correct answer. The other choices, while true, would not affect the animal's chances for survival.

33. c. The passage explains that the same side of the moon always faces Earth because the moon's rotation period equals its period of revolution around Earth. So choice **c** is the correct answer.

34. e. Choice **a** is inaccurate since during the new moon phase, the far side of the moon is in sunlight. Choice **b** is inaccurate since sometimes the far side is completely in darkness or partially in darkness. The far side always faces away from Earth, so choice **c** is incorrect. Choice **d** is also incorrect since during a full moon, the near side is completely lit and the far side still does not face Earth. Choice **e** is the correct answer since the far side faces away from Earth, so it is never seen.

35. c. The phase in which the greatest part of the moon is visible is the full moon phase, in which the side of the moon facing Earth is fully lit. This is point C in the diagram, so choice **c** is the correct answer.

36. d. Choice **a** is factually correct but not an explanation as to how pine trees survive a harsh environment. Nothing in the article suggests that choices **b**, **c**, or **e** are reasons why the trees can survive. The lack of surface area on needle-shaped leaves (choice **d**) is the correct answer because according to the article, it is through the surface of the leaves that trees lose water. If the surface area of the leaves is small, the tree will lose less moisture and will have a better chance for survival in a harsh climate.

37. c. Choices **a**, **b**, and **e** are factually incorrect. Choice **d** deals with an issue unrelated to the question. Choice **c**, which states the fact that the top leaves receive more sunlight, which aids photosynthesis and food production, is the best answer.

38. e. All objects accelerate, or increase their speed, at the same rate as they fall toward the ground. So as they fall, their speed increases to terminal velocity. Thus choice **a** is false. Since the rate of acceleration for all objects is the same regardless of their mass, choices **b** and **c** are false. In a vacuum, there is no air resistance, but objects still fall at the same rate of acceleration. So choice **d** is also false. The lighter an object is, the sooner it will reach its terminal velocity. So, choice **e** is the correct answer.

39. a. Choices **b** and **d** would prove the opposite of your claim that the clump is many one-celled animals. Choice **c** would neither prove nor disprove the claim, since all cells have an outer boundary. Choice **e** is not true of any cell. Choice **a** would prove your claim, since a one-celled organism must be able to function independently.

40. a. In order for fish to adapt to the drying up of swamps and ponds they needed to be able to survive and move about on land as well as in water. Choice **a** describes the two major adaptations needed for doing these things. The other choices describe adaptations of other species to meet other needs.

41. e. Nuclear fission and fusion are both examples of chemical change, so choice **a** is incorrect. Nuclear fission and fusion are controlled reactions, so choice **b** is incorrect. In nuclear fission the atoms split and become lighter, not heavier, so choice **c** is incorrect. Nuclear fission produces waste products, but nuclear fusion does not; therefore, choice **d** is incorrect. Choice **e** correctly states the difference between the two types of nuclear reaction.

42. b. The main advantage of nuclear fusion is that all the fuels needed are found in water, which is a cheap and plentiful resource. So choice **b** is the correct answer. Nothing stated in the article supports any of the other choices.

43. d. The main reason there are no nuclear fusion plants is that scientists have not solved the problem of how to create and maintain the needed high temperatures for the fusion process. So choice **d** is the correct choice. Choices **a**, **c**, and **e** are not supported by evidence in the article. Choice **b** may be factually correct in some locations, but it is not the main reason for why there are no nuclear fusion plants.

44. d. You would avoid sunscreens A, B, and E since they contain PABA, a chemical you are allergic to. You would also not use sunscreen C, since it fails to screen out UV-A, which could result in an allergic reaction to your medication. Thus you would use sunscreen D, which does not contain PABA but does protect against UV-A radiation. The correct answer is choice **d**.

45. d. Sunscreen B has an SPF of 15, which means a person who normally burns in 15 minutes can stay in the sun 15×15, or 225, minutes without burning. Sunscreen D has an SPF of 20, which means the same person could spend 20×15, or 300, minutes sunbathing without burning. This is 75 minutes more than the 225 minutes afforded by sunscreen B. Thus, choice **d** is the correct answer.

46. a. The one advantage that sunscreen E has over the other sunscreens is the number of minutes it takes for the sunscreen to wash off under water. Someone who intends to stay in the pool all day would need a sunscreen that does not wash off quickly in water. Therefore, the correct answer is choice **a**.

47. e. Building underground wells has no effect on soil erosion by wind. Planting rows of trees would help prevent soil erosion by the wind since the trees would provide shelter from heavy winds. Similarly, growing plants with thick roots would help prevent soil erosion by the wind because the roots of the plants would hold the soil in place during heavy winds. Therefore, choice **e**, which includes planting trees and growing plants with thick roots, is the correct answer.

48. b. In order for the sum of the charges to be equal, the positive charges must equal the negative charges. Since Al is 3+ and O is 2–, for every 2 ions of Al you need 3 ions of O, which is represented by the formula Al_2O_3, which is choice **b**. If you check the other formulas, you will find that either the positive charges are greater than the negative charges, as in choices **a** and **d**, or the positive charges are less than the negative charges, as in choices **c** and **e**.

49. e. When the light emanating from the flashlight passes through filter A, only vertical waves pass through. These waves would then all be absorbed by filter B. Thus, no light waves would shine on the box and the box would not be visible at all. So, choice **e** is the correct choice.

50. a. Plants absorb carbon dioxide, so planting a flower (choice **c**) would help reduce the amount of carbon dioxide in the atmosphere, but not to a significant degree. The other choices, **b**, **d**, and **e**, would have no effect on reducing the gases that cause the greenhouse effect. The most effective action to control the greenhouse effect is to develop energy sources that stop releasing air pollutants into the atmosphere. Solar energy power plants use an alternative energy source that would meet this requirement. Thus, choice **a** is the correct answer.

55 ▶ Practice Exam 2, GED Mathematics

▶ Part I

You are about to begin Part I of this exam. You may use your calculator for these questions.

1. A photograph is 5 in. wide and 8 in. long. It is enlarged so that its new length is 20 in. long. Which proportion can be used to find how many inches long the width of the enlarged photograph is?

   a. $\frac{x}{5} = \frac{8}{20}$

   b. $\frac{5}{20} = \frac{8}{x}$

   c. $\frac{5}{x} = \frac{20}{8}$

   d. $\frac{20}{5} = \frac{x}{8}$

   e. $\frac{5}{8} = \frac{x}{20}$

Please use the following to answer questions 2–3.

The following table gives the annual average hourly wages of production workers in the United States in the 1990s. The data is supplied by the U.S. Department of Labor.

AVERAGE HOURLY EARNINGS OF U.S. PRODUCTION WORKERS

Year	Hourly Earnings
1990	$10.01
1991	$10.32
1992	$10.57
1993	$10.83
1994	$11.12
1995	$11.43
1996	$11.82
1997	$12.28
1998	$12.77

2. In which year was the increase in hourly earnings the least from the previous year?
   a. 1992
   b. 1994
   c. 1996
   d. 1997
   e. 1998

3. What was the approximate percent increase to the nearest percent in hourly earnings from 1990 to 1996?
   a. 10%
   b. 15%
   c. 18%
   d. 20%
   e. 120%

4. The following figure shows all of the faces of a rectangular prism that has been unfolded. What is the surface area in square centimeters (cm^2) of the rectangular prism?

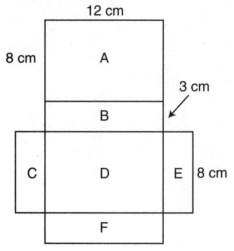

   a. 156 cm^2
   b. 192 cm^2
   c. 252 cm^2
   d. 288 cm^2
   e. 312 cm^2

5. In a jar of coins in which 35% of the coins are pennies, 50% of the pennies were minted before 1975. If there are 245 pennies minted before 1975 in the jar, what is the total number of coins in the jar? Mark your answer in the circles on the grid below.

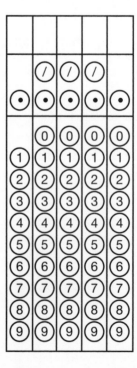

6. Here are test scores for 5 students: 79, 79, 81, 82, and 84. Which statement is true?

 a. The mean and median scores are the same.

 b. The mean score is greater than the median score.

 c. The mean score is less than the median score.

 d. The mode score is the same as the median score.

 e. The mode score is greater than the median score.

7. Bill spends an average of 5 minutes each day waiting in lines. If Bill is typical of the 290 million people in the United States, which of the following expresses the approximate combined amount of time these people spend annually waiting in line?

 a. 1.45×10^9 minutes a year

 b. 14.5×10^8 minutes a year

 c. 1.825×10^3 minutes a year

 d. 0.52925×10^{10} minutes a year

 e. 5.2925×10^{11} minutes a year

8. What is the sum of the areas of the rectangles as a polynomial in simplest form?

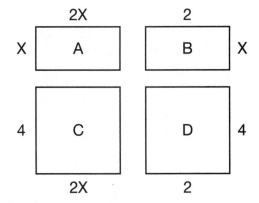

 a. $8x + 4$

 b. $x^2 + 8x$

 c. $2x^2 + 2x + 4$

 d. $2x^2 + 10x + 8$

 e. $4x^2 + 12x + 4$

9. Frank is a salesman for an appliance company. He earns a weekly salary of $500. In addition to his salary Frank earns an 8% commission on the total amount of appliances he sells. If Frank sold $265,000 worth of appliances last year, which expression would give the total amount of money Frank earned last year?

 a. $500 + 0.08(265,000)$

 b. $52(500) + 0.08(265,000)$

 c. $\dfrac{[265,000 + (0.8)500]}{0.08}$

 d. $52(500) + 0.8(265,000)$

 e. $\dfrac{[52(500) + 265,000]}{0.08}$

10. Evaluate the expression $\dfrac{2(a-b)^2}{3}$ if $a = -2$ and $b = 4$.

 a. -24

 b. -4

 c. $\dfrac{8}{3}$

 d. 8

 e. 24

11. The sum of the measures of the angles of a polygon having n sides is $(n - 2)180°$. If the sum of the measures of five angles of a hexagon is equal to $650°$, which expression gives the measure of the sixth angle?

 a. $650 - 3(180)$

 b. $\dfrac{650}{5} - 180$

 c. $650 - \dfrac{180}{3}$

 d. $5(180) - 650$

 e. $4(180) - 650$

Please use the following to answer questions 12–13.

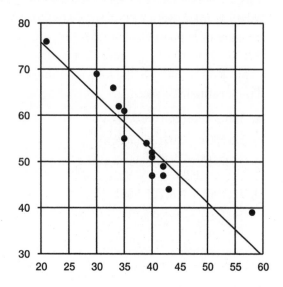

The table lists the latitude and mean April temperature (°F) for 15 cities in the United States. The data is displayed in a scatter plot where a fitted line is drawn.

CITY	LATITUDE (°NORTH)	MEAN APRIL TEMP. (°F)
Albuquerque	35	55
Baltimore	39	54
Charlotte	35	61
Chicago	42	49
Dallas	33	66
Denver	40	47
Detroit	42	47
Hartford	42	49
Honolulu	21	76
Houston	30	69
Juneau	58	39
Little Rock	34	62
Milwaukee	43	44
Philadelphia	40	52
Salt Lake City	40	51

12. San Francisco has a northern latitude of 37°. Based upon the scatter plot, what do you predict as its mean April temperature in °F?
a. 36°F
b. 45°F
c. 56°F
d. 61°F
e. 65°F

13. Which city has an actual mean April temperature that is 9 degrees warmer than predicted by the fitted line of the scatter plot?
a. Baltimore
b. Dallas
c. Houston
d. Juneau
e. Salt Lake City

14. In the diagram below, line *c* intersects lines *a* and *b*, which are parallel. If the measure of ∠4 = 122°, what is m∠7?

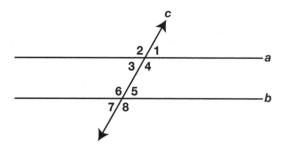

a. 122°
b. 88°
c. 68°
d. 58°
e. Not enough information is given.

15. Bill plans to rent a car while he is on a one-week vacation. The cost of renting the car is $150 per week, plus $0.20 for every mile he drives. What is the greatest number of miles Bill can travel, if he wants to spend at most $300? Mark your answer in the circles on the grid below.

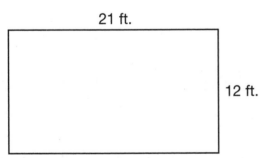

16. Bernice is planning to carpet her living room. She has selected carpeting that costs $12 a square yard. What is the total cost for carpeting Bernice's living room?

21 ft.

12 ft.

Living Room

a. $3,024
b. $1,008
c. $336
d. $252
e. $224

17. The pie graph shows what fraction each kingdom is of the total number of species. If there are a total of 1,424,800 species, about how many protist species are there, to the nearest hundred?

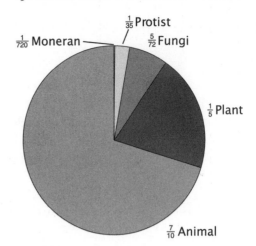

a. 1,980
b. 4,000
c. 19,800
d. 39,600
e. 98,900

Please use the following to answer questions 18–19.

FOOD ITEM	PRICE
Hot dogs	1—$2.25 or
	3—$6.00
Hamburgers	1—$3.50 or
	3—$10.00
French Fries	small size—$2.00
	jumbo size—$3.00
Soda	8–oz. cup—$1.25
	12–oz. cup—$1.50
	20–oz. cup—$2.00

18. Which expression shows the total cost for purchasing two hot dogs, a jumbo size order of french fries, and an 8-oz. cup of soda?
a. $2(3.5) + 3 + 1.5$
b. $2(2.25) + 3 + 1.25$
c. $2(2.25) + 2 + 1.5$
d. $6 + 2(2) + 1.25$
e. $7 + 2 + 1.35$

19. Frank wants to buy four hamburgers, two jumbo size fries, and three 12-oz. sodas. What is the least amount he can spend to buy these items?
   a. $24.00
   b. $25.50
   c. $27.50
   d. $30.00
   e. $31.50

20. Francine and Lucille bowled together and had a combined score of 320. Lucille's score was 24 more than Francine's score. Which system of equations can be used to find Francine and Lucille's bowling scores?
   a. $f + l = 320$
       $f + 24 = l$
   b. $f = 320 + l$
       $f - 24 = l$
   c. $\frac{f+l}{24} = 320$
       $f - 24 = l$
   d. $f - l = 24$
       $f + 320 = l$
   e. $f - l = 320 - 24$
       $\frac{f}{24} = l + 320$

21. If $\overline{BC}$ is parallel to $\overline{DE}$ in the diagram, how many centimeters long is $\overline{BC}$?

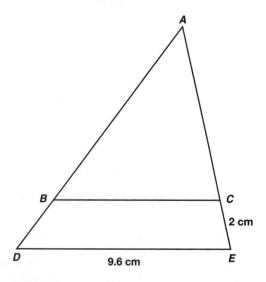

   a. 57.6 cm
   b. 28.8 cm
   c. 12.8 cm
   d. 7.2 cm
   e. 5 cm

Please use the following to answer question 22.

Zone	Weight	Shipping Cost
1	less than 50 lbs.	$1.50
	more than 50 lbs.	$2.50
2	less than 50 lbs.	$3.00
	more than 50 lbs.	$4.50
3	less than 50 lbs.	$4.00
	more than 50 lbs.	$5.50

22. How much more will Sherry pay in shipping costs to ship packages B and D compared to shipping packages A and C?

Package A: 44 lbs. Shipped to Zone 2.
Package B: 83 lbs. Shipped to Zone 3.
Package C: 12 lbs. Shipped to Zone 1.
Package D: 75 lbs. Shipped to Zone 3

   a. $6.50
   b. $5.50
   c. $4.50
   d. $3.50
   e. $3.00

23. For which pair of coordinates would a line that passes through them have the greatest positive slope?
   a. (3,–2) and (8,4)
   b. (–3,1) and (2,9)
   c. (3,2) and (4,7)
   d. (5,–2) and (6,–4)
   e. (–2,3) and (4,8)

24. Which is the sum of $\sqrt{108}$ and $\sqrt{75}$?
   a. $61\sqrt{3}$
   b. $11\sqrt{3}$
   c. $3\sqrt{61}$
   d. $\sqrt{178}$
   e. $\sqrt{3}$

25. The formula for the area of a trapezoid is $A = \frac{1}{2}h(b_1 + b_2)$. If the area of the trapezoid is 45, which expression gives the length of the other base?

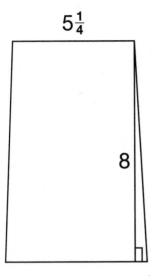

$5\frac{1}{4}$

8

a. $\left[\frac{2(45)}{5\frac{1}{4}}\right] - 8$

b. $\left[\frac{2(45)}{8}\right] - 5\frac{1}{4}$

c. $\left[\frac{2(45)}{5\frac{1}{4}}\right] - \frac{2(45)}{88}$

d. $\left[\frac{(5\frac{1}{4})(45)}{8}\right] - \frac{2(45)}{8}$

e. $\left[\frac{(5\frac{1}{4})(45)}{8}\right]$

▶ Part II

You are about to begin Part II of this exam. In this section, you must answer an additional 25 questions. Unlike Part I, you may NOT use your calculator for these questions, so be sure to put it away to simulate the actual GED testing experience.

26. During a training session, firefighters set up a ladder to reach a window in an upper floor of a building. How many feet from the ground is the window? Mark your answer in the circles on the grid below.

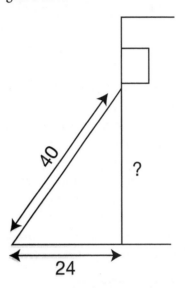

40

?

24

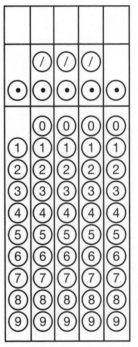

27. Which equation can be used to find four consecutive integers whose sum is 54?

a. $4x + 4 = 54$

b. $4x + 6 = 54$

c. $\frac{4x}{4} = 54$

d. $\frac{4x}{6} = 54$

e. $x + (x + 1) + 54 = (x + 2) + (x + 3)$

28. There are 8 dogs entered in the hunter competition at the Longacre Kennel Club show. Which expression best represents the number of different ways first, second, and third prizes can be awarded in the competition?
a. 8×3
b. $8 + 7 + 6$
c. $8 \times 7 \times 6$
d. $(8 \times 3) + (7 \times 2) + (6 \times 1)$
e. $8 \times (7 + 6)$

Please use the following to answer questions 29–30.

Seismologists use distance–time graphs, like the one that follows, to determine the distance to an earthquake epicenter. In the graph, the distance that waves travel is indicated along the horizontal scale. The time needed for each type of wave to travel a certain distance is indicated along the vertical scale.

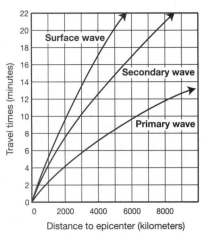

29. How many kilometers per minute is a secondary wave traveling at 2,000 km?
a. 750 km/m
b. 500 km/m
c. 250 km/m
d. 200 km/m
e. 100 km/m

30. Approximately how many kilometers does a secondary wave travel in the same amount of time it takes a primary wave to travel 3,000 kilometers?
a. 3,000 km
b. 2,000 km
c. 1,500 km
d. 1,100 km
e. 500 km

31. The diagram shows the shape and dimensions of the patio at the back of Karen's house. What is the area of the patio to the nearest square foot?

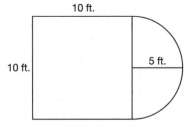

a. 179 ft.^{2}
b. 157 ft.^{2}
c. 139 ft.^{2}
d. 15.7 ft.^{2}
e. 13 ft.^{2}

32. Jerry is 4 years older than his sister Marie. Five years ago, he was twice as old as his sister was. Which pair of equations can be used to solve this problem?
a. $2j - 4 = m$
   $j + 5 = m - 4$
b. $j = m - 4$
   $j - 5 = m - 5$
c. $j - m = 4$
   $j - 5 = 2m - 5$
d. $j = 4 - m$
   $j + 5 = 2m$
e. $j = 4 + m$
   $j - 5 = 2(m - 5)$

33. In the diagram, triangle ABC is isosceles. $\overline{AB} \cong \overline{CB}$. $\overline{BD}$ bisects $\angle ABC$. Which method establishes that $\triangle ABD \cong \triangle BD$?

a. ASA
b. AAS
c. AAA
d. SAS
e. Not enough information is given.

34. Fred buys 2 shirts, each costing $23.99, and a sweater that costs $45.49. He is charged sales tax of 8%. Which of the following expressions represents the total amount he will be charged for his purchases?

a. $2(23.99) + 45.49 + 0.08$

b. $2(23.99) + (45.49)$

c. $2(23.99) + 45.49 + 0.08(45.49)$

d. $1.08[2(23.99) + (45.49)]$

e. $8[2(23.99) + (45.49)]$

Please use the following to answer questions 35–36.

U.S. Car Sales by Vehicle Size and Type, 1983, 1993, 1998, and 1999

Year	Total U.S. Car Sales
1983	9,182,067
1993	8,517,859
1998	8,141,721
1999	8,698,284

35. Approximately how many small cars were sold in the United States in 1998?

a. 500,000

b. 1,000,000

c. 2,000,000

d. 3,000,000

e. 4,000,000

36. In 1999, about how times were more midsize cars sold than luxury and large cars combined?

a. eight times as many

b. five times as many

c. three times as many

d. twice as many

e. the same

Please use the following to answer questions 37–38.

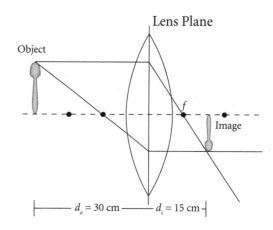

The diagram shows a convex lens, an object, and its image. Notice the position of the object, the lens plane, and the image.

A mathematical formula relates three kinds of distances in lens calculations. The formula is:

$$\frac{1}{f} = \frac{1}{d_o} + \frac{1}{d_i}$$

f = focal length of the lens

d_o = distance from the object to the plane of the lens

d_i = distance from the image to the plane of the lens

37. What is the focal length of the lens in the diagram?

a. 10 cm

b. 15 cm

c. 20 cm

d. 25 cm

e. 40 cm

38. If an object is 20 centimeters from the lens plane and the focal length distance is 10 centimeters, what is the distance between the lens plane and the image?

a. 45 cm

b. 35 cm

c. 20 cm

d. 15 cm

e. 10 cm

39. Factor: $x^2 + 11x + 28$.

a. $(x + 2)(x + 9)$

b. $(x + 4)(x + 7)$

c. $(x + 2)(x + 14)$

d. $(x - 4)(x + 7)$

e. $(x - 4)(x - 7)$

40. Which expression shows how to find the length of $\overline{AB}$?

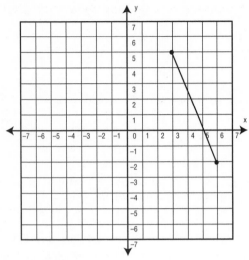

a. $\sqrt{6^2 + -2^2}$

b. $\sqrt{3^2 + -5^2}$

c. $\sqrt{(6-3)^2 + (5-2)^2}$

d. $\sqrt{(6-3)^2 + (-2-5)^2}$

e. $\sqrt{(3-6)^2 + (2-5)^2}$

41. James is playing darts with his friend Kevin. Assuming that each player will hit a spot on the dartboard, and that every spot on the dartboard has an equally likely chance of having a dart land on it, which expression gives the probability of hitting the bull's-eye?

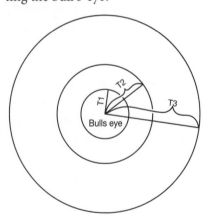

a. $\dfrac{\pi r1^2}{(\pi r2^2 + \pi r3^2)}$

b. $\dfrac{\pi r1^2}{(\pi r2^2 - \pi r3^2)}$

c. $\dfrac{(\pi r1^2 + \pi r2^2)}{\pi r3^2}$

d. $\dfrac{(\pi r1^2 - \pi r2^2)}{\pi r3}2$

e. $\dfrac{\pi r1^2}{\pi r3^2}$

42. Francine took a 5-mile cab ride from the airport to her home. She gave the driver a 15% tip of the fare. How much did the cab ride, including the tip, cost her?

Cab Rates

First $\frac{1}{5}$ mile $ .80

Each additional $\frac{1}{5}$ mile $ .30

a. $8.00

b. $9.20

c. $10.40

d. $11.50

e. $12.00

Please use the following to answer questions 43–44.

**U.S. Higher Education Trends: Bachelor s
Degrees Conferred**

Source: National Center for Education Statistics, U.S. Dept.
of Education Figures for 2009–2010 are projected

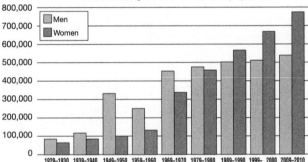

43. In which academic year did the number of women receiving bachelor's degrees exceed the number of men receiving bachelor's degrees for the first time?

a. 1929–30

b. 1939–40

c. 1969–70

d. 1979–80

e. 1989–90

44. Approximately how many more women received a bachelor's degree in 1989–1990 than men?

a. 150,000

b. 120,000

c. 60,000

d. 35,000

e. 15,000

45. A lightbulb study found that in a random sampling of 100 lightbulbs, 3 were defective. Based upon this sampling, how many lightbulbs would you expect to be defective in a sampling of 2,000 lightbulbs?

a. 600

b. 500

c. 250

d. 60

e. 30

46. What is y if $y = 7(x - 9)$ and $\frac{x}{2} - 5 = 4$?

a. 0

b. 9

c. 56

d. 63

e. 189

47. If you reflect $\triangle ABC$ across the y-axis, what will be the coordinates of the image of its three vertices, A', B', C'?

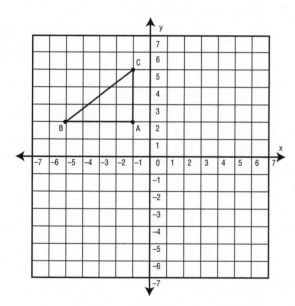

a. A': $(-1,-2)$, B': $(-5,-2)$, C': $(-1,-5)$

b. A': $(1,-2)$, B': $(5,-2)$, C': $(-1,5)$

c. A': $(1,2)$, B': $(5,2)$, C': $(1,5)$

d. A': $(0,2)$, B': $(-4,2)$, C': $(0,5)$

e. A': $(4,2)$, B': $(0,2)$, C': $(4,5)$

48. Kenneth spends 72% of his 40-hour work week on his computer. What fraction of his work week does Kenneth spend NOT working on his computer?

a. $\frac{1}{4}$

b. $\frac{3}{20}$

c. $\frac{7}{25}$

d. $\frac{18}{25}$

e. $\frac{3}{4}$

49. Which of the following equations will have a graph that is parallel to the equation, $y = 3x - 4$?

a. $2x - 4y = 8$

b. $y = 4x - 3$

c. $2y = 2x - 6$

d. $y + x = 3$

e. $6x - 2y = 4$

Please use the following to answer question 50.

June Accounts
Dog walking $10.50
Baby Sitting $15.25
Movies   −$27.00

50. The table shows Brenda's actual earnings and expenses in June. Which signed number describes the sum of her earnings and expenses in June?

a. $5.75

b. $1.25

c. $0.75

d. −$0.75

e. −$1.25

▶ Answers

1. e. Write ratios comparing width to length. Original photo: $\frac{5}{8}$, new photo: $\frac{x}{20}$. Then write the proportion that shows these ratios as equivalent. $\frac{5}{8} = \frac{x}{20}$.

2. a. Subtract hourly earnings of previous year from given year.

a: 1992–1991 = $10.57 – $10.32 = $0.25
b: 1994–1993 = $11.12 – $10.83 = $0.29
c: 1996–1995 = $11.82 – $11.43 = $0.39
b: 1997–1996 = $12.28 – $11.82 = $0.46
b: 1998–1997 = $12.77 – $12.28 = $0.49

Compare differences to find the least difference. $0.25 is the least difference, which means 1992 had the least increase in hourly earnings from the previous year.

3. c. Subtract to find the amount of increase.
1996 hourly earnings – 1990 hourly earnings
$11.82 – $10.01 = $1.81
Write a ratio comparing the amount of increase to the original amount: $\frac{\$1.81}{\$10.01}$.
Change to a percent by first expressing the fraction as decimal, and then changing the decimal to a percent.
$1.81 \div 10.01 \approx = 0.1808$
$0.1808 = 18.08\% \approx 18\%$

4. e. Find the area of each of the six faces, and then add the areas.
Area of A = 8 cm × 12 cm = 96 cm²
Area of B = 3 cm × 12 cm = 36 cm²
Area of C = 8 cm × 3 cm = 24 cm²
Area of D = 8 cm × 12 cm = 96 cm²
Area of E = 8 cm × 3 cm = 24 cm²
Area of F = 3 cm × 12 cm = 36 cm²
Surface Area = 312 cm²

5. 1,400.

Let x = number of pennies in the jar.

50% of x = 245
$0.50x = 245$
$x = \frac{245}{.5}$
$x = 490$ (pennies in the jar)

Let y = total number of coins in jar

35% of y = 490
$0.35y = 490$
$y = \frac{490}{0.35}$
$y = 1,400$ (total coins in the jar)

6. a. Find all three measures of central tendencies:
Find the mean.
$79 + 79 + 81 + 82 + 84 = 405$
$405 \div 5 = 81$
So, the mean score is 81.
Find the median.
79 79 81 82 84 (81 is the middle number)
So, the median score is 81.
Find the mode.
79 79 81 82 84 (79 is the most frequent score)
So, the mode is 79.
The mean and median scores are the same, so choice **a** is correct.

7. e. You can use ratios to solve this problem.

Time spent annually = $\frac{\text{number of minutes}}{1 \text{ day}} \times$

$\frac{\text{number of days}}{1 \text{ year}} \times$ number of people

Substitute the values using scientific notation and then find the product.

$\frac{5 \times 10^0}{1} \times \frac{3.65 \times 10^2}{1} \times (2.9 \times 10^8) = 52.925 \times 10^{10} =$
5.2925×10^{11}

8. d. Find the area of each rectangle.

A: $x \times 2x = 2x^2$

B: $2 \times x = 2x$

C: $4 \times 2x = 8x$

D: $4 \times 2 = 8$

Write it as a sum. Then write it in simplest form by combining like terms.

$2x^2 + 2x + 8x + 8 = 2x^2 + 10x + 8$

9. b. Look for the expression that multiplies Frank's weekly salary by 52 to find his yearly salary. 52(500). This leaves choices **b**, **d**, or **e**.
Then look for the expression that adds on his commission, which is 8% of 265,000.

8% = 0.08

8% of 265,000 = 0.08(265,000)

Choice **b** adds the commission amount to his yearly salary and is the correct answer.

10. e. First replace a with −2 and b with 4. Then simplify the numerical expression using the order of operations.

$2(a - b)^2 = \frac{[2(-2-4)^2]}{3}$

$= \frac{[2(-6)^2]}{3}$ Work within parentheses

$= \frac{2(36)}{3}$ Work with exponents

$= \frac{72}{3}$ Multiply

$= 24$ Divide

11. e. The sum of the measures of the angles of a polygon having n sides is $(n - 2)180°$. A hexagon has 6 sides, so the sum of the measures of the six angles = $(6 - 2)180°$ or $4(180°)$.

Since you know the sum of the measures of 5 angles is equal to 650°, you can subtract 650° from 4(180°) to find the measure of the sixth angle.

12. c. Look at the fitted line. Find where a northern latitude of 37° is on the line. Then look across to see what temperature this corresponds to. 37° corresponds to a temperature 56°F. Therefore, you would predict that 56°F is the mean April temperature for San Francisco.

13. d. Look for points above the fitted line. Find a point 9 degrees higher than the point on the fitted line. Note its northern latitude of 58° and temperature of 39°F. Find the city with these readings on the table. Juneau has these readings.

14. d. A line that intersects a pair of parallel lines is called a transversal. Pairs of angles that are formed by a transversal have special names and relationships.

∠4 and ∠8 are corresponding angles. They are congruent. Thus, if m∠4 = 122°, then m∠8 = 122°.

Supplementary angles form a straight line, or 180°. ∠7 and ∠8 are supplementary angles. Thus, if m∠8 = 122°, then m∠7 = 180° − 122°, or 58°.

15. 750.

The solution requires setting up and solving an inequality.

Let b = number of miles Bill can travel

Key fact: Cost of car rental is at most $300.

Translate these facts into an inequality.

$150 + 0.20b \le 300$

Solve the inequality.

$150 + 0.2b \le 300$

$0.2b \le 300 - 150$

$0.2b \le 150$

$b \le \frac{150}{0.2}$

$b \le 750$

Bill can travel up to 750 miles and still spend $300 or less.

16. c. Find the area of the living room.

$A = l \times w$

$= 21 \times 12$

$= 252 \text{ ft.}^2$

Change square feet to square yards.

$$\frac{\overset{28}{\cancel{252 \text{ ft.}^2}} \times 1 \text{ yd.}}{\underset{1}{\cancel{9 \text{ ft.}^2}}} = 28 \text{ yd.}^2$$

Multiply to find cost.

$28 \text{ yd.}^2 \times \$12/\text{yd.}^2 = \$336$

The cost is \$336.

17. d. Protists represents $\frac{1}{36}$ of the entire circle. Therefore, the number of protist species is $\frac{1}{36}$ of the total. $\frac{1}{36} \times 1{,}424{,}800 = 39{,}577.777\ldots$ 39,577 to the nearest hundred is 39,600. So, there are about 39,600 protist species.

18. b. Write an expression to find the cost of each food item.

two hot dogs: 2(2.25)	Multiply cost of 1 hot dog (\$2.25) by 2.
jumbo size fries: 3	$3.00 = 3$
8-oz. soda: 1.25	

Write an expression that shows the sum of the cost of each item.

$2(2.25) + 3 + 1.25$

19. a. Find the least cost for purchasing each food item. Then find the sum.

4 hamburgers	= 1 set of 3 hamburgers + 1 hamburger
	$= 1(\$10) + \$3.50 = \$13.50$
2 jumbo fries	$= 2(\$3.00) = \$6$
3 12-oz. sodas	$= 3(\$1.50) = \$4.50$

$$\begin{array}{r} \$13.50 \\ 6.00 \\ +\ 4.50 \\ \hline 24.00 \end{array}$$

The total cost is \$24.00.

20. a. Choose variables. Let f = Francine's bowling score and l = Lucille's bowling score. Translate each statement into an equation. Francine and Lucille had a combined score of 320.

$f + l = 320$

Lucille's score was 24 more than Francine's score.

$f + 24 = l$

21. d. Since $\triangle ABC \cong \triangle ADE$, the corresponding sides are proportional. Therefore, $\frac{AE}{DE} = \frac{AC}{BC}$. Substitute and solve for BC.

$$\frac{AE}{DE} = \frac{AC}{BC}$$

$$\frac{8}{9.6} = \frac{6}{BC}$$

$8(BC) = 6(9.6)$

$8(BC) = 57.6$

$BC = \frac{57.6}{8} = 7.2$

So, BC is 7.2 cm long.

22. a. Here is one way to solve this multi-step problem.

Find the shipping cost for each package using the data from the table.

Package A: \$3.00

Package B: \$5.50

Package C: \$1.50

Package D: \$5.50

Add to find the total cost for shipping packages B and D.

$\$5.50 + \$5.50 = \$11.00$

Add to find the total cost for shipping packages A and C.

$\$3.00 + \$1.50 = \$4.50$

Subtract to find the difference.

$\$11.00 - \$4.50 = \$6.50$

23. c. Find the slope for each pair of coordinates. Use the formula: slope $= \frac{y_2 - y_1}{x_2 - x_1}$ (where $x_1 \neq x_2$)

(3,–2) and (8,4): $\frac{[4 - (-2)]}{8 - 3} = \frac{6}{5} = 1$

(–3,1) and (2,9): $\frac{(9 - 1)}{[2 - (-3)]} = \frac{8}{5} = 1$

(3,2) and (4,7): $\frac{(7 - 2)}{(4 - 3)} = \frac{5}{1} = 5$

(5,–2) and (6,–4): $\frac{[-4 - (-2)]}{6 - 5} = \frac{-2}{1} = -2$

(–2,3) and (4,8): $\frac{(8 - 3)}{[4 - (-2)]} = \frac{5}{6}$

5 is the greatest positive slope. A line passing through (3,2) and (4,7) would have the greatest positive slope.

24. b. You can use the property $\sqrt{ab} = \sqrt{a} \times \sqrt{b}$ to simplify radicands allowing you to work with like radicands. Look for perfect squares.
$$\sqrt{108} + \sqrt{75} = \sqrt{36}\sqrt{3} + \sqrt{25}\sqrt{3}$$
$$= \sqrt{36 \times 3} + \sqrt{25 \times 3}$$
$$= 6\sqrt{3} + 5\sqrt{3}$$
You can then add radicals having like radicands as like terms.
$$6\sqrt{3} + 5\sqrt{3} = 11\sqrt{3}$$

25. b. Write the formula for the area of a trapezoid and then solve it in terms of the second base.
$A = \frac{1}{2}h(b_1 + b_2)$
$2A = h(b_1 + b_2)$ Multiply both sides by 2.
$2\frac{A}{h} = b_1 + b_2$ Divide both sides by h.
$\frac{2A}{h} - b_1 = b_2$ Subtract b_1 from both sides.
Substitute the known values.
$A = 45$, $h = 8$, and $b_1 = 5\frac{1}{4}$
$\frac{2(45)}{8} - 5\frac{1}{4}$

26. 32.

You can use the Pythagorean theorem to find x, the distance from the ground.
$a^2 + b^2 = c^2$
$x^2 + 24^2 = 40^2$
$x^2 = 40^2 - 24^2$
$x^2 = 1{,}600 - 575 = 1{,}024$
$x = \sqrt{1{,}024}$
$x = 32$ feet (from the ground)

27. b. Let x = the first consecutive integer. Then
$x + 1$ = second consecutive integer,
$x + 2$ = third consecutive integer, and
$x + 3$ = third consecutive integer.
Use the facts from the problem to write the equation.
$x + (x + 1) + (x + 2) + (x + 3) = 54$
Then simplify the equation by combining like terms.
$4x + 6 = 54$

28. c. For the number of permutations of n things taken r at a time, you can use the following formula carried out to r factors:
$_nP_r = n \times (n - 1) \times (n - 2) \times \ldots$
You need to find the number of permutations of 8 things taken 3 at a time, or $_8P_3$.
$_8P_3 = 8 \times (8 - 1) \times (8 - 2)$
$= 8 \times 7 \times 6$
Thus, $8 \times 7 \times 6$ will give the number of ways first, second, and third prizes can be awarded in the competition.

29. c. Find the time it takes for a secondary wave to travel 2,000 km.
The graph of the secondary wave intersects the time at 8 minutes, when the distance is 2,000 km. Substitute in the distance formula, and solve for r.
$d = rt$
$2{,}000 = 8r$
$\frac{2000}{8} = \frac{8r}{r}$
$250 = r$
So, the rate of speed is 250 km/m.

30. c. Find the time that it takes a primary wave to travel 3,000 kilometers.
At 3,000 kilometers, the primary wave intersects the vertical scale at 6 minutes.
Now find the distance that the secondary wave travels in 6 minutes.
At 6 minutes, the secondary wave intersects the horizontal scale midway between 1,000 km and 2,000 km.
So, we can estimate the distance as 1,500 km.

31. c. Find the area of the square.
$A = s^2$
$A = 10^2 = 100$
Find the area of the semicircle.
$A = \frac{1}{2}\pi r^2$
$A = \frac{1}{2}(3.14)(5)^2$
$= 39.25$
Find the sum of the areas.
$100 + 39.25 = 139.25$
139.25 is 139 rounded to the nearest square foot.
So, the area of the patio is 139 ft.^{2} to the nearest square foot.

32. e. Let j = Jerry's age now, and let m = Marie's age now. Make a chart to show age now and five years ago.

Name	Now	5 years ago
Jerry	j	$j - 5$
Marie	m	$m - 5$

Use the two facts from the problem to write two equations.

Fact 1: Now: Jerry is 4 years older than Marie.
1st equation: $j = 4 + m$
Fact 2: Five years ago: Jerry was twice as old as Marie.
2nd equation: $j - 5 = 2(m - 5)$

33. d. You know that $\overline{AB} \cong \overline{CB}$. Since $\overline{BC}$ bisects $\angle ABC$, $\angle 1 \cong \angle 2$. Also BD is a side of both triangles. Therefore, by the SAS (Side = Angle ≈ Side) test, $\triangle ABD \approx \triangle CBD$.

34. d. The cost of buying 2 shirts is 2(23.99). The cost of buying 1 sweater is 45.49. The sum 2(23.99) + 45.49 is the cost without the sales tax.
8% is 0.08 as a decimal.
1.08 represents 100% for the cost and 8% for the sales tax.
Therefore, 1.08[2(23.99) + (45.49)] represents the total amount Fred will be charged including the sales tax.

35. c. Use the table to find the total number of cars sold in the United States in 1998.
total sales in 1998 = 8,141,721
Use the bar graph to find what percent of total car sales in 1998 small cars represented.
small car sales in 1998 = 24.7%
Estimate 24.7% of 8,141,721 to find the approximate number of cars sold.
$24.7\% \approx 25\% = \frac{1}{4}$
$8,141,721 \approx 8,000,000$
$\frac{1}{4} \times 8,000,000 = 2,000,000$
Approximately 2,000,000 small cars were sold in 1998.

36. d. Use the graph to find the percent of sales for midsize, luxury, and large size cars.
midsize: 52.7%
luxury: 16.5%
large: 7.6%
Find the sum of the percentages of luxury and large size car sales.
$16.5 + 7.6 = 24.1$
Find the ratio of midsize car sales to the sum of luxury and large size car sales.
52.7:24.1
This is about 2 to 1.
About twice as many midsize cars as luxury and large size cars combined were sold in 1998.

37. a. Use the formula to find f, when $d_o = 30$, and $d_i = 15$.

$$\frac{1}{f} = \frac{1}{d_o} + \frac{1}{d_i}$$

$$\frac{1}{f} = \frac{1}{30} + \frac{1}{15}$$

$$30\left(\frac{1}{f}\right) = 30\left(\frac{1}{30} + \frac{1}{15}\right)$$

$$\frac{30}{f} = 1 + 2$$

$$\frac{30}{f} = 3$$

$$f\left(\frac{30}{f}\right) = 3f$$

$$30 = 3f$$

$$10 = f$$

So, the focal length is 10 cm.

38. c. Use the formula to find d_i, when $d_o = 20$, and $f = 10$.

$$\frac{1}{f} = \frac{1}{d_o} + \frac{1}{d_i}$$

$$\frac{1}{10} = \frac{1}{20} + \frac{1}{d_i}$$

$$20\left(\frac{1}{10}\right) = 20\left(\frac{1}{20}\right) + \frac{1}{d_i}$$

$$2 = 1 + \frac{20}{d_i}$$

$$1 = \frac{20}{d_i}$$

$$d_i(1) = d_i\left(\frac{20}{d_i}\right)$$

$$d_i = 20$$

So, the distance between the lens plane and the image is 20 cm.

39. b. Since the coefficient of the linear term is positive, list the positive factors of 28.

Factors of 28		Sum of the Factors
1	28	29
2	14	16
4	7	11

Find the factors whose sum is 11.
Therefore, $x^2 + 11x + 28 = (x + 4)(x + 7)$.

40. d. You can use the distance formula to find the length of $\overline{AB}$.
For points A and B the formula is:

$$\sqrt{(x_a - x_b)^2 + (y_a + y_b)^2}$$

Substitute the x- and y-coordinates of points A and B.

$$\sqrt{(6 - 3)^2 + (-2 - 5)^2}$$

41. e. The probability of an event is the ratio of favorable outcomes to total outcomes. Therefore,

$$P(\text{bull's-eye}) = \frac{\text{area of bull's-eye}}{\text{area of dartboard}}$$

Use the area formula for a circle to express the areas.

bull's–eye: dartboard:
$r = r_1$ $r = r_3$
$A = \pi r^2$ $A = \pi r^2$
$= \pi r_1^2$ $= \pi r_3^2$

Substitute the expressions of the area into the probability ratio.

P(bull's-eye) = area of bull's-eye/area of
dartboard $= \frac{\pi r_1^2}{\pi r_3^2}$

42. b. Find the fare for the first mile.
$\$.80 + 4(\$.30) = \$2.00$
$\frac{1}{5} + \frac{4}{5} = $ 1st mile
Find the fare of the 4 additional miles.
$5(\$.30) = \$1.50$ (each additional mile)
$4(\$1.50) = \$6.00$ (4 miles)
Add to find the total fare.
$\$6.00 + \$2.00 = \$8.00$
Find amount of tip.
$0.15(8.00) = \$1.20$
Add the tip to the fare to find the total cost of the cab ride.
$\$8.00 + \$1.20 = \$9.20$

43. e. Look for the first year in which the bar that represents the number of women receiving bachelor's degrees is taller than the bar that represents the number of men receiving bachelor's degrees.
The first time this occurs is for 1989–90.

44. c. To solve the problem, first find how many women and how many men received bachelor's degrees in 1989–1990.
For women, the height of the bar is a little past the middle between 500,000 and 600,000.
Estimate: 560,000
For men, the bar is just under 500,000.
Estimate 500,000.
Subtract the estimates.
$560,000 - 500,000 = 60,000$
Approximately 60,000 more women received bachelor degrees in 1989–90.

45. d. Write a ratio of defective lightbulbs: total number of lightbulbs.
$\frac{3}{100}$
Write and solve a proportion.
Let x = number of defective lightbulbs in second sampling.
$\frac{3}{100} = \frac{x}{2000}$
$3(2,000) = 100x$
$6,000 = 100x$
$60 = x$

46. d. Solve the second equation for x.
$\frac{x}{2} - 5 = 4$
$\frac{x}{2} - 5 + 5 = 4 + 5$
$2(\frac{x}{2}) = 2(4 + 5)$
$x = 2(9) = 18$
Then substitute 18 for x in the first equation.
$y = 7(x - 9)$
$= 7(18 - 9)$
$= 7(9) = 63$
So, $y = 63$.

47. c. When you reflect triangle ABC across the y-axis, its image triangle $A'B'C'$ will be in the first quadrant. The y-coordinates of the reflected image will be the same as the y-coordinates of triangle ABC. The x-coordinates will be opposites of the x-coordinates of triangle ABC.
A' (1,2)
B' (5,2)
C' (1,5)
So, (1,2), (5,2), (1,5) will be the coordinates of the image of triangle ABC.

48. c. Subtract 72% from 100% to find the percent of time not working at the computer.
$100\% - 72\% = 28\%$
Write 28% as a fraction.
$28\% = \frac{28}{100}$
Write the fraction in lowest terms.
$\frac{28}{100} \div \frac{4}{4} = \frac{7}{25}$
Kenneth spends $\frac{7}{25}$ of his work week not on the computer.

49. e. Write each equation in the slope-intercept form, then look for the line that has a slope of 3.
a: $2x - 4y = 8$
$-4y = -2x + 8$
$y = 2x - 2$, slope is 2.
b: $y = 4x - 3$, slope is 4.
c: $2y = 2x - 6$
$y = x - 3$, slope is 1.
d: $y + x = 3$
$y = -x + 3$, slope is –1.
e: $6x - 2y = 4$
$-2y = -6x + 4$
$y = 3x - 2$, slope is 3.
The graph of equation $6x - 2y = 4$ has a slope of 3 and therefore is parallel to the graph of equation $y = 3x - 4$.

50. e. Add the earnings and expenses.
$\$10.50 + \$15.25 + (-\$27.00)$
$\$25.75 - \$27.00 = -\$1.25$
The sum of Brenda's earnings and expenses is –$1.25.

56▶ Practice Exam 2, GED Social Studies

Directions: Read each question carefully. The questions are multiple choice and may be based on a passage, table, or illustration. Select the one best answer for each question. Note: On the GED, you are not permitted to write in the test booklet. Make any notes on a separate piece of paper.

Questions 1 and 2 are based on the following table.

25 Largest Employers in Douglas County

The University of Kansas	Institution of higher education that offers undergraduate/graduate studies and professional training
Pearson Government Solutions	Information services company for business, educational, financial, and professional assessment markets
Lawrence Public Schools	City school system
City of Lawrence	City government service
Lawrence Memorial Hospital	Acute care hospital with skilled nursing unit and broad outpatient program covering several clinical services

Hallmark Cards, Inc.	Manufactures social expression products
The World Company	Operates the Lawrence *Journal World* daily newspaper and the Sunflower Broadband cable/internet/telephony company
Baker University	Four-year private liberal arts college with a master's degree program
Amarr Garage Doors	Manufacturer of garage door components
K-Mart Distribution Center	Distribution center for K-mart retail stores in the Midwest
DCCCA Center	Alcohol and drug abuse counseling and information
Berry Plastics	Manufacturer of injection molded plastic containers and lids
Douglas County	County government services
Allen Press	Commercial typesetting, printing, and publishing company for clients in the scientific, technical, and medical publishing fields
Lawrence Paper Company	Manufacturer of corrugated cardboard boxes
Community Living Opportunities, Inc.	Provides residential and vocational services for adults with severe and profound developmental disabilities
Hamm Companies	Rock production and sales, highway construction asphalt production, and waste management
Sauer Danfoss	Manufacturer of hydrostatic transmissions and pumps
Cottonwood, Incorporated	Cottonwood, Inc. is a provider of employment, residential, and support services for people with developmental disabilities in Douglas and Jefferson counties in Kansas
Haskell Indian Nations University	Native American university operated by the federal government
Bert Nash Community Mental Health Center	Community mental health services
Astaris	Phosphorus chemicals plant
Westar Energy	Electric utility
DST, Inc.	Financial processing services
Del Monte Foods	Pet food manufacturing plant

1. The table best supports which of the following conclusions?
  a. Douglas County is a major manufacturing center.
  b. Education is a major contributor to the Douglas County economy.
  c. Lawrence is the state capital of Kansas.
  d. There are no farms in Douglas County.
  e. The healthcare system in Douglas County is insufficient for the population.

2. Which of the following would likely have the biggest negative impact on the economy of Douglas County?
  a. severe cutbacks in government spending
  b. a nationwide newspaper strike
  c. an increase in spending on government consultants
  d. a campaign to promote healthy lifestyles
  e. an increase in enrollment at the University of Kansas

Question 3 is based on the following table.

APPORTIONMENT POPULATION AND NUMBER OF REPRESENTATIVES, BY STATE: CENSUS 2000

State	Apportionment Population	Number of Apportioned Representatives Based on Census 2000
Alabama	4,461,130	7
Alaska	628,933	1
Arizona	5,140,683	8
Arkansas	2,679,733	4
California	33,930,798	53
Colorado	4,311,882	7
Connecticut	3,409,535	5
Delaware	785,068	1
Florida	16,028,890	25
Georgia	8,206,975	13
Hawaii	1,216,642	2
Idaho	1,297,274	2
Illinois	12,439,042	19
Indiana	6,090,782	9
Iowa	2,931,923	5
Kansas	2,693,824	4
Kentucky	4,049,431	6
Louisiana	4,480,271	7
Maine	1,277,731	2
Maryland	5,307,886	8
Massachusetts	6,355,568	10
Michigan	9,955,829	15
Minnesota	4,925,670	8
Mississippi	2,852,927	4
Missouri	5,606,260	9
Montana	905,316	1
Nebraska	1,715,369	3
Nevada	2,002,032	3
New Hampshire	1,238,415	2
New Jersey	8,424,354	13
New Mexico	1,823,821	3
New York	19,004,973	29
North Carolina	8,067,673	13

North Dakota	643,756	1
Ohio	11,374,540	18
Oklahoma	3,458,819	5
Oregon	3,428,543	5
Pennsylvania	12,300,670	19
Rhode Island	1,049,662	2
South Carolina	4,025,061	6
South Dakota	756,874	1
Tennessee	5,700,037	9
Texas	20,903,994	32
Utah	2,236,714	3
Vermont	609,890	1
Virginia	7,100,702	11
Washington	5,908,684	9
West Virginia	1,813,077	3
Wisconsin	5,371,210	8
Wyoming	495,304	1
Total Apportionment Population[1]	281,424,177	435

[1]Includes the resident population for the 50 states, as ascertained by the Twenty-Second Decennial Census under Title 13, United States Code, and counts of overseas U.S. military and federal civilian employees (and their dependents living with them) allocated to their home state, as reported by the employing federal agencies. The apportionment population excludes the population of the District of Columbia.

NOTE: As required by the January 1999 U.S. Supreme Court ruling (*Department of Commerce v. House of Representatives*, 525 U.S. 316, 119 S. Ct. 765 (1999)), the apportionment population counts do not reflect the use of statistical sampling to correct for overcounting or undercounting.

Source: U.S. Department of Commerce, U.S. Census Bureau.

3. Which of the following is used to determine the number of representatives each state is allotted in the House of Representatives?
   a. the population of the state
   b. the distance of the state from Washington D.C.
   c. the amount of taxes the state pays to the federal government
   d. the size of the state, in square miles
   e. the number of senators each state is allotted

Questions 4–6 are based on the following campaign poster and paragraph.

In 1872, Ulysses S. Grant ran for the presidency as the incumbent. Grant was the leader of the Radical Republicans, a faction of the Republican Party that felt the South should continue to be punished for its rebellion during the Civil War. His opponent, Horace Greeley, was also a Republican. Greeley believed that the South had suffered enough for the war and that Congress should end Reconstruction, a program under which federal troops occupied the South. Greeley formed the Liberal Republican Party; the Democratic Party also adopted Greeley as its candidate. Greeley's campaign attempted to paint the first Grant administration as deeply corrupt; this strategy failed with voters, and Grant won the election of 1872 in a landslide.

4. The campaign poster suggests that voters in 1872 were most concerned about
   a. the corruption of the first Grant administration.
   b. Grant's record as a Civil War hero.
   c. whether Reconstruction should continue.
   d. which candidate was more patriotic.
   e. which candidates could best relate to their concerns.

5. Greeley's campaign accused Grant of corruption. Based on the campaign poster, how did Grant respond to these accusations?
   a. He accused Greeley of making dishonest accusations.
   b. He argued that he could not be corrupt because he had once been a tanner.
   c. He chose not to address the accusations.
   d. He refuted Greeley's accusation point by point.
   e. He accused Greeley, a newspaperman, of corrupt business practices.

6. People who voted for Grant in 1872 almost certainly expected that a Grant victory would have which of the following results?
   a. Reconstruction would continue.
   b. Grant and Wilson would rebuild the White House.
   c. Horace Greeley would be offered a position in the Grant administration.
   d. The Radical Republicans and Liberal Republicans would split permanently.
   e. Grant would start a new war with the South.

Question 7 refers to the following photograph.

"Following evacuation orders, this store was closed. The owner, a University of California graduate of Japanese descent, placed the I AM AN AMERICAN sign on the storefront after Pearl Harbor."

—Dorothea Lange, Oakland, CA, April 1942

Source: National Archives and Records Administration.

7. Which of the following statements would the photographer most likely support?

a. People of Japanese descent feel loyal to Japan first, the United States second.

b. The store owner felt that his rights as an American citizen were denied.

c. The security of the majority outweighs the rights of a minority.

d. Japanese Americans were not established members of the community.

e. Unusual measures like internment camps are necessary during wartime.

8. Isolationism refers to the national policy of avoiding political or economic relations with other countries. Which of the following is an example of American isolationist policy?

a. the Neutrality Act of 1935, an arms embargo designed to try to keep the United States out of a European war

b. bombing al-Qaeda training camps in Afghanistan after the terrorist attack on the World Trade Center

c. the unsuccessful attempt to overthrow Cuban leader Fidel Castro in 1961

d. joining with 11 nations to form the North Atlantic Treaty Organization (NATO) in 1949

e. the Open Door Policy, a policy that allowed all countries equal trading rights in China in the late 1800s

Questions 9–11 are based on the following passage.

Even though acid rain looks, feels, and even tastes like clean rainwater, it contains high levels of pollutants. Scientists believe car exhaust and smoke from factories and power plants are the main causes of acid rain, but natural sources like gases from forest fires and volcanoes may also contribute to the problem. Pollutants mix in the atmosphere to form fine particles that can be carried long distances by wind. Eventually they return to the ground in the form of rain, snow, fog, or other precipitation. Acid rain damages trees and causes the acidification of lakes and streams, contaminating drinking water and damaging aquatic life. It erodes buildings, paint, and monuments. It can also affect human health. Although acid rain does not directly harm people, high levels of the fine particles in acid rain are linked to an increased risk for asthma and bronchitis. Since the 1950s, the increase of acid rain has become a problem in the northeastern United States, Canada, and western Europe. Some believe it is the single greatest industrial threat to the environment, although most feel that the emission of greenhouse gases is a far larger problem.

9. Which of the following natural resources is least likely to be affected by acid rain?
   a. animal life
   b. plant life
   c. coal reserves
   d. water
   e. forests

10. Which of the following is NOT a cause of acid rain?
   a. human activity
   b. natural phenomena
   c. volcanoes
   d. lakes and streams
   e. traffic

11. Which of the following is an OPINION stated in the passage?
   a. Acid rain is formed when pollutants mix in the atmosphere.
   b. Acid rain damages trees, lakes, and streams.
   c. Acid rain cannot be distinguished from unpolluted rain by sight, smell, or taste.
   d. No industrial pollutant causes more damage to the environment than acid rain.
   e. Acid rain does not directly harm humans, although its effects can contribute to some health problems.

Question 12 is based on the following table.

Free African Americans in the North and South, 1820 to 1860

	1820	1840	1860
United States	233,504	386,303	488,070
North	99,281 (83.9%)	170,728 (99.3%)	226,152 (100%)
South	134,223 (8.1%)	215,575 (8.0%)	261,918 (6.2%)

*Percentages in parentheses represent percentage of total African American population.

12. The data in the table supports which of the following conclusions?
   a. By 1820, there were no more slaves in the North.
   b. Between 1820 and 1860, millions of freed slaves emigrated from the South to the North.
   c. Prior to the Civil War, there were no free African Americans in the South.
   d. Between 1820 and 1860, there were many more African Americans in the South than in the North.
   e. Most free African Americans in the South lived in the state of Virginia.

Question 13 refers to the following campaign poster.

Pro Quarterback Bill Wyoming Says:

"Vote for Sylvia Montanez for Governor. She'll do a *great* job!"

So don't forget:

Vote Montanez on Election Day!

13. Which of the following questions would be most useful in determining the value of the information presented on Governor Montanez' campaign sign?
   a. What is Bill Wyoming's definition of "great"?
   b. What qualifies Bill Wyoming to predict the quality of a future governor?
   c. How good a season did Bill Wyoming have last year?
   d. Does Bill Wyoming live in Sylvia Montanez' state?
   e. What happens if a person forgets to vote on Election Day?

Questions 14–15 refer to the following graph.

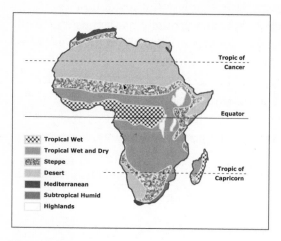

14. According to the map, what is the primary climate of the northern third of Africa?
   a. tropical wet
   b. steppe
   c. subtropical humid
   d. desert
   e. highlands

15. It can be inferred from the map that the Mediterranean Sea borders
   a. the west coast of Africa.
   b. the southern tip of Africa.
   c. the southeastern coast of Africa.
   d. the northeastern coast of Africa.
   e. the northern coast of Africa.

Questions 16–18 are based on the following quotation.

"Today, education is perhaps the most important function of state and local governments. Compulsory school attendance laws and the great expenditures for education both demonstrate our recognition of the importance of education to our democratic society. It is required in the performance of our most basic public responsibilities, even service in the armed forces. It is the very foundation of good citizenship. Today it is a principal instrument in awakening the child to cultural values, in preparing him for later professional training, and in helping him to adjust normally to his environment. In these days, it is doubtful that any child may reasonably be expected to succeed in life if he is denied the opportunity of an education. Such an opportunity, where the state has undertaken to provide it, is a right which must be made available to all on equal terms.

"We come then to the question presented: Does segregation of children in public schools solely on the basis of race, even though the physical facilities and other 'tangible' factors may be equal, deprive the children of the minority group of equal educational opportunities? We believe that it does."

—U.S. Supreme Court Chief Justice Earl Warren in a 1954 decision that ruled that separate schools for African Americans and whites as unconstitutional

Source: Legal Information Institute, Cornell Law School, Brown v. Board of Education of Topeka.

16. Which of the following is NOT a value of education as expressed in the quotation?
   a. to expose children to music and the arts
   b. to explain the government's education budget
   c. to prepare those who might serve the country as soldiers
   d. to produce good citizens
   e. to give children a chance to succeed at life

17. According to the passage, how might the Court define "equal educational opportunity"?
   a. schools with the same quality of teaching
   b. schools with the same quality of facilities and materials
   c. schools that only admit students based on sex
   d. schools that separate minority students to give them a better chance
   e. schools that are of the same quality and welcome all students regardless of race

18. Chief Justice Warren most likely mentions compulsory school attendance and government spending on education in order to
   a. argue that the government should reduce its efforts in the field of education.
   b. support the position that segregated schools are not inherently unequal.
   c. encourage young Americans to remain in school long enough to get a high school diploma.
   d. give examples of situations in which the government can force people to do things they don't want to do.
   e. strengthen the argument that education is a critical function of government.

Question 19 is based on the following passage.

The Sixth Amendment of the U.S. Constitution states, "In all criminal prosecutions, the accused shall enjoy the right to a speedy and public trial, by an impartial jury of the State and district wherein the crime shall have been committed, which district shall have been previously ascertained by law, and to be informed of the nature and cause of the accusation; to be confronted with the witnesses against him; to have compulsory process for obtaining witnesses in his favor, and to have the Assistance of Counsel for his defence[sic]."

19. Which of the following instances is NOT protected by the Sixth Amendment?
   a. a person accused of a crime silently prays before his trial begins
   b. a person accused of drug trafficking hires a lawyer to defend him
   c. a trial is moved to another area because no jurors could be found who had not heard of the crime and had an opinion about who committed it
   d. a lawyer informs an accused person of her charges
   e. a lawyer cross-examines witnesses who testify against her client

Questions 20–21 are based on the following graph and text.

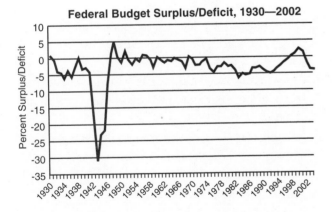

Federal Budget Surplus/Deficit, 1930—2002

Each year the federal government collects revenues in the form of taxes and other fees. It also spends money on such necessary functions as national defense, education, and healthcare. When the government collects more than it spends, it operates at a surplus. In the graph, the government operated at a surplus for every

year in which the line is above 0%. When the government spends more than it collects, it operates at a deficit. In the graph, the government operated at a deficit for every year in which the line is below 0%.

20. In what year between 1930 and 2002 did the federal government operate with the greatest budget deficit?
   a. 1930
   b. 1945
   c. 1951
   d. 1994
   e. 1999

21. In 1932, while campaigning for president, Franklin D. Roosevelt said the following:

"If the Nation is living within its income, its credit is good. If, in some crises, it lives beyond its income for a year or two, it can usually borrow temporarily at reasonable rates. But if, like a spendthrift, it throws discretion to the winds, and is willing to make no sacrifice at all in spending; if it extends its taxing to the limit of the people's power to pay and continues to pile up deficits, then it is on the road to bankruptcy."

In 1981, Ronald Reagan made the following statement during his Inaugural Address:

"For decades, we have piled deficit upon deficit, mortgaging our future and our children's future for the temporary convenience of the present. To continue this long trend is to guarantee tremendous social, cultural, political, and economic upheavals."

Roosevelt was president from 1932 to 1945. Reagan was president from 1981 to 1988. Which of the following conclusions is supported by the graph and the quotations?
   a. All presidential candidates make promises they do not intend to keep.
   b. If a president cares enough about federal deficits, he or she can force the government to operate on a surplus.
   c. Ronald Reagan and Franklin Roosevelt pursued virtually identical agendas during their presidencies.
   d. Despite their best intentions, it is often difficult for presidents to control federal deficits.
   e. If the United States does not end its deficit spending soon, it will be bankrupt by the year 2015.

Questions 22–23 are based on the following photograph and map.

The photograph and map depict the Great Wall of China, built during the late 1400s and early 1500s.

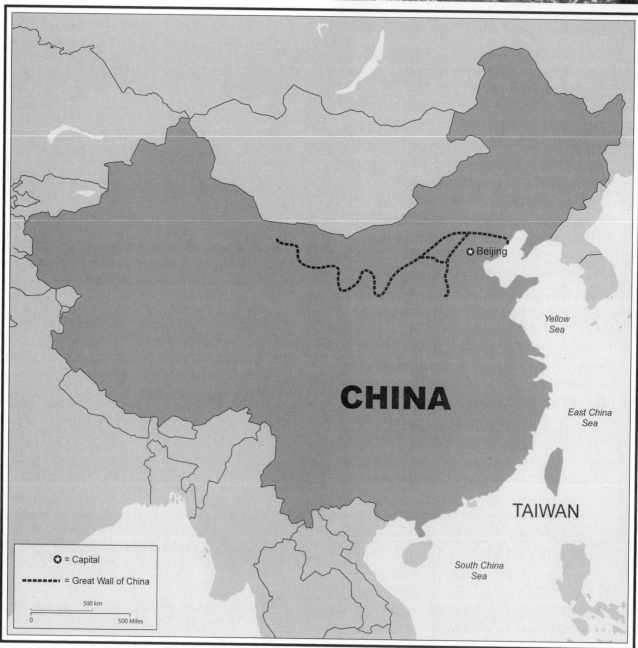

22. What is the approximate total length of all segments of the Great Wall of China?

a. 600 miles

b. 1,000 miles

c. 3,000 miles

d. 6,000 miles

e. 10,000 miles

23. For what purpose was the Great Wall of China most likely built?

a. to provide protection from military invaders from the north

b. to provide protection from military invaders from the south

c. to create a tourist attraction that would bring international travelers to China

d. to protect Beijing from flooding rivers

e. to create jobs for Chinese masons

Questions 24–25 are based on the following passage.

The Aztec empire of the thirteenth and fourteenth centuries was based on an agricultural economy. The Valley of Mexico—a fertile basin with five lakes in its center—provided land for farming. However, as the population of the empire grew, the Aztecs needed to make more land suitable for agriculture. To do this, they developed **irrigation** (a system that carries water through dams and canals to use for farming) and formed **terraces** (a process that cuts "steps" into hillsides to make flat surfaces for farming). They also practiced land **reclamation**, turning swamps and wet areas into land that can be cultivated.

24. What factor caused the Aztecs to develop agricultural innovations?

a. The empire shifted from an agriculture-based economy to an industrial one.

b. Annual flooding created rich soil, but the lakes could not sustain crops the rest of the year.

c. An increase in population created a need for land for more housing.

d. A growing population resulted in increased food demands.

e. Mountain ranges on either side of the central plateau of Mexico made transportation difficult.

25. An island in Southern Indonesia, Bali has a hot and humid climate and volcanic soil that is good for farming rice, but much of the island is hilly. To solve this problem, Balinese rice farmers use which of the techniques also employed by the Aztecs?

a. land reclamation

b. land terracing

c. irrigation

d. landfill

e. deforestation

Questions 26–27 refer to the following passage.

The U.S. Constitution does not explicitly give the power of judicial review to the Supreme Court. In fact, the Court did not use this power—which gives it the authority to invalidate laws and executive actions if they conflict with the Constitution—until the 1803 case of *Marbury v. Madison.* In that case, Chief Justice John Marshall ruled that a statute was unconstitutional. He argued that judicial review was necessary if the Court was to fulfill its duty of upholding the Constitution. Without it, he felt that the legislature would have a "real and practical omnipotence." Moreover, several of the Constitution's framers expected the Court to act in this way. Alexander Hamilton and James Madison emphasized the importance of judicial review in the *Federalist Papers,* a series of essays promoting the adoption of the Constitution. However, the power of judicial review continues to be a controversial power because it allows the justices—who are appointed rather than elected—to overturn laws made by Congress and state lawmaking bodies.

26. Which of the following statements is an implication of judicial review?

a. The Constitution is a historic document with little influence over how the government operates today.

b. The Constitution must explicitly state which branch of government is to have what authority.

c. The framers never meant for the Supreme Court to have this power.

d. If Supreme Court justices were elected, the power of judicial review would be justified.

e. The Constitution is a living document that continues to be interpreted.

27. Which of the following best describes the process of judicial review?
- **a.** to declare a law unconstitutional
- **b.** to follow public opinion polls
- **c.** to determine the country's changing needs
- **d.** to propose new laws
- **e.** to adapt the Constitution to what the Court feels is right

Question 28 is based on the following line graph.

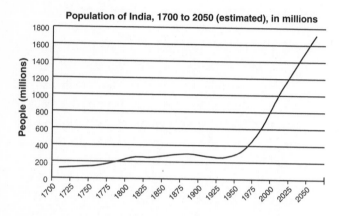

Population of India, 1700 to 2050 (estimated), in millions

28. All of the following might explain the change in India's population from 1950 to 2000 EXCEPT
- **a.** advances in healthcare.
- **b.** improvements to national sanitation services.
- **c.** a dramatic increase in per capita income.
- **d.** a series of severe weather events, such as earthquakes and hurricanes.
- **e.** wide distribution of vaccines for contagious diseases.

Questions 29–31 are based on the following table and text.

INCOME PER CITIZEN, 2006

	Per Capita Income (US Dollars)	PPP Income (US Dollars)
Luxembourg	80,288	69,800
Norway	64,193	42,364
Iceland	52,764	35,115
Switzerland	50,532	32,571
Ireland	48,604	40,610
Denmark	47,984	34,740
Qatar	43,110	29,000
United States	42,000	41,399
Sweden	39,694	32,200
Netherlands	38,618	32,100

Economists use several measures to calculate the income of the average citizen of each country. Data documenting each citizen's personal income is rarely available, unfortunately, so economists must estimate personal income by dividing gross domestic product (GDP)—the value of all the goods and services produced in a country—by the number of citizens. This figure gives an inaccurate picture of how citizens live, however, because it fails to take into account the cost of goods and services in a country. A second measure, called purchasing power parity (PPP), adjusts for the domestic cost of goods to provide a more accurate picture of what each citizen's money will buy him or her. For the sake of comparison, both measures are calculated in U.S. dollars. The table shows the figures for ten of the world's wealthiest nations in 2006.

29. Which of the following would best explain the difference between per capita income and PPP income in Norway?
- **a.** Consumer goods are extremely costly in Norway.
- **b.** Many consumer goods are available in Norway.
- **c.** Norway must import most of its consumer goods from Asia.
- **d.** Services are relatively cheap in Norway.
- **e.** Norway does not produce its own fuel.

30. Which of the following would be an effect of listing nations in descending order by PPP income rather than by per capita income?
   a. Luxembourg would no longer be at the top of the list.
   b. It would be more difficult to determine where citizens can buy the most goods and services with their income.
   c. Countries not currently on the list would have to be included.
   d. The United States would move from eighth on the list to a higher position.
   e. The table would better support the argument that Qatar is the world's wealthiest nation.

31. What is the most likely reason that the author finds it "unfortunate" that "data documenting each citizen's personal income is rarely available"?
   a. The author believes that such data should be private and should never be available.
   b. The author believes that estimates based on gross domestic product are extremely accurate.
   c. The author believes that such data would demonstrate that citizens of the United States are the wealthiest in the world.
   d. The data would eliminate the necessity for economists to calculate purchasing power parity.
   e. The data would provide a more accurate picture of personal income in each country.

Question 32 is based on the following passage.

When European settlers arrived on the North American continent at the end of the fifteenth century, they encountered diverse American Indian cultures—as many as 900,000 inhabitants with over 300 different languages. These people, whose ancestors crossed the land bridge from Asia in what may be considered the first North American immigration, were virtually destroyed by the subsequent immigration that created the United States. This tragedy is the direct result of treaties, written and broken by foreign governments, of warfare, and of forced assimilation.

Source: The Library of Congress, American Memory.

32. What does the author of this passage believe?
   a. The U.S. government was faithful to its treaties with American Indians.
   b. American Indians made up a homogenous group.
   c. The European settlers were responsible for the decimation of native people.
   d. Native cultures were unsophisticated.
   e. The Europeans benefited from contact with native cultures.

Questions 33–34 are based on the following passage.

33. The cartoonist would probably agree with which of the following statements?
   a. The vice presidency is the second-most important position in the government.
   b. Presidents should travel by elephant.
   c. The vice presidency is not an important government office.
   d. Everyone should dress in a top hat and a waistcoat.
   e. Elephants do not belong in Washington, D.C.

34. The cartoon shows Theodore Roosevelt, a presidential candidate in 1904, and Joseph Cannon, a man whom Roosevelt wanted for his vice president. What is the most likely explanation for why Roosevelt is riding an elephant?

   a. The elephant is a universal symbol of wealth and prosperity.

   b. Roosevelt was the Republican candidate for president.

   c. Roosevelt was born in India, a place where it is not unusual for people to ride elephants.

   d. Roosevelt was well known as a champion of animal rights.

   e. Joseph Cannon worked as an elephant keeper in a zoo.

Questions 35 and 36 refer to the following graph.

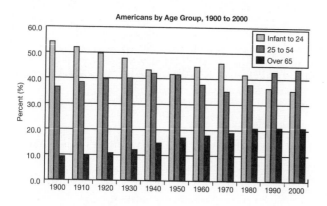

Americans by Age Group, 1900 to 2000

35. Which of the following conclusions is supported by the data in the graph?

   a. Americans are less healthy in 2000 than they were in 1900.

   b. The age of the average American has increased since 1900.

   c. The average American earns more in 2000 than he or she did in 1900.

   d. The number of Americans under the age of 24 has decreased since 1900.

   e. The population of the United States was the same in 2000 as it was in 1900.

36. Which of the following is an opinion based on the data in the graph?

   a. About 40 percent of all Americans were between the ages of 25 and 54 in 1930.

   b. In 1950, the number of Americans under the age of 25 was roughly equal to the number of Americans between the ages of 25 and 54.

   c. The current trend suggests that the population of the United States is growing old too quickly.

   d. More than half of all Americans were under the age of 25 in 1900.

   e. Americans under the age of 25 made up a greater portion of the population in 1970 than they did in 1960.

Questions 37–38 are based on the following map and passage.

The map on page 571 shows the political borders of European nations before the start of World War I (the map on the left) and after the war concluded (the map on the right).

At the end of World War I, Germany was required to sign the Treaty of Versailles, which required Germany to accept responsibility for causing the war. The treaty also required Germany to pay the victor nations over 6 million pounds in reparations and to cede some of its land, including its valuable coal mines on the German-French border. In addition, Germany had to give up all of her colonies, which had provided her with a steady source of income. Finally, strict limitations were placed on the size and weaponry of the German military, and the country was forbidden from entering into an alliance with neighboring Austria.

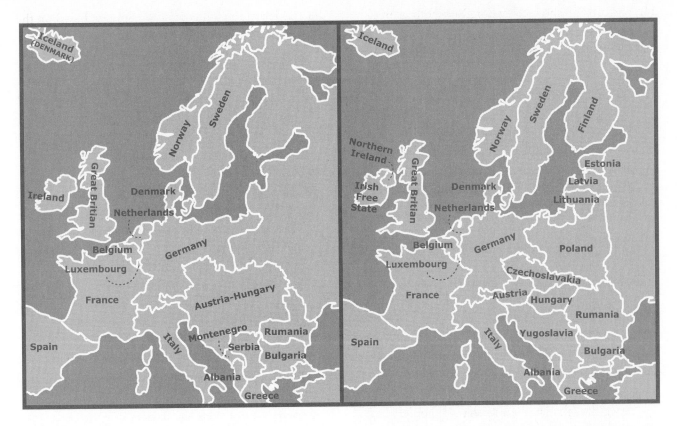

37. Which country increased in size at the conclusion of World War I?
   a. Austria-Hungary
   b. Norway
   c. Rumania (Romania)
   d. Ireland
   e. Serbia

38. Which of the following is a FACT about the Treaty of Versailles?
   a. The Treaty of Versailles harmed the German economy.
   b. Germany deserved the harsh terms of the treaty because Germany started the war.
   c. If the Treaty of Versailles had been fairer to Germany, the Nazis never would have gained power.
   d. The United States was the country that benefited the most from the Treaty of Versailles.
   e. Germany should have been allowed to keep the coal mines along its border with France.

Questions 39–40 are based on the following passage.

Like so many other exploration stories, the Lewis and Clark journey was shaped by the search for navigable rivers, inspired by the quest for Edens, and driven by competition for empire. Thomas Jefferson was motivated by these aspirations when he drafted instructions for his explorers, sending them up the Missouri River in search of a passage to the Pacific. Writing to William Dunbar just a month after Lewis and Clark left Fort Mandan, Jefferson emphasized the importance of rivers in his plan for western exploration and national expansion. "We shall delineate with correctness the great arteries of this great country." River highways could take Americans into an Eden, Jefferson's vision of the West as the "Garden of the World." And those same rivers might be nature's outlines and borders for empire. "Future generations would," so the president told his friend, "fill up the canvas we begin."

Source: Library of Congress, Exhibits, "Rivers, Edens, Empires: Lewis & Clark and the Revealing of America."

39. Which of the following was NOT one of Jefferson's goals in sponsoring the Lewis and Clark expedition?
  a. finding a waterway to the Pacific Ocean
  b. mapping uncharted territory
  c. setting aside vast tracts of land for native people
  d. discovery of unspoiled plant and animal life
  e. creation of an empire

40. Which historical idea best summarizes Jefferson's attitude toward the West?
  a. Separation of Powers
  b. Manifest Destiny
  c. Pursuit of Happiness
  d. Good Neighbor Policy
  e. Separate but Equal

Questions 41–42 refer to the following passage.

About the time of World War I, sharp-eyed entrepreneurs began . . . to see ways to profit from the motorist's freedom . . . Shops could be set up almost anywhere the law allowed, and a wide variety of products and services could be counted on to sell briskly in the roadside marketplace. A certain number of cars passing by would always be in need of gas. Travelers eventually grew hungry, tired, and restless for diversions. Soon gas stations, produce booths, hot dog stands, and tourist camps sprouted up along the nation's roadsides to capitalize on these needs. As competition increased, merchants looked for new ways to snag the new market awheel. Each sign and building had to visually shout: "Slow down, pull in, and buy." Still more businesses moved to the highway—supermarkets, motor courts, restaurants, miniature golf courses, drive-in theaters. By the early 1950s, almost anything could be bought along the roadside.

Source: Chester H. Liebs, excerpt from *Main Street to Miracle Mile.* Little, Brown and Company, 1985.

41. What is the main idea of the passage?
  a. Miniature golf was a very popular sport in the 1950s.
  b. Travelers were looking for sources of entertainment.
  c. Some highway businesses were more successful than others.
  d. Flashy commercial enterprises sprouted along highways, eager to profit from travelers.
  e. The first businesses to flourish along the highways were gas stations and hot dog stands.

42. Given the information in this passage, what appeared to be an important post-World War II trend in the United States?
  a. train travel
  b. car culture
  c. historic preservation
  d. downtown renewal
  e. environmentalism

Question 43 is based on the following map.

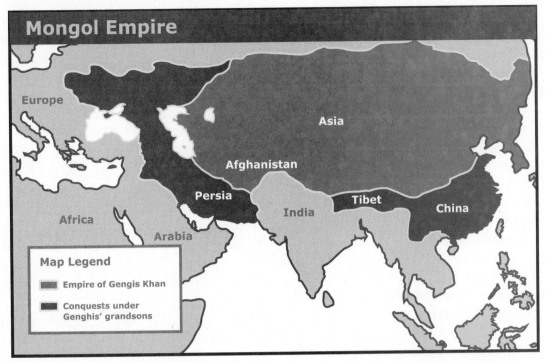

Mongol Empire

Europe

Asia

Afghanistan

Persia

Tibet

India

China

Africa

Arabia

Map Legend

Empire of Gengis Khan

Conquests under Genghis' grandsons

43. The area conquered by Genghis Khan is best described as
   a. Persia.
   b. Europe.
   c. Arabia.
   d. Southeast Asia.
   e. Central Asia.

Questions 44 and 45 are based on the following graph.

President's Proposed Federal Budget, 2008

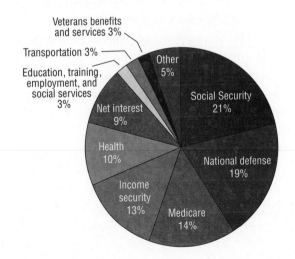

Veterans benefits and services 3%

Transportation 3%

Education, training, employment, and social services 3%

Other 5%

Net interest 9%

Social Security 21%

Health 10%

National defense 19%

Income security 13%

Medicare 14%

44. Which of the following statements is a FACT found in the circle graph?
   a. The United States spends too much on Social Security.
   b. National defense is the single largest expense in the federal budget.
   c. The federal government spends more on health than it spends on education.
   d. Increased spending on public transportation would benefit the environment.
   e. More than half the federal budget is spent on education.

45. The data in the circle graph does NOT support which of the following conclusions?
   a. "Other" expenses include spending on interest on the national debt.
   b. Transportation constitutes a relatively small portion of the federal budget.
   c. National defense is an important priority for the federal government.
   d. The federal government spends more on income security than it spends on net interest.
   e. Social Security, national defense, and Medicare together account for over half the federal budget.

Questions 46–47 are based on the following passage.

The Cuban Missile Crisis began in 1962 when U.S. spy planes spotted Soviet missile installations under construction in Cuba. The missiles were capable of carrying nuclear weapons and were within range of major U.S. cities. A 13-day standoff began, during which President Kennedy imposed a naval blockade of Cuba and demanded that the Soviets remove the weapons. Kennedy stated that any missile attack from Cuba would be regarded as an attack from the Soviet Union and would be responded to accordingly. Khrushchev later conceded, agreeing to remove the weapons if, in return, the United States pledged not to invade the island. Details from U.S. and Soviet declassified files and participants in the crisis have surfaced since the incident. Unknown to the U.S. government at the time, 40,000 Soviet soldiers were stationed in Cuba and armed with nuclear weapons. Although Khrushchev's actions helped to avert nuclear war, they made him appear weak to younger Soviet leaders who ousted him from power. Historians regard the crisis as the world's closest brush with the threat of nuclear war.

46. According to the information given in this passage, it is most likely that President Kennedy
  a. viewed this as a regional crisis solely between the United States and Cuba.
  b. trusted Soviet officials who said there weren't any missiles in Cuba.
  c. believed that the conflict was principally between the United States and the Soviet Union.
  d. viewed the situation as serious but felt it could be managed with diplomacy.
  e. felt confident about how Khrushchev would respond.

47. Which of the following conclusions can you make based on the passage?
  a. Kennedy's first concern during the crisis was the appeal of Communist ideas.
  b. Nuclear war is the only way to win a cold war.
  c. Kennedy knew that Khrushchev would back down.
  d. Khrushchev's popularity increased at home.
  e. The U.S. government did not know the full extent of the Soviet threat at the time.

48. Capital gains tax is money paid to the federal government out of profits from the sale of financial assets, like property (land or buildings) or stocks. For which of the following would you need to pay capital gains tax?
  a. cigarettes
  b. groceries
  c. your mortgage
  d. your wages
  e. a profitable real estate sale

Questions 49–50 are based on the following illustration and text.

In 1754, representatives of the American colonies met to discuss their common defense and strategies for improving relations with American Indian tribes. At the meeting, Benjamin Franklin proposed closer relations among the colonies. His proposal called for a single executive and a colonial legislature to handle such matters of mutual interest as taxes, defense against the French, and American Indian relations. To promote his plan, Franklin printed the illustration in his newspaper, *The Pennsylvania Gazette*. In an accompanying editorial, he complained about "the present disunited State of the British Colonies, and the extreme Difficulty of bringing so many different Governments and Assemblies to agree in any speedy and effectual Measures for our common Defence and Security; while our Enemies have the very great Advantage of being under one Direction, with one Council, and one Purse. Hence, and from the great Distance of Britain, they presume that they may with Impunity violate the most solemn Treaties subsisting between the two Crowns . . . murder and scalp our Farmers, with their Wives and Children . . . which if they are permitted to do, must end in the Destruction of the British Interest, Trade and Plantations in America."

Franklin's plan was rejected by both the King and the American colonies.

49. In Franklin's cartoon, the pieces of the snake represent
a. the French army.
b. various American Indian tribes.
c. the English King and Parliament.
d. various colonial newspapers.
e. the British colonies.

50. In his editorial, Franklin makes all of the following criticisms of the system under which American colonies governed themselves EXCEPT which of the following?
a. The system makes it impossible for the colonies to rebel against British rule.
b. The system is inefficient.
c. The system makes it difficult for the colonies to defend themselves.
d. It is too easy for the French to take advantage of weaknesses in the system.
e. The system is doomed to fail.

▶ Answers

1. b. The University of Kansas and the Douglas Public Schools are among the two top employers in Douglas County. Manufacturing (choice **a**) represents only a small segment of the local economy. The data in the table cannot support choices **c**, **d**, and **e**, because the table tells only how many people are employed by various large employers. Choice **c** is factually incorrect; Topeka is the capital of Kansas.

2. a. A cutback in government spending would have a negative impact on public education (the University of Kansas and Douglas Public Schools) and on the Lawrence city government. Together these employers account for a substantial portion of the Douglas workforce. Spending cutbacks could result in layoffs and pay cuts, which in turn would increase the unemployment rate and reduce the amount of money circulating in the local economy.

3. a. The table shows that apportionment in the House of Representatives is based on population; the larger the population of a state, the larger its delegation to the House of Representatives. Choice **c** is disproven by the example of Alaska; although it is the largest state in terms of square mileage, it has a relatively small delegation in the House of Representatives.

4. e. This campaign poster portrays Grant and Wilson as working people. The subtext of the poster is that Grant and Wilson understand the common American and will represent his or her interests. It also implies that Grant's opponent, Greeley, does not understand the common American, because a campaign poster tries to persuade voters to choose one candidate over another based on the candidate's perceived advantage in a particular area. The poster ignores corruption (choice **a**), Grant's war record (choice **b**), Reconstruction (choice **c**), and patriotism (choice **d**), so it could not suggest that voters were concerned about those issues.

5. c. The poster does not address the issue of corruption, suggesting that Grant's strategy for dealing with the accusations was to ignore them.

6. a. Grant was the candidate of the Radical Republicans, a faction of the Republican Party that supported the continuation of Reconstruction. Thus, voters who chose Grant in 1872 would have expected Reconstruction to continue into his second term.

7. b. Lange's image draws a powerful contrast between the grocery owner's proud statement "I AM AN AMERICAN" and the "SOLD" sign above. It is likely that she felt he was being "sold out" by his country and that his rights as an American citizen were denied.

8. a. An example of American isolationist policy is the 1935 Neutrality Act, because it was an instance of avoiding political and economic alliances with other countries.

9. c. All of these natural resources are negatively affected by acid rain except coal reserves. The passage identifies coal burning as a source of acid rain. It does not say that coal reserves are harmed by acid rain.

10. d. Lakes and streams are affected by acid rain, but do not cause it.

11. d. Choices **a**, **b**, **c**, and **e** are facts stated in the passage. Only choice **d** is an opinion; it draws a comparison that can be reasonably argued. In fact, the passage notes that choice **d** is the subject of some debate. According to the final sentence of the passage, many people believe that greenhouse gas emissions, not acid rain, are the greatest source of concern.

12. d. According to the table, there were more free African Americans in the South than in the North. In the South, free African Americans made up only a small portion of the total African American population; according to the table, over 90% of southern African Americans were slaves. This means that there were well over 1 million African Americans in the South between 1820 and 1860. Therefore, the table supports the conclusion that there were many more African Americans in the South than in the North between 1820 and 1860.

13. b. The campaign poster suggests that voters should choose Governor Montanez because professional quarterback Bill Wyoming thinks Montanez would be a great governor. This is typical of endorsement advertisements, which try to persuade voters by associating the candidate with a popular figure. To determine whether the information on the poster is valuable in determining whether to vote for Montanez, the voter should ask herself whether Wyoming has any expertise in the field of governing. Why should the voter care who Bill Wyoming thinks would make a great governor if Wyoming is not an expert in this area?

14. d. The northern third of Africa appears at the top of the map of Africa. It is made up primarily of desert; more specifically, the Sahara Desert.

15. e. The northern tip of the African continent has a Mediterranean climate. No other part of the continent has such a climate. Therefore, it is reasonable to conclude that the northern coast of the African continent borders the Mediterranean Sea.

16. b. The "value of an education" refers to the benefits an education confers on its recipient. It helps children develop cultural values (choice **a**), prepares them for service in the armed forces (choice **c**), teaches them their civic responsibilities (choice **d**), and provides professional training (choice **e**). The amount of money the government spends on education shows that people care about education; it is not, however, a value of education as previously defined.

17. e. The Court's decision states that a similar level of "physical facilities and other 'tangible' factors" is not enough to offer equal educational opportunity. You can infer that the Court believes schools should also welcome students of all races.

18. e. By pointing out that the government requires students to attend school, Warren makes the point that American society places a strong emphasis on the need for a good education. Similarly, government spending on education indicates that education is a major priority in American society. Both of these facts support the argument that education is a critical function of government.

19. a. Prayer is protected by the First Amendment, which protects the freedom of religion.

20. b. The graph shows that the federal government operated at approximately a 30% deficit in 1945. This is by far the largest deficit shown on the graph.

21. d. Both Roosevelt and Reagan promised to avoid deficit spending, yet both generated budget deficits throughout their presidencies. Thus, the quotes and the data in the graph support the conclusion that presidents have a hard time controlling federal deficits. Choice **a** is incorrect because it indicates that both Roosevelt and Reagan were insincere in their promises to control spending; there is no evidence presented to support that characterization.

22. c. Use the scale to approximate the length of the Great Wall as shown on the map. Use process of elimination to get rid of answer choices that are either too small (choices **a** and **b**) or too large (choices **d** and **e**).

23. a. The most likely explanation for building the Great Wall was to provide protection. The photograph shows that the wall was tall and sturdy and would thus have presented a formidable obstacle to an invading army. Because the Great Wall is built along the northern portion of China (with the city of Beijing to the south of the wall) it is most likely that the wall was built to stop invaders from the north.

24. d. The Aztecs needed more land for farming to produce enough food for the growing population.

25. b. Terracing solves the problem because it creates flat surfaces out of hillsides for farming.

26. e. Through judicial review, the Supreme Court is continually interpreting the limits set by the Constitution.

27. a. According to the passage, judicial review is "the authority to invalidate laws and executive actions if they conflict with the Constitution." Choice **a** is a good paraphrase of the excerpt from the passage.

28. d. The population of India began a rapid increase in 1950 that continued through 2000. Choice **d** describes events that would reduce the population; each of the incorrect choices describes conditions that would promote population growth.

29. a. According to the passage, PPP income adjusts for the cost of living in a given country. The lower the PPP is relative to per capita income, the more expensive it is to live in that country. In Norway, PPP is much lower than per capita income; therefore, it is reasonable to conclude that consumer goods are extremely costly in Norway.

30. d. If the countries in the table were rearranged by PPP, the United States would move to third on the list, right behind Luxembourg and Norway.

31. e. The author's purpose is to measure personal income in various countries in order to compare the countries. The reason he thinks it is unfortunate that personal income data is rarely available is because such data would provide more accurate information on the subject of the table and passage.

32. c. The author states that American Indians "were virtually destroyed by the subsequent immigration that created the United States." Choice **c** is a good paraphrase of that excerpt from the passage.

33. c. The cartoon depicts presidential candidate Theodore Roosevelt offering the vice presidency to Joseph Cannon. The vice presidency is represented by a tiny elephant with a child's chair mounted atop. These details indicate that the cartoonist thinks the vice presidency is an insignificant job.

34. b. The elephant is the symbol of the Republican Party, the party to which Theodore Roosevelt belonged. None of the other answer choices is supported by details in the cartoon.

35. b. The graph provides data about Americans by age group, so it can only support conclusions about the ages of Americans. It cannot support conclusions about health (choice **a**) or income (choice **c**). Because it only provides data about the proportion of the population in each decade, and not on the actual population, choices **d** and **e** are unsupported by the graph. Choice **b** is correct; with a greater proportion of the American public over age 25 than in 1900, the age of the average American in 2000 must be greater than it was in 1900.

36. c. Each of the incorrect choices is a fact that can be confirmed in the graph. Choice **c** is an opinion because it is a point that can be reasonably debated. Some people may reasonably believe that the United States is aging too quickly while others may reasonably believe that not to be the case.

37. c. Of the countries listed, only Rumania increased in size, according to the map. Austria-Hungary (choice **a**) was dissolved; the newly created states of Austria and Hungary together were much smaller than their predecessor. The borders of Norway (choice **b**) did not change as a result of the war. Ireland (choice **d**) was divided into two smaller states when the war ended. Serbia (choice **e**) was also dissolved as a result of the war.

38. a. According to the passage, the Treaty of Versailles imposed huge fines on Germany and stripped the country of valuable property. These provisions harmed the German economy by depriving it of cash and income, which it needed to rebuild the country after an extremely costly war. Each of the incorrect choices is an opinion, not a fact.

39. c. Remember that correct answers must be supported by details from the passage. The passage never states that Jefferson had a plan for setting aside land for native people, so choice **c** does not describe one of Jefferson's goals in sponsoring the Lewis and Clark expedition, according to the passage.

40. b. Manifest destiny is a belief that the United States had a mandate to expand its civilization westward. Jefferson's vision of an empire with future generations filling up "the canvas we begin" most closely resembles the idea of manifest destiny.

41. d. Choice **d** best describes the main idea of the paragraph. Each of the incorrect choices identifies a detail from the passage. The main idea summarizes the entire passage; a detail does not.

42. b. Roadside commercial enterprises flourished with highway construction and car travel.

43. e. The map shows that Genghis Khan conquered very little of Persia (choice **a**), Europe (choice **b**), or Arabia (choice **c**). His conquests primarily cover the central part of the Asian continent. Thus, **e** is the answer.

44. c. Choices **a** and **d** are opinions, not facts. Choices **b** and **e** are untrue, according to the graph. The government spends 10% of its budget on health and 3% of its budget on education; therefore, choice **c** is a fact found in the circle graph.

45. a. The graph includes a section for Net Interest. That is the portion of the budget dedicated to paying interest on the national debt.

46. c. Kennedy proclaimed that any nuclear missile attack from Cuba would be regarded as an attack by the Soviet Union; thus, it is reasonable to conclude that he saw the Cuban Missile Crisis as a conflict between the United States and the Soviet Union.

47. e. According to the passage, the United States did not know how many Soviet troops were present in Cuba. Therefore, the United States did not know the full extent of the Soviet threat at the time.

48. e. A capital gains tax does not apply to your income, a home that you own, or goods and services. It does apply to the profit from the sale of property or other financial assets.

49. e. The snake represents "the disunited State of the British Colonies." Note that the individual colonies are represented by letters (N.C. for North Carolina, N.J. for New Jersey, etc.).

50. a. Franklin never mentions rebelling against the British. This cartoon first appeared in 1754, long before there was any serious feeling among the colonists that the colonies should declare independence from Great Britain. Each of the other answers is identified in the passage.